GW01418260

EXCELLENCE IN TEXTS

Hamlet

Full Play Text with Analysis and Annotation

AND
TWO COMPARATIVE STUDY OPTIONS

Aoife O'Driscoll
of Aoife's Notes

educate.ie

educate.ie

PUBLISHED BY:

Educate.ie
Walsh Educational Books Ltd
Castleisland, Co. Kerry, Ireland
www.educate.ie

PRINTED AND BOUND BY:

Walsh Colour Print, Castleisland

Editor: Caitriona Clarke
Design: Kieran O'Donoghue
Layout: Liz White Designs

ACKNOWLEDGEMENTS:

For permission to reproduce photographs, the author and publisher acknowledge the following copyright holders:

Hamlet

Clive Barda / ArenaPAL; Collection Christophel / ArenaPAL; Donald Cooper / Alamy Stock Photo; Ellie Kurttz © RSC; Entertainment Pictures / Alamy Stock Photo; Freepik; Fritz Curzon / ArenaPAL; Geraint Lewis / ArenaPAL; Helen Murray / ArenaPAL; Johan Persson / ArenaPAL; Keystone / Stringer; Manuel Harlan / ArenaPAL; Manuel Harlan © RSC; Marilyn Kingwill / ArenaPAL; Mark Douet / ArenaPAL; Moviestore Collection Ltd / Alamy Stock Photo HAMLET (1991) HELENA BONHAM CARTER, IAN HOLM HAM 006 MOVIESTORE COLLECTION LTD; Moviestore Collection Ltd / Alamy Stock Photo HAMLET (1991) HELENA BONHAM CARTER HAM 030 MOVIESTORE COLLECTION LTD; Moviestore Collection Ltd / Alamy Stock Photo HAMLET (2000) BILL MURRAY, JULIA STILES HAET 001 MOVIESTORE COLLECTION LTD; Nigel Norrington / ArenaPAL; PA Images / Alamy Stock Photo ARTS Theatre_Hamlet 1; PA Images / Alamy Stock Photo Whishaw & Stubbs Hamlet; Pete Jones / ArenaPAL; Hugo Glendinning © RSC; Manuel Harlan © RSC; Reg Wilson © RSC; Ros Kavanagh / ArenaPAL; Shutterstock; TopFoto / ArenaPAL.

Comparatives

Atlaspix / Alamy Stock Photo; Everett Collection Inc / Alamy Stock Photo Sen. Joseph McCarthy at McCarthy hearings, 1954; Johan Persson / ArenaPAL; Lifestyle pictures / Alamy Stock Photo; Maximum Film / Alamy Stock Photo; Moviestore Collection Ltd / Alamy Stock Photo; Photo 12 / Alamy Stock Photo; Pictorial Press Ltd / Alamy Stock Photo; PictureLux / The Hollywood Archive / Alamy Stock Photo; Shutterstock; Ullstein Bild / ArenaPAL.

The author and publisher have made every effort to trace all copyright owners, but if material has inadvertently been reproduced without permission, they would be happy to make the necessary arrangement at the earliest opportunity, and encourage owners of copyright material not acknowledged to make contact.

ISBN: 978-1-913698-96-6

Contents

Comparative Study

Introduction

The aim of this book is to assist you in your reading of *Hamlet* and your comparative texts and prepare you for the single text and comparative questions on Paper 2 of your Leaving Certificate English exam.

Hamlet

This book contains the full text of the play. Each scene opens with a summary of the action about to take place, a description of the setting and a key image to help you visualise the world of the play.

As the English language has changed so much since the time of William Shakespeare, annotation will help you understand what unfamiliar words and phrases mean and assist you with navigating your way through the action.

At the end of each scene, questions will prompt you to think about how the characters, action and key themes have developed in the section you have just read. They will encourage you to think about what the characters say and do, how they interact with each other and how they express thoughts, feelings and opinions. You will consider common themes and explore images and symbols to contribute to your overall understanding of the play.

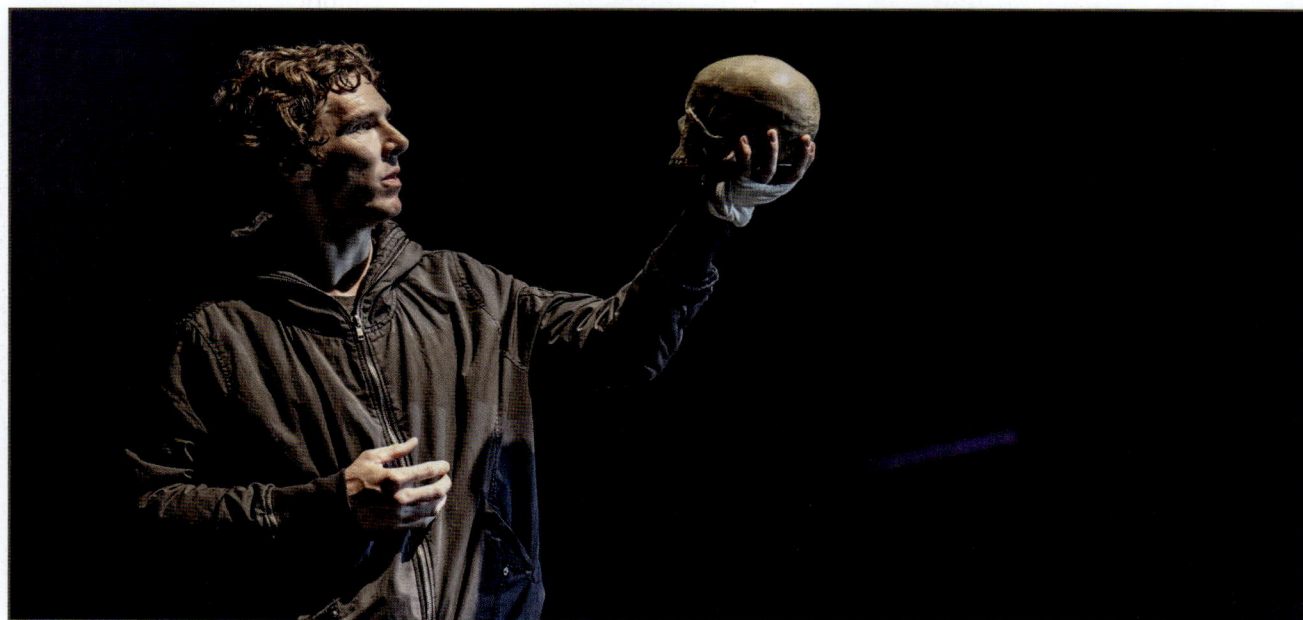

At the end of the play, detailed study notes focusing on character development, key themes, imagery and symbolism will assist you with getting ready for your exam.

You should pay particular attention to quotes from the play. As well as learning key quotes from each scene you will be introduced to more quotes as you move through the analyses of individual characters, themes and dramatic techniques. You may find that when you are researching and writing an essay on a specific theme or aspect of imagery and symbolism, you need to use other quotes. In this case, you should note them carefully and learn them as you use them in your work.

The best way to prepare for any exam question is to know the play inside out. The more familiar you are with the plot and the characters, the more readily you will be able to adapt your knowledge to fit whatever question is asked. There is no definitive 'right' answer: as long as you are honest, well-informed and can make a good case, you will get good marks.

Comparative Study

For the comparative question on your exam, you must use three texts and compare them under particular headings known as the modes of comparison. The modes of comparison for Higher Level for examination in 2024 are: **cultural context**, **literary genre** and **theme or issue**.

In this book, we provide comparative notes for two sets of three texts.

The three texts for Comparative Option One are the novel *Never Let Me Go* by Kazuo Ishiguro, the play *Philadelphia, Here I Come!* by Brian Friel and the film *Lady Bird* directed by Greta Gerwig.

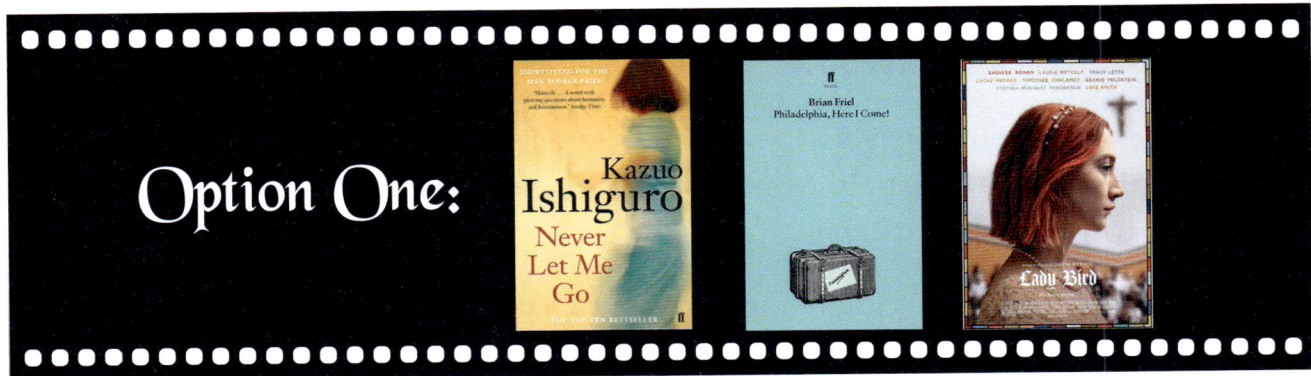

The three texts for Comparative Option Two are the novel *Room* by Emma Donoghue, the play *The Crucible* by Arthur Miller and the film *Casablanca* directed by Michael Curtiz.

You or your teacher may choose which comparative option you will study. You should then use the comparative notes to ensure you know your texts well, understand how to compare and contrast them, and use key comparative phrases.

The Life and Times of William Shakespeare

Shakespeare's life

- William Shakespeare was born in 1564 in Stratford-upon-Avon, England. His father was John Shakespeare, a glove-maker, and his mother was Mary Arden, the daughter of a wealthy farmer. Little is known about his early life. It is thought that he attended King's New School in Stratford.

- At the age of 18 he married Anne Hathaway, who was eight years his senior. They had three children together: Susanna, the eldest, and Hamnet and Judith, who were twins. Their son, Hamnet, died at the age of 11.

- In the 1580s, Shakespeare began a career as an actor and writer in London. There are conflicting theories about why he moved there and how he entered his chosen career. He became part-owner of a theatre group called The Lord Chamberlain's Men. He stayed in London for more than 20 years, writing more than 30 plays and achieving great fame for his work. He is known to have played parts in his own works.

- Shakespeare wrote plays in several genres – comedies, histories and tragedies. The play we will study in this book, *Hamlet,* is a tragedy.

- In or around 1613, Shakespeare retired to Stratford. His work had made him a wealthy man and he bought the second-largest house in the town. He died there in 1616, aged 52. It is thought that his death was sudden, as he was in good health, but he may have contracted a fever. He left most of his estate to his daughter Susanna, on condition that she pass it to her first-born son. Susanna's three children all died without marrying, as did Judith's only daughter, Elizabeth. As a result, there are no direct descendants of Shakespeare living today.

Shakespeare's birthplace in Stratford-upon-Avon

Shakespearean theatre

Reconstruction of Shakespeare's Globe Theatre

- Playhouses offered something for everyone in Shakespeare's England. The plays covered a variety of themes that were not dissimilar to today's soap operas.

- When permanent playhouses first appeared, civic leaders and church authorities did not want them because of the threat of plague, riots and even rebellion.

- The playhouses provided just one of many colourful spectacles for the audience of the time; they also enjoyed public executions, bear baiting, fencing and public processions through the streets.

- Shakespeare's audience would have been hardened to acts of violence in many ways. For example, public executions were crowd-pleasers, and theatre-goers would most likely have seen bodies swinging from gallows as a warning to others not to break the law. What we would consider unbearable cruelty would have been considered entertainment by the audience of the time.

- It was lucky for playwrights in Shakespeare's time that the royals enjoyed the theatre – this fact made their plays far more popular than they might otherwise have been.

- The Globe Theatre was the home of Shakespeare and his acting troupe. It was built in about 1598 in London's Bankside district by Shakespeare's theatre company, The Lord Chamberlain's Men. It could hold up to 3,000 spectators.

- The sets were very simple, with little or nothing by way of effects, so it fell to the playwright to use words to create the images for the audience.

- In 1613, during a performance of *Henry VIII*, a misfired cannonball set the Globe on fire. In less than two hours it had burned to the ground, but fortunately many of the props and costumes were saved. The theatre was rebuilt the following year, this time with a tiled roof instead of a thatched one. The roof did not fully cover the theatre because plays took place during the day and depended on daylight for illumination.

- In 1644, the Puritans, a religious faction, demolished the theatre and built housing on the site.

- In 1997, a reconstruction of Shakespeare's theatre, Shakespeare's Globe, was built about 750 feet from the site of the original playhouse. The design is based on what is known of the 1598 and 1614 buildings.

Did you know?

- In 1572 in England, the Poor Law classed actors in the same category as vagabonds, rogues and wandering beggars.
- Actors had to be good, as audiences booed and hissed and even threw rotten vegetables at the stage if they didn't like what they saw. Women did not act; their parts were taken by young boys whose voices had not yet broken. Many of these boy actors died of lead poisoning because of the presence of this mineral in their make-up.
- There was no copyright; a play was produced as soon as it was written and would be attended by scribes, who would copy the play in order for it to be sold on to other theatre companies and shown elsewhere.
- There was very little rehearsal time and there were no breaks between scenes.
- The majority of plays in the Globe were shown in the summer because the stage was open to the elements.
- Elizabethans said, 'I'm going to hear a play,' as opposed to, 'I'm going to see a play'.

Setting the scene

Shakespeare probably borrowed the idea for *Hamlet* from at least one of several older sources. This was a common enough practice in his time, but what made Shakespeare's plays resonate with his audience was the manner in which they captured universal and timeless themes and tapped into the prevailing mood of the people. At the time that *Hamlet* was written, a pertinent question was whether or not killing or even deposing the king could ever be justified. It is an idea explored in other plays, such as *King Lear* and *Macbeth*, and in each case it would have been seen as a hugely controversial notion. When *Hamlet* was written, Queen Elizabeth was nearing the end of her reign and it was far from clear who would succeed her. European powers always had an eye for the main chance where England was concerned, and Shakespeare's audience would have been keenly aware of their country's potential vulnerability should a strong and capable leader not emerge before Elizabeth died.

'This was the noblest Roman of them all …' The speech that begins with these words is from *Julius Caesar*, the Globe Theatre's first premiere and a huge success for Shakespeare. (He makes reference to it in *Hamlet* when the actors visit Elsinore and Polonius says he once played the role of Julius Caesar.) He had dabbled in tragedy in the past but *Julius Caesar* was his first mature tragedy and doubtless encouraged him to write the lengthy and complex *Hamlet*. It has often been noted that the character of Brutus in *Julius Caesar* is the forerunner of the character of Hamlet. Certainly, there are similarities and it is the characters' inner journeys, as well as their political machinations, that make both plays so absorbing. Revenge plays were popular at the time *Hamlet* was written but it is the main character's introspection that has ensured the enduring popularity of this particular tale of revenge. Rather than simply focusing on a dramatic, exciting plot, Shakespeare takes us with him on a journey through the protagonist's inner turmoil.

At the time that *Hamlet* was written, scholars had been revisiting classical Greek and Roman texts and exploring their relevance to their own lives. Renaissance humanism is the name for the school of thought that held that the moral philosophy of the ancient Greeks and Romans should be the basis for self-knowledge and development. Poetry, and literature in general, grew in importance as scholars delved deep into the realm of human experience and human understanding. Renaissance scholars were encouraged to question and challenge the world around them. They hoped that if they understood more about human nature and reasoning, they would be in a position to know how people should act and thus benefit society as a whole. Hamlet's famous speech beginning 'What a piece of work is a man!' is taken almost directly from *Oration on the Dignity of Man* by an Italian humanist writer.

When viewed this way, Hamlet becomes less a man characterised by inaction and more so a man concerned with the essence of what it means to be human.

List of Characters

HAMLET

Hamlet is the Prince of Denmark. He has been studying at the University of Wittenberg but is back at the Danish court when the play begins. His father is dead and Hamlet's uncle, Claudius, has married Hamlet's mother and is now king. The old king's ghost appears to Hamlet and reveals that Claudius murdered him. He urges Hamlet to seek revenge but the prince does not find it easy to carry out his father's wishes.

CLAUDIUS

Claudius is the King of Denmark, Hamlet's uncle and the late king's brother, as well as his murderer. He has married the widowed Queen Gertrude. Claudius is concerned that Hamlet may suspect his secret and, when this is confirmed, he attempts to have Hamlet murdered as well.

GERTRUDE

Gertrude is the Queen of Denmark and Hamlet's mother. When the play begins, she is married to her late husband's brother, Claudius. Gertrude loves her new husband as well as her son, and is deeply distressed by Hamlet's open dislike of Claudius.

GHOST

The ghost is that of the murdered King of Denmark, Hamlet's father, who appears as a spirit to urge Hamlet to avenge his murder.

HORATIO

Horatio is a close friend of Hamlet. When the play begins, he has just returned from his studies abroad. Horatio is rational and cool-headed and Hamlet greatly respects his wisdom and self-control. Horatio is the one person in whom Hamlet confides his plan to expose Claudius as a murderer.

POLONIUS

Polonius is the king's Lord Chamberlain or counsellor, and the father of Ophelia, Hamlet's love interest. Polonius is a pompous busy-body whose interfering ways lead to his untimely death.

OPHELIA

Ophelia is Polonius's daughter and Hamlet's love interest. She is a beautiful, innocent girl and struggles to cope with the intrigues of the Danish court. Her father uses her to spy on Hamlet on Claudius's behalf. Deeply distressed by her father's murder and Hamlet's cruel treatment of her, Ophelia falls into madness and eventually drowns when she falls into the water while gathering flowers.

LAERTES

Laertes is Polonius's son and Ophelia's brother. At the start of the play, he asks Claudius's permission to return to France and is absent for much of the play. Before he leaves, Laertes warns his sister against believing Hamlet loves her, claiming the prince will marry for political reasons and is only toying with Ophelia.

REYNALDO

Reynaldo is one of Polonius's servants. Polonius tells him to travel to France to spy on Laertes, instructing him to spread rumours about Laertes' behaviour in order to find out if he has been partying, gambling or visiting prostitutes.

VOLTEMAND and CORNELIUS

Voltemand and Cornelius are ambassadors to Norway. Claudius sends them to Norway to tell the king to prevent his nephew, Fortinbras, from attacking Denmark.

MARCELLUS, BARNARDO and FRANCISCO

Marcellus, Barnardo and Francisco are officers of the Watch. At the start of the play, Marcellus and Barnardo bring Horatio with them on their guard duty so that he may see the ghost for himself and prove it was not merely a figment of their imaginations.

ROSENCRANTZ and GUILDENSTERN

Rosencrantz and Guildenstern are courtiers and childhood friends of Hamlet. Claudius uses them to spy on Hamlet but the young prince sees through Claudius's ruse and his old friends' deception. Hamlet discovers that Claudius has arranged for him to travel to England with Rosencrantz and Guildenstern but that they are carrying a letter from Claudius instructing the English king to execute Hamlet. Hamlet changes the letter so that it is Rosencrantz and Guildenstern who will be executed on landing.

OSRIC

Osric is a foolish, pompous courtier. He is sent to tell Hamlet that Laertes is ready for their duel. Hamlet makes fun of Osric, who does not understand and is an easy target for the young prince's wit.

FORTINBRAS

Fortinbras is the prince of Norway. His father was killed in battle by Hamlet's father and Norway had to forfeit land to Denmark as a result. Young Fortinbras is a hot-head and wants to attack Denmark and win back the land and his father's honour. He gathers up a band of mercenaries without his uncle's knowledge. When Claudius learns of his plan, he sends ambassadors to Norway to tell the king, who instructs Fortinbras to cancel his plans. Fortinbras agrees and decides to attack Poland instead. At the end of the play, the dying Hamlet names Fortinbras his successor to the Danish throne.

Other characters in the play include lords, attendants, players from a touring company, gravediggers, sailors, English ambassadors and various followers of Laertes.

The play opens in the Danish royal palace of Elsinore.

Elsinore. A platform¹ before the castle

The setting is the battlements of Elsinore Castle, Denmark. It is midnight, and bitterly cold.

A soldier, Francisco, is on guard alone. Another soldier, Barnardo, arrives to take his place. The men are tense and uneasy. They are joined by Marcellus and Horatio. We learn that a ghost has appeared on the battlements and Marcellus has invited the learned and sceptical Horatio to see it for himself.

The Ghost, which appears to be that of the recently deceased King Hamlet, appears briefly but walks away when Horatio challenges it to identify itself.

While they wait for the Ghost to return, Horatio and the others discuss Denmark's recent preparations for war. Horatio explains that young Fortinbras, nephew of the King of Norway, has gathered up a band of mercenaries. He is threatening to invade Denmark to avenge his late father's death in battle against the old King Hamlet.

The Ghost reappears but still will not speak. A cock crows to signal daybreak and the Ghost vanishes.

The men decide to tell Prince Hamlet, the late king's son, about the ghostly visitation.

1. *A platform: A guard post where cannons were mounted*

FRANCISCO at his post. Enter to him BARNARDO

BARNARDO

Who's there?

FRANCISCO

Nay, answer me. Stand and unfold yourself.[2]

BARNARDO

Long live the King!

FRANCISCO

Barnardo?

BARNARDO

He.   5

FRANCISCO

You come most carefully upon your hour.[3]

BARNARDO

'Tis now struck twelve. Get thee to bed, Francisco.

FRANCISCO

For this relief much thanks.[4] 'Tis bitter cold,
And I am sick at heart. *Possible reference to disease or corruption*

BARNARDO

Have you had quiet guard?[5]   10

FRANCISCO

Not a mouse stirring.

BARNARDO

Well, good night.
If you do meet Horatio and Marcellus,
The rivals of my watch, bid them make haste.[6]

FRANCISCO

I think I hear them. – Stand! Who's there?   15

Enter HORATIO and MARCELLUS

2. *Nay . . . yourself:* No, answer my question. Stop and identify yourself. *Francisco is correct here as Barnardo is the new arrival. Both men are on edge, as is clear in this reversal of the normal convention of a watchman challenging someone approaching his post.*

3. *You . . . hour:* Francisco is grateful for Barnardo's punctuality.

4. *For . . . thanks:* Thank you for coming to take the next shift and giving me a break.

5. *Have . . . guard?:* Have you had a quiet time on watch duty?

6. *The rivals . . . haste:* Barnardo asks Francisco to tell the other night watchmen to hurry up and join him at his post.

HORATIO

Friends to this ground.[7]

MARCELLUS

And liegemen to the Dane.[8]

FRANCISCO

Give you good night.

MARCELLUS

O farewell, honest soldier.

Who hath relieved you?   20

FRANCISCO

Barnardo has my place.

Give you good night.

Exit

MARCELLUS

Holla, Barnardo!

BARNARDO

Say –

What, is Horatio there?[9]   25

HORATIO

 A piece of him.[10]

BARNARDO

Welcome, Horatio. Welcome, good Marcellus.

MARCELLUS

 What, has this thing appeared again tonight?

BARNARDO

 I have seen nothing.

MARCELLUS

Horatio says 'tis but our fantasy,[11]   30

And will not let belief take hold of him

Touching this dreaded sight twice seen of us.[12]

7. *Friends ... ground:* Friends of Denmark. *Horatio is simply letting Francisco know that he and Marcellus pose no threat.*

8. *liegemen ... Dane:* loyal subjects to the King of Denmark

9. *What ... there?:* It is so dark that Barnardo cannot see who is there.

10. *A piece of him:* Critics differ on the meaning of this line. It could mean that Horatio is present, but reluctantly so, or it could mean that it is so dark on the battlements that only Horatio's hand – offered in greeting – can be seen.

11. *fantasy:* imagination

12. *Horatio says ... seen of us:* Horatio doesn't believe in this dreadful ghost that we have seen twice. He says it is a figment of our imagination.

Act 1

13. *entreated:* asked

14. *apparition:* ghost

15. *He may . . . speak to it:* He may confirm what we have seen and speak to the Ghost. *Horatio is a scholar and speaks Latin. It was believed in Shakespeare's time that ghosts spoke Latin and that they would only reply to questions but would not start conversations. Therefore, Horatio – being both a scholar and a sceptical, brave man – would be the ideal person to approach the Ghost.*

16. *Tush:* Nonsense

17. *assail:* attack. *In other words, Horatio will have to listen to them.*

18. *Last night . . . burns:* Last night, at this exact time when the North Star was in the same position it is in now.

19. *Peace . . . off:* Stop talking.

20. *In . . . dead:* The Ghost looks like the dead King Hamlet.

21. *Thou art a scholar:* It was believed that ghosts spoke Latin, so the guardsmen would assume Horatio – an educated man – could speak to it.

22. *Mark it:* Take careful note of it.

23. *harrows:* torments or deeply distresses

Therefore I have entreated[13] him along
With us to watch the minutes of this night,
That if again this apparition[14] come   **35**
He may approve our eyes and speak to it.[15]

HORATIO
Tush,[16] tush, 'twill not appear.

BARNARDO
Sit down awhile,
And let us once again assail[17] your ears,
That are so fortified against our story   **40**
What we two nights have seen.

HORATIO
Well, sit we down,
And let us hear Barnardo speak of this.

BARNARDO
Last night of all,
When yon same star that's westward from the pole   **45**
Had made his course t'illume that part of heaven
Where now it burns,[18] Marcellus and myself
The bell then beating one –

Enter GHOST

MARCELLUS
Peace, break thee off.[19] Look, where it comes again.

BARNARDO
In the same figure, like the King that's dead.[20]   **50**

MARCELLUS
Thou art a scholar[21] – speak to it, Horatio.

BARNARDO
Looks it not like the King? – Mark it,[22] Horatio.

HORATIO
Most like. It harrows[23] me with fear and wonder.

BARNARDO

It would be spoke to.

MARCELLUS

Question it, Horatio.   **55**

HORATIO

What art thou that usurp'st this time of night,

Together with that fair and warlike form

In which the majesty of buried Denmark

Did sometimes march?[24] By heaven, I charge thee, speak.[25]

MARCELLUS

It is offended.   **60**

BARNARDO

See, it stalks away.

HORATIO

Stay, speak, speak, I charge thee speak.

Exit GHOST

MARCELLUS

'Tis gone, and will not answer.[26]

BARNARDO

How now, Horatio? You tremble and look pale.

Is not this something more than fantasy?   **65**

What think you on't?[27]

HORATIO

Before my God, I might not this believe

Without the sensible and true avouch[28]

Of mine own eyes.

MARCELLUS

Is it not like the King?   **70**

HORATIO

As thou art to thyself

Such was the very armour he had on

When he the ambitious Norway combated.

24. *What art thou ... march?:* To usurp is to take possession of something illegally. Horatio asks the Ghost why it has taken possession of the night and why it is dressed in the armour of the dead king.

25. *I charge thee, speak:* I command you to speak.

26. *'Tis gone ... answer:* Some critics believe that the Ghost will not speak to Horatio because it has nothing to say to him. The only person in the play the Ghost will speak to is Hamlet, because he is the only one who can fulfil its demand for vengeance. When the Ghost appears in Gertrude's chamber later in the play, only Hamlet can see it because it has nothing to say to Gertrude. Its purpose in appearing on the castle walls is to summon Hamlet. However, when Horatio tells Hamlet about meeting the Ghost, he says that it appeared as if it were about to speak but then dawn broke and it vanished. If the traditions of ghosts in plays apply to this situation, then all the Ghost would have said to Horatio is that it wanted to speak to Hamlet.

27. *What think you on't?:* What do you think of this?

28. *avouch:* affirmation

29. *He smote . . . ice:* The Polish soldiers were on sleds when they were attacked and defeated by Old Hamlet.

30. *jump:* exactly
31. *martial stalk:* striding in a military manner

32. *in . . . state:* Horatio says his general view of this matter is that it foretells disaster for Denmark.

33. *Why . . . land:* Why are the citizens being made to work all night at the same time as soldiers have to keep a strict watch?
34. *And . . . cannon:* Why are bronze cannons being made every day?
35. *foreign . . . war:* Why are weapons being bought from overseas?
36. *Why . . . week:* Why are shipbuilders being forced to work seven days a week?
37. *toward:* imminent, about to happen
38. *make . . . day:* make people work both day and night

39. *Was . . . combat:* Old Fortinbras, motivated by jealousy and pride, challenged Old Hamlet to fight.
40. *valiant:* brave
41. *sealed compact:* legal agreement

42. *moiety component:* an equivalent amount

43. *gaged:* wagered

44. *carriage . . . designed:* according to the terms of the agreement

So frowned he once when in an angry parley
He smote the sledded Polacks on the ice.[29]   **75**
'Tis strange.

MARCELLUS
Thus twice before, and jump[30] at this dead hour,
With martial stalk[31] hath he gone by our watch.

HORATIO
In what particular thought to work I know not,
But in the gross and scope of my opinion   **80**
This bodes some strange eruption to our state.[32]

MARCELLUS
Good now, sit down, and tell me, he that knows,
Why this same strict and most observant watch
So nightly toils the subject of the land,[33]
And why such daily cast of brazen cannon,[34]   **85**
And foreign mart for implements of war,[35]
Why such impress of shipwrights, whose sore task
Does not divide the Sunday from the week:[36]
What might be toward[37] that this sweaty haste
Doth make the night joint-labourer with the day.[38]   **90**
Who is't that can inform me?

HORATIO
That can I –
At least, the whisper goes so: our last King,
Whose image even but now appeared to us,
Was as you know by Fortinbras of Norway,   **95**
Thereto pricked on by a most emulate pride,
Dared to the combat;[39] in which our valiant[40] Hamlet –
For so this side of our known world esteemed him –
Did slay this Fortinbras, who by a sealed compact[41]
Well ratified by law and heraldry   **100**
Did forfeit with his life, all those his lands
Which he stood seized on to the conqueror;
Against the which a moiety competent[42]
Was gaged[43] by our King, which had returned
To the inheritance of Fortinbras   **105**
Had he been vanquisher, as by the same covenant
And carriage of the article designed[44]
His fell to Hamlet. Now sir, young Fortinbras,

Of unimproved mettle[45] hot and full,

Hath in the skirts[46] of Norway here and there   110

Sharked up[47] a list of lawless resolutes,[48]

For food and diet[49] to some enterprise

That hath a stomach in't,[50] which is no other –

As it doth well appear unto our state –

But to recover of us by strong hand   115

And terms compulsative those foresaid lands

So by his father lost. And this, I take it,

Is the main motive of our preparations,

The source of this our watch, and the chief head

Of this post-haste[51] and romage[52] in the land.   120

BARNARDO

I think it be no other but e'en so.

Well may it sort that this portentous[53] figure

Comes armed through our watch so like the king

That was and is the question of these wars.

HORATIO

A mote it is to trouble the mind's eye.[54]   125

In the most high and palmy[55] state of Rome,

A little ere the mightiest Julius[56] fell,

The graves stood tenantless,[57] and the sheeted dead[58]

Did squeak and gibber[59] in the Roman streets

At stars with trains of fire,[60] and dews of blood,   130

Disasters in the sun;[61] and the moist star,

Upon whose influence Neptune's empire stands,[62]

Was sick almost to doomsday with eclipse.

And even the like precurse of fierce events,[63]

As harbingers[64] preceding still the fates,   135

And prologue to the omen coming on,[65]

Have heaven and earth together demonstrated

Unto our climature and countrymen.

But soft, behold – lo here it comes again!

Re-enter GHOST

I'll cross it[66] though it blast me. – Stay, illusion.   140

If thou hast any sound, or use of voice,

Speak to me.

If there be any good thing to be done

That may to thee do ease and grace to me,

Speak to me: 145

Notes:

45. *Of unimproved mettle:* inexperienced and lacking self-control
46. *skirts:* borders
47. *Sharked up:* snapped up
48. *resolutes:* determined men
49. *For … diet:* This may mean that the men will fight for anyone who will give them food.
50. *That … in't:* an undertaking that requires courage

51. *post-haste:* hurried
52. *romage:* commotion

53. *portentous:* ominous

54. *A mote … eye:* It is as irritating and troubling to the mind as a speck of dust is to the eye.
55. *palmy:* flourishing
56. *Julius:* Julius Caesar, a famous Roman emperor who was assassinated by those close to him
57. *tenantless:* empty
58. *sheeted dead:* dead people wrapped in their burial shrouds
59. *gibber:* speak nonsensically or unintelligibly
60. *At … fire:* comets
61. *Disasters in the sun:* solar eclipses
62. *the moist … stands:* the moon, which influences the tides. Neptune is god of the sea.
63. *Was sick … events:* was eclipsed almost to the darkness, signalling the end of the world. *In the Bible (Matthew 24:29), an eclipse was one of the signs of the end of the world.*
64. *harbingers:* forerunners or signs
65. *prologue … on:* introduction to the dreadful events that will follow

66. *I'll cross it:* This could mean that Horatio will stand in the Ghost's path, or it could mean he will make the sign of the cross (bless himself) in front of it. If the Ghost were an evil spirit, it would react violently both to being halted in its tracks and to the sign of the cross.

Cock crows

67. *If thou art privy:* If you have secret knowledge

68. *uphoarded:* hidden

If thou art privy[67] to thy country's fate,
Which happily foreknowing may avoid, O speak!
Or if thou hast uphoarded[68] in thy life
Extorted treasure in the womb of earth –
For which, they say, you spirits oft walk in death –   150
Speak of it, stay and speak, – Stop it, Marcellus.

MARCELLUS
Shall I strike at it with my partisan?[69]

69. *partisan:* long-handled spear

HORATIO
Do, if it will not stand.

BARNARDO
'Tis here.

HORATIO
'Tis here   155

MARCELLUS
'Tis gone.

Exit GHOST

70. *majestical:* regal or having the bearing of a king

We do it wrong, being so majestical,[70]
To offer it the show of violence,
For it is as the air invulnerable,
And our vain blows malicious mockery.[71]   160

71. *our ... mockery:* Our attempts to strike it are pointless as a ghost can feel nothing, and we were wrong to try to hit something so regal.

BARNARDO
It was about to speak, when the cock crew.

HORATIO
And then it started[72] like a guilty thing
Upon a fearful summons I have heard
The cock, that is the trumpet to the morn,[73]
Doth with his lofty and shrill-sounding throat   165
Awake the god of day, and at his warning,
Whether in sea or fire, in earth or air,
Th'extravagant and erring spirit hies

72. *started:* moved suddenly in surprise and alarm

73. *that is ... morn:* announces daybreak

To his confine;[74] and of the truth herein

This present object made probation.[75]   **170**

MARCELLUS

It faded on the crowing of the cock.

Some say that ever 'gainst that season comes

Wherein our saviour's birth is celebrated[76]

The bird of dawning[77] singeth all night long;

And then, they say, no spirit can walk abroad,   **175**

The nights are wholesome; then no planets strike,

No fairy takes, nor witch hath power to charm,

So hallowed and so gracious is the time.[78]

HORATIO

So have I heard, and do in part believe it.

But, look, the morn in russet mantle clad[79]   **180**

Walks o'er the dew of yon high eastern hill.

Break we our watch up, and by my advice[80]

Let us impart[81] what we have seen tonight

Unto young Hamlet; for, upon my life,

This spirit, dumb to us, will speak to him.   **185**

Do you consent we shall acquaint him with it,

As needful in our loves, fitting our duty?[82]

MARCELLUS

Let's do't, I pray; and I this morning know

Where we shall find him most conveniently.

Exit

74. *Th'extravagant . . . confine:* The Ghost, which has wandered beyond its limits, rushes back to the place in which he is confined.

75. *of . . . probation:* The Ghost's behaviour just now proves this to be true.

76. *Some . . . celebrated:* It is said that, in the lead-up to Christmas

77. *The bird of dawning:* cockerel/rooster

78. *The nights . . . time:* The night air is healthy; the planets have no control over humans; neither fairies' nor witches' spells can have any effect because it is such a holy time.

79. *the morn . . . clad:* Morning appears to be wrapped in a reddish cloak as the sky brightens.

80. *by my advice:* I suggest

81. *impart:* tell

82. *Do you . . . duty?:* Do you agree that we should do this out of both love and duty?

Quotes

> 'Tis bitter cold,
> And I am sick at heart.
>
> (Francisco, lines 8–9)

Francisco's comment may, at first reading, mean he is feeling low, but the phrase 'sick at heart' is an early warning sign that 'Something is rotten in the state of Denmark'. (Marcellus will say this later on in Act 1 Scene 4.) As we will see, Claudius murdered his brother, the king, to gain the throne, and then married the late king's wife. The country, therefore, is ruled by a corrupt leader and the sickness or corruption spreads through the land.

> Tush, tush, 'twill not appear.
>
> (Horatio, line 37)

Horatio is confident that the Ghost is a figment of the guards' imaginations and he is confident he will not see the apparition.

> This bodes some strange eruption to our state.
>
> (Horatio, line 81)

Horatio, shaken by the appearance of a Ghost in whom he did not believe, feels now that the apparition foretells disaster for Denmark.

> Horatio says 'tis but our fantasy,
> And will not let belief take hold of him
>
> (Marcellus, lines 30–31)

Horatio is a sceptic and does not believe in the Ghost. He is an educated, rational man so once he sees the Ghost, the audience will be inclined to believe in it, and Hamlet will be likely to trust his account.

Questions

In each case, support your point with suitable reference to and quotation from the play.

1. What is your impression of Horatio?

2. Why does Horatio make reference to Julius Caesar?

3. What do we learn about the late King Hamlet?

4. Describe what happened between Old Hamlet and Old Fortinbras.

5. Do you think Fortinbras is right to seek revenge? Explain your answer.

Writing Task

Imagine you are Horatio. Write the diary entry you might make after the events of this scene, outlining your thoughts after your encounter with the Ghost.

Essay Building Blocks

'In Hamlet, *Shakespeare makes effective use of language and imagery to create a mood of tension and fear.*'

Write a paragraph in response to this statement, supporting your answer with quotation from and reference to Act 1 Scene 1.

A room of state in the castle

Claudius, King of Denmark, addresses the court. He expresses his grief at the death of his brother, the former king, and his joy at his marriage to Gertrude, the late king's wife. He also sends two ambassadors to Norway to discuss the threat of invasion.

Laertes, son of the king's chief counsellor, requests and is granted Claudius's permission to return to France and resume his studies.

Claudius and Gertrude ask Hamlet why he is still grieving his father's death. They urge him to accept it and move on. Hamlet wishes to return to Wittenberg to study but Claudius and Gertrude ask him to stay. Hamlet grudgingly agrees.

In his first soliloquy, Hamlet expresses his anger and disgust at his mother's hasty remarriage. He is deeply depressed and wishes he were dead. Were it not against God's law, he would take his own life.

Horatio and Marcellus arrive and tell Hamlet about the visitation of the Ghost. Hamlet is excited by the news and arranges to meet them on the battlements later that night to see it for himself.

Enter CLAUDIUS, GERTRUDE, HAMLET, POLONIUS, LAERTES,
VOLTEMAND, CORNELIUS, LORDS, and ATTENDANTS

CLAUDIUS

Though yet of Hamlet our dear brother's death

The memory be green,[1] and that it us befitted

To bear our hearts in grief and our whole kingdom

To be contracted in one brow of woe,[2]

Yet so far hath discretion fought with nature   **5**

That we with wisest sorrow[3] think on him

Together with remembrance of ourselves.

Therefore our sometime sister, now our queen,

The imperial jointress to this warlike state,[4]

Have we as 'twere with a defeated joy,   **10**

With one auspicious and one dropping eye,[5]

With mirth[6] in funeral and with dirge[7] in marriage,

In equal scale weighing delight and dole,[8]

Taken to wife. Nor have we herein barred

Your better wisdoms, which have freely gone   **15**

With this affair along.[9] For all, our thanks.

Now follows that you know young Fortinbras,

Holding a weak supposal of our worth,[10]

Or thinking by our late dear brother's death

Our state to be disjoint and out of frame,[11]   **20**

Co-leagued with the dream of his advantage,[12]

He hath not failed to pester us with message

Importing the surrender of those lands

Lost by his father, with all bonds of law,

To our most valiant brother.[13] So much for him.   **25**

Now for ourself, and for this time of meeting,

Thus much the business is: we have here writ

To Norway, uncle of young Fortinbras –

Who, impotent and bed-rid,[14] scarcely hears

Of this his nephew's purpose – to suppress   **30**

His further gait[15] herein, in that the levies,

The lists, and full proportions, are all made

Out of his subject;[16] and we here dispatch

You, good Cornelius, and you, Voltemand,

For bearers of this greeting to old Norway,   **35**

Giving to you no further personal power

To business with the King more than the scope

Of these delated articles allow.[17]

Farewell, and let your haste commend your duty.

1. *green:* fresh

2. *our . . . woe:* our whole kingdom to be united in mourning; to look like a face wrinkled in sorrow

3. *wisest sorrow:* grief balanced with wisdom

4. *The imperial . . . state:* the joint ruler of the kingdom

5. *one . . . eye:* one happy eye and one eye shedding tears

6. *mirth:* joy
7. *dirge:* sorrow
8. *dole:* grief

9. *Nor . . . along:* We have not ignored your wise advice which has been fully supportive of this marriage all along.

10. *Holding . . . worth:* having a poor opinion of my leadership qualities

11. *disjoint . . . frame:* disorganised and disordered

12. *Co-leagued . . . advantage:* together with his hope of gaining an advantage

13. *Importing . . . brother:* demanding the surrender of those lands his father legally lost to my courageous brother

14. *impotent and bed-rid:* powerless and confined to his bed

15. *to suppress . . . gait:* to stop his progress

16. *in that . . . subject:* The King of Norway has the power to prevent his nephew from proceeding in this matter because all the troops and military supplies belong to Norway.

17. *Giving . . . allow:* They are restricted to the legal and diplomatic terms set out in the documents they carry.

18. *We . . . nothing:* Claudius uses the royal 'We' when referring to himself. He means that he does not doubt the loyalty of Cornelius and Voltemand.

19. *suit:* request

20. *You cannot . . . asking:* If your request is reasonable, you are not wasting your breath by speaking to the King of Denmark. What could you ask for that shall not be freely given without your having to ask for it?

21. *The head . . . father:* The head is not more connected to the heart nor the hand more useful to the mouth than your father is to the throne of Denmark. *This is Claudius's rather long-winded way of saying that Laertes' father has an important role in the Danish court.*

22. *Dread my lord:* The word 'dread' can mean honoured or respected, but it also has connotations of fear, which is appropriate for a ruler like Claudius.

23. *Your leave and favour:* permission

24. *He hath . . . petition:* His constant pleading has worn me down and forced me to give my consent.

25. *Upon . . . consent:* I reluctantly agreed

26. *fair hour:* wonderful opportunity

27. *cousin:* In Shakespeare's time, 'cousin' simply meant a close relative.

28. *A little . . . kind:* Hamlet says Claudius is more than a kinsman (relative) because he is both his uncle and his stepfather, but there is no kindness in the relationship. The word 'kind' can also mean 'type', so Hamlet may also be playing on this word by hinting that Claudius is not the same type of man as he or his late father.

CORNELIUS and **VOLTEMAND**

In that and all things will we show our duty.　　　　40

CLAUDIUS

We doubt it nothing,[18] heartily farewell.

Exit VOLTEMAND and CORNELIUS

And now, Laertes, what's the news with you?
You told us of some suit.[19] What is't, Laertes?
You cannot speak of reason to the Dane
And lose your voice. What wouldst thou beg, Laertes,　　45
That shall not be my offer, not thy asking?[20]
The head is not more native to the heart,
The hand more instrumental to the mouth,
Than is the throne of Denmark to thy father.[21]
What wouldst thou have, Laertes?　　　　50

LAERTES

Dread my lord,[22]
Your leave and favour[23] to return to France,
From whence though willingly I came to Denmark
To show my duty in your coronation,
Yet now I must confess, that duty done,　　　　55
My thoughts and wishes bend again towards France
And bow them to your gracious leave and pardon.

CLAUDIUS

Have you your father's leave? What says Polonius?

POLONIUS

He hath, my lord, wrung from me my slow leave
By laboursome petition,[24] and at last　　　　60
Upon his will I sealed my hard consent.[25]
I do beseech you give him leave to go.

CLAUDIUS

Take thy fair hour,[26] Laertes. Time be thine,
And thy best graces spend it at thy will.
But now, my cousin[27] Hamlet, and my son –　　　　65

HAMLET

[Aside] A little more than kin and less than kind.[28]

CLAUDIUS

How is it that the clouds still hang on you?[29]

HAMLET

Not so, my lord, I am too much in the sun.[30]

GERTRUDE

Good Hamlet, cast thy nighted colour[31] off,

And let thine eye look like a friend on Denmark.   **70**

Do not for ever with thy vailed lids[32]

Seek for thy noble father in the dust.

Thou know'st 'tis common – all that lives must die,

Passing through nature to eternity.

[handwritten notes: Inconsiderate/insensitive / lacks empty / more concerned with power + status / then with empathy / protective of Hamlet with this / political strategy.]

HAMLET

Ay, madam, it is common.[33]   **75**

GERTRUDE

If it be,

Why seems it so particular with thee?[34]

HAMLET

Seems, madam? Nay it is. I know not 'seems'.[35]

'Tis not alone my inky cloak,[36] good-mother,

Nor customary suits of solemn black,   **80**

Nor windy suspiration of forced breath,[37]

No, nor the fruitful river in the eye,[38]

Nor the dejected 'haviour of the visage,[39]

Together with all forms, moods, shows of grief,

That can denote me truly:[40] these indeed 'seem',   **85**

For they are actions that a man might play;

But I have that within which passeth show;

These but the trappings and the suits of woe.[41]

CLAUDIUS

'Tis sweet and commendable in your nature, Hamlet,

To give these mourning duties to your father;   **90**

But you must know your father lost a father;

That father lost, lost his; and the survivor bound

In filial obligation[42] for some term

To do obsequious sorrow.[43] But to persevere

In obstinate condolement is a course   **95**

---

29. *How is it . . . on you?:* Why are you still so depressed?

30. *I am . . . in the sun:* This is a pun, or play on words, on the word 'son' used by Claudius a short time ago. Hamlet does not want to be Claudius's son. Neither does he want to be in the limelight. Finally, he is not in a mood for sunshine because he is in mourning.

31. *nighted colour:* black clothes worn in a time of mourning

32. *vailed lids:* downcast eyes

33. *Ay . . . common:* Gertrude means that death is universal and a normal part of life, but Hamlet plays on the word because 'common' can also mean 'vulgar' and therefore something which should not be accepted by people of culture and sensitivity. He is not really agreeing with her but is putting a sarcastic spin on the word 'common'.

34. *If . . . thee?:* Gertrude responds to Hamlet's sarcastic repetition of 'common' by asking him why, if death is universal, he is so particularly or personally affected by it.

35. *seems:* Hamlet takes offence at his mother's use of the word 'seems', claiming that his sorrow is real.

36. *inky cloak:* black cloak

37. *windy . . . breath:* sighs

38. *the fruitful . . . eye:* the river of tears from my eyes

39. *dejected . . . visage:* the sad facial expression

40. *denote me truly:* truly describe me

41. *trappings . . . woe:* superficial outward appearance of sorrow

42. *filial obligation:* the duties of a son

43. *obsequious sorrow:* mourn in an appropriate manner

44. *But to . . . stubbornness:* But to persist in mourning for so long is irreverently stubborn.

45. *It shows . . . unschooled:* It is offensive to God, showing a weak heart and an ignorant mind.

46. *peevish:* foolish and contrary

47. *Fie:* a mild oath

48. *corse:* corpse

49. *unprevailing woe:* pointless sorrow

50. *You . . . throne:* Claudius publicly states that Hamlet is next in line to the throne.

51. *Wittenberg:* a German university

52. *retrograde:* contrary

53. *beseech you:* beg you

54. *Let not . . . Hamlet:* Let your mother's prayers for you to stay not be in vain.

55. *Be as . . . Denmark:* Enjoy all the privileges of royalty, as if you were the king.
56. *accord:* agreement

57. *in grace whereof:* in celebration of which

58. *No jocund . . . thunder:* Every cheerful toast to which glasses are raised today will be accompanied by the roar of cannon fire which shall echo in the heavens.

Of impious stubbornness,[44] 'tis unmanly grief,
It shows a will most incorrect to heaven,
A heart unfortified, a mind impatient,
An understanding simple and unschooled;[45]
For what we know must be, and is as common   100
As any the most vulgar thing to sense,
Why should we in our peevish[46] opposition
Take it to heart? Fie,[47] 'tis a fault to heaven,
A fault against the dead, a fault to nature,
To reason most absurd, whose common theme   105
Is death of fathers, and who still hath cried,
From the first corse[48] till he that died today,
'This must be so'. We pray you throw to earth
This unprevailing woe,[49] and think of us
As of a father; for let the world take note   110
You are the most immediate to our throne,[50]
And with no less nobility of love
Than that which dearest father bears his son
Do I impart towards you. For your intent
In going back to school in Wittenberg,[51]   115
It is most retrograde[52] to our desire,
And we beseech you,[53] bend you to remain
Here in the cheer and comfort of our eye,
Our chiefest courtier, cousin, and our son.

GERTRUDE

Let not thy mother lose her prayers, Hamlet.[54]   120
I pray thee stay with us, go not to Wittenberg.

HAMLET

I shall in all my best obey you, madam.

CLAUDIUS

Why, 'tis a loving and a fair reply.
Be as ourself in Denmark.[55] Madam, come.
This gentle and unforced accord[56] of Hamlet   125
Sits smiling to my heart; in grace whereof,[57]
No jocund health that Denmark drinks today
But the great cannon to the clouds shall tell,
And the King's rouse the heavens all bruit again,
Re-speaking earthly thunder.[58] Come, away.   130

Exit all but HAMLET

HAMLET

O that this too too solid flesh[59] would melt,

Thaw, and resolve itself into a dew,

Or that the Everlasting had not fixed

His canon 'gainst self-slaughter![60] O God! God,

How weary, stale, flat, and unprofitable   **135**

Seem to me all the uses[61] of this world!

Fie on't! ah fie, fie! 'Tis an unweeded garden

That grows to seed; things rank and gross[62] in nature

Possess it merely. That it should come to this –

But two months dead – nay, not so much, not two –   **140**

So excellent a king, that was to this

Hyperion to a satyr,[63] so loving to my mother

That he might not beteem[64] the winds of heaven

Visit her face too roughly! Heaven and earth,

Must I remember? Why, she would hang on him   **145**

As if increase of appetite had grown

By what it fed on, and yet within a month –

Let me not think on't; frailty,[65] thy name is woman –

A little month, or ere those shoes were old

With which she follow'd my poor father's body,

Like Niobe,[66] all tears, why she, even she –   **150**

O God, a beast that wants discourse of reason[67]

Would have mourned longer! Married with mine uncle,

My father's brother, but no more like my father

Than I to Hercules;[68] within a month,   **155**

Ere yet the salt of most unrighteous tears

Had left the flushing in her galled[69] eyes,

She married. O most wicked speed, to post

With such dexterity[70] to incestuous sheets!

It is not, nor it cannot come to good.   **160**

But break, my heart, for I must hold my tongue.

Enter HORATIO, MARCELLUS, and BARNARDO

HORATIO

Hail to your lordship.

HAMLET

I am glad to see you well.

Horatio – or I do forget myself.

HORATIO

The same, my lord, and your poor servant ever.   **165**

---

59. *O that ... flesh:* In some versions of the play, the word 'solid' is replaced by the word 'sallied', meaning sullied or contaminated. Those who favour 'solid' argue that it makes more sense for Hamlet to mourn the fact that his body is too solid to melt, while those who argue for 'sallied' claim that the idea of contamination runs throughout this soliloquy.

60. *Or ... self-slaughter!:* If only God had not made a canon (divine law) against suicide.

61. *uses:* customs

62. *rank and gross:* rotting and corrupt

63. *Hyperion to a satyr:* Hyperion was the Greek god of the sun and was famously handsome. A satyr is an ugly mythological creature: half-man half-goat and known for lecherous, lustful behaviour.

64. *beteem:* allow

65. *frailty:* weakness

66. *Niobe:* A mother in Greek mythology who wept so much when her 14 children were killed that Zeus turned her into a stone fountain.

67. *wants ... reason:* lacks the ability to reason

68. *Hercules:* son of Zeus, famous for his bravery and strength

69. *galled:* sore and red from crying

70. *dexterity:* speed and skill

[Handwritten notes: misogyny → his mother's marriage has shattered his opinion of woman. Does he see Gertude as weak or does he fail to recognise the political moves she must make to ensure their safety.]

Act 1

71. *I'll change . . . you:* I'll swap my title *(lord)* for yours *(servant)*. Hamlet considers Horatio a friend instead of a subordinate, despite their differences in rank.
72. *And . . . Wittenberg:* What brings you here from Wittenberg?

73. *even:* evening

74. *truant disposition:* desire to stay away from college to avoid work

75. *I . . . truant:* Hamlet says he would not allow Horatio's enemy to call him a truant, so he will not allow Horatio to call himself that. It is worth noting that Hamlet jokingly refuses to allow Horatio to 'do mine ear that violence' by running himself down. Not only is Elsinore a place in which false stories abound, but Hamlet's father died a violent death by having poison poured into his ear.
76. *But . . . Elsinore?:* Hamlet asks Horatio what business he has in Elsinore but he must know that he has come for Hamlet's father's funeral.
77. *We'll . . . depart:* Hamlet is making a sarcastic reference to the partying in the Danish court under King Claudius.

78. *prithee:* pray you, beg you

79. *it followed hard upon:* it happened soon afterwards

80. *Thrift . . . tables:* Hamlet sarcastically claims the royal family saved money (were thrifty) by using the cold, leftover funeral food to feed the wedding guests.
81. *dearest foe:* greatest enemy

82. *mind's eye:* memory or imagination

HAMLET

Sir, my good friend; I'll change that name with you.[71]

And what make you from Wittenberg,[72] Horatio? –

Marcellus.

MARCELLUS

My good lord.

HAMLET

I am very glad to see you. Good even,[73] sir, –   **170**

But what in faith make you from Wittenberg?

HORATIO

A truant disposition,[74] good my lord.

HAMLET

I would not hear your enemy say so,

Nor shall you do mine ear that violence,

To make it truster of your own report   **175**

Against yourself. I know you are no truant.[75]

But what is your affair in Elsinore?[76]

We'll teach you to drink deep ere you depart.[77]

HORATIO

My lord, I came to see your father's funeral.

HAMLET

I prithee[78] do not mock me, fellow-student;   **180**

I think it was to see my mother's wedding.

HORATIO

Indeed, my lord, it followed hard upon.[79]

HAMLET

Thrift, thrift, Horatio! The funeral baked meats

Did coldly furnish forth the marriage tables.[80]

Would I had met my dearest foe[81] in heaven   **185**

Ere I had ever seen that day, Horatio.

My father – methinks I see my father.

HORATIO

O where, my lord?

HAMLET

In my mind's eye,[82] Horatio.

HORATIO

I saw him once. He was a goodly king.

190

HAMLET

He was a man. Take him for all in all,
I shall not look upon his like again.

HORATIO

My lord, I think I saw him yesternight.

HAMLET

Saw? Who?

HORATIO

My lord, the King your father.

195

HAMLET

The King my father?

HORATIO

Season your admiration[83] for awhile
With an attent[84] ear till I may deliver,
Upon the witness of these gentlemen,
This marvel to you.[85]

200

HAMLET

For God's love let me hear!

HORATIO

Two nights together had these gentlemen,
Marcellus and Barnardo, on their watch,
In the dead waste and middle of the night,
Been thus encountered. A figure like your father,

205

Armed at points exactly, cap-a-pie,[86]
Appears before them, and with solemn march
Goes slow and stately by them. Thrice he walked
By their oppressed and fear-surprised[87] eyes
Within his truncheon's length,[88] whilst they distilled

210

Almost to jelly with the act of fear[89]
Stand dumb and speak not to him. This to me
In dreadful secrecy impart they did,[90]
And I with them the third night kept the watch,
Where, as they had delivered, both in time,

215

---

83. *Season your admiration:* Control your astonishment

84. *attent:* attentive

85. *till I may . . . to you:* while I tell, with these men as witnesses, the most astonishing story

86. *cap-a-pie:* from head to toe

87. *oppressed and fear-surprised:* troubled and startled

88. *Within . . . length:* within the length of the king's staff or baton of command

89. *distilled . . . fear:* They were so afraid that they shook with fear, like jelly, and were unable to move.

90. *This to me . . . did:* They confided in me and told me the terrible secret. *'Dreadful'* here means that the secret was something to cause a feeling of dread.

91. *Where . . . good:* Everything they said about the time of the Ghost's appearance and its outward form was proven true.

92. *These hands . . . like:* Presumably Horatio is holding his hands out as he says this. He means that the Ghost resembled the King just as closely as one of Horatio's hands resembles the other.

93. *It lifted . . . sight:* It lifted its head and moved as if it were about to speak, but at that moment the rooster crowed to announce the dawn and it vanished quickly. *Although the Ghost wants to speak to Hamlet, Horatio believes it may have said something to him.*

94. *writ . . . duty:* required of us by our duty

Form of the thing, each word made true and good,[91]
The apparition comes. I knew your father;
These hands are not more like.[92]

HAMLET
But where was this?

MARCELLUS
My lord, upon the platform where we watched.   220

HAMLET
Did you not speak to it?

HORATIO
My lord, I did,
But answer made it none; yet once methought
It lifted up its head and did address
Itself to motion like as it would speak,   225
But even then the morning cock crew loud
And at the sound it shrunk in haste away
And vanished from our sight.[93]

HAMLET
'Tis very strange.

HORATIO
As I do live, my honoured lord, 'tis true,   230
And we did think it writ down in our duty[94]
To let you know of it.

HAMLET
Indeed, indeed, sirs; but this troubles me. –
Hold you the watch tonight?

MARCELLUS and **BARNARDO**
We do, my lord.   235

HAMLET
Armed, say you?

MARCELLUS and **BARNARDO**
Armed, my lord.

HAMLET

From top to toe?

MARCELLUS and **BARNARDO**

My lord, from head to foot.

HAMLET

Then saw you not his face.   **240**

HORATIO

O, yes, my lord, he wore his beaver[95] up.   95. *beaver: visor at the front of the helmet that could be raised*

HAMLET

What looked he? Frowningly?

HORATIO

A countenance[96] more in sorrow than in anger.   96. *countenance:* facial expression

HAMLET

Pale or red?

HORATIO

Nay, very pale.   **245**

HAMLET

And fixed his eyes upon you?

HORATIO

Most constantly.[97]   97. *constantly:* steadily

HAMLET

I would I had been there.

HORATIO

It would have much amazed you.

HAMLET

Very like,[98] very like. Stayed it long?   **250**   98. *Very like:* Most likely

HORATIO

While one with moderate haste might tell a hundred.[99]   99. *While one . . . hundred:* For about the length of time it
                                                                                     would take a person to count to a hundred at a reasonable
                                                                                     speed.

MARCELLUS and **BARNARDO**
Longer, longer.

HORATIO
Not when I saw't.

HAMLET
His beard was grizzled[100] – no?

HORATIO
It was as I have seen it in his life,   **255**
A sable silvered.[101]

HAMLET
I will watch tonight.[102]
Perchance[103] 'twill walk again.

HORATIO
I warrant[104] you it will.

HAMLET
If it assume my noble father's person   **260**
I'll speak to it though hell itself should gape
And bid me hold my peace.[105] I pray you all,
If you have hitherto[106] concealed this sight,
Let it be tenable[107] in your silence still,
And whatsoever else shall hap tonight,   **265**
Give it an understanding but no tongue.
I will requite your loves.[108] So fare you well.
Upon the platform 'twixt eleven and twelve
I'll visit you.

ALL
Our duty to your honour.   **270**

HAMLET
Your love, as mine to you. Farewell.

Exit all but HAMLET

My father's spirit in arms! All is not well.
I doubt[109] some foul play. Would the night were come.
Till then, sit still, my soul. Foul deeds will rise,
Though all the earth o'erwhelm them, to men's eyes.[110]   **275**

Exit

100. *grizzled:* grey

101. *A sable silvered:* black hair with grey running through it

102. *I . . . tonight:* I will join the guard duty tonight.
103. *Perchance:* Perhaps

104. *warrant:* promise or guarantee

105. *I'll speak . . . peace:* Hamlet is determined to speak to the Ghost, even if hell should open wide, like a mouth ready to eat the damned, and order him not to. Hamlet suspects the Ghost may be an evil spirit sent to tempt him. If he speaks to it, he may be damned too.
106. *hitherto:* up to now
107. *tenable:* kept

108. *requite your loves:* return your loyal affection

109. *doubt:* suspect

110. *Foul . . . eyes:* Evil deeds will come to light, no matter how carefully they are hidden.

Act 1 Scene 2
Quotes and Questions

Quotes

A little more than kin and less than kind.

(Hamlet, line 66)

These are Hamlet's first words in the play, and they immediately highlight his dislike of Claudius. He says Claudius is more than a relation because he is his uncle and his stepfather, but there is no kindness in the relationship. The word 'kind' can also mean 'type', so Hamlet may also be playing on this word by hinting that Claudius is not the same type of man as he or his late father.

Hamlet and Claudius are, from the outset, in opposition. Although almost every version of the play prints Hamlet's words here as an aside, some scholars believe Shakespeare originally intended the comment to be spoken directly to Claudius. They argue that the play on words would not make much sense if Hamlet were talking to himself, and that Hamlet wants Claudius to know how he feels. What do you think?

Good Hamlet, cast thy nighted colour off,
And let thine eye look like a friend on Denmark.

(Gertrude, lines 69–70)

Gertrude wants Hamlet to stop mourning so deeply for his late father and to have a better relationship with Claudius than he has had to date.

But I have that within which passeth show;
These but the trappings and the suits of woe.

(Hamlet, lines 87–88)

Hamlet rebukes his mother and says that his dark mourning clothes are merely a superficial outward sign of his deep sorrow.

O that this too too solid flesh would melt,
Thaw, and resolve itself into a dew,
Or that the Everlasting had not fixed
His canon 'gainst self-slaughter! O God! God,
How weary, stale, flat, and unprofitable
Seem to me all the uses of this world!

(Hamlet, lines 131–136)

In some versions of the play, the word 'solid' is replaced by the word 'sallied', meaning sullied or contaminated. Those who favour 'solid' argue that it makes more sense for Hamlet to mourn the fact that his body is too solid to melt, while those who argue for 'sallied' claim that the idea of contamination runs throughout this soliloquy. Either way, these six lines give us an important insight into Hamlet's state of mind. He believes the world to be intolerable and wishes it were not a sin to take his own life. As the play progresses, we will see Hamlet procrastinate when he knows he should act, and descend into madness (whether real or fake is a subject for debate).

> *So excellent a king, that was to this*
> *Hyperion to a satyr*
>
> (Hamlet, lines 141–142)

Hamlet says Claudius cannot possibly compare to the late King, Hamlet's father. Hyperion was the Greek god of the sun and was famously handsome. A satyr is an ugly mythological creature: half-man, half-goat and known for lecherous, lustful behaviour.

> *O most wicked speed, to post*
> *With such dexterity to incestuous sheets!*
>
> (Hamlet, lines 158–159)

Hamlet is disgusted that his mother should have married Claudius so soon after her first husband's death. He calls the marriage incestuous because the two men were brothers. Hamlet's view of women is tainted by his revulsion at his mother's sexuality, and this will cause difficulties in his relationship with Ophelia.

> *Thrift, thrift, Horatio! The funeral baked meats*
> *Did coldly furnish forth the marriage tables.*
>
> (Hamlet, lines 183–184)

Hamlet sarcastically claims the royal family saved money (were thrifty) by using the cold, leftover funeral food to feed the wedding guests. His point is that the wedding happened far too soon after the funeral.

Questions

In each case, support your point with suitable reference to and quotation from the play.

1. What is your first impression of Claudius? Does he appear to be a good ruler?

2. In his opening speech, Claudius tries to convince the court that there is nothing wrong with marrying his brother's wife so soon after the funeral. He does so by combining words such as 'mirth in funeral' and 'defeated joy'. Do you think his speech makes his behaviour acceptable?

3. How do Claudius and Gertrude try to persuade Hamlet to stop mourning his father's death? Do you think their arguments are valid?

4. Having read this scene, what is your impression of Gertrude?

5. Write a summary of Hamlet's soliloquy beginning 'O that this too too solid flesh would melt' (line 131). What do you learn about (a) Hamlet's state of mind and (b) his view of his father?

6. How does Hamlet react when Horatio tells him about the Ghost?

Writing Task

Imagine you are a gossip columnist for a Danish newspaper and were present for the events of this scene, up to Claudius's exit. Write the article that you would submit to your editor. Your article should aim to capture the undercurrents and tensions you witnessed, as well as your impressions of the characters in court. Lay your article out correctly, with a headline, byline, etc. Add illustrations if you like.

Essay Building Blocks

> 'The variety of significant insights that we gain into Hamlet's mind shapes our understanding of his complex character.'

Write a paragraph in response to this statement, supporting your answer with quotation from and reference to Act 1 Scene 2.

A room in Polonius's house

Before he leaves for France, Laertes says goodbye to his sister Ophelia. He is concerned that she has been romantically involved with Hamlet and warns her against compromising her virtue by taking Hamlet's professions of love seriously.

Polonius, Ophelia and Laertes' father, arrives and urges Laertes to hurry aboard his ship, which is ready to sail. He then delays his son by giving him some long-winded and clichéd – if sound – advice.

Alone with Ophelia, Polonius repeats Laertes' warnings about Hamlet and his declarations of love. He tells her not to have any more to do with Hamlet, and Ophelia agrees.

Enter LAERTES and OPHELIA

LAERTES

My necessaries are embarked.[1] Farewell.

And, sister, as the winds give benefit

And convoy is assistant,[2] do not sleep,

But let me hear from you.

OPHELIA

Do you doubt that?   **5**

LAERTES

For Hamlet and the trifling of his favour,

Hold it a fashion and a toy in blood,

A violet in the youth of primy nature,

Forward not permanent, sweet not lasting,

The perfume and suppliance of a minute. No more.[3]   **10**

OPHELIA

No more but so?[4]

LAERTES

Think it no more.

For nature crescent does not grow alone

In thews and bulk, but, as this temple waxes

The inward service of the mind and soul   **15**

Grows wide withal.[5] Perhaps he loves you now,

And now no soil nor cautel doth besmirch

The virtue of his will;[6] but you must fear,

His greatness weighed,[7] his will is not his own,

For he himself is subject to his birth.   **20**

He may not, as unvalued persons do,

Carve for himself, for on his choice depends

The safety and health of the whole state;

And therefore must his choice be circumscribed

Unto the voice and yielding of that body   **25**

Whereof he is the head.[8] Then if he says he loves you,

It fits your wisdom so far to believe it

As he in his particular act and place

May give his saying deed, which is no further

Than the main voice of Denmark goes withal.   **30**

Then weigh what loss your honour may sustain

Handwritten annotation: Her position in society is too low for the future king of Denmark

1. *My . . . embarked:* My luggage is on board.

2. *as . . . assistant:* when the wind is favourable and a ship can sail

3. *For . . . more:* As for Hamlet's affection, which is not serious, view it only as a passing fancy and the sport of youth. It is like a violet which blooms but quickly fades. *Hamlet's affections may be pleasant but they will not last.*

4. *No more but so?:* Is that really all it is?

5. *For . . . withal:* As a person's body grows in strength *(thews)* and size, so the mind grows too. *Hamlet will outgrow Ophelia.*

6. *And . . . will:* At the moment, no fault or deceit stains his goodness

7. *His greatness weighed:* Be aware of his high position in society.

8. *For . . . head:* Hamlet is restricted by his position and cannot choose a wife for himself, as less important people may do. The safety and health of the kingdom depends on his choice. Therefore, he must be guided by the approval of the state that he is to lead.

Act 1

If with too credent ear you list his songs,
Or lose your heart, or your chaste treasure open
To his unmastered importunity.[9]
Fear it, Ophelia, fear it, my dear sister,   35
And keep you in the rear of your affection,
Out of the shot and danger of desire.
The chariest maid is prodigal enough,
If she unmask her beauty to the moon.
Virtue itself scapes not calumnious strokes[10]   40
The canker galls the infants of the spring
Too oft before their buttons be disclosed,[11]
And in the morn and liquid dew of youth
Contagious blastments are most imminent.[12]
Be wary then; best safety lies in fear;   45
Youth to itself rebels, though none else near.[13]

OPHELIA
I shall the effect of this good lesson keep
As watchman to my heart; but, good my brother,
Do not, as some ungracious pastors[14] do,
Show me the steep and thorny way to heaven   50
Whilst like a puffed and reckless libertine
Himself the primrose path of dalliance treads
And recks not his own rede.[15]

LAERTES
O, fear me not.[16]
I stay too long – but here my father comes.   55

Enter POLONIUS

A double blessing is a double grace;
Occasion smiles upon a second leave.[17]

POLONIUS
Yet here, Laertes? Aboard, aboard, for shame!
The wind sits in the shoulder of your sail,
And you are stayed for.[18] There – my blessing with thee,   60
And these few precepts[19] in thy memory
See thou character.[20] Give thy thoughts no tongue,
Nor any unproportioned thought his act.[21]
Be thou familiar but by no means vulgar.

---

9. *Then weigh … importunity:* Consider how your reputation may be damaged if you believe him when you listen to his words of love and lose your heart or the treasure of your virginity to his persistent requests.

10. *The chariest … strokes:* The most careful young woman is reckless if she shows her beauty to the moon. Even the most virtuous person cannot escape slanderous rumours.

11. *The canker … disclosed:* The caterpillar damages young flowers before their buds are opened.

12. *And in … imminent:* In the early morning of life, infectious diseases are most harmful. *In other words, young people are vulnerable to harm.*

13. *Youth … near:* Youth often rebels against what is right, even if there is no temptation.

14. *ungracious pastors:* priests who lack grace or goodness

15. *Show … rede:* Show me the difficult road to heaven while, like a conceited and reckless playboy, he takes the easy road to pleasure and pays no attention to his own advice.

16. *O, fear me not:* Oh, don't worry about me.

17. *A double … leave:* I am doubly blessed by being able to say goodbye a second time.

18. *Yet here … stayed for:* Are you still here, Laertes? Go aboard! The wind is favourable for sailing and those already on-board are waiting for you.
19. *precepts:* principles
20. *character:* inscribe/write *'Character'* is a verb in this instance.
21. *Give … act:* Neither speak nor act rashly.

Those friends thou hast, and their adoption tried,   65

Grapple them to thy soul with hoops of steel,

But do not dull thy palm with entertainment

Of each new-hatched, unfledged comrade.[22] Beware

Of entrance to a quarrel, but being in,

Bear't that the opposed may beware of thee.[23]   70

Give every man thine ear but few thy voice.

Take each man's censure,[24] but reserve thy judgment.

Costly thy habit as thy purse can buy,

But not expressed in fancy; rich, not gaudy;

For the apparel oft proclaims the man,[25]   75

And they in France of the best rank and station

Are of all most select and generous chief in that.[26]

Neither a borrower nor a lender be,

For loan oft loses both itself and friend,

And borrowing dulls the edge of husbandry.[27]   80

This above all – to thine own self be true,

And it must follow, as the night the day,

Thou canst not then be false to any man.

Farewell – my blessing season this in thee![28]

LAERTES

Most humbly do I take my leave, my lord.   85

POLONIUS

The time invites you. Go; your servants tend.[29]

LAERTES

Farewell, Ophelia, and remember well

What I have said to you.

OPHELIA

'Tis in my memory locked,

And you yourself shall keep the key of it.   90

LAERTES

Farewell.

Exit

POLONIUS

What is't, Ophelia, he hath said to you?

22. *Those . . . comrade:* Keep your tried and trusted friends close to you but do not wear out your palm by shaking hands *(making friends)* with every new person you meet.

23. *Beware . . . thee:* Beware of becoming drawn into a quarrel or fight, but if you do, give the man who opposes you reason to fear you.

24. *censure:* judgement

25. *Costly . . . man:* Wear the best clothes you can afford but make sure they are not tasteless or showy because clothes often reveal the wearer's true character.

26. *And they . . . that:* Be guided by the French upper classes, who are known for their taste.

27. *borrowing . . . husbandry:* Borrowing money makes people unlikely to sensibly economise.

28. *my . . . thee!:* Let my blessing help to make this advice grow or mature in your mind.

29. *The time . . . tend:* It is time for you to leave. Go on, your servants are waiting for you.

OPHELIA

So please you, something touching[30] the Lord Hamlet.

POLONIUS

Marry, well bethought.[31]

'Tis told me, he hath very oft of late   95

Given private time to you, and you yourself

Have of your audience been most free and bounteous.[32]

If it be so – as so 'tis put on me,[33]

And that in way of caution – I must tell you

You do not understand yourself so clearly   100

As it behoves[34] my daughter and your honour.

What is between you? Give me up the truth.

OPHELIA

He hath, my lord, of late made many tenders[35]

Of his affection to me.

POLONIUS

Affection, pooh! you speak like a green girl   105

Unsifted in such perilous circumstance.[36]

Do you believe his 'tenders' as you call them?

OPHELIA

I do not know, my lord, what I should think.

POLONIUS

Marry, I'll teach you: think yourself a baby

That you have ta'en these tenders for true pay,   110

Which are not sterling.[37] Tender[38] yourself more dearly,

Or – not to crack the wind of the poor phrase,

Running it thus – you'll tender me a fool.[39]

OPHELIA

My lord, he hath importuned[40] me with love

In honourable fashion –   115

POLONIUS

Ay, fashion you may call it. Go to, go to.

OPHELIA

And hath given countenance[41] to his speech, my lord,

With all the holy vows of heaven.

POLONIUS

Ay, springes to catch woodcocks.[42] I do know,

When the blood burns how prodigal the soul   **120**

Lends the tongue vows. These blazes, daughter,

Giving more light than heat, extinct in both

Even in their promise, as it is a-making,

You must not take for fire.[43] From this time, daughter,

Be somewhat scanter of your maiden presence.   **125**

Set your entreatments at a higher rate

Than a command to parley.[44] For Lord Hamlet,

Believe so much in him, that he is young,

And with a larger tether may he walk

Than may be given you.[45] In few, Ophelia,   **130**

Do not believe his vows, for they are brokers,

Not of that dye which their investments show,

But mere implorators of unholy suits,[46]

Breathing like sanctified and pious bawds

The better to beguile.[47] This is for all –   **135**

I would not, in plain terms, from this time forth

Have you so slander[48] any moment leisure

As to give words or talk with the Lord Hamlet.

Look to't, I charge you. Come your ways.

OPHELIA

I shall obey, my lord.   **140**

Exit

---

42. *springes … woodcocks:* snares to catch woodcocks. *Polonius compares Hamlet's words to snares to catch woodcocks, which were considered to be easily caught birds.*

43. *When … fire:* In the heat of passion, people can say things they do not mean. These passionate impulses are like sudden blazes of fires that do not last and, while they may blaze brightly for a short time, they die out even as promises of love are being given. Do not confuse these blazes of passion with real love.

44. *Be … parley:* Polonius uses military terminology here. He advises Ophelia to be less available to Hamlet's demands to talk to her.

45. *And with … you:* He has a longer leash than you do. *In other words, although he too is restrained, he is freer to behave the way he wants than you are.*

46. *for they … suits:* Hamlet's words are like brokers or middlemen whose words cannot be trusted as they have a hidden agenda.

47. *Breathing … beguile:* Like hypocrites using pious language to charm and deceive

48. *slander:* bring disgrace upon

Act 1 Scene 3
Quotes and Questions

Quotes

For Hamlet and the trifling of his favour,
Hold it a fashion and a toy in the blood

(Laertes, lines 6–7)

Laertes warns his sister that Hamlet does not really love her and that his affection is only a passing fancy. Laertes cares deeply for his sister but he is rather pompous in his manner, lecturing her as if he were a far older, more experienced man of the world than he is. His comments are also insulting, albeit unwittingly. Laertes refuses to believe that Hamlet could truly love Ophelia.

Do not, as some ungracious pastors do,
Show me the steep and thorny way to heaven
Whilst like a puffed and reckless libertine
Himself the primrose path of dalliance treads
And recks not his own rede.

(Ophelia, lines 49–53)

Ophelia shows some spirit when she warns Laertes against hypocrisy. She says that some hypocritical clergymen instruct their congregation on the way to behave if they want to go to heaven, meanwhile they behave like reckless playboys who take the easy road to pleasure and pay no attention to their own advice.

Questions

In each case, support your point with suitable reference to and quotation from the play.

1. Both Laertes and Polonius offer advice to Ophelia in this scene. In each case, discuss the advice they give.

2. How do you imagine Ophelia would feel after hearing this advice from her brother and father?

3. What is your impression of Ophelia from this scene?

4. Do you think this is a serious scene, a comic scene or a mixture of both?

Writing Task

Imagine you are Ophelia. Write a letter to a close friend after the events of this scene. In your letter, outline the advice given to you by Laertes and Polonius, and share your feelings as you reflect on what they said.

Essay Building Blocks

'The play Hamlet *presents us with an overwhelmingly negative view of love.'*

Write a paragraph in response to this statement, supporting your answer with quotation from and reference to Act 1 Scene 3.

The platform

Hamlet waits on the battlements with Horatio and Marcellus for the Ghost to appear. There are loud trumpet and cannon noises offstage as Claudius and his courtiers engage in drunken partying, much to Hamlet's disgust.

The Ghost appears and beckons to Hamlet to follow him. He does so, although Horatio and Marcellus try to prevent him.

Act 1

1. *shrewdly:* bitterly

2. *eager:* sharp

3. *it lacks of:* it is just before

4. *season:* time
5. *held his wont:* was accustomed

6. *takes his rouse:* drinks heavily; carouses

7. *Keeps wassail:* has a drinking party
8. *the swaggering . . . reels:* wild dancing
9. *Rhenish:* German wine from the Rhine region
10. *bray out:* make loud, harsh noises like the braying of a donkey
11. *pledge:* toast

12. *it is . . . observance:* It is a custom which it is more honourable to break than to keep.

13. *This heavy-headed . . . nations:* This drunken partying which leaves the revellers with sore heads leaves us badly disgraced and criticised by other countries.
14. *clepe:* call
15. *Soil our addition:* blacken our reputation

34 Hamlet

Enter HAMLET, HORATIO, and MARCELLUS

HAMLET
The air bites shrewdly,[1] it is very cold.

HORATIO
It is a nipping and an eager[2] air.

HAMLET
What hour now?

HORATIO
I think it lacks of[3] twelve.

HAMLET
No, it is struck.   5

HORATIO
Indeed? I heard it not. Then it draws near the season[4]
Wherein the spirit held his wont[5] to walk.

A flourish of trumpets, and ordnance shot off, within

What does this mean, my lord?

HAMLET
The King doth wake to-night and takes his rouse,[6]
Keeps wassail,[7] and the swaggering upspring reels,[8]   10
And as he drains his draughts of Rhenish[9] down
The kettle-drum and trumpet thus bray out[10]
The triumph of his pledge.[11]

HORATIO
Is it a custom?

HAMLET
Ay, marry is't: 15
But to my mind, though I am native here
And to the manner born, it is a custom
More honoured in the breach than the observance.[12]
This heavy-headed revel east and west
Makes us traduced and taxed of other nations.[13]   20
They clepe[14] us drunkards, and with swinish phrase
Soil our addition;[15] and indeed it takes

From our achievements, though performed at height,[16]

The pith and marrow of our attribute.[17]

So, oft it chances in particular men,   **25**

That for some vicious mole of nature[18] in them –

As, in their birth, wherein they are not guilty,

Since nature cannot choose his origin,

By the o'ergrowth of some complexion,[19]

Oft breaking down the pales and forts[20] of reason,   **30**

Or by some habit that too much o'er-leavens

The form of plausive manners[21] – that these men,

Carrying, I say, the stamp of one defect,

Being nature's livery or fortune's star,[22]

Their virtues else be they as pure as grace,   **35**

As infinite as man may undergo,

Shall in the general censure take corruption

From that particular fault. The dram of evil

Doth all the noble substance over-daub

To his own scandal.[23]   **40**

HORATIO

Look, my lord, it comes!

Enter GHOST

HAMLET

Angels and ministers of grace defend us!

Be thou a spirit of health or goblin damned,[24]

Bring with thee airs from heaven or blasts from hell,

Be thy intents wicked or charitable,   **45**

Thou com'st in such a questionable shape

That I will speak to thee: I'll call thee Hamlet,

King, father, royal Dane. O answer me!

Let me not burst in ignorance, but tell

Why thy canonized bones, hearsed in death,   **50**

Have burst their cerements, why the sepulchre

Wherein we saw thee quietly inurned

Hath oped his ponderous and marble jaws,

To cast thee up again.[25] What may this mean,

That thou, dead corpse, again in complete steel,[26]   **55**

Revisits thus the glimpses of the moon,

Making night hideous, and we fools of nature[27]

So horridly to shake our disposition[28]

---

16. *though … height:* though outstanding

17. *The pith … attribute:* the core or centre of our merits

18. *vicious … nature:* character flaw

19. *o'ergrowth … complexion:* excess of another characteristic

20. *pales and forts:* fences and forts

21. *Or by … manners:* They may have some habit that corrupts their otherwise pleasing behaviour.

22. *Being … star:* A fault of nature or the result of chance

23. *The dram … scandal:* A small measure of evil can ruin a man's noble nature and give him a bad name.

24. *Be thou … damned:* Whether you are a good spirit or a demon from hell

25. *Why … again:* Why your blessed bones, which were buried, have burst from their burial clothes and why the tomb in which we saw you peacefully interred has opened its heavy marble jaws to throw you up again.

26. *complete steel:* full armour

27. *fools of nature:* at the mercy of nature

28. *disposition:* composure

With thoughts beyond the reaches of our souls?
Say, why is this? Wherefore? What should we do? 60

GHOST beckons HAMLET

HORATIO
It beckons you to go away with it
As if it some impartment did desire
To you alone.²⁹

MARCELLUS
Look with what courteous action
It waves you to a more removed ground.³⁰ 65
But do not go with it.

HORATIO
No, by no means.

HAMLET
It will not speak. Then I will follow it.

HORATIO
Do not, my lord.

HAMLET
Why, what should be the fear? 70
I do not set my life in a pin's fee,³¹
And for my soul, what can it do to that,
Being a thing immortal as itself?
It waves me forth again. I'll follow it.

HORATIO
What if it tempt you toward the flood, my lord, 75
Or to the dreadful summit of the cliff
That beetles³² o'er his base into the sea,
And there assume some other horrible form
Which might deprive your sovereignty of reason³³
And draw you into madness? Think of it. 80
The very place puts toys of desperation³⁴
Without more motive, into every brain
That looks so many fathoms to the sea
And hears it roar beneath.

29. *As if ... alone:* As if it wants to tell you something privately

30. *removed ground:* remote spot

31. *in a pin's fee:* the worth of a pin

32. *beetles:* projects or juts out

33. *your sovereignty of reason:* your ability to reason

34. *toys of desperation:* desperate or suicidal thoughts

HAMLET

It waves me still.   **85**

Go on, I'll follow thee.

MARCELLUS

You shall not go, my lord.

HAMLET

Hold off your hand.

HORATIO

Be ruled. You shall not go.

HAMLET

My fate cries out,   **90**

And makes each petty artere[35] in this body

As hardy as the Nemean lion's[36] nerve.

Still am I called. Unhand me,[37] gentlemen.

By heaven, I'll make a ghost of him that lets[38] me.

I say, away! Go on, I'll follow thee.   **95**

Exit GHOST and HAMLET

HORATIO

He waxes[39] desperate with imagination.

MARCELLUS

Let's follow. 'Tis not fit thus to obey him.

HORATIO

Have after.[40] To what issue will this come?

MARCELLUS

Something is rotten in the state of Denmark.[41]

HORATIO

Heaven will direct it.[42]   **100**

MARCELLUS

Nay, let's follow him.

Exit

35. *petty artere:* small artery

36. *Nemean lion:* A mythological beast that was killed by Hercules

37. *Unhand me:* Take your hands off me.

38. *lets:* hinders

39. *waxes:* grows

40. *Have after:* Let's follow him.

41. *Something . . . Denmark:* This quote is often attributed to Hamlet instead of Marcellus. Be sure not to make this mistake!

42. *Heaven will direct it:* Heaven will decide the outcome.

Quotes

> *it is a custom*
> *More honoured in the breach than the observance.*
> *This heavy-headed revel east and west*
> *Makes us traduced and taxed of other nations.*
> (Hamlet, lines 17–20)

Hamlet says the custom of firing cannon and sounding of trumpets to mark the King's drinking is a tradition it would be more honourable to break than observe. He believes the drunken partying which leaves the revellers with sore heads disgraces Denmark and leads to other countries criticising them. Hamlet's disgust shows his moral superiority: unlike Claudius, he has no time for drunken behaviour. Again, the two men are seen to be in opposition. Hamlet's concern for Denmark's reputation shows his royal blood and his potential to rule.

> *The dram of evil*
> *Doth all the noble substance over-daub*
> *To his own scandal.*
> (Hamlet, lines 38–40)

A small measure of evil can ruin a man's noble nature and give him a bad name. This philosophical reflection is important: a tragic hero's flaw can bring about his downfall. Hamlet may be subconsciously analysing himself at the same time as he analyses his country.

> *Be thou a spirit of health or goblin damned*
> (Hamlet, line 43)

Hamlet indicates that the Ghost originates in either heaven or in hell.

> *My fate cries out,*
> *And makes each petty artere in this body*
> *As hardy as the Nemean lion's nerve.*
> (Hamlet, lines 90–92)

Hamlet says the arteries in his body will carry his determination and strength to every part of him, just as the Nemean lion's did. The Nemean lion was a huge beast, killed by Hercules. Hamlet believes it is his fate to do as the Ghost asks, and shows courage in following it, despite the other men's warnings. However, we should also remember that Hamlet has already claimed to place little value on his own life and is in a desperate state.

> *Something is rotten in the state of Denmark.*
> (Marcellus, line 99)

Marcellus believes the appearance of the Ghost is a bad omen and a symbol of the corruption in the country.

Questions

In each case, support your point with suitable reference to and quotation from the play.

1. Why does Hamlet disapprove of Claudius's behaviour?

2. What are Hamlet's views of good and evil?

3. Describe Hamlet's reaction to meeting the Ghost for the first time.

4. Why does Marcellus believe that 'Something is rotten in the state of Denmark'?

Writing Task

If you were directing this scene for a school production of the play, what instructions would you give the actors playing each of the characters? What choices would you make in terms of setting, sound, lighting and costume? Explain your choices with reference to and quotation from the scene.

Essay Building Blocks

'Uncertainty, which features constantly in Shakespeare's play Hamlet, adds significantly to the dramatic impact of the play.'

Write a paragraph in response to this statement, supporting your answer with quotation from and reference to Act 1 Scene 4.

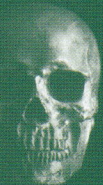

Act 1
Scene 5

Another part of the platform

The Ghost leads Hamlet to a secluded spot and reveals that he is indeed the spirit of the old king, doomed to suffer in Purgatory by day and walk the earth by night until he has atoned for his sins. The Ghost tells Hamlet that he was murdered by Claudius and that he expects Hamlet to avenge his death.

Hamlet is appalled by what the Ghost has to say and vows to take his revenge on Claudius.

Horatio and Marcellus arrive but Hamlet will not tell them what has happened. He makes the two men swear not to tell anyone about the Ghost's appearance. He also warns them that he may appear to be mad in the near future, but he will only be pretending to be so. He asks them not to show by word or deed that they know that his 'antic disposition' is an act.

Enter GHOST and HAMLET

HAMLET

Where wilt thou lead me? Speak. I'll go no further.

GHOST

Mark me.[1]

1. *Mark me:* Pay attention to me.

HAMLET

I will.

GHOST

My hour is almost come,

When I to sulphurous and tormenting flames[2]   5

Must render up myself.[3]

2. *sulphurous and tormenting flames:* the fiery and tormenting flames of purgatory
3. *Must render up myself:* Must return

HAMLET

Alas, poor ghost!

GHOST

Pity me not, but lend thy serious hearing

To what I shall unfold.

HAMLET

Speak, I am bound to hear.[4]   10

4. *I am bound to hear:* Hamlet has a duty to listen to what the Ghost has to say. To be 'bound' in this case means to be obligated to do what is required of him.

GHOST

So art thou to revenge when thou shalt hear.[5]

5. *So art … hear:* When you hear what I have to say, you will have a duty to avenge my death.

HAMLET

What?

GHOST

I am thy father's spirit,

Doomed for a certain term to walk the night,

And for the day confined to fast in fires   15

Till the foul crimes done in my days of nature[6]

Are burnt and purged away. But that I am forbid

To tell the secrets of my prison-house

I could a tale unfold whose lightest word

Would harrow[7] up thy soul, freeze thy young blood,   20

Make thy two eyes like stars start from their spheres,

Thy knotted and combined locks to part,

6. *my days of nature:* the time when I was alive

7. *harrow:* tear or rip

Act 1

Act 1

And each particular hair to stand on end
Like quills upon the fretful porpentine:[8]
But this eternal blazon[9] must not be   25
To ears of flesh and blood. List,[10] Hamlet, list, O list!
If thou didst ever thy dear father love –

HAMLET
O God!

GHOST
Revenge his foul and most unnatural murder.

HAMLET
Murder?   30

GHOST
Murder most foul, as in the best it is,
But this most foul, strange and unnatural.[11]

HAMLET
Haste me to know't, that I, with wings as swift
As meditation or the thoughts of love[12]
May sweep to my revenge.   35

GHOST
I find thee apt,[13]
And duller shouldst thou be than the fat weed
That rots itself in ease on Lethe wharf,
Wouldst thou not stir in this.[14] Now, Hamlet, hear.
'Tis given out[15] that, sleeping in mine orchard,   40
A serpent stung me. So the whole ear of Denmark
Is by a forged process[16] of my death
Rankly abused[17] But know, thou noble youth,
The serpent that did sting thy father's life
Now wears his crown.   45

HAMLET
O my prophetic soul! Mine uncle?

GHOST
Ay, that incestuous,[18] that adulterate beast,
With witchcraft of his wit, with traitorous gifts –
O wicked wit and gifts, that have the power

So to seduce! – won to his shameful lust 50

The will of my most seeming-virtuous queen.

O Hamlet, what a falling-off[19] was there! –

19. *falling-off:* decline in her standards

From me, whose love was of that dignity

That it went hand-in-hand even with the vow

I made to her in marriage, and to decline[20] 55

20. *decline:* lower herself

Upon a wretch whose natural gifts were poor

To those of mine.

But virtue, as it never will be moved,

Though lewdness court it in a shape of heaven,[21]

21. *But virtue . . . heaven:* A truly virtuous person will never be tempted, even if the lustful tempter came in the shape of an angel.

So lust, though to a radiant angel linked, 60

Will sate itself in a celestial bed,

And prey on garbage.[22]

22. *So lust . . . garbage:* However, a lustful person *(Gertrude)* even if married to an angelically virtuous person *(Old Hamlet)* will satisfy their sexual appetite in the marriage bed and then turn to someone disgustingly low *(Claudius).*

But soft, methinks I scent the morning air.

Brief let me be. Sleeping within mine orchard,

My custom always in the afternoon, 65

Upon my secure hour[23] thy uncle stole

23. *secure hour:* time to relax peacefully

With juice of cursed hebenon[24] in a vial,

24. *hebenon: a poisonous plant*

And in the porches of my ears[25] did pour

25. *porches of my ears:* the openings of my ears

The leperous distilment,[26] whose effect

26. *The leperous distilment:* A distilled liquid that caused sores like leprosy to appear on the body

Holds such an enmity with blood of man 70

That swift as quicksilver[27] it courses through

27. *quicksilver:* mercury

The natural gates and alleys[28] of the body,

28. *gates and alleys:* veins

And with a sudden vigour it doth posset

And curd, like eager droppings into milk,

The thin and wholesome blood.[29] So did it mine; 75

29. *And with . . . blood:* And suddenly it curdled the blood as sour drops would curdle milk.

And a most instant tetter[30] barked about,[31]

30. *tetter:* scabs
31. *barked about:* encrusted

Most lazar-like,[32] with vile and loathsome crust,

32. *lazar-like:* like leprosy

All my smooth body.

Thus was I, sleeping, by a brother's hand

Of life, of crown, of queen at once dispatched,[33] 80

33. *dispatched:* deprived

Cut off even in the blossoms of my sin,[34]

34. *the blossoms of my sin:* when I was full of sin *The old king had not had time to pray and repent.*

Unhouseled, disappointed, unaneled,

No reckoning made, but sent to my account[35]

With all my imperfections on my head.

35. *Unhouseled . . . account:* Without receiving communion *(Unhouseled)* or being prepared *(disappointed)* or being anointed in the last rites *(unaneled)*, I had no chance to settle my accounts with God so I died with all my sins unforgiven.

O horrible. O horrible, most horrible! 85

If thou hast nature in thee, bear it not.

Let not the royal bed of Denmark be

A couch for luxury and damned incest.

But howsoever thou pursuest this act,

Taint not thy mind, nor let thy soul contrive 90

Against thy mother aught.[36] Leave her to heaven,

36. *Taint . . . aught:* Do not turn against or scheme against your mother.

And to those thorns that in her bosom lodge

37. *matin:* morning

38. *'gins . . . fire:* begins to let his *(the glow-worm's)* ineffective light fade

39. *couple:* include

40. *while . . . globe:* while my distracted head can retain any memory

41. *trivial fond:* foolish and unimportant

42. *saws:* proverbs and wise sayings

43. *pernicious:* dangerous, deadly

44. *tables:* notebook
45. *meet . . . down:* it is appropriate that I make a note of it

46. *there you are:* Hamlet has finished writing his note.
47. *Now to my word:* now to the promise I have made

To prick and sting her. Fare thee well at once.
The glow-worm shows the matin[37] to be near,
And 'gins to pale his uneffectual fire.[38]   95
Adieu, adieu, Hamlet. Remember me.

Exit

HAMLET
O all you host of heaven! O earth! What else?
And shall I couple[39] hell? O fie! Hold, hold, my heart,
And you, my sinews, grow not instant old,
But bear me stiffly up. Remember thee?   100
Ay, thou poor ghost, while memory holds a seat
In this distracted globe.[40] Remember thee?
Yea, from the table of my memory
I'll wipe away all trivial fond[41] records,
All saws[42] of books, all forms, all pressures past,   105
That youth and observation copied there,
And thy commandment all alone shall live
Within the book and volume of my brain
Unmixed with baser matter. Yes, yes, by heaven.
O most pernicious[43] woman!   110
O villain, villain, smiling, damned villain!
My tables[44] – meet it is I set it down[45]
That one may smile and smile and be a villain.
At least I'm sure it may be so in Denmark.
[*Writing*] So, uncle, there you are.[46] Now to my word:[47]   115
It is 'Adieu, adieu, remember me'.
I have sworn it.

MARCELLUS and **HORATIO**
[*Within*] My lord, my lord.

MARCELLUS
[*Within*] Lord Hamlet!

HORATIO

[Within] Heaven secure him.   120

HAMLET

So be it!

HORATIO

[Within] Hillo, ho, ho, my lord.

HAMLET

Hillo, ho, ho, boy; come, bird, come.[48]

Enter HORATIO and MARCELLUS

MARCELLUS

How is't, my noble lord?

HORATIO

What news, my lord?   125

HAMLET

O wonderful!

HORATIO

Good my lord, tell it.

HAMLET

No, you'll reveal it.

HORATIO

Not I, my lord, by heaven.

MARCELLUS

Nor I, my lord.   130

HAMLET

How say you then, would heart of man once think it?[49]
But you'll be secret?

HORATIO and **MARCELLUS**

Ay, by heaven, my lord.

HAMLET

There's ne'er a villain dwelling in all Denmark
But he's an arrant knave.[50]   135

48. *come, bird, come:* They have been calling one another as a falconer might call a bird.

49. *would . . . it?:* Who would ever have imagined such a thing could happen?

50. *There's . . . knave:* There isn't a villain living in all of Denmark who isn't a downright scoundrel.

HORATIO

There needs no ghost, my lord, come from the grave

To tell us this.

HAMLET

Why, right, you are in the right;

And so without more circumstance[51] at all

I hold it fit that we shake hands and part,   **140**

You as your business and desire shall point you –

For every man has business and desire,

Such as it is – and for mine own poor part,

Look you, I'll go pray.

HORATIO

These are but wild and whirling words,[52] my lord.   **145**

excitable & erratic nervous
& unpredicted from the outset

HAMLET

I'm sorry they offend you, heartily,

Yes faith, heartily.

HORATIO

There's no offence, my lord.

HAMLET

Yes, by Saint Patrick,[53] but there is, Horatio,

And much offence, too. Touching[54] this vision here,   **150**

It is an honest ghost, that let me tell you.

For your desire to know what is between us,

O'ermaster't as you may.[55] And now, good friends,

As you are friends, scholars and soldiers,

Give me one poor request.   **155**

HORATIO

What is't, my lord? We will.

HAMLET

Never make known what you have seen tonight.

HORATIO and **MARCELLUS**

My lord, we will not.

HAMLET

Nay, but swear't.

51. *circumstance:* detail

52. *wild and whirling words:* wildly excited, hysterical words

53. *Saint Patrick:* Saint Patrick was believed to be the keeper of purgatory.
54. *Touching:* concerning/in relation to

55. *For … may:* As for your desire to know what happened between the Ghost and me, do your best to overcome it.

HORATIO

In faith, my lord, not I.   **160**

MARCELLUS

Nor I, my lord, in faith.

HAMLET

Upon my sword.

MARCELLUS

We have sworn, my lord, already.

HAMLET

Indeed, upon my sword,[56] indeed.

56. *upon my sword: Swearing on a sword was taken very seriously because the hilt of the sword forms a crucifix.*

GHOST

[GHOST calls from beneath the stage] Swear.   **165**

HAMLET

Ah ha, boy, say'st thou so? Art thou there, truepenny?[57] –
Come on. You hear this fellow in the cellarage.
Consent to swear.

57. *truepenny: a mining term meaning 'honest man'*

HORATIO

Propose the oath, my lord.

HAMLET

Never to speak of this that you have seen,   **170**
Swear by my sword.

GHOST

[Beneath] Swear.

HAMLET

Hic et ubique?[58] then we'll shift our ground –
Come hither, gentlemen,
And lay your hands again upon my sword.   **175**
Never to speak of this that you have heard,
Swear by my sword.

58. *Hic et ubique?: Latin, meaning 'Here and everywhere'*

GHOST

[Beneath] Swear.

59. *pioneer:* miner. *Hamlet compares the Ghost to a mole or a miner as he appears to be beneath them no matter where they stand.*

HAMLET

Well said, old mole. Canst work i' th' earth so fast?

A worthy pioneer.[59] Once more remove, good friends.   **180**

HORATIO

O day and night, but this is wondrous strange!

HAMLET

And therefore as a stranger give it welcome.

There are more things in heaven and earth, Horatio,

Than are dreamt of in your philosophy. But come;

60. *Here as before:* swear once again, as you did before

Here as before,[60] never, so help you mercy,   **185**

How strange or odd soe'er I bear myself –

As I perchance hereafter shall think meet

To put an antic disposition on[61] –   *excuse for his future actions?.*

coping mechanism to verify his story

That you at such times seeing me, never shall,   *coping mechanism for his grief.*

masks of madness gives

With arms encumbered[62] thus, or this headshake,   **190**

him more

Or by pronouncing of some doubtful[63] phrase

As 'Well, we know,' or 'We could an if we would',

Or 'If we list[64] to speak', or 'There be, an if they might',

Or such ambiguous giving out, to note

That you know aught of me – this not to do,   **195**

So grace and mercy at your most need help you, swear.

61. *How strange ... disposition on:* However oddly I behave, as I may from now on believe it appropriate to pretend to be mad.

62. *encumbered:* folded

63. *doubtful:* unclear

64. *list:* wished

GHOST

[Beneath] Swear.

HAMLET

Rest, rest, perturbed[65] spirit!

65. *perturbed:* uneasy, agitated

They swear

So, gentlemen,

With all my love I do commend me to you,   **200**

And what so poor a man as Hamlet is

May do, to express his love and friending to you,

God willing, shall not lack. Let us go in together,

And still your fingers on your lips, I pray.

The time is out of joint.[66] O cursed spite[67]   **205**

That ever I was born to set it right!

Nay, come, let's go together.

66. *The time is out of joint:* Denmark is in disorder at this time. *Hamlet compares it to a dislocated joint that he will have to heal or 'set'.*

67. *cursed spite:* fate, ill-luck *Hamlet does not want this responsibility.*

Exit

Quotes

> If thou didst ever thy dear father love [...]
> Revenge his foul and most unnatural murder.
>
> (Ghost, line 27/line 29)

The Ghost urges Hamlet to avenge his terrible, unnatural murder.

> Haste me to know't, that I with wings as swift
> As meditation or the thoughts of love
> May sweep to my revenge.
>
> (Hamlet, lines 33–35)

Hamlet is eager to know who is responsible for his father's death so he can swiftly take revenge on them. However, his simile comparing vengeance to 'meditation or the thoughts of love' is unusual in the circumstances. Neither meditation nor love are associated with swift and bloody violence.

> The serpent that did sting thy father's life
> Now wears his crown.
>
> (Ghost, lines 44–45)

The Ghost tells Hamlet that he was killed by Claudius.

> Ay, that incestuous, that adulterate beast,
> With witchcraft of his wit, with traitorous gifts –
> O wicked wit and gifts, that have the power
> So to seduce! – won to his shameful lust
> The will of my most seeming-virtuous queen.
>
> (Ghost, lines 47–51)

The Ghost calls Claudius incestuous because he married his late brother's widow, and condemns Claudius for seducing Gertrude. However, Gertrude does not escape the Ghost's censure either: he suggests her virtue is false and that she is not what she appears.

> Thus was I, sleeping, by a brother's hand
> Of life, of crown, of queen at once dispatched,
> Cut off even in the blossoms of my sin
>
> (Ghost, lines 79–81)

The Ghost tells Hamlet that he lost his life, his crown and his wife in one fell swoop. Because Claudius killed him while he was sleeping, thereby denying him the chance to pray, Old Hamlet must remain in Purgatory until his sins are purged.

> O most pernicious woman!
> O villain, villain, smiling, damned villain!
> My tables – meet it is I set it down
> That one may smile and smile and be a villain.
>
> (Hamlet, lines 110–113)

Hamlet rages against his mother and uncle, calling Gertrude a dangerous woman and Claudius a villain. He vows he will make revenge his first priority and, taking out his notebook, jots down what the Ghost has said. Reaching for his notebook rather than his sword reveals Hamlet as a man more suited to philosophy and scholarly pursuits than the exacting of immediate and bloody revenge.

> The time is out of joint. O cursed spite
> That ever I was born to set it right!
>
> (Hamlet, lines 205–206)

Denmark is in disorder at this time. Hamlet compares the country to a dislocated joint that he will have to heal or 'set'. He calls his fate a 'cursed spite' because he does not want this responsibility.

Questions

In each case, support your point with suitable reference to and quotation from the play.

1. Describe the murder of Old Hamlet.

2. Why is the Ghost doomed to suffer in the 'sulphurous and tormenting flames'?

3. How does the Ghost describe Gertrude's behaviour and how does he want Hamlet to treat her?

4. What is Hamlet's view of both Claudius and Gertrude in this scene?

5. Describe Hamlet's various reactions to what the Ghost tells him.

6. Why do you think Hamlet decides to 'put on an antic disposition'? Are there any moments in this scene in which Hamlet's behaviour seems close to real madness?

Writing Task

Imagine you are Hamlet. Write the diary entry you might make after the events of this scene.

Essay Building Blocks

'The ghost in the play Hamlet *has great dramatic significance.'*

Write a paragraph in response to this statement, supporting your answer with quotation from and reference to Act 1 Scene 5.

A room in Polonius's house

Polonius tells his servant Reynaldo to visit Laertes in Paris and give him money and letters from his father. He instructs Reynaldo to spy on Laertes to see if he can find out if he has been partying, gambling or visiting prostitutes.

Reynaldo leaves and Ophelia enters. She is distressed because she has just had a visit from Hamlet, who was behaving very oddly. His clothes were dishevelled and he did not speak but merely stared at her in a strange way. Polonius is convinced that Hamlet's madness is a result of Ophelia's rejection of him and he rushes straight to the King to tell him this.

Act 2

1. *notes:* letters

2. *Marry:* This is an abbreviation of 'By Mary', meaning Mary, the mother of Jesus.
3. *Danskers:* Danish people

4. *keep:* stay

5. *encompassment:* talking around the topic; not asking directly
6. *drift:* general direction

7. *come you . . . it:* This method will bring you closer to the facts than direct questions could.
8. *Take . . . him:* Pretend you don't know him very well.

9. *mark:* pay attention to; take note of

10. *and there . . . please:* and give whatever false reports of him you like
11. *rank:* awful, foul

12. *wanton:* reckless
13. *usual slips:* typical mistakes

14. *gaming:* gambling

Enter POLONIUS and REYNALDO

POLONIUS
Give him this money and these notes,[1] Reynaldo.

REYNALDO
I will, my lord.

POLONIUS
You shall do marvellous wisely, good Reynaldo,
Before you visit him to make inquire
Of his behaviour.   5

REYNALDO
My lord, I did intend it.

POLONIUS
Marry[2], well said, very well said. Look you, sir,
Inquire me first what Danskers[3] are in Paris,
And how, and who, what means, and where they keep,[4]
What company, at what expense; and finding   10
By this encompassment[5] and drift[6] of question
That they do know my son, come you more nearer
Than your particular demands will touch it.[7]
Take you, as 'twere, some distant knowledge of him,[8]
As thus: 'I know his father and his friends,   15
And in part him' – do you mark[9] this, Reynaldo?

REYNALDO
Ay, very well, my lord.

POLONIUS
'And in part him, but', you may say, 'not well,
But, if't be he I mean, he's very wild,
Addicted so and so'; and there put on him   20
What forgeries you please[10] – marry, none so rank[11]
As may dishonour him, take heed of that –
But, sir, such wanton,[12] wild, and usual slips[13]
As are companions noted and most known
To youth and liberty.   25

REYNALDO
As gaming,[14] my lord?

POLONIUS

Ay, or drinking, fencing, swearing, quarrelling,

Drabbing[15] – you may go so far.

15. *drabbing:* associating with prostitutes

REYNALDO

My lord, that would dishonour him.

POLONIUS

Faith, no, as you may season it in the charge[16]   **30**

You must not put another scandal on him,

That he is open to incontinency.[17]

That's not my meaning – but breathe his faults so quaintly[18]

That they may seem the taints of liberty,

The flash and outbreak of a fiery mind,   **35**

A savageness in unreclaimed blood,[19]

Of general assault.[20]

16. *you may . . . charge:* you can make the accusation in such a way as to make it less insulting

17. *incontinency:* promiscuity

18. *quaintly:* delicately

19. *unreclaimed blood:* passionate, high spirits

20. *general assault:* affecting everyone

REYNALDO

But, my good lord –

POLONIUS

Wherefore[21] should you do this?

21. *Wherefore:* why

REYNALDO

Ay, my lord,   **40**

I would know that.

POLONIUS

Marry, sir, here's my drift,

And I believe, it is a fetch of wit:[22]

You laying these slight sullies[23] on my son,

As 'twere a thing a little soiled in the working,[24]   **45**

Mark you, your party in converse,[25] him you would sound,[26]

Having ever seen in the prenominate crimes[27]

The youth you breathe of guilty, be assured

He closes with you in this consequence:[28]

'Good sir', or so, or 'friend', or 'gentleman',   **50**

According to the phrase or the addition[29]

Of man and country.

22. *Marry . . . a fetch of wit:* By Mary, here is what I am getting at, and I think it is a justifiable trick.

23. *sullies:* things which may damage his reputation; insults or criticisms

24. *a thing . . . working:* something that has been corrupted through use

25. *your party in converse:* the person with whom you are conversing or talking

26. *him you would sound:* the person you wish to sound out about Laertes

27. *prenominate crimes:* previously named misbehaviours

28. *closes . . . consequence:* takes you into his confidence in the following manner

29. *addition:* title

REYNALDO

Very good, my lord.

30. *By the mass:* a mild oath

31. *o'ertook in 's rouse:* overcome by alcohol

32. *Videlicet:* Latin, meaning 'that is to say'

33. *Your bait . . . truth:* Your lie will act as bait and catch the truth. *Polonius is punning here. 'Carp' can mean a type of fish or a criticism.*

34. *windlasses:* approaching indirectly in order to snare or trap *hunting term*

35. *assays of bias:* indirect approaches *bowling term: in lawn bowling, there is a bias on one side of the bowl so it must be bowled in a curved manner in order to hit the jack*

36. *Observe his inclination in yourself:* Judge him yourself.

37. *ply:* play

POLONIUS
And then, sir, does he this – He does – what was I about
to say? By the mass,[30] I was about to say something.   **55**
Where did I leave?

REYNALDO
At 'closes in the consequence', at 'friend, or so',
and 'gentleman'.

POLONIUS
At 'closes in the consequence' – ay, marry;
He closes thus: 'I know the gentleman,   **60**
I saw him yesterday' – or t'other day,
Or then, or then – with such and such, and, as you say,
There was a gaming, there o'ertook in 's rouse;[31]
'There falling out at tennis', or perchance,
'I saw him enter such a house of sale',   **65**
Videlicet,[32] a brothel, or so forth.
See you now,
Your bait of falsehood takes this carp of truth;[33]
And thus do we of wisdom and of reach
With windlasses[34] and with assays of bias[35]   **70**
By indirections find directions out.
So, by my former lecture and advice,
Shall you my son. You have me, have you not?

REYNALDO
My lord, I have.

POLONIUS
God be wi' you. Fare you well.   **75**

REYNALDO
Good, my lord.

POLONIUS
Observe his inclination in yourself.[36]

REYNALDO
I shall, my lord.

POLONIUS
And let him ply[37] his music.

REYNALDO

Well, my lord.   80

POLONIUS

Farewell!

Exit REYNALDO
Enter OPHELIA

How now, Ophelia, what's the matter?

OPHELIA

Alas, my lord, I have been so affrighted.[38]   38. *affrighted:* frightened

POLONIUS

With what, in the name of God?

OPHELIA

My lord, as I was sewing in my closet,[39]   85   39. *closet:* private sitting room
Lord Hamlet, with his doublet all unbraced,[40]   40. *doublet all unbraced:* short jacket, unfastened
No hat upon his head, his stockings fouled,[41]   41. *fouled:* dirtied
Ungartered, and down-gyved to his ankle,[42]   42. *Ungartered . . . ankle:* Without garters to hold the stockings
Pale as his shirt, his knees knocking each other,   up they had fallen to his ankles like gyves *chains or*
And with a look so piteous in purport[43]   90   *manacles used to restrain prisoners, typically placed around*
As if he had been loosed out of hell   *the ankles*
To speak of horrors, he comes before me.   43. *purport:* meaning

POLONIUS

Mad for thy love?

OPHELIA

My lord, I do not know,
But truly I do fear it.   95

POLONIUS

What said he?

OPHELIA

He took me by the wrist and held me hard,
Then goes he to the length of all his arm,[44]   44. *Then . . . arm:* Then he holds me at arm's length.
And with his other hand thus o'er his brow
He falls to such perusal[45] of my face   100   45. *perusal:* examination or study

46. *profound:* deep
47. *bulk:* body

48. *And to . . . me:* And he kept his eyes fixed on me until the last moment.

49. *ecstasy:* madness

50. *property:* quality/nature
51. *fordoes:* destroys

52. *As oft . . . natures:* Just as often as other passions cause us to behave recklessly

53. *repel:* reject, send back

54. *I am . . . him:* I am sorry I did not observe him more closely and with better judgement.
55. *I feared . . . thee:* I was afraid he was only playing around and meant to ruin you.
56. *beshrew my jealousy:* damn my suspicions

57. *it is . . . discretion:* It is as normal for old people to be overly suspicious as it is for young people to be reckless.

58. *This . . . love:* This must be told. If this love remains hidden it may cause more pain than the hatred it would cause by being revealed.

As he would draw it. Long stayed he so.
At last, a little shaking of mine arm,
And thrice his head thus waving up and down,
He raised a sigh so piteous and profound[46]
That it did seem to shatter all his bulk[47]   105
And end his being. That done, he lets me go,
And, with his head over his shoulder turned,
He seemed to find his way without his eyes,
For out o' doors he went without their help,
And to the last bended their light on me.[48]   110

POLONIUS

Come, go with me. I will go seek the King.
This is the very ecstasy[49] of love,
Whose violent property[50] fordoes[51] itself
And leads the will to desperate undertakings
As oft as any passion under heaven   115
That does afflict our natures.[52] I am sorry –
What, have you given him any hard words of late?

OPHELIA

No, my good lord, but, as you did command
I did repel[53] his letters and denied
His access to me.   120

POLONIUS

That hath made him mad.
I am sorry that with better heed and judgment
I had not quoted him.[54] I feared he did but trifle,
And meant to wreck thee.[55]
But beshrew my jealousy![56] By heaven, it is as proper   125
   to our age
To cast beyond ourselves in our opinions
As it is common for the younger sort
To lack discretion.[57] Come, go we to the King:
This must be known, which, being kept close, might move
More grief to hide than hate to utter love.[58]   130

Exit

[handwritten: ↗ feel there is no choice]

Act 2 Scene 1
Quotes and Questions

Quotes

And thus do we of wisdom and of reach,
With windlasses and with assays of bias
By indirections find directions out.

(Polonius, lines 69–71)

Polonius tells Reynaldo that wisdom and knowledge are gained not by directly asking questions but by approaching the topic indirectly. Polonius earlier advised Laertes to always be true to himself, but now he, Polonius, is engaged in devious and underhanded behaviour. Polonius's hypocrisy, unscrupulous behaviour and deceitfulness is a reflection of the corruption and intrigue in the Danish court.

And with a look so piteous in purport
As if he had been loosed out of hell
To speak of horrors

(Ophelia, lines 90–92)

Ophelia was deeply shocked by Hamlet's appearance. She says he looked as if he had been to hell and back. It is not clear if Hamlet was truly in a distressed state or if he was simply pretending to be mad, knowing that news of his behaviour would reach Polonius.

This is the very ecstasy of love,
Whose violent property fordoes itself

(Polonius, lines 112–113)

Polonius believes Hamlet to be driven mad by love, and in such a state of heightened emotion that he may do something desperate.

Questions

In each case, support your point with suitable reference to and quotation from the play.

1. What instructions does Polonius give to Reynaldo?

2. Compare the instructions that Polonius gives to Reynaldo to Polonius's advice to Laertes in Act 1 Scene 3.

3. In this scene, we learn that Ophelia has obeyed her father's instructions to return Hamlet's letters unopened and to refuse to see him. Do you think she was right to do so?

4. How does Hamlet behave when he visits Ophelia?

5. Do you agree with Polonius when he says that Hamlet's behaviour is 'the very ecstasy of love'?

6. Do you think Ophelia truly loves Hamlet?

7. Does Polonius show real concern for Ophelia in this scene?

Writing Task

Imagine that you are a friend of Ophelia and she has come to you, not Polonius, with her tale of Hamlet's behaviour. In modern English, write the dialogue that might take place between you. Your half of the dialogue should reflect your interpretation of Hamlet's behaviour. You should also give Ophelia advice that you think would help her in her current situation.

Essay Building Blocks

'Truth and deception are central themes in the play Hamlet.'

Write a paragraph in response to this statement, supporting your answer with quotation from and reference to Act 2 Scene 1.

A room in the castle

Claudius and Gertrude have sent for Hamlet's old friends Rosencrantz and Guildenstern, hoping that they can discover the reason for Hamlet's recent strange behaviour.

The ambassadors that Claudius sent to Norway return with good news. The king of Norway has spoken to his nephew, Fortinbras, and he is no longer a threat to Denmark.

Polonius is eager to tell Claudius and Gertrude that he knows why Hamlet appears to have gone mad. He takes a long time to get to the point, and Gertrude becomes impatient. Polonius says that he believes that Hamlet has been driven out of his mind by Ophelia's rejection of him. He arranges for himself and Claudius to spy on Hamlet when he next talks to Ophelia.

Polonius sees Hamlet walking towards them and sends Claudius and Gertrude away so that he can talk to the prince alone. Hamlet makes fun of Polonius but Polonius takes the prince's absurd speech as further proof that he is mad.

When Polonius leaves, Rosencrantz and Guildenstern try to find out what is wrong with Hamlet but he guesses the reason for their visit and will tell them nothing. Rosencrantz tries to interest Hamlet in a travelling troupe of actors who are on their way to Elsinore. Hamlet is pleased and when the actors arrive he greets them warmly. He asks them to perform a play called 'The Murder of Gonzago' the following night and to include a speech he has written. Hamlet plans to force Claudius to reveal his guilt by shocking him with a scene closely resembling his murder of the old king.

Alone onstage at the end of the scene, Hamlet berates himself for not having done anything to avenge his father's murder up to this point. He is determined to prove Claudius's guilt once and for all and thereby confirm that the Ghost was telling the truth.

Act 2

1. *Moreover ... you:* besides the fact that we longed to see you

2. *Of Hamlet's transformation:* It seems that Claudius and Gertrude have noticed Hamlet's 'antic disposition'. In Act 1, Scene 5, Hamlet told Horatio that he would 'put an antic disposition on'.

3. *so young days:* since you were all young

4. *since ... haviour:* since you have been so close to him in age and behaviour from an early age

5. *you vouchsafe ... court:* you agree to stay here in the Danish court

6. *draw ... pleasures:* encourage him to have fun

7. *aught:* anything

8. *opened:* revealed

9. *To whom he more adheres:* to whom he is closer

10. *gentry:* courtesy

11. *expend:* spend

12. *For ... hope:* to help us fulfil our hopes

13. *Both ... entreaty:* Both your Majesties have regal power and could have ordered us to obey you, rather than asking us.

14. *full bent:* full intention

Enter CLAUDIUS, GERTRUDE, ROSENCRANTZ, GUILDENSTERN, and ATTENDANTS

CLAUDIUS

Welcome, dear Rosencrantz and Guildenstern.
Moreover that we much did long to see you,[1]
The need we have to use you did provoke
Our hasty sending. Something have you heard
Of Hamlet's transformation[2] – so call it,   **5**
Since not the exterior nor the inward man
Resembles that it was. What it should be,
More than his father's death, that thus hath put him
So much from th'understanding of himself,
I cannot dream of. I entreat you both   **10**
That, being of so young days[3] brought up with him,
And since so neighboured to his youth and haviour,[4]
That you vouchsafe your rest here in our court[5]
Some little time, so by your companies
To draw him on to pleasures,[6] and to gather,   **15**
So much as from occasions you may glean,
Whether aught[7] to us unknown afflicts him thus
That, opened[8] lies within our remedy.

GERTRUDE

Good gentlemen, he hath much talked of you,
And sure I am two men there is not living   **20**
To whom he more adheres.[9] If it will please you
To show us so much gentry[10] and good will
As to expend[11] your time with us a while
For the supply and profit of our hope,[12]
Your visitation shall receive such thanks   **25**
As fits a king's remembrance.

ROSENCRANTZ

Both your majesties
Might, by the sovereign power you have of us,
Put your dread pleasures more into command
Than to entreaty.[13]   **30**

GUILDENSTERN

But we both obey,
And here give up ourselves in the full bent[14]
To lay our service freely at your feet
To be commanded.

CLAUDIUS

Thanks, Rosencrantz and gentle Guildenstern.   35

GERTRUDE

Thanks, Guildenstern and gentle Rosencrantz.
And I beseech you instantly to visit
My too-much changed son. – Go, some of ye,
And bring the gentlemen where Hamlet is.

GUILDENSTERN

Heavens make our presence and our practises[15]   40   15. *practises:* actions
Pleasant and helpful to him.

GERTRUDE

Ay, amen!

Exit ROSENCRANTZ, GUILDENSTERN, and some ATTENDANTS
Enter POLONIUS

POLONIUS

Th'ambassadors from Norway, my good lord,
Are joyfully returned.[16]   16. *joyfully returned:* they bring good news

CLAUDIUS

Thou still[17] hast been the father of good news.   45   17. *still:* always

POLONIUS

Have I, my lord? Assure you, my good liege,[18]   18. *liege:* lord
I hold my duty, as I hold my soul,
Both to my God and to my gracious King.
And I do think – or else this brain of mine
Hunts not the trail of policy so sure   50
As it hath used to do[19] – that I have found   19. *or else . . . do:* or else I have lost my ability to follow a trail
The very cause of Hamlet's lunacy.   and find the truth of the matter

CLAUDIUS

O speak of that, that do I long to hear!

POLONIUS

Give first admittance to th'ambassadors.
My news shall be the fruit to that great feast.[20]   55   20. *My . . . feast:* My news will be like dessert after a great feast.

Act 2

21. *Thyself do grace to them:* Claudius is punning on Polonius's fruit/dessert metaphor. 'Grace' could mean courtesy or it could mean grace before meals.

22. *distemper:* disorder

23. *I doubt ... marriage:* I suspect the main reason is his father's death and our marriage, which took place so quickly after the funeral.

24. *we shall sift him:* we will question him

25. *brother:* fellow king

26. *Upon ... levies:* As soon as he heard our report, he ordered his nephew's forces to stand down.
27. *which ... Polack:* which he had originally thought were being gathered to fight the Poles

28. *whereat ... hand:* whereupon he was displeased to find his nephew had taken advantage of his age and infirmity
29. *arrests:* orders to stop

30. *give th'essay of arms:* take up arms

31. *entreaty:* request

CLAUDIUS

Thyself do grace to them,[21] and bring them in.

Exit POLONIUS

He tells me, my dear queen, he hath found
The head and source of all your son's distemper.[22]

GERTRUDE

I doubt it is no other but the main –
His father's death, and our o'er-hasty marriage.[23]   **60**

CLAUDIUS

Well, we shall sift him.[24]

Re-enter POLONIUS, with VOLTEMAND and CORNELIUS

Welcome, my good friends.
Say, Voltemand, what from our brother[25] Norway?

VOLTEMAND

Most fair return of greetings and desires.
Upon our first he sent out to suppress   **65**
His nephew's levies,[26] which to him appeared
To be a preparation 'gainst the Polack;[27]
But better looked into, he truly found
It was against your highness; whereat grieved
That so his sickness, age, and impotence   **70**
Was falsely borne in hand,[28] sends out arrests[29]
On Fortinbras, which he, in brief, obeys,
Receives rebuke from Norway, and in fine,
Makes vow before his uncle never more
To give th'essay of arms[30] against your majesty;   **75**
Whereon old Norway, overcome with joy,
Gives him three thousand crowns in annual fee,
And his commission to employ those soldiers,
So levied as before, against the Polack,
With an entreaty[31] herein further shown,   **80**

Giving a paper

That it might please you to give quiet pass
Through your dominions for this enterprise

On such regards of safety and allowance

As therein are set down.[32]

CLAUDIUS

It likes us well,[33]   85

And at our more considered time[34] we'll read,

Answer, and think upon this business.

Meantime we thank you for your well-took labour.[35]

Go to your rest; at night we'll feast together.

Most welcome home.   90

Exit VOLTEMAND and CORNELIUS

POLONIUS

This business is well ended.

My liege, and madam, to expostulate[36]

What majesty should be, what duty is,

Why day is day, night night, and time is time,

Were nothing but to waste night, day, and time.   95

Therefore, since brevity is the soul of wit,[37]

And tediousness the limbs and outward flourishes,[38]

I will be brief. Your noble son is mad –

'Mad' call I it, for to define true madness,

What is't but to be nothing else but mad?   100

But let that go.

GERTRUDE

More matter with less art.[39]

POLONIUS

Madam, I swear I use no art at all.

That he is mad, 'tis true; 'tis true 'tis pity,

And pity 'tis 'tis true – a foolish figure,[40]   105

But farewell it, for I will use no art.

Mad let us grant him, then; and now remains

That we find out the cause of this effect[41] –

Or rather say, 'the cause of this defect',

For this effect defective comes by cause.[42]   110

Thus it remains, and the remainder thus.

Perpend.[43]

I have a daughter – have whilst she is mine –

Who in her duty and obedience, mark,

Hath given me this.[44] Now gather and surmise.[45]   115

32. *That . . . down:* That you might allow safe passage of young Fortinbras' army through your lands under the conditions laid down in this document.

33. *It likes us well:* This pleases me.

34. *more considered time:* when there is time to consider

35. *well-took labour:* good job

36. *expostulate:* debate

37. *brevity . . . wit:* To be as brief as possible is the essence of intelligence.

38. *outward flourishes:* embellishments; unnecessary outward appearance or dress

39. *More matter with less art:* Say something of substance using less flowery language: get to the point.

40. *figure:* figure of speech

41. *effect:* result

42. *For . . . cause:* This effect is a defect and it must have a cause.

43. *Perpend:* Consider

44. *this:* this letter

45. *surmise:* draw your own conclusions

Act 2

46. *beautified:* By saying 'beautified' rather than 'beautiful', Hamlet may be suggesting that Ophelia's beauty is not completely natural and that she has beautified herself with make-up.

47. *I will be faithful:* I will read exactly what is in the letter.

48. *numbers:* verses

49. *I have ... groans:* I have not the skill to count, or recount in verse, what makes me miserable.

50. *whilst ... him:* while I have this body/as long as I live

51. *solicitings:* advances

52. *As ... ear:* She told me when, how and where these romantic advances were made.

53. *fain:* gladly

54. *hot love on the wing:* passionate love quickly developing

[Reads] 'To the celestial and my soul's idol, the most beautified[46] Ophelia' –

That's an ill phrase, a vile phrase, 'beautified' is a vile phrase. But you shall hear –

[Reads] 'These in her excellent white bosom, these'.   120

GERTRUDE
Came this from Hamlet to her?

POLONIUS
Good madam, stay a while. I will be faithful.[47]

[Reads] 'Doubt thou the stars are fire,
Doubt that the sun doth move,
Doubt truth to be a liar,   125
But never doubt I love.
O dear Ophelia, I am ill at these numbers.[48]
I have not art to reckon my groans.[49] But that
I love thee best, O most best, believe it. Adieu.
Thine evermore, most dear lady, whilst   130
this machine is to him,[50] Hamlet.'
This in obedience hath my daughter showed me,
And more above hath his solicitings,[51]
As they fell out by time, by means, and place,
All given to mine ear.[52]   135

CLAUDIUS
But how hath she
Received his love?

POLONIUS
What do you think of me?

CLAUDIUS
As of a man faithful and honourable.

POLONIUS
I would fain[53] prove so. But what might you think,   140
When I had seen this hot love on the wing,[54]
As I perceived it – I must tell you that –

Before my daughter told me, what might you,

Or my dear majesty your queen here, think,

If I had played the desk or table-book,[55]   **145**

Or given my heart a winking mute and dumb,

Or looked upon this love with idle sight[56] –

What might you think? No, I went round[57] to work,

And my young mistress thus I did bespeak:

'Lord Hamlet is a prince out of thy star.[58]   **150**

This must not be'. And then I prescripts gave her,

That she should lock herself from his resort,[59]

Admit no messengers, receive no tokens;

Which done, she took the fruits of my advice,

And he, repelled – a short tale to make –   **155**

Fell into a sadness, then into a fast,

Thence to a watch,[60] thence into a weakness,

Thence to a lightness, and, by this declension,[61]

Into the madness wherein now he raves,

And all we mourn for.   **160**

CLAUDIUS

Do you think 'tis this?

GERTRUDE

It may be, very likely.

POLONIUS

Hath there been such a time – I'd fain know that –

That I have positively said ''Tis so'

When it proved otherwise?   **165**

CLAUDIUS

Not that I know.

POLONIUS

[Pointing to his head and shoulder]

Take this from this[62] if this be otherwise.

If circumstances lead me I will find

Where truth is hid, though it were hid indeed

Within the centre.[63]   **170**

CLAUDIUS

How may we try it further?[64]

55. *If . . . table-book:* If I had acted as a go-between for their love letters

56. *Or looked . . . sight:* Or turned a blind eye to their love or not appreciated its seriousness

57. *round:* straight

58. *out of thy star:* of a higher social class than you

59. *resort:* reach

60. *And he, repelled . . . watch:* And he, rejected – in short – became sad, then stopped eating, and then stopped sleeping

61. *Thence to a lightness . . . declension:* Then he became light-headed or dizzy, and as a result of this decline

62. *Take this from this:* Take my head from my shoulders/have me beheaded

63. *though . . . centre:* even if it is very well hidden

64. *How may . . . further?:* How can we test your theory?

65. *four: This may mean several hours rather than exactly four hours.*
66. *lobby: corridor*

67. *arras: tapestry used as a wall covering*

68. *carters: drivers of carts*

69. *I'll board him presently: I'll speak to him right away.*

70. *Well, God-'a'-mercy: Well, thank God.*

71. *fishmonger: Although this word will make Hamlet appear mad, it may also refer to Polonius's fishing for secrets or may be a reference to the Elizabethan slang word for pimp.*

POLONIUS
You know sometimes he walks four[65] hours together
Here in the lobby.[66]

GERTRUDE
So he does indeed.

POLONIUS
At such a time I'll loose my daughter to him.   175
Be you and I behind an arras[67] then.
Mark the encounter. If he love her not,
And be not from his reason fall'n thereon,
Let me be no assistant for a state,
But keep a farm and carters.[68]   180

CLAUDIUS
We will try it.

Enter HAMLET, reading

GERTRUDE
But look where sadly the poor wretch comes reading.

POLONIUS
Away, I do beseech you both, away.
I'll board him presently.[69] O give me leave.

Exit CLAUDIUS, GERTRUDE, and ATTENDANTS

How does my good Lord Hamlet?   185

HAMLET
Well, God-'a'-mercy.[70]

POLONIUS
Do you know me, my lord?

HAMLET
Excellent, excellent well. You are a fishmonger.[71]

POLONIUS
Not I, my lord.

HAMLET

Then I would you were so honest a man.　　　　190

POLONIUS

Honest,[72] my lord?

HAMLET

Ay, sir. To be honest, as this world goes, is to be
one man picked out of ten thousand.

POLONIUS

That's very true, my lord.

HAMLET

For if the sun breed maggots in a dead dog, being　　195
a god kissing carrion,[73] – Have you a daughter?

POLONIUS

I have, my lord.

HAMLET

Let her not walk in the sun.[74] Conception[75] is a blessing,
but not as your daughter may conceive.
Friend, look to it.　　　　200

POLONIUS

[Aside] How say you by that? Still harping[76] on my daughter.
Yet he knew me not at first – he said I was a
fishmonger. He is far gone, far gone, and truly, in my
youth I suffered much extremity[77] for love, very near
this. I'll speak to him again. –　　　　205
What do you read, my lord?

HAMLET

Words, words, words.

POLONIUS

What is the matter,[78] my lord?

HAMLET

Between who?

72. *Honest:* good; virtuous; not corrupt

73. *For . . . carrion:* When the heat of the sun 'kisses' the carcass of a dead dog, the heat and rot allow maggots to breed. *The word 'carrion' was also Elizabethan slang for prostitute, giving Hamlet's words another layer of meaning.*

74. *Let her not walk in the sun: There are layers of meaning to Hamlet's warning. 1. If Ophelia is placed in the centre of events (Polonius will use her to spy on Hamlet in the next scene) harm may come to her. After all, the Danish court is a corrupt and rotten place. 2. Hamlet is the son of a king and the sun is an emblem of royalty. The young prince could be warning Polonius to keep her away from him.*

75. *Conception: 'Conception' has the double meaning of understanding and of conceiving a baby.*

76. *harping:* dwelling on; continuing to talk about

77. *extremity:* distress

78. *matter: Polonius means the subject matter of Hamlet's book, but Hamlet chooses to interpret 'matter' as meaning trouble.*

79. *satirical rogue:* Hamlet is referring to the author of the book of satire he has in his hand.

80. *purging . . . gum:* discharging yellow pus like the yellow resin from trees
81. *hams:* thighs

82. *set down:* written down

83. *for . . . backward:* Hamlet suggests that Polonius would like to crawl backwards in time and be young again.

84. *Though . . . in't:* Although the speech appears mad, there is logic in it.
85. *Will . . . lord?:* Polonius asks Hamlet to come indoors as fresh air was considered bad for those who were insane. The preferred treatment was confinement in a dark room.
86. *Into my grave:* Hamlet is playing with Polonius here and pretending to misunderstand his question. If he literally walks out of the air, he will die.

87. *pregnant:* full of meaning

88. *A happiness . . . of:* Sometimes mad people can express themselves more successfully
89. *delivered of:* brought forth. *Note the furthering of the conception, pregnancy and birth metaphor which Hamlet began.*

90. *You cannot . . . withal:* You cannot take anything from me that I would more willingly part with.

POLONIUS

I mean, the matter that you read, my lord.   **210**

HAMLET

Slanders, sir; for the satirical rogue[79] says here
that old men have grey beards, that their faces are
wrinkled, their eyes purging thick amber and
plum-tree gum,[80] and that they have a plentiful lack of
wit, together with most weak hams.[81] All which, sir,   **215**
though I most powerfully and potently believe, yet
I hold it not honesty to have it thus set down;[82] for
yourself, sir, should be old as I am – if, like a crab,
you could go backward.[83]

POLONIUS

[Aside] Though this be madness, yet there is method   **220**
in't.[84] – Will you walk out of the air, my lord?[85]

HAMLET

Into my grave.[86]

POLONIUS

Indeed, that is out of the air.
[Aside] How pregnant[87] sometimes his replies are! A
happiness that often madness hits on, which reason   **225**
and sanity could not so prosperously be delivered of.[88, 89]
I will leave him, and suddenly contrive the means of
meeting between him and my daughter. – My lord, I
will take my leave of you.

HAMLET

You cannot, sir, take from me anything that I will more   **230**
willingly part withal[90] – except my life, my life, my life.

POLONIUS

Fare you well, my lord.

HAMLET

These tedious old fools!

Enter ROSENCRANTZ and GUILDENSTERN

POLONIUS

You go to seek the Lord Hamlet. There he is.

ROSENCRANTZ

[To POLONIUS] God save you, sir.   235

Exit POLONIUS

GUILDENSTERN

Mine honoured lord.

ROSENCRANTZ

My most dear lord.

HAMLET

My excellent good friends. How dost thou,

Guildenstern? Ah, Rosencrantz – good lads,

how do ye both?   240

ROSENCRANTZ

As the indifferent children of the earth.[91]

91. *As . . . earth:* As any ordinary people do.

GUILDENSTERN

Happy, in that we are not over-happy,

On Fortune's cap we are not the very button.[92]

92. *On . . . button:* We are not at the highest point of fortune.

HAMLET

Nor the soles of her shoe?[93]

93. *Nor the soles of her shoe?:* But you are not at the lowest point of fortune?

ROSENCRANTZ

Neither, my lord.   245

HAMLET

Then you live about her waist, or in the middle

of her favour?[94]

94. *Then . . . favour?:* This remark has sexual undertones, meaning that Rosencrantz and Guildenstern are close to the intimate areas of Lady Fortune's body.

GUILDENSTERN

Faith, her privates we.[95]

95. *Faith, her privates we:* This is a sexual pun: privates may mean private individuals of low rank or it may mean genitals.

HAMLET

In the secret parts of Fortune? O, most true, she

is a strumpet.[96] What's the news?   250

96. *strumpet:* Hamlet compares fortune to a prostitute (strumpet) who gives her favours to all men but cannot be trusted.

97. *doomsday:* the day of judgement

98. *hither:* here

99. *goodly:* sizeable; large

100. *for there is . . . so:* Nothing is truly good or bad. It all depends on how a person views it.

101. *O God . . . dreams:* Hamlet claims he could be totally lacking in ambition and still be troubled by depressing thoughts.

102. *Which . . . dream:* Dreams are ambition because the ambitious man has dreams and his achievements are merely a shadow of those.

ROSENCRANTZ

None, my lord, but that the world's grown honest.

HAMLET

Then is doomsday[97] near. But your news is not true.
Let me question more in particular. What have you,
my good friends, deserved at the hands of Fortune
that she sends you to prison hither?[98]   255

GUILDENSTERN

Prison, my lord?

HAMLET

Denmark's a prison.

ROSENCRANTZ

Then is the world one.

HAMLET

A goodly[99] one, in which there are many confines, wards,
and dungeons, Denmark being one of the worst.   260

ROSENCRANTZ

We think not so, my lord.

HAMLET

Why, then 'tis none to you, for there is nothing either
good or bad but thinking makes it so.[100] To me it is
a prison.

ROSENCRANTZ

Why, then your ambition makes it one; 'tis too narrow   265
for your mind.

HAMLET

O God, I could be bounded in a nutshell and count
myself a king of infinite space, were it not that I
have bad dreams.[101]

GUILDENSTERN

Which dreams indeed are ambition; for the   270
very substance of the ambitious is merely the
shadow of a dream.[102]

HAMLET

A dream itself is but a shadow.

ROSENCRANTZ

Truly, and I hold ambition of so airy and light a
quality that it is but a shadow's shadow.[103]   **275**

HAMLET

Then are our beggars bodies, and our monarchs and
outstretched heroes the beggars' shadows.[104] Shall we
to the court? For, by my fay,[105] I cannot reason.

ROSENCRANTZ and **GUILDENSTERN**

We'll wait upon you.

HAMLET

No such matter. I will not sort[106] you with the rest   **280**
of my servants, for, to speak to you like an honest
man, I am most dreadfully attended. But in the
beaten way of friendship, what make you at Elsinore?[107]

ROSENCRANTZ

To visit you, my lord, no other occasion.[108]

HAMLET

Beggar that I am, I am even poor in thanks, but I thank   **285**
you; and sure, dear friends, my thanks are too dear a
halfpenny.[109] Were you not sent for? Is it your own
inclining? Is it a free visitation? Come, deal justly with
me. Come, come. Nay, speak.

GUILDENSTERN

What should we say, my lord?   **290**

HAMLET

Why, anything – but to the purpose.[110] You were sent for,
and there is a kind of confession in your looks which
your modesties have not craft enough to colour.[111]
I know the good King and Queen have sent for you.

ROSENCRANTZ

To what end, my lord?   **295**

---

103. *Truly … shadow:* Ambition is the least substantial of any dream.

104. *Then … shadows:* Beggars have no ambition and are therefore the only real people. Kings and heroes are full of ambition and therefore merely beggars' shadows stretched out before them.
105. *fay:* faith

106. *sort:* categorise

107. *I am most … Elsinore?:* I have very bad servants. What are you, my tried and tested friends, doing at Elsinore?

108. *occasion:* reason

109. *my thanks … halfpenny:* my thanks are worth a halfpenny more than your friendship *Hamlet realises that Rosencrantz and Guildenstern are not there out of friendship but because they were sent for.*

110. *to the purpose:* to the point

111. *your modesties … colour:* your embarrassment cannot hide

disillusionment man-kind

HAMLET
That you must teach me. But let me conjure you[112] by the rights of our fellowship, by the consonancy[113] of our youth, by the obligation of our ever-preserved love, and by what more dear a better proposer could charge you withal,[114] be even and direct with me whether you were sent for or no? **300**

ROSENCRANTZ
[Aside to GUILDENSTERN] What say you?

HAMLET
[Aside] Nay then, I have an eye of you[115] – if you love me, hold not off.[116]

GUILDENSTERN
My lord, we were sent for. **305**

HAMLET
I will tell you why. So shall my anticipation[117] prevent your discovery, and your secrecy to the King and Queen moult no feather.[118] I have of late – but wherefore I know not – lost all my mirth, forgone all custom of exercise; and indeed it goes so heavily with my disposition[119] that **310** this goodly frame,[120] the earth, seems to me a sterile promontory.[121] This most excellent canopy the air, look you, this brave o'erhanging firmament,[122] this majestical roof fretted with golden fire[123] – why, it appears no other thing to me than a foul and pestilent congregation of **315** vapours.[124] What a piece of work is a man! How noble in reason, how infinite in faculties, in form and moving how express and admirable,[125] in action how like an angel, in apprehension[126] how like a god – the beauty of the world, the paragon[127] of animals! And yet to me what is **320** this quintessence[128] of dust? Man delights not me – no, nor woman neither, though by your smiling you seem to say so.

ROSENCRANTZ
My lord, there was no such stuff in my thoughts.

HAMLET
Why did you laugh, then, when I said 'Man delights **325** not me'?

ROSENCRANTZ

To think, my lord, if you delight not in man what
lenten entertainment[129] the players shall receive from
you. We coted[130] them on the way, and hither are they
coming to offer you service.   330

HAMLET

He that plays the King shall be welcome; his majesty
shall have tribute[131] of me. The adventurous Knight
shall use his foil and target,[132] the Lover shall not
sigh gratis,[133] the Humorous Man shall end his part
in peace, the Clown shall make those laugh whose   335
lungs are tickled o'th' sere,[134] and the Lady shall
say her mind freely, or the blank verse shall
halt for't. What players are they?

ROSENCRANTZ

Even those you were wont to take delight in,[135] the
tragedians[136] of the city.   340

HAMLET

How chances it they travel?[137] Their residence both
in reputation and profit was better both ways.[138]

ROSENCRANTZ

I think their inhibition comes by the means of the
late innovation.[139]

HAMLET

Do they hold the same estimation[140] they did when I was   345
in the city? Are they so followed?

ROSENCRANTZ

No, indeed, are they not.

HAMLET

How comes it? Do they grow rusty?

ROSENCRANTZ

Nay, their endeavour keeps in the wonted pace.[141] But
there is, sir, an eyrie[142] of children, little eyases,[143] that cry   350
out on the top of question and are most tyrannically
clapped for't.[144] These are now the fashion, and so berattle

129. *lenten entertainment:* poor hospitality *Lent is a time of fasting and penance.*
130. *coted:* passed

131. *tribute:* praise or payment

132. *foil and target:* sword and shield

133. *gratis:* without payment

134. *whose . . . sere:* who laugh easily

135. *you . . . delight in:* you used to enjoy

136. *tragedians:* actors in tragedies

137. *How . . . travel:* Why are they touring?

138. *Their . . . ways:* Their reputation and their finances would be better off if they stayed in one place.

139. *I think . . . innovation:* They have been restricted by recent changes. *Shakespeare may be referring to the order forbidding his company to perform for a time in 1601 because one of his plays was considered to have contributed to the Essex rebellion against Queen Elizabeth I.*

140. *estimation:* high regard; esteem

141. *Nay, their . . . pace:* Their standard remains as high as ever.

142. *eyrie:* nest of a bird of prey
143. *eyases:* young hawks

144. *cry out . . . for't:* perform in high, shrill voices and are applauded for it

Act 2

145. *berattle the common stages:* loudly attack public theatres

146. *many . . . quills:* Fashionable young men wore rapiers (a type of sword). The child actors satirise those who have anything to do with the established theatres, so fashionable people will not attend them for fear of ridicule.

147. *escoted:* paid

148. *Will they not . . . succession:* Will these child actors, when they grow up and become adult actors – as they probably will, if they cannot find better work – complain that those who wrote plays for them did them a disservice by making them mock their own future?

149. *tarre:* incite or urge

150. *There . . . question:* For a time there was no money paid for a script unless the plot focused on the fighting between the children's playwrights and the adult actors.

151. *throwing . . . brains:* battle of wits

152. *carry it away:* win

153. *Hercules . . . too:* The sign outside the Globe showed Hercules bearing the world on his shoulders, so this may be a reference to the child actors gaining advantage over the established theatres.

154. *make mows:* grimace/make rude faces

155. *picture in little:* miniature portrait
156. *'Sblood:* a mild oath: By God's blood
157. *more than natural:* abnormal
158. *philosophy:* science

the common stages[145] – so they call them – that many wearing rapiers are afraid of goose-quills,[146] and dare scarce come thither.   355

HAMLET

What, are they children? Who maintains 'em? How are they escoted?[147] Will they pursue the quality no longer than they can sing? Will they not say afterwards, if they should grow themselves to common players – as it is most like if their means are not better – their   360 writers do them wrong to make them exclaim against their own succession?[148]

ROSENCRANTZ

Faith, there has been much to-do on both sides, and the nation holds it no sin to tarre[149] them to controversy. There was for a while no money bid for argument   365 unless the poet and the player went to cuffs in the question.[150]

HAMLET

Is't possible?

GUILDENSTERN

O, there has been much throwing about of brains.[151]

HAMLET

Do the boys carry it away?[152]   370

ROSENCRANTZ

Ay, that they do, my lord, Hercules and his load too.[153]

HAMLET

It is not strange; for mine uncle is King of Denmark, and those that would make mows[154] at him while my father lived give twenty, forty, an hundred ducats apiece for his picture in little.[155] 'Sblood,[156] there is something in this   375 more than natural,[157] if philosophy[158] could find it out.

Flourish of trumpets within

GUILDENSTERN
There are the players.

HAMLET

Gentlemen, you are welcome to Elsinore. Your hands,
come.[159] The appurtenance[160] of welcome is fashion
and ceremony. Let me comply with you in this garb,[161]   **380**
lest my extent to the players – which, I tell you,
must show fairly outward – should more appear like
entertainment than yours.[162] You are welcome. But my
uncle-father and aunt-mother are deceived.

GUILDENSTERN

In what, my dear lord?   **385**

HAMLET

I am but mad north-north-west;[163] when the wind is
southerly, I know a hawk from a handsaw.[164]

Enter POLONIUS

POLONIUS

Well be with you, gentlemen.

HAMLET

Hark you, Guildenstern, and you too – at each ear a
hearer[165] – that great baby you see there is not yet   **390**
out of his swaddling-clouts.[166]

ROSENCRANTZ

Haply[167] he's the second time come to them; for they
say an old man is twice a child.[168]

HAMLET

I will prophesy he comes to tell me of the players.
Mark it. – You say right, sir, o' Monday morning,   **395**
'twas so indeed.[169]

POLONIUS

My lord, I have news to tell you.

HAMLET

My lord, I have news to tell you.
When Roscius[170] was an actor in Rome –

159. *Your hands, come:* Let me shake your hands.

160. *The appurtenance:* the proper accompaniment

161. *comply … garb:* greet you in this polite manner

162. *lest … yours:* in case my behaviour to the players, which, I must tell you will appear very pleasant, seems warmer than my show of hospitality to you

163. *I am but mad north-north-west:* I am only occasionally mad; I am only mad when the wind blows north-north-west.

164. *handsaw:* heron *Birds usually fly in the direction of the wind. If the wind is north-north-west, the morning sun would dazzle a hunter and he would not be able to distinguish one type of bird from another.*

165. *at each ear a hearer:* stand on each side of me

166. *swaddling-clouts:* the blankets in which a small baby is tightly wrapped

167. *Haply:* perhaps

168. *an old man … child: This is a reference to old age being a second childhood.*

169. *You say … indeed: As Polonius approaches, Hamlet pretends to be talking about something else.*

170. *Roscius: a famous actor in Ancient Rome*

171. *Buzz, buzz!: A contemptuous noise meaning 'You are telling me old news'.*

172. *Then . . . ass: This may be a line from a ballad. Hamlet is also mocking Polonius by punning on the word 'ass', which may mean donkey or backside.*

173. *scene individable: a play that consists of a single, long scene*

174. *Seneca: a famous Roman tragic playwright*

175. *Plautus: a famous Roman comic playwright*

176. *For . . . liberty: whether the play is written according to the laws of classical drama or follows no rules*

177. *Jephthah: a character in the Old Testament who sacrificed his daughter to please God*

178. *passing well: extremely well*

POLONIUS

The actors are come hither, my lord.   400

HAMLET

Buzz, buzz!171

POLONIUS

Upon mine honour –

HAMLET

Then came each actor on his ass.172

POLONIUS

The best actors in the world, either for tragedy,
comedy, history, pastoral, pastoral-comical,   405
historical-pastoral, tragical-historical, tragical-
comical-historical-pastoral, scene individable,173 or
poem unlimited. Seneca174 cannot be too heavy, nor
Plautus175 too light. For the law of writ and the
liberty,176 these are the only men.   410

HAMLET

O Jephthah,177 judge of Israel, what a treasure hadst thou!

POLONIUS

What a treasure had he, my lord?

HAMLET

Why,
'One fair daughter and no more,
The which he loved passing well.'178   415

POLONIUS

[Aside] Still on my daughter.

HAMLET

Am I not in the right, old Jephthah?

POLONIUS

If you call me Jephthah, my lord, I have a daughter
that I love passing well.

HAMLET

Nay, that follows not.[179]

420

POLONIUS

What follows then, my lord?

HAMLET

Why,

'As by lot God wot,'

and then you know

'It came to pass as most like it was'[180] –

425

the first row of the pious chanson[181] will show you

more, for look, where my abridgements come.[182]

Enter four or five PLAYERS

You are welcome, masters, welcome, all. – I am glad

to see thee well. – Welcome, good friends. – O, my old

friend! Thy face is valanced[183] since I saw thee last.

430

Comest thou to beard[184] me in Denmark? – What, my

young lady and mistress. By'r Lady, your ladyship is

nearer to heaven than when I saw you last by the

altitude of a chopine.[185] Pray God your voice, like

a piece of uncurrent[186] gold, be not cracked within the

435

ring.[187] – Masters, you are all welcome. We'll e'en

to't like French falconers, fly at anything we see.[188]

We'll have a speech straight. Come, give us a taste

of your quality. Come, a passionate speech.

FIRST PLAYER

What speech, my lord?

440

HAMLET

I heard thee speak me a speech once, but it was never

acted, or, if it was, not above once; for the play, I

remember, pleased not the million. 'Twas caviar to

the general.[189] But it was – as I received it, and others

whose judgments in such matters cried in the top of

445

mine[190] – an excellent play, well digested[191] in the scenes,

set down with as much modesty[192] as cunning.[193] I

remember one said there was no sallets[194] in the lines to

make the matter savoury, nor no matter in the phrase

that might indict[195] the author of affectation, but called it

450

179. *Nay, . . . not:* No, just because you have a daughter it does not necessarily mean you love her. *Hamlet is also playing with the word 'follow' because he could mean that Polonius did not give the lines that follow those he, Hamlet, quoted.*

180. *'As by . . . was':* Hamlet continues quoting from a ballad. *'As by chance God knows, it happened as was most likely'.*

181. *first . . . chanson:* first verse of the religious song

182. *look . . . come:* I am being cut short because the players are approaching.

183. *valanced:* bearded *Hamlet is punning on the word 'beard' here. It can mean 'facial hair' or 'to confront someone'.*

184. *to beard:* confront

185. *the altitude of a chopine:* the height of a high heel *Hamlet addresses the young male actor who plays the role of women in the play, saying he, the actor, has grown taller.*

186. *uncurrent:* illegal

187. *cracked within the ring:* If a coin had a crack that reached to the ring around the stamp of the monarch's head, it was no longer legal currency. Hamlet is referring to the actor's voice. Although he uses the address 'Your ladyship', the actor would have been a young boy, as women were forbidden to act. If the boy's voice had broken or 'cracked', he would be as worthless as a 'piece of uncurrent gold'.

188. *We'll . . . see:* We'll get straight to it. *This is a reference to French falconers, who were thought to be too eager to release their birds at the sight of any prey.*

189. *'Twas caviar to the general:* It was like giving caviar to the general public *(instead of those with tastes refined enough to appreciate it)*

190. *cried . . . mine:* were superior to mine

191. *digested:* constructed

192. *modesty:* restraint

193. *cunning:* skill

194. *sallets:* spicy touches *perhaps rude jokes*

195. *indict:* accuse

Act 2

196. *as wholesome as sweet:* as good as it was lovely

197. *more handsome than fine:* dignified rather than showy

198. *Aeneas' . . . slaughter:* Aeneas, the hero of the Roman poet Virgil's Aeneid, told the Carthaginian Queen Dido about the fall of Troy and the killing of Priam, the king of Troy.

199. *Pyrrhus:* The son of Achilles, Pyrrhus hid in the wooden horse the Greeks used to smuggle soldiers into Troy. Pyrrhus killed Priam to avenge his own father's death.

200. *sable arms:* black armour

201. *When he . . . total gules:* When he lay hidden in the ill-fated (Trojan) horse, has now smeared his terrible, black armour with an even more dreadful coat or arms. From head to toe, he is completely red.
202. *tricked:* Heraldic term meaning 'outlined'
203. *Baked . . . streets:* the blood has baked into a crust in the scorching heat of the burning city

204. *o'ersized . . . gore:* smeared all over with dried blood

205. *carbuncles:* red jewels that were thought to shine in the dark

206. *discretion:* understanding of the lines

207. *Anon:* soon

208. *Striking too short:* failing to hit

209. *Rebellious . . . command:* His sword will not obey his arm and ignores his commands. *In other words, he is not able to lift it.*

210. *whiff . . . sword:* with the breeze created by the sword's cruel (fell) blow
211. *unnerved:* feeble
212. *Ilium:* Troy

213. *Seeming . . . ear:* It seems as if the city's fortress, *which should be 'senseless' or unfeeling,* feels this blow, and crashes to the ground and captures Pyrrhus' attention.
214. *milky:* white

215. *as a painted tyrant:* as still as a tyrant in a picture

216. *neutral . . . matter:* indifferent to both his desire and his task

an honest method, as wholesome as sweet,[196] and by very much more handsome than fine.[197] One speech in it I chiefly loved, 'twas Aeneas' tale to Dido, and thereabout of it especially where he speaks of Priam's slaughter.[198] If it live in your memory, begin at this line – 455
let me see, let me see:
'The rugged Pyrrhus,[199] like th'Hyrcanian beast' –
'tis not so. It begins with Pyrrhus –
'The rugged Pyrrhus, he whose sable arms,[200]
Black as his purpose, did the night resemble 460
When he lay couched in the ominous horse,
Hath now this dread and black complexion smeared
With heraldry more dismal. Head to foot
Now is he total gules,[201] horridly tricked[202]
With blood of fathers, mothers, daughters, sons, 465
Baked and impasted with the parching streets,[203]
That lend a tyrannous and damned light
To their vile murders. Roasted in wrath and fire,
And thus o'er-sized with coagulate gore,[204]
With eyes like carbuncles[205] the hellish Pyrrhus 470
Old grandsire Priam seeks.'
So, proceed you.

POLONIUS

Fore God, my lord, well spoken, with good accent and good discretion.[206]

FIRST PLAYER

'Anon[207] he finds him 475
Striking too short[208] at Greeks. His antique sword,
Rebellious to his arm, lies where it falls,
Repugnant to command.[209] Unequal matched,
Pyrrhus at Priam drives, in rage strikes wide;
But with the whiff and wind of his fell sword[210] 480
Th'unnerved[211] father falls. Then senseless Ilium,[212]
Seeming to feel this blow, with flaming top
Stoops to his base, and with a hideous crash
Takes prisoner Pyrrhus' ear.[213] For lo, his sword,
Which was declining on the milky[214] head 485
Of reverend Priam, seemed i'th' air to stick.
So, as a painted tyrant,[215] Pyrrhus stood,
And, like a neutral to his will and matter,[216]
Did nothing.

But as we often see against[217] some storm

A silence in the heavens, the rack[218] stand still,

The bold winds speechless, and the orb below

As hush as death, anon the dreadful thunder

Doth rend the region:[219] so, after Pyrrhus' pause,

A roused vengeance sets him new a-work;[220]

And never did the Cyclops[221] hammers fall

On Mars[222] his armour, forged for proof eterne,[223]

With less remorse than Pyrrhus' bleeding sword

Now falls on Priam.

Out, out, thou strumpet, Fortune! All you gods,

In general synod,[224] take away her power,

Break all the spokes and fellies[225] from her wheel,

And bowl the round nave[226] down the hill of heaven,

As low as to the fiends!'[227]

POLONIUS

This is too long.

HAMLET

It shall to the barber's, with your beard. Prithee,

say on. He's for a jig or a tale of bawdry, or he

sleeps.[228] Say on, come to Hecuba.[229]

FIRST PLAYER

'But who, O who had seen the mobled[230] queen' –

HAMLET

'The mobled queen'?

POLONIUS

That's good; 'mobled queen' is good.

FIRST PLAYER

'Run barefoot up and down, threatening the flames

With bisson rheum;[231] a clout upon that head

Where late the diadem stood,[232] and for a robe,

About her lank and all o'er-teemed loins,[233]

A blanket, in the alarm of fear caught up –

Who this had seen, with tongue in venom steeped,[234]

'Gainst Fortune's state would treason have pronounced.

But if the gods themselves did see her then,

When she saw Pyrrhus make malicious sport

490

495

500

505

510

515

520

217. *against:* before

218. *rack:* clouds

219. *The bold . . . rend the region:* The bold winds calming, and the earth below as quiet as death, soon the terrible thunder splits the air

220. *A roused . . . a-work:* His reawakened desire for revenge causes him to act again.

221. *Cyclops:* one-eyed giants who helped to make the armour for Mars

222. *Mars:* god of war

223. *proof eterne:* made to provide protection forever

224. *synod:* assembly

225. *fellies:* rim of a wheel *This is a reference to the wheel of fortune.*

226. *nave:* hub

227. *As low . . . fiends!:* Down to hell, to the devils

228. *He's . . . sleeps:* Hamlet mocks Polonius, saying that if a play does not contain comic dances and bawdy stories, he will fall asleep.

229. *Hecuba:* Priam's wife

230. *mobled:* veiled

231. *bisson rheum:* blinding tears

232. *a clout . . . stood:* a cloth on her head where there had been a crown

233. *lank . . . loins:* loins shrunken from bearing so many children

234. *with . . . steeped:* with bitter words

235. *clamour:* noise

236. *Would . . . heaven:* Would have made the heavens weep 'Milch' means to produce milk.

237. *turned his colour:* gone pale

238. *well bestowed:* lodged in good rooms

239. *the abstract . . . time:* a brief recorded summary of events

240. *according to their desert:* as they deserve

241. *God's bodykins:* a mild oath: by God's body

242. *scape:* escape

243. *the less . . . bounty:* The less they deserve, the more merit there will be in your generosity towards them.

In mincing with his sword her husband's limbs,
The instant burst of clamour[235] that she made –
Unless things mortal move them not at all –
Would have made milch the burning eyes of heaven,[236]
And passion in the gods.'   525

POLONIUS
Look, whether he has not turned his colour,[237] and
has tears in 's eyes. Prithee, no more.

HAMLET
'Tis well. I'll have thee speak out the rest soon.
Good my lord, will you see the players well
bestowed?[238] Do ye hear? – let them be well used, for   530
they are the abstract and brief chronicles of the
time.[239] After your death you were better have a bad
epitaph than their ill report while you live.

POLONIUS
My lord, I will use them according to their desert.[240]

HAMLET
God's bodykins,[241] man, much better. Use every man   535
after his desert, and who should scape[242] whipping?
Use them after your own honour and dignity – the
less they deserve, the more merit is in your bounty.[243]
Take them in.

POLONIUS
Come, sirs.   540

HAMLET
Follow him, friends. We'll hear a play tomorrow.

Exit POLONIUS with all the PLAYERS but the FIRST

Dost thou hear me, old friend? Can you play the
Murder of Gonzago?

FIRST PLAYER
Ay, my lord.

HAMLET

We'll ha't[244] tomorrow night. You could for a need study   **545**
a speech of some dozen or sixteen lines which I would
set down and insert in't,[245] could ye not?

FIRST PLAYER

Ay, my lord.

HAMLET

Very well. Follow that lord; and look you mock him not.

Exit FIRST PLAYER

My good friends, I'll leave you till night. You are   **550**
welcome to Elsinore.

ROSENCRANTZ

Good my lord.

HAMLET

Ay, so, God b'wi' ye.

Exit ROSENCRANTZ and GUILDENSTERN

Now I am alone.
O, what a rogue and peasant[246] slave am I!   **555**
Is it not monstrous that this player here,
But in a fiction, in a dream of passion,
Could force his soul so to his own conceit[247]
That from her working all his visage wanned,[248]
Tears in his eyes, distraction in 's aspect,[249]   **560**
A broken voice, and his whole function suiting
With forms to his conceit?[250] And all for nothing.
For Hecuba!
What's Hecuba to him, or he to Hecuba,
That he should weep for her? What would he do,   **565**
Had he the motive and the cue[251] for passion
That I have? He would drown the stage with tears,
And cleave[252] the general ear with horrid speech,
Make mad the guilty and appal the free,[253]
Confound[254] the ignorant, and amaze indeed   **570**
The very faculty of eyes and ears.[255] Yet I,
A dull and muddy-mettled[256] rascal, peak

244. *ha't:* have it

245. *set down and insert in't:* write and insert in it

246. *peasant:* lowly

247. *Could . . . conceit:* could make himself believe in something he had imagined
248. *his visage wanned:* his face grew pale

249. *aspect:* expression

250. *his whole . . . conceit:* all his actions matching his imaginary experience

251. *cue:* cause

252. *cleave:* split

253. *appal the free:* shock and horrify the innocent

254. *Confound:* confuse
255. *amaze . . . ears:* astonish the very senses of sight and hearing

256. *muddy-mettled:* dull-spirited

257. *John-a-dreams: a nick-name for an idle daydreamer*
258. *unpregnant of my cause:* unprepared to do my duty

259. *pate:* head
260. *Plucks . . . face:* To pluck hairs from a man's beard was a terrible insult to his masculinity.

261. *gives . . . lungs:* accuses me of lying
262. *'Swounds: a mild oath: By God's wounds*
263. *pigeon-livered:* Weak and gentle as a pigeon *Pigeons were considered weak and gentle.*
264. *gall:* The liver secretes gall and it was believed that this was the source of a person's anger and bravery.
265. *kites:* birds of prey
266. *offal:* intestine

267. *This is most brave:* Hamlet is speaking sarcastically about himself.

268. *unpack my heart with words:* relieve my feelings with words

269. *drab:* prostitute

270. *scullion:* kitchen maid

271. *About, my brains:* Start thinking, mind.

272. *struck so to the soul:* so moved

273. *proclaimed their malefactions:* confessed their evil deeds

274. *will speak . . . organ:* can speak in miraculous, strange ways

275. *I'll tent . . . quick: This is a reference to probing the sorest point of a person's wound. Hamlet intends to probe Claudius where it will hurt him the most.*
276. *blench:* flinch

277. *perhaps . . . damn me:* perhaps he is taking advantage of my present weakened and depressed state, as ghosts are known to do
278. *I'll have grounds . . . this:* I'll need more proof than the Ghost's word.

Like John-a-dreams,[257] unpregnant of my cause,[258]
And can say nothing – no, not for a king,
Upon whose property and most dear life   575
A damned defeat was made. Am I a coward?
Who calls me villain, breaks my pate[259] across,
Plucks off my beard and blows it in my face, [260]
Tweaks me by the nose, gives me the lie in the throat
As deep as to the lungs?[261] Who does me this?   580
Ha? 'Swounds,[262] I should take it; for it cannot be
But I am pigeon-livered[263] and lack gall[264]
To make oppression bitter, or ere this
I should have fatted all the region kites[265]
With this slave's offal.[266] Bloody, bawdy villain!   585
Remorseless, treacherous, lecherous, kindless villain!
O, vengeance! –
Why, what an ass am I? This is most brave,[267]
That I, the son of the dear murdered,
Prompted to my revenge by heaven and hell,   590
Must, like a whore, unpack my heart with words[268]
And fall a-cursing like a very drab,[269]
A scullion![270]
Fie upon't, foh! – About, my brains.[271] I have heard
That guilty creatures sitting at a play   595
Have by the very cunning of the scene
Been struck so to the soul[272] that presently
They have proclaimed their malefactions;[273]
For murder, though it have no tongue, will speak
With most miraculous organ.[274] I'll have these players 600
Play something like the murder of my father
Before mine uncle. I'll observe his looks,
I'll tent him to the quick.[275] If he but blench,[276]
I know my course. The spirit that I have seen
May be the devil, and the devil hath power   605
T'assume a pleasing shape; yea, and perhaps,
Out of my weakness and my melancholy –
As he is very potent with such spirits –
Abuses me to damn me.[277] I'll have grounds
More relative than this.[278] The play's the thing   610
Wherein I'll catch the conscience of the King.

Exit

Quotes

> *brevity is the soul of wit*
>
> (Polonius, line 96)

Polonius, in a long-winded, rambling speech, says that getting straight to the point is the essence of wisdom. He does not see the irony in his words.

> *More matter with less art.*
>
> (Gertrude, line 102)

Gertrude tells Polonius to get to the point and not to waste time on fancy wordplay.

> *Though this be madness, yet there is method in't.*
>
> (Polonius, lines 220–221)

Polonius believes that there is reason behind Hamlet's madness. He is wrong, however, to believe Hamlet has been driven mad by Ophelia's rejection. Hamlet is pretending to be mad to disguise his true intention: to unmask Claudius as his father's killer.

> *Denmark's a prison. […]*
> *A goodly one, in which there are many confines, wards,*
> *and dungeons, Demark being one of the worst.*
>
> (Hamlet, line 257/lines 259–260)

Hamlet feels trapped and restricted in Denmark. When Rosencrantz says that if Denmark is a prison, then so is the whole world, Hamlet agrees. The world may be a large prison with many dungeons and cells, but Denmark is one of the worst of them.

> *What a piece of work is a man! How noble in reason, how infinite in faculties, in form and moving how express and admirable, in action how like an angel, in apprehension how like a god – the beauty of the world, the paragon of animals! And yet to me what is this quintessence of dust? Man delights not me – no, nor woman neither, though by your smiling you seem to say so.*
>
> (Hamlet, lines 316–323)

Hamlet reflects on the nobility of man and the great potential of humans. However, he is deeply disillusioned with life and knows that even though mankind may rise to angelic heights, all are destined to die and become nothing but dust. He can find no joy in life.

I am but mad north-north-west; when the wind is
southerly, I know a hawk from a handsaw.

(Hamlet, lines 386–387)

Hamlet tells Rosencrantz and Guildenstern that he is only occasionally mad, when the wind blows north-north-west. When the wind blows from the south, he is sane enough to tell the difference between a hawk and a heron. In other words, he can perceive the truth.

Why, what an ass am I? This is most brave,
That I, the son of the dear murdered,
Prompted to my revenge by heaven and hell,
Must, like a whore, unpack my heart with words
And fall a-cursing like a very drab,
A scullion!

(Hamlet, lines 588–593)

Hamlet is disgusted with his own lack of action. He says sarcastically that it is very brave of him, the son of a murdered father, to relieve his feelings with words and curse his fate like a prostitute or a kitchen maid.

The play's the thing
Wherein I'll catch the conscience of the King.

(Hamlet, lines 610–611)

Hamlet is sure that his plan to have the murder of a king acted onstage will make Claudius feel so guilty that he will make it clear he killed Old Hamlet.

Questions

In each case, support your point with suitable reference to and quotation from the play.

1. What is your opinion of Rosencrantz and Guildenstern, based on their actions in this scene?

2. Some directors have had Claudius and Gertrude confuse the characters of Rosencrantz and Guildenstern onstage. Apart from providing a little comic relief, what does such a directorial choice tell us about Rosencrantz and Guildenstern?

3. In your own words, give a detailed account of the ambassadors' report to Claudius upon their return from Norway.

4. Claudius describes Polonius as 'faithful and honourable' in this scene. Do you agree with his assessment of Polonius? Explain your answer.

5. List the various examples of deception in this scene.

6. What do we learn about Hamlet during his meeting with the actors?

7. What does this scene tell us about Hamlet's view of the world?

8. Compare Hamlet's and Fortinbras' plans to seek revenge.

9. Do you believe Hamlet's plan to 'catch the conscience of the King' will work? Why/why not?

Writing Task

Imagine you have recently read a newspaper article calling for the removal of Shakespeare from the school syllabus as the writer considers it irrelevant to young people today. Write a letter to the editor of the newspaper disagreeing with this claim. Base your response on Act 2 Scene 2 of *Hamlet*. You may wish to consider some of the following:

- battle of wits between Hamlet and others
- tension
- drama
- insights into the human condition
- timeless themes of loyalty, love, self-doubt.

Essay Building Blocks

> *'Hamlet loathes himself as much as he loathes Claudius.'*

Write a paragraph in response to this statement, supporting your answer with quotation from and reference to Act 2 Scene 2.

A room in the castle

Rosencrantz and Guildenstern tell Gertrude and Claudius that they have not succeeded in getting Hamlet to confide in them. The only comfort they can offer the royal couple is that Hamlet seemed happy to see the actors arrive and that there is to be a performance of a play that evening.

Claudius sends everyone away except Polonius and Ophelia. He and Polonius hide behind a tapestry and listen in to Hamlet's conversation with Ophelia. Hamlet speaks cruelly and angrily to Ophelia, saying she is like all women, pretending to be something she is not in order to make a fool of men. He claims he never loved her and warns her to go into a convent, where she can do no harm.

Ophelia is heartbroken at what she believes to be proof of Hamlet's madness. Polonius is convinced it proves the Prince has been driven insane by love, but Claudius is far less sure. He considers Hamlet's wild behaviour dangerous and decides to send him to England. Polonius agrees with this plan but he asks that Gertrude speak to Hamlet later that evening after the play, to make one final effort to discover what is the matter with her son.

Enter CLAUDIUS, GERTRUDE, POLONIUS, OPHELIA,
ROSENCRANTZ, and GUILDENSTERN

CLAUDIUS

And can you by no drift of circumstance[1]
Get from him why he puts on this confusion,[2]
Grating so harshly all his days of quiet
With turbulent and dangerous lunacy?[3]

ROSENCRANTZ

He does confess he feels himself distracted,[4]   5
But from what cause he will by no means speak.

GUILDENSTERN

Nor do we find him forward to be sounded,[5]
But with a crafty[6] madness keeps aloof[7]
When we would bring him on to some confession
Of his true state.   10

GERTRUDE

Did he receive you well?

ROSENCRANTZ

Most like a gentleman.

GUILDENSTERN

But with much forcing of his disposition.[8]

ROSENCRANTZ

Niggard of question, but of our demands,
Most free in his reply.[9]   15

GERTRUDE

Did you assay[10] him?
To any pastime?

ROSENCRANTZ

Madam, it so fell out[11] that certain players
We o'er-raught[12] on the way. Of these we told him,
And there did seem in him a kind of joy   20
To hear of it. They are about the court,
And, as I think, they have already order
This night to play before him.

1. *drift of circumstance:* direction of conversation
2. *puts on this confusion:* pretends to be mad
3. *Grating so . . . lunacy?:* disturbing his normal calm with such unstable and dangerous madness?
4. *distracted:* terribly confused
5. *forward to be sounded:* willing to be questioned
6. *crafty:* cunning
7. *aloof:* distant/unapproachable
8. *forcing of his disposition:* forcing himself to be pleasant
9. *Niggard . . . reply:* Not showing interest in beginning a conversation but willing to answer our questions.
10. *assay:* tempt
11. *it so fell out:* it happened
12. *o'er-raught:* overtook

POLONIUS

'Tis most true,

And he beseeched me to entreat your majesties   **25**

To hear and see the matter.[13]

CLAUDIUS

With all my heart; and it doth much content me

To hear him so inclined. – Good gentlemen,

Give him a further edge, and drive his purpose on

To these delights.[14]   **30**

ROSENCRANTZ

We shall, my lord.

Exit ROSENCRANTZ and GUILDENSTERN

CLAUDIUS

Sweet Gertrude, leave us too,

For we have closely[15] sent for Hamlet hither,

That he, as 'twere by accident, may here

Affront[16] Ophelia: **35**

Her father and myself, lawful espials,[17]

Will so bestow[18] ourselves that, seeing, unseen,

We may of their encounter frankly judge,

And gather by him, as he is behaved,

If't be th'affliction of his love or no   **40**

That thus he suffers for.[19]

GERTRUDE

I shall obey you.

And for your part, Ophelia, I do wish

That your good beauties be the happy cause

Of Hamlet's wildness; so shall I hope your virtues   **45**

Will bring him to his wonted way[20] again,

To both your honours.[21]

OPHELIA

Madam, I wish it may.

Exit GERTRUDE

POLONIUS

Ophelia, walk you here. – Gracious, so please you,

13. *And he beseeched ... matter:* And he asked me most earnestly to plead with both of your majesties to come and watch the play.

14. *Give him ... delights:* Give him more encouragement and ensure he is focused on these entertainments.

15. *closely:* privately

16. *Affront:* confront

17. *espials:* spies

18. *bestow:* place

19. *And gather ... suffers for:* And I'll judge, by his behaviour, whether or not it is love which causes him to suffer this way.

20. *wonted way:* usual way of behaving

21. *To both your honours:* to the benefit of both of you *It appears Gertrude may be considering the possibility of a marriage between the young couple, if Ophelia can help cure Hamlet's madness.*

We will bestow ourselves. –   50

[To OPHELIA] Read on this book,

That show of such an exercise may colour

Your loneliness.[22] We are oft to blame in this:

'Tis too much proved that with devotion's visage

And pious action we do sugar o'er   55

The devil himself.[23]

a pawn in her father. → as a daughter + a king's subject, she must obey
+ claudius plan

22. *We will bestow ... loneliness:* We will hide. (Ophelia is given a religious book to hold.) Read this book so that such behaviour (reading) may explain why you are by yourself.

Any hesitation she has may be balanced out by her desire to see Hamlet again + hope that her father is right, that Hamlet is lovesick + than then they can be reunited.

23. *We are oft to blame ... devil himself:* We (people in general) are often guilty of this hypocritical behaviour. It is often the case that a show of holiness can sugar-coat evil behaviour. Polonious is simply reflecting on a common human failing, not realising that he is describing Claudius.

CLAUDIUS

O, 'tis too true.

[Aside] How smart[24] a lash that speech doth give

  my conscience.

The harlot's cheek, beautied with plastering art,

Is not more ugly to the thing that helps it   60

Than is my deed to my most painted word.

O heavy burden![25]

24. *smart:* stinging

25. *The harlot's cheek ... burden!:* A prostitute's face is as ugly under the make-up as my murderous deed is under my fine words. This weighs on my conscience.

POLONIUS

I hear him coming. Let's withdraw, my lord.

Exit CLAUDIUS and POLONIUS
Enter HAMLET

His thoughts about life + death → the only reason the misery of life is endured is because of fear of what will happen if they commit suicide.

HAMLET

To be, or not to be; that is the question: → *Is there something in Hamlet's mind that he is also*

Whether 'tis nobler in the mind to suffer   65

The slings and arrows of outrageous fortune,[26]

Or to take arms against a sea of troubles,

And, by opposing, end them?[27] To die, to sleep –

No more,[28] and by a sleep to say we end

The heartache and the thousand natural shocks   70

That flesh is heir to[29] – 'tis a consummation

Devoutly to be wished.[30] To die, to sleep.

To sleep, perchance to dream. Ay, there's the rub,[31]

For in that sleep of death what dreams may come

When we have shuffled off this mortal coil[32]   75

Must give us pause. There's the respect

That makes calamity of so long life,[33]

For who would bear the whips and scorns of time,

The oppressor's wrong, the proud man's contumely,[34]

The pangs of desprized[35] love, the law's delay,   80

The insolence of office,[36] and the spurns

That patient merit of th'unworthy takes,[37]

26. *slings ... fortune:* hardships of fate

27. *Or to take arms ... end them?:* Or to fight against fate and die in the struggle.

28. *No more:* nothing more

29. *That flesh is heir to:* that is part of being human

30. *'tis a consummation ... wished:* it is a conclusion that would be greatly welcomed

31. *there's the rub:* there's the obstacle

32. *mortal coil:* the troubles of this life

33. *There's the respect ... life:* That's the thought that makes troubles so long-lived. *We are not sure what comes after death so we endure suffering rather than die by suicide.*

34. *contumely:* insulting language/slurs

35. *desprized:* unvalued

36. *insolence of office:* arrogance of those in positions of authority

37. *the spurns ... takes:* the insults that patient people tolerate from those more lowly than themselves

When he himself might his quietus make

With a bare bodkin?[38] Who would fardels bear,[39]

To grunt and sweat under a weary life,   85

But that the dread of something after death,

The undiscovered country from whose bourn

No traveller returns,[40] puzzles the will,

And makes us rather bear those ills we have

Than fly to others that we know not of?   90

Thus conscience[41] does make cowards of us all,

And thus the native hue of resolution

Is sicklied o'er with the pale cast of thought,[42]

And enterprises of great pith[43] and moment

With this regard their currents turn awry,   95

And lose the name of action.[44] Soft you now,[45]

The fair Ophelia! – Nymph,[46] in thy orisons[47]

Be all my sins remembered.

OPHELIA

Good my lord,

How does your honour for this many a day?   100

HAMLET

I humbly thank you, well, well, well.

OPHELIA

My lord, I have remembrances[48] of yours

That I have longed long to redeliver.[49]

I pray you, now receive them.   _A rejection of Hamlet for the 2nd time → hurtful action_

HAMLET

No, no, I never gave you aught.[50]   105

OPHELIA

My honoured lord, you know right well you did,

And with them words of so sweet breath composed

As made the things more rich.[51] Their perfume lost,[52]

Take these again; for to the noble mind

Rich gifts wax poor when givers prove unkind.[53]   110

There, my lord.   _She is able to stand up to Hamlet but does so in a kind & gentle way._

HAMLET

Ha, ha? Are you honest?[54]

---

38. _might his quietus . . . bodkin:_ might settle his debts with a mere dagger _Hamlet means that a person might easily find release from the burden of life by killing himself with a dagger._

39. _fardels bear:_ carry burdens

40. _The undiscovered . . . returns:_ This refers to death, the boundary (bourn) from which no-one can return.

41. _conscience:_ This may mean moral judgement or conscious, rational thought.

42. _And thus . . . thought:_ The natural, healthy colour of resolution is made to look sickly with the pallor of thought. _This means that too much thinking impairs a person's ability to act._

43. _pith:_ importance

44. _With this . . . action:_ Things are diverted from their proper course in this way and are never acted upon.

45. _Soft you now:_ Be quiet.

46. _Nymph:_ beautiful girl

47. _thy orisons:_ your prayers _Hamlet asks Ophelia to remember him in her prayers and to pray that his sins may be forgiven._

48. _remembrances:_ keepsakes – gifts or letters that Hamlet gave Ophelia

49. _redeliver:_ return

50. _aught:_ anything

51. _And with them . . . rich:_ And you gave them with such sweet words that the tokens themselves had more value as a result.

52. _Their perfume lost:_ Their sweetness is gone without your sweet words.

53. _Rich gifts . . . unkind:_ Valuable gifts lose their value when those who gave them act unkindly.

54. _honest:_ This could mean truthful or chaste (virginal).

OPHELIA

My lord.

HAMLET

Are you fair?

OPHELIA

What means your lordship?   **115**

HAMLET

That if you be honest and fair, your honesty should
admit no discourse to your beauty.[55]

OPHELIA

Could beauty, my lord, have better commerce[56] than
with honesty?

HAMLET

Ay, truly, for the power of beauty will sooner   **120**
transform honesty from what it is to a bawd than the
force of honesty can translate beauty into his
likeness.[57] This was sometime a paradox,[58] but now the
time gives it proof. I did love you once.

OPHELIA

Indeed, my lord, you made me believe so.   **125**

HAMLET

You should not have believed me, for virtue cannot
so inoculate our old stock but we shall relish of
it.[59] I loved you not.

OPHELIA

I was the more deceived.

HAMLET

Get thee to a nunnery.[60] Why wouldst thou be a   **130**
breeder of sinners?[61] I am myself indifferent[61] honest,
but yet I could accuse me of such things that it
were better my mother had not borne me. I am very
proud, revengeful, ambitious, with more offences at
my beck[62] than I have thoughts to put them in,   **135**
imagination to give them shape, or time to act them
in. What should such fellows as I do crawling

55. *That if ... beauty:* If you are chaste and beautiful, your chastity should not allow anyone access to your beauty. *Hamlet means that beautiful women should stay away from men if they wish to remain chaste.*

56. *commerce:* dealings

57. *Ay, truly ... likeness:* Yes, for it is easier for beauty to turn chastity into a prostitute than it is for chastity to make beauty chaste. *Hamlet means that beauty is more likely to corrupt a pure woman than purity is likely to make a beautiful woman chaste.*

58. *paradox:* seeming contradiction

59. *for virtue ... it:* Hamlet uses the metaphor of a gardener grafting (inoculating) a piece of a worthy plant (virtue) onto the stem – or stock – of an unworthy plant (corruption and sin). If this is done, some of the flavour or 'relish' of the old plant will remain.

60. *nunnery:* convent *In Elizabethan slang, 'nunnery' could also mean 'brothel'.*

61. *indifferent:* reasonably

62. *beck:* call on; command

63. *arrant knaves:* absolute scoundrels

64. *Where's your father?:* Hamlet may suspect Polonius is spying on him.

65. *plague:* curse

66. *calumny:* slander

67. *Or if ... monsters:* Or if you must marry, marry a fool; because wise men know that you cheat on them. 'Monsters' here means 'cuckolds'. Men whose wives were unfaithful were called cuckolds, and were portrayed as having horns on their heads.

68. *paintings:* make-up

69. *You jig ... ignorance:* You dance, move and speak seductively and use silly nicknames; you claim ignorance as an excuse for such brazenly flirtatious behaviour.

70. *all but one:* Presumably Claudius is the one who will not be permitted to remain married.

71. *Th'expectancy ... state:* the finest flower and hope of Denmark

72. *The glass of fashion:* the picture of fashion

73. *the mould of form:* the model of behaviour

74. *down:* reduced

between heaven and earth? We are arrant knaves,[63] all. Believe none of us. Go thy ways to a nunnery. Where's your father?[64]   **140**

OPHELIA

At home, my lord.

HAMLET

Let the doors be shut upon him, that he may play the fool nowhere but in's own house. Farewell.

OPHELIA

O help him, you sweet heavens!

HAMLET

If thou dost marry, I'll give thee this plague[65] for   **145**
thy dowry: be thou as chaste as ice, as pure as
snow, thou shalt not escape calumny.[66] Get thee to a
nunnery, go, farewell. Or if thou wilt needs
marry, marry a fool; for wise men know well enough
what monsters[67] you make of them. To a nunnery, go,   **150**
and quickly, too. Farewell.

OPHELIA

O heavenly powers, restore him!

making an excellent attempt at fooling Ophelia.

HAMLET

I have heard of your paintings,[68] too, well enough. God
hath given you one face, and you make yourselves
another. You jig, you amble, and you lisp, and   **155**
nickname God's creatures, and make your wantonness
your ignorance.[69] Go to, I'll no more on't. It hath
made me mad. I say we will have no more marriages.
Those that are married already – all but one[70] – shall
live. The rest shall keep as they are. To a nunnery, go.   **160**

Exit   *Despite his cruel words & erratic behaviour, Ophelia refuses to think badly of Hamlet. We sense here that they have been driven apart by circumstances & misunderstanding*

OPHELIA *yet truly in love & meant to be together.*

O, what a noble mind is here o'erthrown!
The courtier's, soldier's, scholar's eye, tongue, sword,
Th'expectancy and rose of the fair state,[71]
The glass of fashion[72] and the mould of form,[73]
The observed of all observers, quite, quite down![74]   **165**

And I, of ladies most deject and wretched,

That sucked the honey of his music vows,[75]

Now see that noble and most sovereign reason

Like sweet bells jangled, out of tune and harsh;

That unmatched form and feature of blown[76] youth   **170**

Blasted with ecstasy.[77] O woe is me,

T'have seen what I have seen, see what I see!

Re-enter CLAUDIUS and POLONIUS

CLAUDIUS

Love? His affections[78] do not that way tend,

Nor what he spake, though it lacked form a little,

Was not like madness.[79] There's something in his soul   **175**

O'er which his melancholy sits on brood,[80]

And I do doubt the hatch and the disclose

Will be some danger;[81] which for to prevent

I have in quick determination

Thus set it down: he shall with speed to England   **180**

For the demand of our neglected tribute[82]

Haply the seas and countries different,

With variable objects,[83] shall expel

This something-settled matter in his heart,

Whereon his brains still beating[84] puts him thus   **185**

From fashion of himself.[85] What think you on't?

POLONIUS

It shall do well.[86] But yet do I believe

The origin and commencement of his grief

Sprung from neglected love.[87] – How now, Ophelia?

You need not tell us what Lord Hamlet said;   **190**

We heard it all. – My lord, do as you please,

But, if you hold it fit,[88] after the play

Let his queen mother all alone entreat him

To show his griefs. Let her be round[89] with him,

And I'll be placed, so please you, in the ear   **195**

Of all their conference. If she find him not,[90]

To England send him, or confine him where

Your wisdom best shall think.

CLAUDIUS

It shall be so.

Madness in great ones must not unwatched go.   **200**

Exit

75. *And I, of ladies . . . music vows:* And I am the most unhappy of all the women who listened to his sweet-sounding promises of love.

76. *blown:* blossoming

77. *Blasted with ecstasy:* blighted by madness

78. *affections:* passions

79. *Nor what . . . madness:* His speech, although a little disjointed, did not sound like the words of a madman.

80. *sits on brood:* broods over, like a hen sitting on eggs to hatch them

81. *And I do doubt . . . danger:* And I believe that when the plot he is hatching is revealed it will prove dangerous.

82. *our neglected tribute:* **money owed to the Danish king by the English**

83. *Haply . . . variable objects:* perhaps the seas and new countries with various different things to see

84. *This something . . . brains still beating:* this thing that is upsetting him and which is constantly on his mind

85. *puts him . . . himself:* causes him to be so unlike his usual self

86. *It shall do well:* It is a good idea.

87. *neglected love:* unrequited love

88. *hold it fit:* think it right to do so

89. *round:* blunt

90. *And I'll be placed . . . find him not:* And I will be hidden where I can overhear their conversation. If she cannot find out what is wrong with him

Act 3 Scene 1
Quotes and Questions

Quotes

'Tis too much proved that with devotion's visage
And pious action we do sugar o'er
The devil himself.

(Polonius, lines 54–56)

As Polonius gives Ophelia a prayer book and tells her to pretend to read it, he reflects that it is common for people to pretend to be religious and devoted to God while actually living sinful lives.

How smart a lash that speech doth give my conscience.

(Claudius, line 58)

Claudius reacts to Polonius's comment about people hiding their evil deeds beneath a mask of piety, remarking to himself that the words make him feel very guilty.

To be, or not to be; that is the question:
Whether 'tis nobler in the mind to suffer
The slings and arrows of outrageous fortune,
Or to take arms against a sea of troubles,
And, by opposing, end them? To die, to sleep –
No more, and by a sleep to say we end
The heartache and the thousand natural shocks
That flesh is heir to – 'tis a consummation
Devoutly to be wished. To die, to sleep.
To sleep, perchance to dream. Ay, there's the rub,
For in that sleep of death what dreams may come
When we have shuffled off this mortal coil
Must give us pause.

(Hamlet, lines 64–76)

In what is undoubtedly his most famous speech, Hamlet thinks about life and death. He treats suicide in a general, philosophical way rather than something he has seriously considered for himself. Hamlet says that to take one's own life would be a way to end the pain and suffering of life, but he accepts that not knowing what happens after death is enough to give people pause for thought.

Thus conscience does make cowards of us all,
And thus the native hue of resolution
Is sicklied o'er with the pale cast of thought

(Hamlet, lines 91–93)

Hamlet observes that thinking too deeply about something can prevent us from acting. His conscience prevents him from taking swift action against Claudius. Hamlet is a typical intellectual of the time: focusing on philosophical ideas and exploring the human condition.

> *Get thee to a nunnery. Why wouldst thou be a*
> *breeder of sinners?*
>
> (Hamlet, lines 130–131)

Hamlet tells Ophelia she should go and live in a convent rather than give birth to sinners. He is disgusted by his mother's sexuality and turns his anger on Ophelia. Of course, he may also be genuinely hurt by her treatment of him.

> *wise men know well enough*
> *what monsters you make of them*
>
> (Hamlet, lines 149–150)

Hamlet's view of marriage is so tainted by his mother's marriage to Claudius that he believes all women are unfaithful to their husbands.

> *O, what a noble mind is here o'erthrown!*
> *The courtier's, soldier's, scholar's eye, tongue, sword,*
> *Th'expectancy and rose of the fair state*
>
> (Ophelia, lines 161–163)

Ophelia mourns what she sees as Hamlet's slide into insanity. She says he was a great debater, a brave soldier and a wise scholar. In short, he was Denmark's great hope for the future.

Questions

In each case, support your point with suitable reference to and quotation from the play.

1. How does Gertrude treat Ophelia in this scene?

2. What happens in this scene to indicate that Claudius has a guilty conscience?

3. What does Hamlet's soliloquy tell us about his state of mind?

4. When Hamlet is talking to Ophelia, are there any indications that he may know they are being overheard?

5. What does Hamlet's conversation with Ophelia tell us about his views of women?

6. How do you think Ophelia felt after her conversation with Hamlet?

7. Do you think Polonius is shown to be a good father in this scene? Explain your answer.

8. What indications are there that Claudius fears Hamlet? What does he plan to do with him after overhearing his conversation with Ophelia?

Writing Task

In your own words, rewrite Hamlet's 'To be, or not to be' soliloquy (line 64).

Essay Building Blocks

'The fascination of the character, Hamlet, lies in the fact that he ranges from subtle reflections on morality and life to cynical, harsh actions.'

Write a paragraph in response to this statement, supporting your answer with quotation from and reference to Act 3 Scene 1.

A hall in the castle

Hamlet instructs the actors on how they should perform the play, warning them against overacting. Alone with Horatio, Hamlet praises his friend's calmness and self-control. He lets Horatio in on his plan to trap Claudius into revealing his guilt and asks him to observe the King closely during the performance.

The court assembles to watch the play. Hamlet sits with Ophelia but distresses her with a series of crude sexual innuendoes.

The play begins with a dumb show in which a man pours poison into a sleeping king's ears and then woos the widowed queen. The spoken version of the play adds more details to the brief, mimed version. The onstage queen professes her love for her husband and promises never to marry again if he should die. Hamlet asks Gertrude what she thinks of the play but she does not seem greatly moved by it. When the poisoner, who is the king's nephew, pours his distilment into the sleeping king's ears, Claudius calls for lights and storms off, followed by the rest of the court except for Hamlet and Horatio. Hamlet is delighted with what he sees as incontrovertible proof of Claudius's guilt.

Rosencrantz and Guildenstern arrive with a message from Gertrude, asking Hamlet to come straight to her room to speak to her. Hamlet is angry with his old friends for spying on him and says they will not succeed in manipulating him.

Polonius enters with a repetition of Gertrude's desire to see Hamlet straight away. He says he will go to her shortly.

Alone onstage at the end of the scene, Hamlet admits to harbouring thoughts of violence but says he will control himself in his meeting with his mother. Although his words may be harsh, he will not physically harm her.

Act 3

1. *pronounced:* delivered; recited

2. *trippingly:* easily or lightly

3. *if you mouth it . . . my lines:* if you overact when reading it, as many of your actors do, I would rather have my lines spoken by the town crier *The town crier was a man employed by the town to deliver public announcements. He did so by shouting them as loudly as possible, so all could hear.*

4. *use all gently:* do everything gently and gracefully

5. *for in the very torrent . . . smoothness:* for even the most stormy, passionate emotions must be delivered with restraint so that they are believable

6. *robustious . . . fellow:* boisterous actor wearing a wig

7. *tear a passion . . . groundlings:* ruin a passionate speech by deafening the poor audience members *Groundlings were audience members who bought the cheapest tickets and stood on the ground in front of the stage, rather than sitting in the seats around the edge of the theatre.*

8. *capable . . . inexplicable dumb shows:* can only appreciate pointless, meaningless mimes

9. *Termagant:* An imaginary god of violent and turbulent character, often appearing in morality plays. His part would have been a loud and boisterous one, difficult to overact.

10. *out-Herods Herod:* Another villainous stage character: the king of Israel at the time of Christ. Like Termagant, his role would have been loud and boisterous.

11. *I warrant your honour:* I guarantee you we will not do that, sir.

12. *that you . . . nature:* to not act in an unnatural manner

13. *from:* against

14. *the very age . . . pressure:* show society its shape and impression

15. *come tardy off:* performed with poor timing; failing

16. *unskilful:* those without taste

17. *censure:* severe disapproval

18. *neither . . . nor no man:* neither speak nor walk like real people

19. *I have thought . . . abominably:* It appeared as if humankind had been made by an unskilled workman, these actors showed humanity in such a bad light.

Enter HAMLET and PLAYERS

HAMLET

Speak the speech, I pray you, as I pronounced[1] it to
you – trippingly[2] on the tongue; but if you mouth it,
as many of your players do, I had as lief the
town-crier spoke my lines.[3] Nor do not saw the air
too much with your hand, thus, but use all gently;[4] **5**
for in the very torrent, tempest, and as I may say
the whirlwind of your passion, you must acquire and
beget a temperance that may give it smoothness.[5]
O, it offends me to the soul to hear a robustious,
periwig-pated fellow[6] tear a passion to tatters, to **10**
very rags, to split the ears of the groundlings,[7] who
for the most part are capable of nothing but
inexplicable dumb shows[8] and noise. I would have
such a fellow whipped for o'erdoing Termagant.[9]
It out-Herods Herod.[10] Pray you, avoid it. **15**

FIRST PLAYER

I warrant your honour.[11]

HAMLET

Be not too tame, neither, but let your own discretion
be your tutor: suit the action to the word, the word to the
action, with this special observance: that you o'erstep
not the modesty of nature.[12] For anything so overdone is **20**
from[13] the purpose of playing, whose end, both at the first
and now, was and is to hold as 'twere, the mirror up to
nature, to show virtue her own feature, scorn her own
image, and the very age and body of the time his form
and pressure.[14] Now this overdone, or come tardy off,[15] **25**
though it make the unskilful[16] laugh, cannot but make the
judicious grieve; the censure[17] of the which one must in
your allowance o'erweigh a whole theatre of others. O,
there be players that I have seen play, and heard others
praise, and that highly, not to speak it profanely, that **30**
neither having the accent of Christians nor the gait of
Christian, pagan, nor no man,[18] have so strutted and
bellowed that I have thought some of nature's
journeymen had made men, and not made them well,
they imitated humanity so abominably.[19] **35**

FIRST PLAYER

I hope we have reformed that indifferently[20] with us, sir.

20. *reformed that indifferently:* corrected that fairly well

HAMLET

O, reform it altogether. And let those that play
your clowns speak no more than is set down for them;
for there be of them that will themselves laugh to
set on some quantity of barren spectators to laugh[21]   **40**
too, though, in the meantime some necessary
question[22] of the play be then to be considered.
That's villanous, and shows a most pitiful ambition
in the fool that uses it. Go make you ready.

21. *set on … laugh:* encourage a number of stupid spectators to laugh

22. *necessary question:* important issue

Exit PLAYERS
Enter POLONIUS, ROSENCRANTZ, and GUILDENSTERN

How now, my lord? Will the King hear this piece of work?   **45**

POLONIUS

And the Queen too, and that presently.

HAMLET

Bid the players make haste.

Exit POLONIUS

Will you two help to hasten them?

ROSENCRANTZ and **GUILDENSTERN**

We will, my lord.

Exit ROSENCRANTZ and GUILDENSTERN

HAMLET

What ho, Horatio!   **50**

Enter HORATIO

HORATIO

Here, sweet lord, at your service.

HAMLET

Horatio, thou art e'en[23] as just[24] a man
As e'er my conversation coped withal.[25]

23. *e'en:* even
24. *just:* balanced; normal
25. *As e'er … withal:* As I have ever met

Act 3

HORATIO

O my dear lord –

HAMLET

Nay, do not think I flatter;   **55**

For what advancement[26] may I hope from thee,

That no revenue hast but thy good spirits,

To feed and clothe thee? Why should the poor be flattered?[27]

No, let the candied tongue lick absurd pomp,

And crook the pregnant hinges of the knee   **60**

Where thrift may follow fawning.[28] Dost thou hear? –

Since my dear soul was mistress of her choice

And could of men distinguish, her election

Hath sealed thee for herself;[29] for thou hast been

As one in suffering all that suffers nothing,[30]   **65**

A man that Fortune's buffets[31] and rewards

Hast ta'en with equal thanks; and blest are those

Whose blood and judgment are so well commingled,[32]

That they are not a pipe for Fortune's finger

To sound what stop she please.[33] Give me that man   **70**

That is not passion's slave,[34] and I will wear him

In my heart's core, ay, in my heart of heart,

As I do thee. Something too much of this.[35]

There is a play tonight before the King;

One scene of it comes near the circumstance   **75**

Which I have told thee of my father's death.

I prithee,[36] when thou seest that act afoot,

Even with the very comment of thy soul[37]

Observe mine uncle. If his occulted[38] guilt

Do not itself unkennel[39] in one speech,   **80**

It is a damned ghost that we have seen,

And my imaginations are as foul

As Vulcan's smithy.[40] Give him heedful note,[41]

For I mine eyes will rivet to his face,[42]

And after, we will both our judgments join   **85**

In censure of his seeming.[43]

HORATIO

Well, my lord.

If he steal aught[44] the whilst this play is playing

And scape[45] detecting, I will pay the theft.[46]

HAMLET

They are coming to the play. I must be idle:[47]   90

Get you a place.

Danish march. A flourish.

Enter CLAUDIUS, GERTRUDE, POLONIUS, OPHELIA,

ROSENCRANTZ, GUILDENSTERN, and others

CLAUDIUS

How fares our cousin Hamlet?

HAMLET

Excellent, i'faith, of the chameleon's dish.[48] I eat the air,[49]

promise-crammed.[50] You cannot feed capons[51] so.

CLAUDIUS

I have nothing with this answer, Hamlet. These words   95

are not mine.[52]

HAMLET

No, nor mine now. *[To POLONIUS]* My lord, you played

once in the university, you say.

POLONIUS

That did I, my lord, and was accounted a good actor.

HAMLET

What did you enact?   100

POLONIUS

I did enact Julius Caesar: I was killed in the Capitol.

Brutus killed me.[53]

HAMLET

It was a brute part[54] of him to kill so capital[55] a calf[56]

there. – Be the players ready?

ROSENCRANTZ

Ay, my lord, they stay upon your patience.[57]   105

GERTRUDE

Come hither, my good Hamlet. Sit by me.

47. *be idle:* pretend to be mad; act the fool

48. *chameleon's dish:* It was believed that chameleons did not eat but survived on air.

49. *air:* This may be a pun on 'heir'.

50. *promise-crammed:* Claudius promised the throne to Hamlet, but Hamlet has also promised the Ghost that he will avenge his death.

51. *capons:* Capons were male chickens castrated and force-fed so they would be tender and fat. Hamlet is probably hinting that Claudius believes he, Hamlet, is a harmless creature who can be killed when required.

52. *These words are not mine:* Your words do not answer my question.

53. *I did enact . . . me:* Shakespeare's Julius Caesar had been a huge success and it is thought that the actor playing Polonius had played the role of Caesar and the actor playing Hamlet had played the role of Brutus. Thus, this short exchange would have had an added meaning for the audience of the time.

54. *brute part:* brutal *a pun of sorts on Brutus*

55. *capital:* Another pun: 'capital' means first-rate but it could also be a reference to the Capitol, the place where Brutus announced the death of Caesar.

56. *calf:* Another pun: a calf in this context could mean that Claudius's role was important and that killing off his character was like killing off a valuable animal. However, 'calf' also meant 'fool' at the time.

57. *stay upon your patience:* wait for you

58. *here's metal more attractive:* This could mean that Ophelia, like a magnetic metal, draws Hamlet to her. It could also be a pun on 'mettle', meaning a person's spirit or moral fibre.

59. *shall I lie in your lap?:* This could simply mean, 'Can I rest my head on your knees?', which would have been quite acceptable at the time, but it also has sexual undertones, which Ophelia recognises.

60. *country matters:* Sex. This is a very crude play on words.

61. *fair:* pleasant

62. *Nothing:* 'Nothing' was Elizabethan slang for vagina. Hamlet is being deliberately ambiguous and offensive.

HAMLET

No, good-mother, here's metal more attractive.[58]

POLONIUS

[To CLAUDIUS] O, ho, do you mark that?

HAMLET

Lady, shall I lie in your lap?[59]

Lying down at OPHELIA's feet

OPHELIA

No, my lord.   110

HAMLET

I mean, my head upon your lap?

OPHELIA

Ay, my lord.

HAMLET

Do you think I meant country matters?[60]

OPHELIA

I think nothing, my lord.

HAMLET

That's a fair[61] thought to lie between maids' legs.   115

OPHELIA

What is, my lord?

HAMLET

Nothing.[62]

OPHELIA

You are merry, my lord.

HAMLET

Who, I?

OPHELIA

Ay, my lord.   120

HAMLET

O God, your only jig-maker![63] What should a man do but be merry? For look you how cheerfully my mother looks, and my father died within's two hours.[64]

OPHELIA

Nay, 'tis twice two months, my lord.

HAMLET

So long? Nay then, let the devil wear black, for I'll have   **125**
a suit of sables.[65] O heavens, die two months ago and not forgotten yet! Then there's hope a great man's memory may outlive his life half a year. But, by'r Lady, he must build churches then, or else shall he suffer not thinking on, with the hobby-horse,[66] whose epitaph is 'For O, for   **130**
O, the hobby-horse is forgot.'

Hautboys[67] play. The dumb-show[68] enters

Enter a King and a Queen very lovingly; the Queen embracing him, and he her. She kneels, and makes show of protestation unto him. He takes her up, and declines his head upon her neck: lays him down upon a bank of flowers: she, seeing him asleep, leaves him. Anon[69] comes in a fellow, takes off his crown, kisses it, and pours poison in the King's ears, and exit. The Queen returns; finds the King dead, and makes passionate action. The Poisoner, with some two or three Mutes, comes in again, seeming to lament with her. The dead body is carried away. The Poisoner woos the Queen with gifts: she seems loath and unwilling awhile, but in the end accepts his love.

Exit

OPHELIA

What means this, my lord?

HAMLET

Marry, this is miching malhecho.[70] That means mischief.

OPHELIA

Belike[71] this show imports[72] the argument[73] of the play.

Enter PROLOGUE

63. *your only jig-maker:* I am your only entertainer

64. *What should . . . two hours:* What else should a person do but be happy? Look how cheerful my mother appears, and my father has only been dead for two hours.

65. *Nay then . . . sables:* As two months is too long to wear mourning clothes, Hamlet says he will let the devil wear them instead and he will wear luxurious furs.

66. *hobby-horse:* A horse costume worn by a Morris dancer during May Day rituals. The hobby-horse was a symbol of continuity and memory. It was also a half-man, half-animal figure. Hamlet may be saying that his father was a symbol of continuity but has been forgotten. He previously referred to Claudius as a 'satyr', a half-man, half-animal figure associated with sexual promiscuity and bestial behaviour.

67. *Hautboys:* high-pitched, wooden instruments

68. *dumb-show:* short mime introducing the play

69. *Anon:* Shortly afterwards

70. *miching malhecho:* sneaky wickedness

71. *Belike:* Perhaps
72. *imports:* indicates
73. *argument:* plot

74. *counsel:* secrets

75. *any show . . . him:* anything you show him *Hamlet is making another sexual pun here, implying that Ophelia may show the actor an intimate part of herself.*

76. *naught:* naughty *meaning 'offensive' in Shakespeare's time*

77. *clemency:* mercy

78. *posy of a ring:* short verse inscribed on a ring

79. *Phoebus:* Phoebus Apollo, the sun god who drove across the sky. The sun was his chariot.
80. *Neptune's salt wash:* the sea *Neptune was the god of the sea.*
81. *Tellus' orbed ground:* Tellus was the god of the earth. His 'orbed ground' is the globe.
82. *borrowed sheen:* reflected light
83. *Hymen:* god of marriage and fertility
84. *commutual:* together

85. *So many . . . be done:* May our love last another 30 years.

HAMLET

We shall know by this fellow. The players cannot   **135**
keep counsel,[74] they'll tell all.

OPHELIA

Will he tell us what this show meant?

HAMLET

Ay, or any show that you'll show him.[75] Be not you
ashamed to show, he'll not shame to tell you what
it means.   **140**

OPHELIA

You are naught,[76] you are naught. I'll mark the play.

PROLOGUE

For us and for our tragedy
Here stooping to your clemency[77]
We beg your hearing patiently.

Exit

HAMLET

Is this a prologue, or the posy of a ring?[78]   **145**

OPHELIA

'Tis brief, my lord.

HAMLET

As woman's love.

Enter two PLAYERS, KING and QUEEN

PLAYER KING

Full thirty times hath Phoebus[79] cart gone round
Neptune's salt wash[80] and Tellus' orbed ground,[81]
And thirty dozen moons with borrowed sheen[82]   **150**
About the world have times twelve thirties been,
Since love our hearts and Hymen[83] did our hands
Unite commutual[84] in most sacred bands.

PLAYER QUEEN

So many journeys may the sun and moon
Make us again count o'er ere love be done.[85]   **155**

But woe is me, you are so sick of late,

So far from cheer and from your former state,

That I distrust[86] you. Yet, though I distrust,

Discomfort you my lord it nothing must.[87]

For women's fear and love holds quantity,[88]   **160**

In neither aught, or in extremity.[89]

Now, what my love is, proof hath made you know,

And as my love is sized, my fear is so.[90]

Where love is great, the littlest doubts are fear;

Where little fears grow great, great love grows there.   **165**

PLAYER KING

Faith, I must leave thee, love, and shortly too.

My operant powers their functions leave to do,[91]

And thou shalt live in this fair world behind,

Honoured, beloved; and haply one as kind

For husband shalt thou[92] –   **170**

PLAYER QUEEN

O, confound the rest![93]

Such love must needs be treason in my breast:

In second husband let me be accurst;[94]

None wed the second but who kill'd the first.[95]

HAMLET

[Aside] Wormwood, wormwood.[96]   **175**

PLAYER QUEEN

The instances that second marriage move

Are base respects of thrift, but none of love.[97]

A second time I kill my husband dead

When second husband kisses me in bed.[98]

PLAYER KING

I do believe you think what now you speak;   **180**

But what we do determine oft we break.

Purpose is but the slave to memory,

Of violent birth, but poor validity,[99]

Which now like fruit unripe sticks on the tree,

But fall unshaken when they mellow[100] be.   **185**

Most necessary 'tis that we forget

To pay ourselves what to ourselves is debt.[101]

What to ourselves in passion we propose,

---

86. *distrust:* am worried about

87. *Discomfort . . . must:* It must not worry you, my lord.

88. *holds quantity:* are balanced

89. *In neither . . . extremity:* either nothing or too much

90. *as my love . . . so:* My fear is as great as my love.

91. *My operant . . . do:* My vital organs are ceasing to work.

92. *haply . . . thou:* perhaps you shall find another husband as kind

93. *confound the rest!:* Damn the rest of your speech!

94. *accurst:* cursed

95. *In second . . . first:* Let me be cursed if I have a second husband; no woman marries a second husband unless she has killed her first husband.

96. *Wormwood:* A bitter medicinal plant. Hamlet is suggesting that Claudius and Gertrude will find this comment a bitter pill to swallow.

97. *The instances . . . love:* The motivations for second marriages are lowly pursuits of money, but not of love.

98. *A second time . . . in bed:* Whenever my second husband kisses me in bed it is as if I am killing my first husband again.

99. *Purpose . . . validity:* Resolutions are only kept if they are remembered. They are born of great passion but lack true feeling and do not last.

100. *mellow:* ripe

101. *Most necessary . . . debt:* We forget to keep the promises we have made to ourselves.

102. *enactures:* acting upon the resolution

103. *Grief . . . accident:* Grief turns to joy and joy to grief on the slightest chance.
104. *aye:* ever

105. *For 'tis a question . . . of enemies:* We still do not have a clear answer on whether love leads to fate or fate leads to love. When the powerful man falls, his friends abandon him; when the poor man rises in the world, even his former enemies become his friends.
106. *hitherto:* up to this point
107. *who not needs:* The person who wants for nothing *(is well off)*
108. *who in want . . . enemy:* A person who is in need finds and tests a friend's generosity and immediately turns him into an enemy.

109. *devices:* plans

110. *ends none our own:* we cannot control the results

111. *die thy thoughts:* your resolution will die

112. *Sport . . . night:* May I have no pleasure during the day nor rest at night.

113. *An anchor's cheer:* a hermit's diet

114. *Each opposite . . . destroy:* Let the opposing forces that wipe out joy cause my happy dreams to be destroyed.
115. *pursue . . . strife:* let endless conflict follow me

116. *break it:* break her vow

117. *fain I would beguile:* I wish to charm away

The passion ending, doth the purpose lose.
The violence of either grief or joy   **190**
Their own enactures[102] with themselves destroy.
Where joy most revels, grief doth most lament;
Grief joys, joy grieves, on slender accident.[103]
This world is not for aye,[104] nor 'tis not strange
That even our loves should with our fortunes change;   **195**
For 'tis a question left us yet to prove
Whether love lead fortune or else fortune love.
The great man down, you mark his favourite flies;
The poor advanced makes friends of enemies.[105]
And hitherto[106] doth love on fortune tend,   **200**
For who not needs[107] shall never lack a friend,
And who in want a hollow friend doth try
Directly seasons him his enemy.[108]
But orderly to end where I begun,
Our wills and fates do so contrary run   **205**
That our devices[109] still are overthrown;
Our thoughts are ours, their ends none of our own.[110]
So think thou wilt no second husband wed;
But die thy thoughts[111] when thy first lord is dead.

PLAYER QUEEN

Nor earth to me give food, nor heaven light,   **210**
Sport and repose lock from me day and night,[112]
To desperation turn my trust and hope;
An anchor's cheer[113] in prison be my scope.
Each opposite that blanks the face of joy
Meet what I would have well and it destroy,[114]   **215**
Both here and hence pursue me lasting strife[115]
If, once a widow, ever I be wife!

HAMLET

If she should break it[116] now!

PLAYER KING

'Tis deeply sworn. Sweet, leave me here a while.
My spirits grow dull, and fain I would beguile[117]   **220**
The tedious day with sleep.

Sleeps

PLAYER QUEEN

Sleep rock thy brain,

And never come mischance between us twain.[118]

Exit

HAMLET

Madam, how like you this play?

GERTRUDE

The lady protests too much, methinks.[119]   **225**

HAMLET

O, but she'll keep her word.

CLAUDIUS

Have you heard the argument? Is there no offence in 't?[120]

HAMLET

No, no, they do but jest, poison in jest. No offence
in the world.[121]

CLAUDIUS

What do you call the play?   **230**

HAMLET

The Mousetrap.[122] Marry, how? Tropically.[123] This play is the
image[124] of a murder done in Vienna. Gonzago is the
Duke's name, his wife Baptista. You shall see anon.[125] 'Tis
a knavish piece of work; but what of that? Your majesty,
and we that have free souls, it touches us not. Let the   **235**
galled jade wince, our withers are unwrung.[126]

Enter LUCIANUS

This is one Lucianus, nephew to the King.

OPHELIA

You are as good as a chorus, my lord.

HAMLET

I could interpret between you and your love if I could
see the puppets dallying.[127]   **240**

---

118. *And never . . . twain:* And may no bad fortune come between us.

119. *The lady . . . methinks:* I believe the lady's vows of love are so overdone that they lack credibility. *In Shakespeare's time, 'protest' did not mean to object to something but to affirm it.*

120. *Have you . . . in 't?:* Do you know the plot? I hope it is not offensive.

121. *No, no . . . world:* Hamlet plays with the word 'poison' here by using it to mean offend, obviously hoping to make Claudius uneasy. He says the actors are only pretending, so there is nothing to offend anyone.

122. *The Mousetrap:* Hamlet has invented this name to fit in with his plan to 'catch the conscience of the king'.
123. *Tropically:* figuratively *A trope is a figure of speech.*
124. *image:* representation
125. *anon:* soon

126. *Let . . . unwrung:* Let the horse with saddle sores wince in pain, our shoulders are not chafed. *In other words, let the guilty feel the sting of this play; we who are innocent will be unmoved.*

127. *I could . . . dallying:* If I could see you and your lover as puppets in a show, I could speak the lines.

128. *keen:* sharp or having the keen edge of desire

129. *It would . . . edge:* Hamlet pretends that Ophelia meant he was full of desire and he says that she would have to groan in lovemaking to take the edge off his desire.

130. *Still . . . worse:* Both wittier and more offensive.

131. *So . . . husbands:* So you take other men for your husbands. Hamlet is playing on Ophelia's 'better and worse' as they resemble the words spoken in a wedding ceremony.
132. *Pox:* curse you
133. *leave . . . faces:* stop pulling faces
134. *'the croaking . . . revenge':* A misquotation from another play: The True Tragedy of Richard III.

135. *hands apt:* hands ready
136. *drugs fit:* the appropriate drug
137. *Confederate season:* the time conspiring to make this the ideal moment
138. *rank:* foul
139. *Hecate's ban thrice blasted:* cursed three times in the name of Hecate *(goddess of witchcraft)*
140. *Thy natural magic . . . immediately:* Use your deadly properties to instantly take away healthy life.

141. *for his estate:* to get his kingdom
142. *extant:* exists in written form

143. *frighted with false fire?:* frightened by blank ammunition?

144. *Give o'er:* stop

OPHELIA

You are keen,[128] my lord, you are keen.

HAMLET

It would cost you a groaning to take off my edge.[129]

OPHELIA

Still better, and worse.[130]

HAMLET

So you mistake your husbands.[131] Begin, murderer.
Pox,[132] leave thy damnable faces[133] and begin. Come: 245
'the croaking raven doth bellow for revenge'.[134]

LUCIANUS

Thoughts black, hands apt,[135] drugs fit,[136] and time agreeing;
Confederate season,[137] else no creature seeing;
Thou mixture rank,[138] of midnight weeds collected,
With Hecate's ban thrice blasted,[139] thrice infected,   250
Thy natural magic and dire property
On wholesome life usurp immediately.[140]

Pours the poison into the sleeper's ears

HAMLET

He poisons him in the garden for his estate.[141] His name's
Gonzago. The story is extant,[142] and writ in choice Italian.
You shall see anon how the murderer gets the love of   255
Gonzago's wife.

OPHELIA

The King rises.

HAMLET

What, frighted with false fire?[143]

GERTRUDE

How fares my lord?

POLONIUS

Give o'er[144] the play.   260

CLAUDIUS

Give me some light. Away!

ALL

Lights, lights, lights!

Exit all but HAMLET and HORATIO

HAMLET

Why, let the stricken deer go weep,

The hart ungalled play,

For some must watch, while some must sleep,   **265**

So runs the world away.[145]

Would not this, sir, and a forest of feathers, if

the rest of my fortunes turn Turk with me, with two

Provençal roses on my razed shoes, get me a

fellowship in a cry of players, sir?[146]   **270**

HORATIO

Half a share.

HAMLET

A whole one, I.

For thou dost know, O Damon[147] dear,

This realm dismantled was

Of Jove himself,[148] and now reigns here   **275**

A very, very – pajock.[149]

HORATIO

You might have rhymed.[150]

HAMLET

O good Horatio, I'll take the Ghost's word for a

thousand pound. Didst perceive?[151]

HORATIO

Very well, my lord.   **280**

HAMLET

Upon the talk of the poisoning?

HORATIO

I did very well note him.

Re-enter ROSENCRANTZ and GUILDENSTERN

145. *Why … away:* Lines from a ballad. The distressed, injured deer must be on his guard while the uninjured one can enjoy himself at his leisure and rest.

146. *Would not … sir?:* Would not this play – along with the feathers an actor wears on his hat, actors' shoes with rosettes and designs engraved on them – get me a partnership in a company of actors if my fortunes abandon me?

147. *Damon:* The legend of Damon and Pythias centres on a devoted friendship.

148. *This realm … himself:* The kingdom was taken from a man like Jove. *Jove was the chief deity.*

149. *pajock:* peacock *insulting term for a vain and worthless man*

150. *You might have rhymed:* If Hamlet had used rhyme, he could have used 'ass' instead of pajock because 'ass' would rhyme with 'was'.

151. *Didst perceive?:* Hamlet wants to know if Horatio noticed the effect the play had on Claudius.

Act 3

152. *belike:* it's likely
153. *pardie:* assuredly *from the French* (par dieu)

154. *vouchsafe me:* grant me

155. *Is in . . . distempered:* Has retired to his room because he is extremely out of sorts. *'Distempered' could mean sick in mind or body.*

156. *With drink:* Hamlet chooses to interpret Guildenstern's words as meaning that Claudius is sickened with drink.

157. *choler:* meaning anger, but it could also mean nauseated, which Hamlet refers to in his reply

158. *Your wisdom . . . doctor:* You would be wiser to tell this to his doctor.
159. *For . . . choler:* For if I were to purge him *(make him vomit)* it might make him even angrier. *Hamlet may also be referring to a spiritual purging or cleansing here, which would of course have a deleterious effect on Claudius's mood.*

160. *put . . . frame:* Put your words in some logical order.
161. *start . . . affair:* Do not shy away from the matter I am trying to discuss.

162. *I am . . . Pronounce:* I am calm. Say what you have to say.

163. *in most . . . spirit:* terribly upset

HAMLET

Ah ha! Come, some music, come, the recorders,
For if the King like not the comedy,
Why then, belike[152] he likes it not, pardie.[153]   **285**
Come, some music.

GUILDENSTERN

Good my lord, vouchsafe me[154] a word with you.

HAMLET

Sir, a whole history.

GUILDENSTERN

The King, sir –

HAMLET

Ay, sir, what of him?   **290**

GUILDENSTERN

Is in his retirement marvellous distempered.[155]

HAMLET

With drink,[156] sir?

GUILDENSTERN

No, my lord, rather with choler.[157]

HAMLET

Your wisdom should show itself more richer to signify
this to his doctor.[158] For, for me to put him to his purgation   **295**
would perhaps plunge him into far more choler.[159]

GUILDENSTERN

Good my lord, put your discourse into some frame,[160] and
start not so wildly from my affair.[161]

HAMLET

I am tame, sir. Pronounce.[162]

GUILDENSTERN

The Queen your mother, in most great affliction of   **300**
spirit,[163] hath sent me to you.

HAMLET

You are welcome.

GUILDENSTERN

Nay, good my lord, this courtesy is not of the right breed.[164] If it shall please you to make me a wholesome[165] answer, I will do your mother's commandment; if not, your pardon and my return shall be the end of my business.[166]

305

164. *this courtesy . . . breed.* Your answer is not appropriate.

165. *wholesome: meaning sensible, but it could also mean healthy*

166. *your pardon . . . business:* Excuse me, and I will return to the Queen and that will be the end of it.

HAMLET

Sir, I cannot.

GUILDENSTERN

What, my lord?

HAMLET

Make you a wholesome answer. My wit's diseased.[167] But, sir, such answer as I can make, you shall command; or rather, as you say, my mother. Therefore no more, but to the matter. My mother, you say?

310

167. *My wit's diseased:* I am not well, mentally.

ROSENCRANTZ

Then thus she says; your behaviour hath struck her into amazement and admiration.[168]

315

168. *admiration:* bewilderment

HAMLET

O wonderful son, that can so astonish a mother! But is there no sequel at the heels of this mother's admiration?[169]

169. *But is . . . admiration?:* But is there nothing to follow her astonishment?

ROSENCRANTZ

She desires to speak with you in her closet[170] ere[171] you go to bed.

170. *closet:* private room
171. *ere:* before

HAMLET

We shall obey, were she ten times our mother. Have you any further trade[172] with us?

320

172. *trade:* business

ROSENCRANTZ

My lord, you once did love me.

HAMLET

So I do still, by these pickers and stealers.[173]

173. *pickers and stealers: meaning hands, which those who read* The Book of Common Prayer *were advised to keep from 'picking and stealing'*

174. *You do . . . friend:* You shut the door on freedom (from the troubles that are driving you mad) if you do not share your problems with your friend.

175. *advancement:* promotion

176. *you have . . . Denmark:* The King himself has named you as his successor.

177. *'while the grass grows . . .':* From a proverb: 'While the grass grows, the horse starves.'
178. *musty:* stale

179. *withdraw:* speak

180. *to recover the wind of me:* Hunting term – a hunter wishing to drive an animal would go upwind of it so that the hunter's scent would be blown to the animal, causing it to run away.

181. *toil:* trap

182. *if my duty . . . unmannerly:* If I am too forward carrying out my duty, it is only because my love of you has led me to forget my manners.

183. *pipe:* recorder

ROSENCRANTZ

Good my lord, what is your cause of distemper? You
do freely bar the door upon your own liberty if you   325
deny your griefs to your friend.[174]

HAMLET

Sir, I lack advancement.[175]

ROSENCRANTZ

How can that be when you have the voice of the King
himself for your succession in Denmark?[176]

HAMLET

Ay, but 'while the grass grows…'[177] – the proverb   330
is something musty.[178]

Re-enter PLAYERS with recorders

O, the recorder! Let me see. To withdraw[179] with you, why
do you go about to recover the wind of me[180] as if you
would drive me into a toil?[181]

GUILDENSTERN

O my lord, if my duty be too bold, my love is too   335
unmannerly.[182]

HAMLET

I do not well understand that. Will you play upon
this pipe?[183]

GUILDENSTERN

My lord, I cannot.

HAMLET

I pray you.   340

GUILDENSTERN

Believe me, I cannot.

HAMLET

I do beseech you.

GUILDENSTERN

I know no touch of it,[184] my lord.

HAMLET

'Tis as easy as lying. Govern these ventages[185] with your
fingers and thumb, give it breath with your mouth, and   **345**
it will discourse[186] most excellent music. Look you, these
are the stops.

GUILDENSTERN

But these cannot I command to any utterance of
harmony; I have not the skill.

HAMLET

Why, look you now, how unworthy a thing you make of   **350**
me! You would play upon me, you would seem to know
my stops,[187] you would pluck out the heart of my mystery,
you would sound me from my lowest note to the top of
my compass;[188] and there is much music, excellent voice,
in this little organ, yet cannot you make it speak.   **355**
'Sblood, do you think I am easier to be played on than
a pipe? Call me what instrument you will, though you
can fret[189] me, yet you cannot play upon me.

Enter POLONIUS

God bless you, sir.

POLONIUS

My lord, the Queen would speak with you, and   **360**
presently.[190]

HAMLET

Do you see yonder cloud that's almost in shape of
a camel?

POLONIUS

By th' mass, and 'tis like a camel, indeed.

HAMLET

Methinks it is like a weasel.   **365**

184. *I know … it:* I cannot play it.

185. *Govern these ventages:* control these stops *(holes in the recorder)*

186. *discourse:* play/speak

187. *stops:* holes in the recorder

188. *sound me … compass:* 1. Play me from the lowest to the highest note in my range 2. Find out all my secrets.

189. *fret:* This is a pun. A fret is a wooden bar to hold the strings of an instrument tight, but it also means to annoy.

190. *presently:* at once

Act 3

POLONIUS

It is backed like[191] a weasel.

HAMLET

Or like a whale.

POLONIUS

Very like a whale.

HAMLET

Then I will come to my mother by and by.[192]

[Aside] They fool me to the top of my bent.[193]   **370**

[To POLONIUS] I will come by and by.

POLONIUS

I will say so.

HAMLET

'By and by' is easily said.

Exit POLONIUS

Leave me, friends.

Exit all but HAMLET

192. *by and by:* This could mean immediately or in due course.
193. *They fool … bent:* They treat me like a fool and try my patience to the limit.

'Tis now the very witching time of night,[194]   **375**

When churchyards yawn,[195] and hell itself breathes out

Contagion[196] to this world. Now could I drink hot blood,[197]

And do such bitter business as the day

Would quake to look on. Soft, now to my mother.

O heart, lose not thy nature![198] Let not ever   **380**

The soul of Nero [199]enter this firm bosom.

Let me be cruel, not unnatural.

I will speak daggers to her, but use none.

My tongue and soul in this be hypocrites[200] –

How in my words somever she be shent,   **385**

To give them seals never my soul consent.[201]

Exit

194. *witching time of night:* The time of night when evil roams.
195. *churchyards yawn:* graves open
196. *Contagion:* disease
197. *Now … blood:* Witches were believed to drink blood.
198. *nature:* natural love of a son for his mother
199. *Nero:* Roman emperor who had his mother executed
200. *My tongue … hypocrites:* I will not say what I truly feel.
201. *How … consent:* However much I rebuke her with my words, I will never put a seal on them by turning my words into actions.

Act 3 Scene 2
Quotes and Questions

Quotes

> *Give me that man*
> *That is not passion's slave, and I will wear him*
> *In my heart's core, ay, in my heart of heart,*
> *As I do thee.*
>
> (Hamlet, lines 70–73)

Hamlet deeply admires Horatio's self-control.

> *The instances that second marriage move*
> *Are base respects of thrift, but none of love.*
>
> (Player Queen, lines 176–177)

The Player Queen says second marriages may be based on money, but never on love.

> *The lady protests too much*
>
> (Gertrude, line 225)

Gertrude says that the lady onstage is overdoing her promise never to remarry. Gertrude may be defending her own remarriage or she may simply be commenting on the quality of the acting. Whether she is cool under pressure or just unaware of the point Hamlet is making, Gertrude certainly does not react the way Hamlet clearly hoped she would.

> *This realm dismantled was*
> *Of Jove himself, and now reigns here*
> *A very, very – pajock.*
>
> (Hamlet, lines 274–276)

Hamlet, who looked up to his father, says that the kingdom was deprived of a god-like ruler and is now in the hands of foolish, vain man.

> *do you think I am easier to be played on than a pipe?*
>
> (Hamlet, lines 356–357)

Hamlet is annoyed that Rosencrantz and Guildenstern have been spying on him for Claudius. He asks Guildenstern to play the recorder and when Guildenstern protests that he does not know how, Hamlet asks if Guildenstern thinks he, Hamlet, is easier to play or manipulate than a musical instrument.

> *Let me be cruel, not unnatural.*
> *I will speak daggers to her, but use none.*
>
> (Hamlet, lines 382–383)

Hamlet says he will be cruel to his mother, but not inhumane. His words will be as sharp as a dagger, but he will not actually use a dagger.

Questions

In each case, support your point with suitable reference to and quotation from the play.

1. How does Hamlet behave and appear when he speaks to the players and Horatio?

2. What is it about Horatio that Hamlet admires?

3. Comment on Hamlet's treatment of Ophelia in this scene.

4. Do you admire Ophelia's response to Hamlet's behaviour? Explain your answer.

5. In what ways does Lucianus resemble (a) Hamlet and (b) Claudius?

6. How does 'The Mousetrap' criticise Gertrude?

7. Describe and comment on the differences between (a) Gertrude's and (b) Claudius's reactions to 'The Mousetrap'.

8. Hamlet arranged the play to trap Claudius into showing his guilt. Based on what has happened, what do you expect Hamlet to do next? Explain your answer.

9. What is your impression of Polonius, based on his behaviour in this scene?

10. What does Hamlet's final speech in this scene tell us about his intentions towards Gertrude?

Writing Task

Imagine you are a gossip columnist for a Danish newspaper and were present for the performance of 'The Mousetrap'. Write the article that you would submit to your editor. Your article should aim to capture the undercurrents and tensions you witnessed, as well as your impressions of the characters in court. Lay your article out correctly, with a headline, byline, etc. Add illustrations if you like.

Essay Building Blocks

'Throughout the play, Hamlet, Shakespeare makes effective use of a variety of dramatic techniques that evoke a wide range of responses from the audience.'

Write a paragraph in response to this statement, supporting your answer with quotation from and reference to Act 3 Scene 2.

A room in the castle

Claudius tells Rosencrantz and Guildenstern to escort Hamlet to England immediately, fearing the danger that Hamlet poses if he is allowed to remain in Denmark any longer.

When Rosencrantz and Guildenstern have left, Polonius arrives to say that he will hide behind the arras in Gertrude's room and eavesdrop on her conversation with Hamlet. He leaves.

Alone onstage, Claudius admits to himself that he has committed a terrible sin. He kneels and attempts to pray for forgiveness but cannot truly repent because he is unwilling to surrender what he gained from his brother's murder.

Hamlet enters and, on seeing the kneeling king, says he will take this ideal opportunity to kill him. However, he reflects before taking action and quickly decides against doing anything there and then. Hamlet reasons that if he kills Claudius while he is at prayer, his spirit will go to heaven. Claudius did not allow Hamlet's father any such mercy, so the prince resolves to avenge his father's murder at a time when Claudius is not in a state of grace so that he may suffer eternal damnation. The irony is that Hamlet does not realise that Claudius is unable to repent and so would go to hell were he to be killed at that moment.

Act 3

1. *nor . . . us:* it is not safe

2. *I your . . . dispatch:* I will have your orders drawn up immediately.

3. *terms of our estate:* my position as king

4. *brows:* threatening looks and madness

5. *provide:* prepare

6. *Most holy . . . it is:* It is our sacred duty.

7. *single and peculiar:* individual and private

8. *noyance:* injury or harm

9. *weal:* well-being

10. *The cease of majesty . . . with it:* The king does not die alone, but he is like a whirlpool that pulls everything down with it. *Rosencrantz wants to stress that the nation's well-being depends on the king's well-being and it is in their interests to protect him.*

11. *It is a massy . . . ruin:* It is like a massive wheel *(like the Wheel of Fortune)* on top of the highest mountain, on the spokes *(of the wheel)* are fastened ten thousand smaller things *(the people)*, and when it rolls down, each little thing attached to it, each insignificant thing, shares in the terrible destruction.

12. *a general groan:* everyone groans

13. *Arm you:* prepare yourselves

14. *fetters:* iron chains

15. *fear:* cause of fear *Claudius wants to control the threat posed by Hamlet who, he feels, has been allowed to run loose.*

Enter CLAUDIUS, ROSENCRANTZ, and GUILDENSTERN

CLAUDIUS

I like him not, nor stands it safe with us[1]
To let his madness range. Therefore prepare you.
I your commission will forthwith dispatch,[2]
And he to England shall along with you.
The terms of our estate[3] may not endure   5
Hazard so dangerous as doth hourly grow
Out of his brows.[4]

GUILDENSTERN

We will ourselves provide.[5]
Most holy and religious fear it is[6]
To keep those many many bodies safe   10
That live and feed upon your majesty.

ROSENCRANTZ

The single and peculiar[7] life is bound
With all the strength and armour of the mind
To keep itself from noyance;[8] but much more
That spirit upon whose weal[9] depend and rests   15
The lives of many. The cease of majesty
Dies not alone, but like a gulf, doth draw
What's near it with it.[10] It is a massy wheel
Fix'd on the summit of the highest mount,
To whose huge spokes ten thousand lesser things   20
Are mortised and adjoined, which when it falls
Each small annexment, petty consequence,
Attends the boisterous ruin.[11] Never alone
Did the King sigh, but with a general groan.[12]

CLAUDIUS

Arm you,[13] I pray you, to this speedy voyage,   25
For we will fetters[14] put upon this fear[15]
Which now goes too free-footed.
Rosencrantz and Guildenstern
We will haste us.

Exit ROSENCRANTZ and GUILDENSTERN

Enter POLONIUS

POLONIUS

My lord, he's going to his mother's closet.[16]

Behind the arras[17] I'll convey myself

To hear the process.[18] I'll warrant she'll tax him home.[19]

And, as you said – and wisely was it said –

'Tis meet that some more audience than a mother,

Since nature makes them partial, should o'erhear

The speech, of vantage.[20] Fare you well, my liege.

I'll call upon you ere[21] you go to bed,

And tell you what I know.

CLAUDIUS

Thanks, dear my lord.

Exit POLONIUS

O, my offence is rank![22] It smells to heaven.

It hath the primal eldest curse upon't,

A brother's murder.[23] Pray can I not.

Though inclination be as sharp as will,[24]

My stronger guilt defeats my strong intent,

And like a man to double business bound[25]

I stand in pause where I shall first begin,

And both neglect. What if this cursed hand

Were thicker than itself with brother's blood,

Is there not rain enough in the sweet heavens

To wash it white as snow?[26] Whereto serves mercy

But to confront the visage of offence?[27]

And what's in prayer but this twofold force,

To be forestalled ere we come to fall,

Or pardoned being down?[28] Then I'll look up.

My fault is past – but O, what form of prayer

Can serve my turn? 'Forgive me my foul murder'?

That cannot be, since I am still possessed

Of those effects for which I did the murder –

My crown, mine own ambition, and my Queen.

May one be pardoned and retain th'offence?[29]

In the corrupted currents of this world

Offence's gilded hand may shove by justice,

And oft 'tis seen the wicked prize itself

Buys out the law.[30] But 'tis not so above.[31]

There is no shuffling,[32] there the action lies

In his true nature, and we ourselves compelled,

Even to the teeth and forehead of our faults[33]

30

35

40

45

50

55

60

65

---

16. *closet:* private rooms
17. *arras:* large tapestry wall-hanging
18. *process:* proceedings
19. *I'll warrant … home:* I guarantee she will scold him severely.
20. *'Tis meet … of vantage:* It is appropriate that someone other than a mother, since mothers are naturally inclined to favour their sons, should listen in on the speech, from an advantageous position, in order to benefit.
21. *ere:* before
22. *rank:* foul
23. *It hath … murder:* In the Bible, Cain killed his brother Abel and was cursed by God as a result.
24. *Though … will:* though my desire is as strong as my intention
25. *like … bound:* like a man who is committed to carrying out two courses of action at the same time
26. *I stand … white as snow?:* I am paralysed, unsure where to start and, therefore, I don't do either task. Even if this cursed hand were covered with my brother's blood, is there not enough rain in heaven to wash it white as snow? *Claudius thinks that heaven can forgive the worst sins.*
27. *Whereto … offence?:* What is the function of mercy if it is not to confront sin?
28. *And what's … down?* What is the point of prayer but to prevent us from sinning before we do so and to pardon us if we do sin?
29. *th'offence:* the things gained through sinning *Claudius wrestles with a dilemma: he does not see how he can truly ask God for forgiveness when he is unwilling to give up the crown, Gertrude and all that comes with being king.*
30. *In the corrupted … law:* In this corrupt world, a sinner's hand that holds out a bribe may escape justice, sometimes using the proceeds of the crime to commit the bribe.
31. *above:* in heaven
32. *shuffling:* trickery
33. *Even to … faults:* face to face with our faults

Act 3

34. *What rests?:* What remains?

35. *Try what repentance can:* Try to see what repentance can do.

36. *limed soul:* A reference to trapping birds by putting a sticky substance on the branches of trees. The more the birds struggle, the more they stick to the branch.

37. *Make assay!:* Make an attempt!

38. *Bow . . . babe:* Bend in prayer, stubborn knees. And may my hardened heart of steel be as soft as a newborn baby.

39. *pat:* easily

40. *That would be scanned:* This must be carefully considered.

41. *this is hire . . . revenge:* This is like the action of a paid assassin rather than a person seeking revenge.

42. *He took . . . May:* He killed my father when he had eaten, rather than when he was fasting and he was unprepared for death with all his sins in full bloom, as abundant as flowers in May.

43. *audit:* spiritual account

44. *But in . . . him:* As far as we can tell, he is in a terrible position.

45. *him:* Claudius

46. *purging:* cleansing

47. *seasoned:* ready

48. *Up, sword . . . hent:* I must put you away, sword, until there is a better occasion to grasp you for a terrible deed.

49. *gaming:* gambling

50. *relish:* taste; trace

51. *stays:* waits

52. *This physic . . . days:* Hamlet is speaking under his breath to Claudius, who cannot hear him and is unaware of his presence. This medicine *(prayer)* simply prolongs your life but cannot save you forever.

53. *My words . . . heaven go:* My words fly up towards heaven but my thoughts remain here on earth. Insincere words of prayer will never make it to heaven.

To give in evidence. What then? What rests?[34]
Try what repentance can.[35] What can it not?
Yet what can it when one cannot repent?   **70**
O wretched state, O bosom black as death,
O limed soul[36] that, struggling to be free,
Art more engaged! Help, angels! Make assay![37]
Bow, stubborn knees; and, heart with strings of steel,
Be soft as sinews of the new-born babe.[38]   **75**
All may be well.

Retires and kneels
Enter HAMLET

HAMLET
Now might I do it pat,[39] now he is praying,
And now I'll do't. And so he goes to heaven,
And so am I revenged. That would be scanned.[40]
A villain kills my father, and for that   **80**
I, his sole son, do this same villain send
To heaven.
O, this is hire and salary, not revenge![41]
He took my father grossly, full of bread,
With all his crimes broad blown, as flush as May;[42]   **85**
And how his audit[43] stands, who knows save heaven?
But in our circumstance and course of thought
'Tis heavy with him.[44] And am I then revenged,
To take him[45] in the purging[46] of his soul,
When he is fit and seasoned[47] for his passage?   **90**
No!
Up, sword, and know thou a more horrid hent.[48]
When he is drunk asleep, or in his rage,
Or in th'incestuous pleasure of his bed,
At gaming,[49] swearing, or about some act   **95**
That has no relish[50] of salvation in't,
Then trip him, that his heels may kick at heaven,
And that his soul may be as damn'd and black
As hell whereto it goes. My mother stays.[51]
This physic but prolongs thy sickly days.[52]   **100**

Exit HAMLET

CLAUDIUS
[Rising] My words fly up, my thoughts remain below.
Words without thoughts never to heaven go.[53]

Quotes

I like him not, nor stands it safe with us
To let his madness range.

(Claudius, lines 1–2)

Claudius is unhappy with Hamlet's behaviour and thinks that he poses a threat. Therefore, he does not want to allow Hamlet to remain in Denmark.

O, my offence is rank! It smells to heaven.
It hath the primal eldest curse upon't,
A brother's murder. Pray can I not.
Though inclination be as sharp as will,
My stronger guilt defeats my strong intent

(Claudius, lines 40–44)

Claudius says he committed a foul murder, just as Cain killed his brother Abel in the biblical story. Although he dearly wants to pray, Claudius's guilty conscience prevents him from doing so.

I am still possessed
Of those effects for which I did the murder –
My crown, mine own ambition, and my Queen.
May one be pardoned and retain th'offence?

(Claudius, lines 57–60)

Claudius knows it is not possible to be forgiven for his sin while he holds onto all he gained when he killed his brother.

He took my father grossly, full of bread,
With all his crimes broad blown, as flush as May;
And how his audit stands, who knows save heaven?
But in our circumstance and course of thought
'Tis heavy with him. And am I then revenged,
To take him in the purging of his soul,
When he is fit and seasoned for his passage?
No!

(Hamlet, lines 84–91)

Hamlet decides he will not kill Claudius while he is praying because Claudius killed Old Hamlet before he could confess his sins. Hamlet does not think it is right that Claudius should go to heaven if he died while asking God to forgive him, while the man he murdered suffers in purgatory.

My words fly up, my thoughts remain below.
Words without thoughts never to heaven go.

(Claudius, lines 101–102)

Ironically, Claudius cannot pray at all because he does not believe what he is saying. Had Hamlet killed him, therefore, he would not have gone to heaven.

Questions

In each case, support your point with suitable reference to and quotation from the play.

1. Where is Claudius sending Hamlet and why?

2. How would you describe Rosencrantz's speech to Claudius about the value of kingship? Is there any irony in it?

3. Why can Claudius not pray?

4. Do you feel any sympathy for Claudius in this scene?

5. Do you agree with Hamlet's reason for not killing Claudius?

6. Do you believe the reason Hamlet gives for not killing Claudius is the only reason he does not act?

7. What is the dramatic significance of the encounter between Hamlet and Claudius?

Writing Task

Your class has decided to perform one scene from Hamlet during an end-of-year school show. Your teacher has asked each student to choose a scene that they believe contains great emotional power, tension and dramatic significance. You have chosen Act 3 Scene 3. Write the text of a short talk you would deliver to your teacher and your classmates in which you try to convince them that this scene meets the criteria.

Essay Building Blocks

'Claudius can be seen as both a heartless villain and a character with some redeeming qualities in the play, Hamlet.'

Write a paragraph in response to this statement, supporting your answer with quotation from and reference to Act 3 Scene 3.

The Queen's closet

Polonius hides behind the arras in Gertrude's room after urging her to speak frankly to Hamlet about his recent bad behaviour.

Gertrude tries to reprimand Hamlet but he turns on her, saying he will force her to face up to the truth about herself. Fearing for her life, Gertrude calls for help. Polonius calls out in response and Hamlet stabs him through the arras, killing him. He is unrepentant, asking if it is the King he has killed, and seems irritated to find it is only Polonius.

Hamlet turns his attention to Gertrude once more, telling her that she should never have entered into an incestuous relationship with Claudius, a man who is not only vastly inferior to her first husband but is also a murderer. Gertrude is deeply distressed by Hamlet's words and begs him to say no more but he continues to berate her.

The Ghost appears in order to remind Hamlet of his duty to avenge his murder. Gertrude cannot see the Ghost and believes Hamlet is truly mad. Hamlet denies this and once again orders Gertrude to repent of her sins and to have nothing more to do with Claudius. He reassures her that his madness is just an act and tells her to keep this fact a secret. Gertrude agrees to do so and Hamlet tells her that he must go to England soon but that he does not trust Rosencrantz and Guildenstern, suspecting them of plotting to lead him into danger. He leaves, dragging Polonius's body away with him.

Act 3

2. *Look . . . him:* Scold him severely for his behaviour.
3. *broad:* unrestrained

4. *Much heat:* Claudius's anger
5. *sconce me e'en here:* be silent now
6. *round:* open and direct

7. *I'll warrant you:* I guarantee I will do as you ask.

8. *Fear me not:* Don't worry about me.

9. *thy father:* Claudius

10. *my father:* Old Hamlet

11. *idle:* meaningless or foolish

12. *Have you forgot me?:* Have you forgotten to whom you are speaking?

Enter GERTRUDE and POLONIUS

POLONIUS

He will come straight.[1] Look you lay home to him.[2]

Tell him his pranks have been too broad[3] to bear with,

And that your grace hath screened and stood between

Much heat[4] and him. I'll sconce me e'en here.[5]

Pray you, be round[6] with him.   **5**

HAMLET

[Within] Mother, mother, mother!

GERTRUDE

I'll warrant you.[7]

Fear me not.[8] Withdraw; I hear him coming.

POLONIUS hides behind the arras
Enter HAMLET

HAMLET

Now, mother, what's the matter?

GERTRUDE

Hamlet, thou hast thy father[9] much offended.   **10**

referring to Claudius

HAMLET

Mother, you have my father[10] much offended.

referring to old king Hamlet

GERTRUDE

Come, come, you answer with an idle[11] tongue.

HAMLET

Go, go, you question with a wicked tongue.

GERTRUDE

Why, how now, Hamlet?

HAMLET

What's the matter now?   **15**

GERTRUDE

Have you forgot me?[12]

HAMLET

No, by the rood,[13] not so.

You are the Queen, your husband's brother's wife.

And – would[14] you were not so! – you are my mother.

13. *rood:* cross on which Jesus was crucified

14. *would:* I wish

GERTRUDE

Nay, then, I'll set those to you that can speak.[15]   **20**

15. *set . . . speak:* send for people who can speak to you

HAMLET

Come, come, and sit you down. You shall not budge.

You go not till I set you up a glass[16]

Where you may see the inmost part of you.

16. *glass:* mirror

GERTRUDE

What wilt thou do? Thou wilt not murder me?

Help, help, ho!   *Subverts the traditional parent/child relationship.*   **25**
Hamlet controls the conversation fully.

POLONIUS

[Behind] What, ho! Help, help, help!

HAMLET

[Drawing his sword] How now, a rat?[17] Dead, for a ducat,

   dead.[18]

17. *rat:* traitor or spy

18. *Dead, for a ducat, dead:* I'll bet you a ducat *(gold coin)* that he will soon be dead.

Makes a pass through the arras

POLONIUS

[Behind] O, I am slain!

Falls and dies

GERTRUDE

O me, what hast thou done?

HAMLET

Nay, I know not. Is it the King?   **30**

Hamlet's first thought has turned to Claudius

GERTRUDE

O, what a rash and bloody deed is this!

HAMLET

A bloody deed – almost as bad, good-mother,

As kill a king, and marry with his brother.

GERTRUDE

As kill a king?

HAMLET

Ay, lady, 'twas my word.[19]   35

Lifts up the arras and discovers POLONIUS

[handwritten: Hamlet showing no remorse (madness)]

Thou wretched, rash, intruding fool, farewell.
I took thee for thy better:[20] take thy fortune;[21]
Thou find'st to be too busy is some danger.[22] –
Leave wringing of your hands. Peace, sit you down,
And let me wring your heart; for so I shall   40
If it be made of penetrable stuff,[23]
If damned custom have not brassed it so
That it is proof and bulwark against sense.[24]

GERTRUDE

What have I done, that thou darest wag thy tongue[25]
In noise so rude against me?   45

19. *'twas my word:* That is what I said.

20. *I took . . . better:* I thought you were the King.
21. *take thy fortune:* accept your fate
22. *Thou find'st . . . danger:* You discovered that to be too much of a busybody is dangerous.

23. *If it . . . stuff:* If it is capable of being reached

24. *If damned . . . sense:* If wicked habits have not hardened it like brass so that it is fortified against proper feeling.

25. *wag thy tongue:* scold

HAMLET

Such an act

That blurs[26] the grace and blush of modesty,

Calls virtue hypocrite,[27] takes off the rose

From the fair forehead of an innocent love

And sets a blister there, makes marriage vows   **50**

As false as dicers'[28] oaths – O, such a deed

As from the body of contraction[29] plucks

The very soul, and sweet religion makes

A rhapsody of words.[30] Heaven's face doth glow,[31]

Yea, this solidity and compound mass[32]   **55**

With tristful visage, as against the doom,[33]

Is thought-sick[34] at the act.

GERTRUDE

Ay me, what act,

That roars so loud and thunders in the index?[35]

HAMLET

Look here upon this picture, and on this,[36]   **60**

The counterfeit presentment[37] of two brothers.

See what a grace was seated on this brow –

Hyperion's curls,[38] the front of Jove[39] himself,

An eye like Mars,[40] to threaten and command,

A station like the herald Mercury[41]   **65**

New-lighted on a heaven-kissing hill;[42]

A combination[43] and a form indeed

Where every god did seem to set his seal

To give the world assurance of a man.

This was your husband. Look you now what follows.   **70**

Here is your husband, like a mildewed ear[44]

Blasting his wholesome brother.[45] Have you eyes?

Could you on this fair mountain leave to feed,[46]

And batten on this moor?[47] Ha, have you eyes?

You cannot call it love, for at your age   **75**

The heyday in the blood[48] is tame, it's humble,

And waits upon[49] the judgment; and what judgment

Would step from this to this?

Sense, sure, you have,

Else could you not have motion; but sure that sense   **80**

Is apoplexed,[50] for madness would not err,

Nor sense to ecstasy was ne'er so thralled[51]

But it reserved some quantity of choice,

To serve in such a difference. What devil was't

[handwritten margin note: Theme of justice & revenge]

26. *blurs:* stains

27. *Calls virtue hypocrite:* makes a mockery of virtue

28. *dicers':* gamblers'

29. *the body of contraction:* the marriage contract

30. *sweet religion . . . words:* makes religion nothing more than a senseless jumble of words.

31. *doth glow:* blushes

32. *this solidity and compound mass:* the earth

33. *With tristful . . . doom:* with a sorrowful face, as on doomsday

34. *thought-sick:* sick at the thought

35. *what act . . . index?:* What act are you about to describe if the introduction is so loud and angry?

36. *this picture, and on this:* Hamlet shows his mother two pictures: one of Claudius and one of Old Hamlet.

37. *counterfeit presentment:* portrait pictures

38. *Hyperion's curls:* the hair of Hyperion *god of the sun*

39. *the front of Jove:* the forehead of Jove *the chief deity*

40. *Mars: god of war*

41. *A station . . . Mercury:* A stance like Mercury *the messenger of the gods and always portrayed as fleet of foot and athletic*

42. *New-lighted . . . hill:* just landed on a high hill *Mercury was often portrayed with wings*

43. *combination:* combination of god-like characteristics

44. *mildewed ear:* like a mildewed ear of grain

45. *Blasting . . . brother:* Infecting his healthy brother

46. *leave to feed:* stop feeding

47. *batten on this moor:* gorge yourself on this barren upland

48. *heyday in the blood:* excitement of sexual appetite

49. *waits upon:* is instructed by

50. *apoplexed:* paralysed

51. *Nor . . . thralled:* Sense was never so enslaved by madness.

52. *cozened you at hoodman-blind?:* cheated you in a game of blind-man's buff

53. *sans:* without (the senses)

54. *mope:* act stupidly or blindly

55. *mutine:* mutiny/rebel

56. *If thou ... fire:* If passion can take over an older woman (as it has you) then what about young people?

57. *Proclaim ... will:* Do not call it shameful when young people give in to their irresistible desires since their elders (the 'frost' of old age is compared to the fire of youth) explain their self-indulgence in reasoned terms.

58. *grained:* ingrained

59. *As ... tinct:* cannot give up the stain of shame

60. *enseamed:* greasy from animal sweat

61. *honeying:* sweet words of love

62. *sty:* pigsty

63. *tithe:* tenth part

64. *your precedent lord:* your former husband

65. *vice:* In morality plays of the time, the character of Vice was presented as a clownish, evil figure. Hamlet also means that Claudius is the epitome of vice or villainy.

66. *cutpurse:* thief *Claudius has stolen the kingdom*

67. *diadem:* crown

68. *shreds and patches:* the ragged costume worn by fools in plays of the time

That thus hath cozened you at hoodman-blind?[52]   85
Eyes without feeling, feeling without sight,
Ears without hands or eyes, smelling sans[53] all,
Or but a sickly part of one true sense
Could not so mope.[54]
O shame! where is thy blush? Rebellious hell,   90
If thou canst mutine[55] in a matron's bones,
To flaming youth let virtue be as wax
And melt in her own fire.[56] Proclaim no shame
When the compulsive ardour gives the charge,
Since frost itself as actively doth burn   95
And reason panders will.[57]

GERTRUDE *Admitting guilt - showing remorse*
O Hamlet, speak no more!
Thou turn'st mine eyes into my very soul,
And there I see such black and grained[58] spots
As will not leave their tinct.[59]   100

HAMLET
Nay, but to live
In the rank sweat of an enseamed[60] bed,
Stewed in corruption, honeying[61] and making love
Over the nasty sty[62] –

GERTRUDE
O, speak to me no more!   105
These words like daggers, enter in mine ears.
No more, sweet Hamlet!

HAMLET
A murderer and a villain,
A slave that is not twentieth part the tithe[63]
Of your precedent lord;[64] a vice[65] of kings.   110
A cutpurse[66] of the empire and the rule,
That from a shelf the precious diadem[67] stole,
And put it in his pocket –

GERTRUDE
No more.

HAMLET
A king of shreds and patches[68] –   115

Enter GHOST

Save me, and hover o'er me with your wings,

You heavenly guards![69] What would you,[70] gracious figure?

69. *heavenly guards:* angels
70. *What would you:* What do you want?

GERTRUDE (Gertrude can't see the ghost)

Alas, he's mad.[71]

71. *Alas, he's mad:* Gertrude cannot see the Ghost so she assumes Hamlet must be mad.

HAMLET Theme of procrastination

Do you not come your tardy son to chide,[72]

That, lapsed in time and passion,[73] lets go by   **120**

The important[74] acting of your dread[75] command?

O, say!

72. *Do you ... chide:* Have you come to scold your procrastinating son?
73. *lapsed ... passion:* having allowed time to pass and passion to cool
74. *important:* urgent
75. *dread:* serious

GHOST

Do not forget. This visitation

Is but to whet[76] thy almost blunted purpose.

But look, amazement[77] on thy mother sits.   **125**

O, step between her and her fighting soul.

Conceit[78] in weakest bodies strongest works.

Speak to her, Hamlet.

76. *to whet:* to sharpen
77. *amazement:* bewilderment
78. *Conceit:* imagination

HAMLET

How is it with you, lady?

GERTRUDE

Alas, how is't with you,   **130**

That you do bend your eye on vacancy,[79]

And with the incorporal[80] air do hold discourse?[81]

Forth at your eyes your spirits wildly peep,[82]

And, as the sleeping soldiers in th'alarm,

Your bedded hair, like life in excrements,   **135**

Start up and stand on end.[83] O gentle son,

Upon the heat and flame of thy distemper[84]

Sprinkle cool patience! Whereon do you look?

79. *bend ... vacancy:* stare at empty space
80. *the incorporal:* bodiless
81. *hold discourse:* converse
82. *Forth ... peep:* you look startled
83. *And, as the sleeping ... end:* And, like sleeping soldiers who were woken by an alarm, your hairs stand to attention as if they had a life of their own.
84. *distemper:* illness/madness

HAMLET

On him, on him. Look you, how pale he glares.

His form and cause conjoined, preaching to stones,   **140**

Would make them capable.[85] Do not look upon me,

Lest with this piteous action you convert

My stern effects.[86] Then what I have to do

Will want true colour[87] – tears perchance for blood.[88]

85. *His form ... capable:* The combination of his appearance and his purpose would make the stones respond if he spoke to them.
86. *Lest ... effects:* In case your pitiful look turns me aside from my stern purpose.
87. *want true colour:* lack its proper appearance
88. *tears ... blood:* cause me to shed tears instead of blood

89. *Nothing ... I see:* I cannot see what you are trying to show me, but I can see everything that is actually there.

90. *habit:* the clothes he usually wore

91. *portal:* doorway

92. *coinage ... brain:* invention of your imagination

93. *This bodiless ... in:* Madness is very clever at creating this kind of hallucination.

94. *temperately keeps time:* beats at a normal rate

95. *Bring me ... from:* Put me to the test and I will say the same thing again, something that a madman would shy away from.
96. *unction:* ointment
97. *trespass:* sin Hamlet tells Gertrude not to try to soothe her conscience by claiming that what is happening is due to his madness rather than her sin.
98. *skin and film:* form a thin covering over
99. *mining:* undermining

100. *ranker:* grow more vigorously but also smell even more foul

101. *pursy:* bloated with self-indulgence

GERTRUDE

To whom do you speak this? 145

HAMLET

Do you see nothing there?

GERTRUDE

Nothing at all, yet all that is I see.[89]

HAMLET

Nor did you nothing hear?

GERTRUDE

No, nothing but ourselves.

HAMLET

Why, look you there! look, how it steals away. 150
My father, in his habit[90] as he lived.
Look, where he goes even now out at the portal.[91]

Exit GHOST

GERTRUDE

This the very coinage of your brain.[92]
This bodiless creation ecstasy
Is very cunning in.[93] "mad in craft'— antic disposition 155

HAMLET

Ecstasy?
My pulse as yours doth temperately keep time,[94]
And makes as healthful music. It is not madness
That I have uttered. Bring me to the test,
And I the matter will reword, which madness 160
Would gambol from.[95] Mother, for love of grace
Lay not a flattering unction[96] to your soul
That not your trespass[97] but my madness speaks.
It will but skin and film[98] the ulcerous place
Whilst rank corruption, mining[99] all within, 165
Infects unseen. Confess yourself to heaven;
Repent what's past, avoid what is to come,
And do not spread the compost o'er the weeds
To make them ranker.[100] Forgive me this my virtue,
For in the fatness of these pursy[101] times 170

Virtue itself of vice must pardon beg,

Yea, curb and woo[102] for leave[103] to do him good.

GERTRUDE

O Hamlet, thou hast cleft my heart in twain![104]

HAMLET

O, throw away the worser part of it,

And live the purer with the other half!   **175**

Good night – but go not to mine uncle's bed.

Assume[105] a virtue if you have it not.

That monster custom, who all sense doth eat,

Of habits devilish, is angel yet in this:

That to the use of actions fair and good   **180**

He likewise gives a frock or livery

That aptly is put on.[106] Refrain tonight,

And that shall lend a kind of easiness

To the next abstinence, the next more easy –

For use[107] almost can change the stamp of nature[108] –   **185**

And either lodge[109] the devil, or throw him out

With wondrous potency.[110] Once more, good night;

And when you are desirous to be blessed,[111]

I'll blessing beg of you.[112] For this same lord,

Pointing to POLONIUS

I do repent. But heaven hath pleased it so *showing remorse* **190**
but believes that God has

To punish me with this, and this with me, *planned this out for me*

That I must be their scourge and minister.[113]

I will bestow[114] him, and will answer well[115]

The death I gave him. So, again, good night.

I must be cruel only to be kind: **195**

Thus bad begins, and worse remains behind.

worst is yet to come

GERTRUDE

What shall I do?

HAMLET

Not this, by no means, that I bid you do:[116]

Let the bloat King tempt you again to bed,

Pinch wanton on your cheek,[117] call you his mouse,   **200**

And let him, for a pair of reechy[118] kisses,

Or paddling in your neck[119] with his damned fingers,

102. *curb and woo:* bow and scrape
103. *leave:* permission

104. *cleft . . . twain:* split my heart in two

105. *Assume:* acquire

106. *That monster . . . put on:* Habit, which can take away our awareness of the evil we do every day, has another good side in that it can also easily make us as accustomed to good practices if we do them regularly.

107. *use:* habit
108. *the stamp of nature:* a person's nature
109. *lodge:* house
110. *potency:* power
111. *desirous to be blessed:* willing to repent; ask God's forgiveness
112. *I'll blessing beg of you:* I'll ask for your forgiveness *(for being so harsh).*

113. *scourge and minister:* heaven's instrument of justice and the one who carries out the punishment
114. *bestow:* dispose of
115. *answer well:* account for/atone for

116. *Not this . . . do:* Do not, by any means, do what I am about to say.

117. *Pinch . . . cheek:* pinch your cheek in a sexually playful manner
118. *reechy:* reeky/filthy
119. *paddling in your neck:* pawing your neck

Act 3

120. *Make . . . out:* persuade you to tell him this truth about me

121. *mad in craft:* cunningly pretending to be mad
122. *'Twere . . . know:* Hamlet is being sarcastic here.

123. *paddock:* toad
124. *gib:* tom cat *Toads, bats and cats were thought to be witches' familiars and know their secrets.*
125. *dear concernings:* important matters
126. *in despite of:* in spite of

127. *Unpeg . . . down:* This seems to be a reference to an old story about an ape who, having released birds from a cage and seen them fly, attempted to imitate them and jumped from a roof to his death. It is a warning that if Gertrude acts foolishly, she may bring about disaster.

128. *Alack:* Like 'alas', this is an expression used to express regret or dismay.
129. *concluded on:* arranged

130. *as I will adders fanged:* as much as I would trust poisonous snakes
131. *mandate:* royal command
132. *marshal me to knavery:* escort me into a trap

133. *Hoist . . . petard:* blown up by his own bomb

134. *I will delve . . . moon:* I will dig under their mines and blow them into the sky.
135. *When in one line . . . meet:* when two plots confront one another
136. *This man . . . packing:* Polonius will force me to leave in a hurry (because I have murdered him and so will be sent away).
137. *lug the guts:* drag the body (Polonius's corpse)
138. *neighbour:* next
139. *This counsellor:* Polonius
140. *grave:* This is a pun: 'grave' can mean 'serious' or 'a burial place'.
141. *prating:* chattering
142. *to draw . . . you:* Another pun. Hamlet could mean 'drawing to an end' or 'dragging away'.

Make you to ravel all this matter out,[120]
That I essentially am not in madness,
But mad in craft.[121] 'Twere good you let him know,[122]   205
For who that's but a queen, fair, sober, wise,
Would from a paddock,[123] from a bat, a gib,[124]
Such dear concernings[125] hide? Who would do so?
No, in despite of [126] sense and secrecy,
Unpeg the basket on the house's top,   210
Let the birds fly, and, like the famous ape,
To try conclusions in the basket creep,
And break your own neck down.[127]

GERTRUDE

Be thou assured, if words be made of breath,
And breath of life, I have no life to breathe   215
What thou hast said to me.

HAMLET

I must to England. You know that?

GERTRUDE

Alack,[128] I had forgot. 'Tis so concluded on.[129]

HAMLET

There's letters sealed, and my two schoolfellows –
Whom I will trust as I will adders fanged[130]–   220
They bear the mandate,[131] they must sweep my way
And marshal me to knavery.[132] Let it work,
For 'tis the sport to have the engineer
Hoist with his own petard;[133] and't shall go hard
But I will delve one yard below their mines   225
And blow them at the moon.[134] O, 'tis most sweet
When in one line two crafts directly meet.[135]
This man shall set me packing.[136]
I'll lug the guts[137] into the neighbour[138] room.
Mother, good night indeed. This counsellor[139]   230
Is now most still, most secret, and most grave,[140]
Who was in life a foolish prating[141] knave. –
Come, sir, to draw toward an end with you.[142] –
Good night, mother.

Exit severally; HAMLET dragging in POLONIUS

Act 3 Scene 4
Quotes and Questions

Quotes

Hamlet, thou hast thy father much offended.
(Gertrude, line 10)

Gertrude refers to Claudius, Hamlet's uncle and stepfather, as his father.

Mother, you have my father much offended.
(Hamlet, line 11)

Hamlet tells his mother that she has offended her first husband, Hamlet's father, by marrying Claudius.

Thou wretched, rash, intruding fool, farewell.
I took thee for thy better
(Hamlet, lines 36–37)

Hamlet addresses the dead Polonius, calling him a foolish busybody. Hamlet thought it was Claudius hiding behind the tapestry.

A combination and a form indeed
Where every god did seem to set his seal
To give the world assurance of a man.
This was your husband. Look you now what
*   follows.*
Here is your husband, like a mildewed ear
Blasting his wholesome brother.
(Hamlet, lines 67–72)

Hamlet forces Gertrude to look at two pictures, one of Old Hamlet and one of Claudius. He praises Old Hamlet as the epitome of perfection. Her second husband, he says, is like a rotten ear of corn, spreading its blight to the corn beside it. Of course, the reference to ear and infection reminds the audience of the way Claudius murdered his brother.

O Hamlet, speak no more!
Thou turn'st mine eyes into my very soul,
And there I see such black and grained spots
As will not leave their tinct.
(Gertrude, lines 97–100)

Gertrude is appalled by Hamlet's words and says she sees now what she has done wrong.

Do not forget. This visitation
Is but to whet thy almost blunted purpose.
(Ghost, lines 123–124)

The Ghost rebukes Hamlet for not avenging his murder. He says he has visited Hamlet again to remind him of his duty.

I essentially am not in madness,
But mad in craft.
(Hamlet, lines 204–205)

Hamlet tells his mother that he is not really mad, but merely acting.

Questions

In each case, support your point with suitable reference to and quotation from the play.

1. Why has Gertrude sent for Hamlet?

2. How does Hamlet gain control of the conversation?

3. Based on her behaviour in this scene, do you think Gertrude was aware of her first husband's murder?

4. Hamlet believes the person hiding behind the arras is Claudius. Compare his reaction here to his behaviour when he comes across Claudius in the prayer scene. Why do you think he behaves so differently in this scene?

5. What is Hamlet's opinion of his late father?

6. What is Hamlet's attitude towards his mother's relationship with Claudius and what does he ask her to do when she is next alone with her husband?

7. Why does the Ghost reappear?

8. Why do you think Gertrude cannot see the Ghost?

9. Discuss Hamlet's attitude towards Polonius in this scene.

Writing Task

Imagine you are Gertrude. Write the diary entry you might make after Hamlet's visit to your room. Your diary entry should reflect your innermost thoughts and fears.

Essay Building Blocks

> 'Horror and disgust at his mother's behaviour, and a spreading and deepening of that horror to include all life, dominates the soul of Hamlet.'

Write a paragraph in response to this statement, supporting your answer with quotation from and reference to Act 3 Scene 4.

A room in the castle

Gertrude tells Claudius that Hamlet killed Polonius in a fit of madness. She exaggerates her son's behaviour in order to protect him. Claudius is deeply concerned to hear of Hamlet's behaviour and fears the danger that he poses to him and everyone in the court. He says he will send Hamlet to England immediately and try to explain and excuse Polonius's death as best he can. Claudius fears that his reputation will be damaged by the murder. He orders Rosencrantz and Guildenstern to find Hamlet and bring Polonius's body to the chapel.

Act 4

[Handwritten: Self-preservation. Aligns herself with the king to preserve her status + safety]

1. *matter:* meaning
2. *profound heaves:* deep sighs
3. *translate:* explain their meaning
4. *'Tis fit . . . them:* It is important that I know what has caused them.
5. *your son:* Claudius pointedly refers to Hamlet as Gertrude's son, not their joint son, even though he is now Hamlet's stepfather. He is trying to distance himself from Hamlet and his increasingly unstable behaviour.
6. *Bestow . . . us:* leave us alone

7. *contend:* argue; fight to prove
8. *lawless:* unrestrained

9. *Behind the arras . . . man:* Hearing something move behind the tapestry, he pulls out his sword and cries, 'A rat, a rat!' and in this deluded state, he kills the good old man *(Polonius)* who was hidden there.

10. *heavy:* grievous; terrible
11. *us:* Claudius is using the royal plural
12. *It had . . . there:* If I had been there, I would have been killed.

13. *answered:* accounted for
14. *It will be laid to us:* I will be blamed for it.
15. *whose providence . . . short:* who should have had the foresight to keep *(Hamlet)* on a short lead/controlled
16. *out of haunt:* out of the company of others
17. *We would . . . fit:* I did not see what should have been done.

18. *To keep it from divulging:* to prevent it from being revealed
19. *pith:* centre *Claudius compares Hamlet to a disease that a person might be ashamed of and keep hidden. This would be a mistake, because the disease, left untreated, would weaken its host more and more. Claudius's imagery makes it clear that he cannot tolerate Hamlet's behaviour or his presence any longer and intends to deal with him immediately.*
20. *draw apart:* drag away

21. *O'er whom . . . done:* His true nature shows itself to be pure, like a precious ore in worthless minerals because he weeps for what he has done.

Enter CLAUDIUS, GERTRUDE, ROSENCRANTZ, and GUILDENSTERN

CLAUDIUS

There's matter[1] in these sighs, these profound heaves;[2]
You must translate.[3] 'Tis fit we understand them.[4]
Where is your son?[5]

GERTRUDE

Bestow this place on us[6] a little while.

Exit ROSENCRANTZ and GUILDENSTERN

Ah, my good lord, what have I seen tonight!   5

CLAUDIUS

What, Gertrude? How does Hamlet?

GERTRUDE

[Handwritten: Trying to protect Hamlet]

Mad as the sea and wind, when both contend[7] *[Handwritten: Theme of madness]*
Which is the mightier. In his lawless[8] fit,
Behind the arras hearing something stir,
Whips his rapier out and cries 'A rat, a rat!'   10
And in this brainish apprehension, kills
The unseen good old man.[9] *[Handwritten: The immediate + frank way she tells Claudius everything could suggest she is allied to the king rather than her son]*

CLAUDIUS

O heavy[10] deed!
It had been so with us,[11] had we been there.[12]
His liberty is full of threats to all –   15
To you yourself, to us, to everyone.
Alas, how shall this bloody deed be answered?[13]
It will be laid to us,[14] whose providence *[Handwritten: Theme of madness]*
Should have kept short,[15] restrained, and out of haunt[16]
This mad young man. But so much was our love,   20
We would not understand what was most fit,[17]
But, like the owner of a foul disease,
To keep it from divulging,[18] let it feed
Even on the pith[19] of life. Where is he gone?

GERTRUDE

To draw apart[20] the body he hath killed,   25
O'er whom – his very madness, like some ore *[Handwritten: Theme of madness. Hamlet showing remorse]*
Among a mineral of metals base,
Shows itself pure – he weeps for what is done.[21] *[Handwritten: she lies for him here]*

CLAUDIUS

O Gertrude, come away!
The sun no sooner shall the mountains touch,[22]   **30**
But we will ship him hence;[23] and this vile deed
We must with all our majesty[24] and skill,
Both countenance[25] and excuse. – Ho, Guildenstern!

Re-enter ROSENCRANTZ and GUILDENSTERN

Friends both, go join you with some further aid.[26]
Hamlet in madness hath Polonius slain,   **35**
And from his mother's closet hath he dragged him.
Go seek him out, speak fair,[27] and bring the body
Into the chapel. I pray you, haste in this.

Exit ROSENCRANTZ and GUILDENSTERN

Come, Gertrude, we'll call up our wisest friends
To let them know both what we mean to do   **40**
And what's untimely[28] done. So haply slander,
Whose whisper o'er the world's diameter,
As level as the cannon to his blank,
Transports his poisoned shot, may miss our name
And hit the woundless air.[29] O, come away!   **45**
My soul is full of discord and dismay.[30]

Exit

22. *The sun ... touch:* dawn
23. *But we ... hence:* We will send him away from here.
24. *majesty:* royal authority
25. *countenance:* face up to
26. *join you ... aid:* get others to help you
27. *speak fair:* speak politely to him
28. *untimely:* has been done before its time
29. *So haply ... woundless air:* So perhaps slander, that has an aim as direct as a cannonball that hits its target even across a distance of half the world, may miss us and hit the invulnerable air instead. *Claudius is desperate to avoid any stories of this murder getting out in case he is in some way implicated in the death of Polonius.*
30. *My soul ... dismay:* I am confused and distressed.

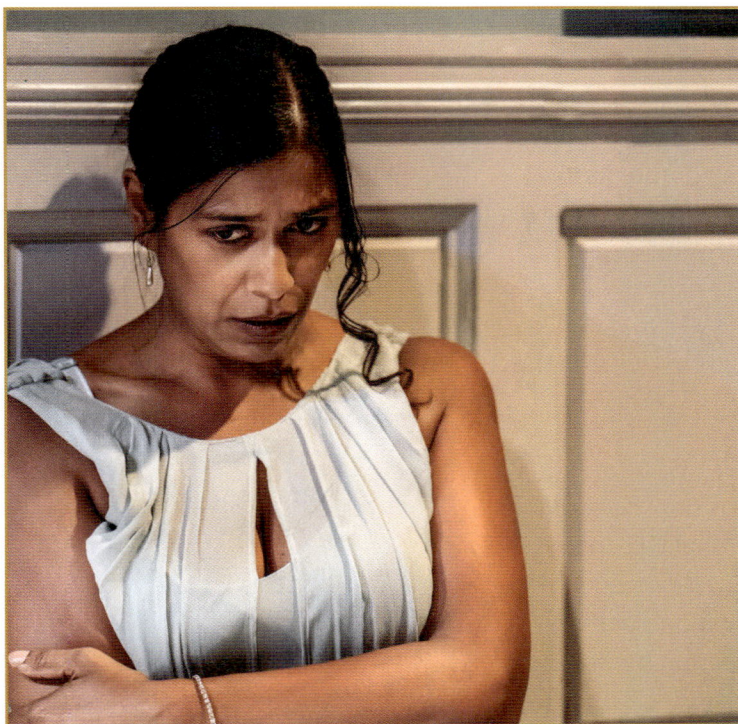

Act 4 Scene 1
Quotes and Questions

Quotes

Mad as the sea and wind, when both contend Which is the mightier.

(Gertrude, lines 7–8)

Gertrude tells Claudius that Hamlet is as mad as the wind and sea when both seem to be competing to see which is stormiest. She tries to protect Hamlet by making it clear he is insane and not responsible for his actions.

It will be laid to us, whose providence Should have kept short, restrained, and out of haunt This mad young man.

(Claudius, lines 18–20)

Claudius is worried that he will be blamed for not controlling Hamlet. In this scene, Claudius is keen to distance himself from Hamlet, calling him Gertrude's son and 'This mad young man'.

To draw apart the body he hath killed, O'er whom – his very madness, like some ore Among a mineral of metals base, Shows itself pure – he weeps for what is done.   (Gertrude, lines 25–28)

Gertrude tells Claudius that Hamlet has dragged Polonius's body away. She lies for Hamlet, saying his true goodness showed through his madness like a precious ore in worthless metal, and that he regretted killing Polonius.

Questions

In each case, support your point with suitable reference to and quotation from the play.

1. How does Claudius react to the news of Polonius's death?

2. Both Gertrude and Claudius lie to one another in this scene. Give a brief account of the lies they tell and why – in your opinion – they tell them.

Essay Building Blocks

'Deception and disloyalty are central to the play, Hamlet.'

Write a paragraph in response to this statement, supporting your answer with quotation from and reference to Act 4 Scene 1.

Writing Task

Claudius says he intends to ask wise friends how he should manage this situation and avoid the slander that will undoubtedly follow when news of Polonius's death becomes known. Write the note that you think Claudius might send one of these friends, explaining the situation and expressing his concerns.

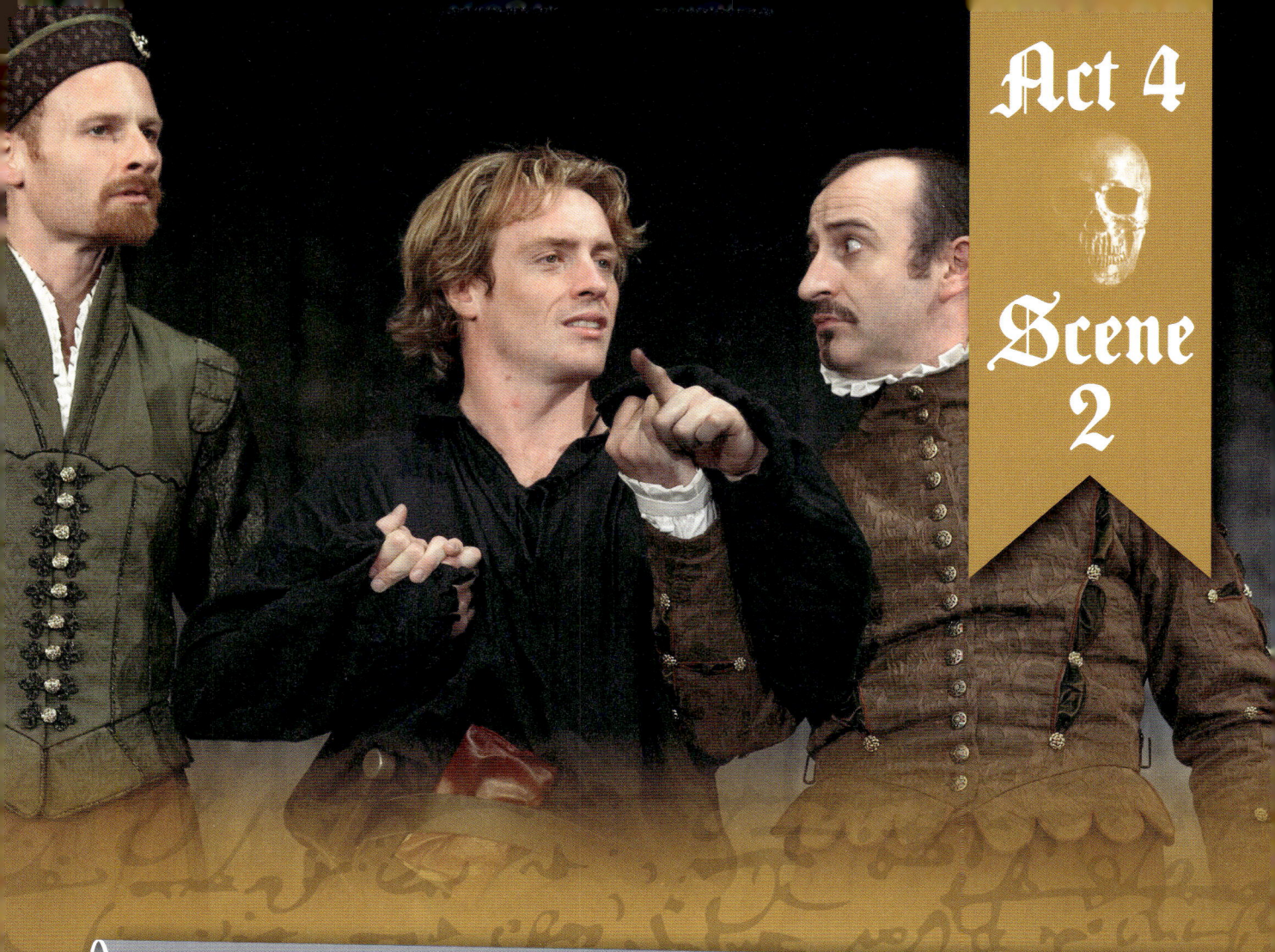

Another room in the castle

Rosencrantz and Guildenstern find Hamlet, but he will not tell them where he has put Polonius's body. He warns his old schoolfriends that Claudius is using them and will not hesitate to dispose of them when they are no longer of value to him. He runs away, forcing Rosencrantz and Guildenstern to follow.

Enter HAMLET

HAMLET
Safely stowed.[1]

ROSENCRANTZ and **GUILDENSTERN**
[Within] Hamlet, Lord Hamlet!

HAMLET
What noise? Who calls on Hamlet?
O, here they come.

Enter ROSENCRANTZ and GUILDENSTERN

ROSENCRANTZ
What have you done, my lord, with the dead body?   5

2. *Compounded:* mixed
3. *whereto 'tis kin:* to which it is related

HAMLET
Compounded[2] it with dust, whereto 'tis kin.[3]

ROSENCRANTZ
Tell us where 'tis, that we may take it thence[4]
And bear it to the chapel.

4. *thence:* from there

HAMLET
Do not believe it.

ROSENCRANTZ
Believe what?   10

HAMLET
That I can keep your counsel[5] and not mine own.
Besides, to be demanded of[6] a sponge –
what replication[7] should be made by the son of a king?

5. *counsel:* secrets
6. *demanded of:* questioned by
7. *replication:* reply

ROSENCRANTZ
Take you me for a sponge, my lord?

HAMLET

Ay, sir, that soaks up the King's countenance,[8] his rewards, his authorities.[9] But such officers do the King best service in the end. He keeps them, like an ape an apple in the corner of his jaw, first mouthed to be last swallowed. When he needs what you have gleaned, it is but squeezing you, and, sponge, you shall be dry again.[10]

15

20

Hamlet warning R & G what Claudius will do.

8. *countenance:* favour

9. *authorities:* power and influence

10. *He keeps . . . again:* He keeps people like you like an ape keeps an apple in the corner of his mouth, which he will swallow when he has squeezed the juice from it. When Claudius has taken everything he needs from you, he will leave you with nothing.

ROSENCRANTZ

I understand you not, my lord.

HAMLET

I am glad of it. A knavish speech sleeps in a foolish ear.[11]

11. *A knavish . . . ear:* A sarcastic speech like mine cannot be understood by a stupid person.

ROSENCRANTZ

My lord, you must tell us where the body is, and go with us to the King.

25

HAMLET

The body is with the King, but the King is not with the body.[12] The King is a thing –

saying Claudius does not deserve to be king

12. *The body . . . body:* Claudius is not part of the body politic. He is not the rightful king and does not embody true kingship.

GUILDENSTERN

A thing, my lord?

HAMLET

Of nothing.[13] Bring me to him. Hide fox, and all after.[14]

13. *Of nothing:* of no importance

14. *Hide fox, and all after:* Hamlet runs away as if he is playing hide and seek. He is the fox and Rosencrantz and Guildenstern are like the King's hounds, chasing him.

Exit

Quotes

> *When he needs what you have gleaned, it is but squeezing you, and, sponge, you shall be dry again.*
>
> (Hamlet, lines 19–21)

Hamlet compares Rosencrantz and Guildenstern to a sponge or an apple kept in the mouth of an ape. He warns them that Claudius is using them, and will squeeze them dry when he has finished with them. In other words, when Claudius has taken everything he needs from the pair, he will leave them with nothing.

> *The body is with the King, but the King is not with the body.*
>
> (Hamlet, lines 26–27)

Hamlet says that Claudius is not part of the body politic. He is not the rightful king and does not embody true kingship.

Questions

In each case, support your point with suitable reference to and quotation from the play.

1. Do you agree with Hamlet's assessment of Rosencrantz and Guildenstern?

2. Do you have any sympathy for Rosencrantz and Guildenstern?

Another room in the castle

Claudius is deeply worried. He fears Hamlet but is reluctant to deal with him harshly in Denmark, as Hamlet is very popular with the people.

Rosencrantz and Guildenstern tell Claudius that they have captured Hamlet but he will not say where he has hidden Polonius's body. Claudius sends for Hamlet and, after mocking his uncle for a time, the Prince tells Claudius where to find the corpse.

Claudius sends Hamlet to the ship bound for England. Alone onstage, Claudius reveals that the letter Rosencrantz and Guildenstern are bringing to the King of England is a warrant for Hamlet's immediate execution.

1. *I have . . . him:* I have sent people to look for him.

2. *the strong law:* impose heavy punishment

3. *distracted multitude:* the irrational people of Denmark

4. *Who like . . . eyes:* Who like him because of his appearance rather than because they have rationally formed an opinion.

5. *scourge:* punishment *The people would focus on Hamlet's punishment rather than the crime he committed.*

6. *To bear . . . even:* to avoid arousing suspicion

7. *Deliberate pause:* a decision reached after careful consideration

8. *Diseases . . . all:* Diseases that are far advanced require desperate remedies or they will not be cured.

9. *what hath befall'n?:* What has happened?

10. *bestowed:* stowed away; hidden

11. *Without:* outside

Enter CLAUDIUS, attended

CLAUDIUS
I have sent to seek him,[1] and to find the body.
How dangerous is it that this man goes loose!
Yet must not we put the strong law[2] on him.
He's loved of the distracted multitude,[3]
Who like not in their judgment but their eyes,[4]   5
And where 'tis so, the offender's scourge[5] is weighed,
But never the offence. To bear all smooth and even,[6]
This sudden sending him away must seem
Deliberate pause.[7] Diseases desperate grown
By desperate appliance are relieved,   10
Or not at all.[8]

Enter ROSENCRANTZ

How now, what hath befall'n?[9]

ROSENCRANTZ
Where the dead body is bestowed,[10] my lord,
We cannot get from him.

CLAUDIUS
But where is he?   15

ROSENCRANTZ
Without,[11] my lord, guarded, to know your pleasure.

CLAUDIUS
Bring him before us.

ROSENCRANTZ
Ho, Guildenstern! Bring in my lord.

Enter HAMLET and GUILDENSTERN

CLAUDIUS
Now, Hamlet, where's Polonius?

HAMLET
At supper.   20

CLAUDIUS

At supper? Where?

HAMLET

Not where he eats, but where he is eaten. A certain
convocation of politic worms are e'en at him.
Your worm is your only emperor for diet.[12] We fat all
creatures else to fat us, and we fat ourselves for   25
maggots.[13] Your fat king and your lean beggar is but
variable service – two dishes, but to one table.[14]
That's the end.

↓ attempts to insult & humiliate
Claudius

CLAUDIUS

Alas, alas!

HAMLET

A man may fish with the worm that hath eat of a   30
king, and eat of the fish that hath fed of that worm.

CLAUDIUS

What dost you mean by this?

HAMLET

Nothing but to show you how a king may go a
progress[15] through the guts of a beggar.

CLAUDIUS

Where is Polonius?   35

HAMLET

In heaven. Send thither to see.[16] If your messenger find
him not there, seek him in the other place[17] yourself. But
indeed, if you find him not this month, you shall nose[18]
him as you go up the stairs into the lobby.

CLAUDIUS

Go seek him there.   40

To some ATTENDANTS

HAMLET

He will stay till you come.

12. *A certain . . . diet:* A gathering of shrewd worms is eating at
him right now. Worms are the emperors of eating. *This is a
reference to the Diet of Worms ('diet' in this case means formal
assembly) in 1521, before which Martin Luther (considered
shrewd) defended his doctrines. The Diet of Worms was called
by Emperor Charles V in the city of Worms, Germany.*

13. *We fat . . . maggots:* We fatten animals to feed us and in so
doing we are fattening ourselves for the maggots that will
eat us when we die.

14. *Your fat king . . . table:* A fat king and a skinny beggar are
just different courses, two dishes that the worms will eat.

15. *progress:* royal journey

16. *Send thither to see:* Send someone there to check.

17. *in the other place:* in hell

18. *nose:* smell *Hamlet means that they will smell Polonius's
decomposing body.*

19. *Hamlet, this deed . . . quickness:* Hamlet, I value your safety as much as I grieve for what you have done, but that deed *(murdering Polonius)* means you must be sent away from here with all speed.
20. *bark:* ship
21. *The associates tend:* Rosencrantz and Guildenstern are waiting
22. *bent:* directed towards

23. *So is it . . . purposes:* If you knew my purposes, you would approve.

24. *cherub:* an angel that knows everything about human affairs *This is another way of saying that heaven is aware of all of Claudius's deeds.*

25. *Follow . . . aboard:* Follow him, and stay so close that you are walking at his heel. Encourage him to board the ship quickly.

26. *Away . . . affair:* Go, because everything about this matter is completed.

Exit ATTENDANTS

CLAUDIUS

Hamlet, this deed, for thine especial safety –
Which we do tender as we dearly grieve
For that which thou hast done – must send thee hence
With fiery quickness.[19] Therefore prepare thyself.   45
The bark[20] is ready, and the wind at help,
The associates tend,[21] and everything is bent[22]
For England.

HAMLET

For England?

CLAUDIUS

Ay, Hamlet.   50

HAMLET

Good.

CLAUDIUS

So is it if thou knew'st our purposes.[23]

HAMLET

I see a cherub[24] that sees them. But come, for England.
Farewell, dear mother.

CLAUDIUS

Thy loving father, Hamlet.   55

HAMLET

My mother. Father and mother is man and wife,
man and wife is one flesh, and so my mother.
Come, for England.

Exit

CLAUDIUS

Follow him at foot. Tempt him with speed aboard.[25]
Delay it not. I'll have him hence tonight.   60
Away, for everything is sealed and done
That else leans on th'affair.[26] Pray you, make haste.

Exit ROSENCRANTZ and GUILDENSTERN

And, England, if my love thou hold'st at aught –
As my great power thereof may give thee sense,
Since yet thy cicatrice looks raw and red   65
After the Danish sword, and thy free awe
Pays homage to us[27] – thou mayst not coldly set
Our sovereign process,[28] which imports at full,
By letters conjuring to that effect,
The present death of Hamlet.[29] Do it, England,   70
For like the hectic[30] in my blood he rages,
And thou must cure me. Till I know 'tis done,
Howe'er my haps,[31] my joys were ne'er begun.[32]

Exit

27. *And, England, . . . homage to us:* And, King of England, if you value my friendship at all, as you should because of my great power, since you still have red, raw battle scars after your defeat by the Danes and you voluntarily pay tribute to Denmark out of respect

28. *thou . . . process:* you may not disregard my royal command

29. *imports . . . Hamlet:* there are full instructions in letters ordering the immediate death of Hamlet

30. *hectic:* fever

31. *Howe'er my haps:* whatever may happen to me

32. *my joys were ne'er begun:* I will never be happy

Act 4 Scene 3
Quotes and Questions

Quotes

He's loved of the distracted multitude,
Who like not in their judgment but their eyes,
And where 'tis so, the offender's scourge is weighed,
But never the offence.

(Claudius, lines 4–7)

Claudius says Hamlet is very popular with the people. While Claudius is scornful of this, calling the public 'distracted', meaning irrational or unstable, he does recognise the danger it poses. The people love Hamlet so would be more likely to be upset by Claudius's punishment of Hamlet than by any crime Hamlet may have committed.

Your fat king and your lean beggar is but
variable service – two dishes, but to one table.
That's the end.

(Hamlet, lines 26–28)

Hamlet reflects on mortality. He says that everybody, whether a fat king or a skinny beggar, ends up as food for worms, and that's all there is to it.

Questions

In each case, support your point with suitable reference to and quotation from the play.

1. What is Claudius's plan for Hamlet?

2. Why is Claudius reluctant to have Hamlet's death sentence carried out in Denmark?

3. What view of life and death does Hamlet express in this scene?

Writing Task

Claudius says that he has sent a letter to the king of England, giving full instructions for the execution of Hamlet. Based on what Claudius says about (a) Hamlet's popularity with the Danish people and (b) his relationship with the English king, write the text of the letter you think Claudius would have sent.

Essay Building Blocks

'It has been argued that in the play, Hamlet, the central figure is Claudius, the King, whose attempts to govern well are hampered by his nephew, Hamlet.'

Write a paragraph in response to this statement, supporting your answer with quotation from and reference to Act 4 Scene 3.

A plain in Denmark

On his way to the harbour, Hamlet meets a Norwegian captain who tells him that Fortinbras is leading an expedition to Poland to capture a tiny, worthless piece of land. Hamlet is struck by the contrast between Fortinbras' willingness to fight and die for a cause that seems pointless and his own delay in avenging his father's death. He vows that from this time forth, he will no longer procrastinate.

Act 4

1. *licence:* permission

2. *conveyance:* escort

3. *rendezvous:* meeting place

4. *If that . . . us:* if Claudius wants to meet with me

5. *express . . . eye:* pay my respects to him face to face

6. *Go softly on:* Proceed carefully.

7. *powers:* troops

8. *How purposed:* What is their purpose; against whom are they marching?

9. *main:* main part of

10. *frontier:* some outlying region

Enter FORTINBRAS, a CAPTAIN, and SOLDIERS, marching

FORTINBRAS
Go, captain, from me greet the Danish king.
Tell him that by his licence[1] Fortinbras
Craves the conveyance[2] of a promised march
Over his kingdom. You know the rendezvous.[3]
If that his majesty would aught with us,[4]   5
We shall express our duty in his eye,[5]
And let him know so.

CAPTAIN
I will do't, my lord.

FORTINBRAS
Go softly on.[6]

Exit FORTINBRAS and SOLDIERS
Enter HAMLET, ROSENCRANTZ, GUILDENSTERN, and others

HAMLET
Good sir, whose powers[7] are these?   10

CAPTAIN
They are of Norway, sir.

HAMLET
How purposed,[8] sir, I pray you?

CAPTAIN
Against some part of Poland.

HAMLET
Who commands them, sir?

CAPTAIN
The nephew to old Norway, Fortinbras.   15

HAMLET
Goes it against the main[9] of Poland, sir,
Or for some frontier?[10]

CAPTAIN

Truly to speak, and with no addition,[11]

We go to gain a little patch of ground

That hath in it no profit but the name.[12]   20

To pay five ducats, five, I would not farm it,[13]

Nor will it yield to Norway or the Pole

A ranker[14] rate, should it be sold in fee.[15]

HAMLET

Why then, the Polack never will defend it.

CAPTAIN

Yes, it is already garrisoned.[16]   25

HAMLET

Two thousand souls and twenty thousand ducats

Will now debate the question of this straw.[17]

This is th'imposthume[18] of much wealth and peace,

That inward breaks and shows no cause without

Why the man dies.[19] I humbly thank you, sir.   30

CAPTAIN

God be wi' you, sir.

Exit

ROSENCRANTZ

Will't please you go, my lord?

HAMLET

I'll be with you straight.[20] Go a little before.[21]

astonished that a war could be fought over such a small piece of land, Hamlet.

Exit all except HAMLET

==How all occasions do inform against me[22]==

==And spur[23] my dull revenge!== What is a man   35

If his chief good and market of his time[24]

Be but to sleep and feed? – a beast, no more.

Sure, he that made us with such large discourse,[25]

Looking before and after,[26] gave us not

That capability and god-like reason   40

To fust[27] in us unused. Now whether it be

Reflects on his own lack of motivation. Reminiscent of his previous soliloques where he reflects on his own failings/shortcomings

---

11. *with no addition:* with no exaggeration

12. *That hath ... name:* The only value to this place is that we will be able to say we conquered it.

13. *To pay ... it:* I wouldn't pay five ducats to rent it as farmland.

14. *ranker:* better price

15. *sold in fee:* sold outright

16. *garrisoned:* defended

17. *Two thousand ... straw:* Two thousand men and 20,000 ducats will hardly be enough to settle the issue of ownership of this worthless piece of land.

18. *th'imposthume:* abscess or ulcer

19. *That inward ... dies:* That burst internally and therefore nobody can see why the man died *Hamlet thinks that Norway and Poland have become corrupt because they have been wealthy and at peace for too long. Now they are willing to engage in a totally meaningless war.*

20. *straight:* straight away

21. *Go a little before me:* Walk a little ahead of me.

22. *How all ... me:* all chance events provide incriminating evidence against me

23. *spur:* urge on

24. *chief ... time:* main way he spends and profits by his time

25. *such large discourse:* impressive powers of reason

26. *Looking before and after:* looking into the future and the past

27. *fust:* go mouldy

28. *Bestial oblivion:* the ignorance/forgetfulness of an animal
29. *craven:* cowardly

30. *Sith:* since

31. *gross:* obvious
32. *exhort:* urge
33. *mass and charge:* size and cost
34. *delicate and tender:* sensitive and young

35. *puffed:* puffed up/inflated

36. *Makes mouths . . . event:* makes scornful faces at the unforeseen consequences

37. *eggshell:* something worthless or trivial/a prize not worth all that is risked to win it
38. *Rightly to be great:* to be truly great
39. *Is not . . . argument:* is not to act without a good reason for doing so
40. *But greatly . . . stake:* but to fight over something insignificant when his honour is at stake
41. *stained:* dishonoured
42. *Excitements . . . blood:* things which should incite both my reason and my passion

43. *fantasy and trick:* illusion and a trifle

44. *Wheron . . . slain:* which is not large enough to serve as a battlefield for those who fight for the cause or to contain the bodies of the fallen dead

---

Bestial oblivion,[28] or some craven[29] scruple
Of thinking too precisely on th'event –
A thought which, quartered, hath but one part wisdom
And ever three parts coward – I do not know   45
Why yet I live to say 'This thing's to do',
Sith[30] I have cause, and will, and strength, and means,
To do't. Examples gross[31] as earth exhort[32] me,
Witness this army of such mass and charge[33]
Led by a delicate and tender[34] prince,   50
Whose spirit with divine ambition puffed[35]
Makes mouths at the invisible event,[36]
Exposing what is mortal and unsure
To all that fortune, death, and danger dare,
Even for an eggshell.[37] Rightly to be great[38]   55
Is not to stir without great argument,[39]
But greatly to find quarrel in a straw
When honour's at the stake.[40] How stand I, then,
That have a father killed, a mother stained,[41]
Excitements of my reason and my blood,[42]   60
And let all sleep while, to my shame, I see
The imminent death of twenty thousand men
That, for a fantasy and trick[43] of fame,
Go to their graves like beds, fight for a plot
Whereon the numbers cannot try the cause,   65
Which is not tomb enough and continent
To hide the slain.[44] O, from this time forth
My thoughts be bloody, or be nothing worth!

Exit

Quotes

How all occasions do inform against me
And spur my dull revenge!

(Hamlet, lines 34–35)

Hamlet says that even chance events show him up and make him realise he has not yet avenged his father's murder. Happening to see Fortinbras' army marching to a pointless battle, Hamlet feels even more keenly that he should act against Claudius, as he has far greater cause to fight than does Fortinbras.

I do not know
Why yet I live to say 'This thing's to do',
Sith I have cause, and will, and strength, and means,
To do't.

(Hamlet, lines 45–48)

Hamlet questions himself, wondering why he has not yet moved against Claudius when he has good reason to do so, and is strong enough to take on the king.

O, from this time forth
My thoughts be bloody, or be nothing worth!

(Hamlet, lines 67–68)

Hamlet, inspired by Fortinbras, vows that he will act. However, it is interesting that he says his thoughts, rather than his actions, will be 'bloody'.

Questions

In each case, support your point with suitable reference to and quotation from the play.

1. Why is Fortinbras in Denmark and what instructions does he give his captain at the start of this scene?

2. What is the significance of having Hamlet meet Fortinbras at this stage in the play?

3. Compare and contrast the characters of Fortinbras and Hamlet.

4. How would you compare Hamlet's state of mind in the soliloquy that ends this scene to his state of mind in the soliloquy in Act 2 Scene 2 beginning 'O, what a rogue and peasant slave am I!' (line 555)?

Writing Task

In your own words, rewrite Hamlet's soliloquy beginning 'How all occasions do inform against me'.

Essay Building Blocks

'Fortinbras plays an important role in the play, Hamlet.*'*

Write a paragraph in response to this statement, supporting your answer with quotation from and reference to Act 4 Scene 4.

Elsinore. A room in the castle

Ophelia has been driven mad by her father's death and Hamlet's treatment of her. She wanders through the court, singing bawdy love songs and grieving for Polonius.

Laertes, accompanied by a band of riotous followers, storms the castle, demanding vengeance for his father's death and ignoble burial. Claudius calms him by promising to help him in his quest for revenge and offering his kingdom and his life in tribute if he cannot convince Laertes that he had no part in Polonius's death.

Ophelia enters once more, handing out flowers to those present. Laertes is heartbroken to see his sister in this state and it reinforces his determination to seek out whoever killed his father and drove Ophelia mad.

Act 4

1. *importunate:* persistent
2. *distract:* distracted; mad
3. *Her mood . . . pitied:* Her state of mind will make you pity her.

4. *What . . . have?:* What does she want with me?

5. *tricks:* deceptions/schemes
6. *hems:* sighs/makes a 'hem' noise as she sighs
7. *Spurns . . . straws:* angrily takes offence at the most trivial things
8. *speaks things in doubt:* what she says is unclear

9. *Yet . . . collection:* The incoherent manner of her speech causes those who hear it to infer their own meaning.
10. *They aim at it:* guess at it
11. *botch . . . thoughts:* interpret her words to fit what they believe she is saying

12. *Which, as her winks . . . unhappily:* Her winks and nods and odd gestures could easily imply that what she says is harmful or malicious.

13. *she may . . . minds:* She may spread dangerous speculations in the minds of people who are prone to think the worst.

14. *To my sick . . . is:* Because my soul is sick from sin, I have a guilty conscience.
15. *Each toy . . . amiss:* Every trivial little thing seems to be a sign of impending disaster.

16. *So full . . . spilt:* Guilt creates paranoia that cannot be concealed and the fear of being found out makes the guilty party behave in such a way that they are more likely to be found out.

Enter GERTRUDE, HORATIO, and a GENTLEMAN

GERTRUDE

I will not speak with her.

GENTLEMAN

She is importunate,[1] indeed distract.[2]

Her mood will needs be pitied.[3]

GERTRUDE

What would she have?[4]

GENTLEMAN

She speaks much of her father, says she hears   **5**

There's tricks[5] i'th' world, and hems,[6] and beats her heart,

Spurns enviously at straws,[7] speaks things in doubt[8]

That carry but half sense. Her speech is nothing,

Yet the unshaped use of it doth move

The hearers to collection.[9] They aim at it,[10]   **10**

And botch the words up fit to their own thoughts,[11]

Which, as her winks and nods and gestures yield them,

Indeed would make one think there might be thought,

Though nothing sure, yet much unhappily.[12]

HORATIO

'Twere good she were spoken with, for she may strew   **15**

Dangerous conjectures in ill-breeding minds.[13]

GERTRUDE

Let her come in.

Exit HORATIO

To my sick soul, as sin's true nature is,[14]

Each toy seems prologue to some great amiss.[15]

So full of artless jealousy is guilt,   **20**

It spills itself in fearing to be spilt.[16]

Re-enter HORATIO, with OPHELIA

OPHELIA

Where is the beauteous majesty of Denmark?

GERTRUDE

How now, Ophelia?

OPHELIA

[Sings]   How should I your true love know

From another one? –   **25**

By his cockle hat[17] and staff,

And his sandal shoon.[18]

GERTRUDE

Alas, sweet lady, what imports this song?[19]

OPHELIA

Say you? Nay, pray you, mark.[20]

[Sings]   He is dead and gone, lady,   **30**

He is dead and gone.

At his head a grass-green turf,

At his heels a stone.

GERTRUDE

Nay, but Ophelia –

OPHELIA

Pray you, mark.   **35**

[Sings]   White his shroud as the mountain snow –

Enter CLAUDIUS

GERTRUDE

Alas, look here, my lord.

OPHELIA

[Sings]   Larded[21] with sweet flowers,

Which bewept[22] to the grave did – not[23] – go

With true-love showers.   **40**

CLAUDIUS

How do you, pretty lady?

OPHELIA

Well, God'ield you![24] They say the owl was a baker's daughter.[25] Lord, we know what we are, but know not what we may be.[26] God be at your table!

17. *cockle hat:* Hat with a cockle shell on it showing the wearer had been on the pilgrimage to Santiago de Compostela. Pilgrims also carried a staff and wore sandals. Lovers were often represented as pilgrims. The idea of a lover on a pilgrimage may be connected to the fact that Hamlet has gone overseas.

18. *shoon:* shoes

19. *what imports this song.* What does this song mean?

20. *mark:* pay attention

21. *Larded:* adorned

22. *bewept:* cried over

23. *not:* Because Polonius was buried quickly without a big funeral, Ophelia has added the word 'not' to the old song.

24. *God'ield you!:* God reward you/Thank you

25. *They say . . . daughter:* This is a reference to an old story in which Jesus turned a baker's daughter into an owl because she scolded her father for giving him a generous amount of bread when he – Jesus – was disguised as a beggar. This may be a reference to Ophelia denying her love to Hamlet.

26. *Lord, we know . . . be:* This may be a reference to the sudden transformation of Hamlet from attentive and kind lover to a cruel, seemingly mad man.

27. *Conceit upon:* thinking about

CLAUDIUS

Conceit upon[27] her father.   **45**

OPHELIA

Pray you, let's have no words of this, but when they

ask you what it means, say you this.

[Sings]   Tomorrow is Saint Valentine's day,

28. *betime:* early

All in the morning betime,[28]

And I a maid at your window,   **50**

To be your Valentine.

29. *donned:* donned; put on

Then up he rose, and donned[29] his clothes,

30. *dupped:* opened

And dupped[30] the chamber-door;

Let in the maid, that out a maid

31. *Let in . . . more:* The girl who entered his room was a virgin but she was not a virgin when she left. *There was an old custom which said that the first person of the opposite sex a person saw on Valentine's Day would become their true love. In this verse, a girl goes to a man's room hoping to be his true love but he takes advantage of her.*

Never departed more.[31]   **55**

CLAUDIUS

Pretty Ophelia –

OPHELIA

32. *Without . . . on't:* I'll finish it without blaspheming

Indeed, la? Without an oath. I'll make an end on't:[32]

33. *Gis:* Jesus

[Sings]   By Gis,[33] and by Saint Charity,[34]

34. *Saint Charity:* Holy Charity

Alack, and fie for shame!

Obsessed with death, beauty + ambiguous sexual desire. Perhaps proof

35. *do't if they come to't:* have sex if they get the opportunity

Young men will do't if they come to't,[35]   **60**

that she had a sexual relationship with Hamlet. Grappling with

36. *Cock:* God *Ophelia promised to end the song without blaspheming, so she does not use God's name. Cock also means penis, so Ophelia's version may not blaspheme but it is still very rude.*

By Cock,[36] they are to blame.

her sexual feelings, discouraged by her father, brother + society?

Quoth she 'Before you tumbled[37] me,

37. *tumbled:* had sex with

You promised me to wed.'

So would I 'a' done, by yonder sun,

38. *An:* if

An[38] thou hadst not come to my bed.   **65**

CLAUDIUS

How long hath she been thus?

OPHELIA

I hope all will be well. We must be patient. But I

39. *him:* Polonius

cannot choose but weep to think they should lay him[39]

in the cold ground. My brother shall know of it.

40. *My brother . . . counsel:* Ophelia is deeply distressed about Polonius's death and his hasty, secretive burial. She says Laertes will hear of it. Thanking the listeners for their good advice – although they have given her none – she leaves.

And so I thank you for your good counsel.[40] Come, my   **70**

coach! Good night, ladies, good night, sweet ladies,

good night, good night. *Shakespeare has demonstrated Ophelia's chaste dependence on men in her life. After Polonius' death + the state of her relationship with Hamlet she finds herself*

Exit abruptly without any of them.

CLAUDIUS

41. *Follow . . . watch:* Follow her closely and keep an eye on her.

Follow her close. Give her good watch,[41] I pray you.

Exit HORATIO

O, this is the poison of deep grief! It springs

All from her father's death. O Gertrude, Gertrude,   **75**

When sorrows come they come not single spies,

But in battalions.[42] First, her father slain;

Next, your son gone, and he most violent author

Of his own just remove;[43] the people muddied,[44]

Thick and unwholesome in their thoughts and whispers   **80**

For good Polonius's death; and we have done but greenly,

In hugger-mugger to inter him;[45] poor Ophelia

Divided from herself and her fair judgment,

Without the which we are pictures or mere beasts;[46]

Last, and as much containing as all these,[47]   **85**

Her brother is in secret come from France,

Feeds on his wonder,[48] keeps himself in clouds,[49]

And wants not buzzers[50] to infect his ear

With pestilent speeches of his father's death;

Wherein necessity, of matter beggared,[51]   **90**

Will nothing stick our person to arraign

In ear and ear.[52] O my dear Gertrude, this,

Like to a murdering-piece,[53] in many places

Gives me superfluous death.[54]

A noise within

GERTRUDE

Alack, what noise is this?   **95**

CLAUDIUS

Where are my Switzers?[55] Let them guard the door.

Enter another GENTLEMAN

What is the matter?

GENTLEMAN

Save yourself, my lord.

The ocean, overpeering of his list,[56]

Eats not the flats with more impetuous haste   **100**

Than young Laertes, in a riotous head,

O'erbears your officers.[57] The rabble call him lord,

And, as the world were now but to begin,

---

42. *When sorrows . . . battalions:* Troubles do not come individually, but all at the same time.

43. *most violent . . . remove:* His violent behaviour was the just cause for his being sent away.

44. *muddied:* confused and stirred up

45. *Thick and unwholesome . . . inter him:* Coming up with dark suspicions and gossiping maliciously about Polonius's death – and we, as thoughtlessly as an inexperienced person, buried him quickly and secretly. *Polonius was an important figure in the Danish court and, under normal circumstances, would have been given a state funeral. Claudius had him buried quickly and without ceremony because he did not want to draw attention to the fact that Hamlet murdered him. However, this undignified, hasty burial dishonours Polonius and would be likely to upset and anger his family.*

46. *Divided from . . . beasts:* removed from her sanity and good judgement, without which we are not fully human and are nothing more than pictures or mere animals

47. *Last . . . these:* finally, and as bad as all the rest of these things

48. *Feeds on his wonder:* feeds on his suspicions

49. *keeps himself in clouds:* remains aloof and suspicious

50. *And wants not buzzers:* and does not lack gossips

51. *of matter beggared:* lacking facts

52. *Will nothing . . . ear:* will stop at nothing and will accuse me *Notice the references to ears again, reminding us of the truth about Claudius.*

53. *murdering-piece:* cannon that fired many shots *(like a shotgun)*

54. *in many . . . death:* The multitude of troubles Claudius has to deal with are more than enough to kill him many times over like the widely scattered shot from the cannon.

55. *Switzers:* Swiss guards *In Shakespeare's time, it was common for European royals to employ Swiss guards, who were known for their good discipline and neutrality. They would remain loyal to their employer.*

56. *overpeering of his list:* rising above its natural level

57. *Eats not . . . officers:* doesn't flood the low-lying land any faster than Laertes, with a rebellious force, overpowers your officers

Antiquity forgot, custom not known,[58]

The ratifiers and props[59] of every word, **105**

They cry 'Choose we! Laertes shall be king.'

Caps, hands, and tongues applaud it to the clouds,[60]

'Laertes shall be king, Laertes king.'

GERTRUDE

How cheerfully on the false trail they cry!

O, this is counter, you false Danish dogs![61] **110**

Noise within

CLAUDIUS

The doors are broke.

Enter LAERTES, armed; DANES following

LAERTES

Where is this King? – Sirs, stand you all without.

DANES

No, let's come in.

LAERTES

I pray you, give me leave.[62]

DANES

We will, we will. **115**

They retire without the door

LAERTES

I thank you. Keep the door.[63] O thou vile King,

Give me my father!

GERTRUDE

Calmly, good Laertes.

LAERTES

That drop of blood that's calm proclaims me bastard,[64]

Cries cuckold to my father, brands the harlot **120**

Even here between the chaste unsmirched brow

Of my true mother.[65]

CLAUDIUS

What is the cause, Laertes,

That thy rebellion looks so giant-like?[66] –

Let him go, Gertrude. Do not fear our person.[67]   **125**

There's such divinity doth hedge a king,

That treason can but peep to what it would,

Acts little of his will.[68] – Tell me, Laertes,

Why thou art thus incensed.[69] – Let him go, Gertrude. –

Speak, man.   **130**

LAERTES

Where is my father?

CLAUDIUS

Dead.

GERTRUDE

But not by him.

CLAUDIUS

Let him demand his fill.[70]

LAERTES

How came he dead? I'll not be juggled with.[71]   **135**

To hell, allegiance! Vows to the blackest devil!

Conscience and grace, to the profoundest pit![72]

I dare damnation. To this point I stand,

That both the worlds I give to negligence,

Let come what comes.[73] Only I'll be revenged   **140**

Most thoroughly for my father.

CLAUDIUS

Who shall stay[74] you?

LAERTES

My will, not all the world's;[75]

And for my means, I'll husband them so well,

They shall go far with little.[76]   **145**

CLAUDIUS

Good Laertes,

If you desire to know the certainty

Of your dear father's death, is't writ in your revenge

66. *giant-like:* huge

67. *Do not fear our person:* Do not be afraid for me.

68. *There's such ... will:* A king is surrounded by God's protection so those who threaten treason can say what they want but cannot carry out their wishes.

69. *incensed:* angry

70. *Let him demand his fill:* Let him ask all the questions he wants to ask.

71. *juggled with:* tricked

72. *profoundest pit:* deepest pit *hell is the deepest pit*

73. *To this ... comes:* I stand by this: I am indifferent to what happens to me in this world or the next.

74. *stay:* prevent

75. *My will, ... world's:* I will do what I want, not what the world wants me to do.

76. *And for ... little:* And as for my resources, I will use them so economically that a little will go a long way.

77. *is't writ . . . loser?:* Will you carry out your revenge in the manner of a sweepstake winner who takes everything; will you destroy friends and enemies indiscriminately?

78. *And, like . . . blood:* In Shakespeare's time, it was believed that the pelican pierced its breast with the hooked end of its long beak and fed its young on its own blood. Laertes intends to show his selfless generosity to those who are on his side.

79. *good child:* Claudius means that Laertes is acting as a son should, in seeking to punish those responsible for his father's death while remaining loyal to his true friends.

80. *sensibly:* feelingly
81. *level:* plainly
82. *pierce:* appear

83. *O heat . . . eye!:* Deprive me of the ability to think or to see.

84. *thy madness . . . beam:* I will take my revenge on whoever drove you mad to the extent that my revenge will outweigh the wrong done to you.

85. *Nature . . . loves:* Human nature is so refined or pure when it is in love that it often sends some precious part of itself *(Ophelia's sanity in this case)* after the one it loves.

That, sweepstake, you will draw both friend and foe,
Winner and loser?[77]   **150**

LAERTES

None but his enemies.

CLAUDIUS

Will you know them then?

LAERTES

To his good friends thus wide I'll ope my arms,
And, like the kind life-rendering pelican,
Repast them with my blood.[78]   **155**

CLAUDIUS

Why, now you speak
Like a good child[79] and a true gentleman.
That I am guiltless of your father's death,
And am most sensibly[80] in grief for it,
It shall as level[81] to your judgment pierce[82]   **160**
As day does to your eye.

DANES

[Within] Let her come in.

LAERTES

How now! What noise is that?

Re-enter OPHELIA

> finally has a voice but it is a disturbing one. Has the pressure to be chaste been partly responsible for her madness?

O heat dry up my brains! Tears seven times salt
Burn out the sense and virtue of mine eye![83]   **165**
By heaven, thy madness shall be paid by weight,
Till our scale turn the beam.[84] O rose of May,
Dear maid, kind sister, sweet Ophelia!
O heavens, is't possible, a young maid's wits
Should be as mortal as an old man's life?   **170**
Nature is fine in love, and where 'tis fine
It sends some precious instance of itself
After the thing it loves.[85]

OPHELIA

[Sings]   They bore him barefaced on the bier,[86]

        Hey non nonny, nonny, hey nonny,   **175**

        And on his grave rained many a tear –

        Fare you well, my dove.

86. *barefaced on the bier:* The coffin was open or Polonius was just carried on a bier without any coffin.

LAERTES

Hadst thou thy wits and didst persuade revenge,

It could not move thus.[87]

87. *Hadst thou … move thus:* If you were sane and asked me to seek revenge, it could not persuade me as much as this does.

OPHELIA

[Sings]   You must sing 'Down, a-down,' and you, 'Call   **180**

        him a down-a'.

        O, how the wheel becomes it![88] It is the false

        steward that stole his master's daughter.

88. *how … it!:* how the refrain suits the song

LAERTES

This nothing's more than matter.[89]

89. *This … matter:* This nonsense is more moving or meaningful than ordinary speech.

OPHELIA

There's rosemary,[90] that's for remembrance. Pray, love,

remember. And there is pansies. That's for thoughts.   **185**

90. *rosemary:* Ophelia's gifts of flowers have symbolic significance but it is not stated to whom she gives each one. She probably gives the flowers representing thoughts and remembrance to Laertes as he is thinking of their late father.

LAERTES

A document in madness – thoughts and remembrance

fitted.[91]

91. *A document … fitted:* A lesson in madness: thoughts and remembrance given to the right person.

OPHELIA

There's fennel[92] for you, and columbines.[93] There's

rue[94] for you, and here's some for me: we may call it

herb-of-grace o' Sundays. O you must wear your rue   **190**

with a difference. There's a daisy.[95] I would give you

some violets,[96] but they withered all when my father

died. They say he made a good end.

[Sings]   For bonny sweet Robin is all my joy.

92. *fennel:* symbol of flattery and deceit
93. *columbines:* symbol of disloyalty
94. *rue:* symbol of grace or repentance

95. *daisy:* symbol of innocence Ophelia does not give this to anyone. Perhaps she keeps it for herself.
96. *violets:* symbol of faithfulness

LAERTES

Thought and affliction, passion, hell itself   **195**

She turns to favour and to prettiness.[97]

97. *Thought … prettiness:* She makes sadness, suffering, passion and hell itself seem charming and pretty.

OPHELIA

[Sings] And will a not come again,

And will a not come again?

No, no, he is dead,

Go to thy death-bed,   **200**

He never will come again.

His beard was as white as snow,

All flaxen was his poll.[98]

He is gone, he is gone,

And we cast away moan.[99]   **205**

God 'a' mercy on his soul.

And of all Christian souls, I pray God. God be wi' ye.

Exit OPHELIA and GERTRUDE

LAERTES

Do you see this, O God?

CLAUDIUS

Laertes, I must commune[100] with your grief,

Or you deny me right. Go but apart,[101]   **210**

Make choice of whom your wisest friends you will,

And they shall hear and judge 'twixt[102] you and me,

If by direct or by collateral[103] hand

They find us touched,[104] we will our kingdom give,

Our crown, our life, and all that we call ours,   **215**

To you in satisfaction. But if not,

Be you content to lend your patience to us,

And we shall jointly labour with your soul

To give it due content.

LAERTES

Let this be so.   **220**

His means of death, his obscure[105] burial –

No trophy, sword, nor hatchment o'er his bones,[106]

No noble rite nor formal ostentation[107] –

Cry to be heard, as 'twere from heaven to earth,

That I must call't in question.   **225**

CLAUDIUS

So you shall;

And where th'offence is, let the great axe fall.

I pray you go with me.

Exit

98. *flaxen was his poll:* his hair was white

99. *And we cast away moan:* This could mean 'we who are left, mourn,' or 'We waste our time mourning'.

100. *commune:* join

101. *Go but apart:* go somewhere private

102. *'twixt:* between

103. *collateral:* indirect

104. *touched:* guilty

105. *obscure:* hidden

106. *hatchment . . . bones:* coat of arms on his tomb

107. *ostentation:* ceremony

Act 4 Scene 5
Quotes and Questions

Quotes

To my sick soul, as sin's true nature is,
Each toy seems prologue to some great amiss.
So full of artless jealousy is guilt,
It spills itself in fearing to be spilt.

(Gertrude, lines 18–21)

Gertrude, having reluctantly agreed to see Ophelia, expresses her guilt and paranoia. She sees disaster around every corner and is anxious that her behaviour will betray the truth about Polonius's murder.

There's such divinity doth hedge a king,
That treason can but peep to what it would,
Acts little of his will.

(Claudius, lines 126–128)

Hypocritically, Claudius claims that a king is surrounded by God's protection so those who threaten treason can say what they want but cannot carry out their wishes. He knows quite well that this is not true. He killed the previous king, after all.

To this point I stand,
That both the worlds I give to negligence,
Let come what comes. Only I'll be revenged
Most thoroughly for my father.

(Laertes, lines 138–141)

Laertes says he doesn't care if he is damned to hell for it, he will avenge his father's death no matter what the consequences. His attitude is the opposite of Hamlet's: Laertes is so angry and so determined to act that he will risk anything.

Questions

In each case, support your point with suitable reference to and quotation from the play.

1. Comment on Gertrude's behaviour in this scene.

2. Laertes says that he will 'be revenged most thoroughly' for his father and does not care what happens to him in this world or the next as a result of his actions. Compare his attitude to revenge with that of Hamlet in his soliloquy beginning 'To be, or not to be' (Act 3, Scene 1, line 64).

3. How does Claudius deflect Laertes' anger? What does this tell us about Claudius's character?

4. Claudius claims that a king has God's protection against treason. Where is the irony in this claim?

5. It is only when she is mad that Ophelia is finally given a voice. What is the dramatic effect of her appearance and her speeches?

Writing Task

Imagine you are Claudius. Write the diary entry you might make after the events of this scene, reflecting on your encounters with Ophelia and Laertes.

Essay Building Blocks

'The theme of honour is prominent throughout the play, Hamlet.'

Write a paragraph in response to this statement, supporting your answer with quotation from and reference to Act 4 Scene 5.

Another room in the castle

Horatio receives a letter from Hamlet, saying that he is back in Denmark. The ship he was on was attacked by pirates who captured Hamlet but released him in return for the promise of a future favour. Hamlet asks that Horatio deliver letters from him to the king and then join him with all speed.

Enter HORATIO and a SERVANT

HORATIO

What are they that would speak with me?

SERVANT

Sailors, sir. They say they have letters for you.

HORATIO

Let them come in.

Exit SERVANT

I do not know from what part of the world

I should be greeted, if not from Lord Hamlet.[1]   **5**

Enter SAILORS

FIRST SAILOR

God bless you, sir.

HORATIO

Let him bless thee too.

FIRST SAILOR

He shall, sir, an't please him. There's a letter for you, sir; it

comes from th'ambassador that was bound for England[2]

– if your name be Horatio, as I am let to know it is.[3]   **10**

HORATIO

[Reads] 'Horatio, when thou shalt have overlooked[4] this,

give these fellows some means[5] to the King. They have

letters for him. Ere we were two days old at sea,[6] a pirate of

very warlike appointment[7] gave us chase. Finding

ourselves too slow of sail, we put on a compelled   **15**

valour,[8] and in the grapple[9] I boarded them. On the

instant they got clear of our ship, so I alone became

their prisoner. They have dealt with me like thieves of

mercy; but they knew what they did.[10] I am to do a good

turn for them. Let the King have the letters I have sent,   **20**

and repair thou to me with as much haste as thou

wouldst fly death.[11] I have words to speak in thine ear will

1. *I do not ... Hamlet:* I do not know anyone who could be writing to me from another part of the world except Lord Hamlet.

2. *th'ambassador ... England:* Hamlet

3. *as I ... is:* as I am told it is

4. *overlooked:* read

5. *means:* means of access

6. *Ere ... sea:* before we had been at sea for two days

7. *warlike appointment:* equipped for war

8. *compelled valour:* forced bravery
9. *grapple:* when the two ships were joined together by grappling irons

10. *They have dealt ... did:* Although they are thieves, they have treated me mercifully, but they knew what they were doing *(because they were aware Hamlet might be of some use to them).*

11. *repair ... death:* Come to me as quickly as you would flee from death.

make thee dumb, yet are they much too light for the
bore of the matter.[12] These good fellows will bring thee
where I am. Rosencrantz and Guildenstern hold their   25
course[13] for England. Of them I have much to tell thee.
Farewell. He that thou knowest thine, Hamlet.'[14]
Come, I will give you way for these your letters,
And do't the speedier that you may direct me
To him from whom you brought them.[15]   30

Exit

12. *much . . . matter:* they inadequately express the seriousness
of the matter

13. *hold their course:* are still on their way

14. *He that . . . Hamlet:* from the man you know is your friend,
Hamlet *Hamlet is simply signing off the letter much as we
might write 'Yours' today.*

15. *I will . . . them:* I will give you the means to deliver these
letters directly to the King, and I will do so quickly so that
you may lead me to Hamlet as soon as possible.

Questions

In each case, support your point with suitable reference to and quotation from the play.

1. In your own words, outline the important information contained in Hamlet's letter to Horatio.

2. Does Hamlet appear more positive and energetic in his account of the sea voyage than he has so far? Explain your answer.

3. Shakespeare had to find a credible way to return Hamlet to Denmark, unharmed. Do you think he succeeded?

Another room in the castle

Claudius has managed to convince Laertes that Hamlet is responsible for the murder of Polonius. He says that he cannot take direct action against Hamlet because it would hurt Gertrude and it would be a very unpopular move. Hamlet is so loved by the people that they would forgive him anything and would turn on Claudius if he harmed him.

A messenger arrives with Hamlet's letter. Claudius is puzzled to hear of Hamlet's return but Laertes is pleased at the thought of being able to take his revenge on the Prince as soon as possible.

Claudius devises a plan to have Hamlet take on Laertes in a fencing match. He will arrange for Laertes to have a sword with a sharpened tip rather than the blunt tip usually used in sporting bouts. Laertes readily agrees but also says he will poison the tip of his sword to ensure Hamlet dies from even the lightest scratch. Claudius thinks this a good plan and suggests the back-up of a poisoned drink to offer Hamlet when he becomes thirsty during the fight.

Gertrude interrupts their conversation to bring news of Ophelia's death. She says the young woman was climbing a tree by the water's edge but a branch broke beneath her and she fell into the stream. She made no effort to save herself but merely sang as she floated. Before long, the weight of her clothes dragged her under.

Laertes weeps to hear the news but says that when he has finished grieving his sorrow will turn to rage.

Act 4

1. *Now . . . seal:* Now you must surely find me innocent *(of any involvement in Polonius's death)*

2. *Sith:* since
3. *knowing:* receptive or capable of understanding

4. *That he . . . life:* The man who killed your noble father was trying to kill me.

5. *proceeded . . . feats:* did not take any action in response to these deeds
6. *capital:* deserving of capital punishment

7. *As by your safety . . . stirred up:* As your concern for your safety, your wisdom and all the other considerations should have motivated you to do.

8. *unsinewed:* weak

9. *The Queen . . . but by her:* The queen, his mother, loves him dearly, and whether it is a good or a bad thing about me, she is so closely joined to my life and soul that, just as a star needs something around which to orbit, I could not live without her. *This refers to a belief that stars orbited the earth.*
10. *public count:* public trial
11. *general gender:* ordinary people
12. *dipping . . . affection:* Their affection for Hamlet is such that they excuse all his faults.
13. *spring . . . stone:* a spring with such a high concentration of lime in the water that it coats any substance placed in it with a covering of limestone *Claudius uses this image of a limestone spring turning wood to water to show that the people of Denmark would turn Hamlet into a hero, despite his crimes.*
14. *Convert . . . graces:* convert his crimes to graces *Gyves are shackles for prisoners and in this context mean crimes which would warrant gyves.*
15. *Too slightly timbered:* made of wood that is too light
16. *so loud a wind:* public opinion
17. *Would have . . . them:* whatever I accused Hamlet of would have rebounded onto me
18. *desperate terms:* desperation/madness
19. *if praises . . . again:* if we could praise her for the way she was before her madness

20. *Stood challenger . . . perfections:* could rival, from on high, the perfection of anyone of her time

21. *Break . . . that:* Don't lose any sleep over that.

Enter CLAUDIUS and LAERTES

CLAUDIUS

Now must your conscience my acquaintance seal,[1]
And you must put me in your heart for friend,
Sith[2] you have heard, and with a knowing[3] ear,
That he which hath your noble father slain
Pursued my life.[4]   5

LAERTES

It well appears. But tell me
Why you proceeded not against these feats,[5]
So crimeful and so capital[6] in nature,
As by your safety, wisdom, all things else,
You mainly were stirred up.[7]   10

CLAUDIUS

O, for two special reasons,
Which may to you, perhaps, seem much unsinewed,[8]
But yet to me they're strong. The Queen his mother
Lives almost by his looks; and for myself –
My virtue or my plague, be it either which –   15
She's so conjunctive to my life and soul
That, as the star moves not but in his sphere,
I could not but by her.[9] The other motive
Why to a public count[10] I might not go
Is the great love the general gender[11] bear him,   20
Who, dipping all his faults in their affection,[12]
Would, like the spring that turneth wood to stone,[13]
Convert his gyves to graces;[14] so that my arrows,
Too slightly timbered[15] for so loud a wind,[16]
Would have reverted to my bow again,   25
And not where I had aimed them.[17]

LAERTES

And so have I a noble father lost,
A sister driven into desperate terms,[18]
Whose worth, if praises may go back again,[19]
Stood challenger, on mount, of all the age   30
For her perfections.[20] But my revenge will come.

CLAUDIUS

Break not your sleeps for that.[21] You must not think

That we are made of stuff so flat and dull

That we can let our beard be shook with danger,

And think it pastime.[22] You shortly shall hear more.   35

I loved your father, and we love ourself.

And that, I hope, will teach you to imagine –[23]

Enter a MESSENGER

How now? What news?

MESSENGER

Letters, my lord, from Hamlet.

This to your majesty; this to the Queen.   40

CLAUDIUS

From Hamlet? Who brought them?

MESSENGER

Sailors, my lord, they say. I saw them not.

They were given me by Claudio. He received them.

CLAUDIUS

Laertes, you shall hear them. – Leave us.

Exit MESSENGER

[Reads] 'High and mighty,[24] you shall know I am set   45

naked[25] on your kingdom. Tomorrow shall I beg leave

to see your kingly eyes,[26] when I shall, first asking your

pardon, thereunto recount the occasion[27] of my sudden

and more strange return. Hamlet.'

What should this mean? Are all the rest come back?   50

Or is it some abuse, and no such thing?[28]

LAERTES

Know you the hand?[29]

CLAUDIUS

'Tis Hamlet's character.[30] 'Naked' –

And in a postscript here he says 'alone'.

Can you advise me?   55

22. *That we are made . . . think it pastime:* That I am so lazy and stupid that I will allow myself to be insulted and threatened and think it unimportant

23. *You shortly . . . imagine –:* You will soon hear more. I cared for your father and I care for myself. And that, I hope, will help you to see – *Claudius expects to receive news that Hamlet has been executed in England. However, the messenger who interrupts him brings unwelcome news.*

24. *High and mighty:* Hamlet is being sarcastic in his address to Claudius. He does not consider Claudius a worthy king in any way.

25. *naked:* unarmed

26. *to see your kingly eyes:* Once again, Hamlet is mocking Claudius.

27. *recount the occasion:* explain the circumstances

28. *Are all the rest . . . such thing?:* Have all the others *(including Rosencrantz and Guildenstern)* returned? Or is it a trick and not true at all?

29. *Know you the hand?:* Do you recognise the handwriting?

30. *'Tis Hamlet's character:* It is Hamlet's handwriting.

31. *I'm lost in it:* I'm bewildered by it

32. *It warms ... diddest thou':* It warms my sick heart that I will be able to look him in the face and tell him, 'Just as you killed my father, so I am killing you'.

33. *If so ... peace:* As long as you don't overrule me and say I must make peace.

34. *As checking his voyage:* because he has turned away from his voyage

35. *I will ... device:* I will manipulate him into going along with a scheme I have worked out.

36. *Under the which ... uncharge the practice:* He will surely die. And nobody will be blamed for his death. Even his mother will not hold me accountable for the plot.

37. *The rather ... organ:* I will be even more willing to go along with your plan if you can work it so that I am your instrument to carry out the plot *Laertes wants to be the one who kills Hamlet.*

38. *It falls right:* That fits in perfectly.

39. *You have been ... shine:* There has been a lot of talk about you, since you left – and Hamlet has overheard it – about something you are really good at.

40. *Your sum of parts ... siege:* The sum total of your accomplishments did not make him as envious as that one did, although I consider it the least important.

41. *very riband:* mere ornament

174 Hamlet

LAERTES

I'm lost in it,[31] my lord. But let him come.
It warms the very sickness in my heart
That I shall live and tell him to his teeth,
'Thus diddest thou'.[32]

CLAUDIUS

If it be so, Laertes –   60
As how should it be so, how otherwise? –
Will you be ruled by me?

LAERTES

If so you will not o'errule me to a peace.[33]

CLAUDIUS

To thine own peace. If he be now returned,
As checking at his voyage,[34] and that he means   65
No more to undertake it, I will work him
To an exploit, now ripe in my device,[35]
Under the which he shall not choose but fall;
And for his death no wind of blame shall breathe;
But even his mother shall uncharge the practice[36]   70
And call it accident.

LAERTES

My lord, I will be ruled,
The rather, if you could devise it so
That I might be the organ.[37]

CLAUDIUS

It falls right.[38]   75
You have been talked of, since your travel, much,
And that in Hamlet's hearing, for a quality
Wherein, they say, you shine.[39] Your sum of parts
Did not together pluck such envy from him
As did that one, and that, in my regard,   80
Of the unworthiest siege.[40]

LAERTES

What part is that, my lord?

CLAUDIUS

A very riband[41] in the cap of youth,

Yet needful[42] too, for youth no less becomes[43]

The light and careless livery[44] that it wears   **85**

Than settled age his sables and his weeds[45]

Importing health[46] and graveness.[47] Some two months since,

Here was a gentleman of Normandy.[48]

I've seen myself, and served against, the French,

And they can well on horseback;[49] but this gallant[50]   **90**

Had witchcraft in't. He grew unto his seat,

And to such wondrous doing brought his horse

As had he been incorpsed and demi-natured

With the brave beast.[51] So far he topped my thought

That I in forgery of shapes and tricks   **95**

Come short of what he did.[52]

LAERTES

A Norman was't?

CLAUDIUS

A Norman.

LAERTES

Upon my life, Lamond.

CLAUDIUS

The very same.   **100**

LAERTES

I know him well. He is the brooch indeed,

And gem, of all the nation.[53]

CLAUDIUS

He made confession of you,[54]

And gave you such a masterly report

For art and exercise[55] in your defence,[56]   **105**

And for your rapier[57] most especially,

That he cried out 'twould be a sight indeed

If one could match you. The scrimers[58] of their nation

He swore, had had neither motion, guard, nor eye

If you opposed them.[59] Sir, this report of his   **110**

Did Hamlet so envenom[60] with his envy

That he could nothing do but wish and beg

Your sudden coming o'er, to play[61] with him.

Now, out of this –

---

42. *needful:* necessary
43. *becomes:* is suited to
44. *livery:* clothing
45. *his sables and his weeds:* his furs and dark clothing
46. *health:* prosperity
47. *graveness:* seriousness or dignity *Claudius is careful to flatter Laertes and suggests that although he, Claudius, thinks Laertes has even more valuable qualities than an ability to fence well, he recognises that such sword fighting is important to young men.*
48. *Here was ... Normandy:* a gentleman from Normandy visited the Danish court
49. *can well on horseback:* rides horses well
50. *gallant:* young man

51. *He grew ... beast:* He sat in the saddle so well and was able to make his horse perform so wonderfully that it looked as if he and the horse were sharing one body, half-horse, half-man.
52. *So far ... did:* He went far beyond anything I could describe or imagine.

53. *brooch ... nation:* jewel/ornament

54. *made confession of you:* acknowledged your superior skill

55. *art and exercise:* theory and practice
56. *defence:* fencing
57. *rapier:* thin, light sword

58. *scrimers:* fencers

59. *had ... opposed them:* would seem unable to attack or defend themselves, would seem blind
60. *envenom:* poison

61. *play:* fence

Act 4

63. *love is . . . time:* love begins at a certain period in time

64. *passages of proof:* evidence that proves my point

65. *Time . . . it:* Time weakens the intensity of it.

66. *There lives . . . abate it:* The wick is the part of the candle that is lit. The snuff is the burnt or charred part of the wick. Claudius claims that love, like a candle, can burn itself out over time.

67. *And nothing . . . still:* Nothing stays at a permanent level of perfection.

68. *plurisy:* excess

69. *We should . . . accidents:* If we intend to do something, we should do it as soon as possible because intentions change and our resolution may be weakened by words, actions and chance events.

70. *And then . . . easing:* Sighs were believed to thin the blood, therefore to sigh like a spendthrift – wastefully and profusely – gives short-term relief but will cause illness or injury in the long term.

71. *the quick of th'ulcer:* the sensitive point of the matter

72. *sanctuarise:* give sanctuary to *Claudius* says that murder is such a terrible crime that Laertes can seek vengeance by killing Hamlet anywhere, even in a church.

73. *We'll . . . excellence:* We will encourage certain people to praise your skill at fencing.

74. *double varnish:* further gloss

75. *in fine:* finally

76. *remiss:* careless

77. *free . . . contriving:* incapable of plotting or scheming

176 Hamlet

LAERTES

What out of this, my lord?   115

CLAUDIUS

Laertes, was your father dear to you?
Or are you like the painting of a sorrow,
A face without a heart?[62]

LAERTES

Why ask you this?

CLAUDIUS

Not that I think you did not love your father,   120
But that I know love is begun by time,[63]
And that I see, in passages of proof,[64]
Time qualifies the spark and fire of it.[65]
There lives within the very flame of love
A kind of wick or snuff that will abate it,[66]   125
And nothing is at a like goodness still,[67]
For goodness, growing to a plurisy,[68]
Dies in his own too much. That we would do
We should do when we would, for this 'would' changes,
And hath abatements and delays as many   130
As there are tongues, are hands, are accidents;[69]
And then this 'should' is like a spendthrift's sigh,
That hurts by easing.[70] But, to the quick of th'ulcer[71] –
Hamlet comes back. What would you undertake
To show yourself your father's son in deed   135
More than in words?

LAERTES

To cut his throat i'th' church.

CLAUDIUS

No place, indeed, should murder sanctuarise.[72]
Revenge should have no bounds. But, good Laertes,
Will you do this? Keep close within your chamber.   140
Hamlet returned shall know you are come home.
We'll put on those shall praise your excellence,[73]
And set a double varnish[74] on the fame
The Frenchman gave you; bring you, in fine,[75] together,
And wager on your heads. He, being remiss,[76]   145
Most generous, and free from all contriving,[77]

Will not peruse the foils;[78] so that with ease,

Or with a little shuffling, you may choose

A sword unbated[79] and, in a pass of practice,[80]

Requite him[81] for your father.   150

LAERTES

I will do't,

And, for that purpose I'll anoint my sword.

I bought an unction[82] of a mountebank[83]

So mortal that but dip a knife in it,

Where it draws blood no cataplasm[84] so rare,   155

Collected from all simples that have virtue[85]

Under the moon, can save the thing from death

That is but scratched withal.[86] I'll touch my point

With this contagion, that if I gall[87] him slightly,

It may be death.   160

CLAUDIUS

Let's further think of this;

Weigh what convenience both of time and means

May fit us to our shape.[88] If this should fail,

And that our drift look through our bad performance,

'Twere better not essayed.[89] Therefore this project   165

Should have a back or second[90] that might hold,

If this should blast in proof.[91] Soft, let me see.

We'll make a solemn wager on your cunnings[92] ... I ha't!

When in your motion you are hot and dry –

As make your bouts more violent to that end –   170

And that he calls for drink, I'll have prepared him

A chalice for the nonce,[93] whereon but sipping,

If he by chance escape your venomed stuck,[94]

Our purpose may hold there.[95] –

Enter GERTRUDE

How now, sweet Queen?   175

GERTRUDE

One woe doth tread upon another's heel,

So fast they follow.[96] Your sister's drowned, Laertes.

LAERTES

Drowned! O, where?

78. *peruse the foils:* examine the fencing swords

79. *unbated:* unblunted *Fencing swords are fitted with buttons at the tip to blunt them and ensure nobody is seriously hurt.*
80. *pass of practice:* treacherous thrust
81. *Requite him:* Take your revenge on him.

82. *unction:* ointment
83. *mountebank:* an illegal seller of medicines

84. *cataplasm:* poultice *a piece of cloth with a hot substance such as clay, herbs or bran applied to an injury to draw out the infection*
85. *simples ... virtue:* medicinal herbs

86. *can save ... withal:* can save from death anything that is even scratched by it
87. *gall:* wound

88. *Weigh ... shape:* Consider what time and place will suit our purposes best.

89. *And that ... essayed:* If our scheme were to become obvious because of our bad performance, then it would be better not to try it.
90. *back or second:* back-up plan
91. *blast in proof:* blow up while being tried
92. *We'll make ... cunnings:* We'll bet on your fencing skills

93. *nonce:* occasion

94. *venomed stuck:* poisoned sword-thrust

95. *Our purpose ... there:* We may still succeed. *Claudius intends to poison a drink to ensure that Hamlet will die one way or another.*

96. *One woe ... follow:* Bad news follows closely behind bad news, as if it steps on the heel of the one that came before.

Act 4

97. *aslant:* slanting over

98. *hoar:* silver-grey

99. *crow-flowers:* flowers resembling buttercups
100. *long purples:* orchids
101. *That liberal . . . name:* free-spoken shepherds call a ruder name
102. *cold:* chaste
103. *maids:* virginal girls
104. *pendent:* hanging
105. *her coronet . . . hang:* She was climbing to put a crown of wild flowers on the branch.
106. *envious sliver:* malicious branch

107. *incapable:* unaware

108. *endued:* adapted

109. *lay:* song

110. *trick:* habit

111. *nature . . . will:* It is a natural custom to weep in the face of such grief, however embarrassing tears may be.
112. *When . . . out:* When I have shed these tears, I will not act as sentimentally as a woman anymore.
113. *I have . . . douts it:* I am eager to express my burning rage but this foolish weeping extinguishes it.

GERTRUDE

There is a willow grows aslant[97] a brook,

That shows his hoar[98] leaves in the glassy stream.   **180**

There with fantastic garlands did she make

Of crow-flowers,[99] nettles, daisies, and long purples,[100]

That liberal shepherds give a grosser name,[101]

But our cold[102] maids[103] do dead men's fingers call them.

There, on the pendent[104] boughs her coronet weeds   **185**

Clambering to hang,[105] an envious sliver[106] broke,

When down her weedy trophies and herself

Fell in the weeping brook. Her clothes spread wide,

And, mermaid-like a while they bore her up;

Which time she chanted snatches of old tunes,   **190**

As one incapable[107] of her own distress,

Or like a creature native and endued[108]

Unto that element. But long it could not be

Till that her garments, heavy with their drink,

Pulled the poor wretch from her melodious lay[109]   **195**

To muddy death.

LAERTES

Alas, then she is drowned?

GERTRUDE

Drowned, drowned.

LAERTES

Too much of water hast thou, poor Ophelia,

And therefore I forbid my tears. But yet   **200**

It is our trick,[110] nature her custom holds,

Let shame say what it will.[111] When these are gone,

The woman will be out.[112] Adieu, my lord.

I have a speech of fire that fain would blaze,

But that this folly douts it.[113]   **205**

Exit

CLAUDIUS

Let's follow, Gertrude.

How much I had to do to calm his rage!

Now fear I this will give it start again;

Therefore let's follow.

Exit

Quotes

> She's so conjunctive to my life and soul
> That, as the star moves not but in his sphere,
> I could not but by her.
>
> (Claudius, lines 16–18)

Claudius says that Gertrude is so important to him that she is like the planet around which he orbits. He says he could not live without her, yet within a few moments, he is suggesting ways to kill her beloved son without her knowledge.

> No place, indeed, should murder sanctuarise.
> Revenge should have no bounds.
>
> (Claudius, lines 138–139)

Claudius tells Laertes that he would be morally justified in killing Hamlet in a church because murder is such a terrible crime that there should be no place of sanctuary for those who carry it out. There is a terrible irony here, of course, because we have already seen that Hamlet was unwilling to kill Claudius when he was at prayer in the chapel.

> I'll touch my point
> With this contagion, that if I gall him slightly,
> It may be death.
>
> (Laertes, lines 158–160)

Laertes has procured a poisoned ointment from an illegal dealer in such items. He says that he will put a little on the tip of his sword so that it will kill Hamlet even if it barely pierces his skin. Laertes appears as corrupt as Claudius here.

Questions

In each case, support your point with suitable reference to and quotation from the play.

1. Do you believe Claudius when he professes his love for Gertrude? Why/why not?

2. In this scene, what does Claudius say about murder and revenge?

3. How do Claudius and Laertes plan to kill Hamlet?

4. Based on the evidence in this scene, what is your opinion of Laertes?

5. Do you believe Gertrude's account of Ophelia's death?

6. Do you think Ophelia's death was an accident or do you think she killed herself?

7. How does Laertes react to news of Ophelia's death?

Writing Task

Imagine that you are a friend of Laertes, in whom he has confided. You are familiar with the Danish court and all the characters who have featured in the play up to this point. Write the dialogue that might take place between you both after the events of this scene, in which Laertes tells you of his meeting with Claudius and the terrible news of Ophelia's death. You are free to give Laertes any advice you think would help him in this situation.

Essay Building Blocks

> 'Although he is often described as a foil to Hamlet, Laertes is far from admirable.'

Write a paragraph in response to this statement, supporting your answer with quotation from and reference to Act 4 Scene 7.

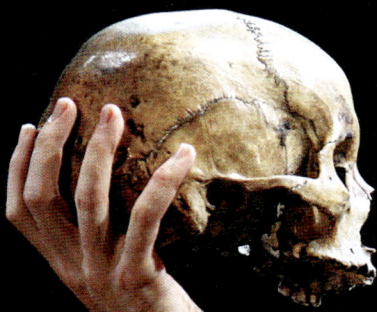

A churchyard

Two gravediggers discuss whether or not a person who has died by suicide should be given a Christian burial. Their language is ridiculously pompous and their misuse of legal terminology provides some light relief at a time of great tension and sorrow. They joke, sing and exchange riddles as they work.

Hamlet and Horatio enter the graveyard and Hamlet is taken aback by the workers' seeming insensitivity. As he looks around at the bones on the ground, Hamlet reflects that everyone, no matter how important, turns to dust in the end.

A funeral procession enters the graveyard and Hamlet is shocked when he realises that it is Ophelia who has died. Laertes curses Hamlet for having driven Ophelia to her death and he leaps into the grave to hold his sister in his arms one last time.

Hamlet steps forward and identifies himself. He and Laertes fight before they are separated on the orders of Claudius. Hamlet claims to have loved Ophelia far more than 40,000 brothers ever could. Gertrude and Claudius try to calm Laertes by saying Hamlet is mad. After Hamlet has left, Claudius reminds Laertes that they have a plan to deal with him before long.

Act 5

1. *she:* Ophelia
2. *willfully . . . salvation?:* took her own life *In times past, a person who had taken their own life was denied a Christian burial.*

3. *straight:* immediately
4. *crowner hath sat on her:* the coroner has judged her case *When the gravedigger says 'sat on her', it also conjures up absurd images.*

5. *unless . . . defence:* A nonsensical misinterpretation of the law, which states that killing someone in self-defence is not a crime.

6. *se offendendo:* In his attempt to mimic the language lawyers use, the gravedigger tries to say se defendo, which is the Latin term for 'self-defence'.
7. *wittingly:* intentionally

8. *Argal:* The gravedigger probably means to say ergo, the Latin for 'therefore'.

9. *but . . . Delver:* Listen, Mr Digger *To delve is to dig*

10. *Give me leave:* Let me finish

11. *will he, nill he:* whether he wants to or not

12. *crowner's quest:* coroner's inquest

13. *Will . . . on't?:* Do you want to hear the truth?

Enter two GRAVEDIGGERS, with spades and picks

FIRST GRAVEDIGGER

Is she[1] to be buried in Christian burial that wilfully seeks her own salvation?[2]

SECOND GRAVEDIGGER

I tell thee she is, and therefore make her grave straight.[3] The crowner hath sat on her,[4] and finds it Christian burial.   **5**

FIRST GRAVEDIGGER

How can that be unless she drowned herself in her own defence?[5]

SECOND GRAVEDIGGER

Why, 'tis found so.

FIRST GRAVEDIGGER

It must be se offendendo,[6] it cannot be else; for here lies the point: if I drown myself wittingly,[7] it argues an   **10**
act; and an act hath three branches: it is, to act, to do, to perform. Argal[8] she drowned herself wittingly.

SECOND GRAVEDIGGER

Nay, but hear you, Goodman Delver.[9]

FIRST GRAVEDIGGER

Give me leave.[10] Here lies the water – good. Here stands the man – good. If the man go to this water and drown   **15**
himself, it is, will he, nill he,[11] he goes. Mark you that. But if the water come to him and drown him, he drowns not himself; argal, he that is not guilty of his own death shortens not his own life.

SECOND GRAVEDIGGER

But is this law?   **20**

FIRST GRAVEDIGGER

Ay, marry, is't crowner's quest[12] law.

SECOND GRAVEDIGGER

Will you ha' the truth on't?[13] If this had not been a

gentlewoman, she should have been buried out o'
Christian burial.

FIRST GRAVEDIGGER

Why, there thou say'st, and the more pity that great   **25**
folk should have countenance[14] in this world to drown
or hang themselves more than their even Christian.[15]
Come, my spade. There is no ancient gentleman but
gardeners, ditchers, and grave-makers; they hold up[16]
Adam's profession.[17]   **30**

SECOND GRAVEDIGGER

Was he a gentleman?

FIRST GRAVEDIGGER

He was the first that ever bore arms.[18]

SECOND GRAVEDIGGER

Why, he had none.

FIRST GRAVEDIGGER

What, art a heathen? How dost thou understand
the Scripture? The Scripture says Adam digged. Could he   **35**
dig without arms? I'll put another question to thee. If
thou answerest me not to the purpose, confess thyself[19] –

SECOND GRAVEDIGGER

Go to.[20]

FIRST GRAVEDIGGER

What is he that builds stronger than either the mason,
the shipwright, or the carpenter?   **40**

SECOND GRAVEDIGGER

The gallows-maker; for that frame[21]
outlives a thousand tenants.

FIRST GRAVEDIGGER

I like thy wit well, in good faith. The gallows does well.
But how does it well? It does well to those that do ill.
Now thou dost ill to say the gallows is built stronger   **45**
than the church, argal the gallows may do well to thee.
To't again, come.[22]

14. *countenance:* permission

15. *even Christian:* fellow Christian

16. *hold up:* uphold/maintain

17. *Adam's profession:* Adam was the first man to dig.

18. *bore arms:* This has a double meaning. 1. Adam was the first man and therefore the first man to have arms. 2. To have a coat of arms such as only a gentleman would have.

19. *confess thyself:* The full saying is 'Confess thyself and be hanged'.

20. *Go to:* This could mean 'be quiet' or 'get to work'.

21. *frame:* gallows *The gallows was a wooden structure from which criminals were hanged.*

22. *I like thy wit . . . come:* I like your humour and intelligent answer, to tell the truth. The gallows does its job well, but how does it do it well? It does well by hanging those who do bad things. However, you are doing wrong by saying that the gallows is stronger than a church. Therefore, the gallows might yet do well by hanging you. Come on, try again.

Act 5

23. *shipwright:* ship builder

24. *unyoke:* This is a reference to unyoking or unharnessing oxen from the cart and was another way of saying 'finish up'.

25. *Mass:* a mild oath meaning 'By the holy Mass'

26. *Cudgel:* beat
27. *for ... beating:* You cannot make a slow donkey walk faster by beating it. The gravedigger means that his companion is stupid and that there is no point in his trying to work it out anymore as he won't become more intelligent.

28. *Yaughan:* probably the name of a local innkeeper
29. *stoup:* tankard

30. *behove:* benefit
31. *In youth ... nothing-a-meet:* This is a version of an old ballad about love and ageing.
32. *there ... meet:* nothing more fitting

33. *Custom ... easiness:* He is so used to doing his job that he is indifferent to it.

34. *'Tis e'en so ... daintier sense:* That's it exactly: those who are not used to such work have more delicate or sensitive feelings about it.

184 Hamlet

SECOND GRAVEDIGGER

'Who builds stronger than a mason, a shipwright,[23] or a carpenter?'

FIRST GRAVEDIGGER

Ay, tell me that, and unyoke.[24]　　**50**

SECOND GRAVEDIGGER

Marry, now I can tell.

FIRST GRAVEDIGGER

To't.

SECOND GRAVEDIGGER

Mass,[25] I cannot tell.

Enter HAMLET and HORATIO, at a distance

FIRST GRAVEDIGGER

Cudgel[26] thy brains no more about it, for your dull ass will not mend his pace with beating;[27] and when you are　**55** asked this question next, say 'a grave-maker'; the houses that he makes last till doomsday. Go, get thee to Yaughan:[28] fetch me a stoup[29] of liquor.

Exit SECOND GRAVEDIGGER

He digs and sings

In youth when I did love, did love,
Methought it was very sweet　　**60**
To contract-O-the-time, for-a-my behove,[30]
O methought there-a-was-nothing-a-meet.[31, 32]

HAMLET

Has this fellow no feeling of his business that a sings at grave-making?

HORATIO

Custom hath made it in him a property of easiness.[33]　**65**

HAMLET

'Tis e'en so; the hand of little employment hath the daintier sense.[34]

FIRST GRAVEDIGGER

[Sings]   But age, with his stealing steps

Hath clawed me in his clutch,

And hath shipped me into the land,   **70**

As if I had never been such.[35]

Throws up a skull

HAMLET

That skull had a tongue in it and could sing once.

How the knave jowls[36] it to the ground as if 'twere

Cain's[37] jawbone, that did the first murder! This

might be the pate[38] of a politician which this ass   **75**

now o'er-reaches,[39] one that would circumvent[40] God,

might it not?

HORATIO

It might, my lord.

HAMLET

Or of a courtier, which could say 'Good morrow,

sweet lord! How dost thou, good lord?' This   **80**

might be my lord-Such-a-One, that praised my

lord-Such-a-One's horse when he meant to beg[41] it,

might it not?

HORATIO

Ay, my lord.

HAMLET

Why, e'en so, and now my Lady Worm's,[42] chapless,[43]   **85**

and knocked about the mazard[44] with a sexton's[45] spade.

Here's fine revolution, an we had the trick to see't.[46]

Did these bones cost no more the breeding but to play

at loggats with 'em? Mine ache to think on't.[47]

FIRST GRAVEDIGGER

[Sings]   A pickaxe and a spade, a spade,   **90**

and a shrouding sheet;

O, a pit of clay for to be made

For such a guest is meet.[48]

Throws up another skull

35. *But age ... such:* But old age crept up on me and caught me in his clutch, and has returned me to the earth, from which I was made.

36. *jowls:* This is a pun. 'Jowls' can mean jaw but it can also mean throws or hurls.
37. *Cain:* Cain – the son of Adam and Eve – is supposed to have used the jaw-bone of a donkey to murder his brother Abel.
38. *pate:* head
39. *this ass ... oe'r-reaches:* This could mean to physically reach over or to rise to a higher office than another person – the aim of politicians. The gravedigger has reached into the grave to pull out the skull but he has also over-reached the dead man in another sense: he lives while the other does not.
40. *circumvent:* get around

41. *beg:* borrow

42. *Lady Worm:* a lady who is now food for worms
43. *chapless:* lacking the lower jaw
44. *mazard:* head
45. *sexton's:* The sexton looks after the church and churchyard and digs graves.
46. *Here's ... see't:* Here's an excellent example of social change if we had the skill to see it.
47. *Did these bones ... think on't:* Were these bones born and reared to become no more than a game? My own bones pain me, thinking about it. *Loggats* was a game in which pieces of wood were thrown at a stake.

48. *A pickaxe ... meet:* A pickaxe and a spade, a spade, a burial sheet, oh, it is appropriate to make a hole in the earth for a guest such as this.

49. *quiddities: from the Latin* quidditas, *meaning subtle arguments*
50. *quillets:* fine distinctions in an argument
51. *tenures:* titles on properties
52. *Why does he . . . sconce:* why does he allow this unmannerly fool to knock him on the head

53. *will . . . battery?:* will not take a case against him for assault

54. *statutes . . . recoveries: These are all legal terms relating to the buying and selling of property.*

55. *Is this the fine . . . dirt?:* Is this the outcome of his legal actions that his handsome head should be full of powdered dirt? *Hamlet is using a play on words here. 'Fine' has four different meanings in this question.*
56. *Will . . . indentures?:* Will all of his contracts guarantee him no more than a piece of land *(his grave)* that is the size of two of these long contract documents joined end to end?
57. *The very conveyances . . . box:* the legal documents relating to all his lands would not fit in this coffin.

58. *They are sheep . . . in that:* Those who feel safe in their ownership of land because the documents are properly drawn up on parchment are as foolish as sheep and calves. *Hamlet is pointing out that nothing lasts forever. No matter what these people owned, it was not permanent.*
59. *sirrah:* sir

60. *You lie . . . mine:* You are lying out of it, and so it is not yours. I am not lying in it, it is mine. *The gravedigger and Hamlet are punning on the word 'lie'. It can mean to tell an untruth or to lie down.*

HAMLET

There's another. Why may not that be the skull of a lawyer? Where be his quiddities[49] now, his quillets,[50] his 95 cases, his tenures,[51] and his tricks? Why does he suffer this rude knave now to knock him about the sconce[52] with a dirty shovel, and will not tell him of his action of battery?[53] H'm! This fellow might be in 's time a great buyer of land, with his statutes, his recognizances, 100 his fines, his double vouchers, his recoveries.[54] Is this the fine of his fines and the recovery of his recoveries, to have his fine pate full of fine dirt?[55] Will his vouchers vouch him no more of his purchases, and double ones too, than the length and breadth of a pair of indentures?[56] 105 The very conveyances of his lands will hardly lie in this box;[57] and must the inheritor himself have no more, ha?

HORATIO

Not a jot more, my lord.

HAMLET

Is not parchment made of sheepskins?

HORATIO

Ay, my lord, and of calf-skins too. 110

HAMLET

They are sheep and calves which seek out assurance in that.[58] I will speak to this fellow. Whose grave's this, sirrah?[59]

FIRST GRAVEDIGGER

Mine, sir.

[Sings]   O, a pit of clay for to be made 115
             For such a guest is meet.

HAMLET

I think it be thine indeed, for thou liest in't.

FIRST GRAVEDIGGER

You lie out on't, sir, and therefore it is not yours. For my part, I do not lie in't, and yet it is mine.[60]

HAMLET

Thou dost lie in't, to be in't and say 'tis thine.   **120**

'Tis for the dead, not for the quick; therefore thou liest.[61]

FIRST GRAVEDIGGER

'Tis a quick lie, sir, 'twill away again from me to you.[62]

HAMLET

What man dost thou dig it for?

FIRST GRAVEDIGGER

For no man, sir.

HAMLET

What woman, then?   **125**

FIRST GRAVEDIGGER

For none, neither.

HAMLET

Who is to be buried in't?

FIRST GRAVEDIGGER

One that was a woman, sir; but, rest her soul, she's dead.

HAMLET

How absolute[63] the knave is! We must speak by the card,[64]

or equivocation[65] will undo us. By the lord, Horatio, these   **130**

three years I have taken a note of it. The age is grown so

picked that the toe of the peasant comes so near the

heel of the courtier he galls his kibe.[66] How long hast

thou been a grave-maker?

FIRST GRAVEDIGGER

Of all the days i'th' year I came to't that day   **135**

that our last King Hamlet overcame Fortinbras.

HAMLET

How long is that since?

FIRST GRAVEDIGGER

Cannot you tell that? Every fool can tell that. It

was the very day that young Hamlet was born –

he that was mad and sent into England.   **140**

61. *Thou dost lie . . . liest:* You are lying in it, being in the grave and saying it is yours. It is for the dead, not the living, therefore you are lying.

62. *'Tis a quick . . . you:* That is a fast-moving, lively lie, sir, jumping from me to you.

63. *absolute:* precise
64. *by the card:* by the book/literally
65. *equivocation:* ambiguity/double meaning

66. *The age . . . kibe:* People have become so sophisticated that the peasant follows so closely on the heels of his betters that he rubs against a sore or chilblain on the heel of the person he is following. *In other words, people from a lower social class are imitating the habits of their social superiors.*

HAMLET

Ay, marry, why was he sent into England?

FIRST GRAVEDIGGER

Why, because he was mad. He shall recover his wits there; or, if he do not, it's no great matter there.

HAMLET

Why?

FIRST GRAVEDIGGER

'Twill, not be seen in him there. There the men **145** are as mad as he.

HAMLET

How came he mad?

FIRST GRAVEDIGGER

Very strangely, they say.

HAMLET

How strangely?

FIRST GRAVEDIGGER

Faith, e'en with losing his wits. **150**

HAMLET

Upon what ground?[67]

FIRST GRAVEDIGGER

Why, here in Denmark.[68] I have been sexton here, man and boy, thirty years.

HAMLET

How long will a man lie i'th' earth ere[69] he rot?

FIRST GRAVEDIGGER

I'faith, if he be not rotten before he die – as we have many **155** pocky corpses,[70] now-a-days, that will scarce hold the laying in[71] – he will last you some eight year or nine year. A tanner[72] will last you nine year.

67. *Upon what ground?:* For what reason?

68. *here in Denmark:* The gravedigger takes Hamlet's question literally.

69. *ere:* before

70. *pocky corpses:* bodies infected with syphillis

71. *scarce . . . laying in:* will hardly last long enough to be buried

72. *tanner:* a worker who cures animal hides and turns them into leather

HAMLET

Why he more than another?

FIRST GRAVEDIGGER

Why, sir, his hide is so tanned with his trade that he   **160**
will keep out water a great while, and your water is
a sore[73] decayer of your whoreson dead body. Here's a
skull, now. This skull has lain in the earth three-
and-twenty-years.

HAMLET

Whose was it?   **165**

FIRST GRAVEDIGGER

A whoreson mad fellow's it was.[74] Whose do you
think it was?

HAMLET

Nay, I know not.

FIRST GRAVEDIGGER

A pestilence on him for a mad rogue[75] – he poured a
flagon of Rhenish[76] on my head once! This same skull,   **170**
sir, was Yorick's skull, the King's jester.

HAMLET

This?

FIRST GRAVEDIGGER

E'en that.[77]

HAMLET

Let me see.

Takes the skull

Alas, poor Yorick! I knew him, Horatio – a fellow of   **175**
infinite jest, of most excellent fancy:[78] he hath borne me
on his back[79] a thousand times; and now, how abhorred[80]
in my imagination it is! My gorge rises at it.[81] Here hung
those lips that I have kissed I know not how oft. Where
be your gibes[82] now, your gambols,[83] your songs, your   **180**
flashes of merriment that were wont to set the table on

73. *sore:* serious

74. *A whoreson . . . was:* It belonged to a wild, crazy man.

75. *A pestilence . . . rogue:* Curse him, the crazy fool.
76. Rhenish: *German wine from the Rhine region*

77. *E'en that:* The very one.

78. *fancy:* imagination

79. *borne me on his back:* gave me piggy-back rides
80. *abhorred:* horrible
81. *My gorge rises at it:* I feel sick at the thought of it.

82. *gibes:* jeers or mocking jokes
83. *gambols:* playful running and jumping about

84. *chap-fallen: This has two possible meanings:. 1. dispirited; 2. the chap, or jaw, has fallen from the skull*

85. *Now get . . . must come:* Go to a lady's room and tell her that even if she cakes herself in make-up an inch thick, she will eventually resemble Yorick. Everybody dies.

86. *Alexander: In Shakespeare's time, Alexander the Great was considered to have been the epitome of perfection.*

87. *To what base uses . . . bung-hole?:* How low we fall when we die, Horatio. Why, you could imagine the dust or clay to which Alexander the Great turned after death used to plug a hole in a cask of beer. A 'bung-hole' is a a hole in a beer barrel which was sometimes stopped up with clay.

88. *curiously:* closely

89. *No, faith . . . thus:* No, I am being reasonable and working out the likelihood of what happened, in this way.

90. *loam: a clay mixture used to make bricks and plaster*

91. *the winter flaw: the winter wind*

92. *But soft . . . a while:* But quiet, be quiet for a moment

190 Hamlet

a roar? Not one now, to mock your own grinning? Quite chap-fallen?[84] Now get you to my lady's chamber and tell her, let her paint an inch thick, to this favour she must come.[85] Make her laugh at that. Prithee, Horatio, tell me one thing. 185

HORATIO
What's that, my lord?

HAMLET
Dost thou think Alexander[86] looked o' this fashion i'th' earth?

HORATIO
E'en so. 190

HAMLET
And smelt so? Pah!

Puts down the skull

HORATIO
E'en so, my lord.

HAMLET
To what base uses we may return, Horatio! Why may not imagination trace the noble dust of Alexander till a find it stopping a bung-hole?[87] 195

HORATIO
'Twere to consider too curiously[88] to consider so.

HAMLET
No, faith, not a jot; but to follow him thither with modesty enough, and likelihood to lead it, as thus:[89] Alexander died, Alexander was buried, Alexander returneth into dust, the dust is earth, of 200 earth we make loam,[90] and why of that loam, whereto he was converted, might they not stop a beer-barrel? Imperial Caesar, dead and turned to clay, Might stop a hole to keep the wind away, O, that that earth, which kept the world in awe 205 Should patch a wall t'expel the winter flaw![91] But soft, but soft; a while:[92] here comes the King.

Enter PRIEST, &c. in procession; the Corpse of OPHELIA, LAERTES and MOURNERS following; CLAUDIUS, GERTRUDE, their trains

The Queen, the courtiers – who is this they follow,
And with such maimed[93] rites? This doth betoken
The corpse they follow did with desperate hand   **210**
Fordo[94] its own life. 'Twas of some estate.[95]
Couch we a while, and mark.[96]

Retiring with HORATIO

LAERTES

What ceremony else?

HAMLET

That is Laertes, a very noble youth. Mark.

LAERTES

What ceremony else?[97]   **215**

FIRST PRIEST

Her obsequies[98] have been as far enlarged
As we have warranties.[99] Her death was doubtful,[100]
And but that great command o'ersways the order
She should in ground unsanctified have lodged
Till the last trumpet.[101] For charitable prayers,   **220**
Shards,[102] flints, and pebbles should be thrown on her;
Yet here she is allowed her virgin crants,[103]
Her maiden strewments,[104] and the bringing home
Of bell and burial.[105]

LAERTES

Must there no more be done?   **225**

FIRST PRIEST

No more be done:
We should profane the service of the dead
To sing sage requiem and such rest to her
As to peace-parted souls.[106]

LAERTES

Lay her i'th' earth: **230**
And from her fair and unpolluted flesh

93. *maimed:* incomplete

94. *Fordo:* take
95. *some estate:* high rank
96. *Couch . . . mark:* We'll hide for a while and watch.

97. *What ceremony else?:* What other funeral rites will be performed? *Hamlet already commented on the brief, incomplete ceremony. Laertes is clearly unhappy with the rites too.*

98. *obsequies:* funeral rites

99. *warranties:* authority
100. *Her . . . doubtful:* The manner of her death was suspicious.

101. *And but . . . trumpet:* And but for the royal command of the king, she should have been buried in unconsecrated ground until the end of the world.
102. *Shards:* pieces of broken pottery
103. *virgin crants:* garlands signifying the dead girl was a virgin
104. *maiden strewments:* flowers scattered on the grave of an unmarried girl
105. *bringing . . . burial:* being brought to her final resting place with the tolling of bells and a proper funeral

106. *We should profane . . . peace-parted souls:* We would disrespect the funeral service if we sang a solemn song of mourning for her as we do for those who died peacefully and did not kill themselves.

107. *And from ... spring:* Violets were associated with the Virgin Mary in Christianity. Laertes says Ophelia was 'unpolluted', meaning she was a virgin. In legends, violets were said to grow from the graves of virgins.
108. *churlish:* rude
109. *A ministering ... howling:* My sister will be an angel in heaven while you lie howling in hell.

→ Hypocritical here?
→ forced to calm Laertes
→ guilty → promised her a happy future?
→ happy she is dead? Eliminates a potential problem for her.

110. *decked:* strewn with flowers

111. *O, treble woe ... thee of!:* Laertes curses Hamlet because it was the killing of Polonius that deprived Ophelia of her excellent and sound mind.

112. *the quick and dead:* the living and the dead

113. *To o'ertop ... Olympus:* Higher than Mount Pelion and Mount Olympus, which is so near the sky that it is blue. Laertes says he wants to be buried alive with Ophelia, he is so distraught.

114. *Bears ... emphasis:* is expressed so strongly

115. *wonder-wounded:* awestruck/astonished

May violets spring.[107] I tell thee, churlish[108] priest,
A ministering angel shall my sister be
When thou liest howling.[109]

HAMLET
What, the fair Ophelia! 235

GERTRUDE
Sweets to the sweet. Farewell!

Scattering flowers

I hoped thou shouldst have been my Hamlet's wife.
I thought thy bride-bed to have decked,[110] sweet maid,
And not t'have strewed thy grave.

LAERTES
O, treble woe 240
Fall ten times treble on that cursed head
Whose wicked deed thy most ingenious sense
Deprived thee of![111] – Hold off the earth a while,
Till I have caught her once more in mine arms.

Leaps into the grave

Now pile your dust upon the quick and dead[112] 245
Till of this flat a mountain you have made
To o'ertop old Pelion, or the skyish head
Of blue Olympus.[113]

HAMLET
[Advancing] What is he whose grief
Bears such an emphasis,[114] whose phrase of sorrow 250
Conjures the wandering stars and makes them stand
Like wonder-wounded[115] hearers? This is I,
Hamlet the Dane.

Leaps into the grave

LAERTES
The devil take thy soul!
Grappling with him

HAMLET

Thou pray'st not well.   255

I prithee take thy fingers from my throat,

For though I am not splenitive[116] and rash,

Yet have I something in me dangerous,

Which let thy wiseness fear. Away thy hand.[117]

CLAUDIUS

Pluck them asunder.[118]   260

GERTRUDE

Hamlet, Hamlet!

ALL

Gentlemen!

HORATIO

Good my lord, be quiet.

The ATTENDANTS part them, and they come
out of the grave

HAMLET

Why, I will fight with him upon this theme

Until my eyelids will no longer wag.[119]   265

GERTRUDE

O my son, what theme?[120]

HAMLET

I loved Ophelia. Forty thousand brothers

Could not, with all their quantity of love,

Make up my sum. – What wilt thou do for her?

CLAUDIUS

O, he is mad, Laertes.   270

GERTRUDE

For love of God, forbear him.[121]

116. *splenitive:* hot-tempered

117. *Yet have I . . . thy hand:* There is something in me that is dangerous and you would be sensible to fear it. Take away your hand.

118. *Pluck them asunder:* Pull them apart.

119. *Until . . . wag:* until my eyelids no longer move *This was considered to be the moment of death.*

120. *O my son, what theme?:* Gertrude asks what is the topic on which Hamlet is willing to fight Laertes to the death.

121. *forbear him:* be patient with him

Act 5

HAMLET

'Swounds,[122] show me what thou'lt do.

Woo't[123] weep, woo't fight, woo't fast, woo't tear thyself,

Woo't drink up eisel,[124] eat a crocodile?

I'll do't. Dost thou come here to whine,   275

To outface[125] me with leaping in her grave?

Be buried quick[126] with her, and so will I.

And if thou prate[127] of mountains, let them throw

Millions of acres on us, till our ground,

Singeing his pate against the burning zone,[128]   280

Make Ossa like a wart.[129] Nay, an thou'lt mouth,[130]

I'll rant as well as thou.

GERTRUDE

This is mere madness,

And thus a while the fit will work on him.

Anon, as patient as the female dove   285

When that her golden couplets are disclosed,

His silence will sit drooping.[131]

HAMLET

Hear you, sir,

What is the reason that you use me thus?

I loved you ever. But it is no matter.   290

Let Hercules himself do what he may,

The cat will mew, and dog will have his day.[132]

Exit

CLAUDIUS

I pray you, good Horatio, wait upon him.

Exit HORATIO

[To LAERTES] Strengthen your patience in our last

night's speech.[133]   295

We'll put the matter to the present push,[134] –

Good Gertrude, set some watch over your son. –

This grave shall have a living monument.[135]

An hour of quiet[136] shortly shall we see;

Till then, in patience our proceeding be.   300

Exit

122. *'Swounds:* by God's wounds
123. *Woo't:* will you
124. *eisel:* vinegar
125. *outface:* outdo
126. *buried quick:* buried alive
127. *prate:* boast
128. *Singeing . . . zone:* burning his head against the sun
129. *Make Ossa . . . wart:* makes Mount Ossa *(mountain in Greek mythology)* appear as small as a wart
130. *an thou'lt mouth:* if you make passionate speeches
131. *Anon . . . drooping:* Soon he will be as quiet as a dove who sees her golden-coloured chicks hatched.
132. *Let Hercules . . . day:* The meaning here is unclear. It may be Hamlet's way of saying that Hercules himself could not stop Hamlet from doing what he wants.
133. *Strengthen . . . speech:* Let the conversation we had last night help you to keep your patience.
134. *We'll put . . . push:* We'll carry out our plan immediately.
135. *This grave . . . monument:* Claudius is assuring Laertes that Hamlet's death will be an enduring monument to Ophelia. It is safe to assume that Gertrude is out of earshot, possibly on her way to keep an eye on Hamlet.
136. *An hour of quiet:* a peaceful time *(once Hamlet is dead)*

194   Hamlet

Quotes

> What is he whose grief
> Bears such an emphasis, whose phrase of sorrow
> Conjures the wandering stars and makes them stand
> Like wonder-wounded hearers? This is I,
> Hamlet the Dane.
>
> (Hamlet, lines 249–253)

Hamlet asks who it is whose grief is so deep and whose words of sorrow make the stars stand still in the skies as if they are amazed and grieved by what they hear. He refers to himself as 'Hamlet the Dane', which would usually mean, 'Hamlet, King of Denmark'. In Act 1, Scene 2, Claudius referred to himself as 'the Dane'. It is significant that Hamlet awards himself this title; it shows that he regards himself as the rightful king.

> I loved Ophelia. Forty thousand brothers
> Could not, with all their quantity of love,
> Make up my sum.
>
> (Hamlet, lines 267–269)

Hamlet claims to have loved Ophelia more than any number of brothers ever could. Hamlet could be genuine in his overblown protestations of grief or he may be trying to show up Laertes' extravagant, hysterical expressions of sorrow.

Questions

In each case, support your point with suitable reference to and quotation from the play.

1. How does the gravediggers' comic exchange contribute to our understanding of the themes of the play?

2. What are Hamlet's views on life and death in this scene?

3. Describe what happens at Ophelia's funeral.

4. What change in Hamlet's character is shown in this scene?

5. How does Laertes behave in this scene?

Writing Task

Imagine you are a gossip columnist for a Danish newspaper and were present for Ophelia's funeral. Write the article that you would submit to your editor. Your article should aim to capture the undercurrents and tensions you witnessed, as well as your impressions of the characters at the graveside. Lay your article out correctly, with a headline, byline, etc. Add illustrations if you like.

Essay Building Blocks

'The Hamlet who returns to Denmark in Act 5 can be at all points distinguished from his earlier passionate, indecisive and unpredictable self. He is a new man.'

Write a paragraph in response to this statement, supporting your answer with quotation from and reference to Act 5 Scene 1.

A hall in the castle

Hamlet tells Horatio that he discovered the execution warrant Claudius had given Rosencrantz and Guildenstern to deliver to the King of England. Hamlet changed the letter so that it ordered the immediate death of Rosencrantz and Guildenstern.

Osric, a foolish courtier, arrives to tell Hamlet the details of the fencing match. Hamlet teases Osric, much as he teased Polonius, but agrees to the contest. Horatio is not sure that it is wise for Hamlet to fight Laertes and urges his friend to pull out of the match if he has any doubts. Hamlet says that it is all in the hands of fate now and what will be will be. If he is to die, what of it?

Before the match begins, Hamlet apologises to Laertes, saying it was not he but his madness that caused him to behave so badly. Laertes accepts the apology up to a point but says his honour must still be satisfied.

The men fight and Claudius tries to encourage Hamlet to take a drink from the poisoned glass of wine but the Prince says he is not yet thirsty. Gertrude takes the cup and drinks to Hamlet, despite Claudius's half-hearted attempt to stop her.

Laertes begins to have pangs of conscience about his underhanded plan to kill Hamlet but he strikes him with the poison-tipped sword nonetheless. There is a scuffle and both swords fall. In the confusion, Hamlet picks up Laertes' sword and strikes him with it.

Gertrude falls to the ground and Claudius tries to pretend she has merely fainted at the sight of blood. Gertrude calls out with her last breath that she has been poisoned. Laertes admits the whole plot to Hamlet who leaps forward and strikes Claudius with the poisoned sword. He takes the poisoned wine and forces Claudius to drink it.

Claudius dies.

Laertes begs and receives Hamlet's forgiveness. Before Hamlet dies, he orders Horatio not to commit suicide as he is needed to tell the approaching Fortinbras what has happened and to pass the throne of Denmark to him. Hamlet dies and Fortinbras becomes the next king.

Act 5

1. *So much ... other:* You know the first part of my story and you will now hear the rest of it.

2. *Remember it, my lord?:* How could I forget it?

3. *mutines in bilboes:* mutineers in shackles *Mutineers are those who rebel against the captain of a ship. They would have been imprisoned in chains until the ship docked.*
4. *Rashly:* on impulse
5. *know:* recognise
6. *Our indiscretion ... pall:* sometimes our impulsive nature helps us out when our plans fail

7. *There's a divinity ... will:* There's a divine force that determines the outcomes of our plans, no matter how much we may try to shape them.

8. *sea-gown:* sailor's coat
9. *scarfed:* wrapped
10. *them:* Rosencrantz and Guildenstern
11. *Fingered their packet:* stole their bundle of letters
12. *in fine:* finally

13. *to unseal ... grand commission:* to open their sealed order from Claudius to the King of England

14. *larded:* padded

15. *Importing:* concerning

16. *With ho! ... off:* With such a list of things to be feared if I were allowed to live, that on reading the letter, without delay, not even waiting to sharpen the axe, my head should be cut off.

Enter HAMLET and HORATIO

HAMLET
So much for this, sir. Now shall you see the other.[1]
You do remember all the circumstance?

HORATIO
Remember it, my lord?[2]

HAMLET
Sir, in my heart there was a kind of fighting
That would not let me sleep. Methought I lay   5
Worse than the mutines in the bilboes.[3] Rashly[4] –
And praised be rashness for it let us know[5]
Our indiscretion sometime serves us well
When our deep plots do pall,[6] and that should teach us
There's a divinity that shapes our ends,   10
Rough-hew them how we will[7] –

HORATIO
That is most certain.

HAMLET
Up from my cabin,
My sea-gown[8] scarfed[9] about me in the dark
Groped I to find out them,[10] had my desire,   15
Fingered their packet,[11] and in fine[12] withdrew
To mine own room again, making so bold,
My fears forgetting manners, to unseal
Their grand commission[13]; where I found, Horatio –
O royal knavery! – an exact command,   20
Larded[14] with many several sorts of reasons
Importing[15] Denmark's health, and England's, too,
With ho! such bugs and goblins in my life,
That on the supervise, no leisure bated,
No, not to stay the grinding of the axe,   25
My head should be struck off.[16]

HORATIO
Is't possible?

HAMLET
Here's the commission. Read it at more leisure.
But wilt thou hear me how I did proceed?

HORATIO

I beseech you.   **30**

HAMLET

Being thus benetted round[17] with villainies –

Ere I could make a prologue to my brains,

They had begun the play[18] – I sat me down,

Devised a new commission, wrote it fair.

I once did hold it, as our statists[19] do,   **35**

A baseness to write fair,[20] and laboured much

How to forget that learning, but, sir, now

It did me yeoman's[21] service. Wilt thou know

The effect[22] of what I wrote?

HORATIO

Ay, good my lord.   **40**

HAMLET

An earnest conjuration[23] from the King,

As England was his faithful tributary,[24]

As love between them like the palm[25] might flourish,

As peace should stiff her wheaten garland wear

And stand a comma 'tween their amities,[26]   **45**

And many such-like 'as'es[27] of great charge,[28]

That on the view and knowing of these contents,

Without debatement[29] further more or less,

He should the bearers put to sudden death,

Not shriving-time[30] allowed.   **50**

HORATIO

How was this seal'd?

HAMLET

Why, even in that was heaven ordinant.[31]

I had my father's signet[32] in my purse,

Which was the model of that Danish seal;

Folded the writ up in form of th'other,[33]   **55**

Subscribed[34] it, gave't the impression,[35] placed it safely,

The changeling never known. Now the next day

Was our sea-fight; and what to this was sequent[36]

Thou know'st already.

---

17. *benetted round:* trapped, as in a net

18. *Ere I . . . play:* Before I could even begin to think about it, my brain had come up with a plan.

19. *statists:* statesmen

20. *A baseness to write fair:* beneath me to write neatly

21. *yeoman:* workman

22. *The effect:* the purport/substance

23. *conjuration:* request

24. *tributary: a country that pays tribute to another country*

25. *palm:* symbol of wealth

26. *As peace . . . amities:* Peace should always wear her garland of wheat *(symbol of the fruitfulness of peace)* and nothing larger than a comma should come between their friendship.

27. *'as'es: Hamlet is mocking the number of clauses in his letter, which began with the word 'as'.*

28. *great charge:* importance

29. *debatement:* debating or discussing

30. *shriving-time:* time for confession

31. *ordinant:* in control of events

32. *signet: A signet ring was used to stamp the writer's personal seal onto the wax holding the letter closed.*

33. *Folded . . . th'other:* folded up the letter in the same way as the other one had been folded

34. *Subscribed:* signed

35. *gave't the impression:* made the impression of the king's seal on the wax

36. *what . . . sequent:* what followed this

HORATIO

So Guildenstern and Rosencrantz go to't.[37]   **60**

HAMLET

Why, man, they did make love to this employment.
They are not near my conscience.[38] Their defeat
Does by their own insinuation[39] grow.
'Tis dangerous when the baser nature comes
Between the pass and fell incensed points   **65**
Of mighty opposites.[40]

HORATIO

Why, what a king is this!

HAMLET

Does it not, think'st thee, stand me now upon[41] –
He that hath killed my king and whored my mother,
Popped in between th'election and my hopes,[42]   **70**
Thrown out his angle for my proper life,[43]
And with such cozenage[44] – is't not perfect conscience,[45]
To quit[46] him with this arm? And is't not to be damned,[47]
To let this canker of our nature[48] come
In[49] further evil?   **75**

HORATIO

It must be shortly known to him from England
What is the issue of the business there.[50]

HAMLET

It will be short. The interim is mine,[51]
And a man's life's no more than to say 'one'.[52]
But I am very sorry, good Horatio,   **80**
That to Laertes I forgot myself;
For by the image of my cause I see
The portraiture of his.[53] I'll court his favours.
But sure, the bravery[54] of his grief did put me
Into a towering passion.   **85**

HORATIO

Peace, who comes here?

Enter OSRIC

Notes

37. *go to't:* go to their deaths

38. *they did make love . . . conscience:* They willingly agreed to do this job. I do not feel any guilt for their deaths.
39. *insinuation:* manoeuvring themselves into a favourable position in Claudius's court

40. *'Tis dangerous . . . opposites:* It is dangerous when men of lower status come between the sword thrusts of angry and powerful opponents.

41. *Does it not . . . upon:* Do you not think the duty to act rests on me now?

42. *Popped in . . . hopes:* had himself elected king before Hamlet could take the throne
43. *Thrown out . . . life:* plotted to kill me *Hamlet uses fishing/ angling imagery here.*
44. *cozenage:* trickery
45. *perfect conscience:* morally correct
46. *quit:* repay by killing
47. *is't not to be damned:* would I not risk damnation
48. *canker of our nature:* cancer of human nature
49. *come in:* grow into

50. *It must . . . there:* He will soon learn from England what happened there.

51. *It will . . . mine:* I will only have a short time *(before the news reaches Claudius)* but I can use that time.
52. *And a man's . . . one:* A man's life can be ended as quickly as the time it takes to say 'one'. *In a duel, the man who made the first hit called 'One'.*

53. *For by . . . of his:* By considering his cause I can see he is in the same situation. *Both men have suffered the loss of a father.*
54. *bravery:* bravado/melodramatic nature

OSRIC

Your lordship is right welcome back to Denmark.

HAMLET

I humbly thank you, sir. *[Aside to HORATIO]* Dost know this water-fly?[55]

HORATIO

No, my good lord. 90

HAMLET

Thy state is the more gracious,[56] for 'tis a vice to know him. He hath much land, and fertile. Let a beast be lord of beasts, and his crib shall stand at the king's mess.[57] 'Tis a chough, but, as I say, spacious in the possession of dirt.[58] 95

OSRIC

Sweet lord, if your lordship were at leisure I should impart a thing to you[59] from his majesty.

HAMLET

I will receive it, sir, with all diligence of spirit.[60] Put your bonnet to his right use; 'tis for the head.[61]

OSRIC

I thank your lordship, 'tis very hot. 100

HAMLET

No, believe me, 'tis very cold. The wind is northerly.

OSRIC

It is indifferent[62] cold, my lord, indeed.

HAMLET

But yet methinks it is very sultry and hot for my complexion.[63]

OSRIC

Exceedingly, my lord; it is very sultry, as 'twere, – I 105 cannot tell how. But, my lord, his majesty bade me signify to you that a has laid a great wager on your head. Sir, this is the matter.

---

55. *water-fly:* small insect/insignificant, vain man

56. *Thy state . . . gracious:* you are better off

57. *Let a beast . . . mess:* If a man who is no better than an animal owns a lot of animals, he can eat at the king's table.

58. *'Tis a chough . . . dirt:* He is little more than a chattering jackdaw but, as I said, he owns a lot of land.

59. *impart a thing to you:* tell you

60. *I will . . . spirit:* I will listen attentively. *Hamlet is mocking Osric's flowery speech.*

61. *Put your . . . head:* Osric has removed his hat as a sign of respect while talking to Hamlet.

62. *indifferent:* somewhat

63. *complexion:* constitution

HAMLET

I beseech you, remember.

HAMLET moves him to put on his hat

OSRIC

Nay, good my lord, for mine ease,[64] in good faith. **110**
Sir, here is newly come to court Laertes, believe me,
an absolute gentleman, full of most excellent
differences,[65] of very soft society[66] and great showing.[67]
Indeed, to speak feelingly of him, he is the card or
calendar[68] of gentry, for you shall find in him the **115**
continent of what part a gentleman would see.[69]

HAMLET

Sir, his definement suffers no perdition in you,
though I know, to divide him inventorially would
dizzy the arithmetic of memory, and yet but yaw
neither, in respect of his quick sail. But in the **120**
verity of extolment, I take him to be a soul of
great article, and his infusion of such dearth and
rareness as, to make true diction of him, his
semblable is his mirror, and who else would trace
him his umbrage, nothing more.[70] **125**

OSRIC

Your lordship speaks most infallibly of him.

HAMLET

The concernancy, sir? why do we wrap the gentleman
in our more rawer breath?[71]

OSRIC

Sir?

HORATIO

Is't not possible to understand in another tongue? **130**
You will do't, sir, really.[72]

HAMLET

What imports the nomination of this gentleman?[73]

64. *for mine ease:* Osric means that he is more comfortable with his hat off.

65. *differences:* distinguishing qualities
66. *soft society:* agreeable manners
67. *great showing:* excellent appearance
68. *card or calendar:* model
69. *continent . . . see:* the container of every quality a gentleman would like to see

70. *Sir . . . more:* His description loses nothing in your telling of it, though I know to make a detailed list of all his qualities would confuse your memory's ability to calculate, and it would make your memory wander off course because he sails so far ahead of everyone else. But, to praise him truly, I believe he is a most important person, and his qualities of such value and rarity that to give a true description of him, the only person like him is his own reflection in his mirror, and anyone who tries to copy him is his shadow, nothing more. *Hamlet continues to mock Osric's affected manner.*

71. *The concernancy . . . breath?:* What is the relevance of this and why are we describing this gentleman in our crude language?

72. *Is't not possible . . . really:* Is it not possible for you to communicate more clearly? You can do it if you try. *Hamlet may be talking to himself or to Osric.*

73. *What imports . . . gentleman?:* What is the significance of mentioning this gentleman?

OSRIC

Of Laertes?

HORATIO

His purse is empty already; all 's golden words
are spent.   135

HAMLET

Of him, sir.

OSRIC

I know you are not ignorant –

HAMLET

I would you did, sir, yet, in faith, if you did,
it would not much approve me.[74] Well, sir?

OSRIC

You are not ignorant of what excellence Laertes is.   140

HAMLET

I dare not confess that, lest I should compare with
him in excellence. But to know a man well were to
know himself.[75]

OSRIC

I mean, sir, for his weapon.[76] But in the imputation
laid on him by them, in his meed he's unfellowed.[77]   145

HAMLET

What's his weapon?

OSRIC

Rapier and dagger.

HAMLET

That's two of his weapons. But well.

OSRIC

The King, sir, hath wagered with him six Barbary[78]
horses, against the which he has imponed,[79] as I take   150
it, six French rapiers and poniards,[80] with their
assigns as girdle, hangers,[81] and so. Three of the
carriages, in faith, are very dear to fancy, very

74. *I would . . . me:* I wish you did know I was not ignorant but even if you did, it would not do me much credit. *Hamlet does not value Osric's opinion.*

75. *I dare . . . himself:* I dare not admit that, lest it be thought I was saying I was equally excellent. But to know a man well, a person has to know himself first.

76. *weapon:* skill as a swordsman

77. *But . . . unfellowed:* According to popular opinion, there is no-one to equal his merit.

78. *Barbary:* North African

79. *imponed:* staked

80. *poniards:* daggers

81. *with . . . hangers:* with their fittings: belt, straps

82. *Three ... conceit:* Three of the straps are very imaginatively designed in a way that corresponds to the design of the hilts.

83. *What ... carriages?:* What do you mean by the carriages?

84. *I knew ... done:* I knew you would need an explanatory comment – such as may be found in the margin of a text – before you were finished.

85. *The phrase ... then:* The term would be more appropriate if we were carrying cannons by our sides. I would prefer we used the word 'hangers' until then.

86. *French:* Laertes has recently returned from France.

87. *laid:* bet

88. *twelve for nine:* These are the odds.

89. *and it ... answer:* The match could begin straight away if you would accept the challenge.

90. *How ... no?:* Hamlet pretends to misinterpret 'answer'. Osric uses it to mean acceptance of a challenge rather than the common meaning of answer to a question.

91. *opposition ... trial:* The challenge to a fencing match.

92. *breathing time of day:* usual time for exercise

93. *an:* if

94. *Shall ... so?:* Will I deliver that message?

responsive to the hilts, most delicate carriages, and of very liberal conceit.[82]   155

HAMLET

What call you the carriages?[83]

HORATIO

I knew you must be edified by the margin ere you had done.[84]

OSRIC

The carriages, sir, are the hangers.

HAMLET

The phrase would be more germane to the matter if   160
we could carry cannon by our sides. I would it might
be hangers till then.[85] But on: six Barbary horses against
six French swords, their assigns, and three liberal-
conceited carriages – that's the French[86] bet against
the Danish. Why is this 'imponed', as you call it?   165

OSRIC

The King, sir, hath laid,[87] sir, that in a dozen passes
between you and him, he shall not exceed you
three hits. He hath laid on twelve for nine,[88] and it
would come to immediate trial if your lordship
would vouchsafe the answer.[89]   170

HAMLET

How if I answer no?[90]

OSRIC

I mean, my lord, the opposition of your person in trial.[91]

HAMLET

Sir, I will walk here in the hall. If it please his
majesty, 'tis the breathing time of day[92] with me. Let
the foils be brought; the gentleman willing, an the   175
King hold his purpose, I will win for him an[93] I can.
If not, I'll gain nothing but my shame and the odd hits.

OSRIC

Shall I re-deliver you e'en so?[94]

HAMLET

To this effect, sir; after what flourish your nature will.[95]

OSRIC

I commend my duty to your lordship.[96]   **180**

HAMLET

Yours, yours.

Exit OSRIC

He does well to commend it himself; there are no
tongues else for 's turn.[97]

HORATIO

This lapwing runs away with the shell on his head.[98]

HAMLET

He did comply with his dug, before he sucked it.[99]   **185**
Thus has he – and many more of the same bevy[100] that
I know the drossy age[101] dotes on – only got the tune of
the time[102] and outward habit of encounter,[103] a kind of
yeasty[104] collection which carries them through and
through the most fanned and winnowed opinions; and   **190**
do but blow them to their trial, the bubbles are out.[105]

Enter a LORD

LORD

My lord, his majesty commended him to you by young
Osric, who brings back to him that you attend him in
the hall. He sends to know if your pleasure hold to
play[106] with Laertes, or that you will take longer time.   **195**

HAMLET

I am constant to my purposes; they follow the King's
pleasure. If his fitness speaks, mine is ready,[107] now
or whensoever, provided I be so able as now.

LORD

The King and Queen and all are coming down.

HAMLET

In happy time.[108]   **200**

95. *after . . . will:* in whatever elaborate manner you choose

96. *I commend . . . lordship:* Osric means that he offers his respects.

97. *He does . . . turn:* Hamlet mocks Osric by pretending that his – Osric's – use of 'commend' meant 'praise'. Hamlet tells Horatio that Osric does well to praise himself as no-one else will do it for him.

98. *This . . . head:* A lapwing is a bird that leaves the nest soon after hatching. Horatio compares Osric's speedy departure to a lapwing chick leaving the nest so quickly that it still has its shell on its head. He may also be poking fun at Osric's elaborate hat or 'bonnet' referred to earlier.

99. *He did . . . it:* He paid his respects to his mother's teat before he suckled. Horatio is mocking Osric's over-the-top flattery and unnecessary, showy manners.

100. *bevy:* group/flock of birds

101. *drossy age:* these frivolous times

102. *only . . . time:* fashions of the time

103. *outward . . . encounter:* out of the superficiality of associating with others in society

104. *yeasty:* frothy/superficial

105. *carries . . . out:* It enables them to bluff their way through conversation with those whose opinions are tried and considered. If you put them to the test, their frothy, empty ideas are shown for what they are.

106. *play:* fence

107. *If his . . . ready:* If he says he is ready, then I am ready too.

108. *In happy time:* At an opportune moment.

109. *use . . . entertainment:* behave courteously

110. *But thou . . . heart:* But you have no idea how troubled I am.

111. *gain-giving:* misgiving

112. *I will . . . hither:* I will put off their coming here

113. *augury:* omens/predicting the future

114. *There's . . . sparrow:* There is divine providence in the fall of a sparrow. *Hamlet is referring to a passage in the Bible in which Jesus, encouraging his followers not to be afraid, said, 'Are not two sparrows sold for a farthing? And one of them shall not fall on the ground without your Father.' This means that God knows everything that happens, even the death of the least of his creatures.*

115. *If . . . come:* If my death is to occur now, it will not occur later. If it is not to occur later, it will be now. If it doesn't occur now, it will occur in the future. *Death is inevitable.*

116. *Since . . . betimes?:* Since no man can know anything about what he leaves behind, what does it matter if he dies early?

LORD

The Queen desires you to use some gentle entertainment[109] to Laertes before you fall to play.

HAMLET

She well instructs me.

Exit LORD

HORATIO

You will lose this wager, my lord.

HAMLET

I do not think so. Since he went into France, I have been   **205**
in continual practice. I shall win at the odds. But thou
wouldst not think how ill all's here about my heart:[110] but
it is no matter.

HORATIO

Nay, good my lord –

HAMLET

It is but foolery, but it is such a kind of gain-giving,[111] as   **210**
would perhaps trouble a woman.

HORATIO

If your mind dislike anything, obey it, I will forestall their
repair hither,[112] and say you are not fit.

HAMLET

Not a whit. We defy augury.[113] There's a special
providence in the fall of a sparrow.[114] If it be now, 'tis not   **215**
to come. If it be not to come, it will be now. If it be not
now, yet it will come.[115] The readiness is all. Since no man
has aught of what he leaves, what is't to leave betimes?[116]

*Enter CLAUDIUS, GERTRUDE, LAERTES, LORDS, OSRIC, and
ATTENDANTS with FOILS, &c*

CLAUDIUS

Come, Hamlet, come, and take this hand from me.

CLAUDIUS puts LAERTES' hand into HAMLET'S

HAMLET

Give me your pardon, sir. I've done you wrong;   **220**
But pardon't as you are a gentleman.
This presence[117] knows,
And you must needs have heard, how I am punished
With sore distraction.[118] What I have done,
That might your nature, honour, and exception[119]   **225**
Roughly awake,[120] I here proclaim was madness.
Was't Hamlet wronged Laertes? Never Hamlet.
If Hamlet from himself be ta'en away,
And when he's not himself does wrong Laertes,
Then Hamlet does it not, Hamlet denies it.   **230**
Who does it then? His madness. If't be so,
Hamlet is of the faction[121] that is wronged.
His madness is poor Hamlet's enemy.
Sir, in this audience
Let my disclaiming from a purposed evil[122]   **235**
Free me so far in your most generous thoughts
That I have shot mine arrow o'er the house,
And hurt my brother.[123]

LAERTES

I am satisfied in nature,
Whose motive, in this case, should stir me most   **240**
To my revenge.[124] But in my terms of honour
I stand aloof, and will no reconcilement
Till by some elder masters of known honour
I have a voice and precedent of peace
To keep my name ungored,[125] but till that time,   **245**
I do receive your offered love like love,
And will not wrong it.

HAMLET

I do embrace it freely,
And will this brothers' wager frankly[126] play. –
Give us the foils. Come on.   **250**

LAERTES

Come, one for me.

HAMLET

I'll be your foil, Laertes. In mine ignorance
Your skill shall, like a star i'th' darkest night,
Stick fiery off indeed.[127]

117. *This presence:* the present company

118. *sore distraction:* serious mental illness

119. *exception:* disapproval

120. *awake:* provoke

121. *faction:* party

122. *disclaiming … evil:* declaring that I was not intentionally evil

123. *Free … brother:* In your generosity of spirit, view me as if I had shot an arrow over the house and injured my brother.

124. *I am … revenge:* My natural feelings, which should urge me to seek revenge, are satisfied.

125. *I stand … ungored:* I remain unapproachable and desire no reconciliation until experts in the matter of honour give me a precedent whereby I can keep my reputation unstained.

126. *frankly:* freely, without any bad feeling

127. *I'll be … indeed:* Hamlet is punning on the word 'foil' here. It can mean a fencing sword or a background against which a jewel is displayed. Hamlet says his lack of skill will act as a foil against which Laertes' skill will contrast brilliantly.

LAERTES

You mock me, sir.   255

HAMLET

No, by this hand.

CLAUDIUS

Give them the foils, young Osric. Cousin Hamlet,

You know the wager?

HAMLET

Very well, my lord.

Your grace hath laid the odds o'th' weaker side.   260

CLAUDIUS

I do not fear it; I have seen you both.

But since he is bettered, we have therefore odds.[128]

LAERTES

This is too heavy, let me see another.

HAMLET

This likes me well. These foils have all a length?[129]

They prepare to play

OSRIC

Ay, my good lord.   265

CLAUDIUS

Set me the stoups[130] of wine upon that table.

If Hamlet give the first or second hit,

Or quit in answer of the third exchange,[131]

Let all the battlements their ordnance[132] fire.

The King shall drink to Hamlet's better breath,[133]   270

And in the cup an union[134] shall he throw

Richer than that which four successive kings

In Denmark's crown have worn. Give me the cups,

And let the kettle[135] to the trumpet speak,

The trumpet to the cannoneer without,   275

The cannons to the heavens, the heaven to earth,

'Now the King drinks to Hamlet.' Come, begin.

And you, the judges, bear a wary eye.

128. *But ... odds:* But since he *(Laertes)* is better than you, the odds are in our favour.

129. *have all a length?:* are all the same length?

130. *stoups:* tankards

131. *Or quit ... exchange:* or acquits himself well by winning the third round

132. *ordnance:* cannon

133. *better breath:* health

134. *union:* pearl *It was a custom for the king to put a jewel in the cup as a present to the person invited to drink. This pearl, however, contains poison.*

135. *kettle:* kettle drum

HAMLET

Come on, sir.

LAERTES

Come, my lord.   **280**

They play

HAMLET

One.

LAERTES

No.

HAMLET

Judgment.

OSRIC

A hit, a very palpable[136] hit.

LAERTES

Well, again.   **285**

CLAUDIUS

Stay. Give me drink. Hamlet, this pearl is thine.
Here's to thy health. –

Trumpets sound, and cannon shot off within

Give him the cup.

HAMLET

I'll play this bout first. Set it by a while. –
Come.   **290**

They play

Another hit. What say you?

LAERTES

A touch, a touch, I do confess.

136. *palpable:* obvious

137. *fat:* unfit
138. *scant of breath:* breathless

139. *carouses:* drinks

CLAUDIUS

Our son shall win.

GERTRUDE

He's fat[137] and scant of breath.[138]

Here, Hamlet, take my napkin. Rub thy brows.   **295**

The Queen carouses[139] to thy fortune, Hamlet. •Accident?
•Protecting Hamlet?

HAMLET

Good madam.

CLAUDIUS

Gertrude, do not drink.

GERTRUDE

I will, my lord, I pray you pardon me.

CLAUDIUS

[Aside] It is the poisoned cup; it is too late.   **300**

HAMLET

I dare not drink yet, madam; by and by.

GERTRUDE

Come, let me wipe thy face.

LAERTES

My lord, I'll hit him now.

CLAUDIUS

I do not think't.

LAERTES

[Aside] And yet 'tis almost 'gainst my conscience.   **305**

HAMLET

Come for the third,[140] Laertes, you but dally,

I pray you pass with your best violence.

I am afeard you make a wanton[141] of me.

LAERTES

Say you so? Come on.

140. *third:* third round

141. *wanton:* spoilt child *Hamlet is afraid Laertes is not fencing at his best and is treating Hamlet like a child.*

They play

OSRIC

Nothing neither way.   310

LAERTES

Have at you now!

LAERTES wounds HAMLET; then in scuffling, they change
rapiers, and HAMLET wounds LAERTES

CLAUDIUS

Part them, they are incensed.[142]   142. *incensed:* enraged

HAMLET

Nay, come again.

GERTRUDE falls

OSRIC

Look to the Queen there, ho!

HORATIO

They bleed on both sides. How is't, my lord?   315

OSRIC

How is't, Laertes?

LAERTES

Why, as a woodcock to mine own springe,[143] Osric.   143. *woodcock ... springe:* a bird trapped in my own snare
I am justly killed with mine own treachery.   Woodcocks were used as bait to lure other birds into a snare
                                                                                      but they often got caught in the snare themselves.

HAMLET

How does the Queen?

CLAUDIUS

She swoons[144] to see them bleed.   320   144. *swoons:* faints

GERTRUDE

No, no, the drink, the drink! O my dear Hamlet,
The drink, the drink! I am poisoned.

Dies

HAMLET

O villany! Ho! Let the door be locked!

Treachery! Seek it out.

LAERTES

It is here, Hamlet. Hamlet, thou art slain.   325

No medicine in the world can do thee good.

In thee there is not half an hour of life.

The treacherous instrument is in thy hand,

Unbated[145] and envenomed.[146] The foul practice[147]

Hath turned itself on me. Lo, here I lie,   330

Never to rise again. Thy mother's poisoned.

I can no more. The King, the King's to blame.

HAMLET

The point envenomed too?

Then, venom, to thy work.

Stabs CLAUDIUS

ALL

Treason, treason!   335

CLAUDIUS

O yet defend me, friends! I am but hurt.

HAMLET

Here, thou incestuous, murderous, damned Dane,

Drink off this potion. Is thy union[148] here?

Follow my mother.

CLAUDIUS dies

145. *Unbated:* unblunted
146. *envenomed:* poisoned
147. *practice:* plot

148. *union:* pearl (which Hamlet now realises was poisoned). This may also refer to the union of Claudius and Gertrude in death.

LAERTES

He is justly served;   340

It is a poison tempered[149] by himself.

Exchange forgiveness with me, noble Hamlet.

Mine and my father's death come not upon thee,

Nor thine on me.[150]

Dies

HAMLET

Heaven make thee free of it![151] I follow thee.   345

I am dead, Horatio. Wretched[152] Queen, adieu!

You that look pale and tremble at this chance,[153]

That are but mutes[154] or audience to this act,

Had I but time – as this fell sergeant[155] Death

Is strict in his arrest – O, I could tell you –   350

But let it be. Horatio, I am dead,

Thou livest. Report me and my cause aright

To the unsatisfied.[156]

HORATIO

Never believe it,

I am more an antique Roman than a Dane.[157]   355

Here's yet some liquor left.

HAMLET

As thou'rt a man,

Give me the cup. Let go. By heaven, I'll ha't.

O God, Horatio, what a wounded name,[158]

Things standing thus unknown, shall live behind me!   360

If thou didst ever hold me in thy heart,

Absent thee from felicity[159] a while,

And in this harsh world draw thy breath in pain,

To tell my story.

March afar off, and shot within

What warlike noise is this?   365

OSRIC

Young Fortinbras, with conquest come from Poland,

To th'ambassadors of England[160] gives

This warlike volley.

149. *tempered:* prepared

150. *Mine . . . me:* May you not be held morally responsible for my death and my father's death, nor may I be held morally responsible for your death.

151. *Heaven . . . it!:* May heaven absolve you of the guilt!

152. *Wretched:* miserable

153. *chance:* event

154. *mutes:* silent spectators

155. *fell sergeant:* cruel officer

156. *Report . . . unsatisfied.* Report the truth of what happened to me to those who look for a satisfactory explanation.

157. *I am . . . Dane:* The ancient Romans viewed suicide as a noble way to die when all was lost.

158. *wounded name:* damaged reputation

159. *felicity:* happiness

160. *th'ambassadors of England:* ambassadors from England reporting that Rosencrantz and Guildenstern have been put to death

161. *o'ercrows:* triumphs over

162. *But I ... voice:* However I predict that Fortinbras will win the election *(to be king).* He has my dying vote.

163. *th'occurrents, more or less:* the great and small occurrences

164. *solicited:* prompted me to do so

HAMLET

O, I die, Horatio!

The potent poison quite o'ercrows[161] my spirit. 370

I cannot live to hear the news from England,

But I do prophesy th'election lights

On Fortinbras. He has my dying voice.[162]

So tell him, with th'occurrents, more and less,[163]

Which have solicited.[164] The rest is silence. 375

Dies

HORATIO

Now cracks a noble heart. Good night, sweet prince,

And flights of angels sing thee to thy rest. –

Why does the drum come hither?

March within

Enter FORTINBRAS, the ENGLISH AMBASSADORS, and OTHERS

165. *Where is this sight?:* Fortinbras has obviously heard the news and knows what sight awaits him.

FORTINBRAS

Where is this sight?[165]

166. *If ... wonder:* If it is anything sorrowful or astonishing

HORATIO

What is it ye would see? 380

If aught of woe or wonder,[166] cease your search.

167. *This ... havoc:* This heap of dead bodies proclaims a merciless slaughter. *To cry havoc meant to give the order to kill everyone without mercy.*

168. *is toward:* is in preparation

FORTINBRAS

This quarry cries on havoc.[167] O proud death,

What feast is toward[168] in thine eternal cell,

That thou so many princes at a shot

So bloodily hast struck! 385

169. *dismal:* dreadful

170. *affairs:* business

FIRST AMBASSADOR

The sight is dismal,[169]

And our affairs[170] from England come too late.

The ears are senseless that should give us hearing

To tell him his commandment is fulfilled,

That Rosencrantz and Guildenstern are dead. 390

171. *Where ... thanks?:* Who will thank us now?

Where should we have our thanks?[171]

172. *his:* Claudius's

HORATIO

Not from his[172] mouth,

Had it th'ability of life to thank you.

He never gave commandment for their death.
But since so jump upon this bloody question[173]   **395**
You from the Polack wars, and you from England,
Are here arrived, give order that these bodies
High on a stage be placed to the view;
And let me speak to th' yet unknowing world
How these things came about. So shall you hear   **400**
Of carnal,[174] bloody, and unnatural acts,
Of accidental judgements casual slaughters,
Of deaths put on by cunning and forced cause;[175]
And, in this upshot, purposes mistook
Fallen on the inventors' heads.[176] All this can I   **405**
Truly deliver.

FORTINBRAS

Let us haste to hear it,
And call the noblest to the audience.
For me, with sorrow I embrace my fortune.
I have some rights of memory in this kingdom,   **410**
Which now to claim my vantage doth invite me.[177]

HORATIO

Of that[178] I shall have also cause to speak,
And from his mouth whose voice will draw on more.[179]
But let this same be presently performed,
Even while men's minds are wild,[180] lest more mischance[181]   **415**
On[182] plots and errors happen.

FORTINBRAS

Let four captains
Bear Hamlet like a soldier to the stage,
For he was likely, had he been put on,[183]
To have proved most royal; and for his passage,[184]   **420**
The soldiers' music and the rites of war
Speak loudly for him.
Take up the bodies. Such a sight as this
Becomes the field, but here shows much amiss.[185]
Go, bid the soldiers shoot.   **425**

*A dead march. Exit, bearing off the dead bodies; after which a
peal of ordnance is shot off*

---

173. *so ... question:* so precisely at the moment of this bloody conflict

174. *carnal:* lustful

175. *put ... cause:* brought about by clever scheming

176. *purposes ... heads:* plots that went wrong turned on those who had planned them

177. *I have ... me:* I have some rights on this kingdom, which my advantageous position allows me to use to claim the Danish throne.

178. *that:* Fortinbras' claim to the throne

179. *his ... more:* Hamlet's final words of support will influence others to support you too.

180. *wild:* distraught or agitated
181. *mischance:* mishaps
182. *On:* on top of

183. *put on:* put to the test

184. *for his passage:* to mark his passing from life to death

185. *Becomes ... amiss:* is appropriate for a battlefield but looks most out of place here

Act 5 Scene 2
Quotes and Questions

Quotes

There's a divinity that shapes our ends,
Rough-hew them how we will –

(Hamlet, lines 10–11)

Hamlet says there's a divine force that determines the outcomes of our plans, no matter how much we may try to shape them.

They are not near my conscience. Their defeat
Does by their own insinuation grow.

(Hamlet, lines 62–63)

Hamlet feels no guilt for the death of Rosencrantz and Guildenstern. He says their plotting led to their deaths. Hamlet's comment is quite ruthless, showing no pity for his old school friends.

I am very sorry, good Horatio,
That to Laertes I forgot myself;
For by the image of my cause I see
The portraiture of his.

(Hamlet, lines 80–83)

Hamlet tells Horatio that he is sorry he fought with Laertes and recognises that Laertes was, like Hamlet, justified in wanting revenge for his father's death.

There's a special
providence in the fall of a sparrow. If it be now, 'tis not
to come. If it be not to come, it will be now. If it be not
now, yet it will come. The readiness is all.

(Hamlet, lines 214–217)

Hamlet says death is inevitable and no man can choose the time of it. All one can do is be prepared.

Now cracks a noble heart. Good night, sweet prince,
And flights of angels sing thee to thy rest.

(Horatio, lines 376–377)

Horatio is heartbroken to say goodbye to Hamlet. His love and loyalty mean he would rather die with Hamlet than live without him, but he agrees to remain alive to tell others what happened.

Questions

In each case, support your point with suitable reference to and quotation from the play.

1. Do you agree with Hamlet's view of Rosencrantz and Guildenstern?

2. Why do you think the character of Osric is introduced in this final act?

3. Compare and contrast the reasons Hamlet and Laertes have to seek revenge and the manner in which they approach the matter.

4. What is your impression of Gertrude in this scene?

5. How does Claudius behave in this scene?

6. What is your final impression of Hamlet?

7. Are you satisfied with the ending of the play? Why/why not?

Writing Task

You have been asked to write a review of *Hamlet* for your school magazine. Your review should include an introduction, description, evaluation and recommendation.

Essay Building Blocks

'Shakespeare's play Hamlet *has been described as "a disturbing psychological thriller".*'

Write a paragraph in response to this statement, supporting your answer with quotation from and reference to Act 5 Scene 2.

Hamlet Study Notes and Analysis

Studying Character

Character checklists

We learn about characters by noting what they **say**, what they **do**, what **others say** about them and **how others act** in their presence. In *Hamlet* the soliloquies are an essential part of learning about the characters.

When you are studying characters in *Hamlet,* it can be helpful to think in terms of the following **checklists**:

Role

✓ In **which scenes** does the character appear? (It is a good idea to make a list of these and note what happens in each as it can give you a clear indication of the challenges the character has to face and how he or she copes with them.)

✓ Does the character **change** as the play progresses?

✓ Do the character's **actions – or inaction – affect the plot outcome**?

✓ Does the character have a **dramatic function** within the play?

✓ Is the character a **hero, heroine or villain**?

✓ Does the character act as a **foil** to another character?

✓ How is the character influenced by the **world of the text**?

Qualities

✓ Make a **list** of the character's qualities.

✓ Divide the list into **positive** and **negative** qualities.

✓ Do these qualities make the character **appealing to an audience**? Why/why not?

✓ Is the character **fully fleshed out** and not **one-dimensional**?

✓ Do we **relate to the character**, perhaps because they are not perfect?

✓ Do the character's qualities/attitudes/values make them vulnerable to manipulation by others?

✓ Do the **character's values change** as the play progresses?

Relationships

✓ **With which characters** does this character have a relationship?

✓ List the **types** of relationship: husband/wife/subject/friend, etc.

✓ Are these relationships **functional or dysfunctional**?

✓ Are the relationships **equal or unequal**?

✓ Who has the **power** in the relationship?

✓ Are the characters **bettered** by being in the relationship?

✓ Does the relationship face **challenges**?

✓ What **threatens** the relationship? Is it **external forces** or **something within the character's personality** that causes difficulties?

✓ Does the relationship undergo **change**?

✓ What are the **key scenes** where we see changes in the relationship?

Structure

When structuring an answer on a character, you should think of the following five questions:

1. How is the character **introduced** and what is our first impression of him or her?

2. Does the character have to face any **challenges**, and if so, how does he or she react to them?

3. Does the character have to deal with a **major crisis** at a turning point in the play?

4. How is the crisis **resolved** and what role (if any) does the character play in the resolution?

5. What is our **final impression** of the character and is it different from our initial impression? Has the character **undergone change**?

Hamlet

Now might I do it pat, now he is praying,
And now I'll do't.

Act 1 Scene 2

- Hamlet listens while Claudius holds court. Hamlet is dressed in black because he is still in mourning for his father.

- Hamlet responds to Claudius's description of him as '**my cousin Hamlet, and my son**' by remarking in an aside that he is '**A little more than kin, and less than kind**'. Hamlet uses wordplay here: he means he is more than a mere relation – '**kin**' – and also that he does not feel kindly towards Claudius.

- Hamlet continues his wordplay when he answers Claudius's question about the clouds – or depression – that seem to surround him, by saying he is '**too much in the sun**'. Hamlet is punning on the word '**son**' used by Claudius a short time ago. Hamlet does not want to be Claudius's son. Neither does he want to be in the limelight. Finally, he is not in the mood for sunshine because he is in mourning.

- Gertrude also rebukes Hamlet for mourning his father for so long, saying, '**Thou knows't 'tis common – all that lives must die**'. Once again, Hamlet picks up on a word with more than one meaning and agrees with Gertrude that it is '**common**', but suggesting it is her behaviour after her husband's death that is '**common**' or promiscuous.

- Hamlet responds explosively to Gertrude when she asks why it seems as though he is the only one grieving. He objects to the word '**seems**', saying his sorrow is real.

- Claudius makes a long-winded speech, encouraging Hamlet to stay in Denmark and not return to Wittenburg. Gertrude, in two brief lines, echoes Claudius's request. Hamlet says he will stay to please his mother: '**I shall in all my best obey you, madam**'.

- Hamlet is left alone onstage. His anguish is clear as he wishes he were dead and that God had not forbidden suicide. Hamlet sees life as meaningless: '**How weary, stale, flat and unprofitable/Seem to me all the uses of this world!**' The world, in Hamlet's view, is a rotten and corrupt place, much like a neglected garden: ''**Tis an unweeded garden/That grows to seed; things rank and gross in nature/Possess it merely**'. He compares Claudius unfavourably to Old Hamlet: '**So excellent a king, that was to this/Hyperion to a satyr**'.

- Hamlet remarks bitterly that despite the love between his parents, his mother did not wait longer than a month before marrying Claudius and her behaviour leads him to extend his disgust to all women: '**frailty, thy name is woman**'.

- Horatio enters with Marcellus and Barnardo. Hamlet is pleased to see his old friend Horatio and roused to excited curiosity by the story of the Ghost. He questions Horatio and the other two men closely and expresses his desire to see the Ghost for himself. He believes the Ghost may have come to tell of some '**foul play**'.

Analysis of Hamlet's character and role in Act 1 Scene 2

- Hamlet stands out as the only person in court dressed in a '**nighted colour**'. He contrasts with the other courtiers who have, to all intents and purposes, moved on from the death of the old king. Hamlet refuses to pretend that all is well and when his mother asks him why he seems to still be grieving so deeply, he replies icily, '**Seems, madam? Nay it is. I know not "seems"**'.

- Hamlet's ready wit is shown when he answers Claudius with a wordplay using the words '**kin**' and '**son**' to make it clear he does not consider himself Claudius's son simply because of his mother's remarriage.

- Despite his sorrow at his father's death and his anger at his mother's hasty remarriage, Hamlet maintains enough self-control to hide the true depth of his feelings until he is alone and able to express himself in his first soliloquy.

- Through his soliloquy, we learn that Hamlet is deeply depressed. He has lost faith in the world and sees little point in living. He wishes he could simply fade away and die, or that God had not forbidden suicide:

  > O that this too too solid flesh would melt,
  > Thaw, and resolve itself into a dew,
  > Or that the Everlasting had not fixed
  > His canon 'gainst self-slaughter! O God! God,
  > How weary, stale, flat, and unprofitable
  > Seem to me all the uses of this world!

- Some critics believe these six lines give an important insight into Hamlet's procrastination and his descent into madness. If he truly believes the world to be so intolerable, then it is not surprising that he should find it so difficult to stir himself to act. What would be the point in going on in a pointless world?

- Hamlet is disgusted by his mother's sexuality and says that even '**a beast that wants discourse of reason/Would have mourned longer**'. Hamlet's view of women is tainted by what he sees as his mother's rush to '**incestuous sheets**'. This negative view of female sexuality will affect his relationship with Ophelia.

- Hamlet's love for his father is clear in this scene. He describes Old Hamlet in his soliloquy as '**so excellent a king**'. He tells Horatio he '**shall not look upon his like again**' and says that he has seen him in his '**mind's eye**'. Yet it seems as though Hamlet feels inferior to his late father. He says Claudius is as like King Hamlet as he, Hamlet, is like Hercules. The late king was a warrior – his ghost appears in full armour – but his son does not believe that he shares his father's physical courage, hence his disparaging remarks about himself in comparison to Hercules.

Act 1 Scene 4

- Hamlet waits for the appearance of the Ghost. As he does so, there is the sound of cannons being fired. Hamlet tells Horatio that cannons being fired as the king drinks is an old custom that had largely fallen out of use before Claudius's ascension to the throne. Hamlet believes such an outward show of drunkenness disgraces the Danes.

- Hamlet says an individual may be damned by a single flaw, just as the Danish people may be damned by being viewed as drunkards.

- The Ghost appears and Hamlet is shocked, wondering if it is a demon or the spirit of his late father. However, he decides to address it as '**Hamlet, King, father, royal Dane**' and begs it to tell him why it has appeared.

- The Ghost beckons Hamlet to come away with it. Horatio and Marcellus advise Hamlet not to go, but he ignores their warnings, saying he does not value his life '**in a pin's fee**', and so has nothing to lose. When Horatio and Marcellus try to restrain Hamlet, he threatens them with violence and follows the Ghost to a secluded spot.

Analysis of Hamlet's character and role in Act 1 Scene 4

- Hamlet's disgust at his uncle's resurrection of the old habit of firing off cannons to signal drunken partying shows his moral superiority: unlike Claudius, he has no time for such '**swinish**' behaviour. He is unhappy that other countries may view the Danes as weak drunkards because of this one tradition. Hamlet's concern for Denmark's reputation shows his royal blood and his potential to rule. This incident also serves to show the contrast between uncle and nephew: while Hamlet is engaged in a serious quest, Claudius is drinking and making merry.

- Hamlet's philosophical reflection that a single flaw may damn a man or a nation is important. Many critics see a tragic hero as having one tragic flaw that brings about their downfall. Hamlet may subconsciously be analysing himself at the same time as he analyses his country.

- Hamlet shows courage in following the Ghost, despite Horatio's and Marcellus' warnings. However, his lack of fear may also be attributed to his desperate state and the lack of value he places on his own life.

- Hamlet is unsure of the Ghost's motives and does not know if the Ghost is good or evil. Although he decides to address it as if it were his late father, Hamlet's doubts about the Ghost remain throughout the play.

Act 1 Scene 5

- Hamlet says he will go no further and commands the Ghost to speak to him.

- Hamlet is horrified to hear his father was murdered and asks the Ghost to tell him more so he can seek revenge.

- Hamlet cries, '**O my prophetic soul!**' as his suspicions of his uncle are confirmed.

- The Ghost vanishes and Hamlet vows to avenge his father's murder. He rages against his mother and uncle, calling Gertrude a '**most pernicious woman**' and Claudius a '**smiling damned villain**'. Hamlet vows that he will make revenge his first priority and, taking out his notebook, jots down what the Ghost has said.

- Horatio and Marcellus re-enter and ask Hamlet about his encounter with the Ghost. Hamlet is in a state of high excitement and agitation and Horatio can make little sense of his '**wild and whirling words**'.

- Hamlet refuses to reveal what the Ghost has said and makes Horatio and Marcellus swear to reveal nothing of the Ghost's appearance. The Ghost joins Hamlet in calling for an oath of secrecy, calling '**Swear**' from beneath the ground. Hamlet seems to find the Ghost's words amusing, calling him '**this fellow in the cellarage**' and '**old mole**'.

- Hamlet tells Horatio and Marcellus he may put on '**an antic disposition**' in the coming days and warns them not to let anyone know his madness is not real.

- In his final speech of the scene, Hamlet calls it '**cursed spite**' that he has to take responsibility for righting the disorder in Denmark.

Analysis of Hamlet's character and role in Act 1 Scene 5

- Hamlet appears bent on avenging his father's murder, but there are some hints he may not actually sweep to his revenge '**with wings as swift/As meditation or the thoughts of love**'. Ironically for one who claims thought and deed will be as one, Hamlet delays over and over as the play progresses, meditating on the Ghost's words and his duty. Hamlet is more a scholar and philosopher than a man suited to seek immediate and bloody revenge. This may be seen in his reaching for his notebook rather than his sword: '**My tables – meet it is I set it down/That one may smile and smile and be a villain**'.

- Hamlet is in a highly agitated state of mind after his encounter with the Ghost. This is hardly surprising, given his despair before the encounter, his horror on hearing the dreadful details of his father's murder, and the burden of duty the Ghost has laid upon him.

- Although the Ghost's visit may initially appear to give Hamlet a sense of purpose, the Prince is overwhelmed by the responsibility. He believes the world is '**out of joint**' and does not believe he is the right person to '**set it right**'.

- It is not clear why Hamlet decides to feign madness but there are moments in this scene when he appears perilously close to genuine madness. His reaction to the Ghost's speaking from under the ground is strange and oddly inappropriate if he believes the spirit to be that of his dead father.

Act 2 Scene 1

- Although Hamlet does not appear in person in this scene, we learn from Ophelia that he has been behaving strangely. He visited her in her room in a dishevelled state, said nothing, stared at her, sighed and left.

Analysis of Hamlet's character and role in Act 2 Scene 1

- Hamlet's behaviour is difficult to interpret here, not least because we do not see him but must rely on Ophelia's account. He may be pretending to be mad and acting this way in front of Ophelia because he knows she will report his behaviour to Polonius. On the other hand, Hamlet may genuinely be distressed because Ophelia, acting on her father's orders, has rejected him and left him more isolated and unhappy than before.

- Polonius believes Hamlet is mad and displaying '**the very ecstasy of love**'. He rushes to tell Claudius the news of his nephew's state of mind.

- If Hamlet is pretending to be mad in this scene, it is difficult to know what he hopes to gain from it.

Act 2 Scene 2

- Several weeks have passed since Hamlet's encounter with the Ghost. Claudius has sent for old school friends of Hamlet – Rosencrantz and Guildenstern – in the hope that they will discover the reason for Hamlet's odd behaviour. Polonius has hatched a plan to spy on Hamlet as he talks to Ophelia and thereby '**find where truth is hid**'.

- Hamlet and Polonius meet. Hamlet seems to speak nonsense, calling Polonius a '**fishmonger**' and talking about the sun breeding maggots in a dog's corpse. Polonius believes he is '**far gone, far gone**'.

- When Polonius says he will take his leave, Hamlet says, '**You cannot, sir, take from me anything that I will more willingly part withal – except my life**'.

- Polonius leaves and Rosencrantz and Guildenstern enter. Hamlet chats to them for a few moments before asking them why they have come to Elsinore. He suspects they have been sent for and they eventually admit the truth.

- Hamlet tells Rosencrantz and Guildenstern that he has lost all joy in life and views the earth as '**a sterile promontory**'; the air and sky no more than a '**foul and pestilent congregation of vapours**'. He takes no joy in others: '**Man delights not me – no, nor woman neither**'. All living things are doomed to die, so Hamlet wonders what the point of life is: '**to me what is this quintessence of dust?**'

- Rosencrantz tells Hamlet that a travelling theatre company is on its way to Elsinore. The news rouses Hamlet from his melancholy, and he shows an interest in news of the players.

- As he takes his leave of Rosencrantz and Guildenstern, Hamlet tells them that he is only pretending to be mad: '**I am but mad north-north-west**'.

- Polonius enters to tell Hamlet that the players have arrived. Hamlet treats him with contempt but greets the players warmly.

- Hamlet asks the players to perform a speech about the murder of Priam, beginning the speech himself. The actor is so moved by the description of Priam's widow's grief that he cries as he delivers the lines.

- Hamlet instructs Polonius to arrange lodgings for the players and dismisses him. Alone with the players, Hamlet asks them if they know the play 'The Murder of Gonzago' and if they would be willing to learn a short additional speech that he will write for the play.

- Alone onstage, Hamlet berates himself for his lack of action. He compares himself unfavourably to the emotional actor who was moved to tears by the plight of Hecuba, Priam's widow. Hamlet lists all the reasons he should have acted before now: his love of and obligation to his father, a command from beyond the grave, and Claudius's villainous nature. He reflects bitterly that he favours words over action and wonders why he must '**like a whore unpack my heart with words**'.

- Hamlet reveals his plan to trap Claudius: he will have the actors perform a scene resembling his father's murder. If Claudius reacts to this, Hamlet will know he is guilty.

- Once again, Hamlet questions the Ghost's origins and motives. He fears it may be '**a devil**' and feels it is important to have more concrete proof than the word of such an uncertain spirit.

Analysis of Hamlet's character and role in Act 2 Scene 2

- Although Polonius believes Hamlet is mad, there is meaning behind the Prince's words. Calling Polonius '**a fishmonger**' may be a veiled reference to Polonius's fishing for secrets, or it may be a reference to the Elizabethan slang word for pimp. Hamlet may suspect Polonius of planning to use Ophelia as bait. Similarly, Hamlet's comment about the sun breeding maggots in a dead dog can be seen as a reflection of his disgust at sexuality because it links death and sex.

- Hamlet asks if Polonius has a daughter, saying, '**Let her not walk in the sun**'. There are layers of meaning to Hamlet's warning. If Ophelia is placed at the centre of events (Polonius will use her to spy on Hamlet in the next scene) harm may come to her. After all, the Danish court is a corrupt and rotten place. Hamlet is also the son of a king and the sun is an emblem of royalty. The young Prince could be warning Polonius to keep her away from him.

- Hamlet is a good judge of character. It appears that he suspects Polonius of planning to use Ophelia to spy on him, and he knows Rosencrantz and Guildenstern were sent to do the same.

- Hamlet is deeply disillusioned with life, telling Polonius he would be happy for his life to be taken from him, and admitting to Rosencrantz and Guildenstern that he is depressed and sees no point in living.

- Hamlet's wit and dark humour in this scene as he toys with Polonius, Rosencrantz and Guildenstern suggest he is sane, as does his comment about being '**mad north-north-west**'.

- His interaction with the players reveals Hamlet's intelligence and learning. Not only does he know the speeches well enough to deliver them himself, but he is able to write an additional speech for 'The Murder of Gonzago'.

- In his soliloquy, Hamlet rails against his inaction and examines the reasons for it. It appears that the players have revived his desire for revenge as he expresses his rage at his own inadequacy. However, he procrastinates once again, saying that he fears the Ghost may be a devil and that it is not a reliable proof of Claudius's guilt. Therefore, he hatches his plot to '**catch the conscience of the King**'.

- This is a long scene but very little happens, although much is discussed. This is an apt reflection of Hamlet's reliance on words rather than action.

Act 3 Scene 1

- Claudius and Polonius have arranged to eavesdrop on Hamlet's conversation with Ophelia.

- Hamlet enters and, in his most famous soliloquy, reflects on the troubles of life. He wonders if it would be better to be dead and comes to the conclusion that people prefer life to death only because they fear the unknown. Most, he believes, would '**rather bear those ills we have/Than fly to others that we not know of**'. Hamlet says that thinking too much can prevent us from acting:

  Thus conscience does make cowards of us all,
  And thus the native hue of resolution
  Is sicklied o'er with the pale cast of thought

- Ophelia interrupts Hamlet's train of thought, telling him she has gifts she wishes to return to him.

- Hamlet claims he never gave Ophelia anything but soon after admits that he did love her once, before immediately contradicting himself again. He asks Ophelia if she is honest as well as beautiful, claiming it is impossible to be both.

- Hamlet attacks Ophelia verbally, telling her repeatedly that she should enter a convent or '**nunnery**'. If she remains in the outside world, she may become '**a breeder of sinners**'. Hamlet says he is '**proud, revengeful, ambitious**' and warns Ophelia against trusting any man.

- Suddenly, Hamlet asks Ophelia where Polonius is and when she answers that he is at home, he calls Polonius a fool.

- Despite Ophelia's distress, Hamlet continues to attack her and all women, saying that they are dishonest and false: '**God hath given you one face, and you make yourselves another**'. He says there must be no more marriages, although of those who are married already '**all but one**' may continue as they are. He leaves Ophelia with a final command to go to a nunnery.

Analysis of Hamlet's character and role in Act 3 Scene 1

- Although Hamlet discusses suicide as an option, he treats it as a general, philosophical idea rather than something he has seriously considered for himself. He is a typical Renaissance intellectual, not particularly interested in action but deeply interested in the human condition.

- Hamlet meditates on the nature of meditation: his conscience prevents him from taking swift action against Claudius.

- Hamlet vents his anger and disgust to Ophelia. Hamlet's cruelty in this scene is open to a number of interpretations.

  1. He is so revolted by his mother's hasty marriage to Claudius that he sees all women's sexuality as a cheap and dirty trick to lure men and then betray them. He is unable to put his mother's behaviour in perspective and condemns all women for her faults.

  2. He may be genuinely hurt and angry by Ophelia's rejection. After all, he came to her room in a state of agitation but she has not relented and wants to return his gifts to her.

  3. Hamlet may be aware that he is being spied upon and his words may be intended for Claudius and Polonius as well as for Ophelia. He refers to both Claudius and Polonius, calling the latter a fool and hinting at a threat to the former: '**I say we will have no more marriages. /Those that are married already – all but one – shall live**'.

- If he does suspect he is being spied upon, Hamlet is likely to feel doubly betrayed by Ophelia for conspiring against him.

Act 3 Scene 2

- Hamlet directs the actors, giving them the new lines he has written for the play and warning them against overacting.

- Horatio arrives and Hamlet greets him warmly, heaping praise upon his friend and insisting it is not mere flattery. He values Horatio's self-control and balanced views: '**Give me that man/That is not passion's slave, and I will wear him/In my heart's core**'. He asks Horatio to watch Claudius's reaction to the play and see whether he appears guilty.

- Claudius, Gertrude, Polonius, Ophelia, Rosencrantz and Guildenstern enter with assorted courtiers. Hamlet deliberately misinterprets Claudius's question about how he '**fares**', pretending to believe Claudius wants to know about his eating habits rather than his general wellbeing. His brief exchange with Polonius about his role in *Julius Caesar* appears similarly meaningless: '**It was a brute part of him to kill so capital a calf there**' but it is actually another play on words. '**Calf**' can mean fool and Caesar was killed in the Capitol, which sounds like '**capital**'. Of course, Brutus and brute are also alike.

- Hamlet declines his mother's request to sit with her, and chooses instead to sit with Ophelia, calling her '**metal more attractive**'.

- Hamlet makes crude comments to Ophelia, asking '**Lady, shall I lie in your lap?**' and when she refuses, asking if she thought he meant '**country matters**' – an extremely rude pun. He comments bitterly that his mother is cheerful despite his father having died only two hours ago and when Ophelia corrects him, saying Old Hamlet died four months ago, Hamlet is even more biting in his criticism, saying all a man can hope for now is that his memory '**might outlive his life half a year**'. When Ophelia remarks that the prologue to the play is brief, Hamlet says, '**As woman's love**'.

- Hamlet follows the play closely and when the Player Queen promises her husband that she would never marry again if he were to die, Hamlet says, '**If she should break it now!**' He asks Gertrude what she thinks of the play and she tells him she feels the Player Queen '**protests too much**'. In answer to Claudius's question about the nature of the play, Hamlet replies that it is inoffensive and merely a joke.

- Hamlet is delighted with the effect the play has on Claudius and believes his walking out at the poisoning scene proves the Ghost was telling the truth: '**I'll take the ghost's word for a thousand pound**'. Alone with Horatio, he asks his friend if he noticed Claudius's reaction.

- Rosencrantz and Guildenstern come to Hamlet with a message from Gertrude, saying that she is bewildered by his behaviour and asking him to come to her room. Hamlet turns on his old friends, asking them why they have tried to manipulate and deceive him. He tells Guildenstern to play the recorder and when he refuses, Hamlet angrily says, '**You would play upon me**'.

- Polonius enters and asks Hamlet to go to Gertrude. Hamlet teases the older man, asking him if he thinks a cloud looks like a camel and, when Polonius agrees, saying that it looks more like a weasel or a whale. Polonius goes along with everything Hamlet says. The Prince dismisses him, saying he will visit his mother '**by and by**'.

- Alone, Hamlet expresses his violent, vengeful thoughts: '**Now could I drink hot blood,/And do such bitter business as the day/Would quake to look on**'. He says he will visit Gertrude but not harm her physically: '**I will speak daggers to her, but use none**'.

Analysis of Hamlet's character and role in Act 3 Scene 2

- Hamlet's love of the theatre, his knowledge of acting and his ability to speak sanely and intelligently are clear.

- Hamlet's conversation with Horatio is clever and coherent, reinforcing the idea that he is rational. He deeply admires his friend and envies him his self-control.

- Hamlet snubs his mother and sits instead with Ophelia, although he insults her. His cruelty and sarcasm foreshadow the way he will speak to his mother when they are next alone together. His attitude to women is bitter and negative.

- Hamlet's response to what he believes is proof of Claudius's guilt shows that he can be violent and ruthless. He wants revenge on Claudius and seems to be poised to kill his uncle, but knows he must first exercise some self-control and refrain from hurting his mother, even though he clearly believes that she deserves to be punished.

Act 3 Scene 3

- In what is generally known as 'the Prayer Scene', Hamlet comes across Claudius praying in the chapel. He knows he could kill his uncle but is reluctant to do so because if he were to kill Claudius at prayer, he would '**this same villain send/To heaven**'.

- Hamlet reflects that Claudius killed Old Hamlet when the latter was '**full of bread/With all his crimes broad blown**'. He does not believe it is right for his uncle to go to heaven while the man he murdered suffers in purgatory.

- Putting away his sword, Hamlet vows instead to kill Claudius when he is drunk, in a rage, committing incest with Gertrude, gambling, cursing or doing anything that will prevent him from dying in a state of grace.

- Hamlet leaves to go to Gertrude, promising that Claudius's prayers have merely postponed his death.

Analysis of Hamlet's character and role in Act 3 Scene 3

- Critics differ over Hamlet's decision not to kill Claudius. Hamlet says he does not do so because he feels it is unfair for his uncle to go to heaven, which an Elizabethan audience would have understood. After all, true revenge means eternal damnation.

- However, some believe this is merely another excuse to avoid taking decisive action. Others say it is Hamlet's sense of fairness that prevents him from murdering an unarmed man. The choice is up to you, of course, but a simple reason may be that if Hamlet were to kill Claudius during this scene, the play would be over!

- There is, of course, a terrible irony in Hamlet's decision. Although he doesn't know it, Claudius is not in a state of grace at all as he is unable to truly repent.

Act 3 Scene 4

- Hamlet visits his mother in her room and she tells him that he has offended Claudius, calling him Hamlet's father. He is Hamlet's stepfather, but the young Prince will not accept the title. He snaps back that Gertrude has offended his father, meaning Old Hamlet.

- Gertrude does not want to talk to Hamlet when he is in this mood, but he forces her to sit and listen. Alarmed, Gertrude cries for help. Polonius, hidden behind the arras, also calls for help. Hamlet, believing the hidden figure to be Claudius, stabs his sword through the tapestry, killing Polonius.

- Hamlet is disappointed that he has not killed Claudius, and calls the dead Polonius '**a wretched, rash, intruding fool**'.

- Seemingly unaffected by the murder, Hamlet tells Gertrude to sit and listen while he tells her of a far worse deed. He claims that she has committed a sin so dreadful that the heavens above are '**thought-sick at the act**'.

- Hamlet forces Gertrude to look at two pictures, one of Old Hamlet and one of Claudius. He praises Old Hamlet as '**A combination and a form indeed/Where every god did seem to set his seal/To give the world assurance of a man**'. By comparison, Claudius is '**like a mildewed ear/Blasting his wholesome brother**'. Hamlet cannot believe his mother could choose to marry Claudius when she had known such perfection.

- Ignoring Gertrude's protests, Hamlet continues his attack, comparing her marriage bed to a '**nasty sty**' and calling Claudius a '**murderer and a villain**'.

- Hamlet breaks off suddenly as the Ghost appears. Gertrude cannot see him and assumes Hamlet is mad. The Ghost reminds Hamlet of his promise to avenge his death: '**This visitation/Is but to whet thy almost blunted purpose**'.

- The Ghost leaves and Hamlet begs his mother to believe he is sane, to repent for her sins and not to sleep with Claudius again. He asks if she knows that Claudius intends to send him to England and tells her that he knows that Rosencrantz and Guildenstern are carrying letters that will seal his doom. However, Hamlet plans to turn the tables on them.

- Now Hamlet turns his attention to the body of Polonius, saying disrespectfully that he must '**lug the guts into the neighbour room**'. He leaves.

Analysis of Hamlet's character and role in Act 3 Scene 4

- Hamlet is furious with his mother in this scene and he confronts her about her marriage. This is the only time in the play that they are alone together.

- This scene is a reversal of the normal parent-child relationship. Hamlet controls the conversation and tries to find out if Gertrude knew about her late husband's murder. Gertrude appears to be shocked by Hamlet's claim and by his attack on her, wringing her hands and begging her son to '**speak no more**'.

- Hamlet is determined to save his mother's soul. He talks to her much as a priest might talk to a sinner, urging her '**for the love of grace**' not to sin anymore and to '**Assume a virtue if you have it not**'.

- The tone of Hamlet's speech to his mother hints that he believes himself to be superior to her. He asks her to forgive his preaching, but immediately says '**For in the fatness of these pursy times/Virtue itself of vice must pardon beg**'. It seems to Hamlet that he is a good person who, in these sinful times, must ask sinners such as his mother to allow him to help them.

- Hamlet's love for his father is clear. He idolises the late King, comparing him to Hyperion, Jove, Mars and Mercury. When the Ghost appears, Hamlet is deeply moved by his appearance and the reason for his visitation: '**His form and cause conjoined, preaching to stones/Would make them capable**'.

- Hamlet's killing Polonius is a hugely significant moment in the play:

  1. It will lead to the madness and death of Ophelia, and the vengeful return of Laertes. Ultimately, it will be this single, impulsive murder that will lead to the death of many of the other characters in the play. Through this spontaneous, violent act, Hamlet has sealed his own fate.

  2. The murder of Polonius raises questions about Hamlet's morality. He does not regret the deed and insults the old man, even in death.

  3. It also shows that Hamlet is capable of acting decisively. However, he can only carry out the '**rash and bloody deed**' because it is on the spur of the moment. In the Prayer Scene, Hamlet has time to stop and think.

  4. The murder lends credence to those who claim Hamlet is genuinely mad. There is no logic behind his belief that Claudius is hiding behind the arras, and his reaction to the murder is extremely odd.

Act 4 Scene 2

- Hamlet enters, saying he has hidden Polonius's body.

- Rosencrantz and Guildenstern enter and ask Hamlet to tell them where he has put the corpse, so they may take it to the chapel.

- Hamlet refuses to answer their questions, giving seemingly meaningless replies.

- Hamlet accuses Rosencrantz of being '**a sponge**' who '**soaks up the King's countenance, his rewards, his authorities**'. He warns Rosencrantz that when Claudius has used him he will squeeze him dry again.

- Still refusing to say where Polonius's body is hidden, Hamlet runs away, forcing the others to chase him.

Analysis of Hamlet's character and role in Act 4 Scene 2

- Hamlet is far too clever for Rosencrantz and Guildenstern. Rosencrantz says '**I understand you not, my lord**' and Hamlet replies that he is '**glad of it**'.

- There is some dark humour in Hamlet's behaviour in this scene. Audiences enjoy his contemptuous outwitting of the disloyal pair. The final moments of the scene, in which Hamlet acts like a hunted fox and runs away, liven up an otherwise dark moment. Polonius may have been a fool but he did not deserve to be murdered and to have his corpse hidden away.

Act 4 Scene 3

- Claudius sends for Hamlet in order to discover where he has hidden Polonius's body.

- Hamlet appears to be mad and says that Polonius is '**At supper**'. However, he goes on to explain that Polonius is being eaten rather than eating, and points out that kings and beggars are the same when they die: both are eaten by maggots and worms and eventually a man may eat a fish that has eaten a worm that has eaten the body of a king. Therefore, '**a king may go a progress through the guts of a beggar**'.

- When Claudius asks again where Polonius is, Hamlet says that he is in heaven and that if he cannot be found there by a messenger, Claudius should '**seek him in the other place**'. The implication is that Claudius will be going to hell, not heaven.

- Eventually, Hamlet tells Claudius where the corpse is, saying rather disrespectfully that Polonius's body will soon begin to smell if it is not found.

- Claudius tells Hamlet that he is to go to England and Hamlet merely responds, '**Good**'. When Claudius replies that Hamlet would approve of his '**purposes**' in sending him away if he knew what they were, Hamlet hints that a guardian angel is aware of the plans.

Analysis of Hamlet's character and role in Act 4 Scene 3

- Hamlet's answers to Claudius's questions are not simply nonsensical. He demonstrates his keen wit, relieves the tension of this section of the play by using dark humour, and makes philosophical observations on the nature of death.

- Hamlet's contempt for Claudius is clear. He insults the King by implying he will go to hell and humiliates him by saying he may eventually '**go a progress through the guts of a beggar**'.

- Hamlet reveals that he suspects Claudius's reason for sending him to England.

Act 4 Scene 4

- On his way to the ship, Hamlet sees the Norwegian prince Fortinbras leading an army to Poland.

- Hamlet asks a Norwegian captain why Fortinbras is going to Poland and is astonished to hear that he intends to fight for '**a little patch of ground/That hath in it no profit but the name**'.

- Hamlet waits behind the others and, when he is alone, expresses his shame that he cannot act as decisively as Fortinbras. He reflects that if all a man does is eat and sleep, he is '**A beast, no more**'. Hamlet believes that Fortinbras' quarrel with Poland is not a worthy cause to fight over but that his own cause – his father's murder and his mother's disgrace – is an honourable one. Yet 20,000 men '**Go to their graves like beds**' over a piece of land too small to hold all their corpses, while Hamlet does nothing.

- Hamlet, inspired by Fortinbras, swears he will act: '**O, from this time forth/My thoughts be bloody, or be nothing worth!**'

Analysis of Hamlet's character and role in Act 4 Scene 4

- Hamlet seems more serious, reflective and less angry than he was in the previous scenes.

- His soliloquy is reminiscent of that in Act 2 Scene 2, in which he berated himself for not being able to show as much emotion as the players, and said that rather than act he tends to, '**like a whore, unpack my heart with words**'.

- Despite his self-criticism and his seeming determination, Hamlet swears his thoughts will be bloody, rather than his deeds.

Act 5 Scene 1

- Hamlet has returned from his voyage. He and Horatio enter a graveyard and overhear two gravediggers chatting as they dig.

- Hamlet reflects that the bones in the graveyard were once living people who could have been important in their time but that death has made their rank and station irrelevant: '**Here's fine revolution, an we had the trick to see't**'.

- The gravedigger provides joking replies to Hamlet's questions about the grave, saying first that it is his own (it is, in a way because he is digging it) and then that no man or woman is to be buried in it but '**One that was a woman**'. He does not recognise Hamlet and tells him that he has been a gravedigger since '**the very day that young Hamlet was born**'.

- The gravedigger shows Hamlet the skull of Yorick, a man who was court jester in Hamlet's youth. Hamlet takes the skull and says he knew Yorick well, '**a fellow of infinite jest, of most excellent fancy**'.

- Hamlet reflects that even the mightiest of men eventually come to nothing more than bones and dust: '**Alexander died, Alexander was buried, Alexander returneth into dust**'.

- Hamlet sees Ophelia's funeral procession arriving and is shocked to learn that she is dead: '**What, the fair Ophelia?**' He steps forward and reveals himself: '**This is I, Hamlet the Dane**'.

- Laertes and Hamlet fight briefly before being separated. Hamlet claims to love Ophelia more than '**forty thousand brothers**' and claims he would '**eat a crocodile**' or be buried alive with her to prove it.

- Hamlet cannot understand why Laertes is so angry with him. He leaves, vowing, '**Let Hercules himself do what he may,/The cat will mew, and dog will have his day**'. Horatio follows him.

Analysis of Hamlet's character and role in Act 5 Scene 1

- Hamlet reflects that everyone, no matter how important they may have been in life, is merely reduced to bones that can be thrown around a graveyard by men such as the gravediggers.

- The gravedigger foreshadows Hamlet's imminent death by remarking that he has been digging graves since Hamlet was born. The gravedigger does not care about social class, nor does he recognise the Prince in front of him. This reinforces the idea that Hamlet will soon be another anonymous set of bones in the graveyard.

- Hamlet's reflections on Yorick and Alexander the Great can be seen as reflections on his own death. Hamlet resembles both in a way; he is a prince and a man who loves to make witty jokes. Yet he, too, will come to dust. Hamlet may also be thinking of his father, whose greatness he has praised so lavishly in previous acts. From this point on, there is little mention of the dead King. Has Hamlet achieved some perspective on his father's importance?

- Hamlet claims the title of '**Hamlet the Dane**'. This is significant as it shows he sees himself as the rightful king.

- Hamlet's behaviour at Ophelia's graveside can be interpreted in a number of ways:

  1. He is genuinely distraught and is telling the truth when he says, ' I loved Ophelia. Forty thousand brothers/Could not, with all their quantity of love,/Make up my sum'.

  2. He is disgusted by Laertes' behaviour and wants to show him up by proving how ridiculous and tasteless Laertes' extravagant shows of grief are. In the next act, Hamlet tells Laertes that the '**bravery**' or showiness and hysteria of Laertes' grief sent him, Hamlet, into '**a towering passion**'.

3. He is <u>jealous of Laertes</u> and wants to regain the limelight himself. He asks Laertes, '**Dost thou come here to whine,/To outface me with leaping in her grave?**'

4. Hamlet is <u>so self-absorbed that he cannot accept that Laertes has an equal or greater right to grief</u>. He appears aggrieved that Laertes is angry with him, even though Laertes has every right to be. Hamlet mistreated Ophelia, murdered Polonius and disrupted the funeral.

5. <u>He is mad.</u> Claudius and Gertrude say he is, but it suits them both to claim that. Claudius wants to stop Laertes from fighting Hamlet until he can be sure Laertes will win, and Gertrude wants to excuse her son's behaviour.

Act 5 Scene 2

- Hamlet explains to Horatio what happened when he was sent to England. He stole the letter Rosencrantz and Guildenstern were bringing from Claudius to the King of England, and discovered that it said that his head '**should be struck off**'. He replaced it with a forged letter of his own, saying Rosencrantz and Guildenstern should be executed instead.

- The ship was attacked by pirates and Hamlet was able to return to Denmark.

- Hamlet asks Horatio if he does not now have good reason to kill Claudius. His uncle, after all, killed Hamlet's father, slept with his mother, took Hamlet's crown for himself and then ordered Hamlet's death.

- Hamlet expresses regret for having fought with Laertes and recognises that the other man was, like Hamlet, justified in wanting revenge for his father's death: '**For by the image of my cause I see/ The portraiture of his**'.

- Osric, a rather foolish courtier, enters and tells Hamlet that Claudius has bet on a duel between Hamlet and Laertes. Hamlet teases Osric much as he used to tease Polonius, forcing the courtier to agree with a series of contradictory opinions and mocking his flowery, long-winded speeches.

- Hamlet agrees to the wager and feels confident that he will win. However, he confesses to Horatio that he is troubled: '**But thou wouldst not think how ill all's here about my heart**'. When Horatio offers to have the duel called off, Hamlet refuses, saying he will not be ruled by presentiments of doom. He says death is inevitable and no man can choose the time of it. All one can do is be prepared: '**If it be now, 'tis not to come. If it be not to come, it will be now. If it be not now, yet it will come. The readiness is all**'.

- Hamlet apologies to Laertes for his behaviour in the graveyard, explaining he was not himself. Laertes appears to accept the apology to a certain extent, but still feels he has been dishonoured.

- Hamlet and Laertes begin the duel. Hamlet hits Laertes twice, and Claudius offers Hamlet a drink from a poisoned cup of wine. Hamlet refuses, but Gertrude takes the cup and drinks from it.

- Laertes wounds Hamlet with the poisoned blade, but Hamlet also wounds Laertes.

- Hamlet is shocked to see his mother fall dying, crying that she has been poisoned.

- Laertes admits that Claudius poisoned the wine and the blade that struck Hamlet. Hamlet stabs Claudius with the poisoned sword and forces him to drink the rest of the poisoned wine.

- Hamlet forgives Laertes: '**Heaven make thee free of it! I follow thee.**'

- As he dies, Hamlet asks Horatio to tell the world his story. He orders the distraught Horatio not to take his own life by drinking the rest of the poison. His final request, on hearing that Fortinbras has arrived, is to elect him King of Denmark.

Analysis of Hamlet's character and role in Act 5 Scene 2

- Hamlet's plot to have Rosencrantz and Guildenstern killed in his place shows that he has a ruthless side. He feels no pity for his old school friends, saying: '**They are not near my conscience**'.

- Hamlet appears to believe that everything that is happening to him is his destiny. He was able to forge the letter of execution on the ship because he happened to have his father's royal ring on him to imprint a seal on the wax: '**Why, even in that was heaven ordinant**'. He also accepts the inevitability of death and faces it calmly.

- Hamlet's killing of Claudius supports the idea of chance taking a hand. It is not planned; Hamlet merely seizes the opportunity when it arises.

- Hamlet dies well, reconciled with Laertes and ensuring that Denmark is left in the hands of a capable ruler. Fortinbras comments on his friend's nobility in the final speech of the play: '**he was likely, had he been put on,/To have proved most royal**'.

Claudius

There's such divinity doth hedge a king,
That treason can but peep to what it would ...

Act 1 Scene 2

- Claudius addresses the court, talking about his late brother, his marriage and the threat of invasion from Norway.

- He claims to be mourning his '**dear brother's death**' but has married Gertrude with great haste.

- Claudius sends ambassadors to Norway to speak to Fortinbras' uncle, urging him to rein in his nephew.

- Laertes asks Claudius for permission to go back to France, and Claudius allows it after checking that Polonius agrees.

- Claudius criticises Hamlet for behaving in an immature, unnatural way by mourning so deeply. At the same time, he tries to win the young man over, calling him '**my cousin Hamlet, and my son**'.

Analysis of Claudius's character and role in Act 1 Scene 2

- Claudius has a <u>high opinion of himself</u>, using the royal 'we' when speaking. He uses this even when talking to Hamlet about personal matters, which shows he and his nephew are not close.

- He speaks in a euphuistic style. (This means that he uses ornate language full of literary devices.) This convoluted language makes him appear pompous.

- He is a <u>skilful manipulator</u>, managing to divert attention away from his recent incestuous marriage by focusing on the threat posed by Fortinbras.

- Claudius is a diplomat: he sends ambassadors as a first recourse to deal with young Fortinbras.

- He is not as warlike a man as Old Hamlet.

- Claudius <u>needs the support of the people</u> and knows that Hamlet is popular with them. Hamlet's dislike of his stepfather could be a problem for Claudius.

- Hamlet believes that Claudius is nothing like as noble as his father, claiming the King is '**no more like my father/Than I to Hercules**'. He says his father was '**So excellent a king, that was to this/ Hyperion to a satyr**'. <u>This imagery would strike a chord with the audience and colour their view of Claudius. Old Hamlet, according to his son, was like a god, while Claudius is like a lecherous satyr: half-man, half-goat.</u>

- <u>There is great tension between Claudius and Hamlet, but the audience cannot be sure who to believe at the start of the play.</u> Hamlet loathes Claudius, but we do not know if his assessment of his uncle's character is correct.

Act 1 Scene 5

- The Ghost tells Hamlet that '**the serpent that did sting thy father's life/Now wears his crown**', and urges his son to avenge his murder.

- Hamlet condemns his uncle as a '**smiling, damned villain**'.

Analysis of Claudius's character and role in Act 1 Scene 5

- <u>The Ghost's revelation introduces the main plot of revenge.</u> Hamlet is duty-bound to kill Claudius.

- The Ghost <u>reinforces Hamlet's negative view of Claudius</u>, calling him '**that incestuous, that adulterate beast**'.

Act 2 Scene 2

- Claudius asks Rosencrantz and Guildenstern, old school friends of Hamlet's, to spy on the Prince in order to find out why he is acting so oddly.
- Voltemand and Cornelius return from Norway with good news: Fortinbras has agreed to make peace with Denmark and turn his attention to fighting "**'gainst the Polack**' instead.
- Polonius airs his theory that Hamlet is sick with love for Ophelia. Claudius agrees to his plan to use Ophelia to spy on Hamlet.

Analysis of Claudius's character and role in Act 2 Scene 2

- Claudius is a skilful liar, pretending he has no idea why Hamlet might be acting so strangely.
- Claudius's behaviour highlights the <u>themes of deception and corruption</u>: he knows Hamlet has good reason to be upset and suspects him to be a danger, and he also admires Polonius, calling him '**faithful and honourable**' for deciding to use Ophelia to spy on Hamlet.
- Claudius is a <u>capable leader</u> and has managed to avert war with Norway.

Act 3 Scene 1

- Claudius interviews Rosencrantz and Guildenstern and learns that Hamlet has met the players and is looking forward to a performance that evening.
- Claudius is <u>pleased to hear his nephew is in a better mood</u>.
- When Polonius remarks that it is easy to lie and '**sugar o'er/The devil himself**', Claudius says in an aside, '**How smart a lash that speech doth give my conscience**'. He refers to his guilt as a '**heavy burden**'.
- Claudius and Polonius eavesdrop on Hamlet's conversation with Ophelia.
- Unlike Polonius, Claudius is not at all sure that Hamlet is driven mad by love. He is <u>worried by his nephew's behaviour</u> and determines to send him '**with speed to England**' as he believes '**Madness in great ones must not unwatched go**'.

Analysis of Claudius's character and role in Act 2 Scene 3

- Claudius is a <u>good judge of human nature</u> and is <u>shrewd</u> enough to know that Hamlet is neither lovesick nor genuinely mad.
- Claudius feels no qualms about spying on Hamlet or using Ophelia as bait.
- Claudius shows that he <u>feels guilt over his brother's murder</u>.

Act 3 Scene 2

- Claudius is <u>startled and upset by the content of the play</u>.
- He calls for light and leaves abruptly.
- Rosencrantz and Guildenstern tell Hamlet that Claudius is '**marvellous distempered**'.

Analysis of Claudius's character and role in Act 3 Scene 2

- <u>Claudius's behaviour during the performance of the play is a key moment</u> in *Hamlet*. Hamlet knows for certain that the King is guilty.

Act 3 Scene 3

- Claudius instructs Rosencrantz and Guildenstern, telling them to accompany Hamlet.

- Alone, Claudius reveals once again that he has a conscience, but this time he is more open about his sins, saying '**my offence is rank! It smells to heaven**'.

- Claudius knows it is unlikely he will be forgiven as his sin '**hath the primal eldest curse upon't**'. In other words, he has killed his brother just as Cain killed Abel.

- It is guilt and fear of hell that drive Claudius to pray; he is not fully repentant. He admits that while his words '**fly up**' to heaven, his thoughts '**remain below**'.

Analysis of Claudius's character and role in Act 3 Scene 3

- In the Prayer Scene, we see Claudius's humanity once again but – more importantly – it is guilt and fear of hell that drive Claudius to pray; he is not fully repentant. He admits that while his words '**fly up**' to heaven, his thoughts '**remain below**'. He is unwilling to renounce what he has gained as a result of his crime: '**My crown, mine own ambition, and my Queen**'. He wonders, '**May one be pardoned and retain th'offence?**'

- Dramatically, this is a hugely significant moment in the play. At last, Hamlet has the means, the motivation and the will to kill his uncle, but ironically he does not do so because he worries that his uncle may go to heaven if he is killed while at prayer.

- It is interesting to note that Claudius acknowledges a time will come when he has to pay for his sins, albeit after he is dead. Immediate, earthly pleasures are more important to him than the promise of heavenly bliss.

Act 4 Scene 1

- Gertrude lies to Claudius, telling him that Hamlet is '**Mad as the sea and wind**,' and that he has killed Polonius.

- Claudius leaps to the conclusion that he could have been the intended victim. He fears Hamlet, and claims the Prince's movements should be curtailed as '**His liberty is full of threats to all**'.

- Claudius declares that he will send Hamlet to England immediately: '**The sun no sooner shall the mountains touch/But we will ship him hence**'.

- Claudius realises he must use all his diplomatic expertise to cover up the truth behind Polonius's murder. He is worried that he will be implicated.

- He orders Rosencrantz and Guildenstern to find Polonius's body and bring it to the chapel.

Analysis of Claudius's character and role in Act 4 Scene 1

- Claudius becomes increasingly worried by Hamlet's behaviour.

- His concerns are selfish: he fears he will be tainted by association with Polonius's death: '**It will be laid to us**'. The pressure on Claudius is mounting.

Act 4 Scene 3

- Claudius says that he has ordered his people to find Polonius's body.

- He worries that Hamlet is a dangerous man who cannot be contained because he is '**loved of the distracted multitude**'.

- Hamlet enters, and Claudius tells him he must go to England.

- When he is alone, Claudius reveals that he has arranged for Hamlet to be killed as soon as he reaches England.

Analysis of Claudius's character and role in Act 4 Scene 3

- Claudius is clever and knows that Hamlet is popular with the people. He makes a smart political move in sending him away while ensuring that his '**sudden sending … away must seem/Deliberate pause**'.

- Claudius is ruthless and devious. He has arranged for Hamlet to be killed, but he will take none of the blame as it will be done in England.

- Claudius claims to love Gertrude, but at the same time he is willing to go behind her back and arrange to have her beloved son murdered in such a way that '**even his mother shall uncharge the practice/And call it accident**'. We have to wonder, therefore, how much Claudius really loves his wife.

Act 4 Scene 5

- Claudius sees Ophelia's madness for himself.

- He appears genuinely upset and instructs his servants to '**Follow her close**'.

- Claudius is disingenuous as he says, '**O Gertrude, Gertrude,/When sorrows come they come not single spies/But in battalions. First, her father slain;/Next, your son gone, and he most violent author/Of his own just remove; the people muddied … poor Ophelia/Divided from herself and her fair judgement …/Her brother is in secret come from France**' as if he had nothing to do with any of these events.

- Laertes returns from France with an angry mob at his heels, demanding justice for Polonius's murder. Claudius remains calm in the face of this threat, telling Gertrude to let Laertes approach him as '**There's such divinity doth hedge a king,/That reason can but peep to what it would**'.

- Claudius asks Laertes if, in his rage, he intends to kill both friends and enemies without stopping to check which is which. He assures Laertes that he – Claudius – is '**guiltless**' and that he will soon uncover the truth of the matter.

- He flatters Laertes, saying that his more reasoned speech is '**Like a good child and a true gentleman**'.

Analysis of Claudius's character and role in Act 4 Scene 5

- Claudius shows <u>intelligence</u> and a certain <u>courage</u> in the way he deals with the angry Laertes. However, the audience cannot miss the irony of <u>Claudius's claim that God will protect him, as he is the anointed king.</u> Claudius is only king because he killed his brother, and he cannot reconcile himself with God, as he is unable to repent.

Act 4 Scene 7

- Claudius tells Laertes that Hamlet not only killed Polonius but also wishes to kill Claudius.

- He gives the dubious Laertes two reasons why he has not brought Hamlet to justice for the murder: he loves Gertrude so much that he could not bear to hurt her, and the young Prince is adored by the '**general gender**'. However, he assures Laertes that he is not taking the affair lightly: '**You must not think/That we are made of stuff so flat and dull/That we can let our beard be shook with danger,/And think it pastime**'.

- A messenger arrives, and Claudius learns that Hamlet has returned to Denmark. The king is faced with a problem as he must control the hot-headed Laertes. He asks, '**Will you be ruled by me**?' and quickly comes up with a plan to further his own ends. He uses the opportunity to manipulate Laertes, asking '**was your father dear to you**?' and '**What would you undertake/To show yourself your father's son in deed/More than in words?**'

- Claudius comes up with a plan for Laertes to challenge Hamlet to a duel and to cunningly switch a blunted blade for a sharp one so that he may kill Hamlet during the fight. Laertes eagerly agrees and says he will tip the scales even further by putting a deadly poison on the tip of the blade. Claudius plans to poison a cup of wine so that even if Hamlet should escape Laertes' '**venomed stuck**', he will be killed when he '**calls for drink**'.

- Gertrude enters with news of Ophelia's death, and Claudius is annoyed, fearing that Laertes might be provoked into ignoring his plans: '**How much I had to do to calm his rage!/Now fear I this will give it start again**'.

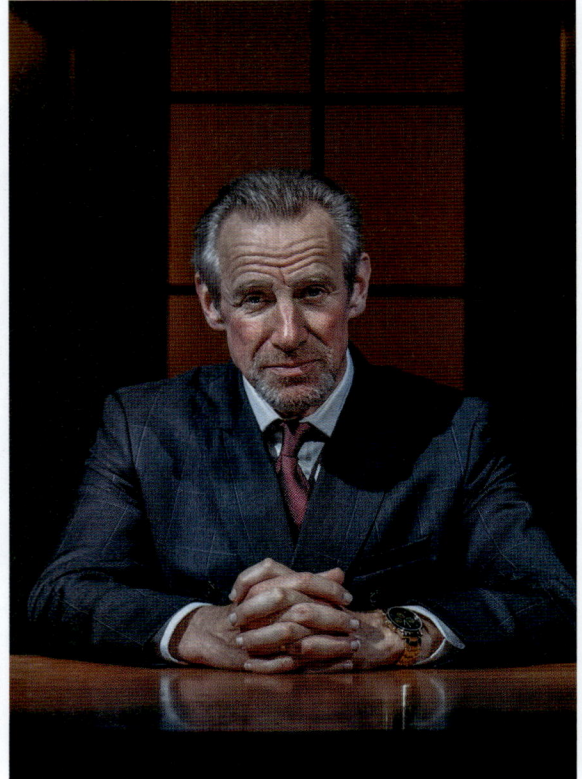

Analysis of Claudius's character and role in Act 4 Scene 7

- Claudius is <u>manipulative, opportunistic and clever</u>. He turns Laertes' rage to his advantage, deflecting the young man's rage from himself and onto Hamlet.

- He is a <u>good judge of human nature</u>, ensuring that Laertes retains a righteous anger but does not become so inflamed with fury that he is out of control.

- Claudius is a <u>cold and calculating man</u> who has no sympathy for Laertes' grief and is unmoved by Ophelia's death. His only concern is how such events will affect his plans.

Act 5 Scene 1

- Hamlet and Laertes fight at Ophelia's graveside and Claudius orders those watching to '**Pluck them asunder**'.

- Hamlet tells Laertes that he loved Ophelia but Claudius is quick to intervene: '**O, he is mad, Laertes**'.

- He urges Laertes to remain patient and promises, '**This grave shall have a living monument**,' before long.

Analysis of Claudius's character and role in Act 5 Scene 1

- There are two possible reasons for Claudius telling Laertes that Hamlet is mad. On the one hand, he may be trying to keep the outraged Laertes calm lest he attack Hamlet in a time and place where the outcome is not certain. On the other hand, he may be trying to keep Laertes from reconciling with Hamlet. If Laertes believes that Hamlet genuinely loved Ophelia, he may not hate him with such intensity. Whichever is the case, the graveyard scene shows once again that Claudius is a quick-witted, cunning manipulator.

Act 5 Scene 2

- As the fencing match is about to begin, Claudius places a pearl in Hamlet's wine cup, saying it is a prize. However, the pearl contains poison.

- Claudius tries to convince Hamlet to have a drink during the match, but Hamlet refuses. Gertrude takes the cup and drinks, despite Claudius calling on her to stop. Claudius knows she has drunk from '**the poisoned cup**,' and that it is too late to do anything about it.

- Gertrude collapses and Claudius assures the watchers that she has merely fainted: '**She swoons to see them bleed**'. However, his attempt at deception is foiled by Gertrude, who cries a warning about the poisoned cup to Hamlet before she dies.

- Hamlet stabs Claudius with the poisoned blade after Laertes reveals the other part of Claudius's scheme. Claudius calls, '**O yet defend me friends! I am but hurt**'. However, Hamlet forces the King to swallow the rest of the poisoned wine: '**Here, thou incestuous, murderous, damned Dane,/ Drink off this potion**'. Claudius dies.

Analysis of Claudius's character and role in Act 5 Scene 2

- Claudius's plan to use the poisoned wine as a back-up in case Laertes should fail to kill Hamlet is a risky one and it adds another layer of dramatic excitement to an already tense scene. The audience is well aware that someone else could drink from the cup, as Gertrude soon demonstrates.

- Claudius's most despicable act is his half-hearted attempt to stop Gertrude drinking the poisoned wine and his desperate efforts to cover up the fact that she is dying. He is self-serving, manipulative and deceitful to the end. It seems unlikely that he ever truly loved Gertrude.

- The audience is likely to agree wholeheartedly with Laertes' comment on Claudius's death: '**He is justly served**'.

Gertrude

O Hamlet, speak no more!
Thou turn'st mine eyes into my very soul,
And there I see such black and grained spots
As will not leave their tinct.

Act 1 Scene 2

- Gertrude urges Hamlet to stop mourning his father and to accept his stepfather: '**Good Hamlet, cast thy nighted colour off,/And let thine eye look like a friend on Denmark**'.
- She explains that it is natural that '**all that lives must die,/Passing through nature to eternity**'.
- Hamlet responds explosively to her question, saying his grief is not a show but is a reflection of his true feeling.
- Gertrude begs Hamlet to remain in Denmark and not to return to Wittenberg. He agrees, but only to please his mother.

Analysis of Gertrude's character and role in Act 1 Scene 2

Gertrude's behaviour is open to a number of different interpretations:

1. She is naïve and does not realise that marrying her brother-in-law so soon after her husband's death is in bad taste. (However, in Act 2 Scene 2, Gertrude says that the main reason for Hamlet's behaviour is his father's death and her '**o'er-hasty**' marriage to Claudius.)

2. She is insensitive and does not take Hamlet's grief for his father's death into consideration.

3. She is in a difficult position because her new husband and her son – both of whom she loves – are at odds with one another.

4. She is a typical Elizabethan wife and mother. She is not in a strong position and must be led by her powerful husband.

5. She is a weak character, unable to do anything but echo her husband's sentiments and afraid to stand up to her son when he speaks harshly to her.

Act 2 Scene 2

- Gertrude and Claudius greet Rosencrantz and Guildenstern, whom Claudius has summoned to spy on Hamlet.

- Gertrude tells Rosencrantz and Guildenstern that Hamlet '**hath much talked**' of them and that they are his greatest friends. She promises them a handsome reward for their cooperation. The two men leave.

- Polonius enters and says he has found '**The very cause of Hamlet's lunacy**', but Gertrude believes she already knows the reason: '**I doubt it is no other but the main –/ His father's death, and our o'er-hasty marriage**'.

- Polonius begins a long-winded explanation of the reason for Hamlet's madness and Gertrude impatiently tells him to get to the point: '**More matter with less art**'.

- Gertrude is surprised to learn of Hamlet's love letters to Ophelia and begins to wonder if he has gone mad because Polonius ordered Ophelia to have nothing to do with him.

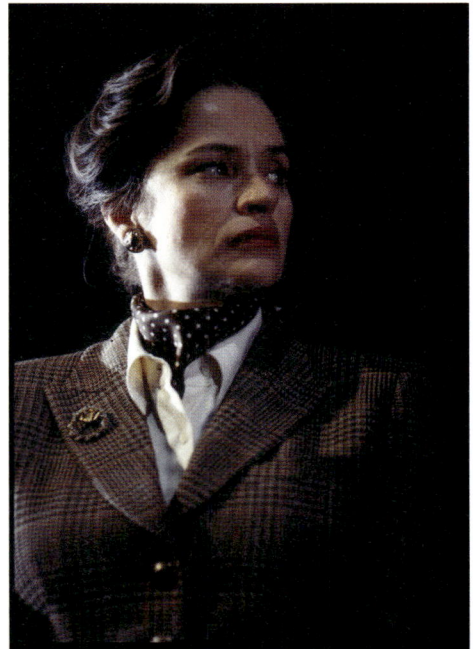

Analysis of Gertrude's character and role in Act 2 Scene 2

- Once again, Gertrude agrees with Claudius and supports his decision to have Rosencrantz and Guildenstern spy on Hamlet. Is she merely a concerned mother or is her behaviour here morally questionable? Later, she goes along with Polonius's plan to use Ophelia as bait for Hamlet, which also paints her in a rather negative light.

- Gertrude makes it clear to Claudius that she believes the reason for Hamlet's odd behaviour is grief at his father's death and anger at her swift remarriage.

- Gertrude loves Hamlet but may not know him as well as she thinks. She thinks that Rosencrantz and Guildenstern are his great friends, but Hamlet, while he greets them warmly, sees through them straight away and sends them to their deaths later in the play without a qualm. She is also surprised to learn of her son's declarations of love for Ophelia.

Act 3 Scene 1

- Gertrude and Claudius question Rosencrantz and Guildenstern about their meeting with Hamlet. Gertrude asks if they managed to get Hamlet to agree to take part in any pastime and Rosencrantz replies that Hamlet was delighted to hear of the arrival of the players.

- At Claudius's request, Gertrude leaves so he and Polonius can spy on Hamlet as he talks to Ophelia. Gertrude says, '**I shall obey you**' and tells Ophelia that she hopes her '**good beauties be the happy cause/Of Hamlet's wildness**' and that she will manage to bring him around to his old self again.

Analysis of Gertrude's character and role in Act 3 Scene 1

- Gertrude is a loving mother who cares for her son and hopes he may soon be himself again.

- Gertrude is also an unquestioningly obedient wife. She does exactly as Claudius asks.

- She speaks kindly to Ophelia and appears to approve of Hamlet's love for her.

Act 3 Scene 2

- Gertrude invites Hamlet to sit with her during the play but he snubs her, sitting with Ophelia instead.

- When the Player Queen declares that she will never marry, should her husband die, Hamlet asks Gertrude what she thinks. She replies, '**The lady protests too much**'.

- After Claudius has walked out on the play, Gertrude sends Rosencrantz and Guildenstern to Hamlet with a message asking him to come to her room. She is, they tell Hamlet, '**in most great affliction of spirit**' and '**struck … into amazement**' by his behaviour.

- Shortly afterwards, Gertrude sends Polonius with the same message because Hamlet has still not been to see her.

Analysis of Gertrude's character and role in Act 3 Scene 2

- Gertrude's reply to Hamlet's question about the Player Queen can be interpreted in two different ways. In Shakespeare's time, '**protest**' meant to vow or promise. Gertrude's comment, therefore, means that the lady is overdoing her pledges never to remarry. She may be saying that such promises are ridiculous, thereby defending her own decision to marry so soon after her husband's death, or she may be simply saying that the Player Queen is losing credibility by overacting and making such wildly elaborate vows. Whether she is commenting on the content or style of the speech, Gertrude does not appear to think very much of it and it certainly doesn't have the effect on her that Hamlet clearly hoped it would when he posed his question. Gertrude remains cool or unaware, depending on your viewpoint.

Act 3 Scene 4

- Gertrude agrees to Polonius hiding behind the arras to eavesdrop on her conversation with Hamlet.

- Gertrude tries to talk to Hamlet about how he has offended his father, meaning Claudius, but Hamlet replies that she has offended his father, meaning Old Hamlet. Gertrude is taken aback by Hamlet's rudeness and says she will send for those to whom he is more likely to speak.

- Hamlet forces Gertrude to stay put, saying that he will force her to see herself for what she is. Alarmed, Gertrude cries for help, and when Polonius responds from behind the arras, Hamlet stabs him. Gertrude is appalled at this '**rash and bloody deed**' and is shocked when Hamlet compares it to her killing the King and marrying his brother.

- Gertrude is forced to endure another verbal attack from Hamlet. He shows her pictures of Old Hamlet and Claudius side by side, asks how she can possibly compare them and accuses her of being lustful. Gertrude claims that Hamlet has made her see '**black and grained spots**' on her soul. She begs him to speak no more and says his words are '**like daggers**'.

- Gertrude does not see the Ghost when it appears and believes that Hamlet is hallucinating: '**This [is] the very coinage of your brain**'.

- When Hamlet urges her to repent for her sins and not to sleep with Claudius again, Gertrude appears to acquiesce. Certainly, she does not argue with her son and, when he tells her to keep their conversation secret, she agrees.

- Hamlet asks Gertrude if she knew he was to be sent to England and she admits she did but had forgotten about it.

Analysis of Gertrude's character and role in Act 3 Scene 4

- There is a reversal of the normal parent-child relationship in this scene. Hamlet lectures Gertrude and forces her to listen to a litany of her sins.

- Gertrude is frightened by Hamlet's behaviour, fearing that he might mean to harm her.

- Gertrude appears genuinely bewildered when Hamlet talks about killing a king. Some critics have wondered if she was complicit in the murder of her husband, but her words here seem to indicate she knew nothing about it.

- Gertrude's reaction to Hamlet's verbal attack may merely be an effort to appease him, or she may be truly repentant and appalled by her behaviour. It would be understandable if Gertrude were to go along with Hamlet rather than argue with him. After all, he has just killed Polonius and his body lies on the floor while Hamlet berates her. She has also seen her son talking to the air, claiming to be speaking to a ghost she could not see. However, her words seem heartfelt and she does more than simply agree with what her son says. She is distressed and cries, '**O Hamlet, thou has cleft my heart in twain**' when he tells her to repent. On the other hand, Gertrude stays with Claudius despite all that Hamlet has told her. Is this because she is not as sorry for her actions as she claims? She does keep Hamlet's secret, as she said she would. Gertrude's behaviour is contradictory at times and it is up to each reader or audience member to make up their own mind about her.

Act 4 Scene 1

- Gertrude tells Claudius that Hamlet has killed Polonius and hidden the body.
- She claims that Hamlet is '**Mad as the sea and wind**' and that '**he weeps for what is done**'.

Analysis of Gertrude's character and role in Act 4 Scene 1

- Gertrude tries to protect Hamlet. She tells Claudius that he killed Polonius in '**a lawless fit**' of madness.
- Gertrude lies for Hamlet, claiming that he regretted killing Polonius and wept when he realised what he had done.

Act 4 Scene 5

- Gertrude does not want to speak to Ophelia, who has gone mad. She agrees to do so when Horatio points out that if Ophelia is not dealt with, she may cause rumours and gossip.
- In an aside, Gertrude admits to having a '**sick soul**' and feeling guilty. She is anxious and paranoid, seeing disaster around every corner.
- When Laertes leads a mob into the castle, Gertrude tries to calm Laertes and quickly assures him that Claudius had nothing to do with Polonius's murder.

Analysis of Gertrude's character and role in Act 4 Scene 5

- It says little for Gertrude's strength of character that she does not want to see Ophelia now that the young woman is distraught and mentally unwell. In Act 2 Scene 1, Gertrude expressed the hope that Ophelia and Hamlet could be a couple, but now she turns her back on Ophelia, only agreeing to see her when Horatio suggests it would be politic to do so.
- Gertrude is still a loyal wife to Claudius. She supports him when he is challenged by Laertes.

Act 4 Scene 7

- Gertrude interrupts Claudius and Laertes as they plot to kill Hamlet. She tells them that Ophelia has drowned. Apparently Ophelia climbed onto a tree to hang a garland of flowers but the branch broke and she fell into the stream. She floated for a time, seemingly oblivious and singing but then her dress became soaked and '**Pulled the poor wretch from her melodious lay/To muddy death**'.

- Gertrude and Claudius follow Laertes when he leaves, in order to calm his rage.

Analysis of Gertrude's character and role in Act 4 Scene 7

- Gertrude's description of Ophelia's tragic but romantic death contrasts sharply with the brutality and ignobility of the scheme Claudius and Laertes had been discussing moments before her arrival.

- Later in the play, it is suggested that Ophelia took her own life. Gertrude's account may not be wholly accurate but rather an attempt to keep the worst from Laertes, perhaps out of sympathy.

- Some have asked if Gertrude witnessed the event she describes so poetically and, if so, why she did nothing to save Ophelia. There are elements of her story, undoubtedly, which make it seem less than credible.

Act 5 Scene 1

- Gertrude attends Ophelia's funeral, saying she wished Ophelia and Hamlet had married so she could have scattered flowers on their wedding bed instead of Ophelia's grave.

- When Hamlet and Laertes fight, Gertrude claims that it is '**mere madness**' that causes Hamlet to behave this way and he will soon be as calm and '**as patient as the female dove**'.

Analysis of Gertrude's character and role in Act 5 Scene 1

- Again, Gertrude's praise of Ophelia and her wish that to see Ophelia and Hamlet married seems at odds with her earlier dismissal of the young woman. Is Gertrude so weak and lacking in moral fibre that she wanted nothing to do with Ophelia when she was mad and troublesome?

- Gertrude continues to defend Hamlet, blaming his actions on madness, even though he is far from mad.

Act 5 Scene 2

- Gertrude supports Hamlet as he fights, giving him her handkerchief to wipe his brow.

- For once, Gertrude does not do as she is told by her husband and drinks a toast to Hamlet, not realising the cup is poisoned. She politely disobeys Claudius's command, '**Gertrude, do not drink**', but she disobeys it nonetheless: '**I will, my lord, I pray you, pardon me**.'

- Gertrude's final words are to say that she is not in a faint, as Claudius claims, but poisoned by the drink.

Analysis of Gertrude's character and role in Act 5 Scene 2

- Some critics believe that Gertrude knew the cup was poisoned, which is why she stubbornly disobeyed Claudius. She may have thought that by drinking it, she would spare Hamlet that same fate.

- Another interpretation is that Gertrude pays the ultimate price for misjudging the man she has married. He was plotting to kill the son she loved so dearly, and even tried to cover up the cause of her collapse: '**She swoons to see them bleed**'.

- Gertrude is a shadowy and often contradictory character. Ultimately, it is up to a director to decide how to portray her: innocent victim; naïve and shallow woman; adulteress and accessory to murder, or a loving wife and mother torn between the two men she loves and unstintingly supportive of both.

Polonius

Give every man thine ear but few thy voice.

Act 1 Scene 2

- Claudius asks Polonius whether he is happy to allow Laertes to return to France. Polonius says that he was reluctant but was won over by Laertes' constant pleading. He asks Claudius to agree to let Laertes go.

Analysis of Polonius's character and role in Act 1 Scene 2

- Polonius has a role in the Danish court. Claudius shows him some respect by checking to see if he has given permission for Laertes to return to France before he, Claudius, agrees to it.
- Polonius appears to care for his son and says he is sorry to see him go, but he also wants the young man to be happy, which is why he gives his '**hard consent**'.

Act 1 Scene 3

- Polonius is surprised to see that Laertes has not yet left for France and he urges his son to hurry. They have said their goodbyes already, but Polonius cannot resist taking the opportunity to give Laertes some more advice, even though he delays him by doing so.

- Polonius tells Laertes to behave prudently, to keep his friends close, to listen more than he speaks, to stay out of fights if possible, but to make his opponents wary of him if he must fight, to dress tastefully but not showily, to avoid borrowing or lending money and, most importantly of all, to be true to himself.

- Laertes takes his leave, reminding Ophelia to heed his advice. Alone with Ophelia, Polonius asks what Laertes said to her. Ophelia tells him he gave her advice about Hamlet. Immediately, Polonius gives his opinion on Hamlet's interest in Ophelia. He dismisses Ophelia's claim that Hamlet cares for her: '**Affection, pooh! You speak like a green girl**' and says Hamlet's vows of love are merely '**springes to catch woodcocks**'.

- Polonius tells Ophelia to have less to do with Hamlet and to remember that the Prince walks with '**a larger tether**' than Ophelia may. He concludes by deciding that Ophelia should not spend any time alone with Hamlet, and she meekly agrees.

Analysis of Polonius's character and role in Act 1 Scene 3

- Polonius is rather pompous and loves the sound of his own voice. Having told Laertes to hurry aboard the ship, he delays him with a long speech on how the young man should behave in France.

- Polonius's advice is sound, even if a lot of it is rather obvious and would have been clichéd even in the sixteenth century.

- There is some irony and hypocrisy in the advice Polonius gives Laertes. For example, he tells his son to '**Give every man thine ear but few thy voice**' and not to rush to judgement. However, Polonius speaks far more than he listens and will soon rush to judgement on the reason for Hamlet's madness.

- Polonius has a cynical view of love. He cannot believe for a moment that Hamlet truly cares for Ophelia, and he assumes that his words of love are merely attempts to lure Ophelia into bed.

Act 2 Scene 1

- Polonius instructs his servant, Reynaldo, to go to Laertes in France and give him money and letters. He also tells Reynaldo to spread rumours about Laertes among those he mixes with, saying that he is a gambler, drinker, fighter, uses bad language and visits prostitutes. Polonius hopes that these rumours will prompt those Laertes socialises with to tell stories of him behaving badly.

- Polonius's instructions to Reynaldo are long and rambling and he loses track of his thoughts part way through, saying, '**By the mass, I was about to say something. Where did I leave?**'

- Reynaldo leaves and Ophelia enters. She is distressed and tells Polonius that Hamlet visited her in his room looking '**As if he had been loosed out of hell/To speak of horrors**'. Polonius immediately jumps to the conclusion that Hamlet has been driven mad by unrequited love. He announces that he will go straight to Claudius with the news.

- Polonius fears he misjudged Hamlet's feelings for Ophelia and now believes that Hamlet does care for Ophelia after all.

Analysis of Polonius's character and role in Act 2 Scene 1

- Polonius is unscrupulous and deceitful. He sends his servant to spy on Laertes and spread false rumours about him to see if he has been misbehaving.

- Again, Polonius's long-winded speech makes him appear foolish. He loses track of what he is saying at one stage, and he gives far too many examples of the sort of things Reynaldo should say and the responses he might receive.

- Polonius has a double standard when it comes to the behaviour of young men and young women. He expects Ophelia to be chaste and to keep herself aloof from Hamlet, but he assumes young men will gamble and visit brothels.

- Polonius's hypocrisy is clear in this scene. In his earlier advice to Laertes he said, '**This above all – to thine own self be true**', but now he is engaged in such devious behaviour that even his servant is reluctant to dishonour Laertes by spreading such lies. Polonius does not seem to see how immoral his behaviour is or how it shows an odd relationship with his son. On the one hand, Polonius appears to care for Laertes, but on the other hand he clearly does not trust him. The father-son relationship is a microcosm of the corruption and intrigue in the Danish court.

- Polonius values his position at court more than his own daughter's happiness. Ophelia is distressed by Hamlet's visit to her room, but Polonius offers her no words of comfort, nor does he apologise for forcing her to stop seeing Hamlet. Instead, he immediately decides to go to Claudius with the news.

Act 2 Scene 2

- Polonius tells Claudius and Gertrude that he has found the reason for Hamlet's madness. He begins to speak in his usual, rambling way while declaring that '**brevity is the soul of wit**'. Impatiently, Gertrude tells him to get to the point: '**More matter with less art**'.

- Polonius reads the letter Hamlet sent to Ophelia and explains that he warned his daughter that '**This must not be**' as Hamlet is of a higher social class than she. Polonius believes that Hamlet has been driven mad by Ophelia's rejection. He is convinced he is right and asks Claudius if he has ever been wrong in the past.

- Polonius hatches a plan to 'loose' Ophelia on Hamlet, using her as bait to trap him into conversation while he and Claudius spy on the couple from behind an arras.

- Hamlet enters, and Polonius asks Gertrude and Claudius to leave him alone with the young Prince.

- Hamlet mocks Polonius but the old man is not astute enough to see what his happening. He believes Hamlet's strange comments are merely further proof of his madness. Polonius takes his leave, plotting to 'contrive the means of meeting between him and my daughter'.

- Later, when the players arrive, Polonius comes to tell Hamlet the news. Hamlet continues to mock him, comparing Polonius to Jephthah, a character in the Old Testament who sacrificed his daughter to please God. Polonius does not understand what Hamlet means, and only picks up on the fact that the young Prince is still talking about Ophelia.

- Polonius watches a little of the players' speeches and then leaves to show them to their rooms.

Analysis of Polonius's character and role in Act 2 Scene 2

- Polonius's foolishness and verbosity are clear when he rambles pointlessly while supposedly telling Claudius and Gertrude why Hamlet has gone mad. There is great irony in his saying 'brevity is the soul of wit' and not realising that he is far from brief, so much so that Gertrude has to interrupt his tedious speech to tell him to get to the point.

- Polonius is sycophantic. He hurries to tell Claudius all about Hamlet, and makes sure the King and Queen know he did not allow Ophelia to suppose she was worthy of Hamlet's attentions: 'Lord Hamlet is a prince out of thy star'.

- Polonius puts self-interest before his daughter's happiness. Not only does he forbid her to see Hamlet, but he also plans to use her as bait to trap the young Prince into speaking freely and revealing the reason for his odd behaviour.

- Polonius may once have been a better politician and judge of character than he is now. He is confident that he is right about Hamlet and when he asks Claudius if he has ever known him to be wrong, the King admits that he has not. However, Polonius is ageing and that may account for some of his loss of mental acuity.

Act 3 Scene 1

- Polonius agrees with Rosencrantz that Hamlet was pleased to see the actors arrive and he adds that Hamlet was most keen for Claudius and Gertrude to attend the performance that night.

- Claudius sends Gertrude away and Polonius tells Ophelia how to behave when Hamlet arrives. Polonius and Claudius hide behind the arras and listen to Hamlet's conversation with Ophelia, in which he verbally attacks her and tells her to take herself to a nunnery to avoid sinning.

- Hamlet leaves, and Polonius and Claudius emerge from their hiding place. Polonius ignores Ophelia, apart from telling her that she '**need not tell us what Lord Hamlet said;/We heard it all**'. He advises Claudius to have Gertrude send for Hamlet to try to find out why he is behaving so oddly. Polonius plans to hide and listen to the conversation between mother and son.

Analysis of Polonius's character and role in Act 3 Scene 1

- Polonius is <u>devious and immoral</u>. He sees nothing wrong in using his daughter to spy on Hamlet and plots with Gertrude to spy on Hamlet again.

- <u>Although Ophelia is distressed by her conversation with Hamlet, Polonius offers her no comfort whatsoever.</u> His only concern is how he might help Claudius get to the bottom of Hamlet's odd behaviour.

Act 3 Scene 2

- Polonius watches the play. He notices when Hamlet wants to sit with Ophelia rather than Gertrude, and comments on it to Claudius: '**O, ho, do you mark that?**'

- After the play, Polonius tells Hamlet that Gertrude wants to speak to him in her room. Hamlet mocks Polonius, forcing him to agree to a series of contradictory observations about a cloud, first saying it is like a camel, then a weasel, then a whale.

Analysis of Polonius's character and role in Act 3 Scene 2

- Polonius's <u>sycophantic agreement with everything Hamlet says provides some comedic relief at a tense moment in the play</u>. He appears a foolish and ridiculous old man and it is hard to take him seriously. However, it must be remembered <u>that his meddling has caused great harm to his daughter</u> and will ultimately cost him his life and Ophelia her sanity.

Act 3 Scene 3

- After the performance of the play, Polonius tells Claudius that he plans to hide behind the arras in Gertrude's room to eavesdrop on her conversation with Hamlet. Polonius says that he agrees with Claudius that a mother cannot be impartial and therefore it would be a good idea to have a third party present to report back.

Analysis of Polonius's character and role in Act 3 Scene 3

- It was Polonius, not Claudius, who suggested hiding in Gertrude's room and listening to her conversation with Hamlet. He <u>fawningly flatters</u> Claudius by saying that it was his idea: '**And, as you said – and wisely was it said**'.

Act 3 Scene 4

- Polonius instructs Gertrude on how to speak to Hamlet when he arrives. He tells her to be firm with her son and '**Tell him his pranks have been too broad to bear with**'.

- Polonius says he will '**sconce me e'en here**' and he hides behind the arras as Hamlet arrives.

- Gertrude is frightened by Hamlet's wild manner and when she cries for help, Polonius repeats her cry from his hiding place. Hamlet hears the noise and stabs through the arras, killing Polonius.

Analysis of Polonius's character and role in Act 3 Scene 4

- Polonius <u>meddles until the end</u>, instructing Gertrude how to deal with her own son. His persistent interference proves his undoing.

- <u>There is an irony in Polonius saying he will be silent behind the arras</u>. He has never managed to stay silent for long, and indeed he proves incapable of doing so now. Hamlet silences him for good when he stabs him.

- <u>Polonius's death has wide-ranging effects</u>. Ophelia is driven mad when she discovers that the man she loves has killed her father, and Laertes arrives home from France vowing to seek vengeance on Hamlet for the murder. Polonius's death sets in motion a chain of events ending with the death of most of the major characters in the play.

Ophelia

O, what a noble mind is here o'erthrown!
The courtier's, soldier's, scholar's eye, tongue, sword,
Th'expectancy and rose of the fair state

Act 1 Scene 3

- First Laertes and then Polonius lecture Ophelia on her relationship with Hamlet.

- Laertes tells her that Hamlet thinks their relationship is '**The perfume and suppliance of a minute./No more**'. He claims Hamlet is too important to the royal court to be permitted to marry a girl of his choosing.

- Ophelia says, '**I shall the effect of this good lesson keep**'.

- However, Ophelia shows that she has some spirit when she warns Laertes against telling her to behave herself while he, '**the primrose path of dalliance treads**'. In other words, Ophelia thinks Laertes may be a hypocrite: telling her to be virtuous while he is misbehaving.

- Polonius also warns Ophelia against taking Hamlet seriously. She obediently tells her father the truth about Hamlet, admitting that he has '**made many tenders/Of his affection to me**'. She believes that Hamlet loves her but her father disabuses her of this notion. Like Laertes, he is convinced that Hamlet simply wants to sleep with Ophelia and that all his words of love are merely '**springes to catch woodcocks**' – designed to lure Ophelia into bed with him.

- Ophelia does not argue with her father at this point.

Analysis of Ophelia's character and role in Act 1 Scene 3

- Ophelia is an intelligent young woman who has enough spirit in her nature to warn her brother against hypocrisy.

- However, although she has some spirit and a mind of her own, Ophelia is essentially a typically passive and obedient Elizabethan woman. Some critics point out that Ophelia is young and unmarried and, as such, is duty-bound to obey her father and brother. Another view is that she is also a rather undeveloped character who allows herself to be ruled by the men in her life, unlike stronger heroines such as Juliet in *Romeo and Juliet* or Portia in *The Merchant of Venice*. This may explain why she seems to so meekly and obediently accept her brother's hurtful assertion that Hamlet does not take their relationship seriously and that she is not a worthy partner for him.

- Ophelia is a kind-hearted girl who loves her father and brother and wants to do as they say.

- Ophelia might understandably doubt Hamlet's love for her after her brother and father have told her that the Prince was merely toying with her.

- Ophelia's language shows how dependent she is on the men in her life to give her guidance. Of course, this was considered right and proper at the time the play was written! When Polonius asks Ophelia if she believes that Hamlet loves her, she meekly answers '**I do not know, my lord, what I should think**'. At the end of Polonius's lecture on the nature of men and his stern instruction to her not to spend any time with Hamlet from now on, Ophelia simply says, '**I shall obey, my lord**'.

- Ophelia is not permitted to voice her true feelings and can only meekly protest that she believes Hamlet loves her before this notion is shot down. It is only when she goes mad later in the play that Ophelia is given a voice, albeit a rather disturbed and disturbing one.

Act 2 Scene 1

- Ophelia tells Polonius that Hamlet visited her but that his behaviour was most odd. His clothes were in disarray and he looked '**As if he had been loosed out of hell/To speak of horrors**'. Hamlet said nothing to Ophelia but held her by the wrist and stared at her intently for some time before leaving.

- Polonius asks his daughter if she has given Hamlet '**hard words**' but she says that she has not. Ophelia claims to have done her duty by refusing to see Hamlet or receive his letters, as Polonius ordered.

- Polonius now believes Hamlet truly loves Ophelia. He tells his daughter that they must go to Claudius to inform him that it may be thwarted love that has driven the Prince mad.

Analysis of Ophelia's character and role in Act 2 Scene 1

- Ophelia's report on Hamlet's behaviour shows us that the Prince has adopted his **'antic disposition'**.

- Ophelia has shown her obedience to her father by breaking off her relationship with Hamlet.

- Polonius now believes that Hamlet has been driven mad by unrequited love. This sets in motion a chain of events that will lead to tragedy, as Polonius decides to spy on Hamlet. We also see that Polonius is more concerned with Claudius's good opinion than his daughter's happiness.

Act 3 Scene 1

- Polonius orders Ophelia to set a trap for Hamlet: he and Claudius will eavesdrop on their conversation.

- Ophelia obeys her father yet again.

- She tells Hamlet that she wants to return his gifts to her, as they mean nothing to her now that he is behaving so badly: **'Rich gifts wax poor when givers prove unkind'**.

- Hamlet denies having given Ophelia anything, tells her he loved her once and then turns on her angrily, claiming that he never really loved her at all. Bitterly, he says **'Get thee to a nunnery'**, claiming all women are untrustworthy. Hamlet tells Ophelia that **'wise men know well enough what monsters you make of them'**.

- Ophelia is deeply distressed by Hamlet's treatment of her and she mourns the change in the Prince: **'O, what a noble mind is here o'erthrown!'**

Analysis of Ophelia's character and role in Act 3 Scene 1

- Hamlet's behaviour towards Ophelia convinces Polonius that unrequited love has driven the prince mad. Claudius disagrees. This is an important moment in the plot as Polonius's insistence on spying on Hamlet a second time to prove he is correct will lead to his death. Hamlet's killing of Polonius will lead Laertes to seek revenge, which, in turn, will lead to Hamlet's death.

- Ophelia clearly loves Hamlet. Her genuine concern for the young man is in stark contrast to the behaviour of Claudius and Polonius, who are only interested in furthering their own causes.

- Through Ophelia, we learn that Hamlet was a very different man before his father's death and his mother's remarriage. He was **'The observed of all observers,'** and **'Th'expectancy and rose of the fair state'**.

- We see how isolated Ophelia is: Polonius uses her as a pawn, telling her how to act in order to trap Hamlet into conversation: **'Ophelia, walk you here'** … **'Read on this book'**. Although Ophelia is very upset after her encounter with Hamlet, Polonius offers her no support.

- The conversation between Ophelia and Hamlet worries Claudius and he decides it is time to get rid of his troublesome nephew, fearing **'something in his soul'** that may **'be some danger'**. Therefore, he resolves to send Hamlet **'with speed to England'**.

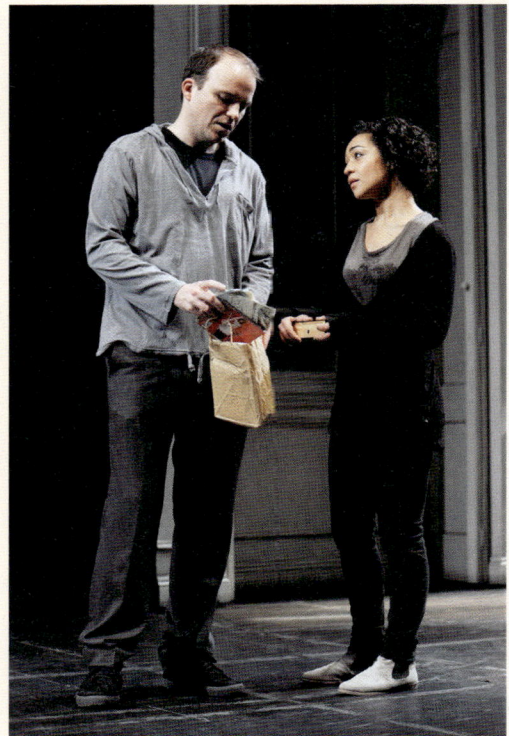

Act 3 Scene 2

- Hamlet chooses to sit by Ophelia during the performance of the play that he has engineered to trap Claudius.

- Hamlet makes crude comments such as '**Lady, shall I lie in your lap?**' and implies Ophelia is sexually sophisticated by asking if she thought he meant '**country matters**' when she refuses. Ophelia merely says, '**You are merry, my lord**'.

Analysis of Ophelia's character and role in Act 3 Scene 2

- Hamlet's sarcastic and cruel treatment of Ophelia is a precursor to his attack on his mother in Act 3, Scene 4. Her patience shows her goodness and innocence and evokes sympathy and admiration.

- Ophelia is patient and tolerant of Hamlet's behaviour towards her, even though he is cruel and crude.

Act 4 Scene 5

- We learn that Ophelia has been driven mad by grief at her father's death and Hamlet's treatment of her. Gertrude is reluctant to see her.

- Ophelia sings about love, seduction and sorrow.

- Laertes enters and is shocked to see his sister's deterioration.

- Ophelia hands out flowers which have symbolic significance (see notes on imagery and symbolism).

Act 4 Scene 7

- Gertrude tells Claudius and Laertes that Ophelia has drowned.
- The descriptions of Ophelia's death are beautiful but the story is a little odd.
- Ophelia was climbing a willow tree when the branch broke and she fell into the water. '**Her clothes spread wide,/And, mermaid-like they bore her up**' for a time, while she floated and sang, but eventually her dress became wet and heavy, dragging Ophelia '**To muddy death**'.

Analysis of Ophelia's character and role in Act 4

- Ophelia's genuine madness contrasts with Hamlet's more ambiguous madness. Both are mourning fathers, but only one is clearly insane.
- Ophelia's madness proves that something really is '**rotten**' in the Danish court. She is innocent but her life has been ruined.
- Ophelia finally has a voice but it is a disturbing one. She sings bawdy songs in front of the royal family. Has the pressure to be chaste been partly responsible for her madness?
- Although she may be mad, Ophelia seems more in control of herself than she was in the earlier part of the play when she meekly obeyed her father and allowed him to control her mind and body.
- We don't know whether Ophelia killed herself or whether she died accidentally. If she did kill herself, her action contrasts with Hamlet's inaction. If she did not, her passivity could be seen as a mirror of Hamlet's passivity.
- Gertrude's moving description of Ophelia's death highlights the girl's purity. She is the tragic, innocent victim in the corrupt world of the Danish court.

Act 5 Scene 1

- Hamlet, recently returned to Denmark, discovers Ophelia is dead.
- The priest suggests Ophelia may have died by suicide: '**Her death was doubtful**'. He believes she does not deserve a proper burial.
- Laertes is angry at these '**maimed rites**'.
- Gertrude expresses her sorrow at Ophelia's death, saying she had hoped Hamlet would marry her.
- Hamlet and Laertes fight, both arguing that they loved Ophelia more. Hamlet claims he loved her more than '**forty thousand brothers**' could do. He even claims he could '**eat a crocodile**' out of love for Ophelia.

Analysis of Ophelia's character and role in Act 5

- The ambiguity of Ophelia's death reinforces the ambiguity of so many of the characters and events in the play.
- Hamlet and Laertes fight over Ophelia but after this scene, they never mention her again. It seems as if they wanted to prove their superiority rather than express genuine love. Ophelia is used as a pawn in death, just as she was in life.

Laertes

That drop of blood that's calm proclaims me bastard …

- Laertes says he came willingly to attend Claudius's coronation but now asks Claudius's permission to return to his studies in France. He is given leave to return after Claudius has checked that Polonius agrees that he may go.

Analysis of Laertes' character and role in Act 1 Scene 2

- This brief introduction to Laertes merely serves to tell us he is Polonius's son and is returning to France to study. Like everyone at court, he is dependent on Claudius's goodwill.

Act 1 Scene 3

- Laertes is preparing to sail to France. He and Ophelia are together in their father's house.

- Laertes warns Ophelia against taking Hamlet's interest in her seriously because, though it may be sweet, it will not last. He urges her to consider it '**The perfume and suppliance of a minute./No more**'.

- Ophelia asks if that is all Hamlet's love for her is, and Laertes replies at length, saying that Hamlet will change his mind and that, furthermore, he is not in a position to choose his wife. As the future King of Denmark, Hamlet's '**will is not his own**' because '**on his choice depends/The safety and health of the whole state**'. Laertes also warns Ophelia against losing her virtue: '**Fear it, Ophelia, fear it, my dear sister**'.

- Ophelia says she will think about what Laertes has said but she also warns him not to behave like a hypocritical priest who tells others how to behave but ignores his own advice.

- Polonius urges Laertes to hurry because his ship is about to sail, but then delays him with a long lecture about how to behave. Laertes respectfully takes his leave of Polonius and says goodbye to Ophelia, telling her to '**remember well**' the advice he gave her.

- Laertes returns to France and does not appear in the action of the play until Act 4 Scene 5.

Analysis of Laertes' character and role in Act 1 Scene 3

- Laertes loves his sister and cares about her reputation and her happiness. However, he is rather pompous in his treatment of her, lecturing Ophelia as if he were her father rather than her brother.

- Laertes talks as if he has great experience of life, but he is a young man. Therefore, he appears a little foolish when he says, '**Youth to itself rebels, though none else near**' as if he were far too mature to ever behave in the self-destructive manner of most young people. Ophelia seems to poke fun at her brother's pomposity when she says that he may behave '**like a puffed and reckless libertine**', while showing her '**the steep and thorny way to heaven**'.

Act 4 Scene 5

- Laertes, at the head of an angry mob who want him to be king, storms Elsinore.

- He tells his followers to wait outside the door while he speaks to Claudius.

- Laertes answers Claudius's plea to be calm by saying that he cannot be his father's son if he does not want to avenge his father's death: '**That drop of blood that's calm proclaims me bastard**'. He vows that come what may, he will be '**revenged/Most thoroughly**' for Polonius's murder.

- Laertes is calmed by Claudius's smooth words and flattery when the latter calls him '**a good child and a true gentleman**'.

- Laertes is distraught on seeing Ophelia's madness. He is more moved by her piteous state than if she had begged him to take revenge for what has driven her to madness: '**Hadst thou wits, and did persuade revenge/It could not move me thus**'.

- Laertes agrees to hear what Claudius has to say about Polonius's death, but he insists that the secretive nature of Polonius's burial be explained as well.

Analysis of Laertes' character and role in Act 4 Scene 5

- Laertes' instant action contrasts with Hamlet's inaction. Where Hamlet overthinks, Laertes is impulsive. Both men want to avenge a murdered father, but Laertes wastes no time in attacking Elsinore. In this way, Laertes acts as a foil to Hamlet.
- Laertes is determined to find the reason for Polonius's '**obscure burial**', which did not befit a courtier who would normally have received an elaborate send-off.

Act 4 Scene 7

- Laertes talks to Claudius alone. He cannot understand why Claudius has not punished Hamlet for his actions.
- Laertes says he will avenge his father's death and his sister's descent into madness.
- Claudius persuades Laertes to '**be ruled**' by him and go along with his plan to have Hamlet killed in such a way that even his mother '**shall … call it accident**'. Laertes agrees, but wants Claudius to engineer matters so that he, Laertes, can be the one to kill Hamlet. Claudius asks what Laertes would be willing to do, and Laertes replies, '**To cut his throat i' th' church**'.
- Claudius says he has heard of Laertes' skill at fencing and suggests that he agree to a match against Hamlet. Claudius suggests that Laertes choose a blade that does not have a blunted tip – as would be normal in a fencing match. Laertes readily agrees but goes one step further and suggests poisoning the tip of his sword so that even the lightest touch '**may be death**'.
- Gertrude enters with news of Ophelia's death. Laertes is heartbroken but more determined than ever to fight Hamlet.

Analysis of Laertes' character and role in Act 4 Scene 7

- Laertes is no match for Claudius. He does not see that he is being manipulated by the devious King.
- Laertes says he is willing to cut Hamlet's throat in church if needs be. This contrasts sharply with Hamlet's unwillingness to kill Claudius in the church.
- Laertes' behaviour is morally questionable. While it might be acceptable for him to fight Hamlet, his plan to poison the tip of the sword is dishonourable.

Act 5 Scene 1

- Laertes is dismayed by Ophelia's low-key funeral. He asks twice: '**What ceremony else?**' and also '**Must there no more be done?**' The priest replies that because it is not certain whether or not Ophelia died by suicide, she is fortunate to be buried in consecrated ground at all: '**Her death was doubtful**'. Laertes calls the priest '**churlish**' or rude and says Ophelia will be a '**ministering angel**' in heaven while the priest will go to hell.

- Laertes, overcome with grief, leaps into Ophelia's grave to hold her in his arms once again and says he wishes to be buried with her.

- On seeing Hamlet, Laertes jumps out of the grave and fights with the young Prince. Hamlet professes to be more distraught over Ophelia's death than Laertes is, and to have loved her more deeply than Laertes did.

- The young men are separated and Claudius persuades Laertes to bide his time as he will soon have the opportunity to deal with Hamlet.

Analysis of Laertes' character and role in Act 5 Scene 1

- It is easy to empathise with Laertes' dismay at the poor funeral rites for Ophelia. After all, his father was murdered and quickly buried without due ceremony, and shortly afterwards his sister is treated in much the same way.

- Laertes' grief may seem over the top. Hamlet certainly seems to think it is, and mocks it with his exaggerated protestations of grief.

Act 5 Scene 2

- Hamlet apologises to Laertes for the wrongs he has done him, but blames his madness. Laertes says he accepts the apology, but with some reservations. He still feels he has been dishonoured.

- Laertes and Hamlet fight. Laertes seems to doubt the morality of what he is doing and says in an aside, '**And yet 'tis almost 'gainst my conscience**'. Laertes injures Hamlet with the poisoned sword but in a scuffle, the swords are exchanged and Hamlet wounds Laertes with the poisoned sword that he has picked up in the confusion.

- Laertes admits that he has been '**killed with mine own treachery**'. Gertrude falls dead, having drunk from the poisoned cup, and Laertes tells Hamlet that Claudius is behind it all.

- Laertes feels Claudius is '**justly served**' when Hamlet kills him. He asks Hamlet to '**Exchange forgiveness**' with him. He will forgive Hamlet for killing Polonius if Hamlet will forgive him for fatally wounding him with a poisoned sword. He calls the young Prince '**noble Hamlet**' in his final speech. Having asked for forgiveness, Laertes dies.

Analysis of Laertes' character and role in Act 5 Scene 2

- Laertes is redeemed somewhat in the final scene. He begins to see that his collusion with Claudius is immoral and he feels pangs of conscience. His final words point the finger of blame at Claudius and beg forgiveness of Hamlet.

- Although he acts as a foil to Hamlet, it would be over-simplistic to say that Laertes is all that Hamlet should be. After all, he allows himself to be corrupted by Claudius into behaving in an ignoble and dishonourable way: poisoning the sword and being complicit in the plot to poison the cup of wine. Revenge is a complex issue.

Horatio

Now cracks a noble heart. Good night, sweet prince,
And flights of angels sing thee to thy rest.

Act 1 Scene 1

- Marcellus has asked Horatio to join the watchmen that night so he can see for himself if '**this dreaded sight twice seen of us**', '**this apparition**' is real or just a figment of their imaginations. Marcellus hopes that Horatio will be able to speak to the Ghost.

- Horatio seems confident he will see nothing: '**Tush, tush, 'twill not appear**'.

- The Ghost appears and Marcellus asks Horatio to speak to it as he is '**a scholar**'. (It was believed at the time that ghosts would understand and speak Latin, and Horatio, being well-educated, spoke Latin.)

- Horatio is filled with '**fear and wonder**' on seeing the apparition for himself, but he questions it, asking why it appears in the guise of the late King. The Ghost leaves, ignoring Horatio's command to stay and speak.

- Horatio, pale and trembling, admits to Marcellus that the Ghost does resemble the King and is wearing the very armour that he wore when he '**smote the sledded Polacks on the ice**'.

- Horatio fears that the Ghost '**bodes some strange eruption to our state**'.

- Marcellus asks why the country is preparing for war. Horatio tells him that young Fortinbras of Norway, son of the late King Fortinbras who was defeated by Hamlet's father, has gathered up a band of '**lawless resolutes**' and threatens to attack Denmark to regain the lands his father lost. Horatio fears that the appearance of the Ghost in full armour at this time is a bad omen that resembles the omens that came before Julius Caesar was murdered.

- The Ghost reappears, and Horatio attempts to speak to it again. He asks if it has any secret knowledge that may help Denmark or if it has returned because it buried stolen treasure when it was alive. The Ghost leaves without answering. Horatio believes it has received a '**fearful summons**' from beyond the grave. He has heard that ghosts cannot walk abroad in daylight, and dawn is breaking.

- Horatio plans to speak to Hamlet about the Ghost, believing that it will talk to Hamlet.

Analysis of Horatio's character and role in Act 1 Scene 1

- Horatio is introduced as a sensible, trustworthy man. Marcellus has sent for him because he believes that Horatio '**will not let belief take hold of him**' and will want proof before he admits the existence of the Ghost.

- Once he sees the Ghost, Horatio acts properly and decisively. He commands it to speak but when it will not, he decides that Hamlet must be told, as the Ghost is sure to speak to him.

- Horatio shows his intelligence and ability to assess situations carefully. He fears that the Ghost's appearance reflects doubts he already has about Denmark's future in these troubled times.

- Horatio acts as a commentator who fills in background details in order to further the plot. He knows why the shipwrights and armourers are working day and night and explains it to Marcellus and, by extension, the audience.

- One of Horatio's roles in the play is to lend credibility to the events and characters in the play, even when they seem fantastical. This early encounter with the Ghost establishes Horatio in that role.

Act 1 Scene 2

- Horatio, along with Marcellus and Barnardo, approaches Hamlet in court and is greeted warmly. Hamlet asks why he returned from Wittenberg, and Horatio answers that he came back to Denmark for Hamlet's father's funeral.

- He tells Hamlet about his sighting of the Ghost. His description is accurate and to the point.

Analysis of Horatio's character and role in Act 1 Scene 2

- Horatio's role as Hamlet's close friend and confidant is established. Hamlet is delighted to see his friend and we learn that they were students together at Wittenberg. Hamlet confides in Horatio that he is distressed at the speed with which his mother remarried: '**The funeral baked meats/Did coldly furnish forth the marriage tables**'.

- Horatio is less emotional than Hamlet. He answers the young Prince's excited questions about the Ghost calmly and precisely. Horatio's self-control and lack of passion make him the perfect foil for the highly-strung Hamlet.

Act 1 Scene 4

- Hamlet joins Marcellus and Horatio on the battlements as they wait for the appearance of the Ghost.

- Horatio suddenly hears several loud noises and asks Hamlet what they are. Hamlet tells him bitterly that it is Claudius's way of celebrating while drinking.

- The Ghost appears and beckons Hamlet to follow it. Horatio advises him not to go, but the Prince insists. Horatio warns that it may be luring him away in order to '**assume some other horrible form**' and drive the Prince to leap off the cliff to his death.

- Hamlet leaves to follow the Ghost, and Horatio and Marcellus follow after.

Analysis of Horatio's character and role in Act 1 Scene 4

- Horatio's caution contrasts sharply with Hamlet's impulsiveness.
- The short exchanges between Hamlet and Horatio when the latter first asks and then tries to order the Prince not to follow the Ghost add greatly to the dramatic tension of this scene.

Act 3 Scene 2

- Horatio and Hamlet converse shortly before the play begins. Hamlet praises Horatio effusively, admiring his self-control and stoicism, saying, '**Give me that man/That is not passion's slave, and I will wear him/In my heart's core**'. He asks Horatio to observe Claudius's reactions to the play and Horatio promises to do so.

- When Claudius walks out in the middle of the play, Hamlet asks Horatio if he noticed Claudius's reaction. Horatio replies twice that he did.

Analysis of Horatio's character and role in Act 3 Scene 2

- Horatio's loyalty to Hamlet never wavers. He supports the Prince in his schemes without playing an active role.
- It is important that Horatio witnessed Claudius's guilty reaction to the play, as he has already been established as a reliable and truthful character.
- Horatio shows none of Hamlet's impassioned excitement on having Claudius's guilt confirmed.

Act 4 Scene 4

- Horatio advises Gertrude to speak to Ophelia. The Queen is reluctant to do so because Ophelia has gone insane.

Analysis of Horatio's character and role in Act 4 Scene 5

- Although Horatio has only two lines in this scene, he <u>speaks sense, as always</u>. He points out that Ophelia, if not dealt with, might '**strew dangerous conjectures in ill-breeding minds**'. In other words, she may draw unwelcome, negative attention to the court and start rumours.

- It is significant that Gertrude agrees immediately when Horatio gives his advice. His <u>trustworthiness, good judgement and common sense are valued by all who know him</u>.

Act 4 Scene 6

- A sailor delivers letters to Horatio. The first is a letter from Hamlet to Horatio, which Horatio reads aloud. Hamlet explains that he was captured by pirates but treated well and returned to Denmark. The other letters are to be delivered to the King.

- In his letter, Hamlet asks Horatio to come to him with all speed because he has '**words to speak in thine ear will make thee dumb**'.

Analysis of Horatio's character and role in Act 4 Scene 6

- <u>Horatio's character is not developed over the course of the play</u>. Once we know that he is <u>truthful, reliable and loyal</u>, we have learned all there is to know about him. In this short scene, Horatio simply <u>serves a dramatic function</u> by reading aloud that Hamlet has returned to shore and has exciting news. He is <u>acting as a commentator</u>, just as he did in Act 1 Scene 1.

Act 5 Scene 1

- Horatio and Hamlet enter the graveyard. Hamlet converses with the gravediggers and muses on the transience of life and the nature of death. Occasionally he looks to Horatio for support and always receives it.

- When Horatio fights with Laertes at Ophelia's burial, Horatio tries to restrain his friend.

- At the end of the scene, when Hamlet leaves vowing vengeance, Claudius asks Horatio to follow him.

Analysis of Horatio's character and role in Act 5 Scene 1

- Horatio acts as <u>sounding board</u> for Hamlet's philosophical comments on life and death. Through him, we learn what Hamlet is thinking. As usual, Horatio merely listens and briefly agrees with Hamlet. He <u>may appreciate the young Prince's wit but he never joins in</u>, leaving the elevated ideas and complex wordplay to Hamlet. However, he <u>shows none of the sycophantic agreement of courtiers</u>, such as Polonius and, later, Osric. Horatio is a <u>true friend to Hamlet</u>.

Act 5 Scene 2

- Hamlet tells Horatio, and by extension the audience, of the way in which he dealt with Rosencrantz and Guildenstern.

- Horatio is shocked to hear that Claudius had plotted to have Hamlet killed: '**Is't possible?**'

- Horatio seems taken aback that Hamlet has contrived to have Rosencrantz and Guildenstern killed in his place: '**So Guildenstern and Rosencrantz go to't**'.

- Horatio warns Hamlet that Claudius will soon learn what has happened.

- Horatio is uneasy about the proposed duel between Hamlet and Laertes, and advises Hamlet to call a halt to it if he suspects that all is not well.

- When Hamlet is mortally wounded, Horatio is distraught. He wants to take his own life, like an '**antique Roman**' but Hamlet orders him not to, telling him that he needs Horatio to tell the world what has happened and to pass the kingdom to Fortinbras.

Analysis of Horatio's character and role in Act 5 Scene 2

- Horatio's <u>good sense and judgement</u> are clear once more in this scene, when he warns Hamlet against the duel.

- Horatio's <u>love for Hamlet is such that he would rather die than live without his dearest friend</u>. However, he <u>loyally obeys Hamlet to the last</u>, and tells Fortinbras what has happened.

- Horatio's final role is that of <u>narrator and commentator</u>.

Rosencrantz and Guildenstern

But we both obey,
And here give up ourselves in the full bent
To lay our service freely at your feet
To be commanded.

Act 2 Scene 2

- Rosencrantz and Guildenstern, friends from Hamlet's youth, are summoned by Claudius to spy on the young Prince and to see if they can find out what is making him behave so oddly.

- Both men readily and humbly agree to do whatever the King and Queen require of them: '**But we both obey,/And here give up ourselves in the full bent/To lay our service freely at your feet/To be commanded**'. (In the National Theatre Live version of *Hamlet*, starring Benedict Cumberbatch, Claudius and Gertrude do not know which of the men is Rosencrantz and which is Guildenstern. The point is that the men are not strong characters or noteworthy individuals. They are mere puppets and a reflection of society at that time.)

- Later in the same scene, Rosencrantz and Guildenstern meet Hamlet. They joke together briefly before Hamlet becomes serious and asks them why they have come, claiming, '**Denmark's a prison**'. They disagree, and Hamlet tells them that he is grateful for their friendship and vows of service for he is, he claims, '**most dreadfully attended**'.

- Hamlet presses Rosencrantz and Guildenstern in an effort to see if his suspicions are founded and they quickly give in and admit the truth: '**My lord, we were sent for**'.

- Rosencrantz and Guildenstern are unable to deal with Hamlet's philosophical musings on life – '**what is this quintessence of dust?**' They try to distract him by telling him of the actors who are on their way to the court. They say the travelling theatre group is struggling because child actors have become the fashion lately.

Analysis of Rosencrantz and Guildenstern's characters and roles in Act 2 Scene 2

- Rosencrantz and Guildenstern may claim to be Hamlet's friends, but their true loyalty is to those in power. They readily acquiesce to Claudius's plan for them to spy on Hamlet, despite his being an old friend of theirs.

- Hamlet sees through his old friends at once, which suggests their loyalty has always been questionable.

- Rosencrantz and Guildenstern act as Shakespeare's commentators on the recent fashion for child actors which, while a novelty, threatened established theatre groups such as Shakespeare's own.

Act 3 Scene 1

- Rosencrantz and Guildenstern report back to Claudius and Gertrude. They say they have found Hamlet hard to read and they felt he struggled to be courteous to them. However, they are pleased to report that when they told Hamlet of the arrival of the actors, '**there did seem in him a kind of joy**'.

Analysis of Rosencrantz and Guildenstern's characters and roles in Act 3 Scene 1

- Rosencrantz and Guildenstern are quick to report to Claudius and Gertrude. It is clear where their loyalties lie. They represent the corruption and sycophantic nature of most of the courtiers in the service of Claudius.

Act 3 Scene 2

- After the performance of the play, Rosencrantz and Guildenstern approach Hamlet to tell him that the King is '**marvellous distempered**'. Hamlet asks if Claudius is drunk (distempered can mean drunk or angry) and Guildenstern replies that he is furious. He also tells Hamlet that Gertrude is upset and wants him to go to her room.

- Rosencrantz reminds Hamlet, '**you once did love me**' and asks him to share his problems with his friends. Hamlet says that he lacks promotion but Rosencrantz says this is not so, as Claudius has named him his heir.

- Hamlet presses Guildenstern to play the recorder and when Guildenstern repeatedly says he cannot, Hamlet angrily asks why his two old friends are trying to play on him as on an instrument.

Analysis of Rosencrantz and Guildenstern's characters and roles in Act 3 Scene 2

- Hamlet's behaviour and refusal to give them straight answers confuse Rosencrantz and Guildenstern.
- Hamlet knows Rosencrantz and Guildenstern are spying on him and their friendship is clearly at an end. Rosencrantz and Guildenstern are out of their depth and are no match for Hamlet's wit or any of the intrigue at the Danish court.

Act 4 Scene 2

- Rosencrantz and Guildenstern ask Hamlet where he has hidden Polonius's body. He refuses to answer, saying that they are working for Claudius and that he will not be interrogated by '**a sponge**'. He warns them that Claudius is using them and will squeeze them dry when he has finished with them.
- Rosencrantz and Guildenstern do not understand Hamlet's point, and he says this is because they are stupid.
- They ask again where the body is and say they must take Hamlet to the King. He runs away, calling for them to chase him in a game of hide-and-seek.
- The next appearance of Rosencrantz and Guildenstern is in Act 4 Scene 4, when they accompany Hamlet to the ship, but they do not do or say anything significant.

Analysis of Rosencrantz and Guildenstern's characters and roles in Act 4 Scene 2

- Rosencrantz and Guildenstern are weak, foolish men and are no match for Hamlet.
- They are a reflection of the sycophantic and corrupt society at the Danish court at the time.

Act 5 Scene 2

- Hamlet tells Horatio that he secretly took the letter Rosencrantz and Guildenstern were delivering to the King of England, and discovered that it ordered his execution. He forged a replacement, saying that Rosencrantz and Guildenstern should be '**put to sudden death**' without even being allowed enough time to pray for their souls first.

- Horatio supposes that is the end for the pair, and Hamlet says he feels no guilt, as '**Their defeat/ Does by their own insinuation grow**'. They were men of low status who became caught up in a fight between '**mighty opposites**'.

Analysis of Rosencrantz and Guildenstern's characters and roles in Act 5 Scene 2

- We do not know if Rosencrantz and Guildenstern knew the content of the letter they bore. Even if they did not, Hamlet says they brought about their own downfall through their meddling and disloyalty. Nobody mourns their deaths.

Fortinbras

Bear Hamlet like a soldier to the stage,
For he was likely, had he been put on,
To have proved most royal ...

Act 1 Scene 1

- Horatio tells Marcellus and Barnardo that Fortinbras is the son of the late King of Denmark. His father lost his life and some land in a battle against Hamlet's father. Young Fortinbras, '**Of unimproved mettle hot and full**', has gathered up a band of '**lawless resolutes**' who are willing to fight for him, and plans to attack Denmark in order to regain the land his father lost.

- The threat posed by Fortinbras is such that the Danes have been preparing for war.

Analysis of Fortinbras' character and role in Act 1 Scene 1

- Fortinbras' threat <u>adds to the tension and anxiety of a court</u> in which the ghost of the dead King walks abroad.

- Fortinbras <u>introduces the theme of revenge</u>. Like Hamlet, he has lost a father and his uncle has taken up the succession, but <u>Fortinbras is a man of action</u> who takes it upon himself to muster an army in order to restore his family honour.

- Fortinbras will be a <u>foil to Hamlet</u> in the play.

Act 4 Scene 4

- Fortinbras' uncle, the current ruler of Norway, has stopped his nephew from attacking Denmark but has allowed him to attack Poland instead.

- Fortinbras sends a captain to ask Claudius's permission to cross Denmark on his way to Poland. He is willing to meet Claudius to '**express our duty in his eye**' if Claudius would prefer it.

- Hamlet is taken aback to find that Fortinbras intends to attack Poland to win what a Norwegian captain describes as '**a little patch of ground/That hath in it no profit but the name**'.

- Fortinbras' actions shame Hamlet, who says that '**a delicate and tender prince**' such as Fortinbras laughs at the unknown future and risks his life – and the lives of his men – for '**an eggshell**'. Hamlet compares himself unfavourably to Fortinbras. Hamlet has more reason to fight than does Fortinbras, and yet he has not acted.

Analysis of Fortinbras' character and role in Act 4 Scene 4

- Fortinbras is obedient to his uncle, the ruler of Norway.

- Fortinbras is <u>honourable and straightforward</u>. He behaves correctly in sending a captain to seek permission to cross Danish land but is also happy to meet Claudius if the King prefers to talk face to face.

- Fortinbras is a <u>man of action and a great leader</u>, whose men are willing to follow him into battle, even when the prize is clearly not worth winning, let alone dying for.

- Fortinbras' <u>decisive and courageous certainty inspires Hamlet</u> to vow: '**O, from this time forth/ My thoughts be bloody, or be nothing worth!**'

Act 5 Scene 2

- Fortinbras, returning victorious after his battle in Poland, enters moments after Hamlet's death. He is shocked to see so much carnage in the court.

- Fortinbras announces that he has '**some rights of memory in this kingdom**' and although the circumstances of his accession grieve him, he makes a claim for the Danish throne. Horatio has already been told by Hamlet to give the crown to Fortinbras and Horatio mentions this.

- Fortinbras calls for Hamlet's body to be carried to the stage with military honour, as he believes Hamlet was a great man who would, had he become king, '**proved most royal**'. He orders that the rest of the bodies be taken away, remarking that the scene would be fitting for a battlefield but has no place in a royal court.

Analysis of Fortinbras' character and role in Act 5 Scene 2

- Fortinbras is decisive to the end. He takes command almost immediately, making a claim for the throne and ordering the bodies be dealt with.

- Fortinbras is a military man through and through. He has been victorious in battle and he comments that the bodies on the floor would suit the battlefield well but are out of place in the palace. He calls for military honours for Hamlet, believing there to be no greater tribute.

- Fortinbras is utterly unlike Hamlet, yet the audience is left feeling that the kingdom is in good hands. After all of the intrigue and corruption, a strong and straightforward ruler is what the country needs.

Studying Theme

Theme checklists

A **theme** is an issue or concern in the text that the writer is trying to explore. When you are reading the text, consider the following **checklists**:

Introduction

✓ How is the theme **introduced**?

✓ Is there a **key moment** that gives us an indication of the **message** the author is trying to convey?

✓ Does one of the **central characters** say or do something that sets us on the **path of understanding** the theme?

Development

✓ How does the author develop this theme?

✓ Is it through a **series of small events**?

✓ Do we see **situations developing** that we know must lead to a **crisis**?

✓ How does the author interest us in the theme? Is it through a **central character** with whom we can **empathise**?

Climax

✓ Is there a moment of crisis or a **turning point** in the text?

✓ Does the central character have to make a **difficult decision**?

✓ Does the character do the **right thing**?

✓ How is this **decision linked** to the theme?

Resolution

✓ How is the theme **resolved**?

✓ Are you very clear on the **author's view** of the ideas explored in the theme?

✓ Have you learned anything about **human behaviour or society in general** from the exploration of this theme?

Gender and sexuality

The women in Hamlet are, according to a critic, '**drawn in fainter lines than their male counterparts**'. Therefore, the audience is forced to make up its own mind as to the purity, motives and history of Gertrude and Ophelia. One of the most commonly asked questions is this: did Gertrude begin an affair with Claudius before her husband was murdered? The Ghost seems to indicate that she may have when he refers to Claudius as '**that incestuous, that adulterate beast**', but we must remember that at the time Shakespeare was writing, '**adultery**' could mean any kind of sexual sin, such as incest. By marrying Gertrude – his late brother's wife – Claudius was certainly committing incest in the eyes of the Elizabethans who based their view on the Old Testament. However, it is much less certain that Gertrude was guilty of any sin.

The role of women in Elizabethan society was complex. On the one hand, they were considered intellectually, physically and socially inferior to men. On the other hand, the country was ruled by a powerful and intelligent queen! In *Hamlet*, the prevailing idea of women being less capable than men is to the fore. Take, for example, the difference in the way Polonius views his son and his daughter. When giving Laertes some parting advice before the young man leaves for France, Claudius says, '**This above all, to thine own self be true**'. He encourages Laertes to trust his better judgement and believes that if he does so, all will be well. However, as soon as Laertes has left and Polonius begins giving advice to Ophelia, the tone changes. He is annoyed that she is seeing Hamlet, and he scolds her: '**You do not understand yourself so clearly/As it behoves my daughter and your honour**'. Ophelia is taken aback and admits, '**I do not know, my lord, what I should think**'. Polonius is not willing to allow Ophelia to trust her own judgement and he tells her, '**I'll teach you: think yourself a baby**'.

The men in the play do their best to restrict the women's sexuality. Hamlet's disgust at his mother's sexuality is clear from the outset. He says that Claudius has '**killed my King and whored my mother**'.

Furious with his mother's betrayal of her late husband by rushing '**With such dexterity to incestuous sheets**', Hamlet announces, '**Frailty, thy name is woman!**'. He is revolted at the thought of his mother lying '**In the rank sweat of an enseamed bed,/Stewed in corruption, honeying and making love/Over the nasty sty**'. When he visits her in her room after the play, Hamlet orders his mother to refrain from sleeping with Claudius again and insists that she must resist all his flattering advances.

Disgusted with his mother and extending this to include all women, Hamlet turns his anger on Ophelia, tarring her with the same brush as Gertrude. As they prepare to watch the play, he asks, '**Lady, shall I lie in your lap?**'. Ophelia is placed in an impossible position when Hamlet talks crudely to her: if she is offended, it proves that she knows more of sexual matters than a pure young maiden should, but if she does not acknowledge it, she must suffer in silence as Hamlet continues to taunt her. A popular belief in Elizabethan times was that once a woman had had sex, particularly outside of marriage, she would become vulnerable to promiscuity and hysteria. Some critics have linked Ophelia's madness and crude songs in Act 4 Scene 5 with possible sexual hysteria, saying it shows she had slept with Hamlet and that it is part of the reason for her behaviour. At the time, it was thought that such women were likely to cheat on their husbands and make cuckolds or '**monsters**' of them. Hamlet accuses Ophelia of being such a woman when he advises her to '**marry a fool; for wise men know well enough what monsters you make of them**'.

Laertes and Polonius are similarly obsessed with women's chastity but do not hold men to the same standards. Laertes lectures Ophelia about her relationship with Hamlet, claiming that the young Prince merely wants to take her '**chaste treasure**' and cannot possibly intend to marry her. There is no criticism of Hamlet implied in these words and Laertes makes it clear that it is up to Ophelia to protect her virtue from the 'natural' urges of young men. Polonius echoes Laertes' fears, saying that Hamlet's vows of love are merely '**springes to catch woodcocks**' and cannot be taken seriously. Polonius, like Laertes, does not blame Hamlet for his behaviour and tells Ophelia that the Prince – being a young man – has '**a larger tether**' and can exercise far more freedom than a young woman. Polonius reinforces this double standard when telling Reynaldo to spy on Laertes in Paris. He appears to assume that Laertes will visit prostitutes but that there is no dishonour in his doing so, provided it is not excessive. Polonius views such '**Drabbing**' as just one expression of '**The flash and outbreak of a fiery mind**'.

Gender inequality in the play is not limited to sexual freedom. In Elizabethan society, men acted while women talked. Hamlet's procrastination makes him appear feminine, something which he recognises when he accuses himself of being prone to '**like a whore unpack my heart with words**'. Claudius also chides Hamlet for his '**unmanly grief**' in mourning his father too deeply and for too long.

Hamlet's treatment of women in the play can be seen as a measure of his state of mind. When he is angry and confused, he turns on them viciously. It could be argued that he has reason to do so, as he has been let down by both his mother and the woman he loves. Gertrude married Claudius soon after her husband's death. When we first meet her, Gertrude shows little real understanding of her son's grief, asking him to '**cast thy nighted colour off**' and tactlessly pointing out that '**all that lives must die**'. Ophelia, similarly, sides with another against Hamlet when she agrees to her father's plan to use her as bait to spy on the Prince. In Hamlet's time of need, the women he loves let him down. This hardly excuses his cruel treatment of Ophelia in particular, but it may go some way towards explaining it.

However, when Hamlet is more content with his lot and less troubled, his view of women is far more positive. On the ship to England, he outwits Rosencrantz and Guildenstern and this is the beginning of a great change in the young Prince. Spurred on by his success and admiring Fortinbras' decisive move against the Poles, Hamlet is determined to act and is, therefore, behaving in a more manly fashion according to the conventions of the time. At this point, he ceases to loathe women, perhaps because he is finally a man of action and no longer in need of the support of the women in his life. On his return to Denmark, Hamlet channels his aggression into his plan to kill Claudius instead of using it to attack the women in his life. Now, at last, because Hamlet is less conflicted, he can view Ophelia as an icon of purity and feminine virtue. At her graveside, Hamlet appears to forget his earlier attacks on the unfortunate young woman and claims to love her more than '**forty thousand brothers**' could do.

Even in the manners of their deaths, the male and female characters differ. Polonius, Hamlet and Laertes die by the sword, while Ophelia drowns and Gertrude drinks poison. King Hamlet died a '**foul, strange and unnatural**' death because he was poisoned. For men of the time, dying in combat possessed a certain honour, and for a soldier of renown to die in this unmanly way would have added another layer of outrage to Claudius's murder of his brother. The Ghost appears clad in '**the very armour he had on**' when he defeated the King of Norway in battle, even though he did not die in his armour. His manliness is linked to his physical strength and bravery, however, so he would want to be remembered in this way. Claudius is wounded by Hamlet's sword but he is not granted a manly death. He claims he is '**but hurt**' and calls for help, but Hamlet forces him to drink from the poisoned cup, denying him any sort of honourable end.

Finally, it is worth comparing the different attitudes towards the men and women in various stage and film productions of *Hamlet*. In his 1990 film version of the play, for example, the director Franco Zeffirelli makes it clear that Claudius and Gertrude were conducting an adulterous affair before the old king was murdered. This interpretation is bound to colour our view of Gertrude and Hamlet's attitude towards her. You should try to see as many versions of the play as possible and make brief notes on differences in the approach to gender and sexuality. You are free to comment on film and stage performances in your Leaving Certificate essay but you must also be prepared to analyse and say whether you agree or disagree with the interpretation of the play.

Revenge

Note: *Before reading these notes on the theme of revenge, you should read the 'Setting the scene' section (p. x) once more as it provides some information on revenge plays in Shakespeare's time.*

The theme of revenge is central to the plot of *Hamlet*. Three sons, Hamlet, Fortinbras and Laertes, all seek to avenge their fathers. However, each man approaches it differently and, through their actions or inaction, we learn the difference between just and lawful vengeance and that which is executed without due consideration or cause. We are also invited to contrast the old, traditional view of revenge with the more philosophical approach embodied by Hamlet. At the time *Hamlet* was written, scholars and learned men were encouraged to consider topics deeply before taking any action, and to take their own feelings on the matter into account. Hamlet's studies at Wittenberg would have played a role in shaping him into a thoughtful young man but would also have meant that he lacked the simple, straightforward attitude of men like Fortinbras.

Fortinbras has no real justification for seeking revenge for his father's death. Old Fortinbras agreed to the trial of combat in which he was killed by Hamlet's father, and the lands that Norway forfeited to Denmark as a result were legally handed over. Horatio tells Marcellus and Barnardo that Fortinbras has '**Sharked up a list of lawless resolutes**' to help him lay claim to the territory that formed part of 'a sealed compact/Well ratified by law and heraldry'. Claudius puts a quick stop to Fortinbras' plan when he sends ambassadors to the young Prince's uncle, advising him of his nephew's actions. Fortinbras seems untroubled that he has been caught in the act and immediately makes '**a vow before his uncle**' never to threaten Denmark again. Instead, he turns his energies to what appears to be a pointless fight with Poland. Fortinbras is often contrasted with Hamlet and held up as a man of action who does what he should do to avenge his father. It is important to remember that Fortinbras has no just cause and fails in his quest to win back his family honour through force of arms. He does succeed to the Danish throne at the end of the play, but in a lawful manner, because he has been nominated by Hamlet.

Fortinbras' attitude serves a purpose in that his actions highlight Hamlet's inaction. Hamlet is astonished and ashamed when he sees Fortinbras' army marching to fight for '**a little patch of ground/That hath in it no profit but the name**' and he reflects that it is right to act decisively '**When honour's at the stake**'. Hamlet has certainly been dishonoured by having '**a father killed, a mother stained**' by Claudius. Moved by Fortinbras' bravery and determination, Hamlet vows, '**O, from this time forth/My thoughts be bloody, or be nothing worth!**'

Laertes is also contrasted with Hamlet but his approach to vengeance is even more flawed than Fortinbras'. When he returns to Denmark on hearing of his father's death, Laertes, like Fortinbras, has gathered a mob eager to do his bidding. He storms the castle and announces that he does not care what happens to him in this world or the next, as long as he can avenge Polonius's death.

> Conscience and grace, to the profoundest pit!
> I dare damnation. To this point I stand,
> That both the worlds I give to negligence,
> Let come what comes. Only I'll be revenged
> Most thoroughly for my father.

On seeing Ophelia's madness, Laertes is even more enraged and immediately swears that his revenge on whoever has driven his sister mad will be so severe that it will outweigh the wrong done to her: '**By heaven, thy madness shall be paid by weight,/Till our scale turn the beam**'.

While Laertes' cause seems just and his anguish and determination relatable and admirable, his readiness to surrender his '**Conscience and grace**' and to '**dare damnation**' makes his approach to revenge morally questionable. In Shakespeare's time, the Church taught that revenge should be left to God, but the classical tradition of revenge plays put forward the idea that when honour was at stake, a man was within his rights to seek vengeance on those who had done him wrong. Hamlet wrestles with the conflict between these two ideals, but Laertes does not. His abandonment of morality leads him to conspire with Claudius in a wicked and deeply dishonourable plot to rig a duel by poisoning both a cup of wine and his own sword tip so that even the lightest touch '**may be death**'. The contrast between Hamlet's morality and Laertes' immorality in the matter of revenge is crystal clear when Claudius asks what Laertes would be willing to do to Hamlet, and Laertes replies, '**To cut his throat i' th' church**'.

Laertes regrets his actions in the final scene of the play. He begins to see that his collusion with Claudius is immoral and he feels pangs of guilt about his underhanded plan to kill Hamlet with a poisoned sword: '**And yet 'tis almost 'gainst my conscience**'. Laertes' final words are to point the finger of blame at Claudius and to beg forgiveness of Hamlet.

Although he acts as a foil to Hamlet, Laertes is not an example of all that Hamlet should be. In his desire for vengeance, Laertes has become corrupted and yet more proof that '**Something is rotten in the state of Denmark**'.

Hamlet's situation is the most complex of all three. Once he learns that Claudius has killed the old king, Hamlet has a clear duty to seek vengeance. The Ghost demands that Hamlet '**revenge his foul and most unnatural murder**'. Hamlet vows that he will act '**with wings as swift/as meditation or the thoughts of love**'. The Ghost is pleased with this: '**I find thee apt**'. However, almost immediately after agreeing to the Ghost's demands, Hamlet expresses his dismay at being put in the position of avenger: '**The time is out of joint. O cursed spite/That ever I was born to set it right!**'

Unlike Fortinbras and Laertes, Hamlet engages in lengthy soul-searching to determine whether and how he should avenge his father's death. Hamlet knows he should act but his conscience rebels against the violent act he must carry out if he is to obey the Ghost. The arrival of the visiting actors causes Hamlet to feel even more conflicted than before. He feels guilty when he sees the actor weep '**in a fiction, in a dream of passion**' for a character in a drama, and wonders what such a man would do had he '**the motive and the cue for passion**' that Hamlet has. He rebukes himself for his inability to act in his soliloquy at the end of Act 2, acknowledging that he is '**Prompted to my revenge by heaven and hell**'. Yet the mention of hell introduces another reason for Hamlet not to act just yet.

Perhaps, he muses, the Ghost is '**the devil, and the devil hath power/T'assume a pleasing shape**'. It seems to Hamlet that he must have greater proof of Claudius's guilt before he moves against him, and so he strikes upon the idea of the play to '**catch the conscience of the King**'.

The success of his adaptation of 'The Murder of Gonzago' invigorates Hamlet and he is convinced at last that Claudius is truly guilty. It is also a form of revenge, and one well-suited to Hamlet's personality because it allows him to use his intellect to achieve his goal. Also, there is no real risk to Hamlet's conscience in this bloodless form of vengeance: if Claudius had not murdered the old king, the play would have passed without incident. Hamlet is delighted with the success of the lines he has written and his first words to Horatio after Claudius has stormed out are to claim that he could get '**a fellowship in a cry of players**' if he wished to do so.

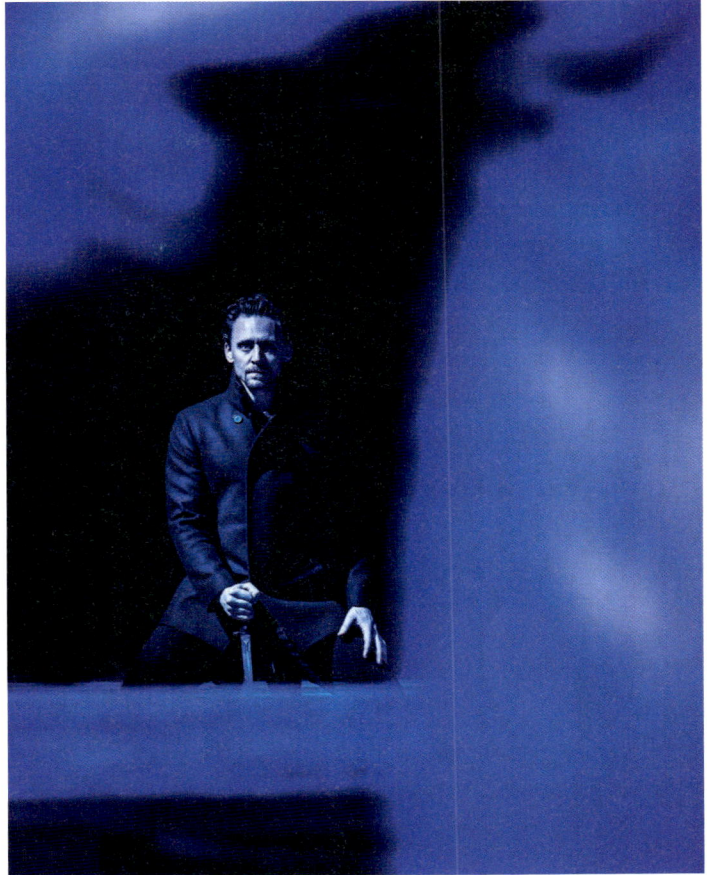

Hamlet's language when he is alone after the performance of the play at court proves that at this stage he harbours violent thoughts of revenge, saying, '**Now could I drink hot blood,/And do such bitter business as the day/Would quake to look on**'. He has to remind himself to exercise restraint when talking to Gertrude: '**I will speak daggers to her, but use none**'.

Shortly after the play, Hamlet comes upon Claudius praying alone and realises that this is the ideal moment to kill him: '**Now might I do it pat … and so I am revenged**'. However, at this moment of heightened tension when the audience might reasonably expect Hamlet to act at last, the Prince once again procrastinates. He begins to analyse the situation and realises that if Claudius dies at prayer, he will go to heaven. Hamlet reasons that Claudius gave his victim no such chance to die in a state of grace, and therefore killing him now would be '**hire and salary, not revenge**'. Shakespeare's audience, while possibly disappointed by Hamlet's sparing Claudius's life and thereby removing the tension and excitement from the scene, would understand his motives. They would have expected the Prince to want a lasting revenge that included eternal damnation, even if they were somewhat shocked to see the depth of Hamlet's vengeful cruelty. Of course, there is great irony in Hamlet's believing that Claudius is engaged in '**the purging of his soul**'. We know that the King cannot repent as he is unwilling to give up what he has gained by his brother's murder: '**My crown, mine own ambition and my Queen**'. This scene, in which we see a more human side to Claudius and a more barbaric side to Hamlet shows just how complex the issue of revenge is.

When Hamlet visits his mother in her chamber after the play, he is once again in his element as he constructs powerful and moving arguments to convince Gertrude that she should not have married '**A murderer and a villain**'. Part of Hamlet's revenge is to force his mother to see the wrong she has done to the memory of her former husband, a man '**Where every god did seem to set his seal/To** give the world assurance of a man'. Gertrude begs her son to say no more and the Ghost reappears, reminding Hamlet not to forget his mission: '**This visitation/Is but to whet thy almost blunted purpose**'. Is the Ghost right to say Hamlet has forgotten his cause? Certainly, he has rushed to tackle Gertrude rather than Claudius once he is convinced of the latter's guilt. This is hardly in keeping with the classical idea of vengeance and is yet another example of how Hamlet has deviated from his vow to act '**with wings as swift/As meditation or the thoughts of love**'. It appears that Hamlet has a far greater need to prick Gertrude's conscience than to kill Claudius, yet it is possible to see why he feels this way. After all, Claudius's death will not bring Hamlet's father back to life and will effect little change on the world, something Hamlet acknowledges later in the graveyard scene. Gertrude, on the other hand, may repent of her hasty and incestuous remarriage and thus Hamlet will have achieved something positive. Gertrude appears appalled by Hamlet's denunciation of her behaviour and claims she can now see '**such black and grained spots**' in her soul, proving that Hamlet's words hit home.

The downside of Hamlet's public exposure of Claudius is that the King must now remove the threat to his rule and his life. Therefore, he sends Hamlet to England with sealed letters ordering his death when he arrives. This puts paid to any chance of Hamlet's avenging his father's death in the immediate future.

Hamlet's soliloquy at the end of Act 4 Scene 4, as he sees Fortinbras' men marching to Poland, expresses his confusion and disgust at his inability to exact revenge:

> *I do not know*
> *Why yet I live to say this 'Thing's to do',*
> *Sith I have cause, and will, and strength, and means*
> *To do't.*

Hamlet now appears determined to revenge his father's death as soon as possible and without any further deliberation: '**O, from this time forth/My thoughts be bloody, or be nothing worth!**' However, although Hamlet may be impressed by Fortinbras' courage and decisiveness, he is not the same sort of man as Fortinbras and this is why his words do not ring true. The audience has heard enough of Hamlet's vows of vengeance which have come to nothing to disbelieve him.

In this soliloquy, Hamlet claims he may be too cowardly or be guilty of '**thinking too precisely on th'event**' to act. Yet he is not a coward and we see he is more than capable of acting bravely, decisively and mercilessly at times. He shows no fear of the Ghost, although he is warned it may be dangerous and is not at all sure that it is not an evil spirit. He cleverly arranges the play to '**catch the conscience of the King**' the moment he meets the players. He kills Polonius and appears unmoved when he realises his error; sends Rosencrantz and Guildenstern to their deaths, and stabs and poisons Claudius in the final scene. It seems thinking '**too precisely on th'event**' is the problem.

Although Hamlet vows instant vengeance at the start of the play and seems on the point of acting a number of times, he does nothing concrete until the very end of the play. When he does, it is impulsive rather than the culmination of a plan. His killing of Claudius at the end of the play is a sudden act: he stabs and then poisons his uncle when he learns that the King has plotted to poison him and has accidentally poisoned Gertrude. At this stage, Hamlet seems to have resigned himself to fate and to the belief that the opportunity to avenge his father's death will present itself at the right time. He believes now that '**There's a divinity that shapes our ends**' and that he can surrender himself to fate. This may be true, as Hamlet does – finally – avenge his father's murder. However, the killing of Claudius comes too late to save Polonius, Ophelia, Rosencrantz, Guildenstern, Gertrude and Laertes. Hamlet's procrastination causes a chain of tragic deaths.

Appearance and reality

Note: *The theme of appearance and reality is closely linked to the theme of deception. If you know one, you know the other. This general approach to the themes is important in the context of the Leaving Certificate exam questions. Students can panic when they see a question on a theme they believe they may not have studied, but the chances are they are more than prepared for the question. For example, if you were asked about deception, you could use your knowledge of appearance versus reality. Similarly, if you were asked about justice, you could draw from your notes on revenge.*

In the opening lines of *Hamlet*, Barnardo questions the guard on duty, even though he is the one arriving to relieve the watch. His nervous '**Who's there?**' introduces the idea of an uneasy, upside-down world in which things are not as they seem. Hamlet searches for the truth about his father's murder, but his quest is not straightforward. The opening scenes of the play, in which the characters are mired in darkness and confusion, reflect the confusion in Hamlet's mind. In order to decide what is real and what is not, the characters should at least be able to see clearly. Horatio's arrival on the battlements in the first scene reinforces the idea that it is impossible to do so. When Barnardo thinks he spots Horatio joining them on the watch, he asks, '**is Horatio there?**' Horatio answers, a little dryly, '**A piece of him**'. In other words, all that is visible is Horatio's hand proffered in greeting, so the guards must take his word that he is who he says he is.

Claudius, the master of deception, has no trouble taking on the mantle of the King of Denmark and he manipulates reality so that all appears well in Denmark. When we first meet Claudius, he pretends to join his subjects in grief and says the kingdom is '**contracted in one brow of woe**'. Later, we learn that Claudius has murdered his brother, so his words of comfort ring exceedingly hollow. However, he does appear to be a competent ruler and a good king at this stage in the play. He is very much in control and more than able to deal with the threat posed by Fortinbras. He seems to care for his wife and stepson and to have the best interests of his country and people at heart. Hamlet, however, cannot believe that the face Claudius presents to the world is an accurate reflection of who he is. When Claudius calls him '**my cousin Hamlet, and my son**', Hamlet responds bitterly in an aside that he is '**A little more than kin and less than kind**'. He may appear to be close to Claudius because he is both his nephew and his stepson, but he does not feel kindly towards him.

In a world in which it is impossible to know the truth, Hamlet's task is hugely complicated. It is clear from outset that he is unhappy with his uncle's assuming the throne and marrying the late king's widow and that he suspects there is something deeper afoot. He replies scathingly to Gertrude's question about why his father's death should appear to affect him so deeply: '**Seems, madam? Nay, it is. I know not "seems"**'. '**O my prophetic soul!**' he cries in deep distress when the Ghost tells him that '**The serpent that did sting thy father's life/Now wears his crown**'. This reinforces Hamlet's view of the hypocrisy in the Danish court. He takes care to note down the Ghost's words, saying they prove that Denmark is a place in which '**one may smile and smile and be a villain**'.

However, the Ghost also poses a problem for Hamlet in terms of appearance and reality. It may be the spirit of his late father seeking revenge for his murder, or it may be '**the devil**' with the power '**T'assume a pleasing shape**'. Therefore, Hamlet decides he needs greater proof of Claudius's guilt than the words of a possibly evil spirit, and he decides to arrange a special performance by the actors in order to '**catch the conscience of the King**'.

The play within the play, also known as 'The Murder of Gonzago' or 'The Mousetrap', is itself an elaborate deception that further blurs the line between appearance and reality. The purpose of the play within the play is not simply to entertain but also to see if Claudius is all he seems to be or if he is hiding a dark secret. The dramatic tension of this scene is heightened by the fact that the audience is watching Hamlet watch Claudius watching a play. This is not the only moment in the play in which the audience might find it difficult to separate life and art. Hamlet compares the earth and sky to a theatre on two different occasions. After his first meeting with the Ghost, Hamlet promises to remember it '**while memory holds a seat/In this distracted globe**'. '**Globe**' here can be interpreted in a number of ways: it could mean Hamlet's head, or the earth, but it could also be a reference to the Globe theatre. Later, when Hamlet is telling Rosencrantz and Guildenstern how weary he is of the world, he draws their attention to '**this brave o'erhanging firmament, this majestical roof fretted with golden fire**'. This could simply mean the sky and the sun and stars, or it may be a reference to the roof of the Globe theatre, which was painted to resemble a sky with stars and planets dotted about. At times, therefore, the audience is drawn into the lives of the characters and seems part of the performance, such as during the 'The Murder of Gonzago', but at other times the audience is reminded that all of the action is a fiction, such as when Hamlet makes veiled reference to the theatre.

The difference between appearance and reality in the Prayer Scene is an example of great dramatic irony, which draws the audience further into the action of the play by allowing them greater insight into the reality than the two characters onstage. Claudius is kneeling in prayer and unaware of the threat approaching him from behind. Hamlet, however, resolves not to kill him at that moment because to do so would mean that the King died in a state of grace and could go to heaven, something Claudius did not afford the old king when he murdered him. What the Prince does not know is that Claudius's prayers are pointless, as he admits he cannot repent his actions. Despite his intelligence and determination to see through Claudius's hypocrisy and deceit, Hamlet is unable to perceive the reality in this instance.

Hamlet's madness is yet another layer of deception in the play that makes it difficult to distinguish between appearance and reality. Although Hamlet claims he is merely putting on this '**antic disposition**' to throw Claudius off the scent, there are times when he comes perilously close to genuine madnes. It is difficult for the audience to decide if the Prince is acting or if he is really struggling with his sanity. Indeed, critics still argue over which is the case.

In a world in which so little is as it appears, it is easy to see why Hamlet finds it hard to trust anyone. The woman he loves goes along with a plan to allow Claudius and Polonius to spy on him, and his two old schoolfriends also conspire with the King to try to find out more about his thoughts and plans. Hamlet reacts to such betrayals with fury. Already disillusioned with women because of his mother's hasty and incestuous remarriage, Hamlet rounds on Ophelia, accusing her of being hypocritical, like all her sex. He tells her that women use make-up and flirtatious behaviour to lure men and hide their true selves: '**I have heard of your paintings, too, well enough. God hath given you one face, and you make yourselves another. You jig, you amble, and you lisp, and nickname God's creatures, and make your wantonness your ignorance**'. Hamlet tells Ophelia she can only spare herself further shame by going to live in a convent.

Hamlet's treatment of Rosencrantz and Guildenstern is even harsher than his treatment of Ophelia. He knows they are spying for Claudius and warns them that they in turn are being deceived. Claudius may appear to value those who serve him but he is merely using them. He keeps them like an ape keeps an apple in the corner of its mouth which it will swallow when it has squeezed all the juice from it. Later, when Hamlet discovers that Rosencrantz and Guildenstern are carrying a letter to the King of England ordering his death, he changes it to a death warrant for his two unwitting companions. Rosencrantz and Guildenstern pay the ultimate price for allowing themselves to be caught up in the deception of the Danish court.

The relationship between Polonius and his children reinforces the hypocritical, corrupt nature of life in Elsinore. When Polonius sends Laertes back to Paris with his blessing, all seems straightforward. However, despite telling Laertes, '**This above all – to thine own self be true**', Polonius deviously instructs his servant to spy on Laertes and spread rumours about his immorality in order to elicit confidences about the young man's partying habits. This father-son relationship is a microcosm of the corruption in the Danish court. Nothing is as it seems. Polonius's jaundiced view of the world is further reinforced in his conversation with Ophelia. He cannot believe for a moment that Hamlet truly cares for Ophelia, and he assumes that his words of love are merely attempts to lure Ophelia into bed. Ultimately, Polonius's deception is his undoing. He spies on Hamlet while the Prince believes he is in private conference with his mother, and is stabbed through the arras as a result.

The tragic end to the play is brought about when Laertes allows himself to be manipulated by Claudius and agrees to an underhanded and deceitful plan to kill Hamlet with a poison-tipped sword. Like all who are caught in Claudius's web of deceit, Laertes pays a terrible price for his moral lapse. He is killed by his own sword, but not before he admits the truth to Hamlet: '**The King. The King's to blame**'. All is revealed, but it is too late for the damage to be undone. Claudius, Gertrude, Ophelia, Polonius, Rosencrantz, Guildenstern, Laertes and Hamlet lose their lives, yet there is a note of hope in the arrival of Fortinbras. He is a straightforward man who readily agrees to Horatio's request to lay all out in the open once and for all: '**Let us haste to hear it,/And call the noblest to the audience**'. At last, appearance and reality have a chance to be one and the same in Elsinore.

Death

Death, one critic remarked, is the cause and consequence of all that happens in *Hamlet*.

All of the deaths, whether they are by poison, the sword or suicide, are unnatural. The murder of the old king sets in motion a train of events which ends in the deaths of most of the main characters. There is great irony, therefore, in Claudius's efforts in Act 1 Scene 2, to persuade Hamlet that death is the most natural thing in the world. He chides the Prince for his **'unmanly grief'**, calling it **'a fault to heaven,/A fault against the dead, a fault to nature'**. The **'death of fathers'** is **'a common theme'**, Claudius points out, and not to accept it is most unreasonable.

Gertrude's view of death is simple and uncomplicated. In the same scene in which Claudius rebukes Hamlet for his **'obstinate condolement'**, Gertrude reminds her son that **'all that lives must die'**. She asks Hamlet why he cannot accept this and why he appears to be taking his father's death so badly. While a modern audience might find Gertrude's attitude callous, it must be remembered that at the time the play was written, life expectancies were far lower than they are today. Plagues swept through cities with devastating consequences. Shakespeare's audience may have found Claudius's and Gertrude's words sensible and correct, at least until they learned of the murder of the old king and the hasty remarriage of his widow.

The treatment of the theme of death reflects the conflict between old and new ideas on the afterlife at the time the play was written. Catholics believed in ghosts and spirits, and held that those who died when they were not in a state of grace were forced to suffer in purgatory until they had paid for their sins. The Ghost in *Hamlet* seems to dwell in this place, even though it is never explicitly stated where he has come from. However, he says he is **'Doomed for a certain term to walk the night,/And for the day confined to fast in fires/Till the foul crimes done in my days of nature/Are burnt and purged away'**. Protestants, however, did not believe in purgatory and thought the dead either went to heaven or hell. Therefore, there was little point in praying for their souls because they had already been judged. The humanist doctrine generally held that ghosts did not exist and were merely figments of the imagination, although some believed they could also be bad omens. Horatio has been educated at Wittenberg and, as an educated man, tries at first to dismiss the Ghost. However, once he has seen it for himself and believes in its existence, he fears it may by the **'prologue to the omen'**, comparing it to those that appeared in the streets of Rome before the murder of Julius Caesar.

Early in the play, Hamlet views death as a welcome release from the troubles of the world. He sees little point in living and, in his first soliloquy, wishes he could simply fade away and die, or that God had not forbidden suicide:

> O that this too too solid flesh would melt,
> Thaw, and resolve itself into a dew,
> Or that the Everlasting had not fixed
> His canon 'gainst self-slaughter! O God! God,
> How weary, stale, flat, and unprofitable
> Seem to me all the uses of this world!

Later in the play, when Polonius takes his leave of Hamlet, the Prince says, **'You cannot, sir, take from me anything that I will not more willingly part withal – except my life'**. Shortly afterwards, Hamlet tells Rosencrantz and Guildenstern that he has lost all joy in life and, as living things are doomed to die, Hamlet wonders what the point of life is: **'to me what is this quintessence of dust?'**

In his most famous soliloquy, beginning 'To be, or not to be', Hamlet wonders if it would be better to be dead and comes to the conclusion that people prefer life to death only because they fear the unknown. Most, he believes, would 'rather bear those ills we have/Than fly to others that we know of'. Although Hamlet discusses suicide as an option and calls death 'a consummation/Devoutly to be wished', he treats it as a general, philosophical idea rather than something he has seriously considered for himself. Hamlet is a typical Renaissance philosopher; he is more interested in the human condition and debating the merits and otherwise of death rather than acting on his words.

Hamlet is also fascinated by the idea of death and decay. He wonders what awaits us when we die. When he kills Polonius, Hamlet tells Claudius that the corpse is 'At supper'. However, he goes on to explain that Polonius is being eaten rather than eating, and points out that there is no difference between kings and beggars when they die: both are eaten by maggots and worms and eventually a man may eat a fish that has eaten a worm that has eaten the body of a king. Therefore, 'a king may go a progress through the guts of a beggar'.

This obsession with decay and what awaits us after death is also clear in the graveyard scene, when Hamlet returns from his sea voyage. Hamlet reflects that the bones scattered about the graveyard were once living people who have all been made equal by death, despite their differing stations in life: 'Here's a fine revolution, an we had the trick to see't'.

One of the gravediggers shows Hamlet the skull of Yorick, a man who was court jester in Hamlet's youth. Hamlet takes the skull and says he knew Yorick well, 'a fellow of infinite jest, of most excellent fancy'. Hamlet reflects that even the mightiest of men eventually come to nothing more than bones and dust: 'Alexander died, Alexander was buried, Alexander returneth into dust'.

Hamlet's reflections on Yorick and Alexander the Great can be seen as reflections on his own death. Hamlet resembles both in a way: he is a prince and a man who loves to make witty jokes. Yet he, too, will come to dust. Hamlet may also be thinking of his father, whose greatness he has praised so lavishly in previous acts. From this point on, there is little mention of the dead king. Has musing on death allowed Hamlet to achieve some perspective on his father's importance?

The graveyard scene foreshadows Hamlet's imminent death. The gravedigger, not recognising the Prince, says that he has been digging graves since Hamlet was born. That the gravedigger knows the Prince's name and age but does not know who he is when he is standing in front of him shows that Hamlet, too, will soon be nothing more than an anonymous set of bones in a graveyard.

For Hamlet, the graveyard scene is a pivotal moment. He realises that all men, from Alexander the Great to his father to Yorick, come to dust in the end. Once he has accepted that everyone will be 'turned to clay', Hamlet becomes more resigned to the fact that death is inevitable.

Ultimately, the death of all the main characters allows the possibility of restoration of order in Elsinore. The murder of the old king is avenged by the death of his killer and all those who conspired with him. Even Rosencrantz and Guildenstern are dead, according to the ambassador who arrives with Fortinbras. Fortinbras observes that the carnage in the court would suit the battlefield well, but is out of place in the palace. This leaves the audience with a note of hope. Claudius, after all, did not hesitate to bring death into the court but Fortinbras, the new King of Denmark, is appalled to see death outside what he considers its rightful sphere.

Madness

Revenge tragedies in Shakespeare's time generally featured a character or characters who had gone mad and, true to form, *Hamlet* contains not one but two characters who appear to have lost their sanity: Hamlet and Ophelia. Ophelia's madness is obviously genuine and brought about by a combination of traumatic incidents. The big question, of course, and one that has divided critics since the play was first discussed, is whether or not Hamlet is truly mad. In revenge plays, it was common for the hero to fake insanity in order to lull his victim into a false sense of security, which is exactly what Hamlet tries to do. However, there are inconsistencies in his behaviour that seem to indicate that there are moments when the Prince has genuinely lost his mind.

For the purposes of these notes (and it is important to remember that notes on a theme or character do not constitute an essay on that theme or character but are merely a collection of points of reference you may draw from), it is easiest to look at Hamlet's madness from both points of view. You will see that several scenes are open to different interpretations. The final decision is up to you! It is worth bearing in mind that question marks over Hamlet's mental state only serve to make him a more intriguing, complex character. Unlike Horatio, who is sane, sensible, unchanging and possibly rather dull throughout the play, Hamlet is mercurial, passionate and fascinating.

Hamlet is genuinely mad

Early in the play, long before he talks of pretending to be mad, Hamlet appears to be in a highly distressed state of mind. In his first soliloquy, in Act 1 Scene 2, he says he has lost faith in the world and sees little point in living. Indeed, he is so depressed that he contemplates taking his own life, only deciding against it because it is a sin.

> *O that this too too solid flesh would melt,*
> *Thaw, and resolve itself into a dew,*
> *Or that the Everlasting had not fixed*
> *His canon 'gainst self-slaughter! O God! God,*
> *How weary, stale, flat, and unprofitable*
> *Seem to me all the uses of this world!*

The appearance of the Ghost is a further strain on Hamlet. His behaviour when he first sees the Ghost is close to true madness. He is determined to follow it wherever it leads him, even though his friends advise against it. Hamlet orders them to stay behind and leave him to follow the Ghost on his own. Horatio remarks that Hamlet '**waxes desperate with imagination**' and Marcellus says '**Let's follow.**

'**Tis not fit thus to obey him**.' Both men clearly believe Hamlet is not in his right mind and should have his orders overruled, despite his being the Prince.

Hamlet's actions, when his friends catch up with him, reinforce the idea that he may be on the verge of true madness. While he says he will put on '**an antic disposition**' in the near future, his treatment of the Ghost when it calls to him from beneath the ground seems to indicate that he is already struggling with his sanity. He appears amused by the Ghost, referring to him as '**this fellow in the cellarage**' and addressing him as '**old mole**'. This tone is most inappropriate, particularly if Hamlet believes the spirit to be that of his dead father. Of course, Hamlet's agitation is hardly surprising, given his despair before the encounter, his horror on hearing the dreadful details of his father's murder, and the burden of duty the Ghost has laid upon him. It may be that he is overwhelmed and on the verge of being driven mad by the responsibility. He believes the world is '**out of joint**' and does not think he is the person to '**set it right**'.

Polonius is convinced that Hamlet has lost his mind when he hears of his visit to Ophelia's room. While he may misinterpret the reason for Hamlet's madness, believing it to be evidence of '**the very ecstasy of love**', Polonius is correct in judging that the Prince's mind is disordered. After all, it is hard to know what Hamlet hopes to gain from appearing in Ophelia's room in a dishevelled state, looking '**As if he had been loosed out of hell/To speak of horrors**'. The more likely reason for Hamlet's behaviour is that he is terribly distressed because Ophelia, acting on her father's orders, has rejected him at a time when he was already isolated, unhappy and weighed down by the dreadful responsibility of having to avenge his father's death.

Claudius also fears for Hamlet's sanity. Although Hamlet announces his intention to '**put on an antic disposition**', Claudius indicates that the young Prince has been behaving oddly for some time. When he sends for Rosencrantz and Guildenstern, Claudius says he is sure they have heard of Hamlet's '**transformation**'. He claims that Hamlet is so changed that he neither looks nor behaves the way he used to and that it is hard to know what else, apart from his father's death, could have '**put him/So much from th'understanding of himself**'. Some critics have taken this to mean that Hamlet's behaviour was erratic even before the appearance of the Ghost.

Hamlet's treatment of his mother after the play within the play, and his murder of Polonius, lend credence to the idea that he is genuinely mad. Hamlet behaves so aggressively and strangely that even his own mother feels sure he is going to murder her. Her cries of help lead to Polonius's making his presence known and Hamlet stabbing him impulsively. There is no logic behind Hamlet's belief that Claudius is hiding behind the arras, and his reaction to the murder is extremely odd. Why should he hide the body and refuse to disclose its location? After all, even though Polonius is an interfering old busybody, Hamlet has no real reason to hate him or to dishonour him in death. He must also know that by doing this he will cause Ophelia great pain.

At Ophelia's funeral, Hamlet acts most irrationally, fighting Laertes over who loved Ophelia more. As he grapples with his former friend, Hamlet warns him that while he is not hot-tempered, '**Yet have I something in me dangerous,/Which let thy wiseness fear**'. This can be read to mean that Hamlet knows he may be filled with a violent, uncontrollable rage and that his erratic and unpredictable behaviour should make Laertes fear him. Gertrude and Claudius both assure Laertes that Hamlet is indeed mad. Gertrude says that Hamlet has such fits but in a short while will be calm and as gentle as a dove. Hamlet supports this notion in the final scene, when he takes Laertes' hand before they duel and claims that he never intended to do him wrong. He says that it was not he, Hamlet, acting at such times, but his madness: '**His madness is poor Hamlet's enemy**'. Speaking of himself in the third person reinforces the idea that there are two distinct personalities at play: Hamlet when he is sane and Hamlet when he is mad.

Hamlet is pretending to be mad

Hamlet tells Horatio and Marcellus that he plans to adopt '**an antic disposition**', and informs Rosencrantz and Guildenstern that he is '**but mad north-north-west**'. Later in the play, he tells Gertrude that he is '**But mad in craft**' and orders her not to let Claudius know he is only acting.

Hamlet's plan is very much in the tradition of revenge plays, in which a character feigned madness to throw others off the scent. By pretending to be mad, Hamlet may hope to appear to be less of a threat to Claudius than a shrewd, sane prince – and legitimate heir – may be. However, if Hamlet's '**antic disposition**' is intended to deceive Claudius into viewing him as harmless, it fails. Claudius is never fully convinced of Hamlet's madness and seems to know that it is all pretence. He asks Rosencrantz and Guildenstern if they have managed to find out '**why he puts on this confusion**'. The words '**puts on**' show that Claudius believes Hamlet is merely faking insanity. Claudius tells Polonius that '**madness in great ones must not unwatched go**', but it is obvious from his plan to have Hamlet sent to England and murdered there that Claudius realises exactly how great a threat Hamlet poses.

Ophelia believes Hamlet to be mad, but she is too close to him to make a judgement. Her assessment of Hamlet's madness when he appears in her room is not to be taken seriously. He may well know she is likely to report back to Polonius who will, of course, rush straight to Claudius with the news. This way, news of his lunacy will spread quickly, just as Hamlet intended. Also, Ophelia's description of Hamlet does not sound anything like the young Prince. She says he has '**doublet all unbraced/No hat upon his head, his stockings fouled/Ungartered, and down-gyved to his ankle**'. In addition, Hamlet says nothing but holds Ophelia's hand while sighing and nodding his head up and down. Such behaviour seems more like exaggerated pretence of madness than genuine insanity, particularly when we consider that Hamlet uses words very freely when he is emotionally agitated. The more distressed he is, the more he says, in fact. Therefore, it appears that he is putting on a performance of his '**antic disposition**' for Ophelia. Even Polonius, who originally believed that Hamlet had been driven mad by his love for Ophelia, is forced to admit that the young Prince's speeches show a quick and able mind: '**Though this be madness, yet there be method in't**'.

The next time Hamlet meets Ophelia, he appears to know he is being spied upon. He makes veiled threats to Polonius and Claudius as if he is aware they can hear every word. He is cruel to Ophelia but even Claudius is forced to admit that Hamlet's speech, though a little disordered, is far from mad: '**what he spake, though it lacked form a little,/ Was not like madness**'. Hamlet's attack on women in general and Ophelia in particular is not surprising, given his view of his mother's hasty remarriage, nor is it a sign he has lost his mind. Ophelia does not see the reason for Hamlet's anger, saying '**O, what a noble mind is here o'erthrown**'. She believes the Prince has been '**Blasted with ecstasy**' and grieves to see him so reduced, but her love for Hamlet blinds her to the possibility that he is simply using her to spread the word that he is mad.

Hamlet's treatment of Gertrude, after his play has angered Claudius, is cruel but not mad. Certainly, Gertrude is frightened at first and is sure Hamlet means to kill her, but once she understands the reason for his anger, she realises why he has been behaving so oddly. Even after the appearance of the Ghost, which Gertrude cannot see and believes to be a hallucination, Hamlet warns her not to let it slip that he is '**not in madness,/But mad in craft**'. After this conversation with her son, Gertrude tells Claudius that Hamlet is '**Mad as the sea and wind, when both contend/Which is the mightier**' but she is simply trying to explain why he murdered Polonius.

Hamlet's conversations with the visiting actors clearly show his rationality and sanity. He directs the actors, giving them the new lines he has written for the play and warning them against overacting. Shortly after his intelligent and astute observations about the theatre, Hamlet greets Horatio. He speaks to him cleverly and coherently, expressing his admiration of Horatio's self-control and balanced views: '**Give me that man/That is not passion's slave, and I will wear him/In my heart's core**'.

Ophelia's madness

Ophelia's genuine madness contrasts with Hamlet's more ambiguous madness. Both are mourning fathers who have been brutally murdered, but only one is clearly insane.

Some critics argue that part of the reason for Ophelia's madness is that she lost her virginity to Hamlet and believes her reputation is ruined because he no longer cares for her. The songs she sings in front of the royal family are rude and seem to show that Ophelia knows more about sexual matters than would be expected of a young, unmarried woman.

We don't know whether Ophelia killed herself or died accidentally. If she did kill herself, her action contrasts with Hamlet's inaction. If she did not, her passivity could be seen as a mirror of Hamlet's passivity. Whatever your opinion, it is impossible not to feel pity for the innocent young woman who loses her mind and her life. Ophelia is yet another victim of the corruption and evil at the heart of the Danish court.

Studying Imagery and Symbolism

Shakespeare's stages would look very bare to a modern audience that is used to elaborate scenery, sophisticated lighting and a multitude of props. It was up to the actors of the time to create the setting and the mood by using language and action. Costumes were the only exception to an otherwise blank canvas and they could be very colourful and well made. Clothing was an important way of defining status and wealth.

Visiting the theatre was popular among people from all walks of life. The poorest stood near the stage and paid a small amount to attend the performance. Such people generally lacked education, so imagery and symbolism would have played an important role in helping them to understand and relate to difficult or abstract ideas.

Imagery and symbolism checklist

When you are studying imagery and symbolism, consider the following **checklist**:

✓ Does the imagery or symbolism help to **bring a scene to life** for us and/or make it **more dramatic**?

✓ Does the imagery or symbolism **create atmosphere**?

✓ Do recurring images or symbols help us to **establish or reinforce themes** in the play?

✓ Does the imagery or symbolism help us to come to an **understanding of certain characters**?

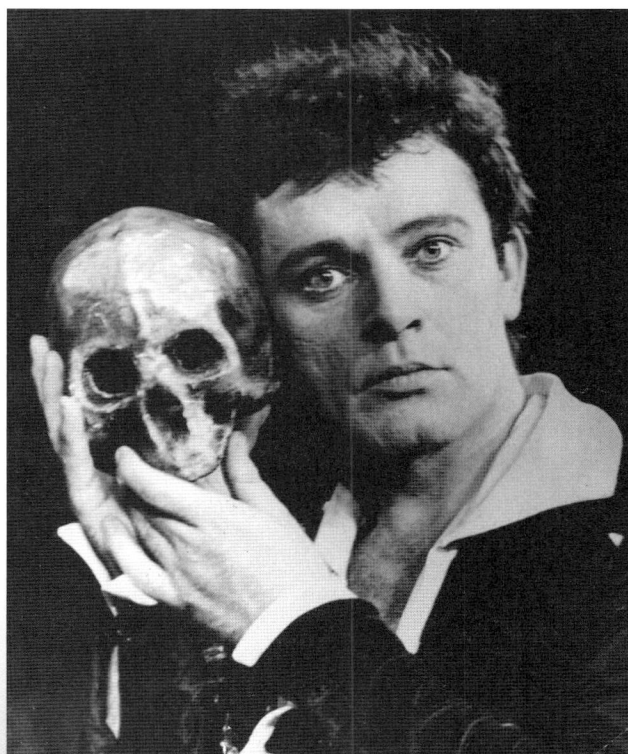

Sickness and disease

In the opening lines of the play, Francisco says that he is 'sick at heart', introducing the idea that all is not well with Denmark. Soon afterwards, Marcellus reinforces this idea when he observes, 'Something is rotten in the state of Denmark'.

The Ghost's description of his murder is particularly gruesome. The effect of Claudius's 'leperous distilment' poured into his brother's ear was to make a 'vile and loathsome crust' cover his body from head to toe. Claudius's poisoning of Old Hamlet's 'thin and wholesome blood' is symbolic of his reign. Claudius is the political and moral disease infecting Denmark, corrupting everything and everyone around him.

Laertes uses imagery of disease and decay when warning Ophelia against the damage to her reputation if she continues in her relationship with Hamlet, saying 'The canker galls the infants of the spring/Too oft before their buttons be disclosed'. Just as the budding flowers on a plant can be destroyed by 'canker' or disease before they have the chance to bloom, so Ophelia's virtue might be tarnished by vicious gossip if rumours about her and Hamlet continue to spread about the court.

Hamlet is as much a victim of the disease that plagues Denmark as anyone else. He tells Rosencrantz and Guildenstern that he considers the very air he breathes 'a foul and pestilent congregation of vapours'. In his soliloquy in Act 3, he muses that he cannot act because his resolution is 'sicklied o'er with the pale cast of thought' and later claims to Rosencrantz and Guildenstern that he cannot explain why he has been behaving so oddly: 'My wit's diseased'.

Hamlet sees his role as that of a doctor charged with curing Denmark of its illness. He compares his country to a dislocated joint that he will have to heal or reset. 'The time is out of joint. O cursed spite/That ever I was born to set it right!' He views Claudius as 'a mildewed ear' of corn, spreading its disease to everything around it. When Hamlet plans the play within the play, he compares himself to a surgeon prodding the patient to find the most painful part of an ulcer or a wound so he might know where to cut: 'I'll tent him to the quick. If he but blench,/I know my course'. After the play, when Hamlet finds Claudius praying, he decides not to kill him but believes this particular 'physic' or cure will simply prolong Claudius's 'sickly days'.

When he tackles Gertrude in her room after the play, Hamlet believes he must be 'cruel only to be kind' if she is to be saved. He tells her that by marrying Claudius, she has replaced the 'rose' of love with 'a blister' and made a mockery of love. He warns her that if she does not admit her sin and do something about it, she will merely be hiding a rot that will spread unseen:

> It will but skin and film the ulcerous place
> Whilst rank corruption, mining all within,
> Infects unseen.

Claudius also sees Hamlet as a disease that threatens his life. He compares Hamlet to a fever for which the only cure is to send him away and have him executed: 'Do it, England./For like the hectic in my blood he rages,/And thou must cure me'. He justifies this drastic action by stating that a disease that is far advanced requires a desperate remedy: 'Diseases desperate grown/By desperate measures are relieved,/Or not at all'.

Flowers

In Act 4, Scene 5, Ophelia hands out flowers to those around her. Ophelia's gifts of flowers have symbolic significance but it is not stated to whom she gives each one. She probably gives the flowers representing thoughts and remembrance to Laertes, as both are thinking about their late father: '**There's rosemary, that's for remembrance. Pray, love, remember. And there is pansies. That's for thoughts**'. The fennel and columbines, which represent flattery, deceit and disloyalty, are most likely intended for Claudius. Shakespeare's audience would have understood the significance of the flowers and the implied insult to the King.

Rue, which Ophelia probably hands to Gertrude, while also keeping some for herself, is a symbol of grace, sorrow and repentance. Ophelia calls it a '**herb-of-grace o' Sundays**' because it was a popular custom to wear it to church and dip it in the holy water for God's blessing or grace. Although both Ophelia and Gertrude are to wear the rue, Ophelia says they must to so '**with a difference**'. Presumably she means that Gertrude is to repent her marriage to Claudius and all that followed, while she, Ophelia, will wear it as a sign of her sorrow and regret at losing both her father and her lover. The daisy, which represents innocence, is not given to anyone. This is appropriate as, bar Ophelia, nobody present is innocent. Violets represent faithfulness but they '**withered all**' when Polonius died. Ophelia loved Hamlet but he betrayed her when he killed her father.

Yorick's skull

Hamlet dwells on the idea of death throughout the play. He contemplates suicide in his fourth soliloquy: '**To be, or not to be**' and regrets that God has '**fixed/His canon 'gainst self-slaughter**'. When Hamlet looks at the skull of the court jester, Yorick, he comes to an important realisation about life and death. Although Yorick was '**a fellow of infinite jest**', who was an important part of Hamlet's childhood, he is now reduced to nothing. Man is insignificant in the greater scheme of things and, Hamlet reflects, great kings like Alexander will, like Yorick, all turn to dust. Hamlet's reflections on Yorick and Alexander the Great can be seen as reflections on his own death. Hamlet resembles both, in a way: he is a prince and a man who loves to make witty jokes. Yet he, too, will become nothing more than bones in a graveyard. Hamlet may also be thinking of his father, whom he idolised and feared he could never equal. After this scene, there is little mention of the old king. Shortly after these reflections on the meaning of life, Hamlet announces himself to the mourners at Ophelia's funeral as '**Hamlet the Dane**'. He appears to view himself as the rightful king at last and to have put his father's achievements and greatness into perspective.

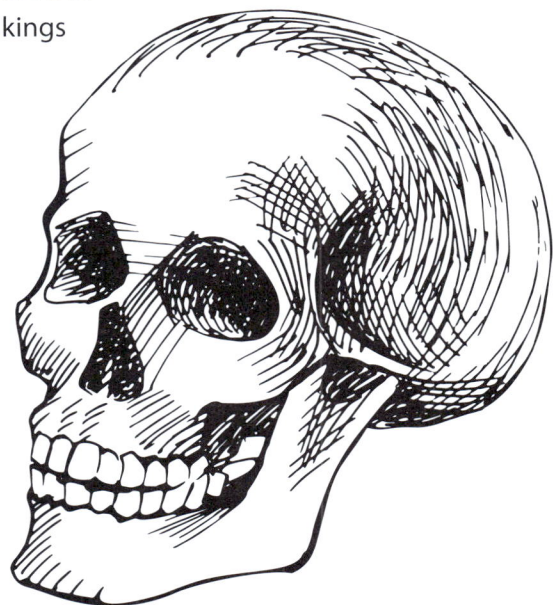

Approaching the Essay

Timing

- The Single Text question is worth 60 marks and you should spend around 55 minutes answering it.
- There is no set length – the size and speed of people's handwriting varies – but most essays will be between four and five pages long.

Types of questions

Questions in the Single Text section tend to focus on the following areas:

Characters

- Be prepared to discuss groups of similar/contrasting characters or relationships between characters.
- Remember, you will never be asked to write a simple character sketch! Think about the character's role, development and relationship with others.

Themes

- Be aware of the main themes in the play and be ready to talk about the manner in which they are conveyed.

Imagery and symbolism

- You will need to have detailed knowledge of the play to answer a question on imagery and symbolism.

Dramatic scenes

- If you are focusing on dramatic scenes, know them in great detail, be able to state the act and scene numbers, and be prepared to refer to a stage or film version of the play you have seen.
- It is a good idea to focus on three key scenes, perhaps from the beginning, middle and end of the play.

General questions

- These tend to focus on the overall impact of the play or on the relevance or appeal of the play to a modern audience.
- Many questions do not fall neatly into one category but require you to discuss aspects of character, themes and dramatic techniques. For example, the following question clearly requires discussion of dramatic techniques as well as character and theme: Discuss how Shakespeare's use of language, including imagery, plays an important part in developing our understanding of one of the following aspects of his play, *Hamlet*: themes; characterisation; setting and atmosphere. Develop your answer with reference to the text.

Analysing the question

- This does **not** mean simply underlining key words, calling to mind everything you know about that character or theme and jotting down your studied notes in some sort of chronological order with regular, forced references to the question.
- The examiner will reward a nuanced answer in which you express genuine viewpoints and frame your essay as a coherent argument.
- Do not focus on one word only – the name of the character or a theme – as Higher Level questions are never as simple as a rehash of notes on character or theme. You will be required to engage with all aspects of the question.
- Be aware of the coding used by the examiners. Try to work out what it might be, and keep in mind that a point that cannot be coded has no place in your answer. Here are examples from past marking schemes:
  - 'Uncertainty, which features constantly in Shakespeare's play, *Hamlet*, adds significantly to the dramatic impact of the play.' Discuss this statement, developing your response with reference to the text.
    - Marking Scheme: Code UD for uncertainty adds significantly to the dramatic impact of the play.
  - Discuss how Shakespeare makes effective use, for a variety of purposes, of the contradictions and inconsistencies evident in Hamlet's character. Develop your discussion with reference to Shakespeare's play, *Hamlet*.
    - Marking Scheme: Code CE for the contradictions and inconsistencies evident in Hamlet's character effectively used for a variety of purposes.

- Shakespeare's play *Hamlet* has been described as 'a disturbing psychological thriller'. To what extent do you agree or disagree with this description of the play? In your response you should deal with all aspects of the statement, supporting your answer with reference to the text.
  - Marking Scheme: Code DT/PT for the play is/is not a disturbing psychological thriller.
- 'Shakespeare makes effective use of both Laertes and Horatio to fulfil a variety of dramatic functions in his play, *Hamlet*.' Discuss this statement, supporting your answer with reference to the text.
  - Marking Scheme: Code LF for makes/does not make effective use of Laertes to fulfil a variety of dramatic functions.

In the 2021 Leaving Certificate exam, students were asked to consider a proposed production of the play in which certain characters do not appear and to reflect on the effect the characters' removal would have on the play. Although this may seem a difficult question, it is simply asking students to think about each character's role in the play, their highlighting of certain themes, their qualities, relationships, etc. Refer to the notes on Studying Character in this book, where you will see relevant checklists.

In 2017, students were asked the following question: '"Shakespeare makes effective use of both Laertes and Horatio to fulfil a variety of dramatic functions in his play, *Hamlet*." Discuss this statement, supporting your answer with reference to the text.'

This question could equally have been framed as follows: 'A production of Shakespeare's play, *Hamlet*, in which the characters of Horatio and Laertes do not appear has been proposed. Discuss the reasons why, in your opinion, the removal of each of these characters would or would not diminish Shakespeare's play, *Hamlet*. Develop your response with reference to the text.'

Both questions are simply asking students to consider the characters' roles in the play.

Planning

- There is no set way to plan an answer. At this stage, you probably have your own style. What follows is a suggested approach, but if you have another method that suits you, stick with it.
- Brainstorm the idea, jotting down everything you can think of in relation to the question.
- Fine-tune your notes, deciding the order in which you will make your points and the key moments/ quotes you will use to support those points.

Structure

- Your essay should flow naturally.
- If it were cut into individual paragraphs and jumbled up, anyone reading them should be able to reassemble them correctly, as there should be clear links between paragraphs.

Introduction

- Give your thesis statement in response to the question. Provide a brief outline of the ideas you will explore in the essay.
- Remember, if you mention something in your introduction, then you MUST deal with it in the body of the essay.

Main body of the essay

- Each paragraph should advance your argument.
- The topic sentence in each paragraph should be linked in some way to the question.
- Use link words or phrases to connect your paragraphs where possible: 'However …', 'It is not only …', 'We can also see …'
- Reference and quotation should be commented on and evaluated. This does not mean explaining the quotation in your own words. You should show how the example reinforces the point you are making.

Conclusion

- Summarise the main points of your argument.
- Restate your thesis.
- If you have an apt quote from or about the play, this is a good time to use it. Make sure you work it into a sentence and evaluate/comment on it rather than simply throwing it down on the page!
- Do not raise any new points in the conclusion, no matter how good they may seem. If you didn't think of a point in time, just leave it out.

Common mistakes

- Not realising there are several elements to the question
- Not planning the essay and therefore wandering off the point or writing contradictory points
- Writing unfocused narrative (telling the story of the play)
- Writing simple character sketches
- Not quoting accurately/sufficiently
- Writing quotes that are too long

Sample Answers

2011 Leaving Certificate

Claudius can be seen as both a heartless villain and a character with some redeeming features in the play Hamlet.

Discuss both aspects of this statement, supporting your answer with suitable reference to the text.

Step 1: Analyse the question

1. What are the key words in this question?

Claudius can be seen as both a <u>heartless villain</u> and a <u>character with some redeeming features</u> in the play Hamlet.

Discuss <u>both aspects</u> of this statement, supporting your answer with suitable reference to the text.

2. Think about the question in some detail.

You do not have to fully agree or fully disagree with any statement. The examiner will reward a nuanced answer in which you really mull over the question and frame your essay as a coherent argument. Ask yourself:

- In what ways is Claudius a heartless villain?
- Are there moments in the play when this aspect of his nature comes to the fore?
- What does he do that you consider particularly heartless?
- Does Claudius have any redeeming qualities? What are they?

Now ask yourself whether those redeeming qualities outweigh his heartless, villainous traits. What conclusion did you draw?

> **Tip**
>
> Ask for some sheets of extra paper at the start of the exam and use these for your plans. That way, you won't have to keep flipping back and forth through your booklet to check your plan when writing your essay.

Heartless villain	Redeeming qualities
Murders his brother/the king	Capable king/diplomat
Marries brother's widow	Does appear to love her
Uses those around him	Bravely faces Laertes
Lets Gertrude die	
Refuses to repent	Knows he should repent
Driven by self-interest	Self-aware
Obs. bad qualities outweigh good qualities	

Evaluation (my thesis/introduction)

Claudius is not a completely heartless villain but he is ultimately self-serving and greedy. Good qualities not enough to redeem him in our eyes. (List reasons)

Step 2: Create a plan

This brainstorming should now be fine-tuned as you decide the order in which you will make your points and the key moments/quotes you will use to support those points.

Structure of essay:

1. Good king: opening speech is impressive/deals with personal and political matters. Clever to show danger of young Fortinbras' rebellious attitude could lead to war

2. Appearance of Ghost shows us other side: lustful and corrupt. Good leadership not enough to make up for crimes

3. Conscience goes small way towards redeeming him: feels guilty (a) when Polonius tells O. about hiding evil (b) in Prayer Scene

4. Will do anything to protect self. Sacrifices others. Is brave when dealing with Laertes but then corrupts him. Lets Gertrude die and lies about poison.

5. Trades soul for throne and queen. Deserves to die: 'is justly served'. Ruled by morally corrupt side of self.

Sample answer

Claudius, like so many of the characters in Shakespeare's *Hamlet* is a complex and fascinating character who excites both admiration and revulsion at various stages in the play. Although he is the villain of the piece, Claudius is not merely an evil sociopath. He is a good king in many ways and a skilled diplomat, and he feels pangs of conscience for his heinous crime against his brother. It does appear that he loves his wife, although his means of procuring her love are utterly despicable. He is brave in facing down Laertes and his angry mob, but a coward in the way he kills his brother and manipulates the lives of others to serve his own ends. He is certainly not likeable, but he is human. However, the positive features of his character are not enough to redeem him and in the end Claudius goes to his grave unmourned by the audience, who see his death as just reward for a man who was ultimately self-serving and ruled by greed.

When we first see Claudius, he appears eloquent, relaxed and in control. His opening speech deals with personal and political matters and is polished, persuasive and carefully structured. The first half of the speech sugar-coats his marriage to his brother's wife, claiming that both he and Gertrude balanced their love for one another with their sorrow for the death of Old Hamlet:

> 'With mirth in funeral and with dirge in marriage,
> In equal scale weighing delight and dole.'

> **Tip**
>
> Your introduction should outline the points that you will discuss during the rest of your answer. Remember, if you mention something in the introduction, you must deal with it over the course of the essay.

Claudius smoothly moves on from the potentially controversial topic of his recent marriage to the threat posed by young Fortinbras' plan to capitalise on the recent change of government in Denmark by 'Importing the surrender of those lands/ Lost by his father'. This is a clever move as it reminds the people that any civil unrest in Denmark could leave them vulnerable to attack from outside. It also shows that he, Claudius, is dealing with the matter decisively by sending his ambassadors to the King of Norway. Yet this is more than a mere show of power. Claudius's actions are well-judged, as we learn later in the play that young Fortinbras is reined in by his uncle and promises 'never more/To give the assay of arms against your majesty'.

However, there is more to Claudius than this diplomatic, public face. The Ghost describes him as 'that incestuous, that adulterate beast' and tells Hamlet that Claudius murdered him in a cowardly and foul way. The 'leperous distilment' Claudius poured into his sleeping brother's ear caused his skin to erupt into a 'vile and loathsome crust'. Hamlet echoes the audience's horror on hearing of this dreadful crime when he calls Claudius a 'smiling, damned villain'. Despite his affable, capable public persona, Claudius is a lustful, corrupt man and no amount of skilled leadership can make up for the fact that he is what is 'rotten in the state of Denmark'. His crimes of fratricide and incest make him unfit to rule.

> **Tip**
>
> Any points you make must be linked back to the question.

An interesting facet of Claudius's character and one that goes a small way towards redeeming him in our eyes when we first learn of it, is that he is troubled by his conscience. When he hears Polonius tell Ophelia that people can hide their wickedness by pretending to be virtuous, Claudius remarks in an aside, 'How smart a lash that speech doth give my conscience!' and refers to his crime as a 'heavy burden'. Similarly, in the Prayer Scene, we see that Claudius is tormented by his guilt, admitting 'my offence is rank! It smells to heaven'. Another aspect of Claudius's nature that gains a certain admiration is his ability to face the truth. He is self-aware enough to know that because he 'cannot repent' his crime and give up what he gained by the murder of his brother, he does not deserve to be forgiven. This evidence of humanity reminds us that Claudius is more than a heartless villain but because he cannot fully repent, we must conclude that this is not enough to redeem him.

It is self-interest that drives Claudius and prevents him from publicly acknowledging or admitting his guilt. This self-interest also means that he will do whatever it takes to protect himself and his position. He is willing to sacrifice the lives of those who stand in his way. That he does so cleverly and coolly does not mitigate the heinous nature of his crimes. Hamlet's play shows that his crime is known and this makes Hamlet a threat to Claudius. He concludes that it is unsafe to 'let his madness range' and arranges for him to go to England with Rosencrantz and Guildenstern, where he will be executed. Even more damningly, Claudius is willing to manipulate the lives of those who pose no threat to him, if doing so will further his own ends. His dealings with Laertes show his bravery and good judgement on the one hand, in that he swiftly suppresses his rebellion and persuades the young man that he is 'guiltless of your father's death'. But they also show just how corrupt he is when he convinces Laertes that it is morally right to kill Hamlet. Most cruelly and selfishly of all, Claudius does nothing to stop Gertrude from drinking the poisoned cup, as he would be implicated in the plot to kill Hamlet if he were to intervene. When Gertrude falls, he even pretends it is because she is distressed by the bloody fight between Hamlet and Laertes: 'She swoons to see them bleed'.

Ultimately, Claudius's determination to live a lie and to trade his soul for the throne and the queen as his wife seals his doom. Laertes remarks that the dead king 'is justly served' when he is both stabbed and poisoned by Hamlet, and it would be difficult to disagree with this assessment. Claudius was neither a heartless villain nor a monster but he chose to suppress the better side of his nature and be led by the morally corrupt side of himself, which was his undoing. We are left, therefore, with a picture of a man whose talents in leadership and shrewdness in judging human nature came to nothing because his public and private life were based on murder and deceit, and such crimes cannot go unpunished.

Sample Question

What is your view of the importance of **either** Gertrude **or** Ophelia in Shakespeare's *Hamlet*?

Support the points you make with reference to the text.

(*Note: You are free to choose either woman. Focus on the role of your chosen character.*)

Sample plan:

> She is Hamlet's love interest: shows us his view of women

> Exploited by others, which is symptomatic of the world of the play

> Her innocence and purity highlight the corruption of others

> She excites our pity and sympathy, as she is torn between two worlds and treated badly by Hamlet

Sample answer

Ophelia's principal role in the play is to be Hamlet's love interest and to show how genuine, honest love can be corrupted in a corrupt world. Her love for Hamlet shows us another side to the Prince's tortured soul. Her innocence and openness contrast with the cruelty and deception of the Danish court and through her, we see how the innocent can suffer when those in power put their own needs before the greater good.

From the start, Ophelia appears to truly care for Hamlet and is wounded by Laertes' assertion that Hamlet's interest in her is 'Forward not permanent, sweet, not lasting', asking sadly, 'No more but so?' She does not want to believe that Hamlet does not love her and her adoration for him remains undiminished. She praises him as 'that unmatched form and feature of blown youth' and is dismayed at his apparent descent into madness: 'O, what a noble mind is here o'erthrown!' It is Ophelia who tells us what Hamlet was like before his father's death and his mother's marriage to Claudius: 'The courtier's, soldier's, scholar's eye, tongue, sword'/Th'expectancy and rose of the fair state'. Her praise of Hamlet shows us not just how much she loves him but also reminds us that the young Prince was once far happier and more admirable than he is when we first meet him. However, their relationship is doomed from the moment Hamlet meets the Ghost, and Ophelia becomes a victim of the plotting and intrigue that mark the Danish court.

Ophelia suffers because Gertrude betrayed Hamlet's late father. Hamlet takes out his rage and disgust with his mother on the innocent Ophelia and blames her for sins she has not committed. He claims only a fool would marry her or any woman because 'wise men know well enough what monsters you make of them'. Later, as they wait to see Hamlet's play performed, he taunts her with the crudest of puns and innuendos, referring to 'country matters' and 'puppets dallying', which confuses and distresses Ophelia. Every time she asks him to explain himself, Hamlet merely attacks her with further hurtful words. Hamlet's treatment of Ophelia is grossly

Tip

It is important to link any point you make about Ophelia back to the question. In other words, you need to comment on her role in the play and why she is important.

unfair but it does serve to highlight his negative and misogynistic views.

It is not just Hamlet who exploits Ophelia's loving and trusting nature. Her inexperience makes her unable to fathom Hamlet's abuse of her and it also makes her unable to stand up to her father and brother when they tell her what to do. She heeds Laertes' advice to hold Hamlet's passion for her as 'a toy in blood'. She shows similar obedience to her father's wishes when she says 'I do not know, my lord, what I should think' in response to his probing questions about Hamlet's intentions. Her exploitation by others highlights how the powerful characters in the Danish court can use and abuse those who are weaker or more naïve than they are.

> **Tip**
>
> It is essential to keep your focus on the question throughout. The question asked you to comment on the importance of your chosen character so you must ensure that every example you use can be linked to the character's role in the play.

Polonius's treatment of Ophelia is particularly unpleasant, and is symptomatic of the corrupt nature of the world of the play. Ophelia turns to her father for help and advice when Hamlet comes to her room in a dishevelled state, acting oddly. Polonius shows no real concern for his daughter but instead leaps to the conclusion that Hamlet is mad with love for her and he wonders how he can use this to his advantage. He uses her as bait to trap Hamlet into admitting the reason for his madness and the obedient and dutiful Ophelia agrees to do as he says. Hamlet's harsh treatment of her: 'I loved you not', wounds Ophelia deeply and she cries 'O woe is me,/T'have seen what I have seen, see what I see!' when he leaves. Polonius and Claudius, who have been spying on the couple, care nothing for her sorrow and Polonius merely says, 'You need not tell us what Lord Hamlet said;/We heard it all' before ignoring her and turning to Claudius to discuss the best way to deal with Hamlet. That a father could abuse his daughter's obedient and trusting nature shows just how rotten things are in the state of Denmark.

Ophelia's innocence and purity highlight the corrupt nature of the court and also elicit the audience's sympathy. Her plight is terrible, and as the play progresses and intrigue follows intrigue, it is the pure and blameless Ophelia who suffers the most. The man she loves turns on her and blames her for all the sins he perceives in women. Her father treats her as bait, telling Claudius, 'I'll loose my daughter to him', and shows no compassion when this scheme leads to Hamlet verbally attacking Ophelia. Finally, the man she loves kills her father and hides his body before it is found and hastily buried without due ceremony. It is no surprise, then, that Ophelia cannot cope with this litany of horrors and that she descends into madness. Her piteous condition appals Laertes and his words, 'Do you see this, O God?', as she wanders through the court singing and handing out flowers to those she meets, echo the audience's dismay on seeing the deterioration in the young woman's mental state.

Ophelia's death is truly tragic. Unlike the deaths of the other characters, all of whom have behaved badly in one way or another, Ophelia was entirely innocent from start to finish. She was too unworldly and too pure to comprehend the plotting, corruption and deceit around her and she could never adapt to such a place as Elsinore has become. Her final role is to show us that purity and goodness can do little when faced with evil.

2011 Leaving Certificate

'Revenge and justice are finely balanced themes in the play, *Hamlet*.'

Discuss this statement, supporting your answer with suitable reference to the text.

*(**Note:** You must deal with both revenge and justice, although not necessarily equally.)*

Sample plan:

> Revenge outweighs justice

> Three sons seek revenge in different ways

> Fortinbras does not have justice on his side

> Hamlet is keen to balance revenge and justice but his procrastination leads to unjust suffering and death

> Laertes seeks revenge for Polonius's death but is not concerned with justice and is corrupted by Claudius

> Ophelia dies because of revenge plot

> Hamlet's revenge at the end of the play is impulsive

Sample answer

The themes of revenge and justice are central to the play, *Hamlet*. However, they are not perfectly balanced. Three sons – Hamlet, Fortinbras and Laertes – seek to avenge their fathers' deaths. Each approaches his quest differently and, through the three men's actions or inaction, we learn the difference between just and lawful vengeance and that which is executed without due consideration or cause. Hamlet, unlike Fortinbras and Laertes, wants to strike a balance between revenge and justice. Tragically, it is his desire to do this that brings about one of the greatest injustices in the play: the death of the innocent Ophelia who is caught in the web of lies, intrigue and violence that result from Hamlet's quest.

Before we meet Hamlet, the themes of justice and revenge are introduced by the conversation between Horatio, Marcellus and Barnardo as they wait for the Ghost to appear. Horatio explains that Denmark is preparing for war because young Fortinbras, nephew of the current King of Norway, wishes to avenge his father's death at the hands of Old Hamlet, the previous King of Denmark. However, Fortinbras does not have just cause to seek revenge. His father agreed to the trial of combat in which he was killed by Hamlet's father, and the lands that Norway forfeited to Denmark as a result were handed over in 'a sealed compact/Well ratified by law and heraldry'. It is because his desire for revenge is not just that Fortinbras has to gather 'a list of lawless resolutes' to help him in his quest. Later in the play we learn that Claudius has put a stop to Fortinbras' plans by sending ambassadors to warn the young man's uncle of his intentions. Fortinbras agrees never to threaten Denmark again and instead turns his energies to what appears to be a pointless war with Poland. Ultimately, Fortinbras does regain the land his father lost when Hamlet names him King of Denmark, but it is important to note the difference between his unjust and failed quest for revenge and his lawful nomination to the throne.

Although Fortinbras is not a model for anyone seeking to balance revenge and justice, he nonetheless plays an important role in that his actions highlight Hamlet's inaction. Hamlet, unlike Fortinbras, has just cause to avenge his father's death. The Ghost has ordered him to revenge his 'foul and most unnatural murder'. Despite vowing that he will act 'with wings as swift/As meditation or the thoughts of love', Hamlet does not kill Claudius straight away. Instead, he engages in lengthy soul-searching to determine whether and how he should act. It is only when he sees Fortinbras and his army on the march to fight for 'a little patch of ground/That hath in it no profit but the name' that Hamlet vows to stop procrastinating and to avenge his father, reflecting that he has 'cause, and will, and strength, and means' to do it. The question is, of course, why has Hamlet not acted until now? The answer lies in the problem of balancing revenge and justice. Hamlet is a scholar and a thoughtful young man who lacks the simple, straightforward attitude of men like Fortinbras. He knows he should act but his conscience rebels against killing Claudius without absolute proof that it is right and just to do so. Although he rebukes himself for this, saying in his soliloquy in Act 2 that he is 'Prompted to my revenge by heaven and hell', Hamlet believes he must be sure of Claudius's guilt before he moves against him. After all, he muses, the Ghost might be 'the devil, and the devil hath power/T'assume a pleasing shape'. This desire to mete out justice and vengeance in equal measure leads Hamlet to strike on the idea of staging a play to 'catch the conscience of the King'.

The success of 'The Murder of Gonzago' invigorates Hamlet and he is at last convinced that Claudius is guilty. The play is also a bloodless form of revenge well-suited to Hamlet's personality because it allows him to use his intellect to achieve his goal and not run the risk of acting unjustly. After all, if Claudius had not murdered the King, the play would have passed without incident. Now, however, Hamlet must act, and the ideal opportunity presents itself when he comes across Claudius kneeling at prayer. Just as he says, 'Now might I do it pat … And so I am revenged', Hamlet decides it would be better not to kill his uncle. His reasoning is based on the balance between revenge and justice: if Claudius dies at prayer, he will go to heaven. Hamlet reasons that Claudius gave Old Hamlet no such chance to die in a state of grace, and therefore killing him now would be, 'hire and salary, not revenge'. For true justice to be served, Claudius must suffer eternal damnation. Soon afterwards, Hamlet believes he might have found the ideal opportunity to kill his uncle when he realises there is an eavesdropper hiding behind the arras while he and Gertrude talk. Believing it to be Claudius, Hamlet stabs the unseen man and is disappointed to find it is only Polonius. This case of mistaken identity will precipitate another son, Laertes, to seek revenge for his father's death, further complicating an already complex situation.

Hamlet's failure to kill Claudius means he is packed off to England and vanishes from the action of the play for some time. However, the themes of justice and revenge are still to the fore. Laertes returns from France, storms the castle and vows bloody vengeance on whoever killed Polonius. Unlike Hamlet, Laertes is not concerned with ensuring justice and revenge are balanced. He rages, 'Conscience and grace, to the profoundest pit! … Let come what comes. Only I'll be revenged/Most thoroughly for my father'. While Laertes' cause is just, his readiness to 'dare damnation' makes his approach to revenge morally questionable. Yet his quest serves to show the rightness of Hamlet's approach. At the time, the Church taught that revenge should be left to God, but the classical tradition of revenge plays implied that when honour was at stake, a man was within his rights to seek vengeance on the wrongdoer.

Hamlet wrestles with the conflict between these two ideals, but Laertes does not. Ultimately, this leads to Laertes being corrupted by Claudius when the pair conspire to kill Hamlet in a rigged and dishonorable duel. Although he repents in the end and is forgiven, Laertes – like Fortinbras – provides us with an example of revenge divided from justice.

Polonius dies because he has become caught up in the struggle between Claudius and Hamlet, and has chosen the wrong side. His death is not warranted, but it is hard to feel any real sympathy for him. Ophelia's death, however, is a far greater example of the injustice that results from Hamlet's quest for vengeance. She is torn between love for her father and Hamlet, and when she allows herself to be used as bait so that Claudius and Polonius can spy on Hamlet, the Prince takes out all his frustrations and anger on her, subjecting her to verbal and emotional abuse. His madness, whether real or feigned, distresses the gentle Ophelia terribly and his cruelty ultimately causes her to lose her own mind. Whether Ophelia falls in the water accidentally or takes her own life, she is undoubtedly an innocent victim of Hamlet's long, drawn out and complex revenge plot.

Hamlet's revenge on Claudius is a long time in coming, but when he does act, everything happens rather quickly and impulsively. He stabs and then poisons his uncle when he learns that the King has plotted to kill him and is responsible for Gertrude's death. Justice is served in that Claudius dies by poison, just as Hamlet's father did, and the Ghost's desire for vengeance has been fulfilled. The audience is likely to agree with Laertes' comment on the King's death: 'He is justly served'. However, the killing of Claudius came too late to save Polonius, Gertrude or Ophelia. Revenge has triumphed over justice in the end.

2020 Leaving Certificate

(ii) Discuss how Shakespeare makes effective use, for a variety of purposes, of the contradictions and inconsistencies evident in Hamlet's character. Develop your answer with reference to Shakespeare's play, *Hamlet*.

Sample plan:

> Danish court corrupts everything, including the relationship between Hamlet and Ophelia. Rosencrantz and Guildenstern reflect this corruption and Hamlet's contempt of them is understandable, given what he know.

> Shakespeare's audience were beginning to explore the theme of mortality/death: did things have to be this way?

> It is easy to relate to Hamlet's struggle to balance duties and feelings

> Hamlet's unpredictability creates and maintains tension in the play right to the end

Sample answer

Hamlet is an enigma. At the end of the play, we are little closer to understanding his nature than we were at the start. We can never say for certain that he is truly mad, that he genuinely loves Ophelia or that he is driven to avenge his father's murder. Naturally, we may feel uneasy when studying a character who is so hard to categorise. The reality, of course, is that life is not straightforward, and people do not always follow clear paths. Hamlet is an 'Everyman', wrestling with exaggerated versions of struggles we all face when we try to balance duties and feelings. Above all, of course, Shakespeare ensures that the contradictions and inconsistencies evident in Hamlet's character provide plot twists and turns that keep the audience on the edge of their seats.

Tip

Your introduction should outline the direction your essay will take. If you raise something in the introduction, you must deal with in the body of the answer.

One of the most intriguing aspects of Hamlet's character is his madness, whether real or feigned. In revenge plays, it was common for the hero to fake insanity to lull his enemy into a false sense of security, which is exactly what Hamlet tries to do. However, there are inconsistencies in his behaviour that seem to indicate the Prince has genuinely lost his reason. Although Hamlet tells his friends he intends to put on 'an antic disposition', at times this madness seems pointless or counterproductive. The first of these is his behaviour when the Ghost calls to him from beneath the ground. He appears amused by his dead father's spirit, referring to him as 'this fellow in the cellarage' and addressing him as 'old mole'. This inappropriate tone signals an agitated, irrational state of mind, which is hardly surprising given Hamlet's despair at his father's death and horror on learning the dreadful details of the murder.

Tip

Aim to support each point with two key moments from the play.

Later in the play, Hamlet again behaves in a puzzling manner. He confronts Gertrude in her chamber, becoming so aggressive that she fears for her life. Her cries of help lead to Polonius making his presence known and Hamlet stabbing him impulsively. There is no logic behind Hamlet's belief that Claudius is hiding behind the arras, and his reaction to the murder is extremely odd. He says he will 'lug the guts into the neighbour room' and continues to treat the body disrespectfully, refusing to disclose its location when asked. Hamlet has no reason to hate or dishonour Polonius this much, and he must know his actions will cause Ophelia great pain. His actions are bewildering, unless we believe he is truly mad. These question marks over Hamlet's mental state recur throughout the play and serve to make him a complex, endlessly fascinating character.

Hamlet's treatment of Ophelia throughout the play highlights the inconsistencies and contradictions in his character. He seems to love her but behaves most cruelly to her on occasion. During the performance of the play, he subjects her to a barrage of crude innuendos meant to shock and insult her, asking if she thought

> **Tip**
>
> Link back to the terms of the question in each section of your essay.

he was talking about 'country matters' when she refused his request to lie in her lap. Hamlet takes out his rage and disgust with his mother on the innocent Ophelia, blaming her for things she has never done. He claims only a fool would marry because 'wise men know well enough/What monsters you make of them'. Hamlet's mistreatment of Ophelia and his killing Polonius eventually drive the poor young woman mad. She dies bewildered and heartbroken, an innocent victim of a corrupt court.

Ophelia's funeral again shows Hamlet at his most mercurial. He claims to have loved Ophelia more than 'Forty thousand brothers' could and jumps into her open grave to fight Laertes. If Hamlet truly cared for Ophelia, would he have treated her as he did in life, and disrespected her so in death? Their troubled relationship keeps the audience on tenterhooks to the very end. And yet, if Hamlet's love is real, why does he never mention Ophelia once after this scene? He muses on death and the afterlife frequently, and is clearly deeply affected by his father's death, so his dismissal of Ophelia seems callous and not in keeping with his character. As is the case with so much of Hamlet's behaviour, more questions are raised than answered.

Hamlet says the reason for his 'antic disposition' is to help him in his desire to avenge his father's murder. He claims he will act 'with wings as swift/As meditation or the thoughts of love' yet he famously procrastinates and questions the morality of vengeance. The contradiction between Hamlet's stated aim and his failure to act raises a number of interesting philosophical questions. Is Shakespeare using Hamlet's moral dilemma to show the folly of reckless, impulsive behaviour? Should we ask ourselves if it is ever acceptable to repay murder with murder? After all, Fortinbras and Laertes seek vengeance without hesitation and are willing to kill to achieve their ends, but neither succeeds. Furthermore, Laertes becomes morally compromised when he conspires with Claudius.

Unlike Fortinbras and Laertes, Hamlet engages in lengthy soul-searching to determine whether and how he should act. His conscience rebels against the violent act he must carry out if he is to obey the Ghost. Over the course of the play, Hamlet veers between determination and hesitation, certainty and doubt. At times, he harbours violent thoughts of revenge. After the performance of the play within the play, he says he could 'drink hot blood/And do such bitter business as the day/Would quake to look on'. Soon afterwards, he comes across Claudius praying alone and realises that this is the ideal opportunity to kill him. However, at this moment of heightened tension when the audience might reasonably expect Hamlet to act at last, he again procrastinates. Once more, he begins to think deeply about the situation, concluding that killing his uncle at prayer would be 'hire and salary, not revenge'. This contradiction of his earlier desire to 'do it pat' is anti-climactic, but it also shows us yet another aspect of Hamlet's character. He is coldly determined to ensure Claudius is doomed to eternal damnation, and this ruthlessness does not seem to align with his thoughtful, philosophical nature.

Ironically, given that Hamlet wrestles so much with his conscience and agonises over what is right to do, his killing of Claudius at the end of the play is a sudden act. He stabs and poisons his uncle when he learns that the King has plotted to poison him and has accidentally poisoned Gertrude. At this stage in the play, Hamlet again contradicts himself. Far from believing that he should exercise careful judgement, the Prince seems to have resigned himself to fate and to the belief that the opportunity to avenge his father's death will present itself at the right time. He claims now that 'There's a divinity that shapes our ends' and that he can simply surrender himself to fate. He seizes this opportunity when it arises, certainly, but his killing of Claudius comes too late to save Polonius, Ophelia, Rosencrantz, Guildenstern, Gertrude, Laertes and Hamlet himself. Yet the action and excitement of this final scene in the play undoubtedly contribute to the audience's enjoyment. The tension is maintained until the last moments, and few could argue but that Claudius is 'justly served' at the end.

Hamlet's behaviour throughout the play is at times frustrating and perplexing, and audiences and critics alike continue to hotly debate his character and his actions. Yet there is no contesting that the enduring popularity of *Hamlet* is due to the complexity of the titular character. 'What a piece of work is man' indeed.

Sample Question

Two approaches to a question - there is no 'right answer'

'Despite her suffering, Ophelia is a weak, passive character who fails to gain our sympathy.'

To what extent would you agree or disagree with this view of Ophelia?

(**Note**: the plans are far longer than you would write in an exam and are given in detail here so they can be easily understood.)

First approach:

Ophelia is weak and passive and fails to gain our sympathy.

- Although she loves Hamlet, Ophelia meekly accepts Laertes' claim that the Prince views their relationship as 'The perfume and suppliance of a minute./No more'. When Polonius reinforces the idea that Hamlet is only toying with her and could not possibly marry someone so lowly, Ophelia does not argue.

  She appears to have no real mind of her own, and when Polonius asks if she really believes that Hamlet loves her, Ophelia replies, 'I do not know, my lord, what I should think'.

- Ophelia allows her father and brother to lecture her and says little in response. As a result, it is difficult to sympathise with her.

- Some argue that Ophelia is duty-bound to obey her father and brother and is neither weak nor passive in nature but simply a typically obedient Elizabethan woman. If that were the case, we might feel sympathy for her. However, Shakespeare was very capable of writing about strong-willed women who took the initiative when it came to love and who were more than capable of defying the men in their lives. Juliet, for example, was only 13 but risked all for love.

- Ophelia's obedience may make her a good Elizabethan daughter, but it prevents her from being an admirable heroine. If she truly loved Hamlet, why did she not show some strength of character and stand up to Polonius when he demanded that she break off all contact with him? 'I did repel his letters and denied/His access to me'

- It is difficult to feel any sympathy for Ophelia here. She has treated Hamlet very poorly indeed, showing no sympathy or understanding when he arrives in her room in a state of great distress. Once again, she stands by passively while Hamlet comes before her 'with a look so piteous in purport/As if he had been loosed out of hell/To speak of horrors'. Worse still, she says nothing when Polonius changes his mind about Hamlet, claiming that he must truly love Ophelia after all and that he has been driven mad by her rejection.

- Ophelia's continued loyalty to her father and ready agreement to his plan to use her to spy on Hamlet is difficult to understand. She knows her father was wrong about Hamlet – he has said so – and she believes that her rejection of him may have driven the Prince mad. Still, she does nothing to help matters but allows herself to be used as a lure to trap Hamlet into revealing his innermost thoughts.

- Polonius's language shows just how passive Ophelia is: 'walk you here … Read on this book'.

- It is hard to feel any sympathy for Ophelia when she merely walks and talks as instructed by her father, and deliberately hurts Hamlet by returning his letters and gifts, refusing to see him, offering him no words of comfort when he visits her in a pitiful state, etc.

- Ophelia's response to her father's death and Hamlet's cruel treatment of her is extreme. She is overwhelmed and loses her mind. Unlike Hamlet's 'antic disposition', Ophelia is genuinely mad and her deterioration is shocking. One may pity her in this state but still reflect that she continued to treat Hamlet cruelly when she believed he was mad, and she went along with Polonius's plans at every turn.

- Ophelia never had the strength to make her own decisions but instead allowed herself to be ruled by the men in her life, doing everything they asked of her.

- Even in the manner of her death, Ophelia appears weak and passive. The story Gertrude tells is an odd one: Ophelia was climbing a willow tree when the branch broke and she fell into the water. She floated for a while before her clothes pulled her down 'to muddy death'. It appears that Ophelia allowed herself to drown rather than actively taking her own life and thus she dies as she lived: passively.

- Ophelia may be a pitiful character at times but her inaction and lack of courage mean she fails to evoke any real sympathy.

Second approach:

Ophelia is not weak and her passivity is a consequence of the time and place in which she lives. She is an innocent whose mistreatment by those who claim to love her causes her to lose both her sanity and her life. There can be no doubt that Ophelia wins our sympathy.

- When we first meet Ophelia, she says little. This is because she is being lectured, first by her brother and then her father. Their words are hurtful: they both claim that Hamlet cannot truly love Ophelia and that he is merely toying with her.

- Ophelia is a good and dutiful young woman and her passivity would have been considered right and proper at the time the play was written. She is young and unmarried and as such, must follow the advice and instruction of the men in the family.

- We feel great sympathy for Ophelia as both her father and her brother assure her that Hamlet is only interested in sleeping with Ophelia and could never seriously consider her as a wife.

(**Note**: *It is perfectly acceptable – indeed desirable – to refer to productions of the play you have seen. The most recent version stars Benedict Cumberbatch as Hamlet. It is a National Theatre Live production directed by Robin Lough.*)

- The National Theatre Live's 2015 production of *Hamlet* portrayed Ophelia as a modern young woman dressed in trousers and a jumper. Interestingly, I felt less sympathy for her when I watched this version than I did when I watched other film adaptations in which Ophelia wore more traditional, long dresses. On reflection, I believe this is because Ophelia's behaviour seems weak and passive when she is viewed as a twentieth- or twenty-first-century woman, but is far more understandable and evokes much more sympathy when she is portrayed as an Elizabethan woman, for example.

- Our sympathy for Ophelia deepens when she tells her father of Hamlet's odd behaviour towards her. She is naturally confused and distressed by his manner but Polonius offers no consolation. Instead, he begins hatching a plan to discover the reason for Hamlet's apparent madness.

- Ophelia is not weak but she is in a weak position at court. She has no mother to turn to, her brother has left for Paris, she has been ordered to end her relationship with the man she loves, and she is left at the mercy of the selfish, uncaring Polonius. Her isolation and deep distress evoke our sympathy.

- Ophelia is an innocent, trusting, kind-hearted girl who truly loves Hamlet and mourns the change in him. She has no choice but to follow her father's commands, even though they are motivated by a desire to ingratiate himself with Claudius rather than help his daughter.

- Hamlet's cruel treatment of Ophelia in Act 3 Scene 2 puts her in an impossible position. His crude innuendos are meant to shock and insult her and we feel deep sympathy for the naïve young girl who is damned if she understands his remarks and damned if she does not. When Hamlet asks if Ophelia thought he meant 'country matters' when he wanted to lie in her lap, she is placed in an impossible position. If she shows that she sees the double meaning in his words, she appears to be sexually sophisticated, which would be most inappropriate for a woman of her time. If she fails to see the double meaning, she must resign herself to tolerating the insults in silence. It is not surprising, then, that Ophelia does not react to Hamlet's comments, merely saying patiently, 'You are merry, my lord'. Ophelia's passivity here is not weakness but a sign of her admirable goodness and patience. That such a kind nature should be so abused evokes our sympathy.

- Ophelia's suffering worsens with Polonius's death. The knowledge that the man she loved killed her father is too much to bear and she is driven mad by grief.

- Ophelia's madness proves the rotten, corrupt nature of the Danish court. She is an innocent but her life has been ruined. She has lost everything. It would be impossible not to feel the deepest sympathy for her at this stage in the play.

- Laertes may have returned, but he is more caught up in his conversation with Claudius than he is concerned about Ophelia. She wanders off, alone again, as Laertes plans revenge on Hamlet.

- Ophelia's tragic death shows that nothing pure and innocent can survive the scheming and dangers of Elsinore. Even her funeral is a shoddy affair conducted by a priest who believes she does not deserve to be buried in consecrated ground.

- Hamlet and Laertes fight over Ophelia but after the funeral, they never mention her again. It seems they wanted to prove their superiority rather than express genuine love. Poor Ophelia is used as a pawn in death, just as she was in life. Caught up in a corrupt world, she had no power and no chance to save herself.

Past questions on *Hamlet*

Most questions do not fall neatly into one category but require you to discuss aspects of character, themes and dramatic techniques.

For example, the following question clearly requires discussion of all three elements: '"Uncertainty, which features constantly in Shakespeare's play, *Hamlet*, adds significantly to the dramatic impact of the play." Discuss the above statement, developing your response with reference to the text.'

Character

2020 Leaving Certificate

Discuss how Shakespeare makes effective use, for a variety of purposes, of the contradictions and inconsistencies evident in Hamlet's character. Develop your discussion with reference to Shakespeare's play, *Hamlet*.

2017 Leaving Certificate

'Shakespeare makes effective use of both Laertes and Horatio to fulfil a variety of dramatic functions in his play, *Hamlet*.'

Discuss this statement, supporting your answer with reference to the text.

2012 Leaving Certificate

'Hamlet's madness, whether genuine or not, adds to the fascination of his character for the audience.'

Discuss this statement, supporting your answer with suitable reference to the play, *Hamlet*.

2011 Leaving Certificate

'Claudius can be seen as both a heartless villain and a character with some redeeming qualities in the play, *Hamlet*.'

Discuss both aspects of this statement, supporting your answer with suitable reference to the text.

2006 Leaving Certificate

'We admire Hamlet as much for his weaknesses as for his strengths.'

Write a response to this view of the character of Hamlet, supporting your points by reference to the text.

2002 Leaving Certificate

'The appeal of Shakespeare's *Hamlet* lies primarily in the complex nature of the play's central character, Hamlet.'

To what extent would you agree with the above statement? Support your points by reference to the play.

Educate.ie Sample Paper

'Hamlet's problem is not that of a man who does not want to do his duty; it is that of a man who cannot find out what his duty is.'

Discuss this statement, supporting your answer with reference to the play, *Hamlet*.

Educate.ie Sample Paper

'Despite her suffering, Ophelia is a weak, passive character who fails to gain our sympathy.'

To what extent would you agree or disagree with this view of Ophelia? Support your answer with suitable reference to the play, *Hamlet*.

Educate.ie Sample Paper

'Claudius is a complex character who excites admiration and disgust in equal measure.'

To what extent would you agree or disagree with this view of Claudius? Support your answer with suitable reference to the play, *Hamlet*.

Theme

2011 Leaving Certificate

'Revenge and justice are finely balanced themes in the play, *Hamlet*.'
Discuss this statement, supporting your answer with suitable reference to the text.

1988 Leaving Certificate

'The interaction of the plot and sub-plot gives pointed emphasis to the theme of filial duty in *Hamlet*.'
Discuss this view, supporting your answer by relevant quotation or reference.

1984 Leaving Certificate

'Loyalty and betrayal are significant themes in Shakespeare's *Hamlet*.'
Discuss, using quotation and reference from the play.

1980 Leaving Certificate

'In the play, *Hamlet*, Shakespeare's portrayal of women is not very flattering.'
Discuss this statement with reference to both Gertrude and Ophelia, supporting your answer by relevant quotation or reference.

Educate.ie Sample Paper

'The theme of conflict, both internal and external, is central to the play *Hamlet*'.

Discuss this statement, supporting your answer with suitable reference to the play.

Imagery and Symbolism

Educate.ie Sample Paper

'Powerful images heighten our experience of *Hamlet*'. Write your response to this statement. Textual support may include reference to a particular performance you have seen.

Educate.ie Sample Paper

'The corruption and deception at the heart of the play *Hamlet* are skilfully presented through a series of dramatic images and symbols.' Discuss this view, supporting your answer with suitable reference or quotation.

Educate.ie Sample Paper

'The vivid imagery throughout the play *Hamlet* enhances our understanding of the characters and themes.' Discuss the part played by imagery in enhancing our understanding of the characters and themes in the play.

Dramatic Scenes

2020 Leaving Certificate

'Uncertainty, which features constantly in Shakespeare's play, *Hamlet*, adds significantly to the dramatic impact of the play.'

Discuss the above statement, developing your response with reference to the text.

Educate.ie Sample Paper

'The enduring popularity of the play *Hamlet* is due to scenes of great emotional intensity.'

Discuss this statement with close reference to at least two scenes from the play.

Educate.ie Sample Paper

'Although it was written over four hundred years ago, the play *Hamlet* is still relevant to an audience today.'

Discuss the above statement, developing your response with reference to the play.

Comparative Study

Option One:

Never Let Me Go
by Kazuo Ishiguro

Philadelphia, Here I Come!
by Brian Friel

Lady Bird
directed by Greta Gerwig

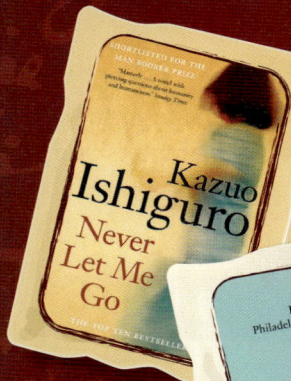

Option Two:

Room
by Emma Donoghue

The Crucible
by Arthur Miller

Casablanca
directed by Michael Curtiz

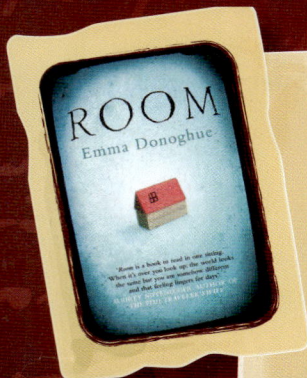

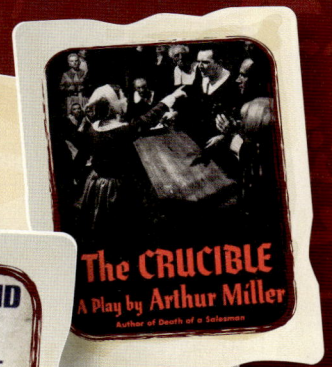

Introduction

What is it?

The comparative study question asks you to compare and contrast **three texts** under **one** of the **three modes of comparison**.

The comparative modes for the exam in June 2024 are:

- **Cultural context**
- **Literary genre**
- **Theme or issue**

Comparative Study

You need to know your comparative text well, but not in the same level of detail as your single text.

Concentrate on *key moments* in each text. (The word 'moment' here can be taken to mean an entire chapter or scene.) A key moment in your text is one that illustrates or helps in the development of one of the chosen modes.

Key moments can overlap: one may be an illustration of both the cultural context and a pivotal moment in the theme, for example.

When you are reading your comparative text, as well as keeping the modes in mind, you should think about your personal response. The examiners will be looking to see how well you engaged with the text. As you read, ask yourself:

- Did I like the characters?
- Would I like to have lived in that time or in that place? Why? Why not?
- Is the theme one to which I can relate?
- Do I like the way in which the author presents the text?

Cultural context

The **cultural context** is the kind of world in which the story takes place or was written.

When you are reading the text and thinking about this mode of comparison, ask yourself:

- In what century or decade is the story set? Does the time matter? Could the story take place now or are things in our society very different?
- Where is the story set? Does the setting matter?
- Do we learn a lot about the social life of that place or time by reading the text?
- What are the protagonists' attitudes and values?
- Are there class distinctions?
- Are there race distinctions?
- Are there gender distinctions?
- Are children treated well?
- What are the manners and customs of that place/time?
- How does the daily life of the characters differ from life in twenty-first-century Ireland?
- What are their attitudes towards religion, money, love, family, etc.?
- Would you like to live in that time or place? Why? Why not?

Past questions have tended to focus on:

- The way in which the world or culture the characters inhabit affects the storyline
- Whether or not attitudes and values in the text are likely to change
- How the characters' lives are restricted or enhanced by the cultural context
- What is interesting about the world or culture of the text
- How the author establishes the cultural context.

Literary genre

Literary genre is the way in which the authors tell their stories.

There is not a finite list of aspects of literary genre, and if you are studying this mode you would be well advised to read the notes on the other modes, as you may find information that you can use. There is overlap between the comparative modes, but as you will only be answering on one mode on the day of the exam, repetition will not be a problem.

When you are reading the text and thinking about this mode of comparison, ask yourself:

- What does the title tell us about the text? Does it deepen our understanding of it before we read or do we not see the full relevance of the title until the end?
- From what point of view is the story told? Does the point of view influence our understanding or enjoyment of the text?
- Is the story told in a linear fashion or are flashbacks used? Which narrative style do you find most effective?
- How are characters created in the text and do we find them believable or likeable?
- Are there moments of tension in the story? How are they created?
- Is humour used to good effect in the text?
- What imagery or symbolism is used? Is it subtle or over-the-top? Does it add to any aspect of the story?

Past questions have tended to focus on:

- How memorable characters are created in the text
- How emotional power is created in the text
- Aspects of narrative and how they contribute to your response to the text
- How the unexpected contributes to the story
- The different ways in which the story is told in the texts you have chosen
- Which of the authors you have studied is most successful in their use of a certain technique.

Theme or issue

A **theme or issue** is a concern in the text which the writer is trying to explore. The theme or issue is not the plot: don't confuse the two. It does not matter what theme you choose, as long as it is central to the text. You will not be able to develop your answer properly if you choose a minor theme.

When you are reading the text and thinking about this mode of comparison, ask yourself:

- How is the theme introduced? Is there a key moment that gives us an indication of the issue the author is trying to explore? Does one of the central characters say or do something that sets us on the path of understanding the theme? Or is it conveyed by the minor characters or even the setting?

- How does the author develop this theme? Is it through a series of small events? Do we see situations developing that we know must lead to a crisis of some sort? How does the author interest us in the theme? Is it through a central character with whom we can empathise?

- Is there a moment of crisis or a turning point in the text? Does the central character have to make a difficult decision? Does the character do the right thing? How is this decision linked to the theme?

- How is the theme resolved? Are you very clear on the author's view of the ideas explored in the theme?

- Have we learned anything about human behaviour or society in general from the exploration of this theme?

- Does the author's or director's use of setting, imagery, motifs, lighting, costumes, special effects or music (if it's a film) add to your understanding of the theme?

Past questions have tended to focus on:

- What you learned about your chosen theme
- How a key moment or moments in the text reveal the theme
- Why you feel that the theme made the text interesting
- How the theme plays an important role in the story
- How the theme affects the life of a character in the text.

Approaching the question

This section is worth 70 marks and should take you around 65 minutes to complete. You will be asked to answer **one** section, A or B. There are two questions within each section, and you must answer **one** of these. You may be asked, in part of a question, to answer on one of your texts separately.

Points to note

- When you read the question, underline the key words, e.g. 'one of the texts', 'key moment', 'describe', 'explain'.
- Think in terms of key moments; this will ensure that you refer to the text and will help you to keep the sequence of events in the right order.
- In your introductory paragraph, name the **text**, the **author** and the **mode** you have chosen. Refer to the question and outline the direction your answer will take.
- You must **compare** your texts and answer on the **mode** you have chosen.
- Do not, under any circumstances, simply summarise the plot.
- Do not write three separate mini-essays. Compare as much as possible. Look at the tables of comparison after each mode in this textbook for ideas on how this can be done.
- Use a selection of the linking words and phrases on the next page when comparing texts. The examiner will be looking for them.

Comparing the texts

Provide the examiner with as many comparative points as you can.

Listed below are some sentence structures you could use when linking texts. In these sentences, T1, T2 and T3 refer to the texts, C1, C2 and C3 refer to the characters and A1, A2 and A3 refer to the authors.

- In all three texts, the pressure placed on women to conform to societal norms is clear.
- We can see in both T1 and T2 that …
- Like C1, C2 resists the pressure to conform.
- The vision of society we are presented with in T1 is far more positive than those presented in T2 and T3.
- I feel that there are many similarities between C1 and C2.
- While the issue of … is highlighted in all three texts, it affects the lives of the principal characters most strongly in T1.
- Unlike C1, C2 …
- The same theme is handled completely differently in T2.
- This scene in T1 is reminiscent of …
- A1 uses humour while A2 treats the theme more seriously …
- Both characters have to deal with … but C1 handles it very differently to C3.
- I was struck by the different ways the issue of … was handled by the protagonists in all three texts.
- In both T1 and T2, the characters face a crisis … but the outcome is very different …

Linking words and phrases

When the texts are similar	When the texts are different
Likewise	Conversely
Similarly	On the contrary
Also	Whereas
In the same way	Differs from
In the same manner	However
Just as	In contrast
Both texts/characters	This is different to
Each text	While

In order to get high marks, you need to:

- Answer the question asked (30%)
- Make sure every paragraph develops that answer (30%)
- Use varied and appropriate language (30%)
- Keep an eye on your spelling and grammar (10%).

Think about the first two points when you are planning your answer.

How should you use this textbook to prepare for the comparative question?

In this textbook, six of the prescribed texts for Comparative Study 2024 have been selected and grouped in options, as follows:

- Option One: *Never Let Me Go* by Kazuo Ishiguro, *Philadelphia, Here I Come!* by Brian Friel and *Lady Bird* directed by Greta Gerwig.
- Option Two: *Room* by Emma Donoghue, *The Crucible* by Arthur Miller and *Casablanca* directed by Michael Curtiz.

You should select **one** option to study.

Each option contains a guide to studying each text in relation to the three prescribed modes for examination in 2024. They will help you to prepare for the written paper by demonstrating how to compare and contrast each text. You will also see past exam questions on each mode.

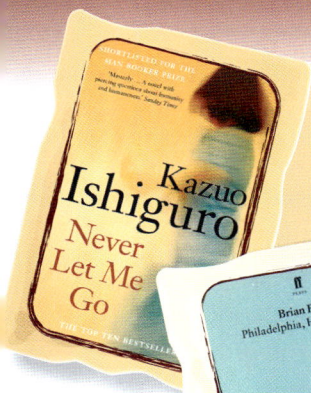

Never Let Me Go
by Kazuo Ishiguro

Philadelphia, Here I Come!
by Brian Friel

Lady Bird
directed by Greta Gerwig

Mode: Cultural context

Cultural context in *Never Let Me Go*

Setting and social class

The novel is set in four main locations in an imaginary version of late-twentieth-century England: Hailsham, the Cottages, the donor recovery centres and the countryside around Norfolk.

Hailsham is situated in the countryside but Kathy is not sure exactly where. When she is older and driving around the country as part of her job, Kathy often sees things that remind her of Hailsham, but she never finds her childhood home again. The students live at Hailsham until they are 16. Life there is all the students know, and they are kept within the grounds by terrifying stories of what happens to those who leave. In one story, a boy wanders off and his body is found in the woods two days later 'tied to a tree with the hands and feet chopped off'. In another story, a girl climbs over the fence to see what it is like outside and is never allowed back in. Now her ghost wanders about the woods, 'pining to be let back in'. Nobody knows where these tales began, although there is a suspicion that they

initially came from the guardians. Whatever the truth, the students are more than willing to spread the rumours to the younger children.

When Kathy and the others move on from Hailsham, they spend two years at the Cottages. Although the Cottages are run-down, Kathy enjoys her time there: 'none of us minded the discomforts one bit – it was all part of the excitement of being at the Cottages'. The Cottages offer Kathy and her friends more freedom than they had at Hailsham, but in many ways their lives there are still quite restricted. Kathy says that while she and the others 'weren't afraid exactly', they 'rarely stepped beyond the confines of the Cottages' in the early days. The students had never been outside the grounds of Hailsham up to that point so were naturally 'just bewildered' to be given greater control of their own lives. Kathy believes that there is a part of all the students that will forever be 'fearful of the world' around them because of the restrictive nature of a childhood spent in a single location.

As the novel progresses, the settings become bleaker, reflecting the characters' fading hopes and opportunities. Kazuo Ishiguro explained in an interview that while he allowed 'a little sun and vibrancy' in the narrator's childhood memories, he wanted 'an England drained of all bright colours' in the later stages of her life. Kathy sees the setting as a reflection of the clones' position in society: the 'dark byways of the country existed just for the likes of us, while the big glittering motorways with their huge signs and super cafés were for everyone else'.

The donor recovery centres, whether modern and bright or old and drab, are the most depressing settings of all in the novel. They are where the clones recuperate after surgery until they 'complete' – in other words, die – after they have given their final donation. The society in the world of the text allows this to happen because it regards the clones as less than human. They are not simply from the lowest social class in society – they have no social class. The clones accept their situation because they have been raised to believe there is no other path for them.

Gender roles

Gender differences are not particularly important in *Never Let Me* Go because the clones are already so unfairly treated that any other inequalities are irrelevant. However, there are certain stereotypes that play out in the story. Women are seen to be either caring and nurturing or sexually predatory, while men are expected to be strong and unemotional. Tommy is unable to cope with the pressure to hide his emotions, and when he does rage or cry, he is subjected to scorn and ridicule by the other students.

Kathy and Ruth epitomise two types of women often found in literature: Kathy is nurturing and maternal while Ruth uses her sexuality to get her way. Ruth knows that Kathy cares for Tommy, but she lures him into a relationship nonetheless. Kathy is unable to compete with Ruth because she is unwilling to use her sexuality to win Tommy over. Unlike Ruth, Kathy fears that her physical desires prove she is a clone of a sex worker or a pornographic actress.

Kathy expresses her caring, maternal nature from an early age. She is sensitive to Tommy's mistreatment at the hands of the other students and tries to calm him down when he loses his temper. As a small girl, she plays the song 'Never Let Me Go' over and over on her tape recorder, imagining that it tells the story of a woman who was told she couldn't have babies but has one against the odds. Young Kathy plays the role of the mother in this situation, lovingly and protectively cradling an imaginary baby to her breast and singing softly to it. Later in life, Kathy becomes an exemplary carer. She channels her nurturing, maternal instincts into helping others, even Ruth, through their donations. As a result of her kindness, she is reconciled with Ruth and begins a relationship with Tommy at the end of his life.

Ultimately, whether the clones are men or women, they are powerless in the world of the text. Unlike many other stories in which there is a patriarchy (men are dominant) or, less commonly, a matriarchy (women are dominant), both genders are subservient to the 'normal' people in the novel.

Love and marriage

In an interview, Kazuo Ishiguro said of love in *Never Let Me Go*, 'The people in the novel believe, irrationally, like we all believe, that love can do all kinds of things that make you exempt from your fate.' However, the love they feel for one another, whether romantic or based on deep and lasting friendships, is far from pointless. In fact, it is what makes their short lives worth living.

Kathy, Tommy and Ruth are caught in a complicated love triangle. From early childhood, Kathy cares for Tommy and understands him in a way the other students do not. Tommy is prone to temper tantrums and his outbursts make him the butt of jokes in the school, but Kathy does her best to help him through these difficult moments. At one stage, the students deliberately goad Tommy into losing his temper by not choosing him for a team game. His predictable performance amuses the children, but Kathy approaches Tommy and puts a hand on his arm. Although Tommy lashes out in his rage and strikes Kathy, her focus is still on helping him. She calms him down and advises him to go inside and get changed because he has mud all over his favourite shirt. This little detail – knowing how Tommy feels about his polo shirt – surprises Tommy and demonstrates Kathy's affection for him. However, despite Kathy's feelings for Tommy, she loses him to Ruth. Ruth's interest in Tommy is not real love, rather it is based on her desire to fit in and have what she believes everybody wants. She is cruel to Tommy at times and Kathy finds it hard to watch her treatment of the boy she cares for.

One of the reasons the clones find it difficult to cope in relationships is because they have been raised in an artificial environment and do not know how adults express their love for one another. When they move to the Cottages, Ruth copies the behaviour of the other couples who, in turn, model their behaviour on what they see on television. Kathy spots this and realises that Ruth does not truly love Tommy but is simply using him.

Comparative Study

Although Ruth has kept Kathy and Tommy apart, she repents of her actions towards the end of her life. She says that as far back as she can remember, 'It should always have been you two' and urges them to find some sort of future together. Ruth believes that Tommy and Kathy's love for one another is so strong that they have a good chance of being granted a 'deferral'. Tommy and Kathy visit Madame and Miss Emily and learn the terrible truth: there are no deferrals, despite all the rumours. It is merely a desperate hope that the young people cling to before they resign themselves to their fate and accept that they can never have a normal, married, family life together. Ultimately, Kathy and Tommy accept that all they can do is spend as much of their remaining time together as possible.

At the end of the novel, Kathy is alone. Ruth and Tommy have 'completed' and she is about to begin her own donation journey. However, love has given her short life a great deal of meaning. She says, 'I lost Ruth, then I lost Tommy, but I won't lose my memories of them.' These precious memories of love are both uplifting and heartbreaking.

Religion

While there is little mention of organised religion in *Never Let Me Go*, the novel nonetheless raises disturbing yet thought-provoking questions about the meaning of life. The most important of these is the ethical and moral dilemma of cloning. The clones in the story are created for one simple purpose: to provide organs that can be harvested for transplant. Naturally, this must be done while the clones are still quite young and healthy, so their lives are short and their fates are sealed. In order for wider society to accept this horrifying reality, it is generally accepted that the clones are not really people because they do not have souls. Hailsham was created as an experiment to show that clones are no different from other people. It is for this reason that Madame takes samples of the students' artwork. As Miss Emily explains to Tommy and Kathy when they visit her at home, she and Madame believed that if they could display the students' artwork publicly, it would 'reveal your souls. Or to put it more finely, we did it to *prove you had souls at all*.' Ultimately, however, people decide it is more convenient to ignore this evidence and continue to say that clones are 'less than human'. If this is the case, society rules that it does not matter if they are killed to provide organs for others.

Although Hailsham is a far nicer place for the young clones than most of the other 'homes', it still indoctrinates the children in a belief system in a similar way to some organised religions. The students are told they are 'special' and must keep themselves 'very healthy inside' because they are chosen for a particular duty. This duty, of course, is to accept the fact that they can never have a normal life and must die to allow others to live. All the Hailsham students eventually come to terms with the path that has been set out for them. Ruth says that after five years as a carer, she is ready to become a donor: 'After all, it's what we're *supposed* to be doing, isn't it?' The clones have no free will. They cannot choose how they want to live or die, but rather have been raised to believe that being a donor is the only option and that by accepting their role as donors, they are fulfilling some sort of higher purpose.

Family

Although they never really discuss it, the clones are keenly aware of their parentless status. When they discuss the 'possibles' – the models from whom they might be cloned – they wonder if the models were likely to be 'normal parent' age. But at that point in the conversation, the clones sense they are 'near territory [they] didn't want to enter, and the arguments would fizzle out'. It is as if they know that if the conversation goes in that direction, it will be too painful for them to bear.

The guardians play a double role in that they are both teachers and, to a limited extent, parents. However, they are raising their charges to die willingly by donating their organs, so they have none of the selfless, unconditional love of real parents. Because the students of Hailsham have no family, they are forced to rely on each other. Their relationships, which may merely have been close in a real boarding school, become incredibly important to them as a result. Hailsham is their home and, like siblings who may squabble but remain connected, the students' shared experiences in Hailsham keep their bond strong throughout their short lives.

Despite their closeness and the guardians' care, the students are always destined to be denied the loving embrace of family. One of the most touching moments in the book occurs when Madame comes across the young Kathy cradling a pillow to her chest, swaying and singing along to 'Never Let Me Go' on her precious tape. Kathy imagines the line 'Baby, baby, never let me go' is about a woman who miraculously has a baby after being told she could never have children. Madame cries as she watches Kathy and it is only a couple of years later that Tommy tells Kathy he believes Madame reacted this way because she thought it was tragic that Kathy was destined to be childless. At the time of the conversation, neither Kathy, Tommy nor any of the other students are 'particularly bothered' at the prospect of not having children. Indeed, some of them view it as a positive in that they can 'have sex without worrying about all of that'. The students are not encouraged to consider family life and lifelong relationships as an option for them. It is only later, when they are older, that some of the students hold out hope that if they can prove they are truly in love, they might be granted an exemption from donation and may be able to stay together. This hope is in vain, however, and the students end their lives as they began them, relying on one another for care, companionship and all that goes with family bonds.

Cultural context in
Philadelphia, Here I Come!

Setting and social class

Gar is a conflicted and troubled young man, and part of the reason for his unhappiness is his divided allegiances in Ballybeg. In the hours before he leaves it for good, Gar examines his complex feelings about life in his home place. On the one hand, he clings to happy memories of his youth in Ballybeg. On the other hand, he realises that Ballybeg is a backwater and that the changes of the latter half of the twentieth century are passing it by. The shop is not doing well, and there is no real future for Gar in running a failing grocery and hardware business. In this small, tight-knit community, Gar is isolated and alienated. His relationship with his home place mirrors his relationships with the people in it. He is torn between love and hatred – a desire to leave and a desperate wish to belong.

Early in the play, Private asks Public if he is fully conscious of 'all the consequences' of his decision to leave 'the country of your birth, the land of the curlew and the snipe, the Aran sweater and the Irish Sweepstakes', in order to go to a 'profane, irreligious, pagan country of gross materialism'. Private uses clichés about Ireland and America, which show that Gar is trying to simplify his situation. These clichés reveal how little he has considered his impending emigration and the realities of both the place he is leaving and his destination.

When Kate visits on the night before Gar's departure, he is both angry and heartbroken. She is married to another man now, and although he knows this is partly his fault for not speaking up and asking for her hand in marriage, Gar launches an extraordinary attack on Ballybeg and Ireland. He is aggressive and unpleasant as he tells Kate that Ballybeg is 'a bloody quagmire, a backwater, a dead-end' in which everybody goes crazy sooner or later. Kate objects mildly by saying Ballybeg is not as bad as all that, but Gar turns on her too, saying that she is bound to defend Ballybeg because she is stuck there. Gar claims that he, on the other hand, is 'Free as the bloody wind!' Of course, this is not true. It is not Ballybeg that has held Gar back but a series of complicated relationships. Leaving Ballybeg will not mean leaving these issues behind – something Gar has yet to discover.

The name Ballybeg comes from the Irish name *Baile Beag*, meaning 'small town'. One of the obstacles Gar fails to overcome in Ballybeg is the strict social hierarchy of the insular town. As the son of the local shopkeeper, Gar's social standing in the town is not sufficient for him to be considered a good match for Kate Doogan. Senator Doogan, Kate's father, is acutely aware of everyone's background and level of education. When Kate leaves Gar alone with her father to ask for her hand in marriage, Senator Doogan immediately takes the upper hand and puts Gar firmly in his place. He mentions Francis King and tells Gar that he and Francis's father were at university together: 'when he did medicine and I did law, we knocked about quite a bit'. Immediately afterwards, he asks how Gar's father is. By enquiring about S.B. straight after his seemingly casual observation about having been at university with Francis's father, Senator Doogan makes it clear that Gar, as the son of the local grocer, is no fit match for his daughter. Kate and Francis, he implies, come from the same social class: one to which Gar does not belong. Gar may be unhappy with this, but he is overawed by Senator Doogan's superior manner. Making his excuses, he leaves without ever mentioning his wish to marry Kate.

Gender roles

The world of the text is overwhelmingly patriarchal. Men and women conform to gender roles of the era, but both are unhappy as a result.

Madge, the O'Donnells' housekeeper, is a selfless, caring woman who has taken care of S.B. and Gar for many years. She also helps her niece with her children, but receives little thanks in return. Gar says Madge 'lives for those Mulhern children, and gives them whatever few half-pence she has'. Yet for all his resentment of the Mulherns for taking Madge for granted, Gar does so too. He never questions all she does for him and, even though he is a grown man, accepts Madge's cooking and cleaning for him and his father. There is an expectation that she will wait on the men and their guests at all hours. Madge is the mother figure in the house, and perhaps neither S.B. nor Gar question her life of drudgery because such selfless toil would have been the norm for wives and mothers of Madge's class at that time. Although Madge is an employee of the O'Donnells, she works ridiculously long hours and is obviously not well paid. Gar mentions the 'few half-pence she has', implying she does not have much. When Madge breaks down on the night before Gar's departure, tearfully telling a bewildered S.B. that she has a mountain of cleaning to do in the house and the shop, it is clear he has never even considered that she might be overworked or feel emotional at the loss of a young man she has raised since he was a baby.

Kate Doogan represents a very different type of woman to Madge in that she is from a far wealthier background; however, she is just as restricted by the patriarchal society. Her father has her life mapped out for her, telling Gar that he and Kate's mother are 'living in hope' that Francis King, who is soon to be the local doctor, will marry Kate. Although Senator Doogan claims Kate can make her own choices and that 'any decision she makes will be her own', this is not the case. Kate loves Gar, but she is incapable of standing up to her father. It is understood that she must have a man to look after her. When Gar does not step up and make a case for his ability to take care of her, Kate's fate is sealed and she marries Francis King.

Even though he loves Kate, Gar is sexist in his view of her. In the flashback of their last intimate conversation, Gar recalls saying, 'Our daughters'll all be gentle and frail and silly, like you; and our sons – they'll be thick bloody louts, sexy goats, like me'. There is no evidence to suggest that Kate is the way Gar describes her. She is practical and sensible, knowing exactly how much money they will need if they are to marry and quickly giving these sums to Gar before he meets her father. Kate may be gentle, but she is far from 'frail and silly'. This description fits Gar better than it does her. He is not the 'thick bloody lout' he claims to be but a sensitive and troubled young man. He does not live up to his own perception of how a man should behave.

This conversation between Gar and Kate is merely one of the indications that men in the text are also restricted by their gender. None of them has the ability to relate to one another honestly and openly. As a result, the majority of the men in the play are unhappy and frustrated. Gar is desperate to open a line of communication with his father before he leaves for America. However, he finds it hard to break the habit of a lifetime and maintains 'a surly, taciturn gruffness' in his father's presence. He acknowledges that he and his father 'embarrass one another' and claims that if one of them were to make a personal remark, the other 'would fall over backwards with embarrassment'. Nonetheless, Gar wants S.B. to say something like, 'Gar, you bugger you, why don't you stick it out here with me for it's not such a bad aul bugger of a place.' However, S.B. does not open up. In fact, he says so little at the dinner table on the night of Gar's departure that Madge gives him 'a hard look' before ironically remarking that, 'The chatting in this place would deafen a body.' This failure to communicate is not only S.B.'s fault. During Gar's last conversation with his father, Private urges Public to speak, telling him to say something unexpected to break the ice. However, all Public can manage is, 'You'll need a new tyre for the van.' Gar wants to break the silence in a meaningful way but is incapable of doing so.

Gar's friends, 'the boys', are further examples of the inability of Irish men of the time to express their feelings. They are full of lies, boasts and blusters, and they avoid any sort of emotional connection with Gar on the night of his departure. Ned, the leader of the group, quickly shuts down any effort to raise the subject of Gar's leaving Ballybeg, despite the fact that he is clearly sorry his friend is leaving. As he turns to go at the end of the visit, Ned awkwardly gifts Gar his belt but avoids any sort of emotional connection with him by boasting about having beaten off attackers by swinging the heavy buckle at them.

Ultimately, Gar is left alone with his regrets and his doubts about leaving. He has nobody in whom he can confide. He doesn't want to go, and his father doesn't want to lose him, but the lack of any real communication between the two men means that both have to live with their sorrow. Madge says it best when she remarks to herself that Gar's heart will break when he leaves and that eventually he will turn out like his father and will have 'learned nothin' in-between times'.

Love and marriage

The view of love and marriage in the text is overwhelmingly negative. *Philadelphia, Here I Come!* is a story of longing, lost love and regrets.

Gar's young mother, Maire, married S.B. because he impressed her. Gar recounts the details of their marriage: 'She was nineteen and he was forty, and he owned a shop, and he wore a soft hat, and she thought he was the grandest gentleman that ever lived'. To a young woman from a poor background, marriage to such a seemingly well-off man was desirable, as it meant she would be supported for the rest of her life. However, such financial security comes at a high price. Although Maire's sister Lizzy says S.B. was good to Maire, it is clear that she was unhappy from the start. Lizzy says Maire's shoulders were 'sorta working' during the marriage ceremony – it wasn't clear whether she was laughing or crying. Shortly after the marriage, however, tears reigned. Maire often cried herself to sleep and yearned to be part of the group of young girls who called into her house 'to dress up on their way to a dance'. Gar reflects bitterly that 'it was good of God to take her away' three days after he was born. Maire's disappointment with S.B. is passed on to her son, who blames his father for his mother's unhappiness.

S.B. was equally disappointed by his marriage to the beautiful, wild girl from Bailtefree. He knows she was miserable for the short time they were married, and he admits to Madge that he may have been 'too old for her'. Although S.B. loved Maire, he could not make her happy and after her death he was left to raise their son alone. The damage caused by the unhappy marriage translates into the dysfunctional relationship between Gar and his father.

Although Gar looks down on S.B. for his views and considers himself to be far less repressed and emotionally stunted than his father, he and his friends are extremely immature and have an adolescent view of love and marriage. Gar jokes that he and his friends are sex maniacs who boast about the 'hot courts' they know. However, despite all their bragging, Gar admits privately that he and his friends are virgins.

Gar's feelings for Kate reflect his immaturity, which ultimately dooms the relationship. His eagerness to marry her as soon as possible is based on lust as much as love. He tells her he will 'bloody-well burst' if he has to wait much longer to sleep with her and begs her to put the wedding forward to 'next month – next week'. Kate has a more realistic view of marriage than Gar, probably because her entire future was dependent on the financial status of the man she married. She has considered the practical aspects of getting engaged and begs Gar to 'be sensible' and focus on their finances. Gar, like an excited child, confides in Kate that he has a secret source of income. Kate is delighted, believing it to be investments like her father's. However, Gar reveals that he earns what is a pittance selling some eggs when he does shop deliveries. Kate knows that this is not enough and advises Gar to lie to her father about his prospects: 'You have £20 a week and £5,000 in the bank and your father's about to retire'. Despite Kate's urging, Gar is too immature and too full of self-doubt to ask Senator Doogan for Kate's hand in marriage. Overawed by the Senator's easy confidence and praise of Francis King, Gar becomes tongue-tied and leaves without saying anything about their engagement. Although Private blames Kate, saying she 'must have known' about her parents' plans for her, the fault is his own. Gar's fantasies about love and marriage are so unrealistic and childish that they cannot sustain him when he comes up against the hard realities of Kate's father and an eminently more suitable suitor. As the flashback in which he recalls this painful episode ends, Private wearily recounts some of the details of Kate and Francis's wedding. He reflects that this memory has 'left a deep scar on the aul skitter of a soul' and was 'a sore hoke on the aul prestige'. We see how heartbroken Gar was by Kate's rejection, and this gives us a greater understanding of his reasons for leaving his home town.

The tragedy for Kate is that, although she loves Gar dearly, she knows the final decision about marriage is not really hers to make. She allows herself to be steered by her father and marries the man he believes will be a suitable husband for her. Although we never hear exactly how the marriage has turned out, Kate does drop a hint that it may not be all roses in the garden. In their last meeting, Gar asks Kate, 'Is Dr King well?' She replies drily, 'I hear no complaints.' The implication is that she has little interest in how her husband feels but would be the first to know if he were in any way unwell or dissatisfied.

Religion

In the play, religion is a repressive aspect of the cultural context. The O'Donnells pay lip service to Catholic beliefs by saying the rosary together in the evenings. However, this is simply a ritual and is not matched by true devotion to the Church's teachings. Canon O'Byrne, S.B.'s friend and the local priest, is the one person who could breach the gap between Gar and his father, yet he avoids such difficult topics in his regular visits to the house. Instead, he seeks refuge behind meaningless phrases and routine acts. Gar can predict the Canon's words almost as easily as he can predict his father's. Private says, 'And how's the O'Donnell family tonight?' a moment before the Canon does. When S.B. asks the Canon which colour draughts he wants to play with, Private says, 'Black for the crows and white for the swans' and, once again, the Canon echoes the words spoken in Gar's head.

S.B. suggests betting more than a half-penny on their first game of draughts, but the Canon resists this change, calling it 'The thin end of the wedge'. It is not surprising that the Canon is content with things as they are. Gar tells us that he goes to Tenerife 'for five weeks every winter', which shows that the Canon has a life of ease and comfort. Although the Canon is as predictable as S.B. in many ways, uttering the same stock phrases each night, Gar also believes that the priest should be able to 'translate all this loneliness, this groping, this dreadful buffoonery into Christian terms' that would make life bearable. Yet the Canon does not say a word. Gar is scornful of the 'arid Canon' for his failure to offer any words of comfort or guidance in a time of crisis.

The Canon is more concerned with his own needs than those of his parishioners. His life is easy and secure because he takes no risks. However, this does not make him a good priest. There are times, such as on the night of Gar's departure, when the Canon should make an effort to say more than his banal stock phrases. The Canon asks when Gar is leaving, but when he hears it is the following morning, he merely repeats, 'Tomorrow morning' and says, 'Powerful the way time passes, too.' The Canon visits S.B. every night but has nothing of any importance to say to his friend and parishioner on the eve of his son's departure.

Family

Although family is hugely important to Gar, S.B., Lizzy (Gar's aunt) and Madge, it is also a source of great pain for them.

The relationship between S.B. and Gar is deeply dysfunctional. They barely communicate, and even on the night before Gar's departure for America, they struggle to say anything meaningful to one another. The tragedy is that both Gar and S.B. love each other but struggle to put their feelings into words. When they make the effort at the very end of the play, it either falls flat or is delivered to the wrong person.

Gar is the first to try to reconnect when he asks S.B. if he recalls 'The fishing we used to do on Lough na Cloc Cor'. Gar remembers this as a time of 'great, great happiness, and active, bubbling joy – although nothing was being said'. Now, however, something needs to be said. Sadly, S.B. is so used to talking to his son of practical matters only that he focuses on unimportant details such as the colour of the boat and the song he might have sung. He misses the emotional significance of the moment. Humiliated and upset, Gar rushes off, leaving S.B. alone.

Later that night, S.B. recalls a touching family moment when Gar was a little boy determined not to go to school but to work in 'my daddy's business' instead. Unfortunately, S.B. is unable to communicate this fond memory to Gar and tells it to Madge instead. He remembers walking Gar to school: 'the two of us, hand in hand, as happy as larks – we were that happy, Madge'. Unlike their interactions when Gar is an adult, father and son had no difficulty communicating when Gar was a child. S.B. tells Madge that 'you couldn't get a word in edgeways with all the chatting he used to go through'. His words remind us of Madge's sarcastic comment, 'A body couldn't get a word in edgeways with you two' as Gar and S.B. sat in silence at the dinner table earlier that night. It is heartbreaking to realise that the possibility for a happy family life was always there but neither Gar nor S.B. was able to make it work in the long term.

His elderly father's reserved manner and the death of his mother have left Gar emotionally stunted. Unable to communicate with S.B., Gar struggles to cope when faced with open displays of fatherly or motherly affection. We see this very clearly when Gar's old schoolteacher, Master Boyle, who retains a fondness for his former pupil, calls to see him the night before Gar's departure. As he goes to leave, Boyle 'embraces Public briefly'. Private shouts, 'Stop it! Stop it!' and as soon as Boyle has left, Gar rushes to his room, where he struggles to control his emotions.

The same inability to handle outward shows of affection with family members plays a large role in Gar's sudden decision to emigrate. When his Aunt Lizzy visits, she is desperate to be a substitute mother to him. Gar gives into her persuasion and impulsively agrees to go to America to live with her and his Uncle Con. Lizzy is overcome with joy and throws her arms around Gar, calling him 'my son'. Private responds with 'happy anguish', saying, 'God . . . my God . . . Oh my God . . .' It is hard to be hopeful about a tenuous family bond built on such a shaky foundation of mutual need and little real understanding.

As she slips money into Gar's coat on his last night at home, Madge reflects that he and S.B. are 'as like as two peas'. She says that when S.B. was Gar's age, he was 'the very same as him: leppin, and eejitin' about and actin' the clown'. Madge believes that when Gar is 'the age the boss is now, he'll turn out the same'. This is a depressing reflection on family life, as it seems to suggest that Gar will inevitably be as taciturn and emotionally repressed a man as S.B.

Cultural context in *Lady Bird*

Setting and social class

Note: There are more detailed notes about Lady Bird's house in the Imagery and Symbolism section of the notes on Literary Genre (page 368). You may find it helpful to refer to them when discussing setting, social class and family life in the film.

Lady Bird looks down on Sacramento because she believes there is no real culture there. She describes it as 'the Midwest of California', meaning it is – in her eyes – a dull place with no thriving artistic or literary centre. She sees her home town as an in-between place and she longs to leave it and attend a college on the East Coast: 'I want to go where culture is, like New York. Or at least Connecticut or New Hampshire.'

Marion, Lady Bird's mother, cannot understand Lady Bird's distaste for Sacramento and sees it as an affectation. She believes she has done the best for her daughter by sending her to a religious school, pointing out that her brother Miguel 'saw someone knifed in front of him' at public school. Lady Bird is unimpressed by her mother's argument, which she sees as parochial and irrelevant. Marion believes that because Lady Bird couldn't pass her driving test, she would be unlikely to pass the tests required for entrance to prestigious East Coast colleges. She scorns Lady Bird's aspirations, wondering, 'How in the world did I raise such a snob?'

Lady Bird dearly wishes she lived in a wealthier neighbourhood. As she and her friend Julie walk home from school early in the film, they pass through an upmarket part of town. They are particularly taken with a beautiful blue house and stop to admire it for a few moments. Lady Bird says if she lived in one of those houses, she would 'have friends over all the time'. Lady Bird's home is quite small and crowded with little opportunity for privacy, as her brother and his girlfriend live there too. Later in the film, Lady Bird discovers that her boyfriend Danny's grandmother owns the blue house and she is delighted to attend Thanksgiving dinner there.

Marion also feels restricted by their rather modest home and dreams of living in a large, spacious house. When Lady Bird is upset after she has had sex with Kyle and discovered, too late, that it did not mean as much to him as it did to her, she cries on her mother's shoulder. Although Marion does not know the details, she attempts to comfort Lady Bird by suggesting they do their 'favourite Sunday activity'. This involves going to open houses and looking around homes they could never afford. Immediately after the montage of mother and daughter admiring beautiful, spacious interiors, we see Lady Bird lying on the worn tartan couch in the family's rather dark and dingy living room. The contrast between what Lady Bird and Marion would love and what they have could not be clearer.

Comparative Study

Even the smallest aspects of Lady Bird's life are affected by her family's social class. While shopping with her mother, Lady Bird asks if she can buy a magazine that is 'only three dollars'. Marion feels this is an unnecessary luxury and says Lady Bird can read it in the library if she wishes. Lady Bird says that is no good, as she would like to read the magazine in bed as a little treat after a hard week. Marion says that such behaviour is 'something rich people do. We are not rich people.'

Lady Bird tells Danny that she is from 'the wrong side of the tracks', and when she is invited to Thanksgiving dinner in Danny's grandmother's house, she has to shop for a dress in Thrift Town. When Danny comes to Lady Bird's house to collect her for Thanksgiving dinner, he seems amused that her comment about her social status was not just metaphorical, telling her parents that he had never realised there are 'actual train tracks' separating his side of town from Lady Bird's. Marion and Larry's faces stiffen into a polite smile, but they are clearly hurt to learn that Lady Bird is ashamed of her background. On cue, Lady Bird enters in the dress her mother bought her in Thrift Town. Marion carefully altered the dress so it would fit her daughter perfectly, and Danny is impressed, saying his grandmother will approve of Lady Bird.

There are a few odd notes during the Thanksgiving dinner in Danny's grandmother's house that highlight the social gap between Danny and Lady Bird. Lady Bird spots a framed poster of the Republican president Ronald Regan on the study wall, and she asks Danny if it is a joke. He tells her it is not. This is clearly a conservative household, unlike Lady Bird's home. Danny's grandmother, who was clearly stiffly surprised by Lady Bird's enthusiastic hug on meeting her, shows Lady Bird how to fashion the table napkins into an elaborate shape. Lady Bird is delighted to feel she is sharing a moment with Danny's grandmother, but when the grandmother asks Lady Bird to do all of the napkins on the dinner table, it is obvious to the audience – if not to Lady Bird – that she views her more as serving staff than a guest.

Lady Bird also alienates her best friend, Julie, in an effort to improve her social standing. She befriends the shallow and judgemental Jenna because Jenna is wealthy and popular. However, being Jenna's friend means Lady Bird cannot be true to herself. In order to fit in with Jenna's social circle, Lady Bird lies about where she lives, pretending Danny's grandmother's house is hers. Jenna says she knows the area, as it was where her family had their 'starter house'.

Lady Bird's parents are aware that she is ashamed of them. Marion tells her how hurt they are by her 'wrong side of the tracks' comment. She points out that they have made great sacrifices to raise Lady Bird with as many advantages as they could afford, such as paying for a private education for her.

As the film progresses, Lady Bird's feelings about Sacramento and her family background undergo some subtle changes. Sister Sarah-Joan tells Lady Bird that her college essay shows she loves her home town: 'You write about Sacramento so affectionately, and with such care.' Lady Bird is a little surprised at this analysis and says that perhaps all she does is 'pay attention'. Sister Sarah-Joan gently asks Lady Bird if she perhaps thinks that love and attention are the same thing.

At the end of the film, when Lady Bird is in New York but not finding college life as easy or as happy as she had imagined, she rings her parents' house and leaves a voice message. She asks her mother if she 'felt emotional' the first time she drove in Sacramento, and admits that she did. Her phone message becomes a voiceover to shots of a smiling Lady Bird driving through her home town as she nostalgically remembers the 'bends I've known my whole life, and stores, and the whole thing'. Jon Brion's 'Reconcile' plays as we see clips of Marion and Lady Bird driving through Sacramento. Although both are alone in the car in these shots, they are united in their, until now, unspoken love for both Sacramento and one another. The film ends with Lady Bird closing her phone and looking up and around her, clearly a little lost and lonely for her family and the life she was so eager to leave behind.

Gender roles

Lady Bird is an unusual coming-of-age film in that the central character's core relationships are with other women – her mother and her friend Julie – rather than a male love interest. The women in the film are strong, independent and ultimately reliable. Marion and Lady Bird clash, but Lady Bird comes to appreciate her mother's love and strength at the end of the film. Similarly, Julie's friendship is, in the end, far more important to Lady Bird than her prom date with the popular and handsome Kyle.

The world of the text is one in which men feel they have to hide their insecurities and anything about them that does not conform to a traditional patriarchal concept of masculinity. Nor do they seem to have a male friend in whom they can confide when they are finding aspects of their life difficult or confusing. After she finds him kissing another boy, Danny opens up to Lady Bird about his sexual orientation and begs her not to tell anyone until he has worked out the best way to break the news to his parents. He cries in her arms as she comforts him and repeats that she will keep his secret. In

the next scene, we see Marion fulfilling a similar role for Father Leviatch as he struggles with his depression. He appears briefly confused when Marion asks him if he has a support system: 'What do you mean?' She rephrases the question: 'Who do you turn to when you feel this way?' There is a pause, and Father Leviatch sighs heavily: 'No one, I guess.' He immediately follows this comment with a plea to Marion not to tell her daughter about his condition. She reassures him, as Lady Bird did Danny.

Larry, Lady Bird's father, also suffers from depression. He loses his job and is devastated not to be able to provide for his family. Marion has to take on extra shifts in order to earn much-needed money. Larry is more fortunate than Danny or Father Leviatch in that he has a wife upon whom he can lean. Larry is a kind and thoughtful father and his relationship with Lady Bird provides her with a positive male role model. He is able to mediate the fights between Lady Bird and Marion, never judging but always trying to show mother and daughter that they love each other despite their personality clashes.

The men and women in the film are complex and imperfect, and as a result are realistic. However, it is the men who suffer most in trying to live up to the expectations of a patriarchal ideology. The women in the story are not defined by men and do not seem to feel the same need to conform to gender roles in the way the male characters do. Lady Bird learns from the men in her life but is not defined by them. She discovers the joys of first love through her relationship with Danny, and when that is shown to be a sham because he is denying his sexuality, she moves on to exploring her own sexual desires with Kyle. Again, this is far from perfect, as Kyle is not the virgin Lady Bird thought he was. She believes that they have 'deflowered' one another, but Kyle claims he has slept with several girls and does not consider this encounter particularly meaningful. Yet Kyle is not an example of toxic masculinity. He is struggling with his own insecurities, and his efforts to appear cool actually come across as the awkward and slightly embarrassing posturing of a teenage boy who is desperate to seem in control of his life and his emotions. A good example of this is when he sits on the bonnet of his car, reading a book while the rest of his gang of friends flirt and chat. As is the case with Danny, Lady Bird finds peace with Kyle. When he does not want to go to the prom, she asks him to drop her at Julie's house instead and he does so, seeming unperturbed. Lady Bird and Julie go to the dance together and rekindle their friendship. Later, when she goes to New York, Lady Bird makes an effort to reconnect with her mother too. The message we are left with is that the bond between women is ultimately stronger and more important than fleeting love affairs. Lady Bird is on a journey of self-discovery, and the young men in her life are merely stopping points on the road rather than the destination.

Love and marriage

Lady Bird's experiences of love are part of her journey into adulthood, but they are not the main focus of the film. Her first boyfriend is Danny, a sweet and gentle fellow member of the school drama cast. He represents innocent and somewhat idealistic love. They dance in a rose garden and lie side by side under the stars. Lady Bird is charmed by Danny's claim to respect her too much to touch her breasts. However, the real reason for Danny's reluctance to become intimate with Lady Bird is revealed when she catches him kissing another boy. Although she is initially devastated and angry, Lady Bird comforts Danny when he reveals his struggle to come out to his family, and the pair become friends.

Kyle, a rather pretentious young man who dearly wants to be considered a rebel, is Lady Bird's second boyfriend. They sleep together but Lady Bird is disgusted to discover that Kyle is not a virgin. She imagined they were sharing a far more meaningful experience than it actually turned out to be and is annoyed that it was not 'special'. Lady Bird's language during this scene is interesting. She looks at a photo of Kyle as a young child and says, dreamily, 'Cut to "ten years later"'. It is as if she is playing a role in a film about her life rather than actually living in the moment. Kyle's revelation ruins the effect she had hoped to achieve, and she seems more annoyed about that than the fact that their sex was unsatisfactory and unimportant.

Lady Bird subverts the traditional love story we associate with romantic comedies and coming-of-age films. The key relationships are not between Lady Bird and either of her boyfriends, but rather between Lady Bird and her mother, and Lady Bird and her best friend. This is brought into sharp focus at the end of the film when Marion and Julie are at the centre of moments more generally given to the two romantic leads in a story. The first of these occurs on prom night, when Lady Bird realises that she and Kyle have nothing in common and he does not even want to go to the dance. She asks him to bring her to Julie's house and the friends tearfully reunite before going to prom together. They dance and laugh and even pose as a couple for the formal photo before walking home, side by side. We are all familiar with these types of scenes, but Gerwig uses them to show the strength of the bond between two friends rather than the typical boy–girl relationship.

Marion's frantic rush to say goodbye to Lady Bird at the airport is another unusual take on a narrative trope. Once again, however, the focus is not on a romantic relationship but on the love between mother and daughter. Marion fails to reach the departure gate in time, and is left heartbroken, crying in her husband's arms as he reassures her that Lady Bird will be back.

Larry's comforting and reassuring Marion at the airport is typical of his role in their marriage. Their relationship is portrayed in a realistic and ultimately positive light. Marion is the stronger of the two, while the gentle, quiet Larry is often left to mediate between her and Lady Bird. Money is a constant worry in the McPherson household and Larry, already suffering from depression, has to cope with losing his job with little hope of finding another. Marion regularly works double shifts at the hospital in order to keep the family afloat, but she never blames Larry for this. When Lady Bird asks about her father's mental health, Marion explains that money 'is not life's report card' and that being successful doesn't mean anything. She does not love or value her husband based on his ability to support his family financially.

Lady Bird's volatile relationship with her mother puts a strain on her parents' marriage at times. Larry and Marion want the best for their daughter and Marion, in particular, is hurt that Lady Bird wants more than they can give her. Larry goes behind his wife's back to help Lady Bird apply for university in New York, and there is a predictable fallout when Marion discovers the truth. Lady Bird asks her father if they are going to get a divorce because of what has happened, but he laughs off the suggestion, saying they can't afford to and reassuring her that he loves his wife.

Ultimately, the film leaves us with the message that true love is not about sweeping romantic gestures or passionate sexual encounters: it is based on understanding, affection, compromise and loyalty.

Religion

Lady Bird attends a Catholic school run by nuns. Her mother believes this gives her a better chance of a good education in a safe environment than if Lady Bird were in public school, but Lady Bird does not agree. In an early conversation with Marion, Lady Bird changes the name of her school from 'Immaculate Heart' to 'Immaculate Fart'. Her irreverent attitude and her resentment of her school is fairly typical teenage behaviour, and the way religion is treated in the film is to view it as just a normal part of life. There is nothing sinister or particularly saintly about the priests and nuns in the film: they are, like everyone, just trying to do their best.

In an interview, Gerwig said that when she was writing the film, she found inspiration in reading about the lives of saints: 'I was always interested in who they were as people and that they both were these people who were divinely inspired, but they were also kind of just annoying teenagers.'

In order to make religion simply a part of Lady Bird's life, religion and secular life are intertwined in many of the shots. The students recite their prayers in church and the Pledge of Allegiance in the same bored, monotonous tones. At the start of the film, a montage of lay teachers, priests and nuns speaking to the students shows a shared commitment to education and student welfare. The clergy in the film are presented as real people rather than religious stereotypes. Sister Sarah-Joan understands Lady Bird and gently tries to guide her towards those areas in which she might do well. Sister Sarah-Joan does not judge Lady Bird for her strange posters when she is running for class president, simply saying that some of the students found them disturbing. She smiles warmly as she notes that Lady Bird has 'a performative streak' and directs her towards the school's theatre programme. Unlike Lady Bird's mother, Sister Sarah-Joan is gentle when broaching the subject of Lady Bird's unrealistic dreams and her weaknesses. When Lady Bird says she would like to take part in Math Olympiad, a highly selective annual maths competition, Sister Sarah-Joan frames her response tactfully. Rather than simply telling Lady Bird that she is not academically capable of such a thing, Sister Sarah-Joan gently says, 'But math isn't something you're terribly strong in?', couching the criticism in a questioning tone that removes its sting and makes Lady Bird feel as if they are having a mature and equal conversation. Lady Bird risks damaging her relationship with Sister Sarah-Joan when she decorates her car as one might for a newly married couple, but the elderly nun takes the prank in her stride and handles the tricky situation with gentle good humour.

The two priests in the film, Father Leviatch and Father Walther, are also presented as individuals rather than religious stereotypes. Father Leviatch is fragile and suffering from depression while Father Walther is a comic figure, enthusiastic but completely at sea when he steps in to direct the school musical.

Lady Bird rails against the restrictions of her life in Sacramento, including the Catholic school she feels she has been forced to attend, but when she is troubled or conflicted, she turns to the unjudgmental and reflective version of religion to which she has been exposed. New York is a lonely and rather bewildering place for Lady Bird. One night, she is brought to the ER after drinking too much at a college party. Walking home from the hospital the following morning, Lady Bird stops at a church and listens to the choir singing 'Rosa Mystica'. Having largely ignored Catholicism and seeing it merely as a backdrop to her education, Lady Bird finally has a truly religious experience in church. She has an epiphany about her relationship with her mother and Sacramento, and comes to realise how deeply she cares about her family and her home.

Family

Lady Bird has a complicated relationship with her mother. Although – or perhaps, because – they are similar in many ways, they frequently clash. Lady Bird does not feel that her mother supports her choices or appreciates her abilities.

The opening shot is of Lady Bird and her mother lying in bed together in a motel room. Their postures mirror one another, hinting at a close connection that Lady Bird will struggle with as she tries to distance herself from her family and her home town. Her first words in the film are addressed to her mother: 'Do you think I look like I'm from Sacramento?' Her mother's matter-of-fact response, 'You are from Sacramento', not only highlights that Lady Bird is rooted in a place she does not wish to call home, but also shows that her mother has no truck with her daughter's aspirations and wants to bring her back to earth.

Lady Bird says her mother does not need to make the motel bed, but Marion says, 'Well, it's nice to make things neat and clean.' As she says this, Marion reaches over and tucks a stray wisp of Lady Bird's hair behind her ears. Clearly, one of the things Marion would like to make 'neat and clean' is her daughter and their relationship. Unfortunately, life is messy, and this scene sets up the conflict between mother and daughter, reality and dreams. The camera captures the silhouettes of Lady Bird and Marion as they sit on the bed, and we see that, for all the differences that will emerge over the course of the film, they are more alike than they are dissimilar.

Early in the film, as the pair drives home, Lady Bird expresses her desire to go to college on the East Coast but her mother refuses to consider this, saying, 'you're not even *worth* state tuition, Christine', and criticising her daughter's work ethic. Lady Bird objects to her mother calling her by her birth name and says she is called Lady Bird. Her mother completely rejects this new name, saying it is ridiculous. The atmosphere becomes increasingly tense as Marion says Lady Bird should just go to city college and then jail. Face set in fury, Lady Bird opens the door and throws herself from the moving car. Marion screams in horror. The next scene opens with Lady Bird at Mass in her school. She is wearing a bright pink cast on the arm she obviously broke in her fall from the car, and on it are written the words 'Fuck you, Mom'. The relationship between mother and daughter is clearly a source of friction in the film.

Lady Bird's relationship with her father is far less fractious than that with her mother. He takes the news that she wants to attend an East Coast college well, simply wondering if it will be very expensive. Lady Bird wants to apply for financial aid and asks her father not to tell her mother about it. He agrees, and arranges everything without telling his wife.

One of the reasons Marion and Lady Bird clash so frequently is that Marion is unable to resist criticising her daughter's choices. Although she does so because she believes she is helping her daughter to improve, the real effect is to drive a wedge between them. A key moment that shows this clearly is when Lady Bird decides to spend her last Thanksgiving before college with Danny's family. Marion tries to be supportive by taking Lady Bird shopping for an appropriate dress for the occasion, but also mentions that she thinks it is 'such a shame you're spending your last Thanksgiving with a family you've never met instead of us'. As they browse the rail of dresses, Marion asks if Lady Bird wants to sit down, as she appears to be dragging her feet. Lady Bird asks her mother why she is being so passive aggressive and infuriating. It appears they are about to have a serious argument when Marion suddenly pulls a dress from the rack that both mother and daughter instantly agree is just perfect.

Comparative Study

This short scene perfectly captures the affection, frustration and unspoken feelings that mark the relationship between mother and daughter.

Although Lady Bird fights with her mother a great deal, she defends her against criticism. Danny tells Lady Bird that he finds Marion scary, with which Lady Bird disagrees. She echoes Shelly's description of Marion, saying, 'She has a big heart. She's very warm.'

Marion hopes that Lady Bird will be content to study in the University of California, Davis, as it is only fifteen minutes from Sacramento. If Lady Bird were to study there, it would mean she could live at home and therefore her education would cost a lot less than if she were to study out of state. However, there is another reason Marion wants Lady Bird to consider Davis, although she cannot express it openly. She loves her daughter dearly and does not want her to leave home just yet. She touts Davis's acting programme: 'You know Davis has a terrific theatre. If you're still interested in theatre. Are you?' This is a poignant moment. Marion's comments show her love for Lady Bird, her desire for her to stay in Sacramento and her lack of familiarity with her almost-adult daughter. She knows Lady Bird *was* interested in acting but is unsure if she still is.

Another exchange between Marion and Lady Bird as they shop for a prom dress shows the tension in their relationship. Lady Bird says she wishes Marion liked her. Marion's reply, 'Of course I love you,' does not hit the mark. Lady Bird persists, 'But do you *like* me?' Cornered, Marion comes up with what she thinks is a compromise between her deep love for her daughter and her disappointment at the choices she is making: 'I want you to be the very best version of yourself that you can be.' Lady Bird asks the unanswerable question, 'What if this *is* the best version?' Marion has nothing to say to this. It is clear that she wants more for and from Lady Bird. She is unwilling to accept her daughter for what she is.

When Lady Bird is offered and accepts a place at a university in New York, Marion is devastated. Too proud to admit to her daughter how much she will miss her, Marion writes and rejects numerous farewell letters. She even refuses to park her car and go into the airport to say goodbye to Lady Bird, but this decision causes her enormous pain. Sobbing heartbrokenly, she finally parks her car and rushes into the departure area, only to find she is too late. Lady Bird has gone.

In New York, Lady Bird unpacks her bag in her dorm room, and she finds all the drafts of letters her mother had wanted to give her. Larry has kept them and ensured Lady Bird saw them because he wants his daughter to know how much her mother loves her. Larry has acted as mediator throughout the film. He may have seemed a rather weak and ineffectual character compared to his strong-willed wife and daughter, but his steadiness and sense of perspective allow him to see that Lady Bird and Marion, though they spark off one another, are more similar than dissimilar. They love one another dearly, even if they struggle to express their feelings. The film ends with a virtual love letter to Sacramento and Marion. Lady Bird leaves a message on her family's answerphone, calling herself 'Christine': 'It's the name you gave me. It's a good one.' As Jon Brion's 'Reconcile' plays, we see Lady Bird coming to terms with her upbringing and realising that her parents supported rather than hindered her personal growth.

Comparative study: Cultural context

Never Let Me Go	*Philadelphia, Here I Come!*	*Lady Bird*

Setting and social class affect the lives of the characters.

The lives of the central characters in *Never Let Me Go* are greatly restricted by their setting and their social class. Because the clones are regarded as less than human, they are raised in homes and kept away from 'normal' people for most of their lives. Although Hailsham is a pleasant home in many ways, it is still a prison of sorts. The children are not locked in but are kept from leaving by horror stories about students who wandered off and were brutally murdered or were forbidden to return and died in the woods. The guardians raise the students to accept that they are considered inferior to 'normal' people. When the students are old enough to live independently, they are moved to run-down cottages in the countryside. Despite having more freedom, the students rarely venture out of the Cottages in the early days of their time there. Kathy believes that there is a part of all of the students that will forever be 'fearful of the world' around them because of the restrictive nature of a childhood spent in a single location. As the novel progresses, the settings become bleaker, reflecting the characters' fading hopes and opportunities. Kathy sees the setting as a reflection of the clones' position in society, reflecting that the 'dark byways of the country' are for 'the likes of us' while 'the big glittering motorways with their huge signs and super cafés were for everyone else'.

Kathy and her friends are not simply from the lowest social class in society – they have no social class. The clones accept their situation because they have been raised to believe there is no other path for them.

Gar in *Philadelphia, Here I Come!* is less restricted than Kathy and the other characters in *Never Let Me Go* because he has a choice. He can decide to live with the restrictions of his social setting, or he can choose to escape them. The characters in *Never Let Me Go* have no such option. However, just because Gar can choose to escape the restrictions of life in his home town does not mean that it is easy. He is torn between a desire to seek a better life and a longing for his father to give him a reason not to go. Gar's father does not openly support his son's moving to America but neither does he oppose it.

In contrast to *Never Let Me Go*, in which the setting changes as the characters move on, nothing changes in *Philadelphia, Here I Come!*, which is part of the tragedy. Gar feels constricted by a world that is not moving with the times, but he does not see that he is just as much at fault as his father and his friends in refusing to change. In his conversation with 'the boys', Gar reverts to his public self and does not challenge their imagined encounters with local and visiting women.

Gar, like Kathy, has to deal with being looked down on by those who feel socially superior. This is a far more serious problem in *Never Let Me Go* than it is in the play because those who despise the clones believe it is acceptable to kill them. In *Philadelphia, Here I Come!* the effects of the difference in social class are far more subtle. Senator Doogan, in the course of a seemingly innocuous conversation, casually but cruelly reminds Gar that he is not in the same class as

Like Gar, Lady Bird is discontented in her home town. She considers it 'the Midwest of California', and makes it clear that she considers it a place without culture. Her situation is far more like Gar's than it is Kathy's in that she has the option to move elsewhere and start a new life. However, like Gar, she is conflicted. For all that she scorns what Sacramento has to offer, there is a part of Lady Bird that simply wishes she could be happy there. Her family's precarious financial situation is a source of shame for her, and she refuses to accept the sacrifices her parents have made to have her privately educated. As Marion says, she and Larry had hoped they would have moved to a nicer house long ago, but they couldn't because they spent all their money on their children. Lady Bird longs to live in one of the wealthier neighbourhoods that surround hers. Walking home from school one day, she stops in front of a beautiful family home and confides in her friend Julie that if she lived in a house like that, she would 'have friends over all the time'. The implication is that she is too ashamed of her own home to invite anyone over.

Gar feels a similar shame when Senator Doogan makes it clear that he, Gar, is not wealthy or influential enough to be seriously considered as a husband for his daughter. The most striking difference between the setting and social class in *Never Let Me Go*, *Philadelphia, Here I Come!* and *Lady Bird* is the fact that neither Gar nor Lady Bird is as deprived as they think they are. Both have a secure home and are loved, even if that is not immediately obvious to either. Kathy is considered the lowest of the low in her society, and her life

→

Never Let Me Go	Philadelphia, Here I Come!	Lady Bird
	Francis King and is therefore not an eligible suitor for Kate. Ultimately, Gar, like the characters in *Never Let Me Go*, is beaten down by the world in which he lives. He is so crushed that we feel sure he will, as Madge says, turn out just like his father: lonely and heartbroken.	is deemed valueless as a result. By contrast, Gar and Lady Bird's problems seem trivial. They have the option of accepting their lot or changing their situation, a luxury that is never afforded to Kathy. As a result, their view of their setting and social class is a matter of their opinion of it, rather than the harsh reality Kathy has to endure.

Never Let Me Go	Philadelphia, Here I Come!	Lady Bird

Gender roles restrict the characters in some texts more than others.

Gender differences are not particularly restrictive in *Never Let Me Go* because the clones are already so unfairly treated that any other inequalities are irrelevant. However, there are certain stereotypes that play out in the story. Women are seen to be either caring and nurturing or sexually predatory, while men are expected to be strong and unemotional. Kathy struggles with her sexual urges because she fears they prove she is cloned from a sex worker or pornographic actress. The implication is that physical desire is not something a woman should feel. Ruth confirms Kathy's worst fears when they are in the Cottages, saying that Tommy could never consider a relationship with Kathy because she had slept with several men. She tells Kathy that 'Tommy doesn't like girls who've been with . . . well, you know, with this person and that'. There is a double standard here, as there is no implication that men are judged by the same standards. Kathy ultimately falls into another female stereotype, that of the nurturing, mother figure. Although she cannot have children, Kathy channels her maternal instincts into helping others, even Ruth, through their donations. Kathy does not feel

Gender roles restrict the lives of the characters in *Philadelphia, Here I Come!* more than they do in *Never Let Me Go*. The world of the play is overwhelmingly patriarchal, and this has a particularly negative effect on the female characters. Madge, the O'Donnells' housekeeper, is a selfless, caring woman who has looked after S.B. and Gar for many years. She also helps her niece with her children, but receives little thanks in return. **Unlike Kathy in *Never Let Me Go*, who is content in her role as a carer, Madge's life of drudgery seems to bring her little joy.** She is briefly happy and excited at the thought of her niece naming the new baby after her, but that does not transpire and Madge is let down once again. She seems resigned to her fate, saying wearily that 'Madge Mulhern' is 'too aul' fashioned or something'.

Kate Doogan is another example of a woman whose life is severely restricted by the gender roles in the world of the text. Although she is a bright, capable young woman, Kate has few choices in life. **Kathy in *Never Let Me Go* has even fewer choices, but she is restricted by being a clone rather than by being a woman.** Kate's father has her life mapped out for her and succeeds in his plan to have her marry Dr Francis King. Senator Doogan tells Gar that 'any decision she makes will be her own', but this is not really the case. Kate has no income of her own and must rely on a man to support her. Therefore, her choices are severely limited. The same was the case for Gar's mother, who married S.B. because he seemed a fine

The women in *Lady Bird* are nothing like as restricted as those in *Philadelphia, Here I Come!* However, there is not the same lack of focus on gender that there is in *Never Let Me Go*. Nor is it women who suffer the most from the expectations and limitations of a patriarchal society. **The men in the film, like those in *Philadelphia, Here I Come!*, feel they have to hide their insecurities and anything about them that does not conform to the traditional view of masculinity.** This means that they are often left with no male friend on whom to rely when they feel emotionally vulnerable. Danny has to turn to his ex-girlfriend, Lady Bird, when he needs someone with whom he can discuss the difficulty of coming out to his parents. He cries in her arms and she comforts him. **The role of carer here is like that assigned to Kathy in *Never Let Me Go*.** Marion fulfils a similar nurturing role when she talks to Father Leviatch about his depression. He admits to her that he has no support system, but he is still anxious that his depression, which he sees as a weakness, not be common knowledge. Larry, too, feels the pressure to conform to the role expected of a male head of the household. He loses his job and can no longer provide for his family. He is already prone to depression and his precarious financial situation simply exacerbates the situation. **This is reminiscent of Gar's burning shame and humiliation in *Philadelphia, Here I Come!* when he feels he cannot measure up to Dr Francis King as a potential husband for Kate Doogan.**

Never Let Me Go	*Philadelphia, Here I Come!*	*Lady Bird*
restricted by this traditional female role; in fact, it allows her to rekindle her relationships with her old friends from Hailsham. Overall, therefore, gender roles do not have a particularly negative impact on the lives of the characters in the text.	gentleman and owned his own shop. **In *Philadelphia, Here I Come!*, therefore, gender roles are a restrictive force in a way they are not in *Never Let Me Go*.** Kathy chooses a traditional female role of carer but she does not feel that this holds her back. Of course, this is because, compared to the horrific control society has over the lives of clones, their gender is an insignificant issue. The men in *Philadelphia, Here I Come!* also suffer because of the strict gender roles. Gar feels impotent because he does not earn enough to provide a good living for Kate. Although she tells him to lie to her father about his income, his paltry egg money and salary from his father's shop pale into insignificance compared to what Dr Francis King can offer her. Gar's friends, 'the boys', are also negatively impacted by the expectations placed upon men. They believe that physical aggression and promiscuity are the signs that one is a 'real' man. Therefore, they lie about their fighting abilities and their sexual conquests. Gar notes wearily that for all their talk, the boys are barely able to take a 'furtive peep' at women. The desire to appear manly means that Gar's friends are unable to express themselves emotionally. Ned awkwardly gives Gar his belt, claiming that he can use it to deal with any 'Yankee scuts' who try to pick a fight with him. **These harmful gender stereotypes are similar to those in *Never Let Me Go*, in which promiscuity in men is acceptable, but women are meant to be more reticent and demure.** **The messages in both texts reinforce the double standards of gender stereotypes, albeit more strongly in *Philadelphia, Here I Come!* than in *Never Let Me Go*.**	The women in *Lady Bird* are far less restricted by gender roles than are the men. Lady Bird learns from the boys she dates, but she is not defined by them. The most important relationships in the text are those between women. Lady Bird rejects the handsome but self-absorbed Kyle and goes to the prom with her best friend, Julie. **This strong female bond is completely absent in *Philadelphia, Here I Come!* and, although Kathy and Ruth in *Never Let Me Go* care for one another, they ultimately fall out over a man.** The message in *Lady Bird* is very different. The rekindled friendship between Lady Bird and Julie is celebrated with the sort of grand romantic gesture usually reserved for the boy and girl in rom-coms. Lady Bird rejects the cool, popular kids and turns up at Julie's house to take her to the prom. The friends dance and laugh the night away and the message is clear: female friendships are more important than fleeting love affairs.

Never Let Me Go	*Philadelphia, Here I Come!*	*Lady Bird*
	The three texts present us with different views of love and marriage.	
Lifelong love and marriage are presented as unachievable goals in *Never Let Me Go*. The characters in the novel are fated to die once they have 'completed' their donations. Therefore, they are raised to believe that they cannot expect to have normal lives and will never be able to marry or have a family. Despite this, the young people have close bonds of friendship and romance, and it	**Although love does not conquer all in *Never Let Me Go*, it still provides the central characters with memories to cherish. In contrast, the view of love and marriage in *Philadelphia, Here I Come!* is entirely negative.** It is a story of longing, lost love and regrets. **The memories Gar has of Kate Doogan at the end of the play do not provide him with the same solace as Kathy's memories of Tommy at the end of *Never Let Me Go*. Instead, Gar is tortured by the knowledge that he let Kate slip away because he was too much of a coward to stand up to her father.** During the flashback in which he recalls the painful meeting with Senator Doogan, Gar recounts some of the details of Kate and Francis's expensive wedding. He reflects that this memory 'has left a deep scar on the aul skitter of a soul' and was 'a sore hoke on the aul prestige'. Gar and Kate's romance is doomed by a society in which women have little choice but to marry for practical reasons, as they need to be supported by their	Love and marriage are presented in a more balanced and realistic way in *Lady Bird* than they are in the other two texts. In *Never Let Me Go*, the clones are raised to believe that they can never have normal relationships because of their short lifespan. In *Philadelphia, Here I Come!*, Gar's unrealistic and immature attitude towards love and marriage means his relationship with Kate Doogan is doomed to failure. In both texts, romantic love plays a central role. In *Lady Bird*, however, the central character has two boyfriends but does not view either as the main

→

Never Let Me Go	Philadelphia, Here I Come!	Lady Bird
is these relationships that makes their short lives worth living. The characters' love for one another adds to the sadness of their situation. Tommy and Kathy are given false hope that if they can prove they are in love, they will be granted a 'deferral' and allowed to have some years together before beginning their donations. However, the world of the text is terribly harsh, and when Tommy and Kathy visit Miss Emily and Madame to ask about the deferrals, their hopes are dashed. Those who want the clones' organs do not care if they are in love or not. The traditional view in stories is that love conquers all, but Ishiguro is at pains to point out that this belief is irrational. At the end of the novel, Kathy is alone. Ruth and Tommy have 'completed' and she is about to begin her own donation journey. However, love has given her short life a great deal of meaning. She says, 'I lost Ruth, then I lost Tommy, but I won't lose my memories of them.' These precious memories of love are both uplifting and heartbreaking.	husbands. Gar is not the only one damaged by this pragmatic and rather unfeeling attitude. Kate, despite her seemingly advantageous marriage, does not seem particularly happy. When Gar asks her, 'Is Dr King well?' she replies drily, 'I hear no complaints.' The implication seems to be that she has little interest in how her husband feels but knows that she would be the first to hear about it if he were in any way unwell or dissatisfied. **This is a far less positive view of love than we are left with at the end of *Never Let Me Go*. In the novel, the message is that love makes life worth living, even if it is not perfect. In *Philadelphia, Here I Come!*, however, love brings nothing but pain and regret.**	**focus of her life.** Danny is her first choice because he appears to represent the chivalric, gallant romantic ideal to which a young girl might aspire. Their love is innocent and sweet. When Danny says he respects Lady Bird too much to touch her breasts, she is charmed. She never for a moment suspects he is gay. When she discovers the truth, she is initially upset but soon forgives Danny, and she becomes a support for him when he admits his struggle to come out. Kyle, Lady Bird's second boyfriend, is edgy and handsome. She loses her virginity to him and reads far more into the moment than does Kyle. Lady Bird is again devastated to learn that her vision of romantic love was not shared by her boyfriend. However, she quickly comes to terms with the reality and is still willing to go to prom with Kyle. Her acceptance of a far from ideal situation indicates that she was never really in love with him. **If we compare her reaction to Kathy, who left the Cottages to become a carer when she could no longer bear to be around Tommy and Ruth, and to Gar, who decided to emigrate to America to be away from Kate and her new husband, we see how clear-headed Lady Bird is on the subject of love.** It is not surprising that Lady Bird should have a balanced and sensible approach to love in the end, despite her being melodramatic and immature at times. After all, her parents model abiding love and loyalty. Marion supports Larry through his depression, and he stands up for his wife while also supporting his daughter: not an easy compromise. Their deep affection for one another provides us with a very positive view of love and marriage.

Never Let Me Go	Philadelphia, Here I Come!	Lady Bird

Religious beliefs affect the lives of the characters in each of the three texts.

Never Let Me Go	Philadelphia, Here I Come!	Lady Bird
While there is little mention of organised religion in *Never Let Me Go*, the students' lives – and deaths – are nonetheless dictated by a belief that the soul is what makes a person human. The 'normals' believe the clones have no souls and therefore can be used as organ donors even though this inevitably leads to their death. Miss Emily and Madame explain to Tommy and Kathy that they set up Hailsham and encouraged the children to be creative in order to 'reveal your souls. Or, to put it more finely,	**Religion is not portrayed in a positive light in *Philadelphia, Here I Come!* but is nothing like as devastating an aspect of the characters' lives as the belief system in *Never Let Me Go*.** In the play, religion is represented by Canon O'Byrne, S.B.'s friend. He is an ineffectual priest, far more concerned with his own needs and comforts than those of his parishioners. He goes to Tenerife 'for five weeks	**The view of religion in *Lady Bird* is far more positive than in the other two texts.** Lady Bird attends a private Catholic school run by nuns, and her experience there is not significantly different to that of high school students in other private schools. The students attend Mass but with no more interest or irritation than students elsewhere attend assemblies. Lady Bird irreverently calls the school 'Immaculate Fart' rather than 'Immaculate Heart', but that is typical teenage behaviour and shows no real malice towards Catholicism or the school itself. **The nuns and priests in the film contribute to the idea that religion is just a normal part of life.** They are not particularly saintly, but they do their best, unlike the Canon in *Philadelphia, Here I Come!* This is most obvious in Lady Bird's interactions with

Never Let Me Go	Philadelphia, Here I Come!	Lady Bird
we did it to *prove you had souls at all*.' Ultimately, however, people decide to ignore the inconvenient evidence and continue to claim that the clones are 'less than human' because they do not have souls. Kathy, Tommy, Ruth and the other students are fated to die because of this deeply flawed belief system.	every winter' and does not want to do anything to rock the boat. Although he is S.B.'s friend, the Canon does nothing to bridge the obvious gap between Gar and his father. Gar believes that the priest should be able to 'translate all this loneliness, this groping, this dreadful buffoonery into Christian terms' that would make life more bearable, but the 'arid Canon' remains silent. There is something very bleak about the Canon's refusal to become involved in what is undoubtedly a difficult situation. He has nothing to say but 'Powerful the way time passes too' when he hears Gar is leaving the following morning, even though it is obvious that there is great unhappiness in the O'Donnell household. **However, the view of religion is not as negative as the belief system in *Never Let Me Go*, in which the clones are seen as sub-human because those in authority find it convenient to say they have no souls.** Religion in *Philadelphia, Here I Come!* is simply like every other aspect of the cultural context in the play: disappointing and depressing.	Sister Sarah-Joan. The elderly nun gently guides Lady Bird through her difficult, rebellious phase and supports her as best she can. The Canon in Friel's play is also aware of the problems in the O'Donnell household, but he does nothing to help. Sister Sarah-Joan directs Lady Bird towards the theatre because she recognises her 'performative streak', laughs off a prank Lady Bird and Jenna play involving her car, and tries to show her wayward pupil that she has a deep affection for her home town, even if she cannot see it yet. **Ultimately, religion in the film offers comfort in a way it does not in the other two texts. In *Never Let Me Go*, the idea of spirituality is used to deny the clones their basic humanity, and in *Philadelphia, Here I Come!*, the 'arid' Canon has nothing of value to offer Gar or S.B.** At the end of the film, however, Lady Bird enters a church in New York and is deeply moved by the choir singing the beautiful 'Rosa Mystica'. At that moment, she has an epiphany and comes to realise how much she cares about her family and her home. In the spirit of reconciliation and forgiveness, she phones her parents and leaves a message expressing her love and gratitude.

Never Let Me Go	Philadelphia, Here I Come!	Lady Bird
Family reflects the cultural context of each text.		
Family life in the traditional sense does not exist in *Never Let Me Go*, and that is part of what makes this dystopian novel so bleak. The guardians in Hailsham double as parental figures to an extent but have none of the selfless, unconditional love of parents raising children in a family setting. Despite their largely loveless upbringing, the students still long for the closeness that comes from a family. They turn to each other to form these bonds, and their	*Philadelphia, Here I Come!* presents us with a rather grim view of the damage that can be caused by dysfunctional family relationships. **In *Never Let Me Go*, the clones create their own version of loving family life for the short time they can, but in *Philadelphia, Here I Come!*, family means pain, longing and loneliness. Gar is faced with the choice between emigrating or staying with his elderly father. The irony is that Gar does not feel shackled by his family bonds and has no real desire to leave home. He would probably stay if only he and S.B. could open up to one another.** Private says, 'There are only the two of us . . . each of us is all the other has; and why can we not even look at each other?' **At the end of the novel and the play, family bonds have been stretched or broken, but the manner in which this**	**Like Gar and S.B in *Philadelphia, Here I Come!* Lady Bird and Marion are similar, and that is what causes the fractious family dynamic. Both are strong-willed and outspoken, and they frequently fall out as a result. However, their ability to at least voice their feelings is different to Gar and S.B., whose relationship is marked by taciturnity and an inability to express their emotions.** **The loving support that a family can offer is evident throughout *Lady Bird* and also, in a slightly different form, in *Never Let Me Go*. The clones in the novel form their own bonds, which are not unlike familial relationships, and they draw comfort from that. However, the world in which they live denies them the opportunity to marry and have families of their own, and it eventually rips them apart with horrific cruelty. The tragedy in *Philadelphia, Here I Come!* is that Gar has a father who loves him but, like Lady Bird and**

→

Never Let Me Go	Philadelphia, Here I Come!	Lady Bird
relationships, which may merely have been close in a real boarding school, become incredibly important to them as a result. Hailsham is their home and, like siblings who may squabble but remain close, the students' shared experiences in Hailsham keep their connection strong throughout their short lives. The cruelty of the world in which the clones are raised becomes clearer as the novel progresses. The students are taught from their earliest days that they can never marry or have children, and although they accept this when they are young, it becomes deeply painful for them when they reach a stage in life when they would love to settle down with a partner. In the Cottages, there are rumours that couples who are truly in love can be granted a reprieve from donations and may even be allowed to live normal family lives. Of course, this is not true, as Tommy and Kathy discover when they visit Miss Emily and Madame. They are crushed but left with no option but to accept their fate. The students end their lives as they began them, relying on one another for care, companionship and all that goes with family bonds in a normal society.	is done and the resultant emotions leave us with a very different understanding of the cultural context in each case. In *Never Let Me Go,* the clones are separated by an unspeakably cruel world that denies them any chance of lasting family life, but Kathy at least has her loving memories of Ruth and Tommy, which nobody can take from her. In *Philadelphia, Here I Come!* Gar prepares to leave S.B. and we have no such sense of comfort. Gar has family waiting for him in America, but he already dreads his Aunt Lizzy's smothering neediness. It is hard to be hopeful about Gar's future family life, either with Lizzy or with a wife and children of his own. After all, Madge says that when S.B. was Gar's age, he was 'the very same as him', and she believes that when Gar is 'the age the boss is now, he'll turn out the same'. This is a depressing reflection on family life in the world of the text as it suggests that Gar will inevitably be as taciturn and emotionally repressed a man as S.B.	Marion, the relationship is strained and awkward. Lady Bird, however, is more fortunate than Gar in that she has her father to mediate between herself and her mother. Madge tries her best to play the same role in *Philadelphia, Here I Come!* but she is not Gar's parent or S.B.'s partner, so her efforts are limited by her position. The view of family life in *Lady Bird* is, ultimately, positive. Larry plays an important part in reconnecting Lady Bird and her mother and keeping the family together. **Unlike the world of the play, in which men struggle to voice their feelings, Larry finds it easy to talk to Lady Bird about how much her mother loves her, and he even ensures that she reads drafts of a letter Marion had been writing to her daughter.** The film ends with Lady Bird leaving a message on her parents' answerphone in which she expresses her love and gratitude for all they have given her. **Family in the film, therefore, is ultimately presented as a nurturing, supportive unit of society in a way it is not in the other two texts.**

Questions

1. **(a)** Identify at least one type of behaviour considered to be unacceptable within the world of one text on your comparative course. Explain why such behaviour is considered unacceptable in this cultural context and discuss the response or responses of society to such behaviour. Support your answer with reference to the text. (30)

   (b) With reference to two other texts on your comparative course, identify at least one type of behaviour considered to be unacceptable in the world of each of these texts. Compare why such behaviour is considered unacceptable in these cultural contexts and the response or responses of society to such unacceptable behaviour. Support your answer with reference to the texts.

   In response to 1. (b) you may refer to the same or different types of behaviour in each of your chosen texts. You may refer to the same or different type(s) of behaviour as those referred to in 1. (a) above. (40)

   OR

2. 'Aspects of cultural context affect the extent to which a character can be happy or successful within the world of a text.'

   Identify a central character in each of three texts on your comparative course. Compare the aspect of the cultural context in each of these texts that, in your opinion, most affects the extent to which your chosen characters are happy or successful. You may refer to the same or different aspects of cultural context in each of your chosen texts. Support your answer with reference to the texts. (70)

1. 'Understanding who holds power and who is powerless helps to reveal the cultural context in texts.'

   Compare how the distribution of power within each of three texts on your comparative course helps to reveal the cultural contexts in these texts. Support your answer with reference to your chosen texts. (70)

   OR

2. 'Central characters can be successful or unsuccessful in challenging aspects of the cultural context in texts.'

   (a) Discuss the extent to which at least one central character is successful or unsuccessful in challenging at least one aspect of the cultural context in one text on your comparative course. Support your answer with reference to the text. (30)

   (b) Compare the extent to which at least one central character, from each of two other comparative texts, is either successful or unsuccessful in challenging at least one aspect of the cultural context in these texts. Support your answer with reference to your chosen texts. You may refer to the same aspect or different aspects of the cultural contexts in your answers. (40)

Mode: Literary genre

Literary genre in *Never Let Me Go*

Note: The song 'Never Let Me Go' is an important symbol in the novel. If you are discussing imagery and symbolism in the novel (page 358), you can also refer to these notes on the title.

One of Kathy's most treasured possessions as a young girl is a cassette tape of an album called *Songs After Dark* by the fictional Judy Bridgewater. Kathy buys the tape at one of the Sales, and one of the songs, 'Never Let Me Go', quickly becomes her favourite. Aged 11, Kathy does not understand the lyrics, believing them to be about a woman 'who'd been told she couldn't have babies, who'd really,

really wanted them all her life'. Then, in young Kathy's imagination, the woman has a baby by a 'sort of a miracle' and she holds it close 'partly because she's so happy, but also because she's so afraid that something will happen' and that she will lose her child. The song is symbolic of love and the fear of loss. Kathy learns in time that she – like all the clones – can never marry or have children, but as a young child she does not fully understand what her future holds.

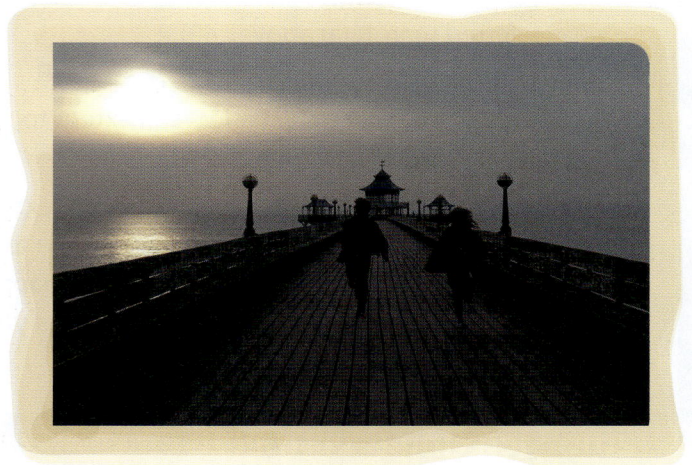

Kathy recalls an incident in which Madame happened to see Kathy cradling a pillow as if it were a baby and softly crooning along with the tape, 'Oh baby, *baby*, never let me go …'. Kathy is bewildered to see Madame sob uncontrollably. It is only years later, when discussing the incident with Tommy, that Kathy comes to some sort of understanding of Madame's reaction. Tommy explains that Madame was probably upset because she knew, long before Kathy did, that the clones were sterile and could never have children, even if society had allowed them that freedom. Madame, however, was more likely to be experiencing even more complex emotions than those attributed to her by Tommy. Kathy's behaviour showed her that the clones were no less human than anyone else and were – despite the public's view of them – deserving of empathy and kindness. Kathy's singing 'never let me go' could have been interpreted as a plea to the wider world not to ignore the basic humanity of the clones. What Kathy was experiencing as she sang a song that seemed relatively straightforward and innocent to her was perceived in a very different way by Madame. Ishiguro reminds us here that our memories are shaped by our perception of them and that a simple incident is rarely simple. Two people might have the same experience, but view it very differently. When Kathy meets Madame again later in life, she says that she, Kathy, had 'her own version' of the song, but Madame says she saw the incident as a little girl desperately wishing that the 'harsh, cruel world' of scientific advances, such as cloning organ donors, could go away. Madame imagined that Kathy was 'holding to her breast the old kind world, one that she knew in her heart could not remain, and that she was holding it and pleading, never to let her go'.

The idea of 'letting go', raised in the title, is a key component of the novel. Kathy has to let go of everything, over time. In Hailsham, she has to let go of the idea that she and Tommy might be together when Ruth claims him as her own. In the Cottages, the three cling to each other because they are 'fearful of the world' around them and therefore 'unable quite to let each other go'. However, they do part when Kathy leaves to become a carer and are only reunited under tragic circumstances. Kathy and Tommy have a brief flicker of hope that they might be allowed to live a little longer than other clones because they are in love, but they have to forsake that dream after a visit to Miss Emily and Madame. After several donations, Ruth and Tommy both die, leaving Kathy alone. In the end, she makes the decision to finally let go and relinquish her claim on life, but not her claim on love. She may have said her final goodbyes to her friends and be about to die, but she is ultimately sustained by her recollections: 'I lost Ruth, then I lost Tommy, but I won't lose my memories of them.' She can be forced to part with her friends and her life, but she will never forego her basic humanity or her love for those closest to her.

Plot/Narrative pattern

The book is not set in an imagined future but rather in an alternative recent past. Kathy, Ruth and Tommy grow up in Hailsham some time from the late 1960s to the 1980s, after which they move to the Cottages. However, Ishiguro does not focus on specific dates, which gives the chronology a rather fluid feel. The advantage of not having the book set in the future is that it allows the reader to relate more easily to some aspects of the novel and makes the shocking parts even more disturbing because they are taking place in a world so similar to our own.

The novel is divided into three parts, with a total of 23 chapters. Part One follows the students through their early years and ends when they leave Hailsham. Part Two covers their time at the Cottages and ends with Kathy leaving to become a carer. Part Three moves from then to the point at the end of the book at which Kathy is finally moving from being a carer to becoming a donor.

Kathy is the narrator of the novel, and she presents the story as a series of memories rather than in a neat, linear framework. This is appropriate, as our recollections of past events are not organised in chronological order. Our minds wander and, as the poet Robert Frost put it, 'way leads on to way'.

The story is bookmarked by Kathy, now aged 31, considering her decision to retire as a carer and become a donor. At this young age, she looks back over her life to date and she treasures her memories as she faces a bleak and terrifying future. The memories she recounts may seem jumbled, but they are cleverly organised by Ishiguro to lead us, step by step, along the path of Kathy's life and its blend of the utterly horrifying and the humdrum of everyday childhood, teenage years and young adulthood. Ishiguro drip-feeds us information to achieve this effect. For example, when Kathy remembers a teacher lecturing them about the dangers of smoking, the normality of this standard advice from an adult is made seem eerily ominous by Miss Lucy's reminder to her nine- or ten-year-old students that although she smoked briefly in her youth, they cannot do so: 'You're . . . *special*. So keeping yourselves well, keeping yourselves very healthy inside, that's much more important for each of you than it is for me.' Miss Lucy looks at the children in 'a strange way' as she says this and they do not know why she is acting so oddly. Yet, they don't ask her. The guardians' way of dealing with teenage sex is equally odd. The students accept that sex cannot lead to pregnancy – the clones are sterile – and they are warned against the emotions that people, particularly those who are not clones, attach to the sexual act. Kathy reflects that this blend of sex and 'the other stuff' was how the clones came to be 'told and not told' that they were created for the sole purpose of donating their organs. As Kathy learns, so do we, the readers. This gradual dissemination of information creates a great deal of suspense and is part of the novel's appeal.

Comparative Study

Kathy is a sympathetic narrator in many ways and succeeds in drawing the reader into her chronicle of events. In Chapter 2, she says, 'I don't know how it was where you were, but at Hailsham we had to have some form of medical almost every week', and later, in Chapter 6, she again invites us into her world, saying, 'I don't know how it was where you were, but at Hailsham the guardians were really strict about smoking.' Kathy's assumption that the reader understands and even shares some of her experiences makes her storytelling appealing and compelling, but it also reminds us that she is not capable of understanding a normal life in which people are not raised simply to donate their organs and die at an unnaturally early age.

Kathy's conversational language and occasional lapses of memory make her an endearing narrator, but they also highlight the limits of her world. She is in an extraordinary situation, but she recounts it in the most ordinary way. She says things such as, 'Maybe I'm remembering it wrong' when recalling Tommy's humiliation on the football field, and peppers her account with phrases like 'I'm not sure' and 'What I do remember is'. Kathy's honesty and self-deprecation show that she has only her own memories to rely on. Most people have family, friends, an extended network to call upon when looking back at their childhood, but Kathy's hesitant and sometimes unsure narration reminds us that she has nobody left with whom she can share anything.

Another aspect of Kathy's narration that adds interest to the story is the question of whether or not she is a reliable narrator. Certainly, she admits to memory lapses and occasional confusion, but she also keeps a part of herself detached from her friends and the reader. She clearly loves Tommy, but she does not share with us the extent of her emotions and seems to take his relationship with Ruth quite calmly. During her time in Hailsham, Kathy discovers that Ruth and Tommy have split up and that the other students consider her, Kathy, the 'natural successor'. Kathy does not go into details about her feelings beyond saying that she was 'in a bit of a confusion' because she had been thinking of sleeping with another boy. However, any hopes Kathy might have had are dashed when Ruth confides in her that she wants to get back with Tommy and, in fact, wants Kathy to act as the go-between. Kathy avoids sharing the depth of her love for Tommy or her disappointment at this news, and this is handled very cleverly in the novel by having the conversation between Ruth and Kathy presented as dialogue rather than reported speech. The only hint we have of Kathy's distress is when Ruth asks, 'What's the matter?' Kathy responds, 'Nothing. I was just a bit surprised, after what's happened.' Because Kathy does not confide in the reader all that much, we have to read between the lines. Some readers enjoy teasing out the hidden messages, while others may find it somewhat frustrating.

Creation of characters

Ishiguro's creation of Kathy's character is so masterful that we become totally immersed in her story from the opening pages. Initially, we are confused as to why she should refer to herself simply as 'Kathy H'. Does she not have a surname? If not, why not? It is these little details that intrigue us.

Kathy's language is informal and idiomatic: in her introduction to herself and her job, she refers to another carer as 'a complete waste of space', and shortly after that she says, 'Okay, maybe I *am* boasting now'. The effect of this relaxed narrative style is to create a sense of intimacy between narrator and reader: it feels as if Kathy is a friend rather than an unknown narrator. This sense of closeness and implied shared understanding is reinforced when Kathy repeatedly addresses the reader, saying things like, 'I don't know how it was where you were'. She seems to assume that the reader will automatically know what 'completing' is and what being a donor means.

Ishiguro has Kathy tell her story in a controlled, sometimes detached manner. Many of her sentences are short and monosyllabic. This has the dual effect of making her seem straightforward but also rather lacking in emotion. However, Kathy's outward self-control masks a compassionate and empathic nature. She has no time for those carers who 'are just going through the motions' in their jobs and she is disgusted by the way so many of them 'can't make themselves speak up on behalf of their donor'. On careful reading, we see how deeply depressing this statement is, not only because it tells us that the donors are not well treated by those harvesting their organs, but because we know Kathy may well be looked after by such an incompetent person when she is too weak to plead her own case or manage her pain and distress. Although Kathy does not tell us outright how dreadful the situation is for most donors, her almost clinical approach shows she has had to cultivate a certain professional detachment in order to cope with the dreadful reality of the clones' lives and in the end she must also try to view her own donations in the same way.

Ruth's character plays an important role in introducing and developing the themes of identity and love in the novel. Ruth is manipulative and, at times, downright cruel. Her bossy nature is revealed early in the story when Kathy remembers playing a game Ruth invented in which she had a stable of imaginary horses. She only allowed Kathy to ride one of the horses, Bramble, on condition that she did not use a whip and that she played the game when and where Ruth wanted to: 'But you're not to use your crop on him. And you've got to come *now*'. While this little incident highlights Ruth's forceful personality, it also paints a poignant picture of children inventing games and scenarios as they would no matter where they live or who they are. This idea of what it means to be human and what makes us who we are is a key theme that is explored throughout the novel.

Ruth is selfish and unlikeable for much of the novel. She forms a relationship with Tommy despite having treated him badly when they were children. Although Ruth knows that Kathy loves Tommy and that the two of them should be together, she denies them that opportunity. She does all she can to drive a wedge between Kathy and Tommy until she is close to death and finally admits that her best friend and her former lover should always have been together.

Closer examination of Ruth's character, however, shows that she is as vulnerable and needy as any of the Hailsham students and her desire for love is so strong that she will do whatever it takes to feel she is the centre of someone's world. This side of Ruth's personality appears at various times, including when she pretends that her new pencil case was a gift from Miss Geraldine. Kathy senses Ruth's distress when the lie is in danger of being revealed, and she saves her friend from the potential embarrassment by telling the other, curious students that she and Ruth 'can't tell you where it came from'.

Comparative Study

As she grows older, Ruth is driven by a desire to find her 'possible'. When she discovers that the woman in Norfolk whom she had briefly believed could be her possible bears only a fleeting resemblance to her, Ruth rages that the clones are all 'modelled from *trash*. Junkies, prostitutes, winos, tramps. Convicts, maybe, just so long as they aren't psychos'. Ishiguro uses Ruth to show the complexity of human nature. We may desire love but behave cruelly towards those closest to us. We all have an innate longing to know who we are and where we fit in.

Tommy is presented as a vulnerable and needy character, and our sympathy for him is immediately aroused by his being mocked and tormented for amusement. In the first chapter, Kathy recalls Tommy being 'humiliated yet again' as the other children gang up and deliberately refuse to pick him for their football team. The description of the young boy's face as he realises he will not be picked is heartbreaking: it ranges from a bright eagerness to 'puzzled concern' and then 'hurt and panic'. Tommy's tantrums may seem extreme but Ishiguro uses them to show an individual railing against a brutally unfair world. Tommy is flawed, but that is part of what makes him human. Everyone around him acts as if the situation they are in is completely normal, but Tommy cannot. Kathy may be able to control her feelings, but Tommy's angry outbursts serve to show us the tension between the genteel calm of Hailsham and the utter chaotic horror that awaits the clones. Although he grows out of these fits of rage as he grows up, Tommy vents his feelings one last time after he and Kathy visit Miss Emily and Madame in the hope of having their short lives briefly extended. They learn that there is no chance of 'deferral' just because they are in love, and, on the way back, Tommy asks Kathy to pull over for a minute. He disappears into the dark and Kathy hears a scream. She runs towards the sound and finds Tommy 'raging, shouting, flinging his fists and kicking out'. Kathy realises then that even at Hailsham, Tommy always knew on some level that their lives were completely out of their control and that they were destined to die before their time. His outbursts are futile, but at least he expresses his anger.

Tommy is given one of the most meaningful lines in the novel. As he nears the end of his life, he asks Kathy to step down as his carer and find him a replacement. She does not want to do so, but he says they are like a couple in a river being pulled apart by a current far stronger than themselves. He says that although they have always loved each other, 'we can't stay together forever'. His observation applies to anyone who loves another: eventually, death will part even the most devoted of couples.

Imagery and symbolism

Note: The song 'Never Let Me Go' is also an important symbol in the novel. If you are discussing imagery and symbolism in the novel, you can also refer back to the notes on the title (page 354).

When Kathy and Tommy visit Miss Emily and Madame, they see a framed picture of Hailsham on the wall. Tommy recognises instantly that the watercolour painting is of the place he and Kathy spent their youth, but she is not so sure. She says, 'the table lamb beneath it had a crooked shade covered with cobweb traces, and instead of lighting up the picture, it just put a shine over the murky glass, so you could hardly make it out at all'. Tommy says the painting shows 'the bit round the back of the duck pond' but Kathy does not share his memory of the layout of Hailsham. This is only a fleeting moment in the novel, but it has a symbolic significance. Ishiguro includes such details for a reason. The murky glass, the dim light and the conflicting memories represent the treacherous nature of recollection and remind us that what we are reading is Kathy's version of events. Her account may or may not be reliable. Everything we read is filtered through her. This is a part of what it is to be human. Our memories may not agree with those of our loved ones, but life is experiential and open to interpretation rather than factual and definite.

The selling of Miss Emily's bedside cabinet may seem like another trivial moment in the novel, but it has a symbolic significance. Miss Emily does not explain why she has to part with an item of furniture she describes as a 'wonderful' and 'beautiful object' beyond mentioning that decorators are working in the house. Miss Emily had the bedside cabinet with her in Hailsham but now, at the same moment that she has to crush Kathy and Tommy's dreams and say goodbye to them forever, she has to let go of something else that matters to her. Although Miss Emily has tried to have the cabinet wrapped to protect it from damage, she acknowledges that the delivery men will 'handle it roughly' and 'hurl it around' if she does not stay with it on its journey. In the same way, she tried to protect the students at Hailsham from the harsh and cruel realities the world had in store for clones, but was unable to be with them throughout their life journeys. Miss Emily leaves her discussion with Kathy and Tommy just after admitting she occasionally felt 'revulsion' for the children at Hailsham and had to fight to overcome such feelings. She becomes so 'preoccupied with her cabinet' that Kathy and Tommy never have a chance to say goodbye to her. She leaves, and does not look back. The cabinet is something Miss Emily can safely admire and protect. It is unchanging and unchallenging, unlike the Hailsham students. The world views the clones as objects, but they are more complicated and difficult to deal with than other objects. Ultimately, even Miss Emily chooses the safer option.

When Kathy and Ruth are reunited towards the end of Ruth's life, Ruth says she would like to see an abandoned fishing boat she has heard about. It is 'stranded in the marshes' on the coast. The trip has echoes of the earlier trip to Norfolk, but the differences are stark and obvious. Chrissie has 'completed' during her second donation, and both Tommy and Ruth are donors. The journey to see the boat is not straightforward. There is barbed wire on the path, much to Ruth's distress. She turns to Kathy for a solution and is not disappointed. Kathy says that they can get under the wire if they 'hold it for each other'. Of course, this symbolises the three friends' journey through life. Through good times and bad in Hailsham and the Cottages, they were there for one another. They have separated since, and Kathy realises that in the car on the way to see the boat, she and Tommy 'ganged up' on Ruth. They both move towards Ruth 'almost as an instinct' and guide her through the fence. Ruth regains a measure of her old confidence as a result of this gesture.

The boat is beached in a marsh of 'dead trunks' and is crumbling away to nothing. Its deterioration reinforces the transience of life and the inevitability of death and decay. Despite all of this, Ruth thinks the boat is 'really beautiful'. This symbolises Ruth's acceptance of her lot and her determination to believe that her early and avoidable death can have beauty and dignity.

Literary genre in
Philadelphia, Here I Come!

Title

Note: The song 'Philadelphia, Here I Come!' is an important symbol in the play. If you are discussing imagery and symbolism in the play (page 364), you can also refer back to these notes on the title.

The title – *Philadelphia, Here I Come!* – is based on the song Gar sings a number of times throughout the play. It is his adaptation of 'California, Here I Come!', a popular 1921 Broadway musical number about the delights of living in sunny California, where – according to the song – life is full of sunshine, flowers and beautiful girls. It is, ostensibly, a cheerful and upbeat song – the exclamation mark in the title implies excitement and energy – but at the heart of the lyrics is the singer's longing to be back home. Gar changes the wording slightly to reflect his intended destination, Philadelphia. The meaning of Gar's song is also different to the original. While in the 1921 version, the singer looked forward to returning to California, Gar is eagerly anticipating leaving his home place. It is significant that the only lines Gar sings include the phrase 'right back where I started from'. As the play progresses, we come to see that Gar is likely to repeat the same mistakes his father made. Madge says father and son are 'as like as two peas' and that Gar is bound to turn out like S.B. Therefore, the song represents an ideal of escape, a dream to which Gar aspires but is unlikely to achieve, and it highlights Gar's inner conflict between a desire to emigrate and a longing to find happiness in Ballybeg.

The titular song is used several times in the play and each instance reminds us of the change in Gar's mood. Gar's entrance in Episode 1 is dramatic and high-spirited. He is 'ecstatic with joy and excitement' on the eve of his departure for Philadelphia, and he sings, 'Philadelphia, here I come' to express his enthusiasm for the impending journey. A short time later, however, he once again sings the lines as he dances into his bedroom, but his exuberance is tempered as he remarks, 'It's all over.'

The song becomes a way for Gar to escape painful memories of the past and hurtful experiences in the present. When Private reflects that S.B. 'must have known' how unhappy Gar's mother was as she cried herself to sleep, Public rushes to the record player, singing 'boisterously as he goes', 'Philadelphia, here I come'. He does the same when remembering his failed relationship with Kate Doogan, which, according to Private, 'left a deep scar on the aul skitter of a soul'. If Gar concentrates on an imagined future in America, the reality of his life in Ireland will not hurt so much. However, this method of distraction only carries him so far. At the end of Episode 1, after Master Boyle has left, Gar struggles to recapture the excitement he felt when he first sang 'Philadelphia, Here I Come!' Now, despite his urgent need to escape the sadness of life in Ballybeg, Gar can only sing 'limply' and half-heartedly.

The arrival of Aunt Lizzy shows just how fanciful Gar's dream of escape is. She represents the reality of life in Philadelphia, and Gar is repulsed by her vulgarity and her overwhelmingly suffocating desire to make him a surrogate son. As Private reminds Public of Aunt Lizzy's neediness, Public 'whistles determinedly' so that the tune of 'Philadelphia, Here I Come!' will drown out the unpleasant truths.

At the very end of the play, after his painful reunion with Kate Doogan, Gar 'attempts to whistle his song' but after the first phrase, 'the notes die away'. Despite his burning need to get away from his failed relationships, Gar is indeed 'right back' where he started from.

Plot/Narrative pattern

Although there are many humorous episodes in the play, *Philadelphia, Here I Come!* is a tragicomedy. Private's amusing commentaries on S.B. may be highly entertaining, but they also draw the audience's attention to the father and son's inability to communicate in any sort of meaningful way.

There is no real plot: the entire play ranges over only a short time between Gar's finishing work on the eve of his departure and his final conversation with his father in the early hours of the following morning. The play is divided into three episodes, and the tension increases in each one as we wonder whether or not Gar will leave and if he and S.B. will have any sort of breakthrough in communication.

Episode 1 ends with Gar, Public and Private, singing 'Philadelphia, here I come' in an effort to escape the painful memories of Kate Doogan, his late mother, and the awkward encounter with Master Boyle. Gar is torn between nostalgia and a resolution not to be 'a damned sentimental fool'. He determinedly focuses on all that he believes America has to offer: 'Great big sexy dames and night clubs and high living and films and dances'.

The ending of Episode 2 is similar to the ending of Episode 1 in that Gar is once more tormented by memories of the past and a yearning to communicate meaningfully with his father. This time, he is less able to blot out his inner torment by thinking of a bright future in America. Whereas Public and Private sang together at the end of Episode 1, now Public can barely whistle a phrase or two of the title song before 'the notes die away'. Private's language is disjointed as he thinks of Kate, Master Boyle, Madge and S.B.: '– a little something to remind you of your old teacher – don't keep looking back over your shoulder, be 100 per cent American . . . seven boys and seven girls'. The strain shows as Public, in a 'whispered shout', desperately wishes for his father to 'say something!'

The structure of the play leads to increasing tension. Gar's urgent need to achieve some sort of breakthrough before it is too late culminates in his final conversation with S.B. There is, even at this eleventh hour, a faint hope that Gar and S.B. will manage to express their feelings for one another. However, although Gar tentatively reaches out, he feels instantly rebuffed by his father's failure to recollect their fishing trip. Timing is key here: Gar withdraws into himself and leaves just as S.B. is struck by a similarly happy memory from the past. He tells Madge about the time he walked Gar to school, 'the two of us, hand in hand, as happy as larks'. The audience is privy to the love that lies underneath the surface of the father and son's relationship, and their utter failure to connect emotionally is heartbreaking.

Friel uses flashbacks to great effect to fill in the background to Gar's reasons for leaving and his conflicted emotions about going. The first flashback centres on Gar's relationship with Kate Doogan. He recalls the night ten months previously when he ruined his chance of a future with her. Because we hear Private's opinion of the encounter, we understand just how embarrassed and disgusted Gar is with his own behaviour. In the flashback, Gar makes childish and unrealistic plans with Kate. He dismisses her fears that they will not have enough to live on and reveals his pathetic secondary source of income – buying and selling eggs. Unsurprisingly, Gar fails to bring up the subject of marriage when confronted by Kate's intimidating father. He is completely unequal to the situation and is humiliated to hear that Senator and Mrs Doogan are hopeful that Kate will soon marry Dr Francis King. As the flashback ends, Private wearily recounts some of the details of Kate and Francis's wedding. He reflects that this memory 'has left a deep scar on the aul skitter of a soul' and was 'a sore hoke on the aul prestige'. We see how heartbroken Gar was by Kate's rejection, and this gives us a greater understanding of his reasons for leaving his home town.

The second flashback concerns Gar's aunt and uncle's visit to Ballybeg on the day of Kate's wedding. Gar, emotionally fragile as Kate marries another man, is stung by his aunt's throwaway comment about the O'Donnells being 'kinda cold'. Despite his misgivings – shown by Private's warning, 'Don't man, don't' – Gar impetuously gives in to Lizzy's smothering affection and desperate need to make him the son she never had. Gar's memory of that fateful day makes it clear that his decision to emigrate to America was an impulsive one rather than a rational, reasoned choice.

Creation of characters

One of the most striking features of *Philadelphia, Here I Come!* is the use of two actors to portray Gar O'Donnell's dual personality. Private is eloquent, witty, mocking and sometimes quite cruel. Public, on the other hand, struggles to communicate with those around him. If it were not for Private, Gar would be a dull, inexpressive and uninteresting character and the stage would be a silent place for much of the play. However, Private gives us an insight into Gar's thoughts and dreams, making him a complex and conflicted character who holds our attention from start to finish.

The silence between the characters onstage highlights the emotional distance between them. Because the audience can hear Private's speeches, it may seem that there is a conversation happening, when in fact Gar and S.B. have little or nothing to say to one another. In Episode 1, Gar and his father exchange the occasional desultory remark about the shop while Private talks incessantly. Private is imaginative, articulate and amusing, whereas Public is almost monosyllabic in his speech. When S.B. goes through his nightly ritual of checking the time, taking off his apron, etc., Private provides a brilliant and highly amusing running commentary on 'the one and only – the inimitable – the irrepressible – the irresistible – County Councillor – S – B – O'Donnell!'

Madge comes into the kitchen and remarks sarcastically that 'The chatting in this place would deafen a body.' Her comment reminds us that, without Private's monologue, the stage would be virtually silent.

Private's dialogue contributes greatly to the humour in the play, particularly when he correctly predicts the actions and words of S.B.'s nightly ritual. There is a deep sadness underlying this humour though, because Private's mockery and witticisms cannot hide Gar's desperate longing to open up a line of communication with his father before he leaves for America. However, he is surly, gruff and inarticulate in S.B.'s presence. In their first conversation onstage, Public is unable to answer S.B.'s simple question about how many coils of barbed wire were delivered to the shop. Public says, 'There were two – no, no, no, three – yes, three – or maybe it was . . . was it two?' Private is disgusted with Public. He shows his annoyance in fluent, expressive language, which contrasts sharply with Public's earlier tongue-tied uncertainty: 'After tomorrow a bloody roll of barbed-wire will be a mere bagatelle to you.' During Gar's last conversation with his father, Private urges Public to speak, telling him to 'Say – say – say –say, "Screwballs, with two magnificent legs like that, how is it you were never in show biz?"' However, all Public can manage is, 'You'll need a new tyre for the van.'

Friel's use of dialogue and stage directions emphasises the contrast between individuals and between the public and private aspects of characters. When Gar's friends, 'the boys', visit, the stage directions tell us that they give 'the impression that they are busy, purposeful, randy gents about to embark on some exciting adventure. But their bluster is not altogether convincing. There is something false about it.' The boys speak in a Donegal vernacular (the language used by ordinary people in a particular region), which adds realism to the play and brings the characters to life. When reminding the others of women they met during the previous year's carnival, Tom asks, 'Mind the night with the two wee Greenock pieces?' Gar speaks like his friends when he is in their company, telling Ned, 'You were never out with big Annie McFadden in your puff, man', but this is not a true reflection of his character. When 'the boys' have left, Gar speaks about his time with them in poetic language: 'Just the memory of it – that's all you have now – just the memory; and even now, even so soon, it is being distilled of all its coarseness; and what's left is going to be precious, precious gold . . .'

In the final episode, the contrast between Public and Private's language again highlights the difference between how Gar feels and his ability to express his emotions. Remembering his childhood fishing trip with his father, Gar says that they felt a joy that was 'so much richer than a content – it was a great, great happiness, and active, bubbling joy – although nothing was being said – just the two of us fishing on a lake on a showery day – and young as I was I felt, I knew, that this was precious, and your hat was soft on the top of my ears – I can feel it – and I shrank down into your coat'. This sensual, evocative description is in stark contrast to what Public actually says when he brings up the topic with his father. The stage directions tell us that he speaks in a 'churlish, off-hand tone' and all he manages is, 'What ever happened to that aul boat on Lough na Cloc Cor', repeating that the boat was 'an aul blue thing'. If it weren't for our knowledge of Gar's inner thoughts, it would appear that this was an insignificant, throwaway remark about something that came to mind.

Private's manner of speaking accurately captures the normal human thought process and reflects his anxiety and uncertainty on the eve of his departure. As the play progresses, Gar's increasing confusion is shown in Private's fragmented, disjointed speech patterns interspersed with snippets from poetry and song. This is particularly evident after Kate Doogan's visit. Tormented by the loss of the woman he loved, Private attempts to control his overwhelming emotions: 'Oh my God, steady man, steady – it is now sixteen or seventeen years since I saw the Queen of France, then the Dauphiness, at Versailles, and surely never lighted on this orb – Oh God, Oh my God, those thoughts are sinful'. Private breaks into song at this point and Public attempts to whistle. Through these monologues, we learn the depth of Gar's suffering and the difference between the face he shows the world and his real self.

Of course, very few people are entirely honest with themselves all the time, and Gar is no exception. Friel has Gar use clichés about Ireland and America when he is thinking about his impending emigration. Early in the play, Private asks Public if he is fully conscious of the consequences of leaving 'the country of your birth, the land of the curlew and the snipe, the Aran sweater and the Irish Sweepstakes' in order to go to a 'profane, irreligious, pagan country of gross materialism'. Gar also adopts a dialect taken from cowboy films of the time when he is packing his case: 'Let's git that li'l ole saddle bag opened and let's git packin''. Towards the end of the play, when Kate Doogan visits, Gar boasts, 'I'll come home when I make my first million, driving a Cadillac and smoking cigars and taking movie-films.' These clichés reveal how little Gar has thought about the realities of both the place he is leaving and his destination.

Gar is not the only character to articulate their inner thoughts through a monologue. Friel also has Madge express herself through a stream of consciousness. As she tidies up before going to bed, Madge voices her thoughts and fears. Like Private's speech, Madge's sentences are fragmented and the pauses marked by ellipses and dashes as she thinks of her little grand-niece and worries about Gar: 'Madge Mulhern – I don't know – it's too aul'-fashioned or something . . . Has he his cap?' Madge's monologue reinforces her selflessness, her common sense and her worldly wisdom as well as giving us an overview of Gar and S.B.'s characters. She reflects astutely that when Gar is S.B.'s age, he will 'turn out just the same' and have 'learned nothin' in-between times'.

Imagery and symbolism

Note: The song 'Philadelphia, Here I Come!' is an important symbol in the play. If you are discussing imagery and symbolism in the play, you can also refer back to the notes on the title (page 360).

Music and literature play an important role in the play, broadening our understanding of the characters and the themes.

Early in the play, in the middle of an imaginary interview with his American employer, Public breaks off and quotes the opening lines of Edmund Burke's 1790 essay, 'Reflections on the Revolution in France': 'It is now sixteen or seventeen years since I saw the Queen of France, then the Dauphiness, at Versailles'. The quote refers to Burke's first sighting of the beautiful Queen of France. Burke first met her when she was the Dauphiness. This means she was married to the Dauphin, the eldest son of the King of France. Later, when the Dauphin became king on his father's death, the Dauphiness became queen. Burke's essay idealises the French monarchy and life before the Revolution. Gar also idealises aspects of the past and is unhappy with the present. He has a difficult relationship with his father and longs for the mother he never knew. Gar believes his life in Ballybeg is going nowhere and that America will be the land of opportunities. At the same time, however, he has doubts about leaving behind a place, a history and a culture to which he is deeply attached, despite his criticisms. Gar repeats this line many times during the play, usually when he is at risk of being overwhelmed by his thoughts or memories.

Like the quotes from Burke's essay, Gar's choice of music reflects a level of culture that is not typical in his home place. Immediately after the imaginary interview, he plays a classical record, accompanying it with an announcement 'in the reverential tones of a radio announcer': 'The main item in tonight's concert . . . in E minor, opus 64, by Jacob Ludwig Felix Mendelssohn.' Although he is merely fooling around, Gar shows that he has a knowledge of culture that his father and the Canon, for example, do not possess. Towards the end of the play, Gar plays the same piece while his father and the Canon play their nightly game of cards. The melody evokes memories of a joyous moment in Gar's childhood. Private tells the unhearing S.B. that the music 'says that once upon a time a boy and his father sat in a blue boat on a lake on an afternoon in May, and on that afternoon a great beauty happened, a beauty that has haunted the boy ever since'. However, the difference between Gar's reaction to the music and that of his father and the Canon shows the cultural and emotional distance between them. The Canon refers to it as 'noise' and S.B. simply says that Gar always plays 'them records'. We know that Gar spent a year studying Arts in UCD, but he dropped out before finishing his degree. His playing classical music and quoting literature may be a way for Gar to convince himself that he is different to the others in Ballybeg and that he is somehow more cultured. At the same time, Gar is also familiar with Irish songs and ballads and sings snatches of them at various stages in the play. They range from the rather raucous 'Give the Woman in the Bed More Porter' to the lyrical and romantic 'She Moved Through the Fair'. Gar is uncertain of his place in the world, and his uncertain cultural identity is reflected in the blend of classical and folk music.

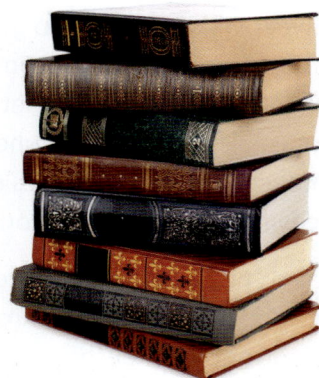

Literary genre in *Lady Bird*

The first mention of the titular name 'Lady Bird' comes early in the film when Marion attempts to dissuade her daughter from applying to colleges in other parts of America. Crushingly, she tells her daughter, 'you're not even *worth* state tuition, Christine'. Lady Bird replies spiritedly, 'My name is Lady Bird!' She sees her name as an integral part of her identity, saying in an audition for the school musical that it is her 'given name': 'I gave it to myself; it's given to me by me'.

Greta Gerwig, writer and director, explained in an interview where the name came from: 'I had been writing all these other scenes, and I couldn't find exactly how it all fit together. I felt like I was – I kept hitting a wall, and then I put everything aside, and I wrote at the top of the page, "Why won't you call me Lady Bird? You promised that you would."'

While initially Gerwig had no idea where this came from, she later remembered the Mother Goose nursery rhyme 'Ladybird, Ladybird', which had 'lodged itself somewhere in [her] brain'. She cited the following version:

Ladybird, ladybird, fly away home,
Your house is on fire and your children are gone.

In the interview, Gerwig described this as 'the creepy, mysterious part of writing.'

Lady Bird's insistence on being called by the name she has seemingly pulled from thin air is part of her rejection of everything her parents have given her. It is only at the very end of the film, when she has grown into a more emotionally secure young woman than she was a year before, that Lady Bird can begin to distance herself from her earlier precocious, rebellious behaviour. Far from her family and a little at sea in New York, Lady Bird reverts to the name Christine, using it to introduce herself to her fellow students and when she leaves a message on her parents' answerphone: 'It's the name you gave me. It's a good one.'

Plot/Narrative pattern

The film takes place over the course of a year in Lady Bird's life. Although the film is a coming-of-age story about Christine 'Lady Bird' McPherson and we see the events from her point of view, the other characters' stories and perspectives are important too. For example, we see Lady Bird clash repeatedly with her mother, and although Marion is harsh to the point of cruelty at times, we come to understand that her comments and actions are founded in deep love for her daughter and an unwillingness to accept that Lady Bird is growing up and moving on. In an interview, Gerwig said that she wanted to look at that mother–daughter dynamic 'from all angles and make something that felt like a kaleidoscope of people and a place'.

Lady Bird centres on the titular character's growth over the course of her final year at school. Gerwig uses a number of driving shots to highlight and link various important moments in Lady Bird's life. At the start of the film, Lady Bird and her mother bicker and then argue hotly during their return from a college visit, culminating in Lady Bird throwing herself from the car and breaking her arm. This darkly comic, melodramatic scene shows both the intensity of the mother–daughter relationship (Gerwig's original working title for the film was 'Mothers and Daughters') and Lady Bird's immaturity. At another key moment in the narrative, Marion collects Lady Bird from Kyle's house after she loses her virginity in an episode that does not live up to her romantic expectations. Lady Bird breaks down in tears and Marion comforts her. Later, when Lady Bird is travelling to prom in Kyle's car, she has an epiphany about love and friendship. The Dave Matthews Band song 'Crash Into Me' comes on the radio and Kyle makes a snide remark about it. The last time that song was used in the film was when Julie and Lady Bird cried and sang together after Lady Bird discovered Danny kissing another boy. Hearing it again, Lady Bird makes a decision. She asks Kyle to drop her at Julie's house. Jenna, sitting in the back seat with her boyfriend, asks who Julie is and Lady Bird replies, 'She's my best friend.' Julie and Lady Bird go to the prom together and their rekindled friendship shows Lady Bird's emotional growth. She is no longer interested in spending time with superficial people who have little interest in her, and she appreciates the value of those who really care about her.

When Lady Bird leaves for college, she and Marion are barely on speaking terms. Marion drives to the airport, stony-faced and uncommunicative as John Hartford's moving song 'This Eve of Parting' plays. Marion refuses to see Lady Bird off in the airport terminal, saying that parking is too expensive. She drives off but almost instantly regrets her decision, turning back and abandoning her car at the airport door. However, Lady Bird's flight has already left, and Marion is left sobbing in Larry's arms as he reassures her that Lady Bird will be back.

The film ends with Lady Bird alone in New York, chastened after a bout of alcohol poisoning. She rings home and, when nobody answers, leaves a voice message in which she asks her mother if she too 'felt emotional' the first time she drove in Sacramento. Her message becomes a voiceover for shots of a smiling Lady Bird driving through her home town as she nostalgically remembers the 'bends I've known my whole life, and stores, and the whole thing'. Jon Brion's 'Reconcile' plays as we see clips of Marion and Lady Bird driving through Sacramento. Although both are alone in the car in these shots, they are united in their, until now, unspoken love for both Sacramento and one another. This is in stark contrast to the car journey at the beginning of the film. Then, resentment, anger and disappointment drove mother and daughter apart.

Creation of characters

The characters in *Lady Bird* are a charming blend of realism and quirky humour. Gerwig uses a number of techniques to highlight Lady Bird's individuality and her teenage awkwardness. For example, although Lady Bird wears the conservative uniform of her Catholic high school, she dyes her hair pink and changes her name to reject her upbringing and assert her independence. Her bedroom (discussed in detail in the notes on imagery and symbolism, page 368) is a shrine to her loves, hopes and dreams as well as being a typical teenage girl's room of the time.

Small details about Lady Bird bring her character to life and make her relatable. For example, when she notices Kyle reading Zinn's *A People's History of the United States*, she begins to read it too. Gerwig's light touch in her use of a simple prop allows us to see Lady Bird's impressionable nature. The same nuanced approach applies to the costumes. Most of the clothes worn in the film were sourced from thrift stores and flea markets in order to reflect Lady Bird's family's financial situation. The school uniforms worn by the students at Immaculate Heart reflect the various characters' personalities. Lady Bird's is a little too large for her and, combined with her gangling, slightly awkward gait, it gives the impression of someone who is not yet totally comfortable in their own skin. Jenna, on the other hand, wears her skirt short and her uniform quite fitted, to show off her figure and make her as attractive as possible. This is perfectly in keeping with Jenna's rather superficial personality and her focus on appearances.

Gerwig uses witty dialogue to great effect in the film. Early on, when Lady Bird tells Julie that she wants to study in New York, Julie wonders about the threat of terrorism there. (The 2001 terror attacks on the World Trade Centre buildings were fresh in people's minds at the time the film was set.) Lady Bird scorns Julie's concerns, telling her not to be 'Republican'. This comment captures the mood of the time and it also gives us an insight into Lady Bird's world view. Later, when she visits Danny's grandmother's house for Thanksgiving and sees the photo of Ronald Regan, Lady Bird's remark comes back to us. We see, even if she does not, that the gap between her family and Danny's is probably too wide to be bridged.

The humour in the film lightens some of the tensest moments and ensures we can retain affection for the characters even when they are behaving badly. A key moment that demonstrates this is when Lady Bird is disgusted to learn she did not get into Berkeley and she turns on her brother, claiming he got into college because of his race rather than his achievements. Miguel calls her 'evil' and asks what is wrong with her. Lady Bird storms out of the room but not before calling back, 'And Miguel and Shelly, you'll never get jobs with all that shit in your face'. Shelly shakes her head, but she and Miguel look at one another with dawning realisation and Miguel frowns as he reaches up to touch one of his facial piercings. This exchange shows the blend of love and frustration that marks the McPhersons' relationships with one another. It also highlights how like Marion Lady Bird is. Her advice is incredibly blunt, but it is good. Miguel and Shelly have removed their piercings when we see them next, and Miguel has applied for a job as a computer programmer.

Larry, Lady Bird's father, is a kind and gentle man torn between his strong-willed wife and daughter. Gerwig's light touch allows us to understand just how miserable and ineffectual Larry feels at times without forcing the issue. An excellent example of this is the confrontation between Lady Bird and Marion when Lady Bird has been suspended from school for her comments to a guest speaker on abortion. Larry sits in a darkened corner of the living room, looking intently at something on the computer screen as Marion berates Lady Bird's selfishness and bad behaviour. She notices Larry on the computer and asks him what he is doing. He is giving the impression of working, but when he turns around, hunched miserably in his chair, he says, 'Nothing'. At that moment, we see he is playing Solitaire. The game represents how alone Larry feels but it also reminds us that he has nothing better to do. He has lost his job and is unlikely to get another in the fast-changing world of computers. Even the game he is playing is old-fashioned and simplistic. Marion begins to tell Lady Bird how 'horrible' she makes Larry feel when she asks him to drop her a block from school because she is ashamed of her family. Larry tries to protest that he does not want to be involved in the argument, but Marion tells him he 'can't just be the nice guy'. He folds his arms and sits silently in the chair while Marion and Lady Bird continue their fight. Larry is struggling to find a place in the outside world and in his family, and this short scene highlights the difficulties with which he has to contend.

Gerwig said that she wanted the characters to be real because she does not know anyone who lives a perfect life. Things can be messy and at the same time wonderful. So, for example, she gives Lady Bird spots yet puts her in a beautiful prom dress. The juxtaposition of imperfect – but normal – teenage skin and a fairy-tale, lacy pink dress captures what Gerwig meant when she said she believed the film would be beautiful if she shot it honestly.

It is Gerwig's careful attention to detail in scenes such as this that brings the characters to life and highlights the complicated dynamics of the family and the love and beauty that can be found in the ordinary and the everyday.

Imagery and symbolism

Lady Bird opens with a frame showing a quote from the author Joan Didion: 'Anybody who talks about California hedonism has never spent Christmas in Sacramento.' (Hedonism is the idea that the pursuit of pleasure is the only goal in life.) Both Didion and Gerwig grew up in Sacramento, so the choice of quote comes from the heart. The film shows that love, loyalty and family prove to be what brings joy, rather than seeking happiness for its own sake. *Lady Bird* actually features a Christmas in Sacramento and it could hardly be further from the hedonistic ideal. The family gathers around a modest Christmas tree and exchanges small gifts. They all express their delight at what they have received. Marion explains that the socks she has given her children and Shelly are expensive and that they 'wick moisture away from your feet'. This slightly disgusting image does not take from the family's good mood. Shelly, to show her gratitude, tells Marion that her feet 'always have moisture', and Lady Bird says she loves her present. Larry is openly delighted with the cheap throw pillow he receives, and they all laugh at the message, 'Golfers Don't Diet, They Just Exist On Greens'. This is a heart-warming moment in a film filled with family tensions and it reminds us of the opening quote. Sacramento is not as cosmopolitan or as wealthy as San Francisco or Los Angeles, but this little interlude and the quote that inspired it show that happiness is not dependent on material things.

Not all of the imagery and symbolism in the film is associated with such simple happiness. In one of the early scenes, Marion and Lady Bird are returning from a trip and just coming to the end of the audio version of Steinbeck's novel *The Grapes of Wrath*. The book is set during the Great Depression and tells of a family who leave their poverty-stricken life in Oklahoma to make a better life in California.

In the film, Lady Bird is eager to leave California for the East Coast. She refuses to see the opportunities that California might have to offer and remains stubbornly determined to make her way in the world far from her home and family. Lady Bird and Marion begin fighting over the issue of college and the atmosphere becomes so fraught with tension and anger that Lady Bird throws herself from the moving car. As the film progresses, we see that the themes in *The Grapes of Wrath*, such as dignity in the face of poverty, the complex nature of family, and the redemptive power of love and friendship, are also explored in *Lady Bird*.

A number of times in the film, Lady Bird and Marion have conversations while looking in a mirror rather than at one another. This symbolises the similarity between them: Lady Bird may resent her mother and Marion may be disappointed with her daughter, but they are reflections of one another in many ways. When Lady Bird is trying on dresses for the prom, Marion stands behind her, offering rather unwelcome comments and advice. The mirror also symbolises Marion's influence on Lady Bird. She is behind her daughter literally and metaphorically, but her efforts to help Lady Bird to improve herself show that she is also behind when it comes to understanding her daughter's needs and feelings. Towards the end of the scene, Lady Bird emerges from the changing room, smiling somewhat self-consciously and wearing the dress she has chosen for the dance. She says, 'I love it' as she looks at her reflection in the mirror. Marion asks if the dress isn't 'too pink'. Lady Bird's face falls and she walks back into the changing room. From behind the door, she asks her mother if she likes her. Marion replies, 'Of course I love you.' Lady Bird opens the changing room door and it blocks the mirror as she steps out and confronts Marion: 'But do you like me?' Face to face, the conversation becomes more serious and awkward. Now they are not looking at reflections but at the real thing, and it is extremely difficult to tackle the obstacles that prevent them from connecting with one another.

Lady Bird's house plays an important role in this coming-of-age story. The house is neat and clean, but the decor and furnishings are quite dark and old-fashioned. The muted colours in the decor hint at the unhappiness in the family.

Comparative Study

Although Lady Bird is ashamed of her parents' precarious financial situation and hurts them deeply when she jokes about living 'on the wrong side of the tracks', Marion and Larry do their best to provide a loving and comfortable home. Yet they too are keenly aware that their slightly shabby, cramped house is a constant reminder that they have not achieved all they had hoped. During an argument with Lady Bird, Marion tells her, 'We didn't think we'd be in this house for 25 years, we thought we would have moved somewhere better'. Marion is hurt because she and Larry have sacrificed a more comfortable life in order to provide for their children as best they could, but it does not seem to be enough for Lady Bird in particular.

Lady Bird's room is an expression of her personality. It is the refuge to which she runs when she has fallen out with her mother. Larry respects this and knocks on the door before entering, something which Marion never does. When Larry brings Lady Bird a cupcake on the morning of her eighteenth birthday, he carefully closes the door after him. He and Lady Bird talk freely in her room and she confides in him how

unhappy she is about the tension between herself and Marion. The bedroom is a safe space for both and a place where they can talk honestly and openly.

The decor in the bedroom shows the transition from child to adult and captures the changes in Lady Bird's life. Similar to the rest of the house, nothing is new or expensive, but it is loved. The walls are pink, like Lady Bird's hair, which is far brighter and more fun than the rest of the colours in the house, and papered with posters of bands that were cool in 2002, which adds realism. Lady Bird's quirky personality is captured in the rather surreal and, as Sister Sarah-Joan points out, disturbing campaign posters she made when running for student president. The posters show the body of a woman with the head of a bird, or vice versa. Lady Bird knows the posters won't win her the student election, but she doesn't care. As she tells Sister Sarah-Joan, it is her tradition to run for office and lose. The posters encapsulate that self-sabotaging part of Lady Bird that we see throughout the film. She is well aware that she rubs others up the wrong way at times, but she doesn't care. However, the posters also reflect Lady Bird's individuality and independence. She is not willing to do whatever it takes to fit in.

Towards the end of the film, Lady Bird clears out and repaints her room before she moves to New York to study. She paints plain white over the playful pink and erases all traces of her former self, including Kyle and Danny's names which she had written on the paintwork when each was her boyfriend. It is as if Lady Bird wants to leave a clean slate and start again in New York. This idea is reinforced when we see, soon after this scene, that Lady Bird calls herself Christine when she begins the next chapter of her life. Clearing the room is also a symbolic gesture of reconciliation with Marion. Lady Bird hasn't really spoken to her mother since her high school graduation and the revelation that she was going away to college, but she shows her consideration by doing the job that Marion would otherwise have had to do.

Comparative study: Literary genre

Never Let Me Go	Philadelphia, Here I Come!	Lady Bird

The title of each text plays an important role in our understanding of the text.

The title *Never Let Me Go* is taken from Kathy's treasured cassette, *Songs After Dark*. As a child, she believes the song is about a woman 'who'd been told she couldn't have babies, who'd really, really wanted them all her life' and then has a baby, against the odds. It is only later in life that Kathy learns that none of the clones can have children.

Madame happens upon the young Kathy singing the song and cradling a pillow as if it were a baby, while softly crooning, 'Oh baby, *baby*, never let me go . . .' Madame, who knows all too well what Kathy's future holds, sobs uncontrollably, much to Kathy's surprise and bewilderment. Madame, of course, is heartbroken to think that the clones are – despite the public's view of them – normal human beings with the same hopes and desires as the rest of society. Kathy's singing 'Never Let Me Go' could have been interpreted as a plea to the wider world not to ignore the basic humanity of the clones. Madame later explains to Kathy and Tommy that she saw the song as a little girl desperately wishing that the 'harsh, cruel world' of scientific advances such as cloning organ donors could go away. Madame imagined that Kathy was 'holding to her breast the old kind world, one that she knew in her heart could not remain, and that she was holding it and pleading, never to let her go'. The fact that Kathy and Madame had such different interpretations of the titular song is Ishiguro's way of reminding us that

Like the title *Never Let Me Go*, the title *Philadelphia, Here I Come!* is based on a song that is mentioned a number of times throughout the text. Just as Kathy makes 'Never Let Me Go' her own, so Gar adapts the tune 'California, Here I Come!' from a popular 1921 Broadway musical number about the delights of living in sunny California to fit his situation. The difference is that Gar's decision is deliberate while Kathy has no idea that she is misinterpreting the song title. However, the effect is largely the same. Both songs – if we take the young Kathy's understanding of hers into account – are about the protagonists' dreams of a better life and, at least in part, an imagined future.

In both cases, other characters in the texts realise how hopeless the dreams are. The only difference is that Madame knows for sure Kathy will never achieve her dreams, while Madge is almost certain Gar will never achieve his. Gar's song includes the phrase 'right back where I started from', and Madge believes Gar is destined to repeat the mistakes his father made and thus end up where he began. She says father and son are 'as like as two peas'. In both texts, therefore, the titular song represents an ideal the characters are unlikely to achieve.

Both titles invite us to explore the nature of memory. In *Never Let Me Go*, the titular song reminds us that memories are subjective and flawed. In *Philadelphia, Here I Come!*, the title becomes a way to escape and even drown out painful memories. When Private reflects that S.B. 'must have known' how unhappy Gar's mother was as she cried herself to sleep, Public rushes to the record player, singing 'boisterously as he goes': 'Philadelphia, here I come'. He does the same when remembering his failed relationship with Kate Doogan, which, according to Private, 'left a deep scar on the aul skitter of a soul'.

The most significant difference between the title *Lady Bird* and the titles of the other two texts is the originality and deliberate precociousness of Lady Bird's choice of name. This perfectly reflects her quirky and independent personality. **Kathy and Gar try to make the words of an existing song their own, but Lady Bird seemingly picks her name out of thin air.**

This may seem a small issue, but the titles of each of the texts reflect the central characters' natures and life choices. In *Never Let Me Go*, Kathy clings to those things that cannot be taken from her. The world in which she lives may deprive her of choices, lasting relationships and ultimately her life, but she draws comfort from the fact that nobody can deprive her of her love for those closest to her. **Like Kathy in *Never Let Me Go*, Gar falls back on the lines of his titular song when he feels most insecure and unhappy. Lady Bird's insistence on being called by the name she has invented is also linked to unhappiness and a determination to reject everything her parents have given her.** It is only at the very end of the film, when she has grown into a more emotionally secure young woman than she was a year before, that Lady Bird can begin to distance herself from her earlier precocious, rebellious behaviour. Far from her family and a little at sea in New York, Lady Bird reverts to the name Christine, using it to introduce herself to her fellow students and when she leaves a message on her parents' answerphone: 'It's the name you gave me. It's a good one.'

→

Never Let Me Go	Philadelphia, Here I Come!	Lady Bird
our memories are shaped by our perceptions of them and that a simple incident is rarely simple. The idea of 'letting go', raised in the title, is a key component of the novel. Ultimately, Kathy has to let go of everything: her friends, her dreams and even her life. Having lost everything else, in the end Kathy makes the heartbreaking decision to let go of life. However, she does not let go of love. The memories of the love she shared with those closest to her sustains Kathy in her final days: 'I lost Ruth, then I lost Tommy, but I won't lose my memories of them.'	If Gar concentrates on an imagined future in America, the reality of his life in Ireland will not hurt so much. **In *Never Let Me Go*, Kathy draws comfort from the thought of never letting go, but Gar derives no such reassurance from the theme of the song he has sung throughout.** At the very end of the play, after his painful reunion with Kate Doogan, Gar 'attempts to whistle his song' but after the first phrase, 'the notes die away'. Despite his burning need to get away from his failed relationships, Gar is indeed 'right back' where he started from.	**The title of *Lady Bird* is as important as are the titles of the other two texts, but the central character's rejection of the name at the end of the film leaves us with a far more uplifting message than either of the other two texts.** Lady Bird outgrows her reliance on her chosen name because she has steered her life onto a better path. **Neither Kathy nor Gar succeed in doing the same: Kathy because of the cruel world in which she lives, and Gar because of his own stubborn nature and inability to connect with his father.**

Never Let Me Go	Philadelphia, Here I Come!	Lady Bird

Certain aspects of narrative structure can add to our enjoyment and understanding of a text.

Never Let Me Go is an unusual dystopian tale. Rather than taking place in an imagined future, the story is set in an alternative recent past. Kathy, Ruth and Tommy spend their youth in Hailsham sometime between the late 1960s and the 1980s, after which they move to the Cottages. There are no specific dates given, which gives the chronology a fluid feel. Even though we may not know exactly when the events in the novel are supposed to be taking place, the fact that it is set in our fairly recent past allows us to relate easily to the familiar aspects of the characters' lives and, at the same time, be deeply shocked and disturbed by those aspects of their childhood and early adulthood that are so vastly different to anything we could ever experience.

Another way Ishiguro helps us to appreciate the horror of the clones' lives is by structuring Kathy's story as a series of memories instead of presenting the events in a neat, linear framework. Kathy's recollections are, like all of our own, jumbled, and linked by emotions rather than chronological order. Ishiguro cleverly selects and

Like *Never Let Me Go*, *Philadelphia, Here I Come!* uses a series of memories to fill in the backstory of a character who is at a turning point in their life when we first meet them. While Kathy's pivotal moment is obviously far more life-changing than is Gar's – she is facing her impending death; he is merely emigrating – both wrestle with painful, bittersweet recollections of episodes in their lives that have brought them to this point. The principal difference between the presentation of memories in the texts is Friel's use of flashbacks to help us to understand Gar's conflicted emotions on the eve of his departure for America. One of the most poignant of these shows us how Gar's relationship with Kate Doogan failed. He recalls the night, ten months previously, when he was too immature, tongue-tied and overawed by Kate's father to fight for her hand in marriage. **The flashback is strikingly effective because we see it acted out onstage and it therefore seems**

Lady Bird follows a more traditional narrative structure than do the other two texts. Memories and flashbacks do not play the same role in the film as in the novel and the play. The film presents us with a series of episodes in the life of Lady Bird McPherson as she finishes high school and prepares for her first year of college.

At the beginning of the novel and the play, we meet the central characters at a turning point in their lives and we gradually learn what has shaped them and led to their current situation. In *Lady Bird*, however, we follow the titular character as she develops from a selfish, resentful girl to a more thoughtful, appreciative young woman. **This chronological structure means that we are unsure of the outcome until the very end of the film, unlike the novel and the play.** Admittedly, there is some hope in *Philadelphia, Here I Come!* that Gar and S.B. may make a connection that would allow Gar to stay at home, but that is at best a slim chance. In *Lady*

→

Never Let Me Go	*Philadelphia, Here I Come!*	*Lady Bird*
organises the 'memories' so that they lead us, step by step, along the path of Kathy's life. The blend of the everyday and the utterly horrifying is striking. For example, Kathy recounts an episode in which Miss Lucy lectured the students about the dangers of smoking. At first glance, this may seem a perfectly normal warning from an adult to a child. However, there is an ominous note in her reminding the clones that they are so 'special' that they must keep themselves 'very healthy inside'. Miss Lucy looks at the children 'in a strange way' as she speaks, and stresses that it is more important for them to stay well than it is for her. In a similar vein, the students are advised not to have sex with those who are not clones because they might attach emotions to the act. The clones are sterile and will never be allowed to marry, so they are free – in the guardians' eyes at least – to view sex as a purely physical expression of desire. Kathy reflects that this gradual dissemination of information means that the clones were both 'told and not told' that they were created for the sole purpose of donating their organs. As Kathy learns the dreadful truth, so do we. This ensures suspense is maintained in the novel and holds our interest from start to finish.	**far more immediate and powerful than Kathy's memories in the novel.** Gar is completely unequal to the meeting with Senator Doogan and his talk of a far more suitable match for Kate: Dr Francis King, who will soon be offered the 'new dispensary job' in Ballybeg. Senator Doogan confides in Gar that he doesn't want to 'raise Kate's hopes unduly', hinting strongly that she and Francis will marry once he is appointed. Gar's heartbreak is obvious, and Friel's use of a second actor to give us a deeper insight into Gar's thoughts heightens the dramatic tension in this flashback. Private reflects bitterly that Kate 'must have known' her parents' plan all along and he is utterly humiliated by the encounter, rushing away as soon as he can. Little moments like this make it increasingly easy for us to understand Gar's reasons for leaving his home town. Through the use of another flashback – this time centred on Gar's aunt's visit on the day of Kate's wedding – we learn that Gar's decision to leave was a sudden impulse rather than a rational choice. Stung by his aunt's observation about the O'Donnells being 'kinda cold', and desperate for love, Gar impetuously agrees when she asks him to come and live with her in Philadelphia. Like *Never Let Me Go*, the use of memories and a gradual drip-feed of information that fills in the background to the characters ensures that we are kept engaged with the text throughout.	*Bird*, **on the other hand, we have far less foreknowledge about the character, so we cannot be sure whether or not she will make the right decision and mend the damaged relationships in her life.** This uncertainty creates some tension in the film, albeit not a huge amount. This is, after all, a relatively straightforward coming-of-age, rom-com structure, so we can be reasonably sure that the main difficulties will be resolved in the end. That proves to be the case. Admittedly, Gerwig subverts the norm of the boy–girl relationship by having Lady Bird reconcile with her best friend in time for prom rather than going to the dance with a romantic love interest, but the pattern of events is one with which we are all familiar. Lady Bird leaves Kyle and Jenna, asking that she be dropped at Julie's house. She and Julie go to the prom, dance, pose for a photo and walk home with their shoes in their hands at the end of the night. This chain of events is one we have all seen in films before, even if it is unusual to see it centred on friendship rather than romance. **The only time Gerwig uses a flashback is in the very last scene. Whereas flashbacks are used to fill in a backstory in the other texts, here the shots of Lady Bird and her mother driving through Sacramento serve to reinforce their shared love and to end the film on a positive note.**

Never Let Me Go	*Philadelphia, Here I Come!*	*Lady Bird*
Authors use a variety of techniques to create credible and interesting characters.		
Ishiguro uses an ordinary person to tell an extraordinary story. Kathy introduces herself in informal, idiomatic language, calling another carer 'a complete waste of space' and admitting – when talking about her own work – 'Okay, maybe I *am*	**Kathy's first-person narration in *Never Let Me Go* allows us an insight into her thoughts and feelings. Usually, the way playwrights provide us with the same information is through monologues, soliloquies or intimate conversations onstage. Friel takes a**	Lady Bird's story is told through a series of small episodes over the course of her final year in high school. **Gerwig uses a blend of realism and quirky humour to create a central character who is, like Gar O'Donnell, immature and infuriating at times, but also**

→

Never Let Me Go	Philadelphia, Here I Come!	Lady Bird
boasting now.' This relaxed and chatty narrative style creates a sense of intimacy between narrator and reader, drawing us into the story from the outset. The sense of shared understanding and closeness is reinforced when Kathy addresses the reader directly, saying, 'I don't know how it was where you were', for example. Despite Kathy's conversational, everyday language, she nonetheless provides the reader with hints that all is not well. For example, she calls herself 'Kathy H' rather than giving an actual surname, and assumes that we will know what she means by 'completing' and by caring for 'donors'. Kathy's controlled, matter-of-fact narration has the dual effect of making her seem straightforward but also rather lacking in emotion. For example, when discussing the donors in her care, she says, 'hardly any of them have been classed as "agitated" even before fourth donation'. Her clinical manner is slightly chilling when we realise that a fourth donation means completion, or death. However, as we learn more about Kathy, we see that she is a loving and empathetic young woman who has had to develop a certain professional detachment in the face of a horrifying reality. At the end of the book, she has to say goodbye to her beloved Tommy as he prepares for his final donation. They avoid a 'big farewell number' and she parts from him with 'a small kiss' before driving away. Ishiguro allows the situation to speak for itself and we do not need Kathy to tell us she is heartbroken: we know. She says that the memories she values	different approach, however, and uses two actors to portray Gar O'Donnell's personality. Private voices Gar's inner thoughts and is far more eloquent, witty and at times cruel than is Public. **Public is even more reserved than Kathy, allowing very little of his real self to shine through. Like Kathy, Public uses language that is practical and matter-of-fact, but he is far less emotionally articulate than she. While Kathy is composed, Public is taciturn and inarticulate, particularly in his father's presence.** He allows little glimpses of his real self when talking to Madge and Kate Doogan, but it is mostly immature silliness. If it were not for Private, Gar would be a dull, inexpressive, sometimes childish character, and the stage would be silent for much of the play. Private, however, allows us to see the complexities of Gar's life and the struggle between his dreams and his unhappy reality, making him a likeable and relatable young man. Private is imaginative and amusing, while Public is gruff and monosyllabic. In Episode 1, when S.B. goes through his nightly ritual of taking off his apron after the day's work, Private comments on his actions as if they were a dazzling stage performance: 'the one and only – the inimitable – the irrepressible – the irresistible – County Councillor – S – B – O'Donnell!' Madge enters shortly afterwards and remarks sarcastically that 'The chatting in this place would deafen a body.' Friel uses Madge in this way a number of times throughout the play to remind us that Private's words go unheard by the other characters onstage and to highlight the deep sadness underlying the humour. **At the end of *Never Let Me Go*, Kathy's self-control and resignation add to the horror and the sadness of the deaths of her loved ones and her own impending donations. It is**	likeable. **Lady Bird is far more outspoken than either Kathy or Gar, but she is also eminently relatable.** Gerwig uses a number of small details to bring Lady Bird to life. For example, when she sees the handsome and cool Kyle reading Zinn's *A People's History of the United States*, she begins to read it too. Gerwig's light touch in her use of a single prop allows us to see Lady Bird's impressionable nature, which is typical of a teenager trying to find their feet in the world and determining who they want to be. Gerwig, like Friel, uses humour to great effect when crafting her characters. Early on in the film, Julie worries that Lady Bird's plans to study in New York might leave her vulnerable to terrorism (the 2001 attacks on the World Trade Centre buildings were fresh in people's minds in 2002, the year in which the film is set). Lady Bird impatiently dismisses Julie's concerns, telling her not to be 'Republican'. This quirky and amusing little comment captures the mood of the time but also gives us an insight into Lady Bird's world view. She sees herself as liberal and has no time for conservative values. That this attitude is rather pretentious and part of who Lady Bird wants to be rather than who she actually is becomes clear in another amusing episode. When she learns that she has not been accepted to study in Berkeley, Lady Bird turns on her brother, claiming he got into college because of his race rather than his achievements. **Although this is a very awkward moment, Lady Bird's parting shot to Miguel and his girlfriend, 'you'll never get jobs with all that shit in your face', reminds us that Lady Bird does care about her family but, like Gar, struggles to express herself in an appropriate manner.** It also shows that, for all her talk, Lady Bird is quite conservative and practical at heart. She realises that Miguel and Shelly's facial piercings are holding them back, and she is later proven right about this when they are shown without the offending jewellery and Miguel applies for a job more suitable to his qualifications than packing bags in the supermarket. **Like Kathy, Lady Bird grows up a great deal over the course of the text. While Gar**

Never Let Me Go	*Philadelphia, Here I Come!*	*Lady Bird*
most will never fade and that she may have lost Ruth and then Tommy, but she will never lose her memories of them. Her self-control and resigned acceptance of the deaths of those closest to her makes Kathy's tale far sadder than if she were to rail against her lot. Even at the very end, Kathy describes her final trip to Norfolk to remember Tommy as 'indulgent' and, although she cries, she points out that she 'wasn't sobbing or out of control'. In a world completely outside of her control, in which even her death is prescribed, Kathy's composure and dignity make her an admirable and memorable character.	**not that Kathy is unable to express her feelings, however, it is that she knows there is no point. Nothing she says now can change the terrible reality. Gar, on the other hand, has an option.** If he manages to open a line of communication between himself and S.B., perhaps he need not leave home forever. Sadly, however, that is not to be the case. During his last conversation with his father, Private urges Public to speak up: 'Now's your time, boy. . . . Put your head on his shoulder and say, "How's my wee darling Daddy?"' Despite the facetious nature of the comment, the intent is deadly serious. However, all Gar can manage is, 'You'll need a new tyre for the van.' Unlike Kathy, who is presented as a dignified, composed character to the end, Gar's complete inability to connect with those closest to him arouses our pity rather than our admiration.	**remains emotionally stunted and unable to express himself, Ishiguro and Gerwig show that their characters have gained a greater understanding of the world and themselves by the end of the text.** *Lady Bird* is a gentle, comedic coming-of-age story rather than a dystopian tale, so this central character's journey is ultimately far more uplifting than that of the novel's central character. Lady Bird's phone call home to her parents at the end of the film is touching and uplifting. Unlike Kathy and Gar, who are left with nothing but precious memories, we are given the impression that Lady Bird has a meaningful and happy future ahead of her as well as her nostalgic recollections of her childhood.

→

Never Let Me Go	Philadelphia, Here I Come!	Lady Bird

Imagery and symbolism contribute to our understanding of the texts.

The trip that Kathy, Tommy and Ruth take to see the old abandoned fishing boat symbolises the value of friendship and the transience of life. The journey to see the boat has echoes of the earlier trip to Norfolk, but the differences are stark and obvious. Chrissie is dead, having 'completed' during her second donation, and both Tommy and Ruth are donors.

Ruth is dismayed by the barbed wire on the path to the boat but Kathy points out that they can get under the wire if they 'hold it for each other'. Of course, this symbolises the three friends' journey through life. Through good times and bad in Hailsham and the Cottages, they were there for one another. They have separated since, and Kathy realises that in the car on the way to see the boat, she and Tommy 'ganged up' on Ruth. They both move towards Ruth, 'almost as an instinct', and guide her through the fence. Ruth regains a measure of her old confidence as a result of this gesture.

The boat is beached in a marsh of 'dead trunks' and is crumbling away to nothing. Its deterioration reinforces the transience of life and the inevitability of death and decay. Despite all of this, Ruth thinks the boat is 'really beautiful'. This symbolises Ruth's acceptance of her lot and her determination to believe that her early and avoidable death can have beauty and dignity.

A boat also plays a significant symbolic role in *Philadelphia, Here I Come!* in highlighting the themes of love and loss. The boat in the play is part of a treasured memory from Gar's childhood. He recalls that 'once upon a time a boy and his father sat in a blue boat on a lake on an afternoon in May' and that there was a 'great beauty' in the moment that has 'haunted the boy ever since'. **Like the beauty of the boat in *Never Let Me Go*, this viewpoint is subjective.** S.B. does not remember the boat or the fishing trip, despite Gar's desperate attempts to make him recall that time when they were happy together. Sadly, the memory of the trip on Lough na Cloc Cor fails to bring Gar and S.B. together. **While the second trip to Norfolk in *Never Let Me Go* cements the friendship between Ruth, Tommy and Kathy, no such unity results from Gar's efforts to revisit the trip he and his father took all those years ago.** Instead, he is left with the bitter realisation that this treasured memory does not appear to mean anything to S.B. He rushes off while S.B. is still talking, hurt and miserable. The next trip Gar will take is to America to start a new life. **Unlike Ruth, who finds a sort of peace as a result of travelling to see the boat with her friends, Gar's revisiting of the fishing trip brings only pain and disappointment.**

In the film *Lady Bird*, journeys also serve to highlight key themes. Driving bookmarks the story and allows us to see how far Lady Bird has come as she negotiates the difficult road from childhood to adulthood. **The symbolism is more similar to *Never Let Me Go* than *Philadelphia, Here I Come!* however, in that it is ultimately linked to a sort of peace and reconciliation rather than sorrow and a failure to connect.**

The first car journey in the film is fraught with tension. Lady Bird and Marion are returning from visiting colleges, and what begins as mild bickering over the radio soon escalates into an angry, heated argument over Lady Bird's life choices. Marion tells her daughter to forget about studying on the East Coast, claiming that city college and jail would be more realistic goals. In the end, Lady Bird throws herself from the moving vehicle, breaking her arm in the process. At the end of the film, Lady Bird is indeed studying in New York, despite her mother's predictions. She is chastened after having been hospitalised for alcohol poisoning, and she decides to reach out to her mother, having left home barely on speaking terms. **Unlike Gar, who fails to connect with S.B., Lady Bird leaves a message on her parents' answerphone that we feel sure will help to heal the rift between her and Marion.** We know from the letters she tried to write and her tears when Lady Bird left that Marion is likely to respond positively to her daughter's words of love and appreciation. Lady Bird uses driving as a way to reconnect with Marion, asking if she too 'felt emotional' the first time she drove in Sacramento. As she speaks, we see images of Marion and Lady Bird at the wheel. Although they are both alone in the car in these shots, they are united in their love for Sacramento and one another. We are reminded of the very different car journey at the start of the film and we see how far the mother–daughter relationship has progressed.

Questions

2018 Leaving Certificate

1. 'The effective use of a variety of techniques can influence how we respond to characters.'

   (a) Identify two techniques which influenced how you responded to a central character in one text on your comparative course. Explain how your response to this character was influenced by the effective use of these techniques. Support your answer with reference to the text. (30)

   (b) Identify at least one technique which influenced how you responded to a central character in each of two other texts on your comparative course. Compare how your response to your chosen characters was influenced by the effective use of your chosen technique(s). Support your answer with reference to the texts.

   In response to 1. (b) you may refer to the same technique or different techniques in relation to each of your chosen texts. You may refer to the same or different techniques to those you referred to in 1. (a) above. (40)

   OR

2. 'Our interest and attention can be captured at the beginning of a text by the effective use of various techniques.'

   With reference to three texts on your comparative course, compare how effectively at least one technique was used to capture your interest and attention at the beginning of each of these texts. You may refer to the same technique or different techniques in each of your chosen texts. Support your answer with reference to your chosen texts. (70)

2015 Leaving Certificate

1. 'Studying a selection of texts helps to highlight how some authors can make more skilful use of the same literary technique than others.'

   Choose one literary technique, common to three texts on your comparative course, and compare how skilful the different authors are in using this literary technique in these texts. Support your answer by reference to the texts. (70)

   OR

2. 'Compelling storytelling can be achieved in a variety of ways.'

   (a) Identify two literary techniques found in one text you have studied. Discuss the extent to which these techniques contributed to compelling storytelling in this text. (30)

   (b) Identify one literary technique, common to two other texts on your comparative course. Compare the extent to which this literary technique contributed to compelling storytelling in these texts. You may select one of the literary techniques identified in 2. (a) above or you may choose to use any other literary technique in your answer. (40)

Mode: Theme or issue

The theme of identity in *Never Let Me Go*

While most young people question their place in the world, Kathy and her friends have to wrestle with a unique problem in terms of their identity. She and all the other donors have been cloned in order to provide organs. Therefore, they must come to terms with the fact that 'normal' people believe the clones have no identity of their own. Kathy spends most of the book struggling with the confusion surrounding her sense of self. Is she merely a copy of the person from whom she was cloned, or does she have the ability to be her own person?

From a young age, the students of Hailsham are raised to believe they are different, but they are not told exactly why. When Miss Lucy warns the children against smoking because they are 'special', they do not ask her to explain further. Looking back on that moment, Kathy thinks that it was because, even at the age of nine or ten, they knew enough to make them 'wary of that whole territory'. The children realise they are not the same as their guardians or the 'normal people outside' but they are unwilling to face who – or what – they really are.

A key moment early in the novel forces the children to face an unpleasant truth about their identities. Kathy and her young school friends are intrigued by the regular visits of a woman known simply as Madame. They believe she comes to the school to view their artwork and select pieces for her 'Gallery'. Madame avoids any contact with the students, and they begin to think she is afraid of them. Kathy, Ruth and some of the other children come up with a plan to swarm around Madame when she next visits. Their scheme works too well, and they are shaken to discover that Madame is genuinely afraid of them 'in the same way someone might be afraid of spiders'. This is a blow to the children's sense of self because, as Kathy says, it had never occurred to them to wonder how they would feel 'being seen like that, being the spiders'. For the first time, the children see themselves through someone else's eyes and they realise that they are truly different from their guardians and 'the people outside'.

The students at Hailsham are encouraged to work on their artistic talents because they are part of Madame and Miss Emily's experiment to prove to the outside world that the clones are 'fully human'. The children do not realise this is the reason they are required to produce artwork, but they are aware that their pieces are an important aspect of their identities. Tommy has very little artistic talent and worries that his lack of ability means he is somehow seen as less of a person than the other students. After he has left Hailsham, Tommy begins to work on his art once more because he wants to prove he has an inner self. He brings his pieces to Madame's house to seek a deferral. He hopes that his art will help her to see he has a soul and that he and Kathy are therefore capable of love and deserving of life. Tragically, proof of their humanity is not enough to spare the young couple their inevitable donations and early death. Madame and Miss Emily explain to Tommy and Kathy that deferrals do not exist and it is not in normal people's interests to see the clones as individuals worthy of life because if they did so, they could not harvest their organs.

Kathy and the others call those from whom they might have been cloned 'possibles'. After they have left Hailsham and are living in the Cottages, the clones have the opportunity to see more of the outside world, and there are occasional, unconfirmed sightings of possibles. There is great excitement whenever one of the clones believes their 'possible' has been spotted. Kathy says that 'Weeks could go by with no one mentioning the subject, then one reported sighting would trigger off a whole spate of others'. The clones naturally want to learn as much as they can about their possibles because they see them as a way of connecting with their identity. They also see their possible as a way of holding out hope for a different life, one in which they might have a place in the 'normal' outside world. Ruth learns from Rodney, one of the other occupants of the Cottages, that her possible may have been spotted working in an office in Norfolk. Rodney organises a trip to see if they can find the woman. Unfortunately for Ruth, the woman only bears a partial resemblance to her, so her hopes are crushed.

Ruth's bitterness turns to anger when Rodney tries to tell her that the search for a possible had been nothing more than a 'bit of fun' anyway. She tells the others that her failure to find her possible living a desirable life has simply confirmed what she always suspected about the clones' identities: 'We're modelled from *trash*'. Ruth says that no respectable person would allow themselves to be cloned, and if the others are looking for their identity through possibles, they should do so in the gutter, rubbish bins and toilets where they might find the 'junkies, prostitutes, winos [and] tramps' on whom they are modelled.

Ruth is not alone in thinking this. Kathy worries that her sexual urges might be too strong and that such feelings must be something to do with the person from whom she is cloned. Kathy searches through pornographic magazines in the Cottages to see if she can find her possible. She explains to Tommy that she doesn't want to find the woman but simply wants an explanation for her feelings. Kathy struggles to determine whether she is simply an exact copy of someone else and therefore must behave a certain way, or whether she is a person in her own right and free to shape her identity and sense of self. She cannot see that by simply reflecting on her place in the world, she is asserting her individuality and humanity.

Ultimately, however, Kathy and the others have to accept their fate. Their destiny has been mapped out for them, and, no matter what they do during their short lives, society will refuse to see them as individuals. At the end of the book, Kathy is about to begin her donations and knows she will soon die. The entire novel is Kathy's reflection on what has been important and valuable in her life: friendship, love and creativity. It is clear that no matter what society thinks of her, Kathy is far more than a cloned organ donor. She is an individual as worthy of life as any of the 'normal' people who continue to deny her humanity and her strong sense of self.

The theme of identity in
Philadelphia, Here I Come!

Gar O'Donnell is a young man torn between a desire to live a meaningful life in Ballybeg and the longing to leave his home place so that he could recreate himself with a new American identity. After facing both internal and external challenges to the development of a consistent and mature identity, he ultimately fails in his effort to establish a strong sense of self.

Gar has a public and a private identity, and he struggles to reconcile the two very different sides of his character. The use of two actors to play the role of one person strikingly portrays this aspect of Gar's personality. Private Gar is eloquent, witty and imaginative, even if he is sometimes cruel and mocking, while Public Gar is far less articulate and generally fails to communicate meaningfully with those around him. For example, Gar is desperate to have a proper adult conversation with his father before he leaves for America. However, he is surly, gruff and inarticulate in S.B.'s presence. In their first appearance onstage together, Public is unable to answer S.B.'s simple question about how many coils of barbed wire were delivered to the shop that day. Public says, 'There were two – no, no, no, three – yes, three – or maybe it was … was it two?' Private is disgusted with Public. He shows his annoyance in fluent, expressive language that contrasts sharply with Public's earlier tongue-tied uncertainty: 'After tomorrow a bloody roll of barbed-wire will be a mere bagatelle to you'.

If it weren't for Private, Gar O'Donnell would be an uninteresting, unimpressive character. Private gives a voice to Gar's inner thoughts and dreams, making him a complex and conflicted character. The problem for Gar's identity is that he cannot blend his public and private selves; therefore, he is constantly torn between them.

As the play develops, we see that one of the main challenges to his development of a consistent adult identity is Gar's childish habit of resorting to foolish daydreams in times of emotional stress. When he is alone, Gar fantasises about being famous, powerful or hugely successful to compensate for his frustration at having achieved little in his life so far and his inability to handle conflict in a mature way. For example, when he is angry and upset that his father forced him to stay late salting pollock on his last night at home, Gar imagines himself piloting a plane and shooting at an Irish boat fishing for 'bloody pollock'. He acts like a young child as he imitates the noise the gun would make, 'Rat-tat-tat-tat-tat …'. Gar's fantasies of being a footballer, pilot or cowboy make him appear far younger than his 25 years. He uses his imagination as an outlet for his overwhelming emotions of anger, bitterness, excitement, frustration and longing, much as a child might do.

Gar's immaturity is a serious obstacle to the development of an adult identity. He wants to marry Kate Doogan but is too childish to cope with the responsibilities of providing for her and asking her father for her hand in marriage. Gar and his friends have an adolescent view of love and marriage and talk like boys rather than men. Gar jokes that he and his friends are sex maniacs who boast about the 'hot courts' they know, but privately he admits that despite all their talk they are virgins. Gar's desire to marry Kate is partly driven by his physical need for intimacy with her. He urges her to get married soon, saying he will 'bloody-well burst' if he has to wait much longer to sleep with her. Gar begs Kate to put the wedding forward to 'next month – next week –'. Kate asks Gar to 'be sensible' and focus on their finances. Gar, like an excited child, confides in Kate that he has a secret source of income. Kate is delighted, believing it to be investments like her father's. However, Gar earns only a pittance selling some eggs when he does shop deliveries. In the flashback to this conversation with Kate, it is obvious to the audience that Gar has little idea of what it means to be an adult.

When he has to speak to Kate's father about the marriage, Gar is unable to say anything. He is overawed by Senator Doogan and the presence of Francis King in the house. Although Private blames Kate, saying that she 'must have known' about her parents' plans for her, the fault is his own. Gar's fantasies are so unrealistic and childish that they cannot sustain him when he comes up against the hard reality of Kate's father and an eminently more suitable suitor. The conflict between his adult desires and his lack of a fully formed adult identity is a serious obstacle to Gar's happiness.

Part of Gar's difficulty in forming a strong sense of self is how conflicted he is about what he actually wants. Emotionally stunted by his mother's death and his elderly father's reserved manner, Gar longs for love but at the same time finds it difficult to cope with open displays of affection. We see this clearly in his dealings with Master Boyle and Aunt Lizzy. Gar's old school teacher, Master Boyle, retains a fondness for his former pupil and calls to see him the night before Gar leaves for America. As he goes to leave, Boyle 'embraces Public briefly'. Private shouts, 'Stop it! Stop it! Stop it!' and as soon as Boyle has left Gar rushes to his room, where he struggles to control his emotions.

When Gar's Aunt Lizzy visits, she is desperate to be a substitute mother. Lizzy says she and her husband want to give Gar 'everything we have', including all their love. Private is terrified, repeating, 'No. No'. Gar impulsively agrees to go to America to live with his aunt and uncle, and Lizzy throws her arms around him, calling him 'my son'. Private responds with 'happy anguish', saying, 'God … my God … Oh my God…' It is hard to see how Gar can develop as a person when he is so unsure of his own feelings.

Although Gar resents S.B.'s remote and even cold manner, he is more like his father than he would care to admit. As the play progresses, we see that it is almost inevitable that Gar will adopt a similar identity to his father in time. Madge says that although S.B. doesn't say much, that 'doesn't mean that he hasn't feelings like the rest of us'. Gar refuses to accept his father's difficulty in expressing his emotions and says, 'If he wants to speak to me, he knows where to find me! But I'm damned if I'm going to speak to him first!' He does not see the irony in his own inability to communicate with the man he blames for a lack of communication.

There are moments when Gar sees the similarity between himself and his father, but he does not possess the strength of character to bridge the gap between them. Gar's demeanour in his father's presence is 'a surly, taciturn gruffness'. He acknowledges that he is like his father when he says they do not talk because 'we embarrass one another'. He believes that if one of them were to make a mildly personal remark, 'the other would fall over backwards with embarrassment'. At the same time, Gar longs for S.B. to say something unpredictable. As they sit together on Gar's last evening at home, Private cries, 'Screwballs, say something! Say something, father!' Madge reflects that he and S.B. are 'as like as two peas'. She says that when S.B. was Gar's age he was 'the very same as him: leppin, and eejitin' about and actin' the clown'. Madge believes that when Gar is 'the age the boss is now, he'll turn out the same', and will have 'learned nothin' in-between times'.

One of the most problematic aspects of Gar's sense of self is how self-destructive he is. He blames Ballybeg for many of his woes, but because he does not accept his own role in how his life has turned out, Gar is destined to keep repeating his mistakes. He tells Kate, 'If I had to spend another week in Ballybeg, I'd go off my bloody head! This place would drive anybody crazy!' He claims Ballybeg is a 'hole', a 'quagmire' and 'a dead-end'. Gar says he wants 'Impermanence – anonymity … a vast restless place that doesn't give a damn about the past'.

Kate says Ballybeg 'isn't as bad' as Gar makes it out to be, and she has a point. As son of the local shopkeeper and county councillor, Gar could have made something of himself and his family business. He was fortunate enough to be sent off to study at University College Dublin, but he dropped out before the end of his first year. He also fell in love with a woman who was willing to marry him if he just spoke up and proved he was a grown man who could take on the responsibilities of married life. However, he could not prove this. Now he boasts in his trademark immature fashion about all he will do when he is in America. Public tells Kate that he will probably study 'law or medicine or something', while Private pours scorn on this idea: 'Like hell! First Arts stumped you!' There is something pathetic about Gar's mention of 'law or medicine'. Kate's father studied law and her new husband is a doctor. Once again, Gar is imagining himself as very different to his real self, rather than accepting who he is and making the most of that. Gar's angry tirade against Ballybeg is also an attack on Kate for moving on with her life without him. Had he more courage and resolve, he could have been the one to marry her. This knowledge is part of the reason for his outburst. Kate's marriage to Francis shows that it is possible to make a good life in Ballybeg. Gar is bright enough to see that he is at fault, but he is not mature enough to face the truth and cope with it in a way that will allow him to grow as a person.

Despite his criticisms, Gar stores up happy memories of his home place, in which 'there was fun and there was laughing'. He knows that even his memory of 'the boys' will be 'distilled of all its coarseness' until all that remains is 'precious, precious gold'. There will always be a part of Gar that longs for Ballybeg when he is in America, just as there is a part of Gar that longs for America when he is in Ballybeg. Based on his words and actions in the play, there seems little hope of a happy resolution to this situation.

In the final lines of the play, Private asks Public, 'Boy, why do you have to leave? Why? Why?' Public answers, 'I don't know. I – I – I don't know'. At the start of the play, Public and Private are strikingly different; at the end of the play, sadly, there has been no change. Gar seems destined to live a life torn between who he wants to be and who he really is, without the emotional wherewithal or strength of character to reconcile these aspects of his identity.

The theme of identity in *Lady Bird*

Lady Bird is at a crossroads in her life when we first meet her. She is filled with a steely determination to carve out her own path, even if that means going against her strong-willed mother's wishes for her. Lady Bird's first words in the film are addressed to Marion, 'Do you think I look like I'm from Sacramento?' Lady Bird regards Sacramento as 'the Midwest of California', meaning it is – in her eyes – a place without culture or history. She does not want her identity to be shaped by living what she fears would be a narrow, stultifying, suburban life. Instead, Lady Bird dreams of studying in a college on the East Coast where, she believes, there is an abundance of progressive thinking and high culture. That is the sort of environment in which she imagines she will thrive, and she rebels against any efforts to tell her otherwise. Lady Bird's uncertainty and desire to be someone other than who she is are clear. However, Marion's matter-of-fact response: 'You are from Sacramento', not only highlights that Lady Bird is rooted in a place she does not wish to call home, but it shows that her mother has no truck with her daughter's aspirations and wants to bring her back to earth.

Although Marion loves Lady Bird, their relationship is far from easy. Lady Bird is keen to establish her independence and her sense of self but to do so, she needs to pull away from her mother's control, and shape her own identity. Marion dismisses her daughter's desire to have a more exciting life. The pair argues about the financial and social implications of Christine attending a college out of state. Crushingly, Marion tells her daughter, 'you're not even *worth* state tuition, Christine'. Lady Bird replies spiritedly, 'My name is Lady Bird'. She sees her chosen name as an integral part of her identity, and later in the film, during an audition for the school musical, explains that it is her 'given name': 'I gave it to myself; it's given to me by me'.

Lady Bird's reaction to her mother's harsh criticism is to throw herself from the moving car, breaking her arm in the process. When we next see Lady Bird, she is at a school Mass, wearing a bright pink cast with the words 'Fuck you, Mom' scrawled on it in black marker. Marion loves her daughter, but she cannot accept her for who she is. When mother and daughter shop for a prom dress later in the film, Marion disagrees with Lady Bird's choice. Lady Bird asks her mother why she can never seem to approve of or even like her. Marion replies that she wants Lady Bird 'to be the very best version of yourself that you can be'. Lady Bird counters, 'What if this is the best version?' and there is an awkward silence.

The problem for Lady Bird is that she does not want to be the 'best version' of herself: she wants to be someone completely different. Sister Sarah-Joan, the principal of the school Lady Bird attends, tries to guide her towards those areas of study in which she might do well. Unlike Lady Bird's mother, Sister Sarah-Joan is gentle when broaching the subject of Lady Bird's unrealistic dreams and her weaknesses. She comments mildly that strange posters Lady Bird hung around the school as part of her bid to be class president are a little disturbing, but doesn't push the issue. She smiles warmly as she notes that Lady Bird has 'a performative streak' and directs her towards the school's theatre programme. When Lady Bird says she would like to be 'on Math Olympiad', a highly selective annual maths competition, Sister Sarah-Joan frames her response tactfully. Rather than simply telling Lady Bird that she is not academically capable of such a thing, Sister Sarah-Joan gently says, 'But math isn't something you're terribly strong in?', couching the criticism in a questioning tone

that removes its sting. Lady Bird takes the kindly nun's advice and auditions for the school play, but she does not accept her academic limitations, despite Sister Sarah-Joan's comments. She steals and throws away her math's teacher's folder of class grades so she can lie about her average. It seems at this stage that Lady Bird struggles hugely to face reality and insists on clinging to an idealised version of herself rather than making the most of who she really is.

Lady Bird continues down this path of delusion for a time. She rejects her best friend, Julie, in favour of the shallow and wealthy Jenna, even though they have nothing in common. Julie understands Lady Bird and supports her through her break-up with her boyfriend, Danny, but Jenna represents the type of life Lady Bird believes she wants. However, being Jenna's friend means Lady Bird cannot be true to herself. To fit in with Jenna's social circle, Lady Bird lies about where she lives, pretending Danny's grandmother's house is hers. The snobbish and shallow Jenna says she knows the area as it was where her family had their 'starter house'.

Lady Bird's desire to move in the same social circle as Jenna is a real threat to her ability to develop a meaningful identity that will allow her to achieve her full potential. Unlike Lady Bird, Jenna is perfectly content to live in Sacramento forever and hopes to marry and reproduce her exact lifestyle for her children. Lady Bird says nothing to this, and her silence speaks volumes. It seems she has accepted that friendship with Jenna is worth the price of independent thought and self-expression. Similarly, Lady Bird's relationship with Kyle is a threat to her sense of self. She is impressed by his pseudo-intellectualism and rather pathetic attempts to appear rebellious and edgy, even losing her virginity to him because she believes they have a deep emotional connection, which is clearly untrue.

However, Lady Bird is strong-willed and determined, like her mother. She eventually comes to see that Kyle and Jenna are shallow and self-absorbed. She realises that she does not want to be like them after all, and that their opinion of her is of little consequence. On prom night, she rejects their plan to 'ditch' the dance and go to a party instead. Lady Bird finally stands up to her new friends and asks to be brought to Julie's house. The pair goes to the dance together and they thoroughly enjoy themselves.

The ending of the film leaves us with a very positive impression of Lady Bird's journey to discover her sense of self. Far from her family and a little at sea in New York, Lady Bird reverts to 'Christine', introducing herself to her fellow students at her first college party in that way. She has managed to move on from her earlier rebellious self and develop a greater understanding of who she really is. Her journey is not over – she is still very young – but she is at least on the right path.

At the party, Lady Bird drinks too much and wakes up in the ER, having been treated for alcohol poisoning. She sees a mother and young son sitting on the next bed. The little boy has a bandage over his eye and his mother is obviously distressed and deeply tired. Lady Bird is clearly moved as she looks at the pair. Perhaps she compares this situation to the pain she must undoubtedly have caused her mother when she leapt from the moving car, breaking her arm. Lady Bird has learned a great deal about herself and is now confident enough about who she is to have a meaningful relationship with her mother. Her story shows us that no matter what difficulties a person faces, if they are true to themselves, they will find inner strength. At the start of the film, Lady Bird was determined to move away from her home and did not want to be identified as somebody from Sacramento. Now, however, she nostalgically remembers her home town and rings home, leaving a touching voice message for her mother. It is significant that Lady Bird calls herself Christine when she rings home. She explains that she is using the name her parents gave her because it's a good one. She does not need a quirky name or a different identity anymore, because she finally knows who she is.

Comparative study: Theme or issue

Never Let Me Go	Philadelphia, Here I Come!	Lady Bird

The theme of identity is presented differently in each text.

Never Let Me Go is a dystopian novel that explores what it means to be human and what determines our identity and sense of self-worth.

The novel is an interesting blend of fantasy and reality. Although the situation is unrealistic, it is Kathy's normality that makes the theme so relatable. The theme of identity is gradually introduced as Kathy recalls her childhood and the moments that have brought her to this point in her life. When we meet her first, Kathy seems composed and quite sure about herself and her place in the world. She is a 'carer' for 'donors', but we are not at all sure what this means at this early stage in the novel. As the story progresses, however, the dreadful truth is revealed. Through Kathy's memories of her time in Hailsham, we gradually come to see that personal identities are denied to the donors by those who believe that their sole purpose is to donate their organs. Kathy's calm acceptance of this shocking reality somehow makes it even worse.

It is the practical way the story is told that makes Kathy's struggle to discover who she truly is, and whether those who say she is nothing and nobody are right, so heartbreaking. For example, as a teenager Kathy worries that her perfectly normal sexual urges may be too strong because all clones may be, as Ruth says, 'modelled from *trash*'. As a result, Kathy searches through pornographic magazines at the Cottages to see if she can find her 'possible' among the women in the pages.

The theme of identity is dealt with very differently in *Philadelphia, Here I Come!* than in the novel. Kathy's desperate situation highlights the importance of an individual fostering a strong sense of their identity to sustain them, but Gar, unlike Kathy, does not develop his identity to any great extent over the course of the play. Instead, he is caught in a sort of limbo between adolescence and adulthood, and there is little indication that he will come to any sort of satisfactory resolution of his dilemma.

The most striking difference between the presentations of the theme in the play and the novel is the use of two actors in the play to represent both sides of Gar's conflicted identity. Private Gar articulates Public Gar's thoughts and feelings. Private is eloquent, witty, mocking and sometimes quite cruel. He reminds us of the humor and the pathos of Gar's desperate need to be loved for who he is and to be able to express his real personality. If it weren't for Private, Gar would be an unsympathetic character, by turns taciturn and immature, and we would have little interest in his struggle to find out who he really is. Private shows us that Gar is a complex and conflicted individual. The problem for Gar's sense of identity is that he cannot blend his public and private selves and is constantly torn between them.

Unlike the novel, which spans a much longer period, the play takes place over the course of a single evening, so it is not surprising that Gar's identity should not develop significantly over this time frame.

Lady Bird **follows a more traditional narrative structure than do the other two texts. At the beginning of the novel and the play, we meet the central characters at a turning point in their lives and we gradually learn what has shaped their identities. In** *Lady Bird*, **however, we follow the titular character as she develops from a selfish, resentful girl to a more thoughtful, appreciative young woman. This chronological structure means that we are unsure, until the very end of the narrative, if Lady Bird will come to terms with who she is and what she wants from life.** There is a degree of uncertainty in *Philadelphia, Here I Come!* too, admittedly, but nothing like as much as in the film. Gar is 25 while Lady Bird is only a teenager, so it seems less likely that Gar will have any great epiphany at this stage in his life.

The film, unlike the novel and play, is a relatively straightforward coming-of-age rom-com, so we feel reasonably sure that Lady Bird will overcome the obstacles in her path to self-knowledge and will ultimately develop a strong sense of self. This proves to be the case. Lady Bird clashes with her mother, but eventually learns that her mother's refusal to except who Lady Bird wants to be is born of love, even if it is sometimes misguided and badly expressed. Gar never makes this leap. His relationship with his father does not move beyond tentative and unsuccessful attempts to bridge the gap between them. One of the most interesting aspects of the presentation of the theme of identity in the film is the author's decision to subvert the norm. We might expect in a narrative of this sort that it would be through her romantic relationships that Lady Bird would find happiness and an acceptance of herself. **Even in the dystopian novel** *Never Let Me Go*, **there is a basic love story of misunderstanding, separation and reunion, which sustains Kathy and forms an integral part of who she is.**

→

Never Let Me Go	*Philadelphia, Here I Come!*	*Lady Bird*
By the end of the novel, the opening makes complete sense. We re-examine the incredible poise, strength of character and sense of self that Kathy displays. She is viewed as less than human by the society in which she lives and is about to die because of this view; yet while she may accept her fate, Kathy does not accept this view of herself. She has a clear sense of her place in the world and a knowledge that her life has been worth living. The way the theme is presented forces us, like Kathy, to examine what it is to be human and to have an individual identity.	**Still, as in the novel, flashbacks and memories of earlier encounters show that Gar, unlike Kathy, does not have the inner resources or the maturity to learn and grow from difficult encounters or challenges to his sense of self.** We fear that Gar is doomed to continue in this vein and to constantly veer between denial and self-loathing. **Kathy, on the other hand, shows grace and dignity as she wrestles with the dilemma of being true to herself in a world that wants to deny her any sort of identity.**	However, Gerwig rejects the typical boy–girl relationship by having Lady Bird reconcile with her best friend in time for prom. She leaves Kyle and Jenna, asking that she be dropped at Julie's house. Lady Bird and Julie go to the prom, dance, pose for a photo and walk home with their shoes in their hands at the end of the night. This chain of events is one we have seen in films before, but it is unusual to see it centred on friendship rather than romance. Danny and Kyle, the two love interests in Lady Bird's story, are stepping stones on her voyage of self-discovery but they are not the destination. **Realising who and what really matters to her is an important part of Lady Bird's growing acceptance of who she is and her development of a clear sense of the sort of person she wants to be in the future.**

→

Never Let Me Go	Philadelphia, Here I Come!	Lady Bird

Characters in each of the texts have a moment or moments of revelation about their identity.

A key moment early in the novel forces the children to face an unpleasant truth about their identities. Kathy and her young schoolfriends are intrigued by the regular visits of a woman known simply as Madame. They believe she comes to the school to view their artwork and select pieces for her 'Gallery'. Madame avoids any contact with the students, which makes them think she is afraid of them. Kathy, Ruth and some of the other children come up with a plan to swarm around Madame when she next visits. Their plan works too well; they are shaken to discover that Madame is genuinely afraid of them 'in the same way someone might be afraid of spiders'. This is a blow to the children's sense of self because, as Kathy says, it had never occurred to them to wonder how they would feel 'being seen like that, being the spiders'. For the first time, the children see themselves through someone else's eyes, making them realise that they are truly different from their guardians and 'the people outside'.

Unlike Kathy, whose moment of revelation occurs quite suddenly during Madame's visit, Gar does not have a single, life-changing moment of revelation about his identity. Instead, he has a series of smaller insights that he fights against and refuses to fully accept, which is why he never grows as a person. These moments are presented by Private's comments and Public's behavior. In each case however, Gar manages to ignore or reject his inner self and continue on his self-destructive path.

For example, in his last meeting with Kate Doogan, Public tells Kate that he will probably study 'law or medicine or something' while Private pours scorn on this idea: 'Like hell! First Arts stumped you!' There is something pathetic about Gar's mention of law or medicine. Kate's father studied law and her new husband is a doctor. Once again, Gar is imagining himself as someone very different to his real self rather than accepting who he is and making the most of that. **Unlike Kathy, who faces the unpleasant truth about her identity and learns from it, Gar resists even his Private self's attempt to tell him the truth.** In his conversation with Kate, Gar doubles down on his fantasies and becomes boastful and aggressive, announcing, 'I'll come home when I make my first million', and saying that he hates everything about Ballybeg and can't wait to be gone.

Lady Bird's situation is more similar to Kathy's than it is to Gar's. Like Kathy, Lady Bird learns from and grows as a result of moments of revelation about herself and her place in the world, while Gar continues to mishandle and sabotage opportunities that come his way. Therefore, it is only Lady Bird and Kathy who develop a strong sense of self. Clearly, Lady Bird's situation is far better than Kathy's, in that she can grow and become her best self, whereas Kathy is denied that chance. Lady Bird possesses a strength of character that Gar does not and, as a result, is able to benefit from facing harsh truths about her life.

One example of Lady Bird's coming to terms with who she really is occurs on the night of the prom. Lady Bird, who has tried to shape a false identity to please Jenna and Kyle, finally realises that there is no point in doing this because they will never really be friends. As they drive to the dance, the Dave Matthews Band song 'Crash Into Me' comes on the radio and Kyle makes a derogatory comment about it. We are reminded that that song was last used in the film when Julie and Lady Bird cried and sang together after Lady Bird's discovery that Danny was gay. Hearing it now, Lady Bird comes to see that Kyle and Jenna are nothing like her and that she is wasting her time by trying to reshape who she is to please them. She makes a decision. She asks Kyle to drop her at Julie's house, which he is happy to do. Jenna asks who Julie is and Lady Bird replies firmly, 'She's my best friend'. **The reunion between Lady Bird and Julie is far more positive and affirming then the reunion between Gar and Kate. Whereas the latter is doomed because Gar has not grown at all and is still the same immature, boastful young man that he was earlier in the play, Lady Bird has developed as a character and can now see what she should prioritise in her life.**

Never Let Me Go	Philadelphia, Here I Come!	Lady Bird

The endings of the texts show that each character has a different degree of success in establishing their own identity.

Despite their struggles to learn who they are and to find their place in the world, Kathy and her friends ultimately have to accept that no matter what they do in their short lives, the society in which they live will never see them as individuals or even human beings. Kathy realises this when she and Tommy visit Miss Emily to ask if they can be considered for a 'deferral'. Miss Emily and Madame explain to the young couple that no matter how much in love they might be or how much they can display their humanity, the 'normal' people will always view them as less than human. However, despite the terrible fate that awaits her, Kathy refuses to sacrifice her own sense of self. She continues her relationship with Tommy and does not give up on life or love. At the end of the novel, Kathy is about to begin her donations and knows she will soon die. The novel is Kathy's reflection on what has been important and valuable in her life: friendship, love and creativity. It is clear that in spite of what society thinks of her, Kathy is an individual who is sustained by her precious memories of all the experiences and relationships that have made her who she is.

Unlike Kathy, whose sense of self is sustained by the memories of the relationships she has had in her short life, Gar is miserably aware that even his memories of his home will prove either false or painful and will contribute to his unrealistic and unsatisfactory sense of who he is. He knows for example, that his time with his friends, the 'ignorant bloody louts', will be 'distilled of all its coarseness' until he is left with a fake memory akin to 'precious, precious gold'. At the very end of the play, Gar watches Madge shuffle off and tells himself to note every detail carefully, as this is 'a film you'll run over and over again'. This yearning contrasts with Gar's inability to tell Madge much how much he cares for her. Both examples show Gar's unrealistic view of life; he persuades himself that he and his friends had only good times, and he makes Madge's exit into a mental film he will cherish. This is a large part of the reason Gar will never have a consistent, strong vision of who he really is and where he belongs.

In this respect, Gar is very different to Kathy, who faces the harsh reality of her life and the fact that the world in which she lives makes every effort to deny her a real identity. Both Kathy and Gar face challenges to their sense of self, but whereas Kathy succeeds, we suspect that Gar does not have the mental and emotional resources to sustain him at the next stage of his life. He is left without any of Kathy's sense of peace. She has come to terms with who she is and with her place in the world, but we suspect that Gar will be forever longing for a different life and a version of himself that he believes he could have become had circumstances been different.

The ending of the film leaves us with a positive impression of Lady Bird's journey to discover her sense of self. She does not quite have Kathy's dignified acceptance of her position in the world, but she has managed to move on and develop in a way that Gar never does. This is clearest when Lady Bird finally goes to college in New York. She drinks too much at a party and wakes up in the ER, having been treated for alcohol poisoning. She sees a mother and young son sitting on the next bed. The little boy has a bandage over his eye and his mother is obviously distressed and deeply tired. Lady Bird is clearly moved as she looks at the pair. Perhaps she compares this situation to the pain she must undoubtedly have caused her mother when she leapt from the moving car, breaking her arm. Lady Bird has learned a great deal about herself and is now confident enough about who she is to have a meaningful relationship with her mother. **In this way, she is very different to Gar, who is running away from his home and his father rather than making his peace with them and himself. Kathy and Lady Bird show us that no matter what difficulties a person faces if they are true to themselves, they will find inner strength.**

At the start of the film, Lady Bird was determined to move away from her home and did not want to be identified as somebody from Sacramento. Now, however, she nostalgically remembers her home town and rings home, leaving a touching voice message for her mother. It is significant that Lady Bird calls herself Christine when she rings home. She explains that she is using the name her parents gave her because it's a good one. She does not need a quirky name or a different identity anymore because she finally knows who she is.

Questions

1. 'The same theme or issue can appear more relevant to life today in some texts than in others.'

   (a) In relation to one text on your comparative course, discuss the aspects of the text that, in your opinion, make your chosen theme or issue appear more or less relevant to life today. Support your answer with reference to the text. (30)

   (b) In relation to two other texts on your comparative course, compare the aspects of those texts that, in your opinion, make your chosen theme or issue appear more or less relevant to life today.

   Support your answer with reference to your chosen texts. (40)

   OR

2. 'There are many reasons why the exploration of the same theme or issue can be more entertaining in some texts than in others.'

   Compare the reasons why you found the exploration of the same theme or issue more entertaining in some texts than in others. Support your answer with reference to three texts on your comparative course. (70)

1. 'Some texts leave readers with a largely idealistic impression of a theme or issue, while others leave readers with a more realistic or believable impression of the same theme or issue.'

   With reference to the above statement, compare the impressions of the same theme or issue you formed when studying three texts on your comparative course. Support your answer by reference to the texts. (70)

   OR

2. 'It is possible for a reader to be surprised or shocked (or both) by aspects of a theme or issue encountered in texts.'

   (a) Discuss the extent to which you were surprised or shocked (or both) by aspects of a theme or issue encountered in one of the texts you have studied for your comparative course. Support your answer by reference to the text. (30)

   (b) Compare the extent to which you were surprised or shocked (or both) by aspects of the same theme or issue encountered in two other texts you have studied on your comparative course. Support your answer by reference to the texts. (40)

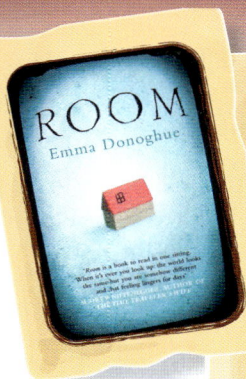

Option Two:

Room
by Emma Donoghue

The Crucible
by Arthur Miller

Casablanca
directed by Michael Curtiz

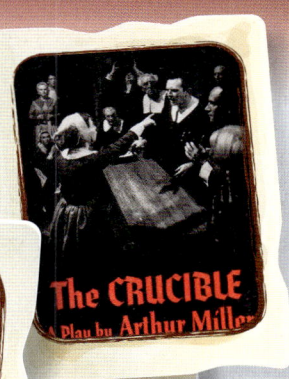

Mode: Cultural context

Cultural context in *Room*

Control and violence

The main source of control and violence is Old Nick, so called because he resembles a devilish character Jack saw in a cartoon. He kidnaps Ma and keeps her in a shed he has converted into a 'twenty-first-century dungeon', repeatedly raping her over the course of the seven years he holds her in captivity. Before Jack was born, Old Nick broke Ma's wrist when she tried to escape and told her that he would abandon her to starve to death if she ever tried to do it again. Ma became pregnant and Old Nick refused to allow her any medical treatment. He 'just stood there' and watched while Ma begged for help and gave birth to a stillborn baby girl. Even when he believes Jack is very ill, Old Nick refuses to take him to hospital, saying he will get him some medicine the next day. He is willing to let his captives die rather than risk getting medical help. It is his deliberate cruelty that makes Old Nick so evil. He knows exactly what he is doing but because he doesn't care about other people at all, he continues to make Ma and Jack suffer.

Old Nick is far from representative of the wider society in the text; he is an aberration. After Ma and Jack's release, Jack reads a newspaper article describing Jack as a 'Garden-shed Ogre'. Dr Clay, normally a composed and calm man, becomes angry as he warns Ma that she must provide all the DNA evidence necessary to convict Old Nick, as 'Monsters are let off on technicalities every day.'

One of the most terrifying things about Old Nick is the way he rationalises his controlling and violent behaviour. For example, his taking Ma was not an impulsive act but rather something he had planned long in advance. He is actually proud of the prison he has created and criticises Ma for the deterioration of the floor and furnishings. Chillingly, he says that a certain amount of wear and tear is 'par for the course'. 'Par for the course' implies something that is to be expected and is typical of this sort of situation. However, there is nothing normal about Room, but Old Nick is incapable of seeing that. He tells Ma that he only designed Room for 'one sedentary user' and feels he is the one being treated badly. The fact that he fathered Jack means nothing to him in this context. This sense of self-righteousness and belief that he is the victim of Ma's inconsiderate and troublesome behaviour makes Old Nick a truly horrifying figure. Although his actions are not normal, far from it, he obviously considers his behaviour not only to be justified, but admirable. We do not know what circles he moves in online or in the real world, but he has clearly had discussions with other captors about the best way to keep a woman or a girl prisoner. When he is chiding Ma at one stage, he tells her that she does not know how fortunate she is. He points out that she lives in a place that is above ground and has natural light, and he seems to feel she should be grateful for these 'luxuries'. There are, he assures her, 'Plenty girls who would thank their lucky stars for a setup like this, safe as houses.' Old Nick believes Ma should be grateful not to have to worry about 'perverts' in the outside world. The irony of his comments is lost on Jack, who listens from Wardrobe, but we find them deeply shocking.

Ma is physically under Old Nick's control and lives in constant fear of him. The only power she possesses over him is her sexuality. Although he rapes her, Old Nick is willing to believe that Ma desires him. She uses this to placate Old Nick when he is angry, hiding her revulsion and terror and asking in what Jack recognises as 'that funny high voice' if he wants to go to bed. At one stage, Old Nick tries to lure Jack out of Wardrobe so he can 'get a good look' at him. He claims Jack has no reason to be afraid of him, pointing out that he 'Never laid a hand on him'. This is a hollow boast, as Ma has protected Jack from Old Nick by hiding him every night, and we know just how violent and cruel Old Nick is. He has no problem imprisoning Jack and threatening to starve him and Ma to death. Ma knows the only way she can keep Jack safe is to distract Old Nick, so she suggests they go to bed. Jack is an innocent, so the implications of Ma's request are lost on him.

Eventually, Old Nick's reign of terror over Ma and Jack ends. He loses his job and Ma fears that he will abandon or kill her and Jack if the bank tries to repossess his house. Her hand is forced, so she hatches a daring escape plan. It succeeds, and she and Jack are freed. Old Nick is arrested shortly afterwards. The novel ends before his court case but the lawyer tells Ma he will spend twenty-five years to life in prison with no parole. However, Ma and Jack will have to live with the repercussions of his violence for the rest of their lives.

During her time in captivity, Ma constantly longs to escape Old Nick's control. Unlike Jack, she knows there is a whole world outside and that 'Room's only a tiny stinky piece of it.' Jack, on the other hand, doesn't wish to be free because he doesn't know he is a prisoner. Ma has to work hard to get him to understand that fact. Even when she succeeds, Jack has mixed feelings about escaping. For him, Room represents security and the only life he has ever known. When Jack manages to escape and bring the police to rescue Ma, she is delighted and tells him they can 'do anything now' because they are free. Jack says he wants to go to bed in Room because he has 'seen the world' and is tired now. When Ma says they are never going back, Jack cries so much he can't stop. Jack felt safe in Room, and Ma felt constantly threatened and in danger. As Ma feels she is gaining control, Jack feels he is losing it.

Jack does not know where his home is when he and Ma escape from Room. He tries to make the hospital room a home and is reluctant to leave it, but Ma is impatient and wants to see more of the world now that she is free. Jack finds the outside world so frightening that he has to breathe into a paper bag to prevent him from hyperventilating and passing out when he goes into the hospital gardens. He felt secure in Room and did not realise how much danger he was in when he was held prisoner there.

Ma is disappointed to discover that escaping Room does not bring the freedom she had imagined. She suffers from the media's prurient interest in her case, their intrusive behaviour and their sensationalist reporting. Even a simple walk in the fresh air has to be cut short suddenly when a photographer in a helicopter tries to get footage of her and Jack. Ma attempts to control the narrative by giving an interview about her ordeal. This is similar in some ways to her selflessness in trying to cajole Old Nick into bed to distract him from Jack. Ma is willing to sacrifice her privacy and speak to the media in order to provide money for Jack's college fund. The interview is a disaster for Ma. She hopes to steer the conversation towards topics of her choosing but she underestimates the sensationalist nature of the press. The interviewer is only interested in lurid details and does not care about Ma's feelings. Ma is emotionally abused and traumatised by the intrusive, hurtful questions. The final straw is when the interviewer asks her if she ever considered asking Old Nick to take Jack to a hospital and leave him there so he could be put up for adoption. She says, 'Every day he needed a wider world, and the only one you could give him got narrower.' Ma had never thought that she was the one keeping Jack imprisoned in Room and she is utterly heartbroken at the suggestion that she was actually Jack's captor. Ma is so devastated at the thought that all her efforts to love and protect Jack were actually acts of selfishness that she takes an overdose the day after the interview. The message is that the exploitative voyeurism of the media and its insatiable appetite for shocking stories, even at the expense of the survivors' mental health, exacerbates the suffering of victims of violence.

Ultimately, Ma and Jack achieve freedom by returning to Room one last time. Ma has gained some authority over her own life by moving into an independent living facility with Jack. It is the first step towards complete independence. Jack, who has at times longed to go back, now sees that Room is a small, dark place and he knows now that the outside world – with all its difficulties – is better. He says goodbye to Room forever and asks Ma to do the same. They walk out the door together, in control of their own lives, at last.

Love and marriage

Traditional views of love and marriage do not play a large role in *Room*. Rather, the focus in on true love in whatever form it comes.

There is no relationship between Ma and Old Nick, although he clearly thinks there is. He views his imprisonment of her as something for which she should be grateful. Bizarrely, he believes he is keeping her safe from 'perverts' in the outside world and repeatedly complains that she does not understand how hard he works to keep her in what he considers luxurious conditions. In his eyes, because she lives 'Aboveground' with 'natural light' and has occasional supplies of fresh fruit and toiletries, Ma is very lucky. He is irritated by her 'hassling' him about renovations when she asks for an extractor fan to remove the smell of cooking, about which he grumbles. In Old Nick's twisted view of the world, he is the hard-working provider and Ma is the nagging wife.

The only other relationships into which we get a brief insight are those between Paul and Deana, and Grandma and Steppa. Paul and Deana seem very happy: Grandma tells Ma that Deana is 'lovely' and their little girl, Bronwyn, is 'almost three and potty trained already'. The normality of Paul and Deana's family is in stark contrast to Ma and Jack's situation.

The strain of Ma's disappearance led to Grandma and Grandpa separating. She 'never stopped hoping' that her daughter would come home one day, but Grandpa 'thought Ma was dead and had a funeral for her'. Their divergent beliefs led to their parting ways and Grandpa moved to Canberra, Australia. Grandma found love again with a gentle, thoughtful and sensitive man whom Jack calls Steppa. His marriage to Grandma is a source of happiness and joy in the family, although Ma does not see that straight away. She is critical of her mother's choice, telling Jack that Steppa is 'nearly seventy and stinks of dope . . . She must have been on the rebound.' Steppa is tactful and kind, recognising potential flashpoints and defusing them as quickly as possible. When Grandma and Ma start arguing in the clinic, Steppa stands up and says to Grandma, 'We should let these folks rest.' Later, when Jack is staying with Grandma and Steppa, he throws a tantrum and Steppa picks him up, carries him to his room and waits until he has stopped crying before asking if he'd like to watch the game and eat pie with him. Steppa and Old Nick are polar opposites, and both show that it doesn't matter whether or not there are marital or biological ties between people: all that ultimately counts is love and kindness.

Gender roles

Room shows the very worst extremes of a patriarchal view that women and children are lesser beings and simply exist for men's convenience. Old Nick believes he has an absolute right to keep Ma as a sex slave and to have the power of life and death over her and Jack. However, Emma Donoghue is keen to point out that Old Nick is not representative of men in general but is rather a perversion of a widely accepted view that women are somehow inferior. That attitude, taken to extremes, can lead to violent abuse. The other males in the novel are generally kind and decent, normal, flawed human beings – just like the women.

Donoghue has said in interviews that she deliberately made Jack male so that people wouldn't think the story was about male versus female. Jack is kind and gentle and Ma loves him dearly. She doesn't associate him with Old Nick at all, insisting he is hers alone. Jack is only five when the story begins, so his gender is not particularly important. However, Ma draws on the male stereotype of bravery and heroism when she needs Jack to go along with her escape plan. She calls him 'my brave Prince JackerJack' and tells him that 'Jack the Giant Killer' would not mind having hot water placed on his forehead to simulate a temperature if it was necessary. Jack rises to the occasion, and despite his terror when he is rolled up in the rug, he tells himself that Ma needs him 'to be Super Prince JackerJack'.

It is only when Jack is in the outside world that he realises that some people expect boys and girls to behave differently. His uncle Paul takes him to a mall and Jack is thrilled to see his beloved TV character, Dora the Explorer, on a backpack in a shop. Paul's wife, Deana, asks if Jack would like the bag but Paul immediately suggests he buy one 'that's not pink'. He holds up a Spider-Man bag and asks Jack if he thinks it is cool. However, Jack is having none of it and insists on taking the Dora bag instead. A passer-by in the mall notices Jack has taken off his shoes (he is not used to wearing them) and returns them to Paul and Deana, asking if they are 'your older daughter's'. Jack is confused and wonders why the woman thought he was a girl. Deana explains that the woman was misled by Jack's long hair and pink Dora bag.

A few moments later, Jack needs to pee, so Paul takes him to the men's toilets and guides him towards a urinal. Jack has never seen such a thing and can't understand why there should be special toilets for boys and men. He is used to being with Ma, so is happier to go to the toilet with Deana and his cousin Bronwyn. This proves a disaster, because Jack knows nothing about 'private parts'. He is curious when he sees that Bronwyn's body is different to his and Ma's, and he touches her inappropriately, although he does not know he is doing anything wrong. Deana slaps him away so hard that she cuts his hand with her ring and Jack is deeply distressed. Having shared such a tiny space with Ma all his life, Jack struggles to grasp the concept of privacy, especially when it relates to gender.

Coming to terms with the fact that some people have stereotypical ideas around gender roles becomes less problematic for Jack over time. Despite the difficult trip to the mall, Paul proves to be a largely positive male influence. He calls Jack 'buddy', which Jack decides 'is man talk for sweetie', and he plays football with him. Steppa is gentle and understanding, helping Jack with everything from Lego to dealing with tantrums. Jack gradually becomes less attached to Ma, although he is still very close to her. When Ma takes an overdose, Jack has to go and stay with Grandma and Steppa. Grandma's child-rearing methods are quite gender-specific. Unlike Ma, she refuses to share a bath with Jack unless she can wear her bathing togs, and when Steppa pulls some of Jack's peeling, sunburnt skin from his shoulder, Grandma considers this slightly disgusting behaviour typical of men. While staying with Grandma, Jack makes the decision to cut off his ponytail and thus he is more easily identifiable as a boy. Very little is made of this in the text: Jack simply takes the scissors and snips off the long ponytail and Grandma tidies up the ragged ends so he has a proper hairstyle. Jack is gradually fitting into a world that has certain expectations of how a boy should look and behave but there is no implication that this is a negative outcome.

Emma Donoghue has said in interviews that she considers *Room* to be a feminist novel. Ma is not simply an example of the resilience of the human spirit but a beacon of female strength. She is also a very real character and not simply a complete innocent snatched away from a perfect life by Old Nick. Ma is a fully-rounded, interesting, flawed character with incredible courage. There are times when she is irritated by Jack and, on occasion, she is overwhelmed by her situation both before and after her escape from Room. However, Ma does her utmost to care for and protect Jack in the most difficult of circumstances. All of this makes her a character we can admire for her honesty, humanity and determination to do the absolute best for her child. Emma Donoghue says that Ma 'turns her pain into something wonderful' and that, despite all she has been through, Ma shines a light on the power and importance of motherhood.

Values

Room is, at heart, a story of the power of parenting and family bonds. Ma's value system is shaped by maternal love and, in spite of the horrific conditions of her imprisonment, she finds meaning in life through caring for Jack. Being a mother to him gives her strength in the darkest hours. Ma tells Jack that before he was born, she had no purpose. She was sunk in abject misery and cried until she 'didn't have any tears left'. She counted not just the days or the hours, but the seconds of her interminable captivity.

Comparative Study

Later in the novel, Ma explains to a television interviewer that Jack 'was everything' to her during her captivity and that when he was born, she felt alive again because she mattered to someone. The message of the novel is that it is in loving and being loved by others that we find our sense of self.

Ma does her best to care for Jack in incredibly difficult circumstances. She educates him, plays with him and showers him with love. Food is precious in Room, but Jack says that when they eat a tub of mandarins, he gets 'the big bits because she prefers the little ones'. When they run low on food and there is only one bagel left, Ma only has a quarter of it and lets Jack believe she is 'not very hungry'. She is willing to sacrifice everything for Jack while ensuring that he does not know she is doing so.

Ma eventually comes to the difficult decision that Jack must escape Room, even if she does not. She believes her fate is irrelevant as long as Jack is alright: 'You're the one who matters, though. Just you.'

Room shows us that there is no single definition of family. Although Jack was born of rape, Ma loves him dearly and says he is 'nobody's son but mine'. Jack and Ma are a family

unit and Old Nick, Jack's biological father, plays no role. His value system is utterly warped and based only on his own perverted desires and twisted view of the world. He does not care for Jack, calling him a freak and keeping him imprisoned in Room with Ma. Old Nick does not hesitate to punish Jack and Ma: depriving them of food, heat and power when they anger him. Ma believes that he would abandon them to starve to death if it suited him to do so. She has good reason for thinking this, as Old Nick also allowed his daughter – Jack's sister – to die because he would not take Ma to hospital to give birth. He did not even bother to do an internet search on delivering babies but just stood and watched the tragedy unfold. His attitude is not representative of the wider world of the text, of course. However, he is an example of what can happen when extreme misogyny and belief in the patriarchy are given free rein. Old Nick sees women as inferiors who are there to serve him as he sees fit.

When Jack and Ma escape, Jack discovers that he has another family. Grandma accepts him immediately and, in her own way, is supportive and loving. Despite her best intentions, Grandma finds Jack a handful sometimes, and when he has a tantrum while staying with her, she asks Steppa to take over because she has had enough. Grandma struggles with how different Jack is to most boys his age. He is articulate and intelligent, but he doesn't know how to use a swing, for example. At the end of the day, however, Grandma is willing to do whatever it takes to care for her daughter and grandson. Grandpa, on the other hand, cannot accept Jack. He is too caught up in the idea of Old Nick being Jack's father to see that the little boy is an innocent in all of this. Steppa fills the gap left by Grandpa. When Steppa catches Jack playing with matches, he does not get angry but just teaches Jack about everything in the kitchen and how to use it. Jack doesn't know how to play with Lego, but Steppa teaches him and says any mistakes Jack makes are 'no problemo'. Steppa is not related to Jack, and this shows that biological ties are far less important than kindness, acceptance, patience and love.

Cultural context in *The Crucible*

Control and violence

The power of the Puritan church lies in its repression of individual voices and its ability to punish anyone who refuses to conform. As their name suggests, the Puritans in the play live by a strict set of communal values. Independent thought is strongly discouraged because the community is the most important aspect of life. In this theocratic society, an outward show of religious observance is essential. In the introduction to Act One, Miller says that at the time the play was set, there was a two-man patrol sent to take the names of those who did not attend church and give the list to the magistrates so that they could be 'accordingly proceeded against'.

A strong, united community had been essential when the Puritans first established themselves in America. Danger was never far away, and the communities that encroached on Native American territories were made up of tough men and women who survived where others did not. Miller describes the early Puritans as 'a communal society which, in the beginning, was little more than an armed camp with an autocratic and very devoted leadership'. This system was essential to their survival. Some in Salem had lost family members to marauding tribes. Abigail Williams tells the other girl that she understands violence very well because of the terrible way in which she was orphaned: 'I saw Indians smash my dear parents' heads on the pillow next to mine, and I have seen some reddish work done at night, and I can make you wish you had never seen the sun go down!'

However, Miller also tells us that by the late 1600s, 'the time of the armed camp had almost passed' and there was not the same need for tight control over the town and its people. For people like John Proctor, 'old disciplines were beginning to rankle'. Another reason Proctor rebels against the church's efforts to control him is because he holds the Reverend Parris in contempt. He dislikes and distrusts Parris's obsession with money and property. Proctor says that he stopped attending church because the last time he heard Parris preach, he 'spoke so long on deeds and mortgages' that Proctor felt 'it were an auction' rather than a religious meeting. Miller's narration reinforces the view that Parris is not a fit person to exercise any sort of power. His need to be in control is portrayed as something petty and slightly ridiculous: 'In meeting, he felt insulted if someone rose to shut the door without first asking his permission'. Parris represents those – past and present - who may have an elevated position in society but lack the moral maturity to be worthy of that post.

Although it is a risky business to stand up to Parris in this way, Proctor stays true to himself, declaring, 'I may speak with my heart, I think' in response to Parris's outrage at his outspokenness. Parris insists that his parishioners accept his control: 'There is either obedience or the church will burn like Hell is burning!' He suspects there is a 'faction and a party' bent on overthrowing him. Thomas Putnam agrees, saying that there is such a movement 'Against him and all authority!' Far from denying this and appeasing Parris, Proctor says he must find this group and join it because he does not like 'the smell of this authority'.

John Proctor's word carries some weight because he is a man and a landowner. The women in the play are not so fortunate. In a world in which women have little control over their lives, Abigail Williams wields what power she has. She has a stronger will than the other girls and is not afraid to both threaten and use violence if it suits her ends. In Act One, she shakes the unconscious Betty Parris and says she will beat her if she does not wake up. When Betty awakes and says Abigail drank blood as part of a curse intended to kill Elizabeth Proctor, Abigail 'smashes her across the face'. She vows she will inflict a 'pointy reckoning' on the other girls if they speak a word about her actions and she assures them she knows how to kill if need be.

Abigail is also cunning enough to manipulate the church rulers. She harnesses the hysteria, fear and hypocrisy of those in her community and uses them to her advantage. The witch trials give Abigail a sense of power. Everyone in Salem and the judges brought in from outside the community uphold her version of events and people live or die based on her testimony and that of the girls she bullies into agreeing with her version of events.

Terrible violence is alluded to throughout the play, but Miller makes the decision not to show it to us directly. This has the effect of allowing us to use our imaginations, which can be far more effective than reading about gruesome scenes. For example, we learn that Giles Cory has been tortured to death, but we do not see the old man's suffering. The torture method of pressing was a terrible death in which a board was place on the person's body and heavy stones laid on top until the person either confessed or was crushed by the accumulation of weight. Similarly, we see the lead-up to and the aftermath of the hangings of those accused of witchcraft, but the executions themselves are not shown on stage.

Ultimately, those who hold power will not tolerate any challenge to their authority. Judge Danforth believes his power is bestowed upon him by God, and he refuses to accept the trials are deeply flawed. Were he to do so, he would have to admit the situation is outside his control. This he is unwilling to do, even if innocent people are sent to their deaths as a result. He takes no notice of Hale's pleas or Proctor's impassioned speech, ordering that those convicted be hanged 'high over the town'. Danforth's power lies in his reputation as a judge – if he admitted that he had made a mistake, he would lose all credibility. Danforth represents those involved in persecuting alleged communists in Miller's America. The abuses of power in the play served to remind us of what some in authority are capable of if they feel threatened.

John Proctor is hanged at the end of the play, but he has far more moral authority than those who condemn and convict him. Even during his final hours in a jail cell, Proctor manages to take control of his destiny to a certain extent. He may lose his life, but he will not lose his reputation. He is unmoved by Danforth's threats and Hale's pleas. While many of those around him choose to capitulate rather than stand up for what is right, Proctor refuses to yield to an oppressive regime. Although he would be spared the hangman's noose were he to allow his signed confession to be shown to the people of Salem, Proctor does not agree to Danforth's demand. Danforth is bewildered but Proctor cries out, 'How may I live without my name? I have given you my soul; leave me my name'. Hale begs Elizabeth Proctor to be her husband's 'helper', asking, 'What profits him to bleed? Shall the dust praise him? Shall the worms declare his truth? Go to him, take his shame away'. Hale does not understand that John does not want to be remembered as a liar; if he were to sign a false confession, he would betray those who were hanged as witches. Elizabeth knows the sort of man her husband is and she tells Hale, 'He have his goodness now. God forbid I take it from him!' In the end, John Proctor has defied those in control and he goes to his death having regained his honour and his courage.

Love and marriage

The Crucible is a love story as well as an allegory of the persecution of suspected communists by the American government in the 1950s. The central relationship in the play is the marriage of John and Elizabeth Proctor. The couple is put under great strain: first by John Proctor's affair with Abigail Williams, and then by the ludicrous accusations of witchcraft levelled against both man and wife.

The love story helps us to relate to the events of the play on a more personal level and ensures that we see how ordinary people's lives can be torn apart when hysteria and self-interest are allowed free rein.

Before we ever meet the Proctors, we learn that their marriage may be in difficulties. Reverend Parris is suspicious because his niece, Abigail, was dismissed by the Proctors seven months ago and no other family is willing to take her on as a servant. He says that Elizabeth Proctor will not come to church any longer because she is unwilling to 'sit so close to something so soiled'. Abigail lashes out that Elizabeth is 'a bitter woman, a lying, cold, snivelling woman'.

John Proctor's first appearance in the play reinforces the impression that the Proctors' marriage is in trouble. Miller says in his narrative that Proctor 'is a sinner, a sinner not only against the moral fashion of the time, but against his own vision of decent conduct'. When Abigail and Proctor are alone (apart from the seemingly unconscious Betty Parris), Abigail reveals her desire for Proctor, asking him to give her 'A soft word'. Proctor says firmly that he is finished with her but she does not take no for an answer, reminding him, 'you clutched my back behind your house and sweated like a stallion whenever I came near'. Proctor continues to insist there is no longer anything between them but Abigail says she has seen him looking up at her window at night. Still, he says that even if he does think of her from time to time, he will never act on it again and he urges her to put the affair from her mind, too. Abigail angrily accuses Proctor of being controlled by a 'sickly wife' and for the first time we see a real flash of anger in Proctor. He is disgusted with Abigail and knows he has been wrong in allowing the situation to develop.

The meeting between Proctor and Abigail gives us an insight into their attitudes towards the relationship. Proctor considers it something shameful that he wishes had never happened, but he also struggles with his physical attraction to Abigail. For her part, Abigail thinks they are in love. She says Proctor 'took me from my sleep and put knowledge in my heart'. She cannot understand how he now expects her to 'tear the light' from her eyes. Abigail is a young girl and Proctor is a married man in his forties, so it is hardly surprising that they should view the relationship very differently. How we view it depends on our attitudes. Some critics see Abigail Williams as a knowing, manipulative young woman who entices Proctor away from his wife. Others see her as a victim who cannot be entirely to blame for clinging to the hope that she might have a future with Proctor. After all, Abigail is an orphan who has only a home of sorts with an uncle who cares far more for his reputation than he does for her.

Abigail's sexual awakening is linked to her social awakening. She says she knows that Salem is a 'pretence' and that she has been taught 'lying lessons' by the Puritan community. Her relationship with Proctor has led Abigail to reject the societal norms of Salem, which is why she finds it easy to turn to witchcraft – a taboo among her neighbours – to eliminate Elizabeth. That plan does not work but

Comparative Study

Abigail is both clever and malicious enough to use the fear it generates to have Elizabeth accused of trying to kill her. Abigail's love for John is entirely possessive and destructive. She is willing to sacrifice others for her own ends.

Eight days after the scene between Proctor and Abigail, we see the reality of the marriage between Proctor and Elizabeth. While Elizabeth is offstage, taking care of the children, Proctor tastes the dinner she has prepared and seasons it without her knowledge. When she appears and serves the meal to him, she asks if he likes it and he replies that it is 'well seasoned'. Elizabeth blushes with pleasure. Although Proctor's comment is a white lie, it is telling. Elizabeth does not know his tastes as well as she thinks, but he wants to cover that up and allow her to believe that she pleases him. They are more like a young couple trying to impress one another than a comfortable, married husband and wife at ease together.

The Proctors are farmers, so it is not surprising that natural imagery should play a role in their relationship. Still uneasy and trying their best to heal the wound caused by his affair with Abigail, Proctor tells Elizabeth that they will have 'green fields soon' as the earth is 'warm as blood' beneath the clods. This can be seen as a metaphor for his hope for the regrowth of their love. Although things may be cold on the surface, there is a core of warmth underneath. Elizabeth is not as receptive as Proctor might wish, and he tells her that she should bring flowers into the house as 'It's winter in here yet'. This is a veiled reprimand because Elizabeth is not responding to his efforts to win her forgiveness. Before long, the subject of the witch trials comes up and Abigail Williams is brought into the conversation. Almost immediately, the real tension in the marriage comes to the surface. Proctor becomes angry that Elizabeth still suspects him of carrying on the affair with Abigail, and accuses her of having 'an everlasting funeral' in her heart. He says he has done all he can to please Elizabeth but that she continues to judge him. Elizabeth lives by Puritan values and Proctor finds this hard to take. He accuses her of hypocrisy and unkindness, traits that have led to the terrible situation in which Salem finds itself. He regrets confessing that he slept with Abigail: 'Some dream I had must have mistaken you for God that day. But you're not, you're not, and let you remember it. Let you look sometimes for the goodness in me, and judge me not'.

The Proctors' marriage is put to the ultimate test during the witch trials. Abigail Williams accuses Elizabeth of witchcraft and John sacrifices his good name by admitting to the court that he slept with Abigail. He hopes that by so doing, he will prove that Abigail is motivated by spite and lust: 'She thinks to dance with me on my wife's grave'. He calls Elizabeth his 'dear good wife' and says he would not have risked his reputation but to save her. Elizabeth is not in court when her husband confesses, and when she is called in to corroborate his story and thus save herself, she refuses to admit that there was ever anything between Proctor and Abigail. She does so out of love and loyalty, just as Proctor confessed the affair for the same reasons.

At the end of the play, Proctor is once again faced with a choice. He can make a false confession and be spared hanging, or he can tell the truth and die. Reverend Hale begs Elizabeth to persuade him to confess but she uses their last moments together to beg him to forgive her. She says she never thought herself worthy of his love and that she kept 'a cold house' because she always suspected he would cheat on her. She admits her love for him now and says she 'never knew such goodness in the world'. Ultimately, both Proctor and Elizabeth want to be worthy of one another's love. He tears up his confession and goes to his death with his honour intact. Elizabeth, though heartbroken, says her husband has 'his goodness now' and refuses to take it from him.

In Salem, hysteria, jealousy and cruelty lead to the breakdown of relationships on a social and personal level. The Proctors' relationship alone shows that people are capable of rising above such sentiments. Both John and Elizabeth Proctor are more self-aware, less judgemental characters at the end of the play. They are bettered by their trials and they ultimately refuse to capitulate to the corruption and lies that reign in their hometown.

Gender roles

Salem is a patriarchal society. The men hold all the power and the women are restricted to servitude, marriage and motherhood. Women who step outside their appointed roles in any way are vulnerable to criticism or worse. It is no coincidence that the majority of those in the play accused of witchcraft are women. If women show an interest in anything apart from their household duties, they are viewed with suspicion. For example, Martha Corey is accused of witchcraft because she reads books. One of her neighbours attributes his failure to raise pigs to Martha's reading. Martha made a derogatory comment about his poor animal husbandry and he manages to convince the court that his pigs' failure to thrive is due to Martha having 'bewitch[ed] them with her books'. Even Martha's husband Giles initially suspects her reading as being a sign of witchcraft, telling Reverend Hale that he is sure it is the reason he struggled to pray the previous evening: 'And then she close her book and walks out of the house, and suddenly – mark this – I could pray again!' Men's literacy, on the other hand, is treated with great respect. Reverend Hale brings a stack of books with him to Salem and the heaviness of the bundle is seen as a sign of his intellectual weight. Giles Corey respectfully calls him 'a learned man' and sees no irony in voicing his suspicions of his wife's 'readin' of a book' to Hale.

There is a clear division in the play between young and old women. The young women are the accusers and those they accuse are middle-aged or older. Those named as witches were, generally speaking, easy targets because they lacked value in a society that judged women by their ability to bear children. The only thing that can save them from execution is pregnancy, and then they are only safe until the child is born.

The initial accusations are made by women who are in a lowly position in society and they save themselves by making an even lowlier woman a scapegoat. When her uncle questions her about their behaviour in the woods, Abigail blames Tituba. Tituba is not only a servant, she is also from Barbados. This immediately marks her out as different to the other members of the community and more vulnerable to suspicion as a result. Tituba, for her part, names Sarah Good, a homeless old woman who begs from door to door. Thomas Putnam has suggested Sarah Good to her, along with another woman, and Tituba shrewdly realises they are even easier targets than she.

There is little solidarity between the women in the play and they are often harsh judges of one another. Ann Putnam turns on Rebecca Nurse, accusing her of killing her children. She is motivated by jealousy: Rebecca has raised a large, healthy family. A woman who could not provide her husband with children was not valued highly, and the Putnams have only one daughter who, at the time the play begins, has apparently fallen ill. Rebecca's role in Salem also makes her vulnerable. Midwives, or any women who showed medical knowledge, were often targeted in witch trials. Their expertise made them suspect, and if anything happened to a child they had helped bring into the world, the finger of blame was pointed at them.

Comparative Study

Women's sexuality is subject to harsh scrutiny in the play. There is a double standard: women who show any signs of their sexuality are presented as evil temptresses who prey on men's natural sexual desire. We see this in the relationship between John Proctor and Abigail Williams. She is a seventeen-year-old girl in the Proctor household and he is a married man in his forties, a landowner and a person of repute in Salem, yet it is she who is blamed for the affair. Religious imagery is used to shape our opinion of Abigail Williams. Abigail tells Proctor the effect their relationship had on her, 'I look for John Proctor that took me from my sleep and put knowledge in my heart'. This is an allusion to the story of Adam and Eve in the Bible. They ate the forbidden fruit in the Garden of Eden and immediately lost their innocence. Eve is the temptress in the story, and the originator of sin on earth, just as Abigail is presented as the reason for Proctor's downfall. Abigail is not sexually experienced; she believes Proctor loves her and knows he is still attracted to her: 'I have a sense for heat, John, and yours has drawn me to my window, and I have seen you looking up, burning in your loneliness'. It is hardly surprising that she should find it so difficult to believe he truly wants nothing more to do with her. Men's dominant position in society means that Proctor can threaten Abigail with physical violence if she criticises his wife. He shakes her and asks, 'Do you look for a whippin'?' when she criticises Elizabeth. In court, Proctor grabs Abigail by the hair and shouts that she is a whore. While there is no doubt that Abigail is in the wrong when she accuses Elizabeth of witchcraft, Proctor's attack on her is unacceptable.

Elizabeth Proctor feeds into the idea that her husband is not really to blame for the sin of adultery. At the end of the play, she and Proctor speak openly in the prison. She says she has had time to look deep into her heart and that she now realises 'It needs a cold wife to prompt lechery'. She claims that in calling himself a sinner, Proctor has nobly taken her sins upon himself and that she kept a 'cold' house because she did not consider herself attractive enough to deserve his love. This attitude allows Proctor to be presented as a tragic hero and a man wronged by both his lover and his wife.

Values

Salem is a theocratic society: a place ruled by religious leaders. The Puritans live by a strict set of communal values and have little tolerance for those who seek to express their individuality. This attitude was both understandable and sensible in the early days of the Puritan community when the people of the area needed to remain united by a strong bond of communal values if they were to survive in a hostile environment. By 1692, however, there was no longer such a need, but those in power were unwilling to give up their authority. Their ancestors had been persecuted in England and they inherited a determination to keep their new home and their version of Protestantism uncorrupted by what they saw as sinful ideas. This intolerant society provides the perfect setting for the witch trials, during which Danforth says 'a person is either with this court or he must be counted against it; there be no road between'.

The repressive society ensures that Puritans, both good and bad, keep their thoughts to themselves as much as possible, creating a great deal of pent-up frustration. The witch trials allow for an explosion of all this resentment and dislike. They are an ideal opportunity for those who want to pursue personal vendettas to do so under the guise of adherence to religious law. Miller says that 'Old scores could be settled on a plane of heavenly combat between Lucifer and the Lord; suspicions and the envy of the miserable toward the happy could and did burst out in the general revenge'. In an interview with *The New Yorker* shortly before the release of the film version of the play, Miller said that the witch trials became 'an invitation to private vengeance, but made official by the seal of the theocratic state'. Thomas Putnam, for example, uses the trials to buy the land of those who are convicted of witchcraft. His wife Ann is jealous of Rebecca Nurse's large family and accuses Rebecca of having used witchcraft to murder the Putnam children: 'You think it God's work you should never lose a child, nor grandchild either, and I bury all but one?'

The witch trials reflect the gross unfairness of the McCarthy hearings in 1950s America in which personal freedoms and rights took second place to what was considered the greater good. In both instances, those who claimed to be on the side of justice were in fact perpetuating terrible injustice, and corruption reigned.

Reputation is important to many of the characters in *The Crucible*. In a small community ruled by a strict set of Puritan principles, a person's good name counted for a great deal. If their reputation were damaged, they risked ostracism or worse. We see this early in the play when Reverend Parris and Abigail Williams are both concerned with the regard – or lack of it – in which they are held by the townsfolk. Parris frets because he worries that the 'three long years' of work he has put into gaining some respect from 'these stiff-necked people' is jeopardised by rumours of his niece's affair with John Proctor and her dabbling in witchcraft. Parris's language when he discusses his parishioners shows no real liking or care for them. He is concerned that there is a faction of local people rising against him, but he does not question why they might dislike his preaching. Similarly, he does seem concerned for Abigail's well-being but wants to ensure that her reputation is 'entirely white'. Abigail, for her part, loses her temper at the suggestion that Elizabeth Proctor has 'soiled' her name, calling the other woman 'a gossiping liar'. Of course, it is Abigail who is the liar as she has slept with John Proctor and still hopes to tempt him away from his wife.

Once the investigations into witchcraft begin, Abigail quickly realises that she can save herself by offering a false confession and at the same time accusing other women. She knows that everything she says is a lie, but she also knows her life and her reputation will be saved if she can eventually persuade the investigators that Elizabeth Proctor is evil and is spreading false rumours about her.

Ultimately, those who choose to protect their reputations do so because they care more for the opinions of others than for their own integrity. Parris only calls for a postponement of the hangings because he fears the tide of popular opinion that is rising up against him. Danforth, who believes himself to be an excellent judge, refuses to countenance any action that may take from his reputation. Neither man shows the slightest genuine concern for anyone else.

There are those who value integrity over reputation. John Proctor is ashamed of his affair with Abigail Williams but is willing to confess it in front of the court if it will prove that Abigail Williams is motivated by hatred of Elizabeth. He urges Danforth to believe him, saying, 'A man will not cast away his good name'. Proctor recognises that people will think less of him, but it is a price he is willing to pay to save his wife. At the end of the play, Proctor is faced with a choice between his reputation in the town and his life. He wrestles with his conscience but chooses to die with integrity rather than live a lie. Refusing to allow his false confession to be shown in public, Proctor cries, 'How may I live without my name? I have given you my soul; leave me my name'. He is taken away to be hanged but Elizabeth believes he has finally redeemed himself for his sin and that he has 'his goodness' back at last.

Cultural context in *Casablanca*

Casablanca was released in November 1942, shortly after America had joined World War II. Therefore, images of Nazi control and the threat of violence predominate. The film opens with credits displayed over a map of Africa and a voiceover explaining the 'tortuous, roundabout refugee trail' for people desperate to escape war-torn Europe. Those who make it as far as Casablanca are far from free, however. They still must contend with a French regime which is sympathetic to the Third Reich, and the audience is repeatedly reminded of the dangers faced by anyone who falls foul of the authorities. We see an example of this early in the film when the police hunt for the killer of the German couriers. A smooth-talking pickpocket explains to an English couple that they are watching the 'customary round-up of refugees, liberals and, uh, of course, a beautiful young girl for Monsieur Renault, the Prefect of Police'. This brief summary of the situation highlights the abuse of power by those in control of Casablanca: the innocent are victimised and sexual violence is also tolerated.

During the round-up, a man whose papers are out of date runs from the police. He is shot down and 'Free France' leaflets prised from his dead hand. All of this takes place beside a poster of Marshal Petain, the puppet ruler of German-occupied France. Petain's slogan, '*Je tiens mes promesses, meme celles des autres*' ('I keep my promises, even those of others'), is meant to imply that Petain and those like him who swore allegiance to the Nazi regime in return for being allowed a semblance of power and control are honourable. The shooting dead of a resistance fighter at this spot highlights the message that nobody is safe from violence, and the real control in Casablanca lies with a cruel, totalitarian regime.

Sexual violence occurs in *Casablanca*, even if it was not regarded as such when the film was made. Captain Renault abuses his power to coerce women into sleeping with him in exchange for freedom. There is little suggestion that this behaviour is reprehensible: Renault is presented as an amusing and likeable rogue. Rick is aware of Renault's activities, but it is only when the young and vulnerable Annina Brandel is clearly distraught at the thought of having to trade sexual favours for exit visas that Rick steps in. He arranges for Annina's husband to win money at the roulette table, much to Renault's disappointment. The captain accuses Rick of interfering with his 'little romances' and hopes he will be more fortunate with the woman he plans to bring to the casino on the following night. The tacit acceptance of Renault's predatory behaviour gives us a revealing insight into the cultural context of the time.

The attitude towards violence in the film seems to indicate that life is cheap. Ugarte's arrest in Rick's café is presented by Renault as something which will amuse the customers. Indeed, he goes so far as to tell Rick that he could have staged the arrest at the Blue Parrot earlier in the evening but is doing it in this café as a token of his 'high regard' for Rick. The arrest itself is messy and distressing. Shots are fired and a loudly protesting Ugarte is dragged away. Rick apologises for the 'disturbance' and tells everybody to sit down and have a good time, which they promptly do.

Major Strasser is the face of the Third Reich in the film. He is a superficially polite, sophisticated man but this veneer slips on occasion and we see the cruelty and violence of which he is capable. Strasser wants Laszlo to betray the other resistance fighters, but Laszlo scornfully refuses, saying he is unlikely to give in to the demands of the Nazi regime as he resisted them for a year in a concentration camp where 'more persuasive methods' were used. Strasser is too polished to openly threaten Laszlo, but it is obvious what he means when he tells Laszlo it would be 'unfortunate' if something were to happen to him while trying to escape. The veiled menace is clear and it is reinforced when Strasser gleefully tells Laszlo and Ilsa that Ugarte is dead. Renault chimes in here, telling the dismayed couple, 'We haven't quite decided whether he committed suicide or died trying to escape'. Although we don't see Laszlo's suffering in the concentration camp or the killing of Ugarte, there is no need for any such graphic depictions of violence. Any audience is more than capable of imagining the violence behind the scenes, but particularly an audience watching the film during wartime when the media was full of the latest news from the front lines.

Although Casablanca may be far from the front lines, war is never far away. The light that shines from the airport tower is a beacon to alert planes arriving in Casablanca, but its sweeping movement and harsh glare are reminiscent of a watchtower searchlight in a prison camp. The light reminds us that the world is at war and everyone is being carefully watched. It sweeps over Rick's café the first time we see it, providing an ominous reminder of the ever-present threat of the Nazi regime. As this shot immediately follows Renault's conversation with Major Strasser in which the latter says that he has already heard of the café 'and also about Mr Rick himself', there is an undercurrent of tension. Strasser does not have to say outright that the Germans are in control in Casablanca: his seemingly casual comment says it for him. Later that evening, as Renault sits outside the café, we see the light sweep across the emerging Rick and then a shot of the tower silhouetted against a dark sky. Through the light, Renault is linked with the sense of danger and the heavy-handed power of a police state. Everyone in Casablanca is under almost constant surveillance.

The ending of the film introduces the idea of a shift in the balance of power. Rick has killed Strasser and ensured Laszlo and Ilsa escape to Lisbon. Captain Renault has decided against having Rick arrested for shooting Strasser and tells his gendarmes to 'round up the usual suspects'. Renault picks up a bottle of water and pours himself a glass. As he does so, he notices the Vichy label. He throws the bottle into a bin that he then kicks over. Vichy France was the German-occupied part of the country, and it was ostensibly self-ruled. As long as it remained neutral, the Germans promised that it would remain free. In fact, that section of France was run by a puppet government that sided with the Germans. Up until the end of the film, Renault has abided by the Vichy government's deal with Germany, despite making a pointed remark to Strasser on his arrival in Casablanca: 'Unoccupied France welcomes you.' Renault has always slightly resented the Germans' show of authority, telling Rick, 'I don't interfere with them and they don't interfere with me. In Casablanca I am master of my fate. I am captain of my –' before being interrupted by a summons from Strasser. By discarding the water bottle in this way, Renault signals his complete break from the Germans. The political message was clear to the audience of the time: Vichy France was a threat that could not be ignored and anyone who sided with the Allies needed to take a firm stance against Petain and any other Nazi sympathisers or pacifiers. Renault suggests that he and Rick leave Casablanca and join a Free French resistance group in Brazzaville. The outcome of the war is still unclear, but in this story at least, good is seen to have triumphed over evil.

Love and marriage

Plainly, the role of women in the text is to be beautiful, gentle and chaste until marriage, after which time they must be loving, loyal, dependent wives. Those who do not adhere to this stereotype are viewed harshly by their contemporaries. Yvonne is portrayed as an immoral drunkard and Rick's callous treatment of her when she asks when they will next spend time together is presented to make him appear cool and controlled while she is hysterical and unstable. Rick's behaviour also seems to indicate that love is not a part of his life and that any relationship he enters into is devoid of emotion.

The arrival of Ilsa Lund and Victor Laszlo in Casablanca shatters Rick's composure and his carefully crafted identity as a hardened cynic. Sam, the piano player, sees Ilsa enter the café, and his apprehension – almost amounting to fear – leads us to believe that whatever her relationship with Rick was, it should not be rekindled. Sam tries to persuade Ilsa that Rick has a girl in the Blue Parrot, but she does not believe this obvious lie. Desperately, Sam begs, 'Leave him alone, Miss Ilsa. You're bad luck to him'.

Despite Sam's efforts, Rick meets Ilsa. She has asked Sam to play and sing 'As Time Goes By'. Rick strides over to the piano, clearly angry. He tells Sam that he told him never to play that song again, and in reply, Sam merely looks towards Ilsa. Rick follows his gaze and two close-ups reveal Ilsa and Rick looking intently at one another. Ilsa's eyes brim with unshed tears. Rick is speechless and can only gulp in astonishment. Rick joins Laszlo and Ilsa at their table, to Renault's surprise. After all, Rick is famously aloof but now he is not only willing to drink with customers, but to foot the bill. Renault's reaction shows that Ilsa must mean a great deal to Rick for him to break with precedent this way. The conversation between Rick and Ilsa is loaded with tension and hints of a difficult past. They recall their last meeting in Paris, on the day the Germans entered the city. Rick says it was 'Not an easy day to forget', but it is obvious he does not simply mean because of the invasion. The tension and undercurrents of anger on Rick's part and sadness on Ilsa's make love appear a destructive and negative force at this point in the film.

The pessimistic mood created by Ilsa's return deepens when she and Laszlo leave the café and Rick sits alone, miserably attempting to drink himself into oblivion. He resists Sam's attempts to get him to leave the café and Casablanca, insisting that he is waiting for Ilsa and that she will return. His cool, cynical façade has crumbled and he sinks his head in his hands, wondering why 'Of all the gin joints in all the towns in all the world,' Ilsa had to walk into his. He forces the reluctant Sam to play 'As Time Goes By' once more. The picture dissolves to a flashback of Rick and Ilsa's time together in Paris.

In the montage of romantic outings at the beginning of the flashback, Rick seems far more carefree and much happier as the couple drive through the Parisian countryside and take a boat trip down the Seine. They are in every way the typical young lovers so familiar to a cinema-going audience. Flowers and champagne abound and all is romantic perfection. Before long, however, the mood changes. Rick and Ilsa are in a café, La Belle Aurore. The name of the café is ironic as it is far from a beautiful dawn for Rick or Ilsa: their relationship is about to end. The Germans will shortly invade Paris and Rick is leaving for Marseille. He believes Ilsa will go with him but, of course, she does not. We see Rick stands in a downpour at the station, reading her letter. The raindrops blur the words, just as falling tears would do. Now at last we know why Rick is so jaded and cynical. His heart has been broken and his bitterness may jeopardise Laszlo and Ilsa's chance of escaping Casablanca. Thus, the relationship takes on a new significance. Rick is so deeply hurt that he finds it difficult to separate the personal and political, and his feelings for Ilsa may place both her and Laszlo's lives in danger as well as jeopardising the war effort by failing to help an important figure in the resistance to the Nazi regime.

Rick refuses to give Laszlo the letters of transit until Ilsa visits him in his apartment. When she does, however, Rick undergoes a transformation. He realises that Ilsa really loved him all along and he understands her reason for leaving him. From this point on, Rick abandons his earlier vow to 'stick [his] neck out for nobody'. He risks all to help Laszlo and Ilsa in their bid for freedom. Rick and Ilsa's relationship has at last become a positive force in their lives and hope dawns once more. Rick's love for Ilsa has rekindled his moral code.

Although *Casablanca* is a typical Hollywood film in many respects, the ending defies convention. The standard happy-ever-after ending would require Ilsa to openly declare her love for one of the men in her life, and for the other to accept her choice, but that does not happen. Instead, we are left with ambiguities and uncertainties.

Part of the reason Ilsa stays with Laszlo even though she loves Rick is that the institution of marriage is more important than personal happiness, and her job is to support her husband in his work. Rick points this duty out to Ilsa, telling her to leave with Laszlo because she is 'part of his work' and 'the thing that keeps him going'. Were Ilsa to follow her heart rather than her duty, the society of the time would frown on her doing so and she would not be worthy of respect as a heroine. Curtiz is careful to acknowledge this viewpoint and ensures, for example, that we never see any direct evidence of Rick and Ilsa doing more than exchanging a kiss once she and Laszlo arrive in Casablanca together.

The main reason that the ending of the film is unclear is because there is no clean merging of the personal and political. On the one hand, Rick's ultimate act of self-sacrifice at the end of the film leaves us in no doubt that he is a true wartime hero. Yet at the same time, his courage and nobility mean an end to his and Ilsa's love. He insists that she and Laszlo escape together and tells her, 'I've got a job to do, too. Where I'm going you can't follow. What I've got to do you can't be any part of. Ilsa, I'm no good at being noble, but it doesn't take much to see that the problems of three little people don't amount to a hill of beans in this crazy world. Someday you'll understand that.'

Rick allows the woman he loves to go away with another man because the war effort is more important than any individual. This is a stirringly patriotic message and impresses even Captain Renault, prompting him to abandon his post and join Rick on his next mission, whatever that may be. However, Rick has lost Ilsa once more. For the second time, they must part ways. The ending of the film reminds us of the railway station scene shown in Rick's flashback. He was heartbroken then, and we can only assume that he is equally so now.

Ilsa's feelings are less clear-cut. Does she truly love Rick? It could be that she simply pretends to in the hope of obtaining the letters of transit, as Rick tells Laszlo. Rick does this to spare Laszlo's feelings and ensure his and Ilsa's marriage survives. If, however, Ilsa truly loves Rick, then being forced to leave him is extremely painful for her and it seems unlikely that she has or will ever achieve fulfillment in her life. She admires Laszlo greatly and realises her importance in his life and his work, but that is not the same as love. As Ilsa tells Rick, she met Laszlo when she was very young and was swept away by his idealism, his courage and the passion of his conviction. Laszlo helped her to grow and to develop a political conscience but is that enough to sustain a loving relationship long term? We are left to speculate on Ilsa's motives and feelings, and this makes the ending of the film open-ended.

There can be no easy answers and no carefree conclusions. Sacrifices must be made, and those who fight and those who are left behind both suffer for the greater good. On a personal level, Rick may have lost the love of his life, but he is not alone in the final moments of the film. He does not have Ilsa, but he has a loyal companion of sorts. The final line in Casablanca is, therefore, somewhat uplifting and cheering as Rick says to Renault, 'Louis, I think this is the beginning of a beautiful friendship,' and the two walk off together into the night.

Gender roles

In the world of Casablanca, men are expected to be largely unemotional, manly providers, decision makers and protectors. This is not surprising given the time in which the movie was made and is set. Stereotypically male issues such as war and patriotism were represented on screen by a film industry dominated by men. Therefore, the masculinity in Casablanca is based on well-established ideas of duty, honour and courage. All of those in power, regardless of their political viewpoints, are men. They are expected to rise to the occasion and take charge of the situation in which they find themselves. Because he seems at ease with this rigid gender stereotype, Rick is not particularly restricted by being expected to conform to the societal norms of the time. His attitude is reflective of the time; during

World War II, it would not have done for a man to be shown as weak, indecisive or overly concerned with private happiness at a time when they were required to subjugate their own personal feelings and instead concentrate on the needs of the majority of their countrymen and allies. Rick, therefore, makes the 'correct' choice at the end of the film and seems sure that what he has decided is best for society as a whole. He tells a tearful Ilsa that he is 'no good at being noble, but it doesn't take much to see that the problems of three little people don't amount to a hill of beans in this crazy world'. Ilsa must go with Laszlo and – like a good and dutiful wife – be there to support him in his great work. Rick's decisive nature, his assumption of responsibilities and his obvious strength make him an admirable figure in the world of the text.

Not all the men in the film are able to take control of their lives and protect those closest to them. The Hungarian couple – Jan and Annina Brandel – are desperate to escape to America, but Jan cannot secure them an exit visa. He lacks money and guile and is no match for the unscrupulous men who run Casablanca. Believing there is no other option, Annina is on the brink of sleeping with Renault in order to get a visa, but she turns to Rick for advice before so doing. Rick is the authority figure: the stoic decision maker, completely in control. In a telling, although affectionately meant comment, Annina tells Rick that Jan is 'such a boy' that she feels she must take charge and keep her intentions secret. Rick, the epitome of manly power, steps up and saves the day by fixing the roulette table so that Jan believes he has won enough money to buy the visas. It is worth noting that Rick does this rather than give the money to Annina; it suggests that the man must be left with his dignity and the belief that he has protected his wife.

Women are far more restricted than men in *Casablanca* by the gender roles imposed on them and are often objectified by the male characters. Rick treats his lover Yvonne with callous disregard, and Renault chides him for being so 'extravagant, throwing away women like that', speaking of women as if they were material possessions that can be kept or discarded on a whim. Renault routinely exploits women, trading sexual favours for exit visas, and Rick seems generally tolerant of such behaviour.

Women have very little power and control in the world of the text. Before he knows the identity of the woman accompanying Laszlo to Casablanca, Rick wonders why he doesn't just leave her and flee alone, as it would be easier. Renault replies that he 'has seen the woman' and implies that she is so lovely that Laszlo will want to keep her with him. The implication, of course, is that a woman's company or presence could only be a hindrance in times of crisis, and a man who was in danger would be better off without her. The only value a woman may have would be her physical attractiveness. Ilsa's beauty is her greatest asset, and the director ensures that we are constantly reminded of this. Her costumes are stylish and elegant, and she is shot in flatteringly soft focus in the close-ups. She, and all the women, are more brightly lit than the men so their features can be easily admired. Ilsa's beauty makes her an object of desire, and the implication is that what little power she possesses stems from her beauty. Attractiveness only carries Ilsa so far, however. She is not free to do exactly as she wishes, and her fortunes are tied to the men in her life. Ilsa herself says as much to Rick, telling him, 'You'll have to think for both of us, for all of us', when she cannot decide whether she should stay with Laszlo.

A rather disturbing insight into the cultural context of the text is revealed when we examine the double standards women are forced to deal with when it comes to morality and sexual freedom. Men are not judged harshly for exploiting women or sleeping with them outside of marriage, but the women most certainly are. Renault is presented as a loveable rogue and a man-about-town for ensuring that women are forced to exchange sexual favours for freedom. Early in the film, we see police herding people into the Palais de Justice. An Englishman asks a European what is going on and is told it is 'the customary round-up of refugees, liberals, and uh, of course, a beautiful young girl for Monsieur Renault, the Prefect of Police'. This news is delivered with a knowing smirk, as if it were understandable rather than abhorrent behaviour. Later in the film, when Rick ensures the Brandels win enough money at the roulette table to buy their exit visas, Renault – who had expected Annina to sleep with him to gain their freedom – chides Rick, accusing him of interfering with his 'little romances'. Once again, there is no suggestion that sexual exploitation of this sort is reprehensible, but rather it is seen as evidence of Renault's roguish charm. Renault says he will forgive Rick but will be back to gamble the next night with 'a breathtaking blonde' and will be 'very happy if she loses'.

Rick may not be as immoral as Renault, but he too feeds into the double standard. He is not judged for sleeping with Yvonne, but she is portrayed as a promiscuous drunk and Rick's complete lack of concern for her feelings when she asks if she will see him again is seen as a natural result of her having made herself available to him. There is a telling moment in the film when Rick instructs his barman, Sacha, to bring the belligerent and intoxicated Yvonne home but warns him to 'come right back'. Sacha's face registers his disappointment as he had clearly planned to take advantage of the drunken, spurned Yvonne. However, he is not portrayed in a negative fashion as a result; the fault – it is implied – would be purely Yvonne's and would be further evidence of her loose morals.

Values

Casablanca is an American film released during World War II. It serves as a political allegory of the war, specifically the US attitude towards joining the Allied forces in Europe. The action of the film takes place in December 1941 (Rick references the date in his conversation with Sam after Ilsa's visit: 'Sam, if it's December 1941 in Casablanca, what time is it in New York?') At first, Rick represents the American isolationist approach to the war. Americans had paid a heavy price for taking part in World War I and there was a strong feeling among the citizenry that they should not intervene in European conflicts again. However, when the Japanese attacked Pearl Harbour in December 1941, America could no longer remain neutral.

In *Casablanca*, Rick symbolises the change in American attitudes as the popular mood swung from isolationism to joining the Allied forces, whatever the cost. Rick's initial isolationist viewpoint shows that he, like many of the American public, has yet to be convinced that self-sacrifice is the noblest course of action. His repetition of the line, 'I stick my neck out for nobody' seems callous and ignoble, and Renault's praise of his 'wise foreign policy' reinforces the idea that Rick is, for the moment, on the wrong side of history.

When Strasser questions a seemingly disinterested Rick about his allegiances, Renault assures him that 'Rick is completely neutral about everything.' Although Rick tells Strasser that he sees the 'point of view of the hound' as well as the fox and seems unwilling to take sides, it is made clear that he actually has a strong moral code. Renault suspects Rick may help Laszlo escape, claiming he is at heart 'a sentimentalist'. Rick denies it, but Renault reminds him that in 1935 he 'ran guns to Ethiopia' and 'fought in Spain on the Loyalist side' in 1936. Renault's comment that Rick 'always happened to be fighting on the side of the underdog' reinforces the idea that Rick is far from the disinterested cynic he pretends to be.

The portrayal of other characters in *Casablanca* is also a political message. Captain Renault initially represents the Vichy puppet state but at the end of the film he leaves with Rick to join a resistance group in Brazzaville. Italy was allied with Germany at the time the film was made, and so in this American film, the Italian characters are shown in a negative light. The Italian officer Tonelli is desperate for Major Strasser's attention but is largely ignored by the more powerful man. The implication is that those who join the wrong side will be used but not treated with any respect.

Casablanca espouses anti-fascist views. Those who were targeted by the Nazi regime are deliberately held up as admirable figures in the film. The customers in Rick's café are culturally diverse and all, bar the Germans, are treated with respect. Signor Ferrari, owner of the Blue Parrot, represents the viewpoint of those who think life is cheap. He offers to buy Sam, but Rick answers stiffly that he does not 'buy or sell human beings'. Ferrari is unapologetic and insinuates that Rick is missing a trick by not engaging in such dealings: 'That's too bad. That's Casablanca's leading commodity. In refugees alone we could make a fortune if you would work with me through the black market.' Ferrari's willingness to prey on the vulnerable shows him, and by extension, his countrymen, in a very poor light.

The ending of the film and Rick's ultimate act of self-sacrifice consolidate the idea that the greater good is more important than personal happiness. Rick ensures that Ilsa and Laszlo escape together and, in one of the most often-quoted lines from the film, tells Ilsa, 'I've got a job to do, too. Where I'm going you can't follow. What I've got to do you can't be any part of. Ilsa, I'm no good at being noble, but it doesn't take much to see that the problems of three little people don't amount to a hill of beans in this crazy world. Someday you'll understand that.' Rick's nobility and patriotism persuade Captain Renault to abandon his post and switch allegiances.

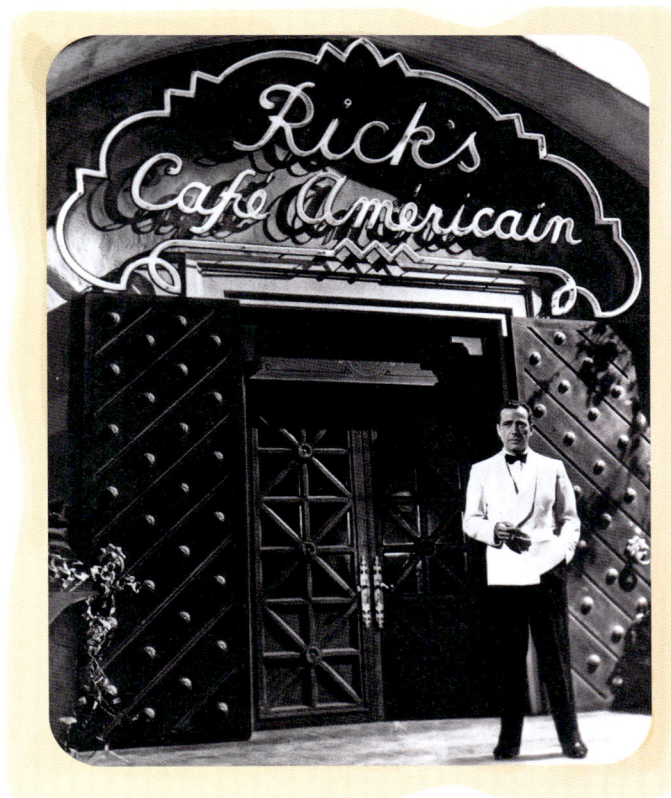

Comparative study: Cultural context

| *Room* | *The Crucible* | *Casablanca* |

Control and violence affect the lives of the characters to different extents in each of the three texts.

Ma is physically and mentally damaged by her incarceration in Room. Old Nick kidnaps Ma, keeps her imprisoned in a 'twenty-first-century dungeon', and repeatedly rapes her over the course of seven years. Before Jack's birth, Ma made an attempt to escape but Old Nick broke her wrist and told her that he would abandon her to starve to death if she ever tried to do that again. Her physical suffering is coupled with intense emotional pain. Her first pregnancy resulted in a stillbirth because Old Nick refused to allow her any medical treatment. He 'just stood there' and watched while Ma begged for help.

One of the most horrifying aspects of Old Nick's violent control over Ma and Jack is that he thinks he is a kind benefactor rather than a vicious monster. He tells Ma that there are 'Plenty girls who would thank their lucky stars for a setup like this,' and complains that Jack hides from him, as he 'Never laid a hand' on the little boy.

Ma is an incredibly strong and brave young woman, and she is determined to spare Jack the horrors she has endured. That is why she hides him from Old Nick and pretends that Room is the entire world, so Jack will not know what he is missing.

One difference between the characters in *Room* and *The Crucible* is that it is obvious from the very start that Ma and Jack are hugely affected by controlling violence. Every aspect of their lives is under Old Nick's control. Early in *The Crucible*, we certainly see that in a societal sense the characters' lives are affected by the Puritan regime. However, it is only as the play progresses that we see the full impact of this. Initially, John Proctor appears to be powerful enough to resist the Puritan control in Salem. He has little time for Reverend Parris and makes his feelings clear. Proctor says that he stopped attending church because the last time he heard Parris preach, he 'spoke so long on deeds and mortgages' that Proctor felt 'it were an auction' rather than a religious meeting. However, as the plot unfolds, we see that John Proctor is not as immune from societal pressure as he might like. Rumours of his affair with Abigail Williams have spread and Proctor has to make some difficult decisions. He misjudges Abigail's feelings for him and, as a result, finds he and his wife are on the receiving end of her vindictive accusations. The theocratic regime is so powerful that Proctor, along with many of his friends and neighbours, are sentenced to death in trials that are a travesty of justice. **In *Room*, on the other hand, Ma and Jack succeed in escaping their captor and have a chance to rebuild their lives.**

In both texts, one of the most horrifying aspects of violent control is that those who wield it believe they are on the side of right. Old Nick, in *Room*, believes he is hard-done-by when Ma is not grateful to him for what he sees as care and protection. In reality, of course, he is an incredibly cruel and evil man who brutalises his victim over many years. However, Old Nick is an aberration and is not reflective of any societal norm. The situation in *The Crucible* is more appalling in that it is those in authority who are torturing and killing innocent victims. Just as Old Nick considers himself a benefactor, so the church leaders and judges in Salem are convinced

Of all three texts, *Casablanca* makes it clearest from the outset that the characters live in a world of violence and oppression. The film opens with credits displayed over a map of Africa and a voiceover explaining the 'tortuous, roundabout refugee trail' for people desperate to escape war-torn Europe. Those who make it as far as Casablanca are far from free, however. They still must contend with a French regime which is sympathetic to the Third Reich, and the audience is repeatedly reminded of the dangers faced by anyone who falls foul of the authorities. We see an example of this early in the film when the police hunt for the killer of the German couriers. During the round-up, a man whose papers have expired runs from the police and is shot dead. **While control and violence gradually decrease over the course of *Room* and increase over the course of *The Crucible*, *Casablanca* never allows us to forget that everyone is in danger in wartime.**

In *Casablanca*, as in *The Crucible*, it is those in authority who pose the greatest risk. A smooth-talking pickpocket explains to an English couple that they are watching the 'customary round-up of refugees, liberals and, uh, of course, a beautiful young girl for Monsieur Renault, the Prefect of Police'. This brief summary of the situation highlights the abuse of power by those in control of Casablanca: the innocent are victimised and sexual violence is also tolerated. **As is the case in the other two texts, those who exert oppressive control over others are convinced that they are on the side of right.** Major Strasser is the face of the Third Reich in the film. He clearly believes he is a civilised, sophisticated man but this veneer slips on occasion and we see the cruelty and violence of which he is capable. Strasser wants Laszlo to betray

→

Room	The Crucible	Casablanca
Eventually, however, Ma has good reason to believe that her life and Jack's are in real danger from Old Nick because he has lost his job and may lose his house. Ma explains to Jack that if the bank forecloses, they could discover Room and Old Nick would 'never let that happen'. Although she doesn't tell Jack exactly what she thinks Old Nick would do, we can imagine. Ma and Jack succeed in escaping Room but the damage Old Nick has caused both is not easily mended. Both find it difficult to adjust to the freedom of the outside world.	**they are good people.** Judge Danforth believes his power is bestowed upon him by God, and he refuses to accept the trials are deeply flawed, even if blameless people are sent to their deaths as a result. Were he to concede that the trials were flawed, he would have to admit the situation is outside his control. He takes no notice of Hale's pleas or Proctor's impassioned speech, ordering that those convicted be hanged 'high over the town'. Danforth's power lies in his reputation as a judge; if he were to admit that he had made a mistake, he would lose all credibility. Danforth represents those involved in persecuting alleged communists in Miller's America. The abuses of power in the play serve to remind us of what some in authority are capable of if they feel threatened.	the other resistance fighters, but Laszlo scornfully refuses, saying he is unlikely to give in to the demands of the Nazi regime as he resisted them for a year in a concentration camp where 'more persuasive methods' were used. Strasser is too polished to openly threaten Laszlo, but it is obvious what he means when he tells Laszlo it would be 'unfortunate' if something were happen to him while trying to escape. The veiled menace is clear, and it is reinforced when Strasser gleefully tells Laszlo and Ilsa that Ugarte is dead. Renault chimes in here, telling the dismayed couple, 'We haven't quite decided whether he committed suicide or died trying to escape'. **Just as Danforth in *The Crucible* is willing to sanction torture and murder if it adds to his power, so Strasser will use any means at his disposal to achieve his ends.**
Jack had never realised he was a prisoner, so there are times when he longs for the security of the only home he has ever known. He felt safe in Room but Ma lived in constant fear. When they leave Room, Ma feels she is gaining some control over her life while Jack feels he is losing it.	**While in *Room*, Jack and Ma succeed in escaping from the controlling, violent situation, the opposite is true in *The Crucible*.** The hysteria generated by Abigail Williams and the other young girls increases dramatically over the course of a few months. When Mary Warren returns from court in Act Two and Proctor asks her if it is true that fourteen women have been arrested on suspicion of witchcraft, she says, 'There be thirty-nine now' and she breaks down as she tells him that some are now being sentenced to death. The witchcraft trials increase the church's control in Salem, and eventually John and Elizabeth Proctor also find themselves accused.	The ending of *Casablanca* introduces the idea of a shift in the balance of power. **Like the other two texts, it shows that people can triumph over adversity, even though such a victory comes at a cost. The ending of the film is more similar to *Room* than it is to *The Crucible* in that the characters may be scarred but they have a chance of a future.** Rick has killed Strasser and ensured Laszlo and Ilsa escape to Lisbon. Captain Renault has decided against having Rick arrested for shooting Strasser and has, in fact, decided to join the Resistance. He suggests that he and Rick leave Casablanca and join a Free French group in Brazzaville. He symbolically throws a bottle of Vichy water in the bin and he and Rick walk off together. The political message was clear to the audience of the time: Vichy France was a threat that could not be ignored and anyone who sided with the Allies needed to take a firm stance against Petain and any other Nazi sympathisers or pacifiers. The outcome of the war is still unclear, but in this story at least, the right side appears to be gaining control. **Like Ma and John Proctor, Rick shows that no regime or individual, however violent and oppressive, can take away a person's integrity.**
The novel ends before Old Nick's court case but Ma's lawyer tells her he will spend most of the rest of his life in jail. That is not the end of the story, however, as Ma and Jack will have to live with the repercussions of his violence for the rest of their lives.	**In *Room*, Ma and Jack are scarred by their experience, but at least they escape Old Nick's clutches and have a chance to start their lives anew. *The Crucible*, on the other hand, ends with Rebecca Nurse and John Proctor being led to their deaths.** However, there is a note of hope. Proctor loses his life, but he has far more moral authority than those who condemn and convict him. Even during his final hours in a jail cell, Proctor manages to take control of his destiny to a certain extent. He is equally unmoved by Danforth's threats and Hale's pleas. While many of those around him choose to capitulate rather than stand up for what is right, Proctor refuses to yield to an oppressive regime. Although he would be spared the hangman's noose were he to allow his signed confession to be shown to the people of Salem, Proctor does not agree to Danforth's demand. Danforth is bewildered but Proctor cries out, 'How may I live without my name? I have given you my soul; leave me my name'. In the end, John Proctor has defied those in control and he goes to his death having regained his honour and his courage.	

→

Room	The Crucible	Casablanca

The three texts present us with different views of love and marriage.

The message of *Room* is that the founding principles of any loving relationship are kindness and care. This is something Old Nick does not understand at all. He believes that he has a relationship of sorts with Ma because he has kidnapped her and held her captive in a soundproof shed. Bizarrely, he thinks he is keeping her safe from 'perverts' and sees himself as her protector and provider. He views her requests for food, clothes or renovations as 'hassling' him and says she should appreciate how lucky she is to be taken care of. In Old Nick's twisted view of the world, Ma is cast in the role of nagging wife while he is the long-suffering husband.

Because the focus of *Room* is the relationship between Ma and Jack, there is little emphasis on other relationships. However, Jack does see functional partnerships when he meets his extended family. Although Grandma and Grandpa separated, Grandma found love once more with the kind and generous Steppa. Initially, Ma is suspicious of this new man in her mother's life, commenting critically that Steppa is 'nearly seventy and stinks of dope . . . She must have been on the rebound.' Steppa, however, proves he has far more to him than Ma gives him credit for. He supports Grandma every way he can and accepts the appearance of Ma and Jack in a way that Ma's own father was unable to do. Steppa is tactful and sensitive, defusing arguments between Grandma and

In both *Room* and *The Crucible*, we see the difference between true, unselfish love and destructive, possessive love.

Abigail Williams and Old Nick demonstrate a damaging, warped view of relationships. Both are willing to do whatever it takes to possess the person they want to be with. However, there is a difference in that Abigail did have good reason to believe John Proctor cared for her, whereas Old Nick merely snatched a stranger from the street. As a result, we have some sympathy for Abigail at the start of the play, though far less so as her malicious, manipulative ways lead to terrible suffering and death.

Abigail was a servant in the Proctors' home when, as she says, Proctor 'took me from my sleep and put knowledge in my heart'. She cannot understand how he now expects her to 'tear the light' from her eyes. Abigail is a young girl and Proctor is a married man in his forties, so it is hardly surprising that they should view the relationship very differently. However, Abigail's reaction to rejection shows that her love for Proctor is deeply possessive and dangerous. **Just as Old Nick's twisted view of relationships makes him believe he is in the right to behave as he does, so Abigail demonstrates that she is willing to do anything, even have Elizabeth killed, if it helps her to get what she wants. Neither Abigail nor Old Nick accept that you cannot force another person to be with you and expect them to view you with anything but loathing.**

Abigail is different to Old Nick in that she has a dual role: she plays a key role in a love triangle, but she also represents those who rip people's lives apart through feeding into hysteria and cruelty. She persuades the other girls

Casablanca, like *Room* and *The Crucible*, focuses on the value of selfless love. Like *The Crucible*, *Casablanca* is a blend of personal and political. In *The Crucible*, we see the terrible damage that can be done when people put their own desires before the greater good.

Just as in the play, there is a love triangle in the film. The key difference is that in *Casablanca*, all three characters act nobly and selflessly in the end. Curtiz, like Miller, is delivering an important political message through the characters' relationships. In *Casablanca*, that message is that 'the problems of three little people don't amount to a hill of beans in this crazy world'.

Rick's nobility and selflessness are not apparent in the early stages of the film. His first meeting with Ilsa in Casablanca is fraught with tension. The conversation between Rick and Ilsa is loaded with hints of a difficult past. They recall their last meeting in Paris, on the day the Germans entered the city. Rick says it was 'Not an easy day to forget', but it is obvious he does not simply mean because of the invasion. The undercurrents of anger on Rick's part and sadness on Ilsa's make love appear a destructive and negative force at this point in the film.

We see an important difference between the three texts emerge as the plot progresses. Abigail is never improved by her feelings for Proctor: she becomes increasingly vindictive and cruel as she realises he will not leave his wife for her. She resembles Old Nick in *Room* in this way: both characters react violently and

→

Room	The Crucible	Casablanca
Ma in the clinic: 'We should let these folks rest,' and coping admirably with the challenge of helping Jack adapt to a strange new world. Steppa and Grandma's relationship is undoubtedly a positive force in Jack and Ma's lives.	to join her in condemning blameless neighbours, simply to achieve her own desires. Because of her determination to be with John Proctor, Abigail is willing to see innocent people tortured and killed. **In *The Crucible*, the focus on the Proctors' marriage demonstrates that marital love can be a positive and nurturing force, just as it is in Grandma and Steppa's relationship. The Proctors' situation is far more extreme than Grandma and Steppa's but in both cases, love is a positive force in troubled times. One couple has to cope with the challenge posed by the return of a traumatised daughter and grandson to the family, while the other is faced with the horrors of the witch trials coming on top of an already troubled marriage.** The Proctors' relationship is put to the ultimate test during the trials. Abigail Williams accuses Elizabeth of witchcraft and John sacrifices his good name by admitting to the court that he slept with Abigail. He hopes that by so doing, he will prove that Abigail is motivated by spite and lust: 'She thinks to dance with me on my wife's grave.' He calls Elizabeth his 'dear good wife' and says he would not have risked his reputation but to save her. Elizabeth is not in court when her husband confesses, and when she is called in to corroborate his story and thus save herself, she refuses to admit that there was ever anything between Proctor and Abigail. She does so out of love and loyalty, just as Proctor confessed the affair for the same reasons. In Salem, hysteria, jealousy and cruelty lead to the breakdowns of relationships on a social and personal level. The Proctors' relationship alone shows that people are capable of rising above such sentiments.	spitefully to anyone who stands up to them. Rick, on the other hand, undergoes a positive transformation. When Ilsa visits him in his apartment, he realises that she really loved him all along and he understands her reason for leaving him. From this point on, Rick abandons his earlier vow to 'stick [his] neck out for nobody'. He risks all to help Laszlo and Ilsa in their bid for freedom. Rick and Ilsa's relationship has at last become a positive force in their lives and hope dawns once more. Rick's love for Ilsa has rekindled his moral code. Laszlo accepts Rick's help even though he knows there is something between the two. Again, he behaves decently and kindly, showing Ilsa he does not blame her for falling for Rick when she believed he, Laszlo, was dead. **While all texts show that those who love one another deeply and selflessly are admirable, *Casablanca* stresses the nobility of people putting the greater good before their own needs.** If that means the end of a relationship, so be it. This was an important message in wartime when people were being asked to part with their loved ones, possibly forever. On the one hand, Rick's ultimate act of self-sacrifice at the end of the film leaves us in no doubt that he is a true wartime hero. Yet at the same time, his courage and nobility mean an end to his and Ilsa's love. He insists that she and Laszlo escape together while he remains behind to join the Resistance. Sacrifices must be made, and those who fight and those who are left behind both suffer for the greater good.

→

Room	The Crucible	Casablanca

Each text presents us with a different view of gender roles.

Because Jack is raised in isolation, with only Ma for company and occasional glimpses of Old Nick through the slats of the wardrobe, he is unaware of any expectations surrounding his gender. The only time Ma uses gender stereotypes is when she is trying to persuade Jack to go along with her escape plan. She taps into the fairytale notion of the brave prince who saves the princess, calling her son 'my brave Prince JackerJack'.

Once the escape has succeeded, Jack has to learn how to cope in the world outside Room. One of the things he finds strange is that some people expect boys and girls to behave differently. On a trip to the shopping mall with his uncle and aunt, Jack spots a backpack with a picture of his beloved Dora the Explorer on it. He is delighted but his uncle tries to convince him to buy a 'cool' Spider-Man bag instead. He is unhappy at the thought of his nephew having a pink bag, although he gives in when Jack insists. A stranger in the mall assumes Jack is a girl and his aunt explains that she was misled by Jack's long hair and pink bag. Through Jack's experience, we see the assumptions made about children from an early age and the limits that might be put on them as a result.

Jack is fortunate to have positive male influences in his life when he leaves Room. Steppa does not consider there to be men's and women's roles in the home and he helps Jack with everything from cooking to playing with Lego. Uncle Paul plays football with Jack and does his best to make him part of the family.

Gender roles in *The Crucible* are more restrictive than in *Room* and strict gender stereotypes prevail. Unlike *Room*, in which Jack gradually comes to understand that there are certain expectations around gender but is not forced to conform to them, the characters in *The Crucible* live in an oppressive, patriarchal society. The men hold all the power and the women are restricted to servitude, marriage and motherhood. If a woman steps outside these roles, she is subject to harsh criticism or worse. The unfairness of the gender roles in the play is obviously evident in the witch trials, where the majority of those accused are women, but we also see it in the double standard when it comes to sexuality. **Unlike *Room*, in which Ma is deliberately shown to have had an active sex life before her abduction and is not judged in the slightest for that, women's sexuality is subjected to harsh scrutiny in the play.** Women in *The Crucible* who are in touch with their sexuality are presented as evil temptresses who prey on men's natural sexual desire. We see this in the relationship between John Proctor and Abigail Williams. She is a seventeen-year-old girl in the Proctor household and he is a married man in his forties, a landowner and a person of repute in Salem, yet it is she who is blamed for the affair. Religious imagery is used to shape our opinion of Abigail Williams. Abigail tells Proctor the effect their relationship had on her, 'I look for John Proctor that took me from my sleep and put knowledge in my heart'. This is an allusion to the story of Adam and Eve in the Bible. They ate the forbidden fruit in the Garden of Eden and immediately lost their innocence. Eve is the temptress in the story, and the originator of sin on earth, just as Abigail is presented as the reason for Proctor's downfall.

In *Room*, Emma Donoghue surrounds Jack with positive and supportive role

Casablanca does not present us with quite as negative or restrictive a view of gender roles as does *The Crucible*, but neither is the attitude as positive and open as in *Room*. Like the play, the world of the film is patriarchal, albeit not quite as strictly so. Both the play and the film reflect the time in which they are set. Stereotypically male issues such as war and patriotism were represented on screen by a film industry dominated by men. All of those in power in the film, regardless of their political viewpoints, are men.

As in *The Crucible*, a rather disturbing insight into the cultural context of *Casablanca* is revealed when we examine the double standards women are forced to deal with when it comes to morality and sexual freedom. Men are not judged harshly for exploiting women or sleeping with them outside of marriage, but the women most certainly are, just as Abigail is subjected to far harsher scrutiny than is Proctor. Renault is presented as a loveable rogue and a man-about-town for ensuring that women are forced to exchange sexual favours for freedom. Early in the film, we see police herding people into the Palais de Justice. An Englishman asks a European what is going on and is told it is 'the customary round-up of refugees, liberals, and, uh, of course, a beautiful young girl for Monsieur Renault, the Prefect of Police'. This news is delivered with a knowing smirk, as if it were understandable rather than abhorrent behaviour.

In *Room*, Ma and Steppa in particular support Jack in being whoever he wants to be, and they reject the notion of gender roles. In the play and the film, however, there is no character who breaks the mould and challenges the gender stereotypes.

→

Room	The Crucible	Casablanca
With very little fuss, Jack cuts off his long ponytail and is thus more easily identifiable as a boy. He is gradually fitting into a world that has certain expectations of how a boy should look and behave, but there is no implication that this is a negative outcome. He makes his own choices. He is surrounded by loving, supportive family members who accept him however he acts or appears, which is ultimately all that matters.	**models who help him to be whatever type of boy he wants to be. In *The Crucible*, there is no such positive message. The negative view of women as leading men astray is reinforced when Elizabeth Proctor feeds into the idea that her husband is not really to blame for the sin of adultery.** At the end of the play, she and Proctor speak openly in the prison. She says she has had time to look deep into her heart and that she now realises 'It needs a cold wife to prompt lechery'. She claims that in calling himself a sinner, Proctor has nobly taken her sins upon himself and that she kept a 'cold' house because she did not consider herself attractive enough to deserve his love. This attitude allows Proctor to be presented as a tragic hero and a man wronged by both his lover and his wife.	Rick may not be as immoral as Renault, but he too feeds into the double standard. He is not judged for sleeping with Yvonne, but she is portrayed as a promiscuous drunk and Rick's complete lack of concern for her feelings when she asks if she will see him again is seen as a natural result of her having made herself available to him. There is a telling moment in the film when Rick instructs his barman, Sacha, to bring the belligerent and intoxicated Yvonne home but warns him to 'come right back'. Sacha's face registers his disappointment as he had clearly planned to take advantage of the drunken, spurned Yvonne. However, he is not portrayed in a negative fashion as a result; the fault – it is implied – would be purely Yvonne's and would be further evidence of her loose morals.

Room	The Crucible	Casablanca

Value systems play an important role in the central characters' happiness and success.

Room	The Crucible	Casablanca
Room is, at heart, a story of the value and importance of parenting. Despite the horrific conditions of her imprisonment, Ma finds the strength and purpose to carry on because she has Jack to take care of. She explains to a TV interviewer, after her release from Room, that Jack 'was everything' to her during her captivity. The message is clear: it is in loving and being loved that we find our sense of self. Ma does her utmost to care for Jack in incredibly difficult circumstances. She puts him first and is willing to sacrifice anything to ensure he has what he needs. Jack believes that she is 'not very hungry' when food runs low because Ma wants him to have what little there is. When escape	**While *Room* centres on family values, *The Crucible* is largely concerned with communal values. This is because, unlike *Room*, *The Crucible* is meant to be an allegory of an important social and political issue at the time it was written. Both texts explore the extent to which a person's value system can help them overcome adversity and bring them happiness. Ma demonstrates that being true to one's own core beliefs gives life a sense of purpose even in the worst of situations. Miller, on the other hand, shows how adherence to a strict and unyielding code of behaviour which has little room for individual beliefs can cause great pain and suffering in any time and place.** The repressive society in Salem ensures that the Puritans keep their thoughts to themselves as much as possible, creating a great deal of pent-up frustration. The witch trials allow for an explosion of all this resentment and dislike. They are an ideal opportunity for those who want to pursue	***Casablanca* is more similar to *The Crucible* than it is to *Room* in that both the play and the film reflect political issues that were relevant at the time they were written. However, there is a difference in that Miller took an existing story and adapted it to fit his message, whereas *Casablanca* is entirely invented. Therefore, the characters are more clearly designed to be representative of prevailing attitudes and values and the message is more heavy-handed than that in *The Crucible*. At the start of the film, Rick – like John Proctor – is not being completely true to himself and is not particularly happy as a result.** In *Casablanca*, Rick symbolises the change in American attitudes as the popular mood swung from isolationism to joining the Allied forces, whatever the cost. Rick's initial isolationist viewpoint shows that he, like many of the American public, has yet to be convinced that self-sacrifice is the noblest course of action. His repetition of the line,

→

Room	*The Crucible*	*Casablanca*
from Room becomes imperative, Ma hatches a plan that has a chance of saving Jack. She knows, and Jack comes to see, that her plan is risky. If Old Nick discovers that Jack is not dead, Ma's life will be in jeopardy if he decides to rush back to Room and exact his revenge. Nevertheless, Ma believes her fate is irrelevant as long as Jack is alright: 'You're the one who matters, though. Just you.'	personal vendettas to do so under the guise of adherence to religious law. Thomas Putnam, for example, uses the trials to buy the land of those who are convicted of witchcraft. His wife Ann is jealous of Rebecca Nurse's large family and accuses Rebecca of having used witchcraft to murder the Putnam children: 'You think it God's work you should never lose a child, nor grandchild either, and I bury all but one?' **At the start of the play, the townspeople are free in a way Ma is not, but their lives are also restricted, and their attitudes dictated to them by an intolerant regime. In both texts, the characters have to fight to live according to their own codes.**	'I stick my neck out for nobody' seems callous and ignoble, and Renault's praise of his 'wise foreign policy' reinforces the idea that Rick is, for the moment, on the wrong side of history. **Whereas Ma is true to her own values from the start of the text, both Rick and John Proctor take some time to do what they know to be right.**
The novel shows us that there is no single definition of family and that a shared value system is more important than biological bonds. Old Nick is Jack's father, but he is unspeakably cruel to his son, calling him a 'freak' and keeping him imprisoned in Room with Ma. He does not hesitate to punish Ma and Jack by depriving them of food, heat and light if they anger him. He is an extreme example of a warped sense of values, of course, but when Ma and Jack escape Room, we see that Grandpa is also unkind to Jack, albeit far, far less so, because he irrationally blames him for the accident of his birth. He shudders when he looks at the little boy, seeing Old Nick every time he does so. Steppa, in contrast, immediately accepts Jack and shows him all the loving support he should have received from Grandpa. Steppa teaches Jack how to navigate his way in a new and confusing world, and never becomes angry when he makes mistakes. Like Ma, he values kindness, acceptance, patience and love above all else.	**Unlike Ma, who is willing to sacrifice anything if it helps and supports her beloved son, the characters in Salem are expected to give up a great deal to maintain the communal, Puritan values.** John Proctor finds this attitude difficult to take. He is expected to attend church regularly but is unwilling to do so because he believes Reverend Parris is a hypocrite who pays lip service only to the values he espouses. He stands up for his personal beliefs, accusing Parris of hardly mentioning God anymore and being too concerned with material things. **Proctor, like Ma, has a strong set of core values and he does his best to maintain them despite the restrictions of the world in which he lives. Like Ma, he is put to the test. Ma is forced to make a choice between her own life and a chance for Jack to escape Room. She puts her love for her son before her own needs and, happily, both she and Jack are freed. Proctor also has to choose between himself and a loved one.** He has a terrible secret: he cheated on his wife with their servant, Abigail Williams, and he does not want this to become public knowledge. However, when his wife is charged with witchcraft, Proctor sacrifices his reputation in an effort to save her. He tells the court that Abigail falsely accused Elizabeth in an effort to remove her rival.	**Rick, like John Proctor, is living under an oppressive and corrupt regime. Both chafe at the attitudes of those around them and become increasingly dissatisfied.** Although Rick does not openly rebel in the early stages of the film, the signs are there. We see an example of this when Signor Ferrari, owner of the Blue Parrot, offers to buy Sam, but Rick answers stiffly that he does not 'buy or sell human beings'. Ferrari is unapologetic and insinuates that Rick is missing a trick by not engaging in such dealings: 'That's too bad. That's Casablanca's leading commodity. In refugees alone we could make a fortune if you would work with me through the black market.' **Rick, however, is not willing to go along with the status quo to that extent. Like John Proctor, he is not as concerned with material things as he is with his own moral code.** **In each of the three texts, the characters are faced with a difficult decision and in each case, they make a selfless choice.** The ending of the film and Rick's ultimate act of self-sacrifice consolidate the idea that the greater good is more important than personal happiness. Rick ensures that Ilsa and Laszlo escape together and, in one of the most often-quoted lines from the film, tells Ilsa, 'I've got a job to do, too. Where I'm going you can't follow. What I've got to do you can't be any part of. Ilsa, I'm no good at being noble, but it doesn't take much to see that the problems of three little people don't amount to a hill of beans in this crazy world. Someday you'll understand that.' Rick's nobility and patriotism persuade Captain Renault to abandon his post and switch allegiances.

→

Room	The Crucible	Casablanca
	Whereas Ma's selflessness leads to a chance of a better life for her and Jack, Proctor has no such luck. In fact, his values are tested to the limit in the final moments of the play. He is faced with a dilemma: if he signs a false confession, his life will be spared but his integrity will be destroyed. **Like Ma, Proctor is ultimately willing to give up his life for what he believes in.** He knows he will be hanged, but he also believes he has found 'some shred of goodness' in himself at last. In *Room*, we learn that those who live by a worthy set of values will win through in the end. **In *The Crucible*, the message is rather different. If the world in which you live is corrupt, then your values may not be enough to save you. However, it is better to die with your integrity intact than live a lie.**	The final message in *Casablanca* is more uplifting than that in *The Crucible*. While Rick has lost Ilsa, he still has a chance of a meaningful and successful life. **In that respect, the film is more similar to the novel than the play. There is no perfect happy ending but Ma and Rick are left with both their integrity and some hope for the future.**

Questions

2018 Leaving Certificate

1. **(a)** Identify at least one type of behaviour considered to be unacceptable within the world of one text on your comparative course. Explain why such behaviour is considered unacceptable in this cultural context and discuss the response or responses of society to such behaviour. Support your answer with reference to the text. (30)

   (b) With reference to two other texts on your comparative course, identify at least one type of behaviour considered to be unacceptable in the world of each of these texts. Compare why such behaviour is considered unacceptable in these cultural contexts and the response or responses of society to such unacceptable behaviour. Support your answer with reference to the texts.

   In response to 1. (b) you may refer to the same or different types of behaviour in each of your chosen texts. You may refer to the same or different type(s) of behaviour as those referred to in 1. (a) above. (40)

   OR

2. 'Aspects of cultural context affect the extent to which a character can be happy or successful within the world of a text.'

   Identify a central character in each of three texts on your comparative course. Compare the aspect of the cultural context in each of these texts that, in your opinion, most affects the extent to which your chosen characters are happy or successful. You may refer to the same or different aspects of cultural context in each of your chosen texts. Support your answer with reference to the texts. (70)

2016 Leaving Certificate

1. 'Understanding who holds power and who is powerless helps to reveal the cultural context in texts.'

   Compare how the distribution of power within each of three texts on your comparative course helps to reveal the cultural contexts in these texts. Support your answer with reference to your chosen texts. (70)

   OR

2. 'Central characters can be successful or unsuccessful in challenging aspects of the cultural context in texts.'

   (a) Discuss the extent to which at least one central character is successful or unsuccessful in challenging at least one aspect of the cultural context in one text on your comparative course. Support your answer with reference to the text. (30)

   (b) Compare the extent to which at least one central character, from each of two other comparative texts, is either successful or unsuccessful in challenging at least one aspect of the cultural context in these texts. Support your answer with reference to your chosen texts. You may refer to the same aspect or different aspects of the cultural contexts in your answers. (40)

Mode: Literary genre

Literary genre in *Room*

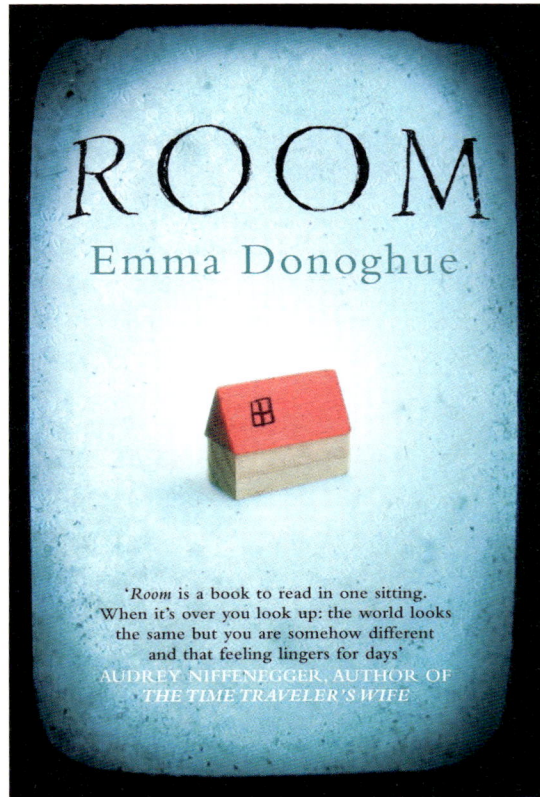

'Room' is Jack's name for the only world he ever knows until he is five years of age. The title of the book shows Room's importance in his life, both when he lives there and when he eventually escapes. Jack's mother, Ma, was kidnapped and held in Room by Old Nick. There she gave birth to two children, of whom only the second – Jack – survived.

Ma, in order to protect Jack, tells him that Room is the world and he believes her. He thinks everything he sees on television is fake, and he finds a certain contentment in his confinement. Because Jack has no knowledge of the world outside his 11-foot-square prison, he forms attachments to Room and the objects within it as a substitute for any other company or stimulation. He loves Meltedy Spoon, Table, Plant and the other objects in his little prison, talking about and to them as if they were sentient beings. He even strokes Table's scratches 'to make them better' as if Table were a living thing that could heal.

Ma does not share Jack's view of Room and she becomes increasingly aware that he cannot stay there forever. Two things prompt her to make an escape bid: Old Nick loses his job and will not be able to keep her and Jack hidden if the bank forecloses on his house, and Jack is rapidly growing up. Their situation is unsustainable, and she must do something. She tells Jack the truth about Room, but he does not want to accept it. Ma says that Room is 'only a tiny stinky piece' of the real world, but he is angry and upset by her claim. He loves Room and cannot see why she does not.

Comparative Study

Although Ma and Jack succeed in escaping Room, its importance in Jack's life does not diminish for a long time. He is bewildered and frightened by the outside world at first, and he struggles to cope. He wants to go back to bed in Room because it represents safety and familiarity. To Ma, it represents the exact opposite. Noreen, a nurse in the Cumberland Clinic, suggests Jack might be 'a bit homesick' and Ma is appalled, saying Room 'wasn't a *home*, it was a soundproofed cell'.

Room has shaped Jack physically and emotionally: he bumps into furniture because he cannot cope with different room layouts, and he finds it hard to interact appropriately with anyone other than Ma.

The novel begins and ends in Room. After they have lived in the outside world for a time, Jack wants to go and see Room one last time. Ma reluctantly agrees. Jack is surprised by how small Room is, and he realises he has forgotten details about it even in the short time since he and Ma escaped. He bids it farewell forever and he and Ma walk out the door.

Narrative style

All of Jack's narration is in the present tense, which is appropriate and effective. Small children live in the here and now, and Jack simply tells us what he is going through at any given moment. His narration voices his internal monologue and his limited language reflects his limited understanding of what he is going through.

Donoghue cleverly uses a light touch to show us the horror of Jack and Ma's imprisonment. Jack believes Room is the whole world, and Ma has done her utmost to spare him the reality of his situation. Therefore, he is a cheerful, chatty little boy who derives great pleasure from the simplest things. Like all children, he exaggerates the importance of what he is doing, claiming he and Ma have 'thousands' of tasks to complete every morning. His delight at playing with old eggshells and exercising in the confinement of Room only serves to make his situation more heartbreaking.

When Jack leaves Room, his narration falters a little. In Room, the vast majority of the dialogue took place between himself and Ma, and she obviously tailored her speech to suit him. Occasionally, he has to report Old Nick's words, but they are simple enough, by and large, even if the meaning is lost on Jack in most cases. Once in the outside world, Jack has to cope with a myriad of new experiences and strange people. As narrator, he faithfully reports what he witnesses but it stretches our imaginations a little thin at times. For example, he hears a television panel discussing his situation and recounts details such as one panellist saying, 'I would have thought the more relevant archetype here is Perseus – born to a walled-up virgin, set adrift in a wooden box, the victim who returns as hero'. Grandma turns off the TV and tells Jack it is time for 'pj's and teeth' before reading him *The Runaway Bunny*. The juxtaposition of the adult dialogue alongside the children's book is oddly jarring. It seems as if there is a second narrator now, filling in those bits of the outside world that Jack could not possibly comprehend, and it does not work as well as the seamless narration in the first half of the book.

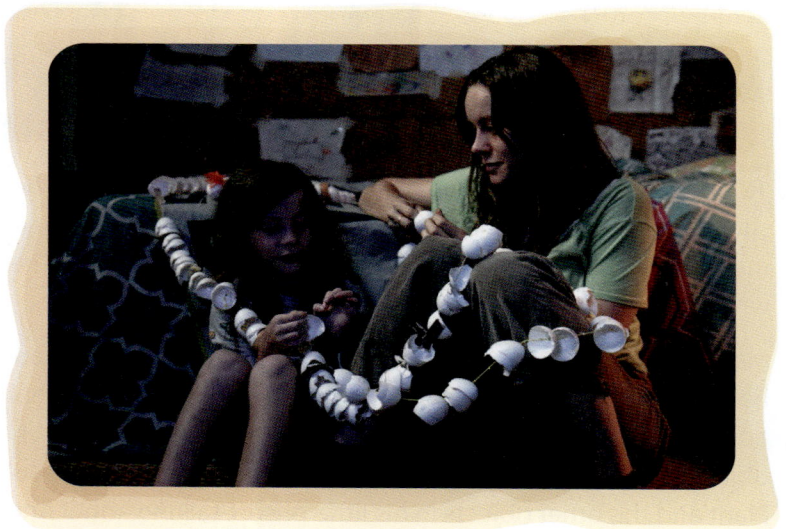

The decision to have the novel narrated by a five-year-old is not the only interesting aspect of style in *Room*. The structure of the story is not what we might originally have expected: leaving Room is not the end but a new beginning. It does not provide Ma and Jack with the perfect resolution to all their woes: it simply brings new obstacles for them to overcome. Because Jack was happy in Room, thanks to Ma's heroic efforts to spare him the knowledge of his confinement, he is initially unhappy in the outside world. Ma, on the other hand, is delighted to be out of the cell in which she had to endure seven years of rape, deprivation and abuse.

Creation of characters

In Jack, Emma Donoghue creates a little boy who is oddly typical of all young children, despite the terrible conditions he and his mother have to endure in Room. Jack finds wonder and joy in the simplest things, naming the objects around him – Table, Lamp, Wall – and giving them human characteristics.

Jack is a cute little boy but he is not cloyingly sweet: he has tantrums and is irritating at times, which is perfectly normal. He is angry that there are no candles on his fifth birthday cake and shouts that it is 'Stinky' and he doesn't want it. Ma tries to explain that she could not ask Old Nick for candles 'for Sundaytreat' because she needed painkillers for her tooth instead. Jack doesn't care, saying she needed the pills, not him. He comes around quite quickly and eats the cake with obvious enjoyment. Jack's imperfections are a large part of what make him a realistic and relatable character.

One of the limitations of Jack's narration is that he must record adult dialogue in such a way as to allow us to gain an understanding of their characters while still maintaining a five-year-old's speech patterns and reflecting an appropriate level of maturity. We can only experience the world through Jack, but even his narrow comprehension does not prevent us from grasping the subtler nuances of interactions, though they escape Jack completely. Jack does not realise, for example, Ma's concerns about his future. Yet Donoghue manages to convey Ma's anxiety by having Jack note that her face goes 'flat' when he says cheerfully that he will 'grow up to be a giant' some day. He knows he has said something wrong, but he does not know what, and he doesn't dwell on it. His simple comment, however, tells us a great deal about Ma's inner life. We can easily see how horrified and helpless she must feel as she is forced to face the dreadful reality: she cannot keep Jack with her or protect him forever. Jack knows there are days when Ma's face goes 'all blank' but he does not understand that she is sunk in the depths of depression on those occasions. He merely plays quietly, takes care of himself, and waits until Ma has recovered enough to interact with him again.

Ma is presented as a complex, well-developed character. Emma Donoghue said she did not want to make Ma a 'pure' innocent, stolen away before she could have experienced much of life. Ma mentions having had an abortion before she was kidnapped, for example, and indicates that her relationship with Grandma was not always plain sailing. When the pair argue after Ma's release from Room, Ma confides in Dr Clay that she would like to slap her mother sometimes. Dr Clay asks if she ever wanted to do that before she was kidnapped, and Ma says, 'Oh, sure.' Ma's reintegration into the world outside Room is difficult. She struggles with depression and, after an insensitive TV interviewer asks if she ever thought she was selfish in not asking her captor to leave the infant Jack at a hospital so he could be adopted into a family, Ma tries to take her own life. She recovers from the attempt and eventually manages to take Jack to live with her in an independent living facility. We do not know how Ma's life will be in the years after the book ends, but she is clearly damaged by her horrific ordeal. Donoghue's refusal to allow a simple, fairy-tale, happy-ever-after ending for Ma after her escape from Room leaves us with the impression of a credible, interesting character doing her best to cope in horrific circumstances.

A character like Old Nick is, perhaps, the hardest to convey effectively in a novel like this. Donoghue does not try to explore his mindset or give him any story outside that of his interactions with Jack and Ma. However, Old Nick's lurking in the shadows does not make him any less frightening. Before we ever meet him, we know he is to be feared. Jack has to hide from him at night, and he remarks that the air is different when Old Nick has been in Room. On the occasions where Jack reports Old Nick's speech, we hear the man's anger, petulance and sense of self-righteousness. When Ma asks Old Nick for vitamins, he complains about her whining and says he has been laid off for six months, asking, 'and have you had to worry your pretty little head?' On another occasion, he tells Ma she should be grateful to live in a place that is above ground with natural light. He says she is 'safe as houses' there and does not have to worry about drug pushers, drunk drivers or perverts. Jack is aware of the tension in the dialogue between Ma and Old Nick, but the irony of his captor's words is lost on him. Ma tries to placate Old Nick when he is angry, asking in what Jack recognises as 'that funny high voice' if he wants to go to bed. Jack is an innocent, so the implications of Ma's request are lost on him. However, Ma's anxious, apologetic responses to Old Nick's angry questions and her efforts to cajole him into bed to prevent him from taking a look at Jack in Wardrobe, help us to form an accurate picture of the terror Old Nick inspires in her.

Humour

There is nothing at all humorous about Ma and Jack's situation. It is a horrifying tale of abduction, rape, torture and suffering. But, at the heart of it, there is the relationship between mother and son, and the young boy's growing awareness of the outside world. Jack is an innocent child with a vivid imagination fuelled by Ma's efforts to provide as much stimulation and education as she possibly can in the limited confines of Room. For the first five years of Jack's life, Ma spares him the knowledge that he is imprisoned and, remarkably, he finds his own sort of happiness despite their terrible situation. O'Donoghue allows Jack's naïve narration to lighten what would otherwise be an unbearably dark and depressing tale.

Jack's inadvertent humour provides brief flashes of happiness for Ma. On his birthday, Jack is unhappy that she drew a picture of him while he slept, as he prefers them to always be awake and asleep together. He amuses Ma by saying he would 'prefer a surprise and me knowing'. Another time, Ma explains to Jack that the plant in Room is not flowering because it doesn't have enough food and he suggests it could be given his broccoli. This cunning attempt to avoid eating a food he dislikes shows that Jack is at heart just a typical small boy, and his suggestion makes Ma laugh.

Even in their darkest moments, Jack's ability to be happy astonishes Ma. After Ma annoys Old Nick by screaming at him to stay away from Jack, he cuts off the power to Room for several days. Ma explains to Jack that Old Nick wants to punish them. Jack is frightened and asks how he will do this. Ma is taken aback by the question, pointing out that he has forced them to endure cold, darkness and rotten food. Jack is relieved, saying that he thought Old Nick might try to separate them. Ma is delighted with his response, telling him he is wonderful. After the power cut, Ma decides they must escape Room and she explains her risky plan to Jack. He is being very serious when he says he will be 'scave', meaning a mixture of 'scared' and 'brave', but his 'word sandwiches' always amuse her. Jack and Ma have little to laugh about, but their ability to find joy and humour even in desperation shows the resilience of the human spirit.

Another function of humour in the novel is to show Jack's lack of understanding of the outside world. All children are unintentionally amusing at times, but Jack is even more so because he is unusually articulate, but also unusually ignorant of the simplest things. Grandma, after their first meeting, asks Jack if he knows the word 'bye-bye' and he says solemnly, 'Actually I know all the words'. This, he notices, makes her 'laugh and laugh', removing a little of the tension from her heartbreaking reunion with her daughter. Jack asks Ma why Grandma laughed when he wasn't making a joke, and she tells him it doesn't matter and it is 'always good to make people laugh'. Humour breaks the tension, not only for the characters in the book, but also for us, the readers. There are no laugh-out-loud moments, certainly, but there are enough gently amusing incidents to allow us to see the ordinary in the extraordinary.

Imagery and symbolism

Teeth may seem an unusual symbol, but they play an important role in *Room*. At the start of the book, Jack scrubs his carefully as part of his morning routine. Ma jokingly covers her eyes when he is finished, telling him that his teeth are so clean that they are 'dazzling' her. Ma's, on the other hand, are 'pretty rotted' because she didn't brush them for a long time. Ma's neglect of her dental hygiene is symbolic of a time in her life when she believed there was nothing worth living for. She began brushing them again when Jack was born because he gave her a sense of purpose and a reason to take care of herself. Still, despite her renewed attention to her teeth, they are badly damaged, as is she. Jack, on the other hand, is bursting with youth and potential, symbolised by his 'dazzling' teeth.

Ma loses one of her rotten teeth – Bad Tooth – and Jack is fascinated by it, carrying it with him as a symbol of Ma. When he is about to play dead in order to escape Room, Jack takes Tooth and tucks it down his sock. It is a piece of Ma that he can carry with him when he is without her for the first time ever. As Old Nick carries what he believes to be Jack's body to his truck, Jack talks to his mother's tooth, drawing comfort from the fact that it is 'a bit of Ma, a little bit of Ma's dead spit riding along with me'. Ma once told him that he was 'made of me, like my spit is', and he believes her tooth is therefore a part of their shared identity that unites them, even when they are apart. Jack succeeds in escaping Old Nick, and when he is in the police car, he tells Officer Oh that the dead tooth is his mother's. Jack doesn't know why the officer's face 'gets all hard' when she looks at Tooth close up, but it is because she sees the rotten tooth as a sign that Ma has been mistreated.

When Ma takes an overdose and Jack has to stay with Grandma, the tooth brings him some consolation. He keeps it with him so that he is linked with her in some way. Towards the end of the book, Jack realises that he has swallowed Tooth and is very distressed. Ma thinks it is 'just a thing', but to Jack, Tooth is a part of her and represents their connection and his identity. To Ma, it is a symbol of a time in her life when she was at her lowest ebb, physically and emotionally. She encourages Jack to forget about it, laughingly saying, 'Bye-bye rotten old tooth. End of story.' The story that is ending is not just Jack's possession of the tooth, however. Ma's willingness to say farewell to everything associated with Room is still at odds with Jack's need to hold on to the familiar. Jack is not yet ready to let go of the intense closeness they shared in Room, but the fact that Ma is gives us some hope that he too will reach that point in his life where he is ready to move on completely. Jack wonders if Tooth will pass through his system or if it will be 'hiding inside me in a corner forever'. Although the tooth may be gone, what it symbolises – his love for his mother and their strong bond – will certainly be with him forever.

The television is another important symbol in the novel. When he lives in Room, Jack believes that everything and everyone he sees on the television is fake. Sometimes he struggles with the comparisons between what he sees on the screen and what he observes in his limited world. For example, when snow falls on the skylight, Jack notices that 'TV snow's white but the real isn't'. Jack thinks everything outside room is 'Outer Space' and what happens there has no bearing on him. No matter how lifelike they may appear, objects and people on the screen are illusions. He enjoys a show called *The Runaway Bunny* and says that 'Bunnies are TV, but carrots are real'. He has eaten carrots, so he has a physical experience on which to base this belief. Bunnies, on the other hand, have never been in Room.

Jack uses what he has seen in programmes to make sense of some aspects of his captivity. For example, he calls their captor 'Old Nick' because he 'saw a cartoon about a guy that comes in the night'. Ma eventually decides Jack needs to know about the outside world but has great difficulty persuading him that much of what he sees on TV exists. She tries to explain that what he sees are 'pictures of real things' but Jack is incredulous and confused. He does not know why Ma should trick him this way, and it is too much for him to take in. He has lived his whole life in a world that is 11 foot square, and he cannot understand how all the things he has seen on the screen would fit in these narrow confines. Ma needs Jack to understand that she did not always live in Room, but when she describes her childhood home, Jack thinks she 'actually lived in TV one time'. Ma is frustrated by Jack's refusal to see that the television depicts the actual world outside Room, but his struggle to do so is symbolic of the difficulties all children face when they reach the end of their childhood. In Jack's case, his growing up is sudden and harsh: Ma fears for their lives and has to debunk all the myths she allowed Jack to believe for the first five years of his life if he is to escape successfully.

When Ma and Jack try to make their way in the world outside Room, television becomes an antagonistic force. The media intrudes on their privacy and they are plagued by paparazzi. Jack sees himself and Ma on a news report, accompanied by sensationalist commentary: 'The malnourished boy, unable to walk, is seen here lashing out convulsively at one of his rescuers.' Although Jack is excited to see himself on television, Ma and those who care for her know the damage that invasive and speculative coverage can do. In an effort to control the narrative once and for all, Ma agrees to a television interview, even though she doesn't want to do it. Her lawyer persuades her that if she appears on a popular show, she will have money for her and Jack's future. The interview, however, is exploitative and deeply damaging to Ma's fragile sense of self. The 'puffy-haired woman' conducting the interview veers from questions which anger Ma, such as asking her if she ever misses being behind a locked door to asking why Ma did not have Old Nick give Jack up for adoption and allow him the chance of a normal childhood. This line of questioning is clearly designed to feed the public's voyeuristic needs rather than a genuine effort to allow Ma to tell her story. The results are devastating: Ma is so traumatised by the suggestion that she denied Jack happiness that she tries to take her own life. This shows the power of television and the media in general: people's lives can be utterly destroyed in order to feed the public's need for drama and sensation.

Literary genre in *The Crucible*

There are two definitions for the word 'crucible' and both are relevant to the title of the play. A crucible is a container in which metals or other substances are heated to an extremely high temperature. It is also a metaphorical term for an intense situation or trial which results in the forging of something new. The play itself is a metaphor for the actions of the House of Un-American Activities Committee, led by Senator Joe McCarthy, which was dedicated to exposing communists in the public and private sectors. There is an obvious parallel between the anti-communist hysteria and the Salem witch trials.

In the play, the town of Salem becomes a crucible. Tempers flare, passions burn and residents are subjected to severe trials. Through all of this, something new is forged. The trials are intended to serve the same function as a crucible that can separate and remove impurities in metal by subjecting it to great heat. Danforth tells Proctor, 'We burn a hot fire here; it melts down all concealment.'

Obviously, there are no witches or demons in Salem and nobody will truly be purified by trial and torture. And yet, as the play progresses, we see that the trials expose different truths to those they were intended to uncover. John and Elizabeth Proctor's relationship is subjected to fierce pressure, and they are transformed as individuals and as a couple at the end of the play. Proctor sees the harm his affair with Abigail has caused, but he is not willing to sacrifice his sense of self or dishonour his neighbours with a false confession. He is, in a sense, purified by the trials he endures over the course of the play. Elizabeth sadly acknowledges that she was cold to her husband and, in a final act of love and loyalty, defends his last act of bravery when he will not sign his name to the confession, despite this making his execution inevitable.

Not everyone is changed for the good, of course. Salem is a melting pot from which old grudges emerge as new accusations of witchcraft and hostility between neighbours is given legitimacy by a court all too eager to find ungodly witches in the small community. If the purpose of a crucible is to separate the pure from the impure, then it is, perversely, the impurities that remain when the trials are over. Even Reverend Hale is transformed by the events he has been largely responsible for putting in motion, but he is not greatly improved by what he undergoes. He chooses to capitulate rather than stand up for what is right, advising those accused of witchcraft to confess so that their lives, if not their reputations, can be saved. Hale begs Elizabeth Proctor to be her husband's 'helper', asking, 'What profits him to bleed? Shall the dust praise him? Shall the worms declare his truth? Go to him, take his shame away'. Hale does not understand that John Proctor does not want to be remembered as a liar and an adulterer; if he were to sign a false confession, he would betray those who were hanged as witches. Proctor's character is reshaped in the crucible of the witch trials and he goes to his death, having regained his honour and his courage.

Narrative style

The structure of the play is relatively straightforward. The action is broken into four acts and the events onstage are continuous within each act. The continuous action within each creates a steady build-up of tension. Act One takes place in Reverend Parris's house. We meet the principal characters and the tension and acrimony between them becomes clear. John Proctor's affair with Abigail is introduced, bringing a personal dimension to what has, up to now, been a community matter. Throughout the play, Miller intertwines the public and the personal. Some time elapses between each act and the pace of each act differs. The second act opens with a quiet conversation between John and Elizabeth Proctor. They discuss the beauty and harmony of life on the farm in spring but then Proctor notices that Elizabeth seems sad. Although the stage directions tell us Elizabeth 'doesn't want friction', she cannot avoid talking about the witch trials any longer. More characters enter with ever more disturbing news about arrests and convictions, culminating in Cheever and Herrick arriving to arrest Elizabeth for the attempted murder of Abigail Williams. Act Three is largely concerned with affairs in court, while Act Four takes place in Salem jail and concludes with John Proctor's struggle with his conscience.

One of the most unusual aspects of *The Crucible* is Miller's decision to include narration at various stages throughout the play. This changes the point of view from third person limited to third person omniscient. Because the characters do not have soliloquies, the narration is often our only insight into their thoughts and fears. The narrative is judgemental and cynical at times but it does give us insights into the characters that we would not gain otherwise. For example, before we hear a word from Parris's character we learn that 'there is very little good to be said for him' and that he 'believed he was being persecuted wherever he went'. Tiny but significant details such as 'he felt insulted if someone rose to shut the door without first asking his permission' help us to put Parris's subsequent behaviour into context and inform our opinion of him and his relationships with others.

The narration also gives us an understanding of the setting and the character of the community as a whole. Miller refers to historical accounts of life in Salem at the time the play was set, noting for example that a 'two-man patrol' recorded the names of those who did not attend church and gave their names to the magistrates, 'whereby they may be accordingly proceeded against'. Miller gave his personal opinion that such an oppressive theocracy would be 'one of the things that a John Proctor would rebel against'.

At times, the narration teases us with snippets of information that we would like to know more about. The brief introduction to John Proctor tells us he lacks an 'untroubled soul' and is 'a sinner not only against the moral fashion of the time, but against his own version of decent conduct'. As soon as Abigail Williams sees Proctor, she stands 'as though on tiptoe, absorbing his presence, wide-eyed'. The stage directions combined with the earlier narration mean we can easily jump to the conclusion that Proctor has had an affair with

Abigail. We know too that he regards himself 'as a kind of fraud', which adds tension to his interaction with Abigail. The narration allows us to feel we share the playwright's intentions in a way we might not were we to simply hear the characters' words.

The narrative sections are not generally included in stage productions of the play but serve to help the director and actors to understand the characters' motivations and put their behaviour in the context of the social commentary provided. Therefore, there is a great deal of difference between watching a performance and reading the play.

Dialogue in *The Crucible* is reflective of the language spoken by the Puritan community in New England in the 1600s. The educated people in the play speak more formally and precisely than do most of their neighbours. Reverend John Hale describes his books in eloquent terms: 'Here is all the invisible world, caught, defined and calculated. In these books the Devil stands stripped of all his brute disguises.' Thomas Putnam asks Hale, 'Mr Hale, I have always wanted to ask a learned man – what signifies the readin' of strange books?' The word order – 'what signifies the readin' – and the dropping of the final 'g' in 'reading' show the time period in which Putnam lived as well as his lack of education. Archaic words such as 'poppet', 'Goody', 'gibbet', 'augur bit' and 'harlot' add authenticity to the dialogue throughout the play. The vocabulary is generally simple, but unusual use of tenses and sentence structure serve to remind us that the characters in the play live in a different world and time. In Act One, Rebecca Nurse says, 'There is hard sickness here, Giles Corey, so please to keep the quiet'. When Ann Putnam tells Rebecca that her daughter will not eat, Rebecca replies, 'Perhaps she is not hungered yet'. The simplicity of the ordinary citizens' language also means that each was ill-prepared to argue his or her case in court when faced with judges raised in relative privilege. Miller's clever use of dialogue highlights the period, the place and the class of the characters.

Creation of characters

Our understanding of the characters in *The Crucible* depends, to a certain extent, on whether we read the play or watch a performance of it. In a staged version, we slowly come to understand the background and motivations of the characters. If we read the text, however, we are also privy to Miller's extending narrative, which changes the point of view from third person limited to third person omniscient. We learn about the characters through Miller's narration, their actions in the play and the regard in which they are held by other members of the community.

It is important to remember that the witch trials are intended to be an allegory of the American anti-communist hysteria exemplified by the McCarthy hearings in the 1950s. Both were travesties of justice, and Miller uses characters like Reverend Parris, Abigail Williams and John Proctor to show us how people react to a moral dilemma.

Reverend Parris is an unsympathetic figure. One critic describes him as 'A graphic personification of the surrender of conscience as a method for survival'. Miller uses various techniques to guide us in our judgement of Parris. In his narration, he tells us that 'there is very little good' to be said for Parris and goes on to describe him as someone who 'believed he was being persecuted wherever he went'. Parris's need to be in control is portrayed as something petty and slightly ridiculous: 'In meeting, he felt insulted if someone rose to shut the door without first asking his permission.'

The reactions of others to Parris also inform our opinion of him. John Proctor has not attended church for some time because he claims Parris hardly ever mentions God but is instead concerned with money and securing the title deeds to his house. Proctor says scornfully that at the last meeting he attended, Parris 'spoke so long on deeds and mortgages' that Proctor thought he was at an auction rather than at church.

Miller uses Parris's cowardice and self-serving nature to show that those who behave selfishly and cruelly are likely to become victims of injustice themselves. Although Parris eventually pleads for the hangings to be postponed for a time, it is not because he has come to see how unjust they are but because he is frightened by the threats against his own life. He claims he does not dare to leave his house at night and heard a dagger falling to the ground when he opened his door. Parris unleashed hysteria in Salem and has now become a victim of it.

Reverend Parris is not a complex character: he does not develop over the course of the play. In contrast, Abigail Williams, the antagonist in *The Crucible*, is less straightforward and more interesting as a result. It would be easy to view Abigail as an evil, monstrous young woman who is capable of bearing full responsibility for her actions. However, Miller shows her to be a pathetic figure who is, in her own way, a victim of a harsh and unforgiving world. Abigail occupies a lowly position in Salem society. She has no immediate family and relies on her uncle's charity to survive. She had been working as a servant in the Proctor household but lost that job seven months before the play begins. In addition, there are rumours that she has had an affair with John Proctor and she is shunned by many of the townsfolk as a result. Parris tells Abigail that he has heard Elizabeth Proctor will not attend church because 'she will not sit so close to something soiled' and he is concerned that since she left the Proctors, Abigail has not been employed by another family.

Abigail Williams's situation deepens our understanding of the world of the text. In that time and place, women had little control over their lives. Abigail wields what power she has. She has a stronger will than the other girls and is not afraid to both threaten and use violence if it suits her ends. In Act One, she shakes the unconscious Betty Parris and says she will beat her if she does not wake up. When Betty awakes and says Abigail drank blood as part of a curse intended to kill Elizabeth Proctor, Abigail 'smashes her across the face'. She vows she will inflict a 'pointy reckoning' on the other girls if they speak a word about her actions, and assures them she knows how to kill if needs be. 'And you know I can do it; I saw Indians smash my dear parents' heads on the pillow next to mine, and I have seen some reddish work done at night, and I can make you wish you had never seen the sun go down!' Abigail's reference to her parents' terrible death is a reminder of the harsh lives the Puritans lived in that part of North America. Danger was never far away and the communities that encroached on Native American territories were peopled by tough men and women who survived where others did not.

Abigail is mean-spirited and selfish, certainly, but much of her behaviour is typical of any adolescent who has been mistreated. She is only seventeen and, when John Proctor begins an adulterous affair with her, Abigail misreads the situation. She believes Proctor loves her and that they have a future together. The Puritans repressed their desires, but Abigail Williams refuses to adopt that particular mindset. She tells Proctor that she was taught 'lying lessons' by 'all these Christian women and their covenanted men'. Proctor has awakened her sexuality and she refuses to simply become a subservient Puritan woman once again. She says that Proctor's insistence that she forget about their time together is the equivalent of asking her to 'tear the light' out of her eyes. She begs, 'John, pity me, pity me!' Her words may be seen to be addressed to the audience as much as to Proctor.

Abigail is also cunning enough to manipulate the church rulers. She harnesses the hysteria, fear and hypocrisy of those in her community and uses them to her advantage. Everyone in Salem and the judges brought in from outside the community uphold her version of events and people live or die based on her testimony and that of the girls she bullies into agreeing with her version of events. Her character flaws are embraced and magnified by the witch trials and the situation soon spins out of control. Ultimately, Abigail gains nothing. She steals her uncle's money and runs away from the horror of Salem.

John Proctor, like Abigail Williams, is a complex and interesting character. He represents those who must make a choice between right and wrong, even if taking the side of right will result in great personal suffering. Proctor's situation would have been of particular significance at the time the play was written: the McCarthy hearings in America meant many people were faced with a similar dilemma. In an interview given before the first performance of *The Crucible*, Arthur Miller said, 'Nobody wants to be a hero. You go through life giving up parts of yourself – a hope, a dream, an ambition, a belief, a liking, a piece of self-respect. But in every man there is something he cannot give up and still remain himself – a core, an identity, a thing that is summed up for him by the sound of his own name on his own ears. If he gives that up, he becomes a different man, not himself.' This is certainly true of John Proctor. While many of those around him choose to capitulate rather than stand up for what is right, Proctor refuses to pretend to be someone he is not. Although he would be spared the hangman's noose were he to allow his signed confession to be shown to the people of Salem, Proctor refuses to agree to Danforth's demand. Danforth is bewildered but Proctor cries out, 'How may I live without my name? I have given you my soul; leave me my name'. Hale begs Elizabeth Proctor to be her husband's 'helper', asking, 'What profits him to bleed? Shall the dust praise him? Shall the worms declare his truth? Go to him, take his shame away'. Hale does not understand that John does not want to be remembered as a liar; if he were to sign a false confession, he would betray those who were hanged as witches. Elizabeth knows the sort of man her husband is and she tells Hale, 'He have his goodness now. God forbid I take it from him!'

Ultimately, John Proctor comes to a deeper understanding of himself over the course of the play. He realises that in isolating himself from the church and staying largely silent despite his disapproval of Parris, he has abdicated his social responsibility. Now, too late, he sees that it is not enough to say nothing; those who recognise evil are morally obliged to speak out. He calls out to Danforth, 'For them that quail to bring men out of ignorance, as I have quailed, and as you quail now when you know in all your black hearts that this be fraud – God damns our kind especially, and we will burn, we will burn together!' Proctor's character is reshaped in the crucible of the witch trials and he goes to his death having regained his honour and his courage.

Humour

The Crucible is far from a comedy, dealing as it does with torture, executions and false allegations of satanic rituals. However, the overblown hysteria could be viewed with a certain degree of amusement if seen as a satirical comment on the McCarthy hearings in America at the time the play was written. Arthur Miller found the investigations into alleged communist activities ridiculous and ironic. After all, a country that claimed to champion freedom was clamping down on liberal ideologies they considered dangerously close to viewpoints espoused by oppressive communist regimes. Miller hoped that *The Crucible* would 'illuminate the tragic absurdities' of the surreal situation in his home country. He was shocked by how swiftly attitudes could change and people could turn against those they had until recently viewed as allies. *The Crucible* explores this absurdity but, in order for the dark humour in the situation to be fully appreciated, the audience needs to be aware of and, to a certain extent, in agreement with Miller's views.

The people of Salem had little to laugh about and were, in any case, actively discouraged from frivolity or jollity. As Miller says in his introduction to the play, 'the people were forced to fight the land like heroes for every grain of corn, and no man had very much time for fooling about'. While Miller acknowledges that there were 'some jokers' who did not regularly attend church, they were reported to the magistrates and 'accordingly proceeded against'. Overall, as Miller says, the people observed 'a strict and sombre way of life' in general.

There is a certain wry humour in Miller's narrative sections of the play. For example, he describes Reverend Parris as a paranoid and perpetually indignant man who 'felt insulted if someone rose to shut the door without first asking his permission'. Similarly, his description of Reverend Hale portrays him as a man of little judgement. Miller shows this lack of self-awareness and common sense when he says that before Hale's arrival in Salem, the witch he had been investigating turned out to be 'a mere pest' and her victim had soon 'recovered her normal behaviour after Hale had given her his kindness and a few days of rest in his own house'.

While Miller might be cynical at times, he is never openly mocking, nor does he poke fun at the seriousness of the issue. Ridiculous though the premise might be, people were tortured and executed on the foot of the hysteria that gripped Salem in 1692. Miller's play serves to remind us all that it takes little for societies to fall into such patterns of hysterical accusation, self-serving corruption and astonishing cruelty.

Comparative Study

Imagery and symbolism

Note: The crucible is an important symbol in the play. If you are discussing imagery and symbolism in the play, you can also refer back to the notes on the title (page 428).

Salem is a theocratic society: religious authority is the law, and the characters are well-versed in biblical matters. The characters' use of religious imagery gives us an insight into their natures and motivation.

Hale is troubled by the direction the witch trials take, particularly when he hears Martha Corey and Rebecca Nurse have been accused, but he clings to his belief that 'the Devil is alive in Salem'. The ridiculousness of his claim angers Proctor who asks how anyone can believe the women guilty. Hale replies 'until an hour before the Devil fell, God thought him beautiful in heaven'. This diabolical image gives the charges of witchcraft a solemnity and validity they do not deserve. That the comparison is utterly ludicrous is shown moments later when Giles Corey explains that Walcott, the neighbour who accused Martha, has been angry with her for a long time because a pig she sold him died soon after he bought it. Martha refused his demand for a refund, pointing out that he didn't know how to feed pigs properly. She was proven right when Walcott's pigs failed to thrive over the years. Now he claims his bad animal husbandry is because Martha – a reader – did 'bewitch them with her books'.

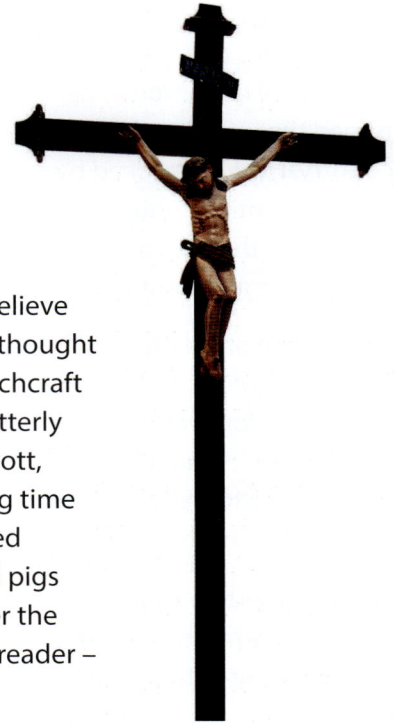

Religious imagery is used to shape our opinion of Abigail Williams. Abigail tells Proctor the effect their relationship had on her: 'I look for John Proctor that took me from my sleep and put knowledge in my heart.' This is an allusion to the story of Adam and Eve in the Bible. They ate the forbidden fruit in the Garden of Eden and immediately lost their innocence. Eve is the temptress in the story, and the originator of sin on earth, just as Abigail is presented as the reason for Proctor's downfall. Elizabeth Proctor says that where Abigail walks, 'The crowd will part like the sea for Israel'. This is a reference to Moses leading his people through the Red Sea when they were fleeing Egypt. Elizabeth recognises that Abigail now wields incredible power in Salem and has a large following.

John Proctor uses religious imagery to show the hypocrisy and evil of the witch trials. When Danforth asks him if he is 'combined with anti-Christ', Proctor says, 'I say – I say – God is dead!' While Parris and Danforth see this as proof of Proctor's guilt, what he actually means is that there is no Christianity, no goodness or decency in the proceedings. Proctor uses diabolical imagery to drive home his point. He says, 'A fire, a fire is burning!' and claims to see and hear Lucifer close by. Proctor means that the courtroom and Salem itself have become like hell. He also says that both he and Danforth are agents of the devil in that they both ignored the truth at different times and did not 'bring men out of ignorance'. Danforth knows, Proctor says, that the trials are a fraud and, as a result, he will burn in hell along with Proctor and all who have conspired to condemn innocent men and women.

The Proctors are farmers, so it is not surprising that natural imagery should play a role in their relationship. Still uneasy and trying their best to heal the wound caused by his affair with Abigail, Proctor tells Elizabeth that they will have 'green fields soon' as the earth is 'warm as blood' beneath the clods. This can be seen as a metaphor for his hope for the regrowth of their love. Although things may be cold on the surface, there is a core of warmth underneath. Elizabeth is not as receptive as Proctor might wish, and he tells her that she should bring flowers into the house as 'It's winter in here yet'. This is a veiled reprimand because Elizabeth is not responding to his efforts to win her forgiveness.

Literary genre in *Casablanca*

The original title of *Casablanca* was *Everybody Comes to Rick's*: the film is based on a play of that name. However, shortly after the bombing of Pearl Harbour in 1941, the Warner Bros. film studio changed the title to *Casablanca*. As America had just joined World War II, public interest in films about the conflict was high. The film was released in November 1942, a few weeks after American and Allied forces landed in French-held territories in North Africa. Two months after this, the US President, Franklin D. Roosevelt, and the British Prime Minister, Winston Churchill, held a conference in Casablanca to plan their strategies. As a result, the title would have resonated with American and European audiences.

Casablanca was particularly relevant to audiences at the time because Rick symbolised the changing attitude of America from isolationism to choosing a side. Although the film was made and released after America had joined the Allies, it is set in a time just before that. Shortly after his first meeting with Ilsa in Casablanca, Rick asks Sam, 'if it's December 1941 in Casablanca, what time is it in New York?' This ensures that the audience retains some sympathy for Rick when he says, 'I stick my neck out for nobody' and tells Strasser that he sees the 'point of view of the hound' as well as the fox. If Rick had espoused these opinions after Pearl Harbour, he would have been a far less sympathetic character.

The exotic location also piqued the interest of the audience. In 1938, the film *Algiers* had been a box office hit and Warner Bros. wanted to cash in on the public appetite for films set in North Africa. Therefore, *Casablanca* was a suitably exotic title and location to capture the public's attention.

Narrative style

The film opens with the credits displayed over a map of Africa. Music that the audience would recognise as Moroccan plays until close to the end of the credits, when it is replaced by the French national anthem, La Marseillaise. A voiceover explains the 'tortuous, roundabout refugee trail' from Europe to Casablanca that those who want to flee to America must follow. This type of voiceover would have been familiar to audiences from newsreels played in cinemas before the main feature, so this narrative technique would have added realism and increased the tension in the film. The scene is now set, and the story can begin.

The story of *Casablanca* is mostly told from Rick's perspective, although we do see other characters' points of view from time to time. Rick, however, is central to the narrative and his experiences are given the most attention.

Our introduction to Rick neatly establishes his importance in the film. The first shot of him is merely of his hand authorising a cheque brought to him by a deferential employee. He is clearly a powerful, authoritative figure, in his own café, at least. A champagne glass rests beside a chessboard. The props – champagne and chess – create the impression that Rick is both affluent and intelligent. The camera pans up to Rick's face as he smokes his cigarette and looks intently at the solitary game of chess he is playing. The doorman looks to Rick for permission to grant or refuse entry to the café. A German is outraged when Rick denies him admission to the casino, but Rick is unmoved by his bluster and threats.

Curtiz's decision to show the events largely from Rick's perspective ensures that Rick is viewed as the hero, rather than the more uncomplicatedly heroic and admirable Victor Laszlo. Laszlo's character is never fully developed in the same way as is Rick's, thereby ensuring we remain firmly on Rick's side, despite his character flaws.

The story is told in chronological order apart from one important flashback to Rick and Ilsa's time together in Paris. The flashback fills in much of the background detail of their love affair. They drive in the countryside, take a boat trip down the Seine, dance and drink champagne together. Later, however, the mood changes. They are in a café, La Belle Aurore (The Beautiful Dawn). The name of the café is ironic, as it is not a beautiful dawn for Rick or Ilsa: their relationship is about to end. The Germans will shortly invade Paris, and Rick is leaving for Marseille. He believes Ilsa will go with him but, of course, she does not. The mood changes as Rick stands in a downpour at the station, reading her letter. Now at last we know why Rick is so jaded and cynical. His heart has been broken and his bitterness may jeopardise Laszlo and Ilsa's chance of escaping Casablanca. Thus, the tension in the film increases.

For the first half of the film, Rick is indeed an obstacle to Ilsa and Laszlo's efforts to reach America. He refuses to give Laszlo the letters of transit until Ilsa visits him in his apartment. That evening, Rick undergoes a transformation. He realises that Ilsa really loved him all along and he understands her reason for leaving him. From this point on, Rick abandons his earlier vow to 'stick [his] neck out for nobody'. He risks all to help Laszlo and Ilsa in their bid for freedom.

The ending of the film is typical of a Hollywood film of the time in many ways in that there is a dramatic, deeply emotional closure to the narrative. However, there is a subversion of the norm in that the romantic leads do not live happily ever after. Instead, Rick nobly sends Ilsa away with Laszlo, telling her, 'You're part of his work, the thing that keeps him going.' When the plane has left, it is Rick and Renault who walk away together, planning to embark on a new adventure and the start of 'a beautiful friendship'.

Creation of characters

Casablanca is both a love story and a political allegory of World War II. Therefore, several characters play a dual role. On the one hand, they provide us with romance and excitement, but they also symbolise different attitudes to the war at the time and convey a message about the importance of patriotism.

The action of the film takes place in December 1941. (Rick references the date in his conversation with Sam after Ilsa's visit: 'Sam, if it's December 1941 in Casablanca, what time is it in New York?') At first, Rick represents the American isolationist approach to the war. Americans had suffered heavy losses in World War I and there was a popular feeling that they should not intervene in European wars again. However, after the attack on Pearl Harbour in December 1941, America could no longer remain neutral. Rick's changing attitude to the political situation in Casablanca reflects this. It took the attack on Pearl Harbour for many Americans to decide that they needed to join the war; it takes Rick's reunion with Ilsa to rekindle his moral code. He opts for self-sacrifice in the same way as those who enlisted at the time. Over the course of the film, there are several unsubtle links between Rick and American political views. When Renault tells Rick that Ugarte will be arrested in his bar and that he should not interfere with the process, Rick says, 'I stick my neck out for nobody.' Renault approvingly calls this 'A wise foreign policy.' When Strasser questions a seemingly disinterested Rick about his allegiances, Renault assures him that 'Rick is completely neutral about everything.'

Rick is not the only character who undergoes change over the course of the film. Captain Renault is initially compliant with the Nazi regime, and he conspires with them against Victor Laszlo and any supporters of the French Resistance. Renault, indeed, chooses the path of least resistance every time and, despite claiming to Rick that he is a free agent and answerable to nobody, he jumps to Strasser's command in the early stages of the narrative. This is exemplified in his conversation with Rick while the latter takes money from the café's safe early in the film. Renault claims, somewhat pompously, 'I don't interfere with [the Germans] and they don't interfere with me. In Casablanca I am master of my fate. I am captain of my –' before being interrupted by a summons from Strasser. Renault's growing sympathy with the Allied cause symbolises the relationship between America and its European allies in World War II.

The portrayal of minor characters in *Casablanca* is also a political message. The Italians were German allies at the time the film was made, and so in this American film, the Italian characters are all portrayed as unsavoury in their own way. When Major Strasser arrives in Casablanca, the Italian officer Tonelli is desperate for his attention but is only briefly acknowledged before being ignored. It is clear that Tonelli is not a character in his own right, but a symbol of the American view that the Italians were being used, but not respected, by the Germans. Ugarte, the reprehensibly obsequious criminal, is also a political symbol rather than a fully fleshed out character, as is Signor Ferrari, owner of the Blue Parrot. Ferrari places little value on human life. He makes Rick an offer for Sam but Rick answers stiffly that he does not 'buy or sell human beings'. Ferrari is unapologetic and insinuates that Rick is missing a trick by not engaging in such dealings: 'That's too bad. That's Casablanca's leading commodity. In refugees alone we could make a fortune if you would work with me through the black market.' Ferrari's willingness to prey on the vulnerable shows him, and by extension, his countrymen, in a very poor light.

Of course, there is more to the central characters than mere political symbolism. Rick and Ilsa's love story is central to the film. Ilsa is portrayed as a stunningly beautiful but ultimately quite weak character. Her looks are the most important thing about her. Close-ups of Ilsa are often shot in soft focus, giving her beauty an almost ethereal quality. Her costumes are invariably elegant, and she is always immaculately turned out, with perfect hair, make-up and jewellery. She is the archetypal cinematic heroine of the time in many ways.

Ilsa's character is more problematic than her looks. She deceives both Rick and Laszlo, and we are left unsure of her true feelings for either. For example, when she confronts Rick in his apartment, Ilsa first pleads with Rick to give her the letters of transit, and when that fails, she produces a gun and tries to force him to hand them over, saying, 'I tried to reason with you. I tried everything.' Rick tells her to shoot him if she likes, but Ilsa cannot. Instead, she tells him she loves him, and they embrace passionately. Ilsa claims that she will never leave Rick again, and her earlier strength of character seems to have deserted her when she asks Rick 'to think for both of us, for all of us'. However, only a short time before, Ilsa was gazing at Laszlo with intense admiration and love as he led a rousing rendition of La Marseillaise in order to drown out the German soldiers' singing.

Rick's love for Ilsa and the flashbacks to their time in Paris allow us to see his depth of character. There is far more to him than a cynical barkeeper whose catchphrase is 'I stick my neck out for nobody.' In Paris, Rick seemed younger, happier and carefree. However, when he read Ilsa's letter at the train station, everything changed for Rick. The pouring rain blurred the ink, bringing to mind tears falling on the page. Rick's hard-bitten cynicism makes sense in the context of his great pain. Of course, we are allowed other glimpses into Rick's true nature during the film. One seemingly irrelevant incident is Rick's reaction to Emil, the croupier, telling him that a customer has had a big win at the casino. Rick takes the news calmly and assures Emil that he does not mind. Rick cares about his staff. We see the same decency in the way Rick treats Sam. He refuses to 'sell' him to Ferrari and insists that they ask Sam if he would like to switch employment. Sam refuses, reinforcing the idea that Rick is an admirable man who inspires loyalty and gratitude in those close to him. Similarly, Rick's generosity to Annina Brandel, rigging the roulette table so her husband wins enough money to allow them passage to America, is a kind and selfless act. All these small moments build up a picture of a man who may well be capable of heroism, despite his desire to appear indifferent to the plight of others.

Rick's ultimate act of self-sacrifice at the end of the film leaves us in no doubt that he is a true hero. He insists that Ilsa and Laszlo escape to America together and, in some of the most often-quoted lines from the film, tells Ilsa: 'I've got a job to do, too. Where I'm going you can't follow. What I've got to do you can't be any part of. Ilsa, I'm no good at being noble, but it doesn't take much to see that the problems of three little people don't amount to a hill of beans in this crazy world. Someday you'll understand that.' Rick's political and romantic sides merge in the final scene. He allows the woman he loves to go away with another man because the war effort is more important than any individual. This is a stirringly patriotic message and impresses even Captain Renault, prompting him to abandon his post and join Rick on his next mission, whatever that may be.

Humour

Humour relieves the tension in the film. However, much of what is intended to be light-hearted fun in the film is quite dated, and the running gag of Captain Renault's attitude to women, in particular, would not be considered amusing today. This is particularly the case when he is discussing the women who are coerced into having sex with him in order to gain exit visas or release from custody. Early in the film, a pickpocket explains to an English couple that, in their hunt for the killer of the German couriers, the police are carrying out the 'customary round-up of refugees, liberals, and uh, of course, a beautiful young girl for Monsieur Renault, the Prefect of Police'. Shortly after Laszlo and Ilsa have their meeting with Captain Renault in his office, an officer tells the captain that 'Another visa problem has come up' and Renault tells him to 'Show her in'. He looks in the mirror and straightens his tie, clearly viewing the meeting as a form of seduction.

Much of the humour in the film is delivered through wisecracks: snappy one-liners that were typical in films of the time. When Annina Brandel tells Rick that Renault invited both her and her husband to join him in the café, Rick observes dryly that 'Captain Renault is getting broadminded'. Towards the end of the film, Rick tells Renault to ring the airport and reminds him that there is a gun pointed at his heart. Unruffled, Renault quips, 'That is my least vulnerable spot.' These one-liners are always delivered by the male characters and are often a way of showing how they can keep their cool, and their cynicism, in moments of tension. An example of this is Rick's use of wisecracks to show how unintimidated he is by the Germans. Strasser has a dossier on Rick but, despite the obvious menace implied in such information being collected by the Nazis, Rick picks up on the least important aspect of what they have written about him: 'Are my eyes really brown?' Delivering this one-liner while remaining deadpan throughout makes Rick seem in control of the situation.

There are also some more obvious and less subtle examples of humour in the film, such as when we meet a German couple who have decided to practise their English so they will be ready for life in America. Their terrible grasp of English and their obvious pride in their abilities lightens the mood.

MR. LEUCHTAG   Liebchen, uh, sweetness heart, what watch?
                She glances at her wristwatch.

MRS. LEUCHTAG   Ten watch.

MR. LEUCHTAG   *(surprised)* Such much?

Carl, who is well aware how poor their translations are, assures them that they will 'get along beautifully in America'. The absurdity of this light-hearted little moment is a welcome contrast to the ominous tone in the conversation moments before between Renault and Strasser in which the latter mused that it was dangerous to let Laszlo live.

Imagery and symbolism

Music and song play an important role in the film. They help to broaden our understanding of the characters and themes as well as adding to the atmosphere of the film.

As the opening credits roll, we hear music with a distinct Moroccan flavour, complementing the map of Africa on-screen. This symbolises Casablanca as it was before French occupation. This music is replaced by notes from the French national anthem, La Marseillaise. As the narrator's voice – mirroring a newsreel announcer of the time – tells of the plight of the refugees, the soundtrack becomes both melancholy and tense, with string instruments adding to the pathos. The music changes once again as the narrator says those in Casablanca 'wait – and wait – and wait'. Shots of Casablanca are accompanied by music and sounds of the bazaar. Within seconds, the tension is built again by a series of striking chords leading to the policeman's announcement to 'all officers' about the murder of the German couriers. Tense chords, whistles and sirens follow as the police round up 'suspicious characters'.

Certain songs play an important role in the film. 'As Time Goes By' is Rick and Ilsa's song. When Ilsa arrives in Casablanca, she asks Sam to play the song for her. The song is an example of diegetic music, as the characters hear and experience it: the melody is part of the world of the film. 'As Time Goes By' becomes inextricably linked to Rick and Ilsa's love affair and is a reminder of happier times in Paris before the German occupation and their subsequent separation. Whenever the melody is played, it is a sign that the narrative is shifting from public to private and we are about to gain another insight into Rick and Ilsa's complicated relationship.

The French national anthem, La Marseillaise, symbolises freedom and resistance to the Nazi regime. We hear it early in the film, during the opening credits, but it becomes part of the diegesis during the Battle of the Anthems, when Laszlo tells the band to play the song to drown out the German soldiers singing 'Die Wacht am Rhein' (The Watch on the Rhine). This is an important moment in the film because the band leader looks to Rick to see if he should comply. Rick gives a small nod and they strike up. Rick, who has cynically insisted he is not on anyone's side, is beginning to be won over by Laszlo's courage and idealism. Laszlo leads the staff and customers of Rick's in a rousing rendition of La Marseillaise even though he is aware that doing so will enrage Strasser.

The fictional 'letters of transit' play an important role in driving the narrative forwards. (No such document ever existed and, even if it did, it would be highly unlikely that the Germans would honour a document signed by General De Gaulle, despite Ugarte's claiming they 'cannot be rescinded, not even questioned'.) However, in the context of the film, those who hold the letters, hold the power. A German courier is murdered and the letters of transit he holds are stolen. The disreputable Ugarte asks Rick to guard the letters for him and Rick, after some initial reluctance, agrees. While Rick has the letters, he has power over Ilsa and Laszlo. If he refuses to give them up, they will be taken prisoner by the Germans.

Both Ilsa and Laszlo try to persuade Rick to hand over the letters. He resists at first, but is eventually moved by a combination of admiration for Laszlo's principles, and his own love for Ilsa. Although he is bitter about the way his relationship with Ilsa ended, Rick cannot but be impressed by Laszlo's love for her. The letters of transit play an important role in convincing Rick that Laszlo's feelings for Ilsa are more important to him than anything else. Laszlo, when he realises that Rick will not part with the letters, asks him to use them to take Ilsa away from Casablanca so she will be safe. Rick is taken aback by the degree of sacrifice implicit in such a request, asking Laszlo if he really loves Ilsa enough not only to part with her for her own sake, but to send her away with his rival. Laszlo tells Rick that he is 'not just the leader of a cause' and that he does indeed care for Ilsa that much.

In the end, Rick insists that Ilsa and Laszlo take the letters. At the airport, he tells an astonished Renault to fill in the names of 'Mr and Mrs Victor Laszlo'. In one fell swoop, Rick relinquishes both Ilsa and any power he might have had in Casablanca. By giving the letters to Laszlo so that he may escape, Rick has ensured that he will be hunted by the Nazis. However, Rick has one noble act of self-sacrifice to come. Once again, he uses the letters, but this time to convince Laszlo that there is nothing between him and Ilsa. He tells the other man that Ilsa came to his apartment at night simply to get the letters and that any love she may have felt for Rick 'was over long ago'. Rick wants Ilsa and Laszlo to have every chance of happiness together, and he wants to make it clear that he is no part of their future. He has also decided at last that he will stand up to the Germans and abandon his tenuous grasp of isolationism. Laszlo understands the subtext of Rick's word and Rick hands him the letters, symbolising both his complete separation from Ilsa and his allegiance to Laszlo's cause.

The light that shines from the airport tower may be a beacon to alert planes arriving in Casablanca, but its sweeping movement and harsh glare are reminiscent of a watchtower searchlight in a prison camp. The light reminds us that the world is at war and everyone is being carefully watched. Our first sighting of Rick's café is an exterior shot, at night. The light sweeps across the café's façade in an ominous reminder that, for all the glamour of Rick's the threat of the Nazi regime is never far away. As this shot immediately follows Renault's conversation with Major Strasser in which the latter says that he has already heard of the café 'and also about Mr Rick himself', there is an undercurrent of tension despite the upbeat swing music and Sam's cheerful rendition of 'It Had to Be You'. Later that evening, as Renault sits outside the café, we see the light sweep across the emerging Rick and then a shot of the tower silhouetted against a dark sky. The regular appearance of the spotlight as Rick and Renault talk underscores the serious nature of their relationship, despite the amusing wisecracks they exchange. Through the light, Renault is linked with the sense of danger and the heavy-handed power of a police state.

After his tense reunion with Ilsa in his café, Rick sits drinking at the bar when the customers have left. Ilsa returns, alone. She opens the door and stands there for a brief moment as Rick looks up. The light from the tower sweeps behind Ilsa, framing her briefly in the doorway and surrounding her in an almost angelic aura. Ilsa's clothes, white coat and gauzy headscarf, contribute to the image of ethereal, saintly perfection. The effect is to combine the idea of Ilsa as a heroine in the spotlight, but also to remind the viewer that the couple can never really be alone. They, like everyone in Casablanca, are under almost constant surveillance.

Rick and Ilsa may love one another, but circumstances have conspired to ensure they can never be together for good. The spotlight plays a role in reinforcing this idea. After Ilsa comes to Rick's apartment to demand the letters of transit but ends by falling into his arms and kissing him passionately, Rick moves to the window and watches the revolving beacon light. Their relationship is always in the spotlight and Rick knows in his heart that parting is inevitable.

The Cross of Lorraine was the symbol of Free France during World War II. When France was occupied by the Germans, General Charles de Gaulle fled to Britain and led the French Resistance from there. Morocco, with its capital city of Casablanca, was theoretically unoccupied by the Germans, even though it was a French colony. Captain Renault stresses this distinction when he meets Major Strasser at the airport, greeting him with the words, 'Unoccupied France welcomes you to Casablanca.' In reality, the Germans have a great deal of power, and anyone who supports the Resistance is in great danger. The Cross of Lorraine, as a symbol of the Resistance, features regularly in the film.

We first see it during a 'customary round-up' of 'suspicious characters' by the police. A man whose papers are not in order runs from the police. He is shot down and leaflets displaying the Cross of Lorraine prised from his dead hand. The cross, which resembles an upper-case letter F, forms the first letter of 'Free France' on one of the pages, while the other shows the cross with the French words '*France Libre*' (Free France) and a picture of a gunboat. As the policemen look at the leaflets, La Marseillaise plays and the camera cuts to the words on the wall above the police headquarters: '*Liberté, Égalité, Fraternité*' ('Liberty, Equality, Fraternity'). This is the national motto of France, and the irony is clear as a man has just been killed for his adherence to that belief and others are being herded into the police station on flimsy pretexts. This irony is reinforced by the fact that the man carrying the 'Free France' literature was shot beside a poster of Marshal Petain, the puppet ruler of German-occupied France. Petain's slogan, *Je tiens mes promesses, meme celles des autres'* ('I keep my promises, even those of others'), is meant to imply that he and those like him, who swore allegiance to the Nazi regime in return for being allowed the semblance of power and control, are more honourable than those who resist occupation. Of course, a man being killed beneath the poster is intended to show how false these promises are. The message is that nobody is safe under German rule.

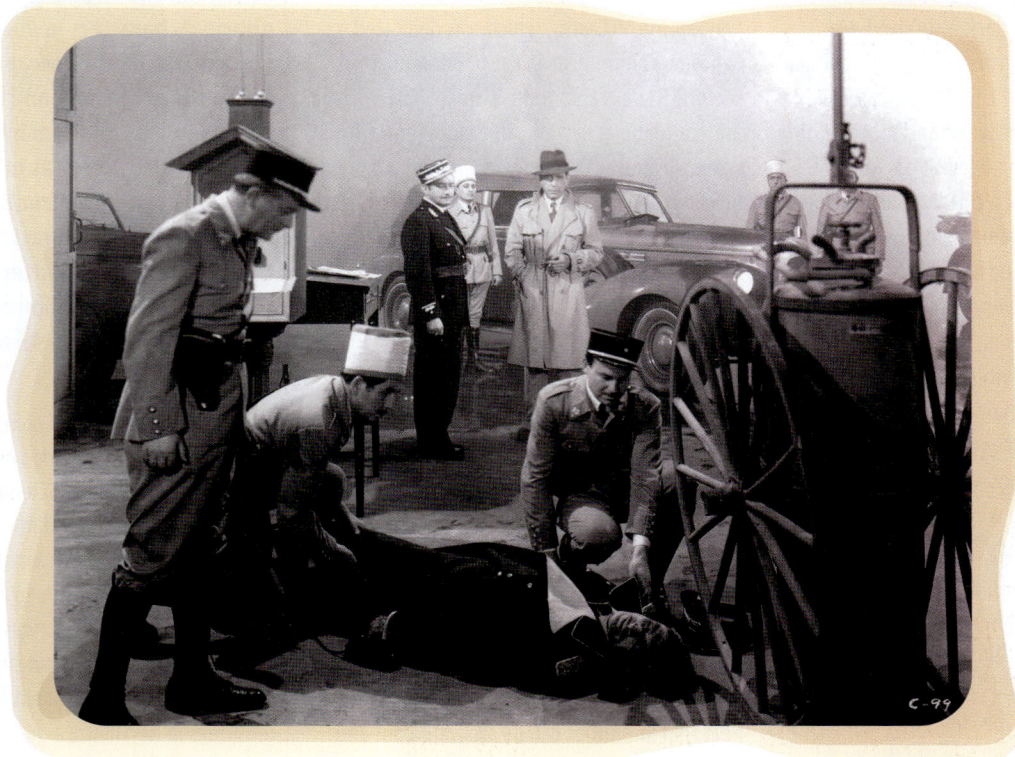

The final symbol used in the film is the bottle of Vichy water that Captain Renault throws into the bin at the airport before deciding to join forces with Rick and abandon his neutrality. Vichy France was the German-occupied part of the country, and it was ostensibly self-ruled. As long as it remained neutral, the Germans promised that it would remain free. In fact, that section of France was run by a puppet government that sided with the Germans. Up until the end of the film, Renault has abided by the Vichy government's deal with Germany, despite making a pointed remark to Strasser on his arrival in Casablanca: 'Unoccupied France welcomes you.' Renault has always slightly resented the Germans' show of authority, telling Rick, 'I don't interfere with them and they don't interfere with me. In Casablanca I am master of my fate. I am captain of my –' before being interrupted by a summons from Strasser. By dropping the Vichy water in the bin and then kicking it over, Renault signals his complete break from the Germans. The political message was clear to the audience of the time: Vichy France was a threat that could not be ignored and anyone who sided with the Allies needed to take a firm stance against Petain and any other Nazi sympathisers or pacifiers.

Comparative study: Literary genre

Room	The Crucible	Casablanca

The title of each text plays an important role in our understanding of the text.

The simple title of the novel captures Room's importance in Jack and Ma's lives. That it is a short, one-word title is appropriate for a novel narrated by a small child. Room is the only world Jack has ever known until he is five years of age. His mother, Ma, was kidnapped and held in Room by Old Nick. There she gave birth to two children, of whom only the second – Jack – survived. Ma decides to protect Jack by telling him this 11-foot-square prison is the whole world and that anything he sees on television is not real. Jack finds a certain contentment in his confinement as a result. Because he has no company besides Ma, and very little stimulation, he forms strong attachments to Room and everything in it. The fact that Room is named as if it is a proper noun shows this. Jack treats the furnishings and objects in Room the same way, showing affection for Meltedy Spoon, Table, Plant and the few other items that he and Ma possess. Ma loathes Room, although she hides this from Jack until it is time to tell him the truth and plan their escape. She says Room is 'only a tiny stinky piece' of the world, much to Jack's distress. Although Ma and Jack succeed in escaping Room, it is an important part of Jack's life for a long time, and he misses it on occasion. He wants to go back to bed there when he is tired because it represents safety and familiarity. One of the nurses in the Cumberland Clinic suggests

The meaning behind the title of *The Crucible* is less immediately obvious than that of *Room*. It is over the course of the play that we come to understand the dual meaning of the word 'crucible': a container in which metals or other substances are heated to an extremely high temperature. It is also a metaphorical term for an intense situation or trial which results in the forging of something new. The play itself is a metaphor for the actions of the House of Un-American Activities Committee, led by Senator Joe McCarthy, which was dedicated to exposing communists in the public and private sectors. There is an obvious parallel between the anti-communist hysteria and the Salem witch trials. Obviously, there are no witches or demons in Salem and nobody will truly be purified by trial and torture. And yet, as the play progresses, we see that the trials expose different truths to those they were intended to uncover.

Both titles relate to control and confinement. While the characters in The Crucible may initially seem unrestricted compared to Ma and Jack in Room, we soon learn that their lives are not their own. The town of Salem becomes a crucible. Tempers flare, passions burn and residents are subjected to severe trials. Through all of this, something new is forged. The trials are intended to serve the same function as the crucible in a laboratory which subjects metals to such intense heat that impurities can be separated out and removed. Danforth tells Proctor, 'We burn a hot fire here; it melts down all concealment'.

At the end of both texts, we reflect on the titles once more and appreciate their significance. The main characters in the novel and the play have been greatly changed: Ma and Jack by their escape from Room and reintegration into society, and John Proctor by the witch trials. John and

As in the other two texts, the title of *Casablanca* links to the idea of people being shaped by their experiences and, perhaps, being able to move past their limitations. The difference between the title of *Casablanca* and that of the novel is that the title of the film immediately brings to mind a far more global issue than the struggles of the principal characters in *Room*. Jack and Ma have to escape the confines of Room and the horrors visited on them by Old Nick but *Casablanca* has more in common with *The Crucible* in that the principal characters' trials are not just a matter of personal safety or happiness but are linked to wider social and political issues.

The film is set at a pivotal point in World War II, at a time when American isolationist policy was challenged by the bombing of Pearl Harbour. The attack resulted in the Americans joining the Allies in Europe to fight Nazi Germany. *Casablanca* was released shortly after American and Allied forces landed in French-held territories in North Africa. Audiences would have appreciated the strategic importance of Casablanca in the war effort and would have been primed to see the connection between Rick and the American attitude to the war.

At the end of the text, we come to a greater understanding of the effect Casablanca has had on the characters. **They may move on, as do the**

→

Room	The Crucible	Casablanca
Jack might be 'a bit homesick' and Ma is appalled at the thought, saying Room 'wasn't a *home*, it was a soundproofed cell'. The novel begins and ends in Room. After they have lived in the outside world for a while, Jack wants to go back to Room one last time. Ma bravely but reluctantly agrees. Jack is surprised by how small Room is and he has already begun to forget parts of the layout. He says goodbye to it one last time and he and Ma walk out the door.	Elizabeth Proctor's relationship is subjected to fierce pressure, and they are transformed as individuals and as a couple at the end of the play. John Proctor sees the harm his affair with Abigail has caused, but he is not willing to sacrifice his sense of self or dishonour his neighbours with a false confession. He is, in a sense, purified by the trials he endures over the course of the play. Elizabeth realises that she was cold to her husband and she takes his side at the end, defending his final act of bravery when he will not sign his name to the confession, despite this making his execution inevitable. John's character is reshaped in the crucible of the witch trials and he goes to his death, having regained his honour and his courage.	characters in *Room*, **but they have been deeply affected by their time in the city.** Rick tells Ilsa that he thought they had lost the love they shared in Paris, 'until you came to Casablanca. We got it back last night'. Their parting in Paris was marred by deception and misunderstanding, but their leaving of Casablanca is dignified and mutually accepted. Both know they must make a personal sacrifice for the greater good but, just as they 'will always have Paris', so Rick and Ilsa will have bittersweet memories of their reunion in Casablanca.

Room	The Crucible	Casablanca
Authors employ a variety of narrative styles.		
The most striking and unusual aspect of style in *Room* is that it is the five-year-old Jack who narrates the story. The book is written in the present tense, which is appropriate because small children live in the moment. Jack's language is quite limited and grammatically incorrect, but that accurately captures his limited understanding of the world. He says Ma's teeth are 'pretty rotted because she forgetted to brush them'. He doesn't fully grasp, obviously, the depths of despair into which Ma sank before he was born. There is little action in the 'Presents' and 'Unlying' sections of the novel. Jack says he and Ma have 'thousands' of tasks to complete every morning but all they actually do are routine and mundane chores and games. Jack's cheerful acceptance of his limited opportunities makes his situation even more heartbreaking. The 'Dying' section of the novel, in which Jack escapes, is the only	***The Crucible* contains far more action and excitement than does *Room*. Part of the reason for this is that so many characters are involved in the plot, whereas *Room* centres on Jack and Ma for a great deal of the storyline. Certainly, Jack and Ma's escape is full of drama and tension, but once they have escaped the focus turns to their integration into society. Both texts are broken into sections but there is continuous action in each act of the play, something which does not happen in the various sections of the novel.** This continuous action creates a steady build-up of tension. For example, the second act opens with a gentle conversation between John and Elizabeth Proctor about the beauty of Massachusetts and the farm in springtime. However, the mood changes when Proctor notices that Elizabeth seems sad. Although the stage directions tell us Elizabeth 'doesn't want friction', she cannot avoid talking about the witch trials any longer. More characters enter with ever more disturbing news about arrests and convictions, culminating in court officials arriving to arrest Elizabeth for the attempted murder of Abigail Williams.	***Casablanca*, like *The Crucible*, is full of drama and action. It is typical of films of the era in which wise-cracks, a beautiful heroine and the threat of violence were par for the course. Like *The Crucible*, *Casablanca* is a blend of the political and the personal.** Therefore, the threat of Nazi invasion, the shooting dead of a refugee, the arrest and subsequent death of Ugarte and the constant danger posed by Major Strasser and his men ensure the audience is kept on the edge of their seat. The opening of the film reinforces this aspect of the plot: the map of Europe showing the refugee trail to Casablanca accompanied by a tense voiceover of the style associated with serious newsreels of the time set the mood. **At the same time, the story of Rick and Ilsa's love affair is every bit as gripping as the central characters' stories in *Room* and *The Crucible*.** ***Casablanca* has an advantage over *Room* and *The Crucible* in that the medium of film allows for a**

Room	The Crucible	Casablanca
thrilling part of the novel. Jack's present tense narration helps to heighten the tension and drama of this part of the novel. It might be supposed that once Jack and Ma escape from Room, the book would end but, in fact, the second half of the book is taken up with their attempts to adjust to life in the outside world. Again, little really happens. Jack narrates events such as meeting new people and discovering how to integrate into society. The most dramatic moment is when Ma attempts suicide because she is overwhelmed by guilt and depression after an interviewer suggests she was selfish not to ask Old Nick to put Jack up for adoption. Even then, however, Jack is unaware of the full circumstances and simply thinks Ma is unwell and needs time in hospital to recover. Jack's narration falters a little when he leaves Room. He reports all that he hears, but it becomes increasingly hard to believe that a five-year-old could, on any level, take in conversations like those he hears between panellists on a television show, one of whom says the 'more relevant archetype' for Ma and Jack's story is the myth of Perseus. The second half of the novel, as a result, is less effective than the first.	**It is more difficult for us to judge the authenticity of the dialogue in *The Crucible* than it is in *Room*.** Obviously, the average reader or audience member cannot judge whether or not Miller accurately captures the speech patterns of New England in the 1600s. What we can be sure of, however, is that the dialogue sets the characters apart from modern-day people and therefore helps to establish the setting and time period. **Both the play and the novel face a difficulty, however. In order for us to fully appreciate the complexity of Jack's situation in *Room*, we have to suspend disbelief and accept that he is capable of absorbing and repeating incredibly difficult concepts. This stretches our credibility to breaking point at times.** In the play, Miller has to find a balance between writing dialogue that is authentic for the time and ensuring it is easily understood. **He is, overall, more successful than is Donoghue in *Room*.** The vocabulary in the play is generally simple, but unusual use of tenses and sentence structure serve to remind us that the characters live in a different world and time. In Act One, Rebecca Nurse says, 'There is hard sickness here, Giles Corey, so please to keep the quiet'. When Ann Putnam tells Rebecca that her daughter will not eat, Rebecca replies, 'Perhaps she is not hungered yet'. Archaic words such as 'poppet', 'Goody', 'gibbet', 'augur bit' and 'harlot' are used sparingly but add authenticity to the dialogue throughout the play. There is enough difference between the characters' language and modern-day English to make it credible but still accessible. **Unlike the first person narrative in *Room*, which allows Jack to express his feelings to the reader, the third person limited narrative in a performance of play does not naturally afford us the same level of insight into the characters' emotional states. However, one of the most unusual aspects of *The Crucible* is Miller's decision to include narration at various stages throughout the play.**	flashback which fills in Rick and Ilsa's backstory. Miller does use narrative effectively to fill in the social, historical and personal context but that relies on a reading of the play rather than watching a performance. Jack in *Room* repeats what he has heard adults saying about him and Ma, but the effect is rather stilted and unnatural. The film has no such limitations. We see a completely different side to Rick in a montage which shows him and Ilsa driving in the countryside, taking a boat trip down the Seine and generally behaving like carefree young lovers. Later, however, the mood changes as the German forces reach the outskirts of Paris. Rick and Ilsa are in a café, La Belle Aurore, when the news reaches them. The name of the café is ironic as it is not a beautiful dawn for Rick or Ilsa: their relationship is about to end. Rick arranges tickets to Marseille for them both but Ilsa does not turn up at the train station, instead sending him a letter with a partial explanation which leaves Rick heartbroken and bitter. The flashback shows the audience why Rick is so jaded and cynical and why he is so shocked to see Ilsa arrive in Casablanca. **It is an effective technique and more convincing than Jack's parroting of media stories or having to choose between a staged and read version of the play.** *Casablanca*, like *The Crucible*, is a limited third person narrative. The story is mostly told from Rick's perspective, although we do see other characters' points of view from time to time. Rick, however, is central to the narrative and his experiences are given the most attention. Our introduction to Rick neatly establishes his importance in the film. The first view of him is merely a hand

→

Room	The Crucible	Casablanca
	It is an effective technique which changes the point of view from third person limited to third person omniscient. There are no soliloquies, so the narration is often our only insight into the characters' thoughts and fears. The narrative is judgemental and cynical at times but it does give us insights into the characters that we could not gain from other means. For example, before we hear a word from Parris's character we learn that 'there is very little good to be said for him' and that he 'believed he was being persecuted wherever he went'. Tiny but significant details such as 'he felt insulted if someone rose to shut the door without first asking his permission' help us to put Parris's subsequent behaviour into context and inform our opinion of him and his relationships with others. **Stage versions of the play do not generally include the narration, but if we read the play, we can gain as deep an understanding of the characters' motivations and histories as we do in the first person narrative of the novel.**	authorising a cheque brought to him by a deferential employee. He is clearly a powerful, authoritative figure, in his own café at least. A champagne glass rests beside the chess board. The props – champagne and chess – create the impression that Rick is both affluent and intelligent. The camera pans up to Rick's face as he pulls on his cigarette and looks intently at the solitary game of chess he is playing. Curtiz's decision to show the events largely from Rick's perspective ensures that he is the hero, rather than the more obviously heroic Victor Laszlo. Laszlo's character is never fully developed in the same way as is Rick's, thereby ensuring we remain firmly on Rick's side, despite his character flaws. **The central character in all three texts is not what we might immediately think of as a heroic protagonist but through their presentation in the text, we come to admire them and care deeply about their fate.**

Room	The Crucible	Casablanca
Different techniques of characterisation are used in each text.		

Room	The Crucible	Casablanca
In Jack, Emma Donoghue creates a little boy who is oddly typical of all young children, despite the terrible conditions he has to endure in Room. Jack is a cute child but he is not cloyingly sweet: he has tantrums and is irritating at times, which is perfectly normal. He is angry that there are no candles on his fifth birthday cake and shouts that it is 'Stinky'. Ma tries to explain that she couldn't ask Old Nick for candles 'for Sundaytreat' because she needed painkillers for her tooth. Jack doesn't care, saying she needed the pills, not him. Jack's imperfections and very natural childish selfishness are a large part of what make him a realistic and relatable character. Ma is presented	**The characters in *The Crucible*, unlike the characters in *Room*, convey a political message. The Salem witch trials are intended to be an allegory of the American anti-communist hysteria exemplified by the McCarthy hearings in the 1950s. Both were travesties of justice, and Miller uses characters like Reverend Parris, Abigail Williams and John Proctor to show us how people react to a moral dilemma.** **The novel and the play rely on different methods of characterisation. The first person narrative in *Room* allows us to share Jack's thoughts and fears, but in *The Crucible*, the characters do not have soliloquies, so a performance of the play requires us to study their actions and their**	**While the characters in *Room* struggle with personal and social restrictions, those in *Casablanca*, as in *The Crucible*, deal with serious social and political issues.** Therefore, several characters in the film play a dual role. On the one hand, they provide us with romance and excitement but they also symbolise different attitudes to the war at the time and convey a message about the importance of patriotism. Early in the film, Rick's attitude seems a little odd. He is a decent man who appears to care for his staff, but his insistence that he sticks his neck out for nobody jars. This is particularly true when he stands impassively by and watches Ugarte arrested in his café, despite the latter's pleas for help. Renault approvingly calls this 'A wise foreign policy'. When Strasser questions a seemingly disinterested Rick about his allegiances,

→

Room	The Crucible	Casablanca

as a complex, well-developed character. Emma Donoghue said she did not want to make Ma a 'pure' innocent, stolen away before she could have experienced much of life. Ma mentions having had an abortion before she was kidnapped, for example, and indicates that her relationship with Grandma was not always plain sailing. When the pair argue after Ma's release from Room, Ma confides in Dr Clay that she would like to slap her mother sometimes. Dr Clay asks if she ever wanted to do that before she was kidnapped, and Ma says, 'Oh, sure.' Even in short snippets of conversation, Donoghue creates a credible, interesting character doing her best to cope with extraordinarily challenging conditions. A character like Old Nick is, perhaps, the hardest to convey effectively in a novel like this. Donoghue does not try to explore his mindset or give him any story outside that of his interactions with Jack and Ma. However, Old Nick's lurking in the shadows does not make him any less frightening. Before we ever meet him, we know he is to be feared. Jack has to hide from him at night, and he remarks that the air is different when Old Nick has been in Room.

On the occasions where Jack reports Old Nick's speech, we hear the man's anger, petulance and sense of self-righteousness. When Ma asks Old Nick for vitamins, he complains about her whining and says he has been laid off for six months, asking 'and have you had to worry your pretty little head?' Ma tries to placate Old Nick when he is angry, asking in what Jack recognises as 'that funny high voice' if he wants to go to bed. Jack is an innocent, so the implications of Ma's request are lost on him. However, we can imagine how Ma feels in Old Nick's

relationships with others in order to form an opinion on them. If we read the play rather than watching it onstage, however, we can benefit from Miller's regular narration. For example, he tells us that 'there is very little good' to be said for Reverend Parris and goes on to describe him as someone who 'believed he was being persecuted wherever he went'. Parris's need to be in control is portrayed as something petty and slightly ridiculous: 'In meeting, he felt insulted if someone rose to shut the door without first asking his permission'.

Just as Emma Donoghue presents us with a complex, flawed but admirable person in Ma, so does Miller catch and hold our interest with his portrayal of John Proctor. Ma shows us that a victim does not have to be a complete innocent to be worthy of our sympathy and respect, while Proctor represents ordinary people who must make a choice between right and wrong, even if taking the side of right will result in great personal suffering. Proctor's situation would have been of particular significance at the time the play was written: the McCarthy hearings in America meant many people were faced with a similar dilemma. Ultimately, John Proctor comes to a deeper understanding of himself over the course of the play. He realises that in isolating himself from the church and staying largely silent despite his disapproval of Parris, he has abdicated his social responsibility. Now, too late, he sees that it is not enough to say nothing; those who recognise evil are morally obliged to speak out. His rebuke to Danforth can easily be read as a scathing commentary on the anti-communist hearings taking place in America in the 1950s. Proctor cries, 'For them that quail to bring men out of ignorance, as I have quailed, and as you quail now when you know in all your black hearts that this be fraud – God damns our kind especially, and

Renault assures him that 'Rick is completely neutral about everything'. However, once we realise that Rick's refusal to intervene is meant to represent American isolationism before the bombing of Pearl Harbour, his behaviour makes more sense. **Miller also uses his characters to comment on issues that were relevant to the time in which the text was written. However, because the play, unlike the film, is set in the past and based on a true story, there are not the same issues with credibility as there are at times in *Casablanca*. Miller's touch is less heavy-handed and no one individual is as much of a symbol of a political viewpoint as is Rick.**

As in the other two texts, some characters are portrayed as more complex than others. Rick is not perfect but he gains our sympathy as we learn – through the use of a flashback – that he and Ilsa were very much in love in Paris but that she abandoned him on the day they were meant to leave for Marseille together. His jaded cynicism and seemingly callous lack of care for the fate of others makes sense once we learn how deeply he has been hurt. Ilsa, on the other hand, is portrayed as a stunningly beautiful but ultimately quite weak character. Her looks are the most important thing about her. Close-ups of Ilsa are often shot in soft focus, giving her beauty an almost ethereal quality. Her costumes are invariably elegant and she is always immaculately turned out, with perfect hair, make-up and jewellery. She is the archetypal cinematic heroine of the time in many ways. **Unlike Proctor, who becomes a heroic figure by the end of the play, Ilsa remains problematic.** She deceives both Rick and Laszlo and we are left unsure of her true feelings for either. For example, when she confronts Rick in his apartment, Ilsa once again tells him she loves him and they embrace passionately. However, only a short time before, Ilsa was gazing at Laszlo with intense admiration and love as he led a rousing rendition of 'La Marseillaise' in order to drown out the German soldiers' singing.

→

Room	The Crucible	Casablanca
company and through her anxious, apologetic responses to his angry questions and her efforts to cajole him into bed to prevent him from taking a look at Jack in Wardrobe, we form an accurate picture of the terror he inspires in her.	we will burn, we will burn together!' **Neither Ma nor Proctor is perfect but their very ordinariness helps us to relate to them and to appreciate the depths of the horrors they are forced to endure.**	**Of all three texts, there can be no doubt that the dialogue in *Casablanca* is the most memorable in terms of creation of characters. In both *Casablanca* and *The Crucible*, central characters choose noble self-sacrifice and explain their choices in impassioned speeches at the end of the texts. While Proctor's defence of his good name and scathing criticism of the witch trials is moving, it is not quite as memorable or impressive as Rick's famous speech at the airport in *Casablanca*. This may be because the language in *Casablanca* is more contemporary, or because Rick blends the personal and the public.** Rick's ultimate act of self-sacrifice at the end of the film leaves us in no doubt that he is a true hero. He insists that Ilsa and Laszlo escape together and, in one of the most often-quoted lines from the film, tells Ilsa, 'I've got a job to do, too. Where I'm going you can't follow. What I've got to do you can't be any part of. Ilsa, I'm no good at being noble, but it doesn't take much to see that the problems of three little people don't amount to a hill of beans in this crazy world. Someday you'll understand that.' Rick's political and romantic sides merge in the final scene. He allows the woman he loves to go away with another man because the war effort is more important than any individual. This is a stirringly patriotic message and impresses even Captain Renault, prompting him to abandon his post and join Rick on his next mission, whatever that may be.

Room	The Crucible	Casablanca
Humour is used in different ways in each text.		
There is nothing even remotely humorous about Ma and Jack's situation. However, it is not all tragic, as at the heart of the story is the loving relationship between mother and son, and the lengths to which a parent will go to keep their child safe and happy. Jack's narration provides us – and Ma – with brief flashes of	***The Crucible*, unlike *Room*, is delivering a powerful political message. It does so through satire: comparing the anti-communist hysteria in 1950s America to the travesty of justice that was the Salem witch trials. That satire can provide us with moments of**	***Casablanca*, like *Room* and *The Crucible*, is not a comedy but humour is used to lighten the tension on occasion. At times, the humour is gentle, as are the amusing moments in Jack's innocent narration.** An example of this occurs shortly after a highly ominous conversation between Renault and Strasser in which the latter muses that it is dangerous to let Laszlo live. A sweetly absurd

→

Room	The Crucible	Casablanca
joy. He is completely unaware of the danger and horror of his captivity, so he expresses many of the typical concerns of any small child. For example, he is unhappy that Ma drew a picture of him while he slept, saying that he would 'prefer a surprise and me knowing'. His innocent lack of understanding of the nature of surprises is endearing. On another occasion, Ma explains to Jack that the plant in Room is not flowering because it does not have enough food, and he suggests it could have his broccoli. This cunning attempt to avoid eating a food he dislikes shows that Jack is like any small child at heart, and Ma cannot help but laugh. Another function of humour in the novel is to break the tension in what could otherwise be an unbearably distressing, heart-wrenching story. All children are unintentionally amusing at times, but Jack is even more so because he is highly articulate yet knows very little about social interaction. Grandma, after their first meeting, asks if he knows the word 'bye-bye' and he says solemnly, 'Actually, I know all the words.' Grandma begins to 'laugh and laugh' at this, to Jack's bewilderment. He cannot understand that he has changed the mood and provided Grandma with another outlet for her emotions. Jack asks Ma why Grandma laughed even though he wasn't joking, and she tells him that it is 'always good to make people laugh'. That is as true for us, the readers, as it is for the characters in the book. There are no laugh-out-loud moments in this novel, certainly, but there are enough injections of gentle humour to show us the ordinary in the extraordinary and to highlight the incredible resilience of the human spirit.	**humour, but the judgemental tone and the seriousness of the topic means that there is little that is likely to make us laugh aloud. Neither does the humour relieve the tension, as it does at times in *Room*. In fact, Miller's wry comments in the narrative sections of the play add to our dislike of the characters and highlight the ludicrous nature of the witch hunt.** For example, he describes Reverend Parris as a paranoid and perpetually indignant man who 'felt insulted if someone rose to shut the door without first asking his permission'. Similarly, his description of Reverend Hale portrays him as a man of little judgement. Miller shows this lack of self-awareness and common sense when he says that before Hale's arrival in Salem, the witch he had been investigating turned out to be 'a mere pest' and her victim had soon 'recovered her normal behaviour after Hale had given her his kindness and a few days of rest in his own house'. **The humour in *The Crucible* is different to that in *Room* because it relies on the audience understanding the comparisons Miller draws between a terrible period in American history and the time in which he lived.** Miller hoped that *The Crucible* would 'illuminate the tragic absurdities' of the surreal situation in his home country. *The Crucible* explores this absurdity but, in order for the dark humour in the situation to be fully appreciated, the audience needs to be aware of and, to a certain extent, in agreement with Miller's views. An example of the foolishness is seen when Martha Corey and Rebecca Nurse are accused. Hale says that, despite	conversation between a German couple in the café lifts the mood. The Leuchtags are practising their English so they will be ready for life in America. Their terrible grasp of English and their obvious pride in their abilities is heartwarming and entertaining. Mr Leuchtag asks his wife, 'Liebchen, uh, sweetness heart, what watch?' She glances at her wrist and says proudly, 'Ten watch'. The head waiter Carl, who is well aware of how poor their translations are, assures them they will 'get along beautifully in America'. **Their childlike delight and their mistaken belief that their dreadful English will help them to fit in is a welcome relief from Strasser's darkly threatening tone, just as Jack's innocence and his pleasure in the simple things goes some way to relieving the atmosphere of *Room* when it becomes almost too dark to bear. There is absurdity in *The Crucible*, but it does little to lighten the tension. Miller's highlighting of the disturbing parallels between the Salem witch trials and the McCarthy hearings is far from gentle. It reinforces the harsh brutality that can result from ignorance, selfishness and spite.** **Whereas the gentle humour in *Room* is relatable because it is based on the timeless innocence of a child, *Casablanca* and *The Crucible* are a little more problematic in terms of what the audience might find amusing. American audiences living through the 'Red Scare' (fear of the rise of communism) did not necessarily sympathise with Miller's satirising the political system. The play opened to mixed reviews as some critics were wary of being seen to support Miller. Nowadays, an audience might not recognise the political significance of the satire because the McCarthy trials are a thing of the past.** **Changing attitudes also affect the perception of humour in *Casablanca*. Captain Renault's behaviour would not be quite so entertaining to a modern viewer.** Much of what is intended to be light-hearted fun in the film is quite dated, and the running gag of Captain Renault's attitude to women would not be considered amusing today. This is particularly

Room	The Crucible	Casablanca
	her excellent reputation, Rebecca may well be a witch because, 'until an hour before the Devil fell, God thought him beautiful in heaven'. This image gives the charges of witchcraft a solemnity and validity they do not deserve. That the comparison is utterly ludicrous is shown moments later when Giles Corey explains that Walcott, the neighbour who accused his wife, Martha, has been angry with her for a long time because a pig she sold him died soon after he bought it. Now he claims his bad animal husbandry is because Martha – a reader – did 'bewitch them with her books'. It is clear that the witch trials are little more than an excuse to seek petty vengeance on neighbours, and the implication is that the anti-communist hearings were similarly ridiculous. However, for the dark humour to be fully enjoyed, the political comparisons need to be understood. **The gentle humour in *Room* is far more relatable because it is centres on the amusing things a small child says and does.**	the case when he is discussing the women who are coerced into having sex with him in order to gain exit visas or release from custody. In what he calls 'a gesture to love', Rick helps Annina Brandel's husband win money at his rigged roulette tables so she will not have to sleep with Renault in order to obtain an exit visa. Renault is put out, complaining to Rick that he is interfering with his 'little romances'. In a manner that would have seemed simply roguish rather than sexually predatory to an audience at the time, Renault warns Rick that he will be coming to the casino the following night 'with a breathtaking blonde', and he expects her to lose all her bets, with predictable results for him. In both the play and the film, the director's choices matter when it comes to humour. In some performances of *The Crucible*, Ann Putnam hovers over Betty's bed lest she fly away, much to the audience's amusement. *Casablanca* has not been remade, so, unlike stage versions of *The Crucible*, we are left with the original presentation of Renault and must make up our own minds as to whether or not we find him humorous.

Room	The Crucible	Casablanca
Imagery and symbolism contribute to our understanding of the texts.		
Teeth may seem an unusual symbol, but they play an important, recurring role in *Room*. At the start of the book, Jack scrubs his teeth carefully as part of his morning routine. Ma jokingly covers her eyes when he is finished, telling him that his teeth are so clean that they are 'dazzling' her. Ma's, on the other hand, are 'pretty rotted' because she didn't brush them for a long time when she believed there was nothing worth living for. She began brushing them again when Jack was born because he gave her a sense of purpose. Still, despite her renewed attention to her teeth, they	**Recurring imagery and symbolism are important in helping us to understand the themes and characters in *The Crucible*. Unlike *Room*, in which the treatment is quite subtle, *The Crucible* relies on repeated religious images to deliver a clear message.** This is natural in a theocratic society: religious authority is the law, and the characters are well-versed in biblical matters. **One of the main differences in the way imagery and symbolism is used in both texts is the emphasis on the public rather than the personal in *The Crucible*. In *Room*, the symbolism of Tooth helps us to understand the**	**In both the play and the film, the imagery and symbolism are less subtle than in the novel. Perhaps this is necessary in order to convey an important message, and both *Casablanca* and *The Crucible* are intended to drive home the necessity of standing up to injustice and oppression. Miller's use of Giles Corey's pig story to ridicule Hale's reference to fallen angels shows up the ludicrous nature of both the witch trials and the hunt for communists in 1950s America. Curtiz delivers a similarly clear message through his use of**

→

Room	The Crucible	Casablanca
are badly damaged, as is she. Jack, on the other hand, is bursting with youth and potential, symbolised by his 'dazzling' teeth. Ma loses one of her rotten teeth – Bad Tooth – and Jack is fascinated by it, carrying it with him as a symbol of Ma. When he is about to play dead in order to escape Room, Jack takes Tooth with him. As Old Nick carries him to the truck, Jack talks to Tooth, drawing comfort from the fact that it is 'a bit of Ma, a little bit of Ma's dead spit riding along with me'. Ma once told him that he was 'made of me, like my spit is', and he believes her tooth is, therefore, a part of their shared identity that unites them, even when they are apart. When Ma takes an overdose and Jack has to stay with Grandma, the tooth brings him some consolation. He keeps it with him so that he is linked with her in some way. Towards the end of the book, Jack realises that he has swallowed Tooth and is very distressed. Ma thinks it is 'just a thing', but to Jack, Tooth is a part of her and represents their connection and his identity. She encourages Jack to forget about it, laughingly saying, 'Bye-bye rotten old tooth. End of story.' The story that is ending is not just Jack's possession of the tooth, however. Ma's willingness to say farewell to everything associated with Room is still at odds with Jack's need to hold on to the familiar. Jack is not yet ready to let go of the intense closeness they shared in Room, but the fact that Ma is gives us some hope that he too will reach that point in his life where he is ready to move on completely. Jack wonders if Tooth will pass through his system or if it will be 'hiding inside me in a corner forever'. Although the tooth may be gone, what it symbolises – his love for his mother and their strong bond – will certainly be with him forever.	bond between Jack and his mother but has no wider significance than that. In the play, however, Miller is making a political point about the hypocrisy and foolishness of the anti-communist movement. A good example of this is in Act Two, when Hale is becoming a little troubled by the witch trials, particularly when he hears Martha Corey and Rebecca Nurse have been accused, but he clings to his belief that 'the Devil is alive in Salem'. The ridiculousness of his claim angers Proctor who asks how anyone can believe the women guilty. Hale replies 'until an hour before the Devil fell, God thought him beautiful in heaven'. This diabolical image gives the charges of witchcraft a solemnity and validity they do not deserve. That the comparison is utterly ludicrous is shown moments later when Giles Corey explains that Walcott, the neighbour who accused Martha, has been angry with her for a long time because a pig she sold him died soon after he bought it. Martha refused his demand for a refund, pointing out that he didn't know how to feed pigs properly. She was proven right when Walcott's pigs failed to thrive over the years. Now he claims his bad animal husbandry is because Martha – a reader – did 'bewitch them with her books'. Miller uses religious imagery for satirical purposes in this key moment, and the humour is effective in mocking those who are self-righteous and deluded. Nobody reading or watching the play could be in any doubt about Miller's intentions. **There is no such political commentary in _Room_, where Donoghue uses a light touch and relies on our picking up on the symbolism of Tooth.** **In both texts, the authors use imagery and symbolism to signal a significant change in the characters' lives. In _Room_, the impression we are left with is positive, as the loss of Tooth marks Jack and Ma moving forwards with their lives while maintaining their bond. In _The Crucible_, imagery and symbolism foreshadow a more**	the bottle of Vichy water at the end of the film. Renault deliberately throws the bottle into the bin at the airport before deciding to join forces with Rick and abandon his neutrality. Before he does so, we are given a clear shot of the label as 'The Marseillaise' plays, so there is no doubt about the meaning behind the gesture. Up to this point in the film, Renault has abided by the Vichy government's deal with Germany despite making a pointed remark to Strasser on his arrival in Casablanca: 'Unoccupied France welcomes you.' Renault has always slightly resented the Germans' show of authority, telling Rick, 'I don't interfere with them and they don't interfere with me. In Casablanca I am master of my fate. I am captain of my –' before being interrupted by a summons from Strasser. By dropping the Vichy water in the bin, Renault signals his complete break from the Germans. The political message is clear: Vichy France was a threat that could not be ignored and anyone who sided with the Allies needed to take a firm stance against Petain and any other Nazi sympathisers or pacifiers. Aspects of imagery and symbolism can help the audience to recognise a character's development over the course of the narrative. **In _Room_, Jack's parting with Tooth represents his changing relationship with his mother, while in _The Crucible_, Proctor uses images of hell to demonstrate his disgust with the witch trials and his refusal to accept the lies any longer.** In _Casablanca_, the fictional 'letters of transit' play an important role in showing how much stronger and nobler Rick has become. While Rick has the letters, he has power over Ilsa and Laszlo. If he refuses to give them up, they will be taken prisoner by the Germans. At first, Rick is too bitter and angry to give the letters to Laszlo, but he is eventually

→

Room	The Crucible	Casablanca
	negative turn of events. We see this when John Proctor uses religious imagery to show the hypocrisy and evil of the witch trials. He finally realises that the truth is powerless in court and, when Danforth asks him if he is 'combined with anti-Christ', Proctor says 'I say – I say – God is dead!' While Parris and Danforth see this as proof of Proctor's guilt, what he means is that there is no Christianity, no goodness or decency in the proceedings. Proctor uses diabolical imagery to drive home his point. He says, 'A fire, a fire is burning!' and claims to see and hear Lucifer close by. Proctor means that the courtroom and Salem itself have become like hell. He also says that both he and Danforth are agents of the devil in that they both ignored the truth at different times and did not 'bring men out of ignorance'. Danforth knows, Proctor says, that the trials are a fraud and, as a result, he will burn in hell along with Proctor and all who have conspired to condemn innocent men and women. **Just as Jack's swallowing Tooth is a pivotal moment, so Proctor's passionate denunciation of the trials marks a turning point in the text. However, the outcome in the play is far more negative than in the novel. Proctor may be on the path to a better understanding of himself and those around him, but he is dragged away to jail because of his outburst.**	moved by a combination of admiration for Laszlo's principles and his own love for Ilsa. **Like John Proctor, Rick is starting to see that he must make a choice between right and wrong, even if it is at great personal cost.** In the end, Rick insists that Ilsa and Laszlo take the letters, telling an astonished Renault to fill in the names of 'Mr and Mrs Victor Laszlo' just in time for them to board the plane to Lisbon. In one fell swoop, Rick lets go of both Ilsa and any power he might have had in Casablanca. He assures Laszlo that Ilsa came to his apartment at night simply to get the letters and that any love she may have felt for Rick 'was over long ago'. Rick now wants Ilsa and Laszlo to have every chance of happiness together, and has no wish to come between them. He hands Laszlo the letters, symbolising both his complete separation from Ilsa and his allegiance to Laszlo's cause. **In *Casablanca*, as in the play and the novel, relinquishing a symbol is a way of metaphorically relinquishing an aspect of identity. The cynical, jaded Rick, who sticks his neck out for nobody, is a thing of the past, and while his parting from Ilsa is sad, his bravery and commitment to what is right are admirable.**

→

Questions

2018 Leaving Certificate

1. 'The effective use of a variety of techniques can influence how we respond to characters.'

   (a) Identify two techniques which influenced how you responded to a central character in one text on your comparative course. Explain how your response to this character was influenced by the effective use of these techniques. Support your answer with reference to the text. (30)

   (b) Identify at least one technique which influenced how you responded to a central character in each of two other texts on your comparative course. Compare how your response to your chosen characters was influenced by the effective use of your chosen technique(s). Support your answer with reference to the texts.

   In response to 1. (b) you may refer to the same technique or different techniques in relation to each of your chosen texts. You may refer to the same or different techniques to those you referred to in 1. (a) above. (40)

   OR

2. 'Our interest and attention can be captured at the beginning of a text by the effective use of various techniques.'

   With reference to three texts on your comparative course, compare how effectively at least one technique was used to capture your interest and attention at the beginning of each of these texts. You may refer to the same technique or different techniques in each of your chosen texts. Support your answer with reference to your chosen texts. (70)

2015 Leaving Certificate

1. 'Studying a selection of texts helps to highlight how some authors can make more skilful use of the same literary technique than others.'

   Choose one literary technique, common to three texts on your comparative course, and compare how skilful the different authors are in using this literary technique in these texts. Support your answer by reference to the texts. (70)

   OR

2. 'Compelling storytelling can be achieved in a variety of ways.'

   (a) Identify two literary techniques found in one text you have studied. Discuss the extent to which these techniques contributed to compelling storytelling in this text. (30)

   (b) Identify one literary technique, common to two other texts on your comparative course. Compare the extent to which this literary technique contributed to compelling storytelling in these texts. You may select one of the literary techniques identified in 2. (a) above or you may choose to use any other literary technique in your answer. (40)

Mode: Theme or issue

The theme of identity in *Room*

When we first meet Ma and Jack, they live in a tiny shed in which Ma has been held captive for seven years. She gave birth to Jack in Room and in the five years since his arrival, Ma has shaped her identity around being the best mother to him that she can be, under the circumstances. This gives Ma a sense of purpose. She tells Jack that before he was born, she was sunk in abject misery and cried until she 'didn't have any tears left'. Later in the novel, Ma explains to a television interviewer that Jack was everything to her during her captivity and that when he was born, she felt alive again because she mattered to someone. We never learn Ma's real name because to Jack, for a long time that is all she is: his mother. That she might have another identity and be someone's daughter, sister or friend is shocking to Jack when he and Ma eventually escape, and Ma too struggles to regain a sense of herself and her place in the world.

Escaping from Room is not the end of Ma and Jack's problems. The confines of the shed have been Jack's home for so long that the place is an essential part of his identity. He wonders, when he is in the outside world, if he is 'still me'. In the Cumberland Clinic, Jack reads a front-page newspaper story titled 'HOPE FOR BONSAI BOY'. He is astonished to read a sensationalist description of himself as a 'pint-sized hero' and a 'haunting, long-haired Little Prince'. The figurative language confuses Jack, and he tells Ma, 'I'm not a tree, I'm a boy' and insists he cannot be 'haunting' because 'that's what ghosts do'. The newspaper story is puzzling to Jack because he cannot understand that others may see him differently to the way he sees himself. Until he gained his freedom, Jack had only ever seen himself reflected in Ma's loving gaze.

Comparative Study

Jack is luckier than Ma in that he is, as Dr Clay tells Ma, 'plastic'. In other words, he is still young enough to learn and to develop a sense of self that is not connected to Room and his overly dependent relationship with Ma. Still, his journey of self-discovery is far from straightforward. Jack may be adaptable, but he has been damaged by his time in Room and is far behind a typical five-year-old in many ways. He finds it difficult to interact with other people and can only cope with them 'if they don't touch me'. He behaves inappropriately at times: staring at a breastfeeding mother and touching his cousin's private parts in the bathroom. Jack is shocked and distressed when his aunt slaps his hand away from his cousin and bewildered when she says, 'we don't touch each other's private parts, that is not OK'. Jack 'doesn't know private parts' because he has never had to consider anyone but himself and Ma until his escape. Their lives were so closely intertwined and so intimate that there was no such thing as privacy. Now Jack must discover not only who he is, but also learn to recognise that others are different to him, physically and emotionally.

Unlike most children, Jack has only known one other significant person in his life: Ma. Once he and Ma reunite with their family, Jack has to come to terms with the fact that he is not just a son, but he is also a cousin, a nephew and a grandson. His mother, he learns, is not just his alone, but is also a daughter, a sister and an aunt. Jack must accept the complexities of all these relationships in one fell swoop. In order for him to do so, he has to develop a strong sense of self far more suddenly than a child would normally have to do. This is particularly evident when Ma takes an overdose after an upsetting television interview. Grandma takes Jack to stay with her, and her no-nonsense but loving approach to childrearing helps Jack to find his feet and to cope with separation from Ma for the first time in his short life. Grandma allows Jack to make mistakes and learn from them. She helps him to see that he is capable of surviving and growing without being coddled. In Ma's absence, Jack can finally find his own place in this new world.

Although Ma, unlike Jack, has lived in the outside world before her time in Room, she too finds it extremely difficult to come to terms with who she is when she escapes. She had longed for freedom for seven years, but it proves to be less than she had hoped for. In Room she was just 'Ma', but now she is a person in her own right again and must behave in a way that is seen as acceptable by society . For example, she is still breastfeeding Jack, and she is angry and upset when others find this unacceptable.

Ma has moments where she finds Jack's demands too much, telling him, 'I keep messing up. I know you need me to be your ma but I'm having to remember how to be me as well at the same time'. She is not the same person she was when she was kidnapped, and she cannot simply pick up the pieces of her old life. In the Cumberland Clinic, Ma logs onto Facebook and searches for her friends. She is taken aback that they look 'so different' and by the evidence that they have moved on with their lives in the seven years that she was unable to move on with hers. Jack says that Ma mutters things like 'South Korea' or 'Divorced already, no way' as she looks at the pictures of people she knew 'a long time ago'.

Another challenge to Ma's identity in the novel is the fact that when she was kidnapped she was a young student, but now she is a 25-year-old mother. Grandma struggles to build a new relationship with the daughter she does not really know anymore, and Grandpa cannot deal with the reality that his daughter is the mother of a child conceived through rape.

The biggest blow to Ma's sense of self comes about when she allows herself to be interviewed for a television show. The interviewer asked her if she ever considered asking Old Nick to take Jack to a hospital and leave him there so he could be put up for adoption, claiming, 'Every day he needed a wider world, and the only one you could give him got narrower'. Ma had always considered herself a good mother and had shaped her identity for five years around the belief that she was doing the best she could for Jack. Until the interview, she had never thought that she was the one keeping Jack imprisoned in Room and she is utterly heartbroken at the suggestion that, far from being a good parent, she was possibly no better than Old Nick in her own way. She is so distressed by this view of herself that she attempts to take her own life.

When Jack and Ma are reunited, they both learn that they need one another a little less than they did when they first escaped from Room, and that is a good thing. If they are to lead fulfilling lives and to have a clear sense of their individuality, they need to pull apart a little. The visit to Room at the very end of the book is a significant moment for Jack and Ma. Ma sees Room from the outside in daylight, and although she is distressed, she rises to the occasion because she knows Jack needs this experience. Jack realises that he can let go of his former emotional attachment to Room. They leave, ready to move on with the next chapter of their lives.

The theme of identity in *The Crucible*

The Crucible is set in a Puritan town in New England during the late seventeenth century and was written in reaction to the McCarthy hearings which took place in America in the 1950s. Many eminent people, including Miller, were accused by Senator McCarthy of being communist spies. There is, of course, a strong link between the hysteria and unfounded allegations in both the McCarthy hearings and the Salem witch trials. In both cases, individual freedom and personal identity took second place to what was considered the greater good.

As their name suggests, the Puritans in the play live by a strict set of communal values and have little tolerance for those who seek to express their individuality. Independent thought is strongly discouraged because the community is the most important aspect of life. In this theocratic society, an outward show of religious observance is essential. In the introduction to Act One, Miller says that at the time the play was set, there was a two-man patrol sent to take the names of those who did not attend church and give the list to the magistrates so that they could be 'accordingly proceeded against'.

Naturally, simply disapproving of individual identity does not abolish it, and Puritans both good and bad merely keep their thoughts to themselves as much as possible, creating a great deal of pent-up frustration. The witch trials allow for an explosion of all this resentment and dislike. They are an ideal opportunity for those who want to pursue personal vendettas to do so, and equally a chance for those who had remained aloof to stand up for their values and refuse to allow themselves to be labelled and condemned by hypocritical or hysterical neighbours.

John Proctor's personal integrity is vital to his sense of self. He refuses to appease those in authority by living a lie and being untrue to himself. Yet he has tainted his view of himself by his 'single error': an affair with Abigail Williams. Proctor is tormented as a result and it is not until the end of the play, when he is about to die, that he regains his sense of identity and can be at peace at last.

Early in the play, John Proctor has little interest in the accusations of witchcraft but makes his dissatisfaction with Reverend Parris clear. He has stopped attending church because he is disgusted by Parris's attempts to secure more money for himself and to own the minister's house outright. Proctor says that the last time he heard Parris preach, he 'spoke so long on deeds and mortgages' that Proctor felt 'it were an auction' rather than a religious meeting. Although it is a risky business to stand up to Parris in this way, Proctor is true to himself and says, 'I may speak with my heart, I think', in response to Parris's outrage at his outspokenness. Rebecca Nurse urges Proctor to make peace with Parris but Proctor says he has 'a crop to sow and lumber to drag home'. In other words, he believes he has more practical and important matters to deal with. He is unwilling to pretend to be someone he is not merely to conform to the societal norm.

Proctor's determination to keep his private life private and maintain his strong sense of individuality and integrity is undermined his adultery. In his introduction to John Proctor, Miller says that the seemingly respectable farmer 'has come to regard himself as a kind of a fraud'. By cheating on Elizabeth, Proctor has not only sinned 'against the moral fashion of the time, but against his own vision of decent conduct'. He is troubled by his affair with Abigail, but for now he maintains a public air of 'quiet confidence and an unexpressed, hidden force'. He knows he has done wrong by his wife and his own moral code, and he tries to make up for that by claiming he will never again touch Abigail. He tells her as much: 'Abby, I may think of you softly from time to time. But I will cut off my hand before I'll ever reach for you again. Wipe it out of your mind. We never touched, Abby'. It may be possible for John Proctor, who is older and more sexually experienced than Abigail, to put their affair from his mind, but he is naïve if he thinks the young girl will be able to do the same.

Abigail does not share John Proctor's concern for personal integrity. She is strong-minded and independent, and she rejects the Puritans' repression of sexual desire. At the same time, she is an isolated young woman who believes that John Proctor loves her because he has slept with her. Tearfully, she tells him, 'I look for John Proctor that took me from my sleep and put knowledge in my heart'. It is easy to regard Abigail as a villain, and indeed she is in many ways, but she is also a vulnerable individual who believes she has found a purpose and an identity as John Proctor's lover. She feels sure she will replace his 'sickly wife' in his affections. In another context, she would be seen as the victim, but in the play she is presented as a knowing, manipulative woman who is responsible for the deaths of nineteen of her community. The witch trials give Abigail a sense of power. Everyone in Salem and the judges brought in from outside the community uphold her version of events and people live or die based on her testimony and that of the girls she bullies into agreeing with her version of events.

Abigail is not simply an evil young woman who brings death and ruin to her town. Miller shows her to be a pathetic figure who is, in her own way, another victim of the hypocrisy and injustice that sweeps through Salem. Abigail is mean-spirited and selfish, certainly, but much of her behaviour is typical of any adolescent who has been mistreated. Her character flaws are embraced and magnified by the witch trials and the situation soon spins out of control. Ultimately, Abigail gains nothing and learns nothing. She steals her uncle's money and runs away from the horror of Salem. It was never a place that would accept her for who she was or allow her to elevate her status. The repressive nature of the theocracy in Salem contributed greatly to Abigail's confused and destructive sense of self.

Despite knowing that he has sinned by sleeping with Abigail, Proctor has a strong sense of right and wrong, and cannot hold himself aloof from the witch trials for long. He is horrified to learn that his neighbours are being accused, and when his wife is accused of witchcraft Proctor decides to sacrifice his reputation in an effort to save her. To prove Abigail has an ulterior motive, he tells Danforth, 'I have known her, sir. I have known her'. Proctor knows that his standing in Salem will be irreparably damaged by his admission and does not tell the story lightly: 'A man will not cast away his good name […] I have made a bell of my honour! I have rung the doom of my good name.'

In an interview given before the first performance of *The Crucible*, Arthur Miller said, 'Nobody wants to be a hero. You go through life giving up parts of yourself – a hope, a dream, an ambition, a belief, a liking, a piece of self-respect. But in every man there is something he cannot give up and still remain himself – a core, an identity, a thing that is summed up for him by the sound of his own name on his own ears. If he gives that up, he becomes a different man, not himself'. This is certainly true of John Proctor. While many of those around him choose to capitulate rather than stand up for what is right, Proctor refuses to pretend to be someone he is not. Although he would be spared the hangman's noose were he to allow his signed confession to be shown to the people of Salem, Proctor refuses to agree to Danforth's demand. Danforth is bewildered but Proctor cries out, 'How may I live without my name? I have given you my soul; leave me my name'. Hale begs Elizabeth Proctor to be her husband's 'helper', asking, 'What profits him to bleed? Shall the dust praise him? Shall the worms declare his truth? Go to him, take his shame away'. Hale does not understand that John does not want to be remembered as a liar; if he were to sign a false confession, he would betray those who were hanged as witches. Elizabeth knows the sort of man her husband is and she tells Hale, 'He have his goodness now. God forbid I take it from him!'

Ultimately, John Proctor comes to a deeper understanding of himself over the course of the play. He realises that in isolating himself from the church and staying largely silent despite his disapproval of Parris, he has abdicated his social responsibility. Now, too late, he sees that it is not enough to say nothing; those who recognise evil are morally obliged to speak out. He calls out to Danforth, 'For them that quail to bring men out of ignorance, as I have quailed, and as you quail now when you know in all your black hearts that this be fraud – God damns our kind especially, and we will burn, we will burn together!' Proctor's character is reshaped in the crucible of the witch trials and he goes to his death, having regained his honour and his courage.

The theme of identity in *Casablanca*

Rick Blaine is an enigmatic figure at the start of the film. Before we meet him, there are hints that Rick is important and well-known in wartime Casablanca. Captain Renault tells Major Strasser, the Third Reich representative who has recently arrived in the city, that 'Everybody comes to Rick's' and the German replies that he has already heard about Rick's café and 'about Mr Rick himself'. The sense of intrigue increases when the action moves to the interior of the café. We hear that Rick never drinks with customers and that he is indifferent to wealth or status. A customer suggests to Carl, the head waiter, that Rick might be willing to join them at their table if he knew that he, the customer, used to run 'the second largest banking house in Amsterdam', but Carl assures him that Rick would not be in the least impressed.

Our first view of Rick is merely a hand authorising a cheque brought to him by a deferential employee. He is clearly a powerful, authoritative figure, in his own café, at least. The first shot of Rick's face shows him looking intently at the solitary game of chess he is playing. The doorman looks to Rick for permission to grant or refuse entry to the café. A German is outraged when Rick denies him admission to the casino, but Rick is unmoved by his bluster and threats. He does not need the validation or approval of others and is very sure of himself.

It quickly becomes clear that Rick deliberately cultivates this aloof, mysterious identity. Ugarte, a local criminal, tries to flatter Rick by saying his handling of the arrogant German was

so effortless that it seemed Rick had been doing that sort of thing all his life. Rick asks sharply, 'what makes you think I haven't?' and Ugarte vaguely implies that Rick was different when he first came to Casablanca. Rick, who has remained deadpan and calm throughout his exchanges with staff and customers, appears irritated for the first time, and Ugarte quickly backs off. It suits Rick that others know little about him and he resists any efforts to categorise him or to get to know him better.

Later that evening, Major Strasser visits the café and attempts to intimidate Rick by claiming to know all about him. He produces a dossier that German intelligence agents have gathered, and through it, we learn more about the mysterious Rick. Strasser hints that Rick did something in Paris that meant his position there was untenable once the Germans occupied the city. Rick appears unmoved by the revelation of his anti-German sympathies and, on glancing at the dossier, merely asks in a dryly amused manner, 'Are my eyes really brown?' Again, we see that Rick is self-assured and unshakeable in the face of disapproval.

Shortly after this exchange, Rick excuses himself, telling Strasser, 'Your business is politics. Mine is running a saloon.' Rick does not want to be identified with any particular cause and when, a short time later, Ugarte is arrested, Rick stands by impassively despite Ugarte's desperate plea for help: 'Rick, hide me. Do something! You must help me, Rick. Do something!' A customer who has observed the arrest says, 'When they come to get me, Rick, I hope you'll be more of a help,' but Rick replies, 'I stick my neck out for nobody.'

Rick may seem callous here, but his identity is inextricably linked to the American attitude towards World War II. In the early part of the film, he represents the American isolationist approach. Having suffered heavy losses in World War I, Americans were reluctant, understandably, to intervene in European affairs again. Therefore, Rick will not take a side when Ugarte is arrested, and he repeatedly states his refusal to involve himself in the troubles of others. Renault calls Rick's attitude a 'wise foreign policy' and assures Strasser that Rick is 'completely neutral about everything'.

Despite his best efforts to appear uncaring, Rick cannot conceal his true nature completely. His basic decency is revealed in a few key moments in the film. One of these occurs when Emil, his croupier, admits that he has not manged to prevent a customer from winning a large amount of money in the casino. Rick takes the news in his stride and calmly assures Emil that there is nothing to worry about. We see the same respect for others in the way Rick treats Sam. He refuses to 'sell' him to Ferrari and instead asks Sam if he would like to move to the Blue Parrot. Sam declines the offer because of his loyalty to Rick, reinforcing the idea that Rick's identity is more complex than his public face. Similarly, Rick's generosity to Annina Brandel, rigging the roulette table so her husband wins enough money to allow them to buy passage to America belies his earlier claim that he will not stick his neck out for anybody. Of course, Rick is careful in the way he carries out these acts of kindness. He is reluctant to do anything that might publicly show him to be other than he appears, and he dismisses thanks and praise with some embarrassment.

The arrival of Ilsa Lund and Victor Laszlo in Casablanca shatters Rick's composure and his carefully crafted identity as a hardened cynic who has little interest in the affairs of others. Through a flashback, we learn that Rick's identity was not always that of a cynical, detached observer. He was, and is, more than a mere symbol of a political standpoint. When in Paris with Ilsa, he was far more carefree and much happier: a true romantic hero. However, when Ilsa abandoned him, everything changed for Rick and he internalised his pain, becoming reserved and seemingly unreachable.

The timing of Ilsa's reunion with Rick is important: Rick mentions to Sam after her visit to the café that it is December 1941: the month that Pearl Harbour was bombed and America entered the war. Rick's changing attitude and the rekindling of his moral code reflects the shift in the American stance. After he meets Ilsa in Casablanca, Rick gradually moves from an isolationist viewpoint to one of self-sacrificing idealism.

Comparative Study

At the end of the film, Rick embraces his heroic side and merges his political and romantic identities. He allows Ilsa to leave with another man because the war effort is more important than any individual. In some of the most famous lines from the film, Rick tells Ilsa, 'I've got a job to do, too. Where I'm going, you can't follow. What I've got to do, you can't be any part of.' Rick claims that he is 'no good at being noble' but his actions prove otherwise.

Ilsa's identity is, for the most part, inextricably linked to the men in her life. She tells Rick why she fell for Laszlo, asking him to imagine her as a young girl meeting Victor for the first time: 'He opened up for her a whole beautiful world full of knowledge and thoughts and ideals. Everything she knew or ever became was because of him.' When she reunites with Rick, Ilsa struggles with who she wants to be: Laszlo's wife or Rick's mistress. Unable to decide, she tells Rick he has to 'think for both of us'. Rick does so, and ultimately asks Ilsa to sacrifice her own needs to be a help and support to Laszlo in his work. The message is clear: in wartime, a person's individuality and sense of self must come second to the common good.

Captain Renault, like Rick, symbolises a political viewpoint. Initially, he represents the Vichy French government: ostensibly self-ruling but, in reality, a German puppet state. As long as it remained neutral, that part of France would not be occupied officially by the Nazis. At the start of the film, Captain Renault is willing to be whatever the Germans want him to be, although there are hints that this does not sit well with him at times. For example, Renault welcomes Strasser to 'Unoccupied France' in order to make it clear that he is not under German rule. However, this façade quickly crumbles. At one stage, Renault tries to assert his independence, assuring the sceptical Rick, 'In Casablanca I am master of my fate. I am captain of my –' before being cut off mid-sentence as one of his aides tells him that Major Strasser has arrived in the café. Renault hurries off and Rick smiles cynically at his eagerness to please the Nazi official.

Like Rick, Renault's identity in the film changes in order to make a political point. At the end of the film, he sides with Rick and turns his back on the Vichy regime. This is symbolised in a very unsubtle way: Renault drops a bottle of Vichy water in the bin and then kicks the bin over. He tells Rick that he will join him in his resistance to German rule, and the pair leave together.

Comparative study: Theme or issue

Room	The Crucible	Casablanca

Each of the characters has a moment of revelation.

The biggest blow to Ma's sense of who she is comes about when she allows herself to be interviewed for a television show. The interviewer asked her if she ever considered asking Old Nick to take Jack to a hospital and leave him there so he could be put up for adoption, claiming, 'Every day he needed a wider world, and the only one you could give him got narrower'. Ma had always considered herself a good mother and had shaped her identity for five years around the belief that she was doing the best she could for Jack. Until the interview, she had never thought that she was the one keeping Jack imprisoned in Room and she is utterly heartbroken at the suggestion that, far from being a good parent, she was possibly no better than Old Nick, in her own way. Ma, of course, is so vulnerable at this stage in the text that she is incapable of separating her sense of self from the interviewer's analysis of her situation. Not only has she made Jack the focus of and reason for her life, but she has never had that belief challenged up to this point. Ma is so distressed by this view of herself that she attempts to take her own life.

Both John Proctor and Ma have made great efforts to hold on to their sense of self in difficult circumstances. The difference is that Proctor knows he has been living a lie while up until the interview, Ma has genuinely believed she was doing the right thing. Proctor's reputation in Salem is an important part of his identity and it is extremely hard for him to give this up. He does so, however, because another key aspect of his character is his strong sense of right and wrong. When Elizabeth is charged with witchcraft, Proctor is faced with a dilemma: in order to prove Abigail's accusations are false and aimed at eliminating the woman she sees as her rival, he must 'cast away his good name' and admit in a public forum that he has cheated on his wife. **Proctor's moment of revelation is different to Ma's in that he is his own accuser. Ma never thought for a moment that she had been shaping her identity around a falsehood. Proctor, on the other hand, knew all along that he was allowing others to see him as something he was not. Like Ma, he is tormented by the challenge to his sense of self and his dramatic language in court shows the depth of his anguish: 'I have made a bell of my honour! I have rung the doom of my good name'. Whereas Ma is so deeply shocked and distressed by the suggestion that she has not been the good mother she considered herself to be, Proctor's emotional pain comes from being forced to publicly admit to being an adulterer.** The stage directions tell us that he is 'breathless and in agony' and 'trembling, his life collapsing around him' as he prepares to admit the truth.

Perhaps because the revelation is less sudden than Ma's, Proctor is better able to cope with the situation.

Rick's moment of revelation is more similar to Proctor's than Ma's in that it is the culmination of an idea that has been gradually building in his mind rather than a bolt from the blue. His reunion with Ilsa slowly rekindles Rick's moral code and he moves from an isolationist viewpoint to one of self-sacrificing idealism. The turning point for Rick comes when Ilsa visits his apartment to get the letters of transit and tells him that she loves him still and that she will 'never have the strength' to leave him again. After their conversation, Rick knows why Ilsa had to abandon him in Paris, but he is also keenly aware that without her, Laszlo will struggle to carry out his resistance work. Both these facts bring out the best in Rick. He once again becomes the man of whom we caught glimpses earlier in the film: the 'sentimentalist' who ran guns to Ethiopia in 1935 and fought on the Loyalist side in Spain in 1936. **Rick's re-embracing of his heroic identity is less traumatic for him than Ma or John Proctor's examining of their sense of self.** This is because his revelation leads to him seeing himself as a better person. **Like Proctor, Rick had been living a lie for some time.** Now he knows exactly who he is, at last. **Of the characters in the three texts, Rick alone achieves some measure of success as a result of coming to a deeper understanding of himself.**

→

Room	The Crucible	Casablanca
	He places himself at the mercy of the court and waits to see what will result from his admission. Sadly for him, Elizabeth is unaware he has confessed his sin and therefore does not support his story. Knowing how much he values his identity as a good, upstanding man, she loyally refuses to admit that her husband cheated on her. Tragically, Proctor's public dismantling of his reputation achieves nothing in the end.	He devises a plan to help Laszlo and Ilsa escape together, even at great risk to his own life and at the cost of his personal happiness. It is not an ideal situation, but the alternative would have led to his continuing to live a lie.

Room	The Crucible	Casablanca
The ending of each text contributes to our understanding of the theme.		

When Jack and Ma are reunited after her overdose and subsequent stay in hospital, they both learn that they need one another a little less than they did when they first escaped from Room, and that is a good thing. The novel shows that in order for people to have a clear sense of their identity, they need to pull apart a little. Jack, during his time with Grandma, has learned that he is capable of living without Ma, and she is coming to terms with her adult self in the world outside Room. The title of this last section of the book is 'Living', and both Jack and Ma discover who they are and who they want to be. Both have had their development stunted by their captivity and must now pull away from their reliance on each other in order to be strong, independent individuals with a clear sense of self. Ma is not the same person she was when she went into Room and is concerned that she has become reclusive and content with Jack's company only. However, as Dr Clay and Noreen tell her, she 'had to change to survive' and 'wouldn't have stayed the same' even if she hadn't been imprisoned. Because Room was the place in which Jack's identity was formed and Ma experienced life-changing events, the visit to their former prison at the

The ending of *The Crucible* is far less optimistic than that of *Room*. While Ma and Jack have faced terrible hardships, there are clear indications that they are moving on and shaping new identities in a new environment. Proctor, however, has no hope of any sort of future. However, there are some positive aspects to Proctor's voyage of self-discovery. He has always cared deeply about his reputation and viewed himself as a decent and honourable man. That vision of himself was tainted by his affair with Abigail and is challenged once again when he is asked to sign a confession which accuses his neighbours of witchcraft. Were he to do so, he would go free. **Like Ma and Jack, Proctor has grown in self-awareness over the course of the text and now, when faced with the choice between remaining true to himself or saving his life, he opts for the former.** In an interview, Arthur Miller said that 'in every man there is something he cannot give up and remain himself – a core, an identity'. Miller wrote the play in response to the McCarthy hearings which he likened to the Salem witch trials. **Therefore, Proctor, unlike Ma, is making a political point. He exemplifies the courage it takes to stand up to corrupt authority.** While many of those around him capitulate, Proctor

As in the other two texts, it takes time for Rick to fully come to terms with who he is meant to be. Like Ma and Jack, Rick has allowed his sense of self to be too closely tied to another person. Ilsa's apparent rejection wounds Rick so deeply that he adopts a bitter, cynical façade to hide his pain. Until Ilsa arrives in Casablanca and explains matters, Rick has no idea why she abandoned him in Paris and his sense of self is dealt a huge blow when he thinks that the woman he loves does not care for him. However, he eventually comes to see that Ilsa loves him still and that he has a difficult choice to make.

The endings of *The Crucible* and *Casablanca* are intended to make political points about individuality and identity. Proctor is linked to the McCarthy hearings, Rick's identity is intertwined with the American position during World War II. Therefore, his decision at the end of the film is not just personal but also represents the American shift from isolationism to solidarity with the Allied cause.

At the end of the film, Rick embraces his heroic side and merges his political and romantic identities. He allows Ilsa to leave with another man because the war effort is more important than any individual. In one of the most famous lines from the film, Rick tells Ilsa, 'I've got a job to do, too. Where I'm going, you can't follow. What I've got to do, you can't be any part of'. Rick claims that he is 'no good at being noble' but his actions prove otherwise.

Room	The Crucible	Casablanca
very end of the book is a significant moment for both. Ma sees Room from the outside in daylight, and although she is distressed, she rises to the occasion because she knows Jack needs this experience. Jack realises that he can let go of his former emotional attachment to Room. They leave, as free as they can be in body and spirit, and ready to move on with the next chapter of self-discovery.	refuses to pretend to be someone he is not. Although he would be spared the hangman's noose were he to allow his signed confession to be shown to the people of Salem, Proctor refuses to agree to Danforth's demand. Danforth is bewildered but Proctor cries out, 'How may I live without my name? I have given you my soul; leave me my name'. Hale begs Elizabeth Proctor to be her husband's 'helper', asking, 'What profits him to bleed? Shall the dust praise him? Shall the worms declare his truth? Go to him, take his shame away'. Hale does not understand that John does not want to be remembered as a liar; if he were to sign a false confession, he would betray those who were hanged as witches. Elizabeth knows the sort of man her husband is and she tells Hale, 'He have his goodness now. God forbid I take it from him!' **Ma and Jack's future together is uncertain but they at least have the chance to continue developing as individuals and seem likely to continue their personal growth. John Proctor has no such hope, and yet his behaviour at the end of the text leaves us with the sense that he has made the right choice.** His character is reshaped in the crucible of the witch trials and he goes to his death having regained his honour and his courage.	**In all three texts, the characters have to make sacrifices if they are to be the best possible versions of themselves and be content with their sense of self. Jack and Ma are luckier than Proctor and Rick in that they can continue to develop their identities together. Both Rick and Proctor have to make greater sacrifices and abandon any hope of personal happiness if they are to be true to themselves. Proctor goes to the gallows and Rick says goodbye to the woman he loves.** He knows that he must put the greater good before his personal needs if he is to do what is right. Rick explains this to Ilsa in their moving goodbye scene: 'I'm no good at being noble, but it doesn't take much to see that the problems of three little people don't amount to a hill of beans in this crazy world'. **In *Casablanca*, as in *Room*, what happens next is far from clear. Jack and Ma have a long road ahead and will surely struggle in their quest to find a clear identity in the new and strange world in which they find themselves. Rick too heads into the unknown, and symbolically walks off into the World War II-equivalent of a sunset – a foggy airport – with an uncertain but surely more personally and politically fulfilling future ahead. The one thing all the principal characters share is the belief that facing reality and standing on your own two feet is an essential part of establishing a strong sense of identity.**

Room	The Crucible	Casablanca
The theme of identity is presented differently in each text.		
Room presents us with an original but disturbing view of the theme of identity. It shows us how difficult it is to develop an identity without being part of a wider community. Jack grows up and forms his sense of self in an entirely artificial environment until he is five years of age. He believes the tiny world in which he lives is the real world, and everything	**Unlike *Room*, in which the wider community is an integral part of the characters' developing sense of self, the community in *The Crucible* represses individuality and independent thought. Jack struggles to understand and adapt to the fact that others are different to him and that he must learn to fit in.**	**The presentation of the theme of identity in *Casablanca* is more similar to *The Crucible* than *Room* because both the film and the play present a political as well as a personal message.** Rick may seem callous when we first see him, but his identity is inextricably linked to the American attitude towards World War II.

→

Room	The Crucible	Casablanca

Room

else is 'outside'. Emma Donoghue thus explores what it is that makes us who we are and shapes our sense of self. Ma and Jack's identities are intertwined. Everyone needs a sense of purpose to give their life meaning, and Jack's birth – albeit in horrific circumstances – provides that for Ma. In the five years since Jack's arrival, Ma has shaped her identity around being the best mother to him that she can be, under the circumstances. She tells Jack that before he was born, she was sunk in abject misery and cried until she 'didn't have any tears left'. Later in the novel, Ma explains to a television interviewer that Jack was everything to her during her captivity and that when he was born, she felt alive again because she mattered to someone. We never learn Ma's real name because that is all she is to Jack for a long time: his mother. That she might have another identity and be someone's daughter, sister or friend is shocking to him when he and Ma eventually escape, and Ma too struggles to regain a sense of herself and her place in the world. Jack is equally shocked to discover that he is not the centre of a small universe but just one among many. However, he is at least young enough to learn and to develop a sense of self that is not connected to Room and his overly-dependent relationship with Ma. Still, his journey of self-discovery is far from straightforward. Jack may be adaptable, but he has been damaged by his time in Room and is far behind a typical five-year-old in many ways. Now Jack has to discover not only who he is but also learn to recognise that others are different to him, physically and emotionally.

The Crucible

John Proctor, on the other hand, struggles to conform. Of course, his battle with the theocracy is representative of the conflict and controversy surrounding the McCarthy hearings in America at the time the play was written. There is, of course, a strong link between the hysteria of the unfounded allegations in both the McCarthy hearings and the Salem witch trials. In both cases, individual freedom and personal identity took second place to what was considered the greater good. Proctor is presented as a flawed but relatable man who becomes the victim of a corrupt and hypocritical theocracy. **Therefore, the theme takes on political significance that does not exist in *Room*.**

Both Arthur Miller and Emma Donoghue show us blatantly cruel and obviously appalling settings in which characters have great difficulty in finding and maintaining a sense of self. In both texts, deviation from a set code of behaviour carries great risk. Obedience is key. In Salem, an outward show of religious observance is essential. In the introduction to Act One, Miller says that at the time the play was set, there was a two-man patrol sent to take the names of those who did not attend church and give the list to the magistrates so that they could be 'accordingly proceeded against'. Naturally, simply disapproving of individual identity does not abolish it, and Puritans both good and bad merely keep their thoughts to themselves as much as possible, creating a great deal of pent-up frustration. **Like Ma when she tries to appease Old Nick, the citizenry of Salem find it best to do as they are told by their church leaders.** The witch trials allow for an explosion of all this resentment and dislike. They are an ideal opportunity

Casablanca

In the early part of the film, he represents the American isolationist approach. Having suffered heavy losses in World War I, Americans were understandably reluctant to intervene in European affairs again. Therefore, Rick will not take a side when Ugarte is arrested and he repeatedly states his refusal to involve himself in the troubles of others. Renault calls Rick's attitude a 'wise foreign policy' and assures Strasser that Rick is 'completely neutral about everything'.

Rick's situation is nothing like as restrictive as that endured by the characters in *Room* or *The Crucible*. Certainly, he has to preserve a façade of detachment and neutrality in order to evade unwelcome attention from the authorities in Casablanca, but he is not personally affected by those in authority, unlike the characters in the novel and the play.

In order to show the shift from American isolationism to siding with the Allied cause, Rick has to have a change of heart. This switch from neutral to anti-German is presented through Rick's love for Ilsa Lund and his eventual rekindling of a moral code after his reunion with her. Through this meeting, we also learn that Rick has an identity beyond that of a representative of the American stance early in the war. The arrival of Ilsa Lund and Victor Laszlo in Casablanca shatters Rick's composure and his carefully crafted identity as a hardened cynic who has little interest in the affairs of others. Through a flashback, we learn that Rick's identity was not always that of a cynical, detached observer. He was, and is, more than a mere symbol of a political standpoint. When in Paris with Ilsa, he was far more carefree and much happier: a true romantic hero. However, when Ilsa abandoned him, everything changed for Rick and he internalised his pain,

→

Room	The Crucible	Casablanca
	for those who want to pursue personal vendettas to do so, and equally a chance for those who had remained aloof to stand up for their values and refuse to allow themselves to be labelled and condemned by hypocritical or hysterical neighbours. Proctor's refusal to subjugate his identity leads to his execution, but he is at least confident that he has remained true to himself. He demonstrates that a person's integrity and honour are worth the ultimate sacrifice, an important message in America of the 1950s.	becoming reserved and seemingly unreachable. **While Rick's situation may seem on the surface more restrictive than Nora's and almost as dangerous as those accused in the Salem witch trials, he has more freedom than any of them and, therefore, a greater chance of realising and expressing his true identity.** This is clearly shown in film's conclusion when Rick embraces his political side and sacrifices his love affair with Ilsa for the greater good. **Like Proctor, Rick pays a price for regaining his integrity, but he at least has a future. In the same way that** *The Crucible* **sent a strong message about standing up to evil and corruption,** *Casablanca* **was intended to make it clear to a wartime audience that a clear set of values and a strong sense of self is worth any price.**

Questions

2017 Leaving Certificate

1. 'The same theme or issue can appear more relevant to life today in some texts than in others.'

   (a) In relation to one text on your comparative course, discuss the aspects of the text that, in your opinion, make your chosen theme or issue appear more or less relevant to life today. Support your answer with reference to the text. (30)

   (b) In relation to two other texts on your comparative course, compare the aspects of those texts that, in your opinion, make your chosen theme or issue appear more or less relevant to life today. Support your answer with reference to your chosen texts. (40)

OR

2. 'There are many reasons why the exploration of the same theme or issue can be more entertaining in some texts than in others.'

   Compare the reasons why you found the exploration of the same theme or issue more entertaining in some texts than in others. Support your answer with reference to three texts on your comparative course. (70)

2015 Leaving Certificate

1. 'Some texts leave readers with a largely idealistic impression of a theme or issue, while others leave readers with a more realistic or believable impression of the same theme or issue.'

   With reference to the above statement, compare the impressions of the same theme or issue you formed when studying three texts on your comparative course. Support your answer by reference to the texts. (70)

OR

2. 'It is possible for a reader to be surprised or shocked (or both) by aspects of a theme or issue encountered in texts.'

   (a) Discuss the extent to which you were surprised or shocked (or both) by aspects of a theme or issue encountered in one of the texts you have studied for your comparative course. Support your answer by reference to the text. (30)

   (b) Compare the extent to which you were surprised or shocked (or both) by aspects of the same theme or issue encountered in two other texts you have studied on your comparative course. Support your answer by reference to the texts. (40)